Escape from North Korea

Paul G. Petredis

© Copyright 2005 Paul G. Petredis
All rights reserved. No part of this publication may be reproduced, stored in a retrieval system, or transmitted, in any form or by any means, electronic, mechanical, photocopying, recording, or otherwise, without the written prior permission of the author.

Note for Librarians: A cataloguing record for this book is available from Library and Archives Canada at www.collectionscanada.ca/amicus/index-e.html
ISBN 1-4120-7244-1

Printed in Victoria, BC, Canada. Printed on paper with minimum 30% recycled fibre. Trafford's print shop runs on "green energy" from solar, wind and other environmentally-friendly power sources.

Offices in Canada, USA, Ireland and UK
This book was published *on-demand* in cooperation with Trafford Publishing. On-demand publishing is a unique process and service of making a book available for retail sale to the public taking advantage of on-demand manufacturing and Internet marketing. On-demand publishing includes promotions, retail sales, manufacturing, order fulfilment, accounting and collecting royalties on behalf of the author.

Book sales for North America and international:
Trafford Publishing, 6E–2333 Government St.,
Victoria, BC v8t 4p4 CANADA
phone 250 383 6864 (toll-free 1 888 232 4444)
fax 250 383 6804; email to orders@trafford.com
Book sales in Europe:
Trafford Publishing (uk) Limited, 9 Park End Street, 2nd Floor
Oxford, UK ox1 1hh UNITED KINGDOM
phone 44 (0)1865 722 113 (local rate 0845 230 9601)
facsimile 44 (0)1865 722 868; info.uk@trafford.com
Order online at:
trafford.com/05-2139

10 9 8 7 6 5 4 3

DEDICATION

To the untold thousands of young United Nations soldiers
who died needlessly and lie in final fraternity
on the snow-swept hills and valleys
of North Korea.

And to Mr. Kim.(Walk with God)
김 그리고 씨에.(신과 도보)
KIM GRIGO SIEGE (SIN KWGA DOBO)

CONTENTS

PART I

1. PRELUDE TO DISASTER ----------------------------------- 2
2. ANUI --- 11
3. THE SCHOOLHOUSE -------------------------------------- 21
4. BREAKOUT! -- 31
5. CHINJU PASS -- 40
6. THE HOSPITAL --- 55
7. THE GRAVEYARD -- 65
8. ASSAULT OF THE HILL ---------------------------------- 76
9. REVENGE -- 87
10. THE DAY AFTER -------------------------------------- 106
11. REMINISCENCES OF THE HILL, PART I ------------- 118
12. REMINISCENCES OF THE HILL, PART II ----------- 128
13. INCHON --- 138
14. YALU OR BUST --------------------------------------- 144
15. THE CALM BEFORE THE STORM ------------------------- 162
16. THE CHINESE CARD ---------------------------------- 174
17. THE WITHDRAWAL ------------------------------------ 333
18. CAPTURE! -- 186
19. MY BUDDY AND ME ---------------------------------- 199
20. THE LONG MARCH ------------------------------------ 220
21. THE CAMPGROUND ------------------------------------ 237
22. THE ICEMAN COMETH --------------------------------- 246
23. SLEEPING WITH THE ENEMY -------------------------- 257
24. HELLO MR. KIM ------------------------------------- 269
25. THE INNOCENTS ------------------------------------- 278
26. THE DAY OF THE PLANES ---------------------------- 293
27. PYONGYANG AND BEYOND ----------------------------- 305
28. CHINNAMPO --- 317
29. DAY FOURTEEN -------------------------------------- 326

PART II

30. THE BATTLE RAGES --------------------------------- 348
31. MACARTHUR -- 371
32. HISTORY AND OTHER CONTENTIOUS ISSUES -------- 388
33. THE COMMANDERS --------------------------------- 408
34. BIBLIOGRAPHY ------------------------------------- 439
35. ABOUT THE AUTHOR ------------------------------- 442
35. INDEX --- 444

Dedication --------------- i	Editor's note ----------- x
Introduction ------------- iv	Map of Korea ---------- xi
Acknowledgments ---- viii	Chronology ----------- xii
POW Escapees --------- ix	Photos --------------- 339

PHOTOS

- Taejon, September 1950—South Korean civilians killed by retreating North Korean People's Army
- Yalu River, October 1950. Fifteenth Chinese Field Army crosses the Yalu
- Iconic Korean War photo
- Civilians fleeing south over destroyed Pyongyang bridge across Taedong River, December 1950. Pulitzer Prize-winning photo by Max Desfor
- Chinese Communist Forces casualties resulting from a major battle
- Typical line of Korean refugees fleeing to South Korea
- Author's display of campaign ribbons and medals by Allen Davis

Back cover photo of author in 2005 by Allen Davis

INTRODUCTION

I am neither a writer nor an author. Professionals seldom start their work with the word *I* at the beginning of a story.

The City of Clovis, a nice town in central California, initiated a class on veterans' military experiences with the concept of compiling real-life military stories from veterans residing there, for the purpose of publishing a book.

As a veteran of the Korean War, I attended simply because I *needed* to tell my story about my experiences when I was an eighteen year young infantryman. In truth, I wanted to relate my story to someone, anyone, as a method of starting a healing process from those nightmares that have been locked in my mind for over 50 years. Now, after so many difficult days and nights that have evolved into years, I have come to realize that this earlier emotional trauma is embedded in my psyche, and it will plague me forever.

Veterans came and went. They shared their stories, sometimes mundane, often times gripping; but the majority of them, having achieved catharsis, moved on with their lives. I couldn't. There was a need within me to continue to be a part of this experience.

I never considered writing my story until I attended this class.

One day as I sat in class, the way to begin was shown to me. My guide was the instructor, Mrs. Janice Stevens, the most gifted person whom I have ever had the honor to know. Through her encouragement and insight, she became my counselor, my editor and my friend. Without Janice, these memoirs could not have been written, for she is the one person who not only has the expertise and the understanding to so skillfully point me in the right direction, but to shepherd me through this writing process as well. And in the process, I discovered that I was not alone. I have come to realize that the unbelievable time and dedication she gave me is not unique. Mrs. Stevens, for reasons I will never grasp, has the capacity to share her time equally among all of her students. She is unique and I am truly blessed by knowing her.

In order to write a story, one must begin to write an experience at the beginning, or so I was taught. But what is the beginning? When one dissects the question, it is easy to discover that there are many places that a narrative may begin, be it fact or fiction. Janice had the answer.

"Write about your capture and work up and down from there."

It was as simple as that. I had not seen the forest for the trees.

As I sat at my keyboard that very day, I began to put down on paper those awful events that transpired so many years ago. As I wrote, I experienced the demons locked in my psyche for over a half century trickle from my brain, flow down my arms and drip from my fingers, spewing forth on the computer keyboard.

My combat experiences pale in comparison to the horrors endured by my fellow combatants, the few who survived the Korean War—fortunately or not, depending upon their perspective. Nevertheless, my unique experiences disabled me physically and emotionally, just as other appalling adventures similarly affected my friends.

Now, when we few survivors meet bi-annually and relive our respective traumatic events, recall takes the form of impersonal dissection, allowing a minute portion of the bound-up memories to gradually escape from the mind, the keeper of these horrific nightmares.

During the documentation of my experiences as an 18-year-old infantryman during the early stage of the Korean War, I concurrently assembled a large database from contemporary sources in respect to various intrigues of the Korean War.

It electrified me to be able to review information relative to the *other side*, in terms of dissecting the political proceedings leading to the onset of The Korean War. That data enabled me to determine the cause of how and why these tragic events ultimately unfolded.

War tactics of the enemy, formerly closed to western analysts, are now open for analysis. The Chinese Communist government cooperates with peers on the American side in a cordial exchange of military information, not at all possible during the *Bamboo Curtain* years.

Contemporary western journalists have access to Chinese military records, veterans, researchers and on some occasions, North Korean *provocateurs* to help them explain and define specific events of this terrible conflict from their perspective.

The Freedom of Information Act has similarly proved to be a vital source of information that opened the door to reveal answers to many enigmatic questions haunting survivors on both sides of this terrible struggle that transpired more than half a century ago.

The Democratic People's Republic of North Korea remains a closed society today, as it was before and during the war; nevertheless, a great deal of information is now common knowledge among the civilized peoples of the world. While the army is well fed, well armed and well trained, the rural inhabitants starve. The North Korean government is closed to all foreigners except those approved by President Kim Chong-il. Production is state regulated, and the faltering economy has collapsed.

It was imperative to record certain events that altered the course of history so dramatically. These interweaving, terrible incidents affecting major world powers throughout the globe, involved victims who were marred by this bloody, three year *forgotten* conflict.

It is my earnest hope that this narrative will cast a degree of enlightenment relative to the cause and effect of this terrible, ill-conceived armed conflict. Those young, deceased United Nations soldiers, whose hallowed skeletal remains lie abandoned on the battlefields of North Korea, buried by the sands of time, deserve nothing less.

Many major leaders of modern history were involved in this terrible carnage on opposing sides to some degree or another. The footprints of Truman, MacArthur, Stalin, Mao Tse-tung, Kim Il-sung and many others altered the course of history then, as now.

It was my intent to place the record of these episodes in perspective by putting a chronological history of events prior to the war at the beginning of this publication. It is that order of events that propelled the United States of America into this tragic armed conflict. A political autopsy is necessary to ascertain why the world's mightiest nation chose to engage in armed conflict in a primitive, diminutive Asiatic country of which the majority of Americans had never heard.

The past is prologue. The tactical and political errors made in the Korean War became the catalyst to compel the United States to rush to judgment and to repeat the same dreadful errors in the Vietnam War, a conflict that our country became inextricably tied to by virtue of failing to gain the victory of the unification of Korea. An understanding of these particulars is crucial to the future curtailment of these misguided adventures, and to that end, it is my fervent aspiration that I have provided adequate data to bring to question America's controversial foreign policy.

As mentioned, my plan was to begin with the history and the cause of the conflict; but alas, I have been overruled by more scholarly minds than mine. It has been explained to me that the publication should open first with the *memoir*, rather than the military history. Therefore, the chapters in the book relative to the Truman/MacArthur incongruity and history have been relegated to the conclusion of the book rather than at the beginning. The reader will decide in which order to read the two parts, and which is the duller of the two segments.

For purposes of clarity, I have taken the liberty of omitting the many punctuation marks so common to the Korean Language. As an example, *P'yong-song* simply becomes Pyongsong. The exception to this usage will be when I quote an author verbatim.

As to quotations—the author makes frequent use of direct quotations of many authorities for purposes of clarification and validation. I have been informed that this usage may cause a distraction, but since the quotations are an integral component of a given passage, I judge them to be consequential, and I apologize for any disruption. At the same time, it is my view that references from these authors can illustrate a point by way of their flair for writing that I lack. I ask for your indulgence.

Additionally, I have kept certain Asian names as they were spelled during this time period. *Mao Zedong*, for example, is *Mao Tse-tung*. The latter form of spelling and pronouncements is understood as the Wade-Giles system, which is generally considered passé today, while *Mao Zedong* is the accepted form of the contemporary Pinyin system. Again, the exception to this principle will be when I quote an author directly.

Through research, I have discovered some disagreement among various authors in respect to specific issues. As an example, I noted several conflicting accounts as to who commanded the Chinese Communist Forces in Korea. For clarification, I defer to contemporary authors who, with the passage of time, were able to review documents and interview adversaries directly involved in the conflict.

This is not to discount these earlier authors. Indeed, they researched and recorded admirably, given the closed society with which they had to deal. In fact, our government was likewise baffled, during this period, by these same mysterious chains of events that not only escalated the conflict, but nearly inexorably propelled the world into World War III.

But, this is for the most part, my narrative. It is the only one I have. And, it is a true story.

Paul G. Petredis

ACKNOWLEDGMENTS

In addition to Janice Stevens, there are a myriad of gracious people who have contributed greatly to the advancement of this essay. Sharon Deter, my Northwest editor, took the reins subsequent to my relocation to delightful Gig Harbor, Washington. I had the pleasure of meeting Sharon at an informal writers' group in the community. Sharon, as well as all of the members, patiently listened, and offered direction, suggestions and encouragement in response to various passages I read aloud to the group. When I inquired as to whether any had an interest in assisting me in the editing process, Mrs. Deter showed by her words "I would consider it an honor and for me it would be a labor of love" that she truly is a lady of her word.

She formatted the text to page size, indexed, edited, inserted maps and photos and most of all devoted many tedious hours revising the author's stilted writing.

Judy Courtwright spent days on end correcting a *faux pas* that only an inexperienced computer user could formulate. The writer was erroneously advised to utilize *save as* during the composition of the manuscript, which ultimately led to a gargantuan problem of having multiple chapters of duplicated work. Working over 18 hours a day, Judy successfully eliminated duplication of passages to present a readable form.

I am grateful to Gail Williams of Clovis, California, a close friend and confidante, who devoted many hours to editing and was gracious enough to direct me into the self-editing process.

My thanks also go to Allen and Cindy Davis for their encouragement and direction. Allen was kind enough to volunteer to take a contemporary photo of me. My lifelong friend from grammar school days, Dick Barrymore, who successfully authored two books, gave me encouragement and direction toward my endeavor. Hyunsook (Anna) Lee called upon her Korean background to translate the dedication.

Lastly I wish to gratefully acknowledge the input from the few survivors of Baker/King Company who came forth with graphic descriptions of their experiences in this war. I humbly have inserted correspondence of their individual heroic actions, which in fact further illustrate the horrors of this conflict.

POW ESCAPEES

American prisoners were marched to the death camps of North Korea, sited near the Manchurian border; there is no record of any escapes. Those who *escaped* did so by starvation, frostbite and/or torture. when bodies were unceremoniously discarded on the b*urial pile*, the ground too frozen to excavate graves.

United States military recognized one other American soldier by the name of Townsend, captured on 12 February 1951 who successfully escaped from Chinese captors and returned safely to military control on 26 May 1951.

First Lieutenant Alexander G. Makarounis, company commander of Ida Company, 29th Infantry Regiment, was captured at the disaster of Hadong, 27 July 1950. He and two other American POWs escaped in the vicinity of the North Korean capitol, Pyongyang, during October, when the din of approaching American artillery was heard in the distance. The prisoners had been housed in an abandoned schoolhouse for the night, during one leg of their forced march to prison camps in the north. Once they escaped, they fled to nearby mountains to await the arrival of UN troops.

The author petitioned the Department of Defense, POW/Missing Personnel Office in the hope of ascertaining if other American soldiers were as fortunate to escape. As of this writing, there is no official report of any successful escapees other than the author during the initial Communist Chinese offensive.

Editor's note:

Writers Gig of Gig Harbor welcomed Paul Petredis in 2003. The first time he came to one of our meetings, he explained he had written a book about his Korean War experiences. His anxiety showed when we asked him to read a selection aloud, but we insisted and he obliged. Within a few pages, he nervously was apologizing for his display of emotion—he was shaken and tearful. The reading of the passage he selected obviously brought back intense feelings. Within a year, as Paul continued to read from his memoir, we noticed he was becoming more comfortable.

"I wrote this to effect a catharsis," he said. The horrific trials he and his fellow soldiers endured obviously had darkened his days and brought torment to his dreams. Nowadays Paul seems more comfortable in his skin than when first he began soliciting our advice on how to rework his book.

While helping get the text ready, I have tried to keep the sound of Paul's voice in my mind. When talking to us in our meetings, or on the phone, he uses a voluminous vocabulary and occasionally convoluted sentences. He writes just as he speaks. He can be wickedly funny, and I think that wryness shows through occasionally in his writing.

Trauma from the war has scrambled the timeline of some of Paul's wartime memories; he has tried to retrieve erased names and hidden place names. He has scrabbled painfully through his memory and persevered to bring us a gripping account.

Sharon Duane Deter

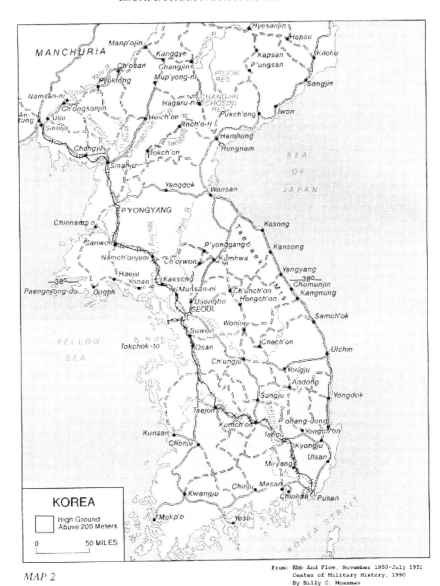

Map of Korea
Map from http://www.army.mil/cmh-pg/books/maps.html

CHRONOLOGY
From 25 June 1950 to 12 December 1950

25 June	North Korea invades South Korea. United Nations Security Council meets in emergency session; calls for end of aggression.
27 June	UN requests member nations to go to aid of South Korea.
28 June	Seoul, capitol of South Korea, captured by North Korean People's Army.
30 June	President Truman orders American ground forces to South Korea.
5 July	Task Force Smith, first United States Infantry unit deployed to South Korea.
7 July	UN authorizes General MacArthur as UN Commander, appointed by President Truman.
24 July	Two-battalion 29th Infantry Regiment lands in South Korea.
27 July	First Battalion 29th Infantry Regiment annihilated at Anui. Third Battalion destroyed at Hadong.
3 August	Twenty-ninth Infantry Regiment at battle of Chinju Pass.
4 August	Pusan Perimeter established in southeastern South Korea.
4 August to 18 September	Heaviest battles of war. Defensive Pusan Perimeter holds.
3 September	B Company, 29th Regiment holds against heavy attack. Awarded first company level Presidential Unit Citation.
6 September	Survivors of 1st Battalion 29th Regiment assimilated into 35th Regiment, and 3rd Battalion to the 27th Regiment, both components of 25th Infantry Division.
15 September	MacArthur lands UN forces at Inchon Harbor.
18 September	UN forces break out of Pusan Perimeter.
26 September	Seoul recaptured by UN forces.
29 September	President Rhee orders Republic of Korea units into North Korea.
9 October	First UN forces cross into North Korea.
12 October	First contingent of Chinese Communist forces enter North Korea.
15 October	Truman and MacArthur meet at Wake Island.
19 October	North Korean capitol, Pyongyang, captured by UN forces.

25 October	Chinese Communist Forces destroys three ROK Divisions.
26 October	X Corps lands at Wonson Harbor.
1-4 November	CCF ambushes US 1st Cavalry Division at Unsan. Eighth Cavalry Regiment effectively destroyed.
24 November	MacArthur orders all UN forces to advance to Yalu River.
9-26 November	X Corps advances toward Yalu River in east, 8th Army in west.
26 November	CCF strikes 8th Army along entire front.
26 November	Second and 25th Divisions defeated at Chongchon River. Total retreat commences.
27 November	CCF attacks US 1st Marine Division and Army 7th Division at Chosin Reservoir.
27 November	CCF attacks and surrounds 35th Regiment.
27 November	X Corps retreats to Hungnam. First Marines break out of Koto-ri.
28 November	Two-thirds of King Company killed or captured. Remainder of company escapes but with heavy losses.
12 December	Author returns to military control. Last of UN forces abandon all of North Korea.
22 December	General Walker killed, replaced by General Ridgway.
24 December	Author air-evacuated to hospital in US.

PRELUDE TO DISASTER

> So ended the second week of American ground combat in Korea. The NKPA had gained another twenty-five air miles (from the Kum River to Okchon) making the total gain for the two weeks seventy-five air miles. Yet another American Regiment, the 19th, had been chewed to pieces; the 34th Infantry had been mauled for the third time - this time decisively. The loss of 24th Division equipment over the two weeks, according to the Army historian was sufficient to equip a full American Division. The loss included a total of thirty-one 105-mm howitzers and five 155-mm howitzers. Blair, p. 141.

When I was eighteen, I killed a man, a living, breathing human being. And more than one. The blood won't go away. It just won't go away. After 50 years it is still there. Same for scars on the mind. They never go away either. Try as I might, the blood doesn't wash away, nor have the demons left my mind.

I was caught up in the Korean War, a phase of history now known as The Forgotten War. The adventure began on 27 July 1950.

~~

Our under strength, two-battalion, 29th Infantry Regiment had just stepped off the commandeered, rickety Japanese ship onto Pusan, South Korea's major seaport. We believed we were going to be thrown on the front lines at any moment.

"Hey, Sarge, I could use some help." The supply sergeant had just issued brand new M-1 Garand Rifles after we were ordered to scrap the ones we carried from Okinawa. Troops stood in line, single column, and unceremoniously discarded the rifles in a heap as they were marched past the trash pile. No one understood the rationale for it. My previous rifle was well used and not subject to jamming because the parts were worn smooth enough to work effectively. If the weapon became dirty, I was confident that it would perform, even though I had never fired my issued rifle.

"What's your problem, soldier?" he sneered sarcastically.

"I need a replacement M-1. A field cleaning tip is jammed in the barrel of my rifle because of the Cosmoline."

"Don't sweat it. The first round will clear the barrel."

"But. . . ." I protested.

"You heard me, soldier! Now, get out of my face. I got other things to worry about."

"But, Sergeant…" I lamented.

"You heard me the first time! Now get the fuck out of here!"

The M-1 rifles, new and covered with Cosmoline, a heavy, loathsome grease used to protect the weapon from rust, required an all-day task to make the weapon operable. There wasn't any solvent available to penetrate the grease, just rags and hours of tedious work. There were arguments over the few cleaning rods available.[1]

There were five cleaning rods dispensed and 235 soldiers fighting over them. As soon as one recruit slid the rod down the barrel, the rod was wrested from the user by another soldier. From the process of using the rigid aluminum cleaning rod, soldiers moved to the field cleaning rod, stored in a small compartment in the butt of the rifle. It contained the same tip as the rigid rod, but the field cleaning device was equipped with twine in place of the rigid aluminum rod. One inserts the line from the end of the barrel into the opened chamber, attaches a cotton cleaning patch through the slot in the aluminum tip, and pulls upward and out, capturing any residue Cosmoline, making the weapon safe to fire. That was the theory. The aluminum tip, with cloth patch attached, had broken the cord and remained stuck in the barrel of my rifle, rendering it into a lethal pipe bomb. I was going to be sent to battle with something inferior to no weapon at all.

I intended to grab one of the discarded rifles, but the temporary supply sergeant was watching, and I could sense his censure.[2] That's how the peacetime Army was then. No training. No consideration.

Following issuance of weapons, we marched to an abandoned high school in Pusan, as a United States Army marching band welcomed our unit to *The Land of the Morning Calm*. Once in the school yard, we were oriented as to the present military situation by young second lieutenants,

---

[1] These two battalions had come from the 29th Infantry Regiment on Okinawa. Until alerted for movement on July 5, both units were at half strength (about 500 men each) and had received no field training other than simulated deployment to protect the Strategic Air Command (SAC) on Okinawa. Both had brand-new commanders with no prior combat experience. Blair, pp. 165-166.

[2] More than a half century later, I learned that the usual supply sergeant had been sent ahead to our destination, the Chinju school house, which was an overnight stop on the way to the front. He was the well-respected Sergeant Edward E. Roslof. Sergeant Roslof, son of White Russians, whose parents fled Russia during the Bolshevik Revolution, barely escaping the charging Red Army. Roslof's family immigrated to the United States. Edward enlisted in the United States Army, having developed into a staunch and ferociously loyal American as a result of his parent's fearful experiences in totalitarian Communist Russia.

Roslof surrendered his comfortable, secure supply sergeant position in Pusan, turning the responsibility and coordination over to the sergeant who had refused to exchange my rifle. Author.

just two or three years older than most of us. The lieutenants were bombastic tyrants when we were stationed in Okinawa. Now they unexpectedly became humane and friendly. Troops were informed that this armed conflict was little more than a native uprising and that as soon as American troops were deployed, the invaders would retreat in fear, back to North Korea. The enemy would not dare challenge the might of the United States Army. We wondered if we were being told the whole story. No one informed us of the tragic results of *Task Force Smith,* an undermanned, poorly-equipped unit that held out against overwhelming odds and then had been overrun by NKPA.

Some noticed one little item of interest. The four lieutenant-grade officers removed their shoulder-holstered Army 45-caliber pistols and donated them to their platoon sergeants. It was learned later that enemy guerrillas would single out and fire upon those carrying pistols, knowing them to be officers.

Many of the soldiers had been seasick on the voyage from Okinawa to Korea, causing the majority of company personnel to turn in early, though the orders were to be ready to move to the front at dawn. It seemed that we had no sooner closed our eyes, than the thunderous resonance of shouting from many voices suddenly awakened us.

Company assignees were ordered to fall in on the double in formation on the school yard for roll call. Once that exercise was summarily accomplished, someone shouted:

"All present and accounted for, Sir!"

It was a platoon leader who thundered to company commander Lieutenant John C. Hughes, who in turn passed an order down the ranks. In time, a sergeant implemented the order by shouting:

"Saddle up!"

Followed by:

"Load Up!"

Troops scrambled hastily aboard general-purpose trucks. There were approximately ten of the vehicles, referred to colloquially as deuce-and-a-halfs, based upon the maximum load capacity (two and one-half tons). The drivers must have been selected for their degree of sadism. I had ridden in a cab of a truck in Okinawa whose driver demonstrated to me how he purposely aimed for every rut, every pothole in the road just to anger the riders.

The regiment was scheduled to be transported at dawn on the first leg of a journey to a city identified as Chinju, where the 29th Infantry Regiment would separate into two battalions for their first assignment.³

The convoy motored north from Pusan Harbor where asphalt and oiled dirt roads abruptly terminated at the edge of the city. From then on, the vile, filthy dust from the dirt road started to churn and cascade from the wheels of every truck, depositing heavy layers of obnoxious grime, coating passengers. Each subsequent driver punched a hole through the enveloping, heavy wall of silt thrown up by the preceding vehicle, hoping the one ahead would not slow or stop because of limited visibility churned by the filthy dirt.

It was a miserable two-hour ride made worse by oversized field packs strapped to our backs. Initially we attempted to sit, but gradually, more and more troops elected to stand to ease the discomfort. Eventually all were standing rigidly, unable to move because of the heavy, bloated packs. Even with the semi-portable benches raised, there was insufficient room to move. The choking clouds of dust continued, but the punishing blows of the potholes were more easily absorbed, because the erratic jolts through our legs were absorbed by our knees as we stood. We wanted to rinse parched mouths with water from canteens, but were unable to retrieve them because of extreme overcrowding.

What seemed to be a lifetime later, the transports arrived at the destination, another abandoned schoolhouse in the center of this town called Chinju. We were to spend the second night here in this squalid school house, similar to the one in the port city of Pusan.

Trucks rolled to the ancient school yard at Chinju and screeched abruptly to a lurching stop, spitefully challenging the resultant clouds of choking road dust.

"Everybody off! Into the yard and line up by company! First Battalion on the left, 3rd Battalion on the right! Let's go! Now! Now! Now!"

There was a mad scramble to comply. Young troops leaped from trucks and poured through the wide-gated portal of the school, searching frantically for fellow members of nine-man squads, and then for associates of the 43-man platoons.

"A company line up here! B Company, over here!"

As authoritative voices shouted, others took up the call. Soldiers

---

³ The 29th Infantry Regiment, as all units in the United States military at the time, was approximately half strength due to draconian budget cuts, particularly to military expenditures following Word War II. As a result, the 2nd Battalion of the regiment was cannibalized of personnel and reassigned to the 1st and 3rd Battalions. These two battalions, augmented by 400 new personnel who arrived the night before, were dispatched to the war zone as a two-battalion regiment. Author.

formed by squads first.

"First platoon, Baker Company here!"

The squad leader held his right arm high. Baker Company fell in formation rapidly, as did the two battalions. Once the battalions lined into precision formation, just as they performed in garrison life, each company commander sounded off to the two implacable, stiff-faced battalion commanders, standing tall in front of their respective battalions:

"A Company all present and accounted for, Sir!"

"B Company all present and accounted for, Sir!"

And so it went down the line. The 1st and 3rd Battalion commanders returned salutes from respective company commanders, simultaneously turning a smart about face, followed immediately with right-hand salutes to the regimental commander Colonel Wilson, and in numerical order, each battalion commander shouted:

"First Battalion all present and accounted for, Sir! Third Battalion all present and accounted for, Sir!"

All this was historic tradition. The entire drill had been accomplished in about two minutes. Recruits were subjected to hours and hours of practice during basic training. The purpose was to instill discipline, coordination and cooperation among the troops. Recruits could have been exposed to combat training at the same time, but who ever opined that our country would be returning to a war footing in five short years? It was the date of infamy for the Republic of Korea when the NKPA smashed across the de facto border, the intractable, 38th Parallel on 25 June 1950.[4]

"Remove field packs!" shouted Regimental Commander Wilson. Respective company commanders, in turn, ordered their platoons to remove packs. The awkward, cumbersome, heavy packs, now appreciatively removed, were placed on the school yard ground in front of each individual. Each squad leader, positioned at the end of each row, aligned each pack by eye, directing soldiers, one at a time, by hand motion, to move the pack until the packs' formation was properly straight.

There was a purpose for this apparently insignificant military tradition. When units returned from this minor skirmish in the so-called native uprising, it would take less time to repeat this drill and every man would automatically stand at attention in front of his individual equipment.

---

[4] The date of the North Korean invasion was, coincidentally, 74 years to the day that General George A. Custer (1839/1876) was slain as were those of the 7th Cavalry troop at his side at the Battle of Little Big Horn during the Anti-Lakota Expedition. Author

The order came to fall out, with the rest of the afternoon designated as leisure. Once inside the school house, some new recruits opened C-Rations and sampled them for the first time. Others knew what they were like and were revolted by them.[5]

The evening, quietly spent in the schoolhouse, was devoted to writing letters to families and friends back home. The young soldiers were too young to drink, vote, or be married, but they were judged sufficiently mature enough to die.

Baker Company was aroused at dawn, again without eating, and ordered into roaring trucks, troops having no concept of where they were heading. Trucks jerked forcefully forward as if they were energetic beasts of burden anxiously straining at tethers to proceed. There was a sense of urgency, reminiscent of movies of the Battle of the Bulge, when reinforcements were haphazardly and speedily rushed to the front in desperate confusion.

The convoy motored forward at deliberate speed, the rolling fleet appearing to be heading in a northwest direction. Later, we learned the objective was to be a village known as Anui, approximately 35 miles northwest of Chinju. The 3rd Battalion would be dispatched to near a town called Hadong, due west of Anui, and 1st Battalion would set up close to the town. The two battalions were to return to Chinju, subsequent to completing the insignificant mission. The regimental support group remained at the schoolhouse. Cooks, supply, medical and others were left behind at Chinju, to be called upon as needed.

The countryside flew rapidly by as apprehensive soldiers watched from speeding trucks. We noted abandoned rice fields, one after another, interspersed occasionally by a small village. The regiment was now an integral component of a great civil war in a poor, miserable country that had literally no assets worth the blood being spilled.[6]

---

[5] While we were stationed in occupied Okinawa, the principal objective was security of various military facilities, equipment and supplies. A devastating typhoon, designated Gloria, razed the island prior to my posting, resulting in the loss of most buildings, which now required huge tarpaulins to protect military supplies. Okinawa inhabitants stealthily entered the restricted area and broke into cases of C-Rations. Posted American sentries, out of curiosity, sampled contents from broken cases. Author.

[6] When World War II began, Korea was regarded by the Allies as a victim of, not a party to, Japanese aggression. One of the earliest signs that the Allied Powers were concerned about Korea appeared in a Joint statement by the United States, China, and Great Britain in December 1943, after the Cairo Conference, which said: The aforesaid three great powers, mindful of the enslavement of the people of Korea, are determined that in due course Korea shall become free and independent." Dept. of State, p.448.

Two autocratic dictators vied for complete power over this miserable, politically-divided peninsula while hundreds of thousands of innocent people trapped in the middle were being slain. And the people? Troops were struck by the absence of people. By now Koreans had a sense the war would personally spread to them, and they fled in terror. Our unit's task was to try to stem the tide of barbarian invaders from the north.

The protracted convoy crossed a green-painted trestle bridge spanning a vast, deep, narrow gorge. Primitive houses were sited near a meandering river that from the great distance appeared to be little more than a rivulet. The countryside was lush with native vegetation and immaculate, terraced hills where crops were growing from ancient, patchwork fields carved and leveled from the mountain sides. The greenness was different than the mile after mile of monotonous, fallow rice fields. No one had the slightest notion that by the end of this day these same banal fields would spring alive and have such a terrible effect on our future.

Shortly thereafter, the convoy braked in such an abrupt manner that the sudden stop threw riders off balance, slamming occupants forward in one mass to the cab of the transport.

"God damn it! Where did you get a driver's license, Sears and Roebuck?" someone shouted angrily. A loud chorus of demeaning shouts rose from occupants of the trucks in support of the initial protester, cursing the poor driving ability of the driver. Nerves were frayed.

"Disembark!" someone screamed, and I thought, wouldn't it be just as easy to say "Get off."

The disgorged trucks hurriedly turned to the right at a crude intersection, quickly reversed, and rushed headlong in the direction whence they came. It was clear that the drivers wanted no part of a probable forthcoming melée.

"What's happening, sergeant?"

The sergeant was Willie Musselwhite of Baker Company, normally a gentle, smiling, soft-spoken man who served in the Pacific Theater during World War II, and who remained during the occupation of Japan. Musselwhite was handsome, short, dark and genuinely liked by everyone. Sergeant Musselwhite responded, "You know about as much as me. I just follow orders. All I know is that we are going to relieve the 19th." (19th Infantry Regiment of the 24th Infantry Division)

"Where are they?"

"How the hell do I know? Do I look like a God-damned Gypsy fortuneteller?" Musselwhite responded sarcastically. He had reached his limit of patience, obviously concerned about what might transpire very shortly. The others were too inexperienced to appreciate what might happen. Sergeant Musselwhite was a gregarious person, but by his strong words he was clearly emphatic that he didn't want to hear any more questions. The sergeant was in his own world. Sergeant Musselwhite was impatient, but at least he didn't put me in harm's way by denying me a simple cleaning rod to clear my rifle barrel.

It must have been midmorning as we lingered around this ancient dirt intersection. Loose-knit groups of inexperienced soldiers ambled forth in clusters of two or more, standing idly about, smoking. Having had nothing to eat since mounting the trucks hours before, the need for sustenance grew. The sun was high in the cloudless sky, and the weather turned from warm to unbearably hot and humid.

About two hours had passed without any orders. Soldiers fatigued from standing gradually sat by the side of the road, continuously smoking to quell appetites while attempting to be nonchalant, but in unspoken nervousness as to what the immediate future would bring.

Approximately at noon, someone shouted excitedly, "Hey! Here comes somebody down the road!"

Idle soldiers leaped up to stare at the road north near the subtle horizon, and the outline of a person was discerned slowly walking south toward the unit. Eventually, the figure loomed larger and larger until he became recognizable a few hundred yards away from the intersection as an American soldier.

The warrior was a ragged, unkempt, teen-aged Mexican-American, carrying his M-1 rifle, and brandishing a week's growth of beard. His helmet was missing as well as his ammo belt. His deep-set eyes betrayed a terror despite his machismo facade. Someone anxiously asked him, "Are you from the 19th?"

"Man, I AM the 19th," he replied with mock bravado. Clearly the trooper was in deep shock, chuckling mockingly, perhaps more for himself than for the rest of the group who, to a person, were in wide-eyed awe.[7]

"Anybody got a cig?" he asked nonchalantly.

One soldier from the 29th pulled out two Camel cigarettes from his pack, placed both between his lips, lit them and passed one to the survi-

---

[7] On the following day, July 20, the NKPA 3rd and 4th divisions encircled, overran, and utterly shattered the American infantry standing before Taejon. In effect, the 34th Infantry and McGrail's attached 2/19 ceased to exist as organized fighting units. The battalions flew apart; little groups of soldiers fought incohesive and desperate battles to escape the trap. Blair, p. 135.

vor, a common gesture of friendship among soldiers.

"Thanks, man."

"What happened?" someone inquired timidly. It seemed more of a plea than a question.

"Man, those gooks went through us like shit through a goose! They are some tough mother-fuckers!"

He blew a smoke ring, watched it waft in the air and dragged on the cigarette again, exhaling fumes, smiling an oily, artificial, forced smile.

"We heard in Okinawa that they had a couple of rifles but mostly spears, and they weren't very organized, just a bunch of rebel gooks," one of the group mouthed plaintively.

"Spears, huh! Try tanks, man. Huge mother fuckin', T-34 Russian tanks. Big as houses and nothin' stops them. Our chicken shit bazookas bounce right off."

I looked around our group and noticed that we were all wide-eyed and stunned. The Army never told us the truth when they obviously knew what was really happening. Soon, it would be our turn. But more importantly, we were lied to.

The wandering soldier finished his cigarette and field stripped it (shredding the butt of the cigarette) as if he were still posted in Japan. It was one of the few rules of the Occupation. Shredding the cigarette eliminated an unsightly cigarette butt normally tossed carelessly on the ground. Habits are hard to break.

"See ya."

And with that the straggler continued his solitary walk down the road, to who knows where? The group stood quietly in open mouth disbelief, watching him in his battle-shock mode, meandering unconcernedly down the road without purpose. No one said anything.

Little did we know what was in store for the unit. It was our turn next.

ANUI

> Half a league, half a league
> Half a league onward,
> All in the valley of Death
> Rode the six hundred.
> Cannon to right of them
> Cannon to left of them
> Cannon behind them
> Volleyed and thundered.
> Into the jaws of Death,
> Into the mouth of hell
> Rode the six hundred.
> Charge of the Light Brigade, 1854
> Alfred Lord Tennyson

Past noon after the solitary soldier wandered off, someone shouted, "Baker Company, fall in!"

Able Company was left to guard the road. None in Baker Company knew the whereabouts of C and D companies until later when it was assumed both companies were held in temporary reserve at the rear of this village. Four companies comprised the 1st Battalion. Lieutenant Hughes, our company commander, marched 235 of us into a village called Anui, about two and a half miles east of where the T-section road joined the main highway. Hadong, the sector where the 3rd Battalion was dispatched, was west.

Meanwhile, Able Company was given the objective to defend the main highway north from encroachment. They were placed near where the battalion was dropped off. Ken Moats, assigned to Able Company, related in essence that two American jeeps armed with soldiers were dispatched north on a jeep reconnaissance mission in a desperate attempt to discover the location of the main body of enemy troops of the dreaded North Korean 6th Division. Later in the day, according to Moats, a jeep was sighted heading back (south) at a high rate of speed.

"Hold fire!" someone shouted, "It's one of ours!"

It was not. It was a contemporary Russian-made jeep driven by a grim-faced North Korean soldier and an equally implacable-looking passenger who also was an NKPA soldier. The jeep suddenly swerved in front of the American guard unit, churned up the dust, making a sliding U turn, the centrifugal force rolling two American teenage soldiers from the jeep onto the dirt road. The North Korean Army driver and his escort drove back north at the same high rate of speed.

The young American victims were dead, hands tied behind them with commo (communications) wire, and shirtless. They died of insidious torture—countless minute slashes to every portion of their upper bodies, inflicted by a razor blade or other sharp instrument. The nipples of each man had been sliced off. The other missing soldiers and the two jeeps were never found. That was the type of enemy young, untrained American soldiers were to face.

~~

Baker Company moved forward toward an unnamed objective. It was difficult going because most were laden with extra loads of heavy cans of 30-caliber machine gun ammunition carried from Okinawa. Surplus from World War II, it had been used to successfully capture the fortified island in 1945, and now it would be put to good use in Korea.

Once in the center of the village, Lieutenant Hughes halted, and barked, "Break ranks!"

Troops shuffled nervously around him to listen, most lighting cigarettes, as Hughes solemnly instructed us to do our duty and to hold firm; but the Lieutenant spoke in vague terms because he apparently didn't understand what we were to encounter, or really, what our objective was. Then Hughes called on Sergeant Pappert, who was known to all as *Sergeant Pappy*. Lieutenant Hughes singled out the sergeant to reinforce what he had just articulated. The company personnel wondered silently and anxiously why Sergeant Pappy was hesitant to respond to the oration. His reaction was just the opposite of what Hughes had wanted. Pappy shook his head ever so deliberately from side to side slowly, and then he uttered soberly, "I don't know, Skipper, this may be awfully big," meaning obviously, the imminent mission might not be an effortless operation.

Lieutenant Hughes ignored Pappert's response; a barely perceivable scowl crossed his face as he stared at the outspoken sergeant. Then Hughes went about the business of separating the four-platoon company into two platoons each. "Platoons Three and Four, follow me. Lieutenant, take charge of platoons One and Two."

Lieutenant Hughes advanced the 3rd and 4th Platoons north, to embed a defensive position. Platoons One and Two were marched further east, under the direction of a lieutenant (name unknown), along with Sergeant Pappy. Shortly thereafter, we halted and were ordered to break ranks and fall out in the east sector of the village.

Sergeant Pappy wandered around inspecting the area of his responsibility before sitting on the ground with his back against the wall, in the shade of a dilapidated shanty in the village. He was obviously saving his strength for what was to come. An infantryman prior to World War II, he knew the terrible horror of battle that is impossible to convey to anyone, particularly to immature rookies.

Thirty-six years old, Pappy appeared to be 50. That is what close-up war does to a man. He had a permanent limp, and was equipped with a walking cane. His physical impairment was a result of a severe leg wound from ground combat in World War II. The Army permitted him to continue to serve, provided the sergeant did not apply for service-connected compensation for his disability.

He was always Sergeant Pappy to us, while the generic title, *The Old Man*, was reserved for Lieutenant Hughes, and every other company commander. Lieutenant Hughes was only 28 years old at the time, though he was a veteran infantryman of World War II. Actually, Hughes held the permanent rank of 1st lieutenant during his assignment in Okinawa. Because of the rush to downsize the armed forces immediately following the war, he continued as an acting captain during the last five years. Once again, the outlandish budget reductions, following the conclusion of World War II, ruled supreme.

Hughes, like Pappy, was short—perhaps five feet, five inches—but strong and a very mature, tough soldier. A handsome, clean-cut man, the skipper wore a neatly-trimmed mustache, probably to appear older than his 28 years. He was always smoking a pipe. He had light brown hair, kept trimmed neat and close, as was the tradition of the infantry. Lieutenant Hughes, now deceased, holds the distinction of being the most decorated soldier in the 100-plus years' history of the 29th Infantry Regiment.

The notoriously brutal North Korean 6th Infantry Division was on a blitzkrieg, having steamrolled over the important rail junction of Taejon, situated in the north central section of South Korea. A town named Osan, north of Taejon, the site of the initial armed clash between both armies, was quickly conquered by the NKPA. The defending unit, Task Force Smith, reeled in retreat from the crushing enemy attacks in defense of Taejon.

From that juncture, the enemy raced south into Kwanju, near the west coast, where the enemy division separated into three components; Regiments 13th, 14th and 15th. As individual units, they deployed widely, and massacred everyone who stood in their path. Upon successful completion of several key objectives in southwest Korea, the enemy regiments regrouped, united once again as the Sixth Division, and marched on Chinju, and thence to Masan. Elements of the 29th Regiment were blocking their way at Anui and Hadong, and they had to destroy our unit first.

~~

That was the essence of Baker Company—untrained and ill-equipped. There was not one hand grenade among the entire company, nor any to be had in the entire skeletal regiment. Rifle grenades? None. Ammunition? Each rifleman's individual ammunition belt contained about 80 paltry rounds, hastily issued to each man and not nearly sufficient to make a dent in staving off armies of natural-born killers, the 4th and 6th North Korean Army Divisions.

Out of profound boredom, three of us rummaged through a decrepit, abandoned house that had partially burned some time ago.

"I wouldn't be poking around in there, boys, if I were you. It might be booby trapped," Sergeant Pappy sniffed.

"Aw what does he know anyhow, he's just an old man," one whispered cockily under his breath. Nevertheless, we obeyed, and had left the shack when our attention was caught by a shout from someone on top of one of the hills, where a machine gun was recently emplaced.

"Hey, guys, bring the ammo (machine gun) up here. We need it now!"

We now had a purpose, so several began carrying the heavy metal cans of 30-caliber machine gun, belt form ammunition up the hill where a soldier had just placed the 1st Platoon's 30-caliber, air-cooled machine gun. The weapon was mounted to give a commanding field of fire over a panoramic vista, including the bridge we crossed over earlier.

The gunner, obviously inexperienced, was firing rounds erratically and nonstop. In his eagerness to test fire, he did not allow the barrel to cool by firing short bursts. The sustained, continuous firing of the rounds soon melted the rifling or what are called lands of the barrel, the purpose of which is to spin each projectile as it leaves the barrel. Unfortunately, there were no spare barrels, but what was really needed was someone who knew how to fire. Incendiary tracer rounds wafting through the air, soaring as if they were out of control butterflies, were an indisputable sign of an ineffectual barrel ruined by an ineffectual machine gunner.

A machine gun barrel, if one was miraculously to be had, could have been replaced by unscrewing the defective barrel from the body of the machine gun, and attaching the replacement in its place. Many were hoping that someone else would take the gunner's place because no one sensed the need to expend a complete belt of ammunition so quickly without a target after we had carried the ammunition so far. Better to wait for the enemy.

More than two dozen metal boxes of ammunition had been lugged to the summit of the hill where the machine gun emplacement was situated, enough to hold off an enemy division at short range for an extended time. One of the guys on the hill opened the first box of ammunition.

"Rotten! Worthless! Why in hell didn't somebody check this out before we brought it so far? The other cans better be OK, or we are in deep shit."

No one said a word.

Troops stared, mouths agape in disbelief, at the ruined, unusable ammunition. It was stored for so long in the humid, tropical jungle climate of Okinawa that it completely decomposed. The brilliant, shiny brass cartridges that at one time so proudly carried the iridescent, lustrous copper clad bullet on their path to destiny were now a dismal mass of muck. There was not even a slight green patina to the brass cartridges, but rather a heavy coat of corrosive slime. The black iron links that made up the belt of the ammunition long ago rusted away to powder and sifted to the bottom of the steel ammo boxes. Utterly worthless.

Ammo cans were frantically torn open in desperation and every box contained the same, gooey, slimy substance that once was ammunition. A future skirmish would be left to the 100 or so of us in our group, now alone with just rifles, and mine didn't count as one of them, having an obstructed barrel.

The backbreaking labor of ammo transport was for naught. The only usable belt was the original one that was with the machine gun, but that belt had been needlessly fired off. I was in hope of trading rifles with the machine gunner because the inexperienced operator would be occupied with the function of his automatic weapon. No luck. Baker Company was armed with only rifles for defense—frontier fighting at its most basic. We had no mortars, hand grenades or automatic weapons, and now we were pitted against the best-trained and best-equipped army in the world. While the soldiers had nothing of substance for comparison, they could never comprehend how an infantry unit could be so ill-equipped and ill-trained and be called upon to stop the surge of the formidable enemy.

The group of three wandered off the hill, dejected, and rejoined Sergeant Pappy, still sitting, conserving his strength. A glance at his unsmiling face reflected his concern, but none could relate to it, because there was no earlier exposure to the dread of armed conflict before. He was more resourceful than all others in the company melded together. Sergeant Pappy knew how to take charge of any situation no matter the predicament. I wanted to stick by him at all cost. Pappy would show everyone how to perform in battle.

At Pappy's suggestion we wandered about the ancient village, inspecting houses, not knowing what the late afternoon and night would bring. During this adventure, the residents of the village of Anui were mingling around and very friendly to us. The Americans were there to save them.

The ancient village was built on a gradual rise composed of numerous dilapidated houses sited one next to another, facing a footpath wandering in front of the shacks. The narrow trail in front of the houses meandered down to the base of the slope where it leveled off into flatland. Some spaces between the houses were fashioned into small plots of vegetable gardens, while the center part of the road was rocked and carried raw sewage down the hill, where somehow it diverted, to avoid being soaked on the ground where the dirt path abruptly vanished.

At the bottom of the hill loomed a huge wood and mud adobe-style building covered with a traditional Korean tule-thatched roof, surrounded on three sides by eight-to-ten feet high walls.[8] A huge opening between the walls in the front revealed a mammoth building inside, a schoolhouse. Beyond the building to the south, lay a wide field, no doubt a playground for young students and just beyond the playground, the ever-present crazy quilt patchwork of lush, green rice fields.

Luxurious emerald green mountains rose dramatically from the earth, forming the south mountain backdrop of this narrow valley, blending harmoniously with the green, serene, water-filled rice fields. An azure blue sky dappled with large cumulus clouds completed a near perfect picture postcard of serenity.

~~

Sometime around three in the afternoon, someone ordered an advance up the north mountain slope, opposite the mountains behind the schoolhouse, which was serenely nestled in a typical small valley between two mountain ranges. Unexpectedly, the friendly residents of the village of Anui quickly, silently and mysteriously vanished.

Once atop the hill, a group of our riflemen observed what appeared to

---

[8] Tule is a reed-like grass that grows in marshy areas. Author

be a South Korean farmer toiling in the fields east of our position. Believing him to be a spy or a North Korean soldier in disguise, acting as a lookout, they began shooting at him. The unfortunate individual began dancing in terrified, wild gyrations to avoid the enfilade of death, bullets swarming like angry hornets about him.

No one was ever instructed on whom to fire, and some lamentable tragedies might have been prevented had infantrymen been exposed to appropriate combat training. Those sent to the combat zone were just a bunch of frightened adolescents lacking direction.

The firing ceased when someone gave an order to dig in. None had ever dug a foxhole before, and there was no one to offer the slightest bit of advice on what to do, in respect to size, depth and so on. Sergeant Pappy was not in the immediate vicinity, so we simply sat on the south side of the hill, while unbeknownst to us the enemy was swarming up the north side of the hill.

I saw him first and I froze in terror. A chill ran up my spine as I witnessed up close and personal the very first enemy soldier I had ever seen. Standing on the skyline, displaying a menacing glare, he was looking right and left and down the hill for the Americans. We were no farther than seven feet from him, lying on stomachs. He would have to look at his boots to see us. His image is burnished in my mind forever. Short, perhaps five-foot four, stocky, and slightly bowlegged. Dark of skin with the fiercest stare I have ever seen. He was outfitted in the standard, mustard-green colored, North Korean army uniform with a field cap bearing the bright red star, symbol of Communism. His wide-set eyes were in search of American soldiers to kill, as he projected the embodiment of all that is evil.

His eyes mirrored a lust to kill everyone and his weapon empowered him to do just that. He was armed with an AK-47, an automatic submachine gun that spat death at the unbelievable rate of over 600 rounds per minute. Recipients of a burst from the gun wouldn't have time for a dying prayer at this close range.

I felt as if I was a child again at the Saturday matinee watching a World War II movie about the campaign in the Pacific Theater. This was real, so real that I couldn't speak because of my overwhelming fear. I nudged the guy who was lying next to me, and pointed to the enemy, who was so close that one could almost smell the traditional fermented cabbage, kimchi, on his breath. My ally fired a wild round at the enemy soldier, who, despite his nearness, was not struck, as the soldier hastily scurried to safety behind the north side of the hill.

All of a sudden the world seemed to come to an end, exploding in our faces. The main bridge we drove over earlier was blown to bits by the enemy, effectively isolating our company. We were now a gift to the NKPA. Gunfire and mortar fire erupted from the tranquil mountain behind the schoolhouse. It was an ambush—a very well thought out plan to kill all in a pincer movement. When the first enemy soldier appeared, it may have been a signal for the enemy soldiers deployed in the mountains south to commence firing.

Commence firing was apparently the order given to the North Korean 6th Division and fire they did. Rounds were stabbing, singing, and ricocheting among the two platoons, and there was nowhere to hide. Troops fled en masse, terrified, down the hill between the rickety shanties.

I was running behind a large group of young soldiers lagging a few feet, when suddenly from the corner of my left eye, I glimpsed a small burst of light. It emanated from a house just vacated by the South Korean owners.

Simultaneously, I felt the bullet smash into my body, tearing tissue near the left rib cage, ripping flesh and muscle before miraculously exiting through the left side of my back. The pain was minimal. Others who have been shot say the same thing. Little to no immediate pain. The excruciating burning of my body by the red-hot projectile was another matter entirely and so piercing. I know now how helpless cattle react to branding.

The force of the gunshot spun me around as it knocked me to the ground, where I fell into the raw sewage draining down the slope. It took no more than a second to digest the gravity of this matter. I had been shot and I had no notion of how I would be affected. I just as quickly recovered, for if I lingered, a second round would ring out, and the enemy would certainly be luckier with a second shot.

Rifle fire was screaming in from all directions, and no one knew where it was coming from, except when an occasional muzzle flash was sighted from the tranquil south mountain. The peaceful harmony and serenity of the mountain proved to be a façade.

I felt raw, unadulterated terror. My heart raced so rapidly I felt faint. I dove face first into the pepper patch in a garden, feigning death and praying to Almighty God that the rifle fire would cease. It didn't.

For the first time in my immature life I felt the ungodly sensation of out-of-control panic—an immense block of ice which was no less than paralyzing, frigid fear in my stomach, growing in proportion to the terror that was inflicted on me.

As I lay prostrate, I sensed an enormous rate of rifle fire tearing beside and over my body. The rounds were missing my body by inches, as I felt the dirt under my boots yield and surrender to the massive amount of lethal gun fire.

I wanted to leap up and run again for my life. Yet I continued to feign death, knowing that if I stirred ever so slightly, it would bring the wrath of their entire arsenal at me. I didn't know if they were tormenting me, or making sure that I was dead before they would opt to move in on the disorganized, incoherent soldiers. Still, despite my panicked state of mind, I had the presence not to move. More correctly, I was petrified by fear.

My head was turned away from the enemy, yet I clamped my eyes closed in dread in an abortive attempt to block out this horrendous nightmare. As I lay, my body rigid and unmoving, I ever so slowly and surreptitiously, reached for a nearby pepper from a small bush in the garden. I just had to extinguish the block of ice of terror that had invaded my stomach. With that, I ever so slowly put the entire unripe pepper in my mouth and bit down. Now, I confronted a dual problem. My mouth seemed to be on fire. The pepper burned so acutely, I could almost visualize awful scar tissue forming, as the flavor seared the taste buds of my tongue and mouth.

Now, I possessed a blistered mouth, while at the same time, the icy feeling of fear in my stomach continued to expand. My gunshot wound was the most trivial of my troubles. Despite a rapidly beating heart, I sensed no rattle or wheezing of my lungs and I seemed to breathe without impediment, albeit in gasps of naked fright. Good. I did not suffer a perforated lung. If I were to die, it would not be as a result of this minor flesh wound. There were so many other deadly gunshots now filling the quiet, sleepy village of Anui that fateful and terrible evening of 27 July 1950.

I dare not tarry. No one would save me. I had to save myself or die where I lay. I was down to the basic instinct of survival.

Could I scream for a corpsman? Not at all. The medics were still in the rear at Chinju, awaiting future orders. Fear motivates a mind to compute instant methods of relief, and I reacted in kind by fleeing for my life toward the would-be sanctuary of the school. Survival took precedence over a gunshot wound. I ran to catch up with my comrades.

In hindsight we wondered where the rest of the American Army was.[9]

---

[9] That same day July 27, Moore sent the other Okinawa battalion…toward Anui to replace Robert Rhea's 1/29, … The relief… was a shambles. Blair, p. 166.

Surely they wouldn't send teenagers to absolute slaughter, without dispatching reinforcements to save us. Where was the cavalry? Every western movie I ever saw, the United States Cavalry arrived at the last moment to save the beleaguered, out-manned and out-gunned settlers in their circled covered wagons. Our Army was the biggest and the best in the world, so where were the reinforcements?

THE SCHOOLHOUSE

The enemy troops that had closed on Anui were advanced units of the N. K. 4th Division. They were well aware that a mixed force of American and South Korean troops was only a few miles below them. To deal with this force, elements of the division turned south from Anui early on 28 July. Appleman, p. 224.

It was a prodigious slaughter. Soldiers were screaming and moaning as the red-hot shards of steel found living targets and drove mercilessly into bodies of boys wearing the uniforms of men.

Teenage soldiers were stumbling and collapsing by the score from scathing, unceasing gunfire. Bullets were pouring in from every direction, except from American rifles. No one could determine where the gunfire was coming from because the firepower seethed from everywhere. Enemy forces on the north mountain from whence we fled were now closing in to complete the pincer movement in concert with their brothers emplaced in the hills to the south of this very narrow, steep valley. Their mutual goal? To slay every American trapped within the net of the well-planned and well-executed ambush.

Nearly all of the panicky troops from the two fragmented platoons fled to the schoolyard, with the exception of a few who apparently sensed the danger of attempting to find protection there, and tried to hide the best they could in other places. Others sought shelter behind a primitive stone wall to the east of the besieged school. I caught up with the fleeing throng in the frenzied, hysterical run for the schoolyard.

Once inside the yard, terrified soldiers quickly discovered that the front entrance had two gigantic ancient wooden solid doors which when closed could be barred from the inside. There seemed to be no purpose, given the schoolyard lacked a gate and walls to the rear (south) near the school play field. Several frightened soldiers joined in closing the ancient creaking doors and securing them with a heavy wooden bar that crashed noisily into place, nesting in primeval iron fittings bolted to the gates.

Now, about 90 terrified soldiers were milling crazily about in the courtyard, bumping and jouncing wildly against one another like steers tightly confined to a small cattle slaughtering holding pen. Soldiers' eyes reflected wild fear; they were pushing against one another, crazed, confined beasts, harboring a deep sense of ominous foreboding. Suddenly, naked reality was brought to bear, soldiers realizing that they were hopelessly trapped. Nervous heads were dipping like out of control bobble dolls, on necks craning to see if there was a way over the towering wall, because escape by any other means was now impossible. Condemned troops painted themselves into an impossible, fatal corner.[10]

It was realized without comment we weren't safe at all. On the contrary. We foolishly trapped ourselves by imprudently seeking shelter in this primitive schoolyard, now metamorphosed into an inescapable prison. It would be only a matter of time when the North Korean Army would enter and kill, torture, or if we were at all fortunate, take prisoners. The latter hypothesis was very unlikely at best, and, even if it was true, the brutal treatment accorded to prisoners of the North Korean Army was unthinkable. Our fate was sealed.

Without warning, a shrill, piercing scream pulsated through the air when someone shrieked, *Grenade!*

A North Korean soldier tossed a fragmentation hand grenade over the approximately ten-foot high, white-washed adobe school wall into a group of trapped soldiers milling about nervously near the east wall. I was among them. Did we hit the ground to escape the bomb that in a brief moment would shatter into a thousand lethal pieces of shrapnel and kill innumerable young soldiers? No. Surrounded young Americans stared stupidly at the metal container of steel about to spew death, unable to react to the imminent danger. We were fixated and mesmerized. I saw it—a shiny gray-colored item with a torpedo type body. I couldn't study it further, because then it transformed into a deadly explosion, disintegrating into innumerable slivers of death in one thunderous, horrific roar.

The ground shuddered, uniting with the ear piercing blast, the mammoth explosion knocking adolescent soldiers down as if they were so many bowling pins. Few rose. Most could not. Blood and body parts were strewn everywhere. This was our baptism of fire by grenade. Those who survived, particularly me, would not be staring ignorantly at a lethal object like that again. Instead, we would instinctively dive to the relative shelter of the ground. I was fortunate not to be struck, luckily standing behind soldiers who absorbed the brunt of the violent detonation along

---

[10] Meanwhile at Anui, Lieutenant Hughes, B Company, 29th Infantry was under attack from superior numbers closing in on three sides, and by nightfall had been forced back into the town. Hughes made plans to withdraw across the upper Am River to a high hill east of the town. Two officers and sixteen men got across before enemy automatic fire cut off the rest. After vainly trying to help the rest of the company to break out eastward, the eighteen men went over the hills to the 34th Infantry position at Koch'ang. In Anui the cutoff troops engaged in street fighting until midnight. Those who escaped walked out through the hills during the next several days. Appleman, p. 224.

with the resultant lethal shrapnel.

Momentarily stunned, and temporarily deaf, I fell to the ground, then rose to the dissonant concert of acute ringing in my ears, a dreadful consequence of the violent, gigantic explosion and concussion. I slipped headlong into shock.

Many young men were pulverized by the deadly grenade. Pieces of pale, gray, grisly flesh adhered to the whitewashed wall, splattered in stark contrast to the bright crimson-colored blood. The air was choked with an ongoing choir of off-key screams and moans. When one moans, death is imminent, whereas casualties, who scream although seriously wounded, generally survive, provided they are evacuated to a medical facility in due course. There would be no evacuation from this hellhole, dead, alive, or wounded.

The 1st Sergeant lay prostrate on the ground and was dying before our eyes. Holding the highest non-commissioned rank of sergeant major, he was a very well-known, politically-connected man. Broad shouldered and built like a bull, he could vanquish anyone. He was a ferocious infantryman in World War II, where he earned his stripes the hard way, by being the toughest soldier in the company. He looked like a member of the Nazi Gestapo with his aloof bearing, and his steely-eyed glare, thin-rimmed eyeglasses and close-cropped, prematurely-gray hair. He was not generally admired because of his despotic and tyrannical ways. Soldiers were in awe and fear of him, and he bullied recruits unmercifully.

Still, he was believed to be immortal. In dying gasps, he begged someone, anyone, to shoot him to put him out of his misery. If he was dying, what about me and the others? What is the feeling of dying? Or death. Life was hemorrhaging from the Sergeant where he lay. The wall nearest him appeared as if someone splashed a bucket of red paint that coursed leisurely down the surface of the wall dripping lazily to the ground. But, of course, it wasn't paint. It was blood. The forbidding cloud of ominous smoke, when at last it dissipated, revealed the apocalyptic crater born of the missile.

Our hearts poured out to our Sergeant. Even though he was a bully and a tyrant, he was a brave soldier to the bitter end, and, he was in death throes. He was an honorable man to accept that which he dispensed. He pitifully begged no one in particular to put a bullet in his head before the North Koreans would take control. None could bring himself to do that despite the constant forlorn, weakened pleas of the Sergeant. He was not afraid to die, but he wanted to die on his terms, not at the hands of the atrociously brutal North Koreans, who lacked any capacity of civilized behavior.

Sergeant Riley Bruner walked up and picked up the Sergeant Major's damaged rifle, and my immediate conviction was that he was pointing the rifle at the dying sergeant's head.

"Oh, my God! He's going to kill him," I whispered in horrified shock.

Instead, Sergeant Bruner cradled the rifle on the 1st Sergeant's right shoulder, muzzle up, near the victim's chin with the trigger mechanism close to the sergeant's right hand. All the mortally wounded soldier had to do was move the muzzle under his chin, and squeeze the trigger. After Sergeant Bruner placed the M-1 rifle with the victim, he lit a cigarette, and placed it between the lips of the dying 1st Sergeant, as he whispered something to him that was out of our hearing.

Minutes later a loud report from an M-1 rifle resonated from the area where our wounded first sergeant lay. No one looked.

In the interim, the dreaded 6th Division of the NKPA apparently had determined the coordinates of the schoolhouse for their gun-sights, and they methodically proceeded to unleash heavy preparation mortar fire into the yard and the primitive thatched roof sheltering the schoolhouse.[11] They were softening us up. The rounds were hurtling in, but the murderous shrapnel was minimal, apart from the savage explosions on the grounds. The mortars striking the thatched roof of the schoolhouse buried themselves in the tule reed, which absorbed a great deal of the concussion and shrapnel of the explosions.

The stench of cordite and death hung heavily in the sticky, humid afternoon air without reprieve.

For some unknown reason the tule reed that made up the thatch did not burn readily, but smoldered throughout, making it impossible to extinguish. The fires were cancerous cysts, crawling ever so slowly, feasting on healthy tule in an ever widening, venomous expanse. The roof was burning in about eight different areas, the smoke emitting a toxic, odious smell, particularly as it filtered down from the roof into the building. No one was concerned about roof fires. There were far more pressing problems to address.

"What happened to Petredis?" someone asked, as I lay prostrate in terror on the dirt field, eyes clamped tightly shut to block out this horren-

---

[11] There is disagreement among authorities whether it was the 4th or 6th Division of the North Korean People's Army the UN forces were facing at this point. Author.

dous nightmare.

"Nothing, he's just scared."

"Aren't we all?" said Sergeant Bruner, casually and empathically, as he approached my quivering, supine body. With that, the sergeant nudged me in the rib cage gently with his boot, and said, "Get up, Pete; we have to figure out how to get out of this mess."

Riley muttered it so matter-of-factly, that I became deeply ashamed of my cowardice.[12] I couldn't believe that I could lose such control over myself, to the point that someone would notice, but I did, and it was Sergeant Bruner who noticed. I wanted to die a thousand deaths in shame that someone perceived I was so very terrified. Yet the sergeant was so understanding and empathetic that he transformed me into a soldier that day.

Sergeant Bruner, of American Indian descent, was tall, lanky, olive skinned and muscular, with coal black hair barbered in a crew cut. Dark and agile, he embodied the very essence of confidence, and he would be the one to accept the challenge to neutralize the present terrifying situation. I would follow him to the ends of the earth.

"OK, Sarge, what do you want me to do?" I asked, trying my best to exhibit some semblance of composure as I picked up a rifle lying near a dead young soldier.

"Hang tight, and we'll think of something."

~~

The torrid afternoon sun of over one hundred degrees of blast furnace heat faded ever so gradually to dusk, which in turn devolved into night without anyone noticing the darkened sky, because of our preoccupation with saving our lives. Sergeant Bruner darted into the main section of the schoolhouse through a large opening created by an open sliding shoji door. Three of us followed. We ran illogically from room to room in the schoolhouse, trying to find a safe haven from the lethal mortar fire. Enemy on the south edge of the mountain now, in concert with the mortars, raked the side of the school building with machine gun fire, from end to end and back again.

We prostrated ourselves on the wood floor trying to compress our bodies as flatly as possible to avoid the continuous, high-velocity rounds

---

[12] When Lieutenant Hughes returned to his company position, he attempted to withdraw but found two of his platoons had frozen in their foxholes and would not move. These were young men who had not been trained in advanced infantry combat conditioning. With the best NCO's having combat experience during World War II…this company was our most experienced and had the best combat-experienced leadership in the battalion. But this was not enough. Gamble, p. 89.

crashing just over our heads. The white-hot machine gun fire ripped through interior wood walls, tearing and shredding wood to bits like kindling. Large chunks of hardened, cement-like adobe spewed forth from the interior wall, crashing noisily to the floor, while on the outside, where the deadly rounds entered, only small holes were left as evidence of impact. It was the same for the bodies. Young kids slain by random shots through the exterior wall of the building displayed the same small penetration hole. The exit hole ripped flesh from bone in grisly fashion so that there was no way to save the wounded, unless they were as fortunate as I to receive a minor flesh wound that avoided vital organs.

Dust, smoke and bodies lay everywhere. The heavy, detestable stench of gunpowder wafted lazily in the hot, sticky, summer night air, while the smoldering roof resembled slow moving white hot lava, as fire ever so gradually crept in all directions, consuming the ancient thatched roof, and spitting noxious ash and dense smoke in the wake. Whenever the fire burned through the roof, clouds of foul smoke and fumes mingled with despicable dust in a macabre duel. The heat continued unabated, unbearable, stifling, humid, leaving us weak and our field uniforms sopping wet from perspiration.

~~

Outside of the school wall, just before sunset, survivors sought shelter against the medieval stone wall near the schoolhouse. The wall initially shielded them against the enemy who were now pouring fire down from the north hill against those trapped in the school. The terrified soldiers huddling behind the wall didn't realize until it was much too late that they were caught in an inescapably lethal crossfire from enemy in the south hills together with the enemy now firing from the ridge to the north, whence we originally fled.

A panicked new, young, inexperienced lieutenant hid behind the stone wall on the far right, involuntarily curled tightly in fetal position on the ground, cradling his rifle in his arms, rocking slowly to and fro, as he ever so softly whimpered, "Mama, help me... Mamma, please help me... Mamma, Mamma..."

A predestined enemy bullet ended his mournful plea, as others urinated in field trousers, a common wartime reaction to uncontrollable fear. Still others made unsuccessful panicky attempts to escape by darting for a safer haven elsewhere, but scores of enemy weapons firing in regimented unison cut them down. There were no safe havens.

~~

A survivor of those 20 or so soldiers hiding along the wall was shot seriously in the foot that afternoon, yet he managed to feign death throughout this dreadful ordeal on that extraordinary late afternoon. When it turned dark, he secretly removed *buddy blood* from the dead on each side of him, and under cover of night, he clandestinely wiped blood on his face and uniform, enough to perhaps pass as a cadaver himself. At dawn, when he heard enemy footsteps from the north side running for the wall, he opened his mouth and eyes, gazing upward, lifeless. A North Korean soldier vaulted the wall, peeked momentarily at him, and believing him to be dead, continued on to slay the remaining pitiful souls trapped in the school. Later that day, when the enemy moved south in pursuit of their next objective, the survivor limped through an arduous, ten-day journey to the safety of the disoriented and bewildered American Army. He became the odd man out, being the 21st survivor. However, company records subsequent to the bloody sacrifice at Anui explicitly listed a total of only 20 survivors, including wounded, from the original complement of 235 committed to battle. Unknown to personnel of our company at the time, there was this 21st survivor.

One officer (Lieutenant Hughes) and two sergeants (Bruner and Pappy) were the sole leaders to survive this ghastly ordeal.

~~

The room on the west side of the schoolhouse was the largest—obviously the assembly room for the rural student population. The other smaller rooms lacked inside doors or walls and instead alcoves had been built to divide the floor space. An imaginary hall ran through the length of the building, but one could enter any room simply by turning into an alcove. These partitions appeared to be for lessons of different age levels for students. Very large windows faced south to the pastoral view of the playground just outside of the schoolhouse, the wooden window frames void of glass. The generally mild temperature, tradition and poverty of the country did not allow for glass in this rural village.

Near the west wall of the assembly room, a speaker's platform was placed on the floor, measuring approximately eight feet by eight feet, by about eighteen inches high. Sergeant Bruner suggested hiding under it, before the North Korean sadists would enter the school at dawn to exact reprisals from survivors. The four of us lifted the platform, and one by one we crawled under, face up, lowering the platform over us and then back to the floor. While the platform accommodated us, the stifling high temperature was suffocating and intolerable. None of us could have endured until the next morning because of the intense heat emanating from the smoldering roof.

Then came the spiders. They remained docile and concealed all of these years, and now they menacingly crawled over us—treating us as intruders who dared to invade their sanctuary. The spiders crawled across faces, because our bodies and arms were pinned to our sides by the limited space between the floor and bottom of the platform. We simply endured the creeping creatures because we could not brush them away. The question of toxicity of the spiders' bite was the least concern, given that retribution by the North Korean sadists was our prime apprehension.

While concealed under the dais, a thought occurred to me that I didn't dare share, primarily because of my recruit status. I was fearful to speak in the presence of experienced infantrymen. When we raised the rostrum to crawl under, it would have been physically impossible to replace the platform exactly where had been sited before. It would clearly leave an obvious line of dirt from where it had been positioned for so many years. When the aggressors entered at dawn, it would be obvious that the platform had been recently moved. They would merely fire their Russian submachine guns, the AK-47's, through the entire platform without bothering to move it, and then laugh as they watched American blood seep from under.

My apprehension didn't matter. Soon Sergeant Bruner's muffled voice grunted, "This isn't going to work," and without a word, the four, in unison pushed the platform up and crawled out. I believed that I was going to die that night or at the latest, the next morning, but if need be, I would die right next to Sergeant Bruner. I stayed very close to my mentor.

I made a decision that I was not going to die by torture. I had it in mind, when captured, to make a break for it, knowing I would be shot down, but capture would not culminate into a slow, tortuous death.

As we fled into the east classroom to escape the constant automatic gunfire, I noticed that the school building itself was now on fire. An incendiary tracer round found a haven of rest embedded in one of the structural posts near the southeast corner of the schoolhouse. The fire idly smoldered, then gained fiery strength in an obsessive quest to consume the building.

Hours inched dreadfully slowly, as we four sprinted back and forth from various rooms to escape the murderous fusillade of machine gun fire. The mortars had ceased firing sometime earlier. There were about four hours until daylight. We hadn't much time left. At approximately one in the morning, the enemy rifle and machine gun fire gradually ceased.

I peeked out of a corner of a window; and it was safe to do so, because now it was as dark outside as in. I discerned hundreds and hundreds of miniature luminescences in the nearby southern hills molding this small valley. The innumerable spots of lights were the glow of cigarettes. The enemy must have been given an order to cease fire. Now, they were most likely on a rest break, and it appeared that most of them were smoking. I stumbled from the schoolhouse to the walled yard where abject sorrow surrounded and gripped me. We knew what would happen in just a few hours. The soldiers of the North Korean Army were by far the most brutal warriors in the world, and they would march in on us in the morning. None could grasp just how inhumane they could be, but all heard the unspeakable horror stories, and in most cases, the revolting accounts were vastly understated.

Survivors sat on the ground, backs resting against walls. The grounds of the schoolyard were cratered and pock marked with large fragments of debris and body parts scattered from earlier mortar barrages. No one spoke, everyone contemplating what the morrow would bring. We were unofficially sentenced to death by torture, and we knew that it would come. It was just a matter of time. There was no way out.

We were teenagers, all of us in our formative years—adolescents who had never attended school or who quit to become soldiers to see the world and to decide later what life's future vocation was to be. The bodies were abandoned to rot in the scorching, humid heat of summer.

The ebbing sands of the hourglass were rapidly falling. There were perhaps two to three hours of night left before the rising sun would eliminate any chance of survival. The NKPA most likely, even at this late hour, must have posted sufficient sentries to prevent any escapes. They had a strangle hold around the school to prevent any Americans from eluding the tightening net of their carefully-laid ambush.

We were dumb animals confined in a pen, awaiting slaughter. No. Dumb animals are oblivious of their imminent doom. We were not.

God, we needed help.

We thought—and Sergeant Bruner, with his formidable infantry experience knew—that our dire predicament would end in death if escape were not possible.

Drenched with depression, I returned to the building with trepidation in my soul, as I observed Bruner and the other two sitting casually on the floor in a small circle, cross-legged, silent, smoking. I joined them and cautiously lit up as well. No one spoke. We just sat on the schoolhouse floor, deeply engrossed in separate thoughts, smoking cigarettes, cupping each in our respective hand to reduce the glow. Bruner was gazing around the room, his eyes darting from one place to another. There was no fear radiating from his eyes, but rather he appeared to be consumed in thought. Shortly thereafter, he arose silently and slowly ambled through the classrooms alone for some time and when he returned a few minutes later, he said just two words firmly, without equivocation, "I'm going."

The manner in which Bruner articulated those two short words implied we were free to make the attempt with him.

Riley sucked in a long, last drag on his cigarette, exhaled through his mouth and nose, ground his cigarette butt on the floor, and determinedly strolled to a small window void of glass about three feet wide and three feet from the ground, on the west side of the building. He seemed to know exactly what strategy he had in mind, and whatever his plan, the three of us would unhesitatingly follow.

BREAKOUT!

> Even for the better American Regiments, the first encounter with the Communist manner of making war in Korea was disturbing, confusing, demoralizing, brutalizing. It was a common experience to see a herd of refugees shuffle toward an American position and, then sweep aside at the last moment to reveal the North Korean infantrymen sheltering among them. Hastings, p. 81.

Riley Bruner clearly realized the dire quandary, as he boldly and unhesitatingly stepped on the lecturer's platform, having improvised it as a rudimentary stepladder braced against the west wall just beneath the small window. Then without an iota of hesitation, he climbed to the frame of the small opening and skillfully adjusted his balance. Bruner quickly dropped noiselessly to the ground and crept forward a few feet, bent over to lower his silhouette. Shortly thereafter, as Bruner patiently waited, the three of us silently, surreptitiously followed. I was last. Joining Bruner, we four crept forward, imitating the sergeant, bent over, single file and close together. When we turned the corner of the schoolhouse, we remained concealed by deep, ebony shadows. Riley stopped in the approximate outside center of the schoolhouse where we joined him. Concealed by the indulging shadows, we were standing immediately facing thousands of enemy soldiers who were oblivious of our presence.

Without a uttering a word or giving a hand signal, Sergeant Bruner suddenly and unpredictably bolted in a full run, racing across the wide, sparse, playground, a soccer field, sliding face first, his momentum carrying him to the near edge of rice paddies abutting the playground. The two others followed in like manner, sprinting one at a time across wide, barren ground headed directly towards the enemy.

Now, it was my turn. I had neither rifle nor gun belt. I had thrown my ammunition belt away at the school as so much excess baggage. Realizing that the water canteen hanging from the ammo belt was bulky, I deferred to the sage wisdom of Sergeant Bruner, who had discarded his belt earlier. I should have thrown my helmet away as well.

My heart was racing with anticipation as I lined up, ready to make my solitary sprint to freedom. I began my race as fast as my legs could carry me, but when I was approximately half way across the field I suddenly perceived the distinctive, recognizable soft explosion.

Oh my God! A flare!

Instantly the black moonless night transformed into high noon at Anui as I instinctively and spontaneously froze in the exact position that I was running. My right foot was high in the air, my left foot on the ground, ready to push off again. My arms were rigid at a 45-degree angle in a pumping action to accelerate my speed. My days at basic training came flooding back to me in an instant, as I bet my life on ingrained Army training, even though it was now bright as day. My first inclination was to slam my body to the protection of Mother Earth, but instead, I continued to stand solitarily and immobile, feeling naked, in front of thousands of enemy soldiers.

I recalled with clarity our training courses on camouflage. It was fascinating to confirm the tenets of concealment:

"Whenever a flare is fired, freeze right on the spot! Never move your position! Do not fall to the ground! Any movement by you will result in your death, and you will be responsible not only for your death, but for the death of others," solemnly intoned the training sergeant.

Now, as I remained in my inflexible posture on the barren soccer field, I reflected on two of the principles of camouflage I learned during basic training, the first being that of *shape*. The round shape of my helmet was out of conformity with the environment. By remaining motionless, I might have a chance to deceive the enemy, but I sincerely believed my round helmet would unquestionably give me away.

Nevertheless, despite a sense of being exposed to enemy fire, I continued my motionless, inanimate position, the hair of my head bristling, as I imagined hundreds of enemy soldiers training their rifles on me. I was anxious, yet determined to remain analytical. I had to believe in what the Army instructed in the way of minimal, basic survival, as I very, very slowly lowered my head to reduce the reflective shine of my face. I wondered if the distinct shape of my helmet would give my position away to the enemy.

The element of *shine* came to me. During garrison duty in Okinawa, our standard-issue helmets were worn from excessive use, producing an ever so slight sheen to the exterior. Could the enemy detect the shiny finish, as I stood alone, bathed in the naked light of the flare?

Surely the enemy was awake as there had to be a reason for firing the flare. I glimpsed, without moving my head, at my companions lying motionless dead ahead, prostrate on the ground, faces down, situated very close next to each other near the edge of the rice paddy.

None of them moved a muscle either. If I erred, the enemy would no doubt saturate the entire field with mortar and machine gun fire and in the process, kill the others as well. I suspected that my companions were praying that I wouldn't make a mistake of judgment and that I could successfully pull this off. I wouldn't disappoint them.

Yet, in my frozen stance I wondered if just one enemy out of the many thousands would realize something that hadn't been there before now was frozen in the middle of the wide-open vacant playground. My stomach turned queasy, and my mind ran rampant with anxious thought. My gunshot wound, just a few hours old, began to throb, apparently from the strain of maintaining immobility for this protracted duration. The pain in my mouth, recently seared by the hot pepper, joined in conspiracy with my wound to taunt me, as I stood helplessly static. I envisioned being shot down by a burst of enemy machine gun fire, and with the inevitable impending collapse to the ground, the enemy would certainly realize that there also were other escapees.

There was a reason for the flare. Someone obviously perceived they discerned movement of men bolting across the field and they decided to concentrate fire there if the slightest motion was detected. When a flare is activated, the primary detection of enemy is by *motion*. Eyes play tricks, especially at night, and as long as I remained immobile, hopefully I appeared to the enemy to be a bush or other inanimate object.

The flare seemed to last a lifetime. Supported by two small parachutes, the pyrotechnic flickered, wafted, sputtered and drifted in the air for what seemed to be an eternity. There was no breeze to carry the artificially induced light away from my position. My right leg began to cramp from holding it in my original running position. My friends in front of me were an extension of my responsibility as well. If I failed, they failed.

When the beacon eventually faded, I once again was shrouded by the protective, black as molasses night. I resumed my sprint, ending up sliding alongside of the three, never uttering a word. Even though I could sense my heart racing, my breath was not accentuated. The NKPA might distinguish gasps for air, but I prayed they couldn't hear my heart.

We remained woodenly motionless for some time, ruminating on what Sergeant Bruner had just accomplished, realizing that it was nothing short of a miracle for us to have come this far undetected. Without a doubt, the first highly dangerous hurdle, escaping from the schoolhouse, was so phenomenally successful because it was so audaciously brazen.

Sergeant Bruner now shifted tactics. He said not a word. He relied on us to do exactly as he did, silently and with sure foot. It was an unspoken pact, and we put our trust in him. He was heading directly toward the thousands of waiting enemy straight in front of us.

Now, he slithered into the first sour, water-filled rice paddy as silently as a water moccasin and crept noiselessly on his stomach. We three emulated his actions. Our entire bodies were submerged, mouth and nose under water, with only eyes held above the surface. It forced us to periodically rise just high enough to reconnoiter the forward escape area and grasp a rapid, silent breath of air before half submerging again. When Bruner was confronted by a rice paddy dike, he slid silently over the dike into the next paddy of water. The three of us followed noiselessly, still in single file. I continued to bring up the rear. Occasionally, Sergeant Bruner would sense something amiss, and he would back up in the obnoxious, fetid, water-filled basin to take another tack. We instinctively slid backwards in response to his movements. Riley was slow, silent, deliberate, and methodical. We were blessed with a moonless night, for the rippling water would shimmer and draw attention to us during a bright moon.

Worse was yet to come. Now we must penetrate the enemy line of defense and crawl through a ring of hundreds or thousands of enemy. Could it be done? Only with Sergeant Bruner leading.

Eventually the saturated slimy rice paddies terminated and we reached terra firma. Sergeant Bruner started to slide from the water, only to hear or see enemy positions near or adjacent to him. He slithered noiselessly back in the water and shifted ten feet or so. Once he was satisfied that he could breach their first line of defense he moved. Bruner's rhythm remained the same, silent, deliberate, on his stomach at all times. Our soaking bodies blended with the fresh growth of vegetation as we slithered on stomachs between enemy positions. I hoped that the odor on us from the foul water would not alert the enemy and expose our position.

Occasionally, Sergeant Bruner would freeze and nod, either right, left or ahead as he spied enemy troops perhaps a mere ten feet from us. Fortunately for us, with the late hour the enemy began to take sleep.

I could smell the odor of burning tobacco, but I couldn't see the source. The effort became more tedious as we continued our painstaking crawl forward, conquering the gradually elevating hill in the middle of the enemy.

About an hour later, near dawn, Sergeant Bruner arose, and again not uttering a word, confidently started to climb up and along the mountain. We did the same, and from his actions we realized that we were at last clear of the enemy.

The four of us were the only ones to escape the schoolhouse. Others could have attempted, but they were too terrified of the probable consequences. The four of us were too terrified of the consequences of staying. About 70 to 80 young soldiers remained. All are dead.

Sergeant Musselwhite also was not among the few fortunate escapees. After surviving the dread of World War II in the horrific Pacific Theater as an infantryman, he was killed in action this night of awful nights.

I crossed the threshold from boyhood into manhood that extraordinary night.

~~

We never discussed the escape Sergeant Bruner engineered for us, and I often wondered why he elected to penetrate those enemy positions that were so heavily manned and fortified. The thought later occurred to me that perhaps his purpose of crawling through the most concentrated enemy positions was because that was the area where the enemy was so confident that they would discount any attempt of enemy intrusion.

~~

We ran through the hills during the day and returned to the main dirt road at night, where we made better time. There was no sleep. Bruner imposed a strict deadline to get back before another major retreat was put in place by the American 8th Army. The trek in the mountains was relatively easy as Sergeant Bruner led us quickly along ancient, primitive footpaths. We never talked, except in guarded whispers when we momentarily stopped to rest.

Very late on about our second night out, as we walked single file along the road, we heard faint, low voices far to the rear. Sergeant Bruner said not a word as he noiselessly slipped from the road, where he hid in the undergrowth, and we duplicated the Sergeant's actions. The oncoming voices became louder, and we deduced that it had to be either enemy movement or escaped American stragglers. No rural inhabitants would be out on this road at this late hour. As the two closed on us, marching abreast so they could converse, Sergeant Bruner allowed them to pass from our concealed area, ostensibly to decipher if they were enemy or friendly troops. Apparently observing nothing unusual, he hailed them, just above a whisper.

"Psst, Hey, Americans!"

The two soldiers were startled beyond words. Their initial impulse was to bolt for their lives, but then they recognized us as friendly. The two had escaped from another area of our embattled, surrounded company, given that no one else escaped from the schoolhouse. After hushed greetings and strong embraces, Sergeant Bruner continued our exodus once again, but in single file with absolute silence.

Through the years I wondered how the two stragglers managed to escape from the village of Anui surrounded by the enemy, where we initially readied our so-called defensive positions. The subject was never addressed because of the powerful emotions associated with the disastrous rout of Baker Company.

An impressive and valuable lesson was learned from Sergeant Bruner that fateful night, which was to never talk at night. Voices and sounds carry a very long distance in the still of the night.

About the third day out from the dizzying heights of the mountain, Riley Bruner spied a farmhouse below, abutting the base of the mountain. There was a field, but it was not rice, but some type of vegetables in full growth. We quietly crept from the summit, and eventually approached the edge of the field. Some type of turnip or huge radish was ready to be harvested, but the caretakers had abandoned their farm in the face of the swift, marauding enemy. Silently, we pulled our individual share of the bountiful food and furtively returned to the mountains. Sitting in a circle, we wiped dirt from the food on our filthy rice-water stained field trousers and devoured the roots ravenously. It was our first sustenance in over three days.

I learned the hard way through numerous incidents that the third day of fasting was the most difficult. After the fourth day, the hunger pangs seem to subside. We learned that we could live without food, but water was a necessity. The new stragglers carried canteens on their belts and ample trickles and pools of water in the mountains satisfied our needs. Our six-day journey was somewhat uneventful, though I frequently wondered where we were, and where the remnants of our out-fought and beaten Army were. However, the most demanding experience was the element of sleep deficit. I was in a fog-like trance, literally walking and sleeping simultaneously.

Aside from Sergeant Bruner, an experienced, combat infantryman, the rest of our young, inexperienced group were in some form of arrested shock, and any discussion relating to the massacre was avoided. It was a counterfeit non-emotional facade we displayed to one another.

From our vantage point, trudging through the mountains during the day, we observed what appeared to be rural Korean citizens wandering aimlessly about farms and villages in the vast valley below. Firmly believing that any could be guerilla or enemy spies, even though they appeared to be unarmed, and having recalled many nightmare episodes of enemy infiltration wearing the garb of the peasantry, Sergeant Bruner concluded that it would be unwise to confront anyone.

The arduous struggle to locate our battalion, or rather what was left of it, was successful when we strolled into the company perimeter in late afternoon. I was astonished by the anti-climatic mood. Others managed to escape from the village ahead of us, but none realized the horrific losses at the time. Someone nonchalantly tossed a can of C-Rations to each of us, but surprisingly we were not hungry. We were advised by Lieutenant Hughes to get some sleep as the company was moving back to confront the enemy again the next morning before dawn. It was an emotionless home-coming. The date: 2 August 1950.

~~

Sergeant Pappy made it out, and I was gratified to see him. From his demeanor, I perceived that he still wanted to avoid conversation. He must have had a premonition of what would happen if he ran for the school-house, and he obviously avoided that trap. No one spoke of the events of Anui, so appalling. Yet, we were so very fortunate to be alive, but out of deference to the many dead and missing, no one articulated that.

Furthermore, Sergeant Pappy obviously had his personal thoughts as to what the next morning's struggle would bring. Everyone kept his own counsel. Baker Company lost every lieutenant, save Lieutenant Hughes and every sergeant except 1st Class Sergeants Pappert and Bruner. The company was devoid of leadership, and there were no replacements. I made an inquiry about medical attention for the gunshot wound to my left side and back, and I was told in less than polite terms that I was fit enough to face the enemy again the next morning,

With that, I wandered over to Supply, and selected a brand new M-1 rifle. The first thing I did was to slide the bolt open and gaze down the barrel to see if there were any obstructions in the barrel or chamber. Not viewing any impediments, I selected a new helmet, gun belt with canteen, first-aid pack and entrenching tool. Two bandoleers of M-1 ammunition completed my outfitting, as there were no hand grenades available. I tossed the remaining half of the loathsome C-Ration away. Despite the lack of food for six days, I had no appetite.

We lay down without bedding on the uncompromising hard ground, having nothing other than the uniforms we wore, to await the morning assault by the remaining survivors from the 1st Battalion.

Where to tomorrow?

It was rumored we were heading back to defend Chinju, where the battalion abandoned field packs in the school grounds prior to the Anui and Hadong massacre. If that were true, that meant we yielded approximately 35 miles of territory and almost the entire complement of the two-battalion regiment to the North Korean Army in one night.

I slept well that night, considering all. Six days with no sleep was without precedence. It was unbelievable that I was still alive.

Thank you God!

~~

More than 50 years later, retired Colonel John C. Hughes and I had an ecstatic meeting, having not seen each other since that inauspicious night when he was severely wounded during the initial Chinese Communist attack. We sat down together over a glass of beer at a 29th Infantry Regiment reunion, and between the two of us, we calculated the true number of survivors from Baker Company that awful night of 27 July 1950. Army historians have bandied about many ludicrous numbers over the years, but it was unofficially finalized by two acknowledged survivors who endured and survived that awful night.

"Pete, how many of you escaped from the schoolhouse that night?" the Colonel, with his razor sharp memory, inquired matter-of-factly. Veterans tend to deal with disaster in impersonal ways.

"Four of us, skipper, and we picked up two more from the company on the road about two days out." I took a deep swallow from my glass in a fruitless effort to blot out the dreadful memory. In later life, it was much more painful to revisit awful nightmares than endure the experience of dreadful actions when they actually took place. The memories now are cast into reminiscences forever. I am not at all convinced one enemy soldier was killed or even wounded during that terribly-doomed night.

"Well, let's see. I brought out 13, not counting me. Fourteen and your count of six is 20, so that was not very good odds at all," the colonel softly lamented, as I watched his eyes beginning to mist. The skipper was an empathetic soul who cared deeply and passionately for the safety and welfare of his men. He was proud of his company, and to lose the vast majority of his command in one disastrous combat operation shattered him. Our beloved commander, Colonel John C. Hughes, was at the vanguard of every vicious battle that the company endured. And that is precisely why the skipper earned seven Purple Heart Medals.

Author Joseph C. Goulden, in his book, *Korea: The Untold Story of the War*, recorded for posterity the fate of the two battalions of the 29th Infantry Regiment during the battles of Anui and Hadong:

> The 3rd Battalion had gone into battle with some 757 men on its rolls. When American troops retook the Hadong area two months later, graves registration teams found of the bodies of 313 slain Americans, most along the rivers and in the rice paddies. A North Korean POW reported that his comrades took about 100 more Americans captive. Goulden p.139

While author Goulden focused primarily on the disaster of the 3rd Battalion at Hadong, the extreme loss of American life of Baker Company at Anui was the highest loss of any company in the regiment, verified by Killed in Action (KIA) statistics. Additionally, the annihilation of the two battalions of the Regiment on 27 July 1950 was recorded as the second highest loss of life of one unit in one battle during the entire Korean War.

As of this writing, to my knowledge, only a few authors have chronicled the disastrous and horrific events that unfolded as consequences of the battles of Anui and Hadong. Finally, in the 50-year anniversary edition of June/July 2000, the VFW magazine printed author Gary Turbak's two page article titled "Hell at Hadong", in reference to the Regiment. Author Turbak terminated his story thus: "The 29th Infantry ceased to exist in Korea after that day, and accounts of the war generally ignore this unit entirely."

I am the last survivor of the schoolhouse debacle and one of but very few who live today that survived that terrible slaughter during the Korean War. I recorded this event from recollection as a surviving participant, for the benefit of the history of Baker Company and the 29th Infantry Regiment who incurred such terrible losses.

On the night of 27 July 1950, during this brutal conflict, the 29th Infantry Regiment ceased to exist as a unit. Almost all military historians of the Korean War fail to mention the commitment of the 29th Infantry Regiment—the date had taken another meaningful significance. On 27 July 1953, exactly three years later to the day, the guns of Korea fell silent. The 10 p.m. armistice was officially emplaced. While millions can recall with clarity that momentous day in 1953 with relief and equanimity, there are but a handful of survivors who remember that it was just three short years earlier, on that very same day, the 29th Infantry Regiment became a *ghost regiment* in a matter of hours.

CHINJU PASS

> After the disasters of July, General Walker's troops were used up, discouraged and resentful. The strength of the American units had been sharply reduced by sickness and causalities, and replacements, when they did arrive, were often young and inexperienced. Donald Knox, p. 79.

"OK, let's get with it! Get ready to load up! Get the lead out! Let's go! Now!"

It was long before dawn when the company was brusquely ordered awake, stirring sluggishly, gathering combat gear from attendant surroundings. We were still clad in the same filthy uniforms with boots still damp from slithering through flooded rice paddies.

Yet the murky, algae-laden pools were sanctuary from enemy discovery, and we would never have been able to get out alive otherwise. One of the guys who walked out of Anui alive murmured barely under his breath, "Hey Sarge, why don't you go screw yourself." It was an unheard of rejoinder to a noncommissioned officer in those days, yet understandable, given the emotional consequences of Anui. No one recalled who said it but it was of little concern given the sergeant in charge didn't hear it either. None knew the sergeant. We had Sergeants Bruner and Pappy, the only two non-coms who escaped Anui, but no one knew from where the replacement came so suddenly. Someone hazarded a guess that he may have been ordered on line from a cushy rear echelon job. Good. He would join us at our next rendezvous. Bullets are nondiscriminatory, unless an enemy sniper discerns a uniform bearing rank insignia, and then that unlucky person is singled out for preferential treatment.

~~

It seemed as if we had just closed our eyes to purge images of the dread of the past six days when we were unceremoniously awakened and ordered to mount trucks. The night before, my friend and I hurriedly scooped out a small and shallow foxhole, pushed beyond the limit of endurance, unable to dig any deeper. We were simply too exhausted to continue, even though we were in an area that would be overrun by massive enemy forces at any time. The next morning, my surviving comrade mentioned that in my exhaustive stupor, I subliminally twitched in reaction to the thunder of artillery fire. It was an embarrassment to me to realize that I deprived my buddy of necessary sleep.

It was true. American artillery fired in defiant defense all night in a desperate effort to hold the enemy at bay until the 1st Battalion could form a more substantial defensive position. The North Korean 6th Division was on an exhilarating, unstoppable mission. They were swiftly and steadfastly triumphing, slaying American and ROK soldiers and confiscating huge parcels of South Korean real estate. They were killing all who stood in opposition, while sustaining little or no casualties. The American and ROK units were gripped in a far more traumatic and different situation altogether. The acute loss of Allied soldiers reached an appalling, unsustainable level, predicated upon the piece-meal deployment of American armed entities. Send one unit in, have the NKPA grind them up, spit them out, and then send in yet another to meet the same disastrous fate.

Survivors of Anui didn't have access to the repulsive C-rations, and even if they were available, there was no time to eat, given the command to rush aboard transport trucks. I struggled to awaken sufficiently from a tortuous daze following those earlier terrible days, and to gear up emotionally for yet another disastrous battle for our lives.

The skeletal number of Baker Company survivors, equipped with newly-replaced combat gear, and recently reissued M-1's slung over shoulders, scrambled aboard the patiently waiting deuce-and-a-half transport trucks, There was no hint from where the replacement troops came, but for us, the remnants of Baker Company, it was sufficient to fill only one transport truck. Before, when we were unceremoniously committed to Anui, it would have taken a minimum of a ten-truck fleet to transport the company. Now one vehicle sufficed. The pivoting side benches of the truck were raised to bar troops from sitting, forcing the 20 survivors to be crowded standing together without respite.

The bulky, cumbersome field backpacks abandoned earlier at the schoolyard, seemingly years past, were not replaced—truly a blessing. Tents and other nonessential equipment, appropriate for non-combat situations, were impracticable for our new, hostile environment, and ancillary combat gear really designated for garrison duty was a useless waste of time, supply, and weight. Troops carried minimal combat equipment, particularly ammunition, because of acute shortages. It was unfortunate that unnecessary field packs could not be exchanged for the essential, inadequate supply of ammunition. To date not one hand grenade was available and this imminent clash with the notorious 6th North Korean Division was when American defenders should have been sufficiently equipped.

~~

Baker Company was en route to Chinju. The date: 3 August 1950. In this instance, rather than staging in the town of Chinju proper, the unit learned that the anticipated mission was to confront and repel the North Korean tidal advance from the main north-south road, east of town, now infamously remembered as The Battle of Chinju Pass. It seemed this objective was not unlike what we were instructed to undertake at Hadong and Anui. Engage, and drive back the invaders, *Part Deux*.

Despite the anguish of the ordeal of Anui, no one complained. The reason was the few survivors were psychologically numb. Moreover, even though it was nothing short of miraculous to barely escape the clutches of death at the hands of the brutal enemy, there was a solemn mood of intense depression, co-mingled with profound culpability among the survivors for leaving behind those who were dead or could not escape. Anui and Hadong left the surviving soldiers in abysmal despair. *Brutal* was the only name that could stick to the inhumane NKPA.[13]

Prior to the armed engagement, the notion that all would die in this awful conflict was never addressed, even though that wretched thought played over and over in the schoolhouse at Anui.

Those who engage in war at close range generally do not think of dying in battle, but whenever the body of an American soldier is beheld, the cold reality of death is driven forcefully home.

The bullet wound through my left side and back began to tingle slightly, a positive sign of healing. Wounds such as mine were thought of derisively as *band-aid* wounds, accepted as a small part of the hazardous occupation. To flaunt a minor wound is to open the door to disparaging comments. The torment is heartless. Infantrymen save empathy for those who rightfully earn it, the dead and the dying. There were other immediate and urgent concerns.

Rather than being transported to the hospital for treatment, I was on my way to the ensuing battle, the only person to be wounded and still survive Anui. I counted my blessings for existing six additional, precious days

---

[13] A bit of background in respect to the enemy is warranted: The NKPA was composed primarily of enemy who were seasoned, well-trained combat veterans of World War II. They confronted the Japanese in Korea and China, and later warred against the Chinese Nationalist Army, allied with the Chinese Communist regime. The NKPA 4th and 6th Divisions, la crème de la crème, with lightning speed and ferocious determination, attacked swiftly and largely unopposed across the South Korean border. The enemy struck through Seoul, Taejon and soon thereafter, swept unopposed, driving southwest through the lower peninsula, before pivoting east toward Chinju.

The NKPA 6th Division, the unit the 29th Regiment was destined to challenge at Chinju, was the same victorious division that destroyed, in one night, the 29th Infantry Regiment. at Anui and Hadong. They relished the thought of fallen boys in their persuasive victories, as American and ROK resistance crumbled effortlessly in front of their massive siege. Author.

when we were isolated in enemy territory. Thanks to the Herculean efforts of Sergeant Bruner, six more soldiers survived the initial call to battle. That is more than could be said of the more than 200 soldiers destined to rot in perpetuity in that hellhole.

It was still dark when the battalion convoyed through the usual biting grit, toward the Pass, rather than the town proper, where all of this madness began. The Pass meant nothing to the returnees, other than wondering if they would again be sacrificed on some god-forsaken hill and end up as just another blip in the annals of military history.

A grieving mother would bear the burden of guilt for the remainder of her life. Guilt, induced because a mother succumbed to the persistence of her 17-year-old son to sign mandatory documents so an anxious teenager could enlist in the Army. An ensuing telegram from the Department of Defense would simply read:

"The Secretary of the Army regrets to inform you that your son.........died in the line of duty in the vicinity of ....on ...."

Fill in the blanks.

Some reasoned the company was heading in a general northwesterly direction as dawn ultimately broke, seemingly to awaken the usual hordes of bothersome flies to torment troops.

Soon thereafter, the convoy stopped abruptly in the middle of the dirt road. Troops were ordered from the trucks and directed to proceed north, in two single files, on each side of the grimy trail. The road ever so gradually rose to an astounding elevation. The primitive route continued in a rather straight line until nearing the apex, where the road slithered from view. At the summit, the road made a rather sharp, hazardous turn to the right, straightened, and once again resumed the same maddening pattern of steep descent from the north side duplicating the ascent from the south side. At the very top of the mountain, a deep gouge of earth had been laboriously excavated years ago in a dedicated effort to level the abrupt grade of the topography. Contemporary military analysts and historians aptly dubbed the apex the *Notch*, in reference to the wide area hacked from the summit.

One may imagine the primitive road being constructed hundreds of years prior, by means of the raw manual labor of those tormented conscripted toilers of Korea. Moreover, it was certain that few, if any, motor-driven vehicles had utilized this passage earlier, given the sparse poverty of this uncivilized, backward, country. The road had most likely been put to use by ox-led carts since ancient times. But there may have been another explanation.

During the despotic, tyrannical 40-year Japanese occupation of Korea, the Japanese improved the infrastructure of the country by construction of roads, bridges, railways, reservoirs and the like. Chinju Pass may have been such an enterprise the Japanese colonists commanded to be built. It may have been constructed by forced Korean manual labor, the unfortunate workers toiling incessantly in steaming, tropical weather, under degrading servitude, to insure the affluence of the Japanese occupiers.[14]

At the apex, a narrow, shallow furrow was excavated following the natural contour of the hill on the east side, ostensibly to capture the summer's swollen torrent of monsoonal deluge, allowing the water to flow unobstructed within the ditch, down the side of the elevated mountain, as opposed to overflowing and flooding the road. The approximately eight-inch deep by 12-inch wide dry gutter would contain more than rainwater in the immediate future.

The view from the east side of the pass was unobstructed for approximately one hundred yards, with natural knolls rising from each end of the open territory. The serene view would soon metamorphose into a grisly gauntlet of death when American soldiers would be forced to sprint through, terrifyingly exposed to heavy enemy fire. For now, the 1st Battalion held the southern end and the level portion of the road unopposed, even though the American force later discovered they were under constant enemy surveillance.

By strategic planning, the notorious North Korean 6th Division deployed earlier, and was now locked in mortal combat with the weakened battle-exhausted remnants of the American 19th Infantry Regiment, the first American infantry unit dispatched to the ground war in Korea.

At the same time, the enemy put in place the Chinju Pass Ambush against the 1st Battalion, 29th Regiment. American military leaders committed inexperienced boys in a desperate effort to staunch the irreversible flood of seasoned enemy. All were brave soldiers marching in lock-step under the banner of the United Nations, to the fields of glory, to the fields of honor, to the sounds of guns and to certain death.

Hard lessons learned through the earlier, humiliating ambush were

---

[14] The Japanese proceeded to declare a protectorate over Korea in 1905, and five years later they formally annexed it as a colony, justifying the move by claiming that the insufficiently advantageous terms of the Treaty of Portsmouth left them no choice if their economy was to recover from the recent war. Over the succeeding years Japanese investments developed the tremendous industrial and agricultural potential of Korea and Manchuria to serve Japan's needs. Whelan, p. 16.

disregarded.[15] The sometimes post-battle critique became irrelevant. Now North Korean forces were pushing their forces arduously in order to achieve final victory—the conquest of Pusan and the ultimate collapse of the American effort.

Beleaguered remnants of the 1st Battalion, 29th Infantry Regiment were a petty annoyance at best, subject to annihilation by the ravaging combatants. Once the enemy was entirely militarily engaged, they retained sufficient manpower and firepower to destroy both the ill-fated 19th Infantry Regiment, as well as the recently arrived, decimated 29th Infantry Regiment.

A sound of a convoy of three American medium tanks with powerful, rumbling, clanking, steel treads, which normally portended disaster to enemy, fell on unconcerned ears. The NKPA was equipped with awesome retaliatory armor as well, the behemoth, much-feared T-34 heavy, well-armed tank. The tank, the pride of the Soviet Army and the bulwark against the Third Reich during the European Campaign, was considered the foremost armored vehicle in that war region.

Charlie Company of the 1st Battalion, 29th was in the vanguard, in ancillary support of newly arrived American armor, preceding the remnants of Baker Company. The tank-led convoy clanked boldly and noisily to the summit, and skillfully maneuvered around the bend, where the procession of American tanks and unsuspecting support troops in transport trucks disappeared from sight.

Without warning, it appeared as if the whole world imploded. The notorious enemy cunningly concealed in the dense brush west of the Pass, supported by heavy weapons, now brought them to bear against the unsuspecting convoy. The resultant devastation was horrific. Machine guns,

---

[15] Maj. Gen. Pang Ho San, commanding general of the North Korean 6th Division, much decorated for the exploits of his division thus far, issued an order calculated to improve troop morale. He said the mission of the division was "to liberate Masan and Pusan within a few days." He demanded stricter discipline and more perseverance than ever before, and stated that tactics must adjust to the changes "this epoch-making conflict has introduced into the art of warfare." He summed up the battle lessons: "Our experience in night combat up to now shows that we can operate only four or five hours in the dark since we start night attacks between 2300 and 2400 hours, and, therefore, if the battle continues until dawn, we are likely to suffer losses. From now on, use daylight for full combat preparation, and commence attacks soon after sunset. Concentrate your battle actions mostly at night and capture enemy base positions. From midnight on, engage enemy in close combat by approaching to within 100 to 150 meters of him. Then, even with the break of dawn, the enemy planes will not be able to distinguish friend from foe, which will enable you to prevent great losses. This is the most valuable battle experience we have gained from the Chinju operation." Appleman, p. 458.

intense rifle fire, mortars and anti-tank weaponry rained havoc on the surprised Americans from out of nowhere, and no one was able to determine the location of the concealed enemy. Survivors of Baker Company dove for the sanctuary of the shallow run-off ditch, oblivious that the shallow depth would protect only the lower half of a supine body.

The enemy swept the road with precision machine gun fire, rounds tearing ruthlessly in the dirt road in the enemy's quest to kill. Trembling young American soldiers frightfully compressed prostrate bodies into the bottom of the shallow gully, hopefully to bond with mother earth, until they were one. Stomachs deflated, pressing against spines, but that wasn't good enough. Survivors had to drop lower.

Minute wisps of dust crazily agitated by lethal rounds were striking the road just in front of partially exposed bodies. Someone screamed harshly, and then just as suddenly, the terrifying sound fell silent. Another survivor of Anui was no longer a survivor. The rounds pouring from enemy guns ricocheted from the road, just above quivering bodies to spend themselves in a dirt embankment barely above defender's heads, spilling dirt from the impact onto shuddering bodies. At the same time, enemy riflemen zeroed in on Baker Company troops with massive fire, apparently realizing the company had not spotted the locations of enemy positions.

Still, soldiers were heartened by the fact that they were reinforced with tank support. None from Baker Company realized that supporting armor was a target of this assault, and when they did, it no longer was a morale booster. Regretfully, there are downsides to every situation, and this event was no exception.

The close proximity of armor almost always draws an inordinate amount of heavy weapons fire from the adversary. There was no exception on that terrible day. The enemy was prepared. In this instance the NKPA was primarily intent on the destruction of American armor, and the ancillary infantry in support was merely an added bonus to covet.

Baker Company was the second unit to be committed to this battle. The company had not reached the forward, downhill, enemy-held position as yet, to bear witness to the horrific carnage and inferno of Charlie Company soldiers and vehicles that awful morning. At that time Baker Company personnel were dangerously exposed to hostile enemy fire. Simultaneously, Allied tanks and trucks rumbled daringly forward, maneuvered across the man-made plateau, and initiated a sharp right turn before descending steeply onto the enemy side of the pass, out of sight. The two forward moving tanks and a convoy of trucks were stranded immobile, deep on the north side of the apex of the Notch, clearly in enemy-held territory.

It was a matter of predetermined destiny that the enemy deployed shortly before the arrival of the 1st Battalion, when they swiftly and methodically put in motion the planned Chinju Pass ambush. The enemy division was already engaged in a desperate five-hour running gun battle against the pathetically few survivors of the American 19th Regiment, who were battling to stem the tide of the advancing North Korean Army. When the enemy recognized the intimidating deep growl of American tanks, special elements of the enemy division disengaged from the siege against the 19th to man heavy weapons against the approaching, unsuspecting 1st Battalion convoy.

Meanwhile the surviving troops of the 19th Regiment broke out in unrestrained, jubilant cheers upon hearing the roar of American tanks approaching the battle site, escorting Charlie Company, intent on rescuing the embattled 19th. It was reminiscent of the United States Cavalry arriving just in time to save ill-fated settlers defending their surrounded, circled wagons in the frontier days of yore.

The cavalry *did* indeed arrive.

The first American tank and trucks were struck by direct hits, killing crews and destroying vehicles as soon as the convoy rounded the bend of the Notch after descending the steep slope of the pass out of Baker Company's view and into the gun-sights of the patiently waiting enemy. The odds of a direct hit by a mortar into the hardened steel belly of a tank, demolishing it, are exceptional, yet there were many eyewitnesses who confirmed the tragic event.

The Sherman tanks' arsenal of 30-caliber machine gun ammunition and countless rounds of deadly 76-millimeter cannon, co-mingled with the detonation of the enemy blast, united as one, and then erupted in a monstrous, horrendous explosion. The NKPA quickly employed a follow-up blast from an antitank gun, striking and destroying a troop transport truck further to the rear of the convoy. The strategic maneuver not only immobilized the convoy, but by that deadly tactic, the enemy prevented the convoy from withdrawing to safety. The many motorized conveyances, laden with young, frightened troops, were now hopelessly and dangerously stranded, blocked between the two destroyed vehicles. The helpless convoy, now in the gun sights of the enemy, was to be destroyed piecemeal.

Enemy small arms fire growled viciously, spitting death and destruction on trapped vehicles and soldiers, inflicting devastating fire, zeroing in, intentionally aiming to strike reserve fuel tanks strapped to the rear section of the tanks.

Raw gasoline gushed from jerry cans, flowed across the cut off convoy, the road, and the ditch when it unexpectedly ignited. The Notch exploded into a flaming, impervious wall of fiery holocaust, everything in its path consumed by a hurricane of searing flames. The ceaseless spillage of fuel delivered a thick, greasy concoction of bilious flames that energized and embellished the wall of fire. The appalling carnage was nourished by the vast firepower from the North Korean Army sweeping heavy machine gun fire, murdering everyone in its path.

Teenage troops of Charlie Company, caught unaware in the transport truck, were instantly killed, wounded or set afire as a result of the fatal strike by enemy anti-tank weapons. Soldiers, uniforms, boots, hair, and flesh on fire, tumbled from tank and truck, thrashing panicky and futilely in the silt of the road in a hopeless attempt to douse their flaming bodies. Shrill screams of intense pain penetrated the air, fusing with the dissonant sounds of mortar, rifle, machine gun fire, explosions, and the roar of the out-of-control, fiery holocaust. Others ran for the false sanctuary of the shallow culvert, only to be shot dead by North Korean troops previously deployed to lie in wait to kill the unsuspecting American victims.

Abhorrent, thick, black smoke belched offensive fumes from burning gasoline, destroying vehicles and bodies, spewing acrid, offensive vapors. Ferociously out of control, it caused a stomach-turning response to the nauseating haze. The surging fires were to become as mighty as a gigantic forest fire, but rather than the somewhat neutral gray hue of a wood fire, this ghastly conflagration was casting colossal black plumes of insidious gasoline-based smoke that pin-pointed exact locations of the tragic loss of men and materials. This terrible battle was the epitome of the reincarnation of *Dante's Inferno.* And so it went—a firestorm of war in all its horror.

Hell was reincarnated on that terrible day, and directors of realistic war film dramas would be envious of the macabre sight of this unspeakably terrible real-life combat struggle.

Lieutenant Suddaby, then assigned to C Company, witnessed the origin of the mammoth inferno, seeing the carnal birth of the horrendous fire begin as flames initially whispered low, then burst into an out of control disaster.

While Baker Company personnel were pinned down by enemy fire in that shallow rain gully, other elements of the enemy 6th Division were zeroing in on half-exposed bodies as soldiers lay prone in absolute terror.

Incredibly, enemy gunfire ratcheted to a higher and even more intense, deadly level. It was as if every rifle in the world was bombarding Baker Company. The bank behind quivering troops was a virtual backstop for a weapon range, ceaselessly absorbing enemy rounds, while young victims, cowering in fright, were the ten spot, the bull's eye of a target, now placed directly in front of the implacable backstop.

Trembling in fear, defensive soldiers glanced up to see the most bizarre sight, and the prime reason for the sudden, ponderous rain of rifle and machine gun fire. A solitary GI, clearly exposed to enemy observation, was wandering aimlessly south on the level section of the pass, completely oblivious to the concentrated enemy fire attempting to kill him. He was stark naked. The unclad soldier escaped the flaming funeral pyre of the tank, and in the process, every item of clothing, including his combat boots, was burned from his body, leaving him deep red in color. He was obviously in severe shock, meandering on the road as if he was strolling noncommittally in some serene park.

The victim, oblivious to the maelstrom of machine gun and rifle fire attempting to cut him down, disregarded the withering fire as if it was merely swarms of pesky, irritating flies. With a greeting to all, who were lying fearfully prostrate, half exposed in the shallow ditch, he matter of factly expressed in a heavy, southern drawl, "Howdy men, I'm Tex. What's your name? How's it going with you? Hey, nice day, ain't it?"

All the while, Tex was sporting a wide grin accompanied with befuddled amusement.

"Get Down! Get Down! You're drawing fire! You're drawing fire! You're fuckin' gonna get us all killed," everyone screamed.

Tex, oblivious to the phobic, plaintive outcries, continued his unconcerned, nonchalant amble down the road, as if walking some young lady to school. He maintained his leisurely stroll, without once being struck, all the way to the Battalion Aid Station, far to the rear, where he reported in and then died.

Bob Jones, 1st Squad, Baker Company, further to the rear, was not immune to enemy firepower. Jones was shot three times: once in the right calf, once in the right thigh, and once in the right buttocks. He was bought down immediately, collapsing and bleeding profusely from multiple gunshot wounds oozing an exorbitant quantity of warm blood in the gritty dirt road.

During the time the first squad was pinned down by unremitting enemy machine gun fire, God was in Jones' corner that day. The North Korean sub-machine gunner miraculously eased off of the trigger so no other rounds burst into Jones's upper body. The recoil of an automatic weapon always forces the barrel upward, causing the trajectory of the rounds to rise in concert. Jones's life was spared only because the sub-machine gunner elected to stop firing.[16] He apparently thought he killed Jones.

Jones earned several Purple Heart medals, but he was only awarded one for this awful incident. Despite multiple gunshot wounds to his body, they were considered, by the military, to be one wound inflicted by enemy. Those are the rules—one medal per encounter.

Members of 3rd Squad, rigid with fear in the shallow ditch, pinned down by enemy machine gun fire, heard a tremendous explosion, as if the world was coming to an end. I peered to my left, from my shallow grave and witnessed some of the bravest soldiers that I have ever encountered. A gun crew of four, silhouetted against the sky, in clear view of the enemy, was emplaced on the knoll to the south.

The crew was methodically firing the 75-mm Recoilless Rifle, a devastating and formidable weapon that was more like a cannon. It is considered a rifle because it fires in a straight trajectory, but it is as powerful as cannon. The crew, in order to search a target, must fire the weapon point blank, silhouetted against the sky, thus exposing themselves to the enemy.[17]

The operation of this weapon is deadly in itself, owing to the nomenclature of the projectile, as well as the weapon itself. The casing of the explosive is perforated, allowing the discharge to spew from the rear of the gun by way of an open breach, as is required to dispatch the missile on

---

[16] The only weapon that could produce such rapid and devastating firepower would be the crudely manufactured, yet highly effective, Russian AK-47 "Burp Gun." It was so nicknamed because the rate of fire was so fast one could not discern individual rounds fired; rather, the sounds melded together, into a type of "brappp."
Considered one of the most reliable submachine guns fabricated in the world, the reliability arose from its being a sloppily and crudely-manufactured weapon. The mechanism was so slack and ill fitting, that it seldom misfired or jammed. Conversely, the American made Garand M-1 Rifle was manufactured with such precision the rifle had to be kept constantly clean in order for the weapon to respond. Author.

[17] As soon as the enemy machine gun positions were located, recoilless rifles took them under fire and either destroyed them or caused the enemy gunners to abandon them. But enemy fire in turn killed three of four crew members of the recoilless rifle on the west side of the Notch. The fourth member, Evert E. (Moose) Hoffman, stayed with the gun and fired at every available target throughout the day. He won a battlefield commission. Appleman, p.241.

its mission. That is why it is identified as a recoilless rifle. The weapon is constructed with lands and grooves in the barrel, indicating that the projectile has a spin, as does a rifle, allowing deadly accuracy at great distances.

Additionally, the firing crew faces instant death from the blast at the rear, should anyone stand near the open breach when the weapon is fired. Added to that is the horrendous noise it emits when fired. Four men are required to carry it into the mountains, by use of four steel handles, two to a side. The enormously heavy weight of the ammunition requires a dedicated crew indeed.

Deep shock following on the heels of the initial enemy encounter at Anui, coupled with this ongoing disaster, and with only one night's sleep in seven days, added to my anxiety. The last thing I remember was that I was continuously exhaling deep breaths in order to compress my body deeper in that shallow gully to avoid the devastating machine gun and rifle fire immediately over prostrate bodies.

The next thing I recall was that I was emplaced, along with surviving squad members, on top of the mountain, east of the Notch, in a skirmish line facing north, and firing west at enemy. To this day I have no recall of how I moved from the shallow ditch to the top of the rise. I was positioned in the eastern-most position, and no one advised me, nor did I realize at the time, that I should have concentrated my attention on the right flank.

Battles customarily are won or lost dependent on flanking maneuvers by warring entities. One of the most basic tactics of infantry warfare is to have enemy slip behind and attack from the side or the rear. I would have been the person responsible had my unit been destroyed for not keeping the right flank under surveillance. And I would have been the first to be killed. Whenever my thoughts return to The Pass, I ponder how I placed my unit in harm's way by my failure to concentrate on the east side. My only justification was that during this intense, bloody battle, the enemy 6th Division was dug in and firing from the extreme west side of the pass. They could not have positioned to the east without being detected, as they would have been required to cross the road. Or so I thought.

It was a regular nine-to-five battle. Punch the time clock and begin shooting. Take breaks and lunch; begin the slaughter again and then clock out at five. In the interim, many hundreds of pathetic souls on both sides had bequeathed their lives in a cause each fervently believed in.

In the late afternoon and while still positioned on the hill, I glanced back at the deuce-and-a-half truck parked facing south, ready to evacuate in case of enemy overrun of the defensive position. I felt sorrow because the truck, one of many that brought living young soldiers to this God-awful place, now bore another cargo. The truck with the same sideboards was now ordained as the official funeral conveyance for the naked and the dead. Lieutenant Hughes and another officer were unceremoniously heaving corpses over the railing and onto the bed of the truck. One of them would grab the body by the ankles, the other by the wrists and swing.

"OK. On the count of three. One... two... three" and another body flailed through the air and fell among fallen comrades, twisted, contorted and intermingled, as arms and legs protruded grotesquely through side railings of the truck. I wondered how the bodies would separate when rigor mortis set in—how would they be untangled? The powder-laden road was speckled with spots of blood from indifferent American dead still oozing as a result of the sweltering, sticky heat.

One of the dead soldiers was a dear friend whom I had come to know in my short stay in the Occupation of Okinawa. Stevens was a quiet, soft-spoken teenager from New Mexico, who sang and played country guitar as beautifully and softly as he spoke. I was deeply saddened by his unpropitious death, and I wondered why the Lord took him, when the world is so saturated with corrupt, dishonest, evil people who should have taken his place. The world would be a better place for that.

"God bless and keep you, Stevens."

While still in emotional trauma, I somehow must have returned to the road, but I had no conscious recollection of that or of any subsequent events. I remember being at the top of the mountain firing at enemy; I do not remember returning to the dreadful road where earlier we were so dangerously pinned down. It was a subtle, indirect form of suppression of the sub-consciousness.

Troops were informed that four captured American soldiers, hands bound by *commo* wire, were methodically shot at the base of the skull where they were discovered on the road. I must have seen them, sprawled erratically in death's repose, but I have no recall of this act of butchery.

~~

Throughout my adult years, I had been tormented with appalling, vivid dreams of the Battle of Chinju Pass, constantly bolting wide awake with racing heart and profusely perspiring, my sleep shattered by these same grotesque, interwoven, nightmares.[18]

In every nightmare, I envisioned scores of dead North Korean soldiers, sprawled about in awful, contorted positions on the level part of the pass. Rifles and AK-47s were strewn about the road, and the road ran red with blood. That couldn't be real, I believed, as my squad was on this very same road just hours before, pinned down by concentrated enemy firepower. My mental fabrications during these terrifying nightmares always contained this central theme:

I consistently dreamed that I stood idly by and observed a bulldozer blade pushing scores of slain enemy from the road, filling the ditch with corpses. In my nightmares, the bulldozer was not painted in the customary bright yellow, but rather, cloaked in the standard, olive drab color used by the Army.

Invariably, my tortured reverie would revert to where I was stranded alone in a position near the bottom of the enemy-held hill, on the north side of the pass. A huge convoy of enemy Soviet T-34 tanks and troop transport trucks were stopped. In my ensuing nightmares, I was lost behind enemy lines, and I was frantically trying to return to the American side. I envisioned being surrounded by North Korean soldiers, methodically searching for me. I would hide in or under enemy vehicles, holding my breath in terror that I would be discovered. As the enemy closed in on my concealment, I would surreptitiously slip away to another hiding site, only to have the enemy close in on me again and again. That frightful scenario would startlingly awaken me gasping and shaking in fear, heavy perspiration dripping from my body. Those awful nightmares consumed my entire life, generally visiting me three or four times a week.

In 1995, I heard about a reunion of the 29th Infantry Regiment, to be hosted at Fort Benning, Georgia. At the reunion, Colonel Hughes and I discussed our experiences, especially the Anui affair.

I told Colonel Hughes about my frequent nightmares in respect to the Battle of Chinju Pass. He listened intently and earnestly and in a short while, he removed his ever-present corncob pipe from his mouth and slowly and deliberately replied, "Pete, you are almost right. But it wasn't a bulldozer we had; it was one of our three Sherman tanks, one with a *dozer* blade attached and you're right. He was pushing dead North Koreans in the ditch where your squad was pinned down that morning. And, you are right about the trucks. There was a big convoy of enemy tanks and trucks

---

[18] Appleman, p. 242.

on the other side of the pass. The North Koreans abandoned them when they took off running. We sent the South Korean Army in and they brought them all back or destroyed them there, so you were correct."

The colonel finished by saying, "We won that one big that day!"

If that were so, then, in my subconscious, I must have seen the four American captured youth, their hands tied behind them, each murdered by a shot to the base of the skull. Everyone one else saw them.

I never had those specific nightmares again.

Later, when I recalled that dreadful conflict, I wondered how the South Korean Army could have accomplished the mission of confiscating or destroying the convoy, given that the First Battalion apparently withdrew from the Pass.

The enemy was still in the process of driving victoriously into Pusan, to liberate the thriving port in the name of The Democratic People's Republic of Korea, whether South Korea liked it or not. The 1st Battalion apparently stopped them cold.

They deserved it.

THE HOSPITAL

> The programme presented a ribald and irreverent view of the 1950-53, conflict through the eyes of colourful medics such as Hawkeye and "Hotlips" Houlihan. It showed the protagonists over-coming the horrors of war with japery and an acerbic wit. In their mobile Army Surgical Hospital (M*A*S*H) alcohol and madcap antics flowed...BBC News, 24 July 2003.

This 4 August 1950 began as usual, unbearably hot and muggy as well—over 100 degrees as the sun roared through the eastern sky. The maddening flies awoke with the first light, but Baker Company had been up for some time, since well before dawn. I have a memory lapse on where and how the company spent the night. The shock of Anui followed rapidly by the Chinju Pass debacle was the culprit.

Baker Company quietly withdrew from Chinju Pass about 5 p.m. the night before, after being savaged once again by the North Korean 6th Infantry Division. But this time Lieutenant Hughes' Baker Company marched out in an orderly manner rather than fleeing in panic. As a consequence of the battle at Chinju, the company lost half of the 21 original survivors who escaped from Anui. However, on this occasion, other companies in the 1st Battalion sustained heavier losses—particularly members of Charlie Company, decimated by the enemy ambush on the north side of the Pass.

Each day, from each company, a Morning Report is to be submitted to battalion headquarters about the status of the unit and the individuals assigned to the particular company. The reports were long overdue— not tendered because of the debacle at Anui, followed by the Battle of Chinju Pass. Now it was deemed essential that the reports be brought up to date and forwarded to battalion headquarters. The status of the company was eight days behind, an unheard-of time span by contemporary Army standards. It was just as well. The terrible loss of the vast majority of company personnel during the eight days of fighting would have made the reports irrelevant in any case.

The company was temporarily bivouacked somewhere south of Chinju, where Sergeant Pappy assembled surviving company members at the periphery of a dirt road near a local village. They congregated under a sparse tree that afforded no respite from the broiling sun and absolutely no relief from the soaring humid heat. Troops huddled informally around Pappy, as he knelt on one knee on the ground with a company roster and a crudely sharpened stub of a pencil to check the names of missing or dead. The few survivors were asked to reply with any information relative to the status of a member of the company, as Pappy softly called off names of Baker Company personnel in alphabetical order.

Responses from the survivors were non-emotional and matter-of-fact. Secretly, all were thankful for being alive. A similar comparison would be as when a friend discovers his or her acquaintance to be afflicted with a terminal illness. The party is dispirited for the friend's sake, but at the same time, he or she is relieved they are not the party afflicted. After each name was called, someone generally responded.

"Sergeant Musselwhite's dead. I saw him get it at..." Another name, and another would chime in, "Yeah, Smith got it, too. He took one to the head..." And so on down the roster.

Whenever a name was called that did not elicit a response, awkward silence prevailed. Subsequent to each verbal confirmation, Sergeant Pappy dutifully scratched a line through the name of the slain soldier. Because of the high volume of dead, it was easier than to scribble KIA (Killed in Action). Sergeant Bruner filled in those he remembered were left in the schoolhouse, and I recalled a few Sergeant Bruner overlooked. Survivors named those they knew as definitely dead, such as the 1st Sergeant. Others unaccounted for would be listed as MIA (Missing in Action), even though it was a justifiable assumption that those alive were captured and subsequently murdered by North Korean soldiers, sadists all.

Following the completion of the Morning Report, troops fell out to rest, consume a can of unpalatable C-Rations, smoke a cigarette, and wait. Waiting was an unfailing commodity in the army—it never required rationing.

Late on this morning I boarded the hospital train at the nondescript village Hamm, northwest of Pusan, where the main hospital was situated. The battalion was positioned generally southeast of Chinju, where the next defensive site was to be established.

Other severely wounded soldiers were carried aboard the same train by stretcher, signifying that they had to live with severe wounds for over 24 hours, pending triage at the hospital in Pusan. Bob Jones, who sustained three bullet wounds, was one of many severely wounded, although I didn't know Jones at the time. He was assigned to the 2nd Battalion in Okinawa, which had been abruptly and unceremoniously stripped of personnel, and reassigned to the 1st and 3rd Battalions.

In addition to his gunshot wounds, Jones developed a ruptured appendix, and underwent an emergency operation on the train ride to Pusan under very trying and primitive conditions. Concurrently, he contracted a serious case of hepatitis, most likely as a consequence of the filthy conditions during the operation. Some people have all the luck.

I was ambulatory, or *walking wounded*, as indicated on a large manila colored tag everyone wore tied by a string to a button on the field shirt. The tag, in addition to routine information and identification of the individual, described the wound and the priority of treatment in numerical order. Tags represented *triage,* the process where the most seriously wounded are treated first.

Wounded boarded a relic that supposedly passed as modern transportation. The entire ancient passenger compartment was constructed of wood, painted outside in a dull, deep red that had faded considerably over the many years. The seats were likewise constructed of wood, fashioned with a flat seat and an equally flat backrest that was extremely high, considering the average height of the population. The seats were most likely built to protect the head and neck of passengers who were subjected to the many abrupt sudden lurching starts and impulsive stops.[19]

Notwithstanding, there was one redeeming factor of the normally uncomfortable vertical high seat backs. Two of the seat backs comfortably accommodated one litter, which effectively raised the severely wounded to an elevated, more secure level to be attended to more easily. Additionally, the frequent, hazardous lurching of the train seemed to affect a patient in a litter somewhat less than those who were ambulatory.

The toilet was a hole in the floor, cordoned off by a wall, open to public view on the side. The entire passenger compartment reeked with a foul and nauseating stench resulting from multitudes of passengers who over the years elected to urinate or defecate behind the floor space in back of the last wooden seat. Both areas had deep revolting stains and a repulsive smell to corroborate usage. It was impossible to evade the vomit-inducing odor that made the entire compartment seem a public toilet. The toilet itself was open to use by anyone, including pedestrian traffic, when the train stopped at a station.

Toilet paper was unknown in Korea. Inhabitants used their hands. There was no washbasin. Disease was rampant and parasitic infestation in the population was common. No one was immune. It appeared that eve-

---

[19] The first recorded history of the accepted and defined Post Traumatic Stress Disorder occurred during the beginning of The Industrial Revolution. Clear evidence of stress was discovered in train passengers as a result of sudden and frequent stops and starts in the primitive train system. Constant lurching, braking, whip wrenching movements, and over-turned compartments all inflicted a serious emotional toll on early passengers who dared to ride. Author.

ryone who served in the Koreas contracted *ascaris,* a serious intestinal parasite resulting from food contaminated with human waste.

Two huge cloth banners depicting a bright red cross superimposed on a white background were secured to each side of the train, in the vain hope that enemy would honor the insignia. Those of us who faced the North Korean Army knew better. No one was considered safe in any sector of the Koreas.[20]

The journey began with neck-snapping starts, followed by abrupt stops that pitched everyone forward, then backward, cracking backs of heads against the high, wooden seat backs. Unfortunately the spasmodic, aberrant, movements continued for some time as the ancient locomotive surged in an effort to gain sufficient momentum for the archaic steel wheels to break from stationary mode. After numerous brusque starts and stops at the same velocity, the primitive train's motion eventually became smoother and in due course the train attained a relatively steadfast speed of about 30 miles an hour.

Powered by steam and fed by coal, this was yet another artifact of the Japanese occupation of Korea from 1905 until 1945. The primitive locomotive belched a perpetual cloud of obnoxious, black smoke that erupted from the primal smoke stack, resembling an active fiery volcano. There was no escape from the loathsome soot that completely covered everyone with a black coat of heavy grime.

The protracted, arduous trip was one of total boredom, to the extent that even the consumption of my one issued can of C-Rations offered diversion. With that I opened my C-ration can of pork and beans just as the train plunged into a long, dark tunnel. With the lack of lighting, the train pitched headlong into dismal ebony. In time, the locomotive escaped from the clutches of the dingy dungeon of the tunnel, and as the train erratically chugged into sunlight, the soot captured in the tunnel made the situation worse than ever. The insidious smoke captured in the tunnel, having no space to escape, billowed out of control directly into the cars. The abominable food, me, and other wounded, were covered with black coal cinders and coal dust.

The trip was an all-day, tortuous, grueling train ride. We traversed perhaps a total of 40 miles. During the journey, passengers were subject to attack by organized guerrillas trying to blow up the train, or at the least, to fire upon it in order to maximize behind-the-lines terror in this so-

---

[20] Appleman, p.383.

called *safe* sector.[21]

It was a unique train ride. The velocity of the locomotive was slow enough for us to avoid being wind-blown. At the same time, we could lean out of the glassless window and find for the first time the flies were helpless, unable to crawl on our hands and faces—a wondrous experience.

On arrival at the RTO (rail transportation office) in the overcrowded, bustling Port of Pusan, the last citadel of freedom for the defenders against the northern insurgents, patients were off-loaded into three-quarter-ton ambulances that ferried them across primitive, oil-coated dirt roads. In a short while they arrived at the hospital, a large former high school, commandeered by Army medical staff as the most viable building for their immediate needs. Designated the 8209th Mobile Army Surgical Hospital (MASH), it was the first and only military hospital in the country at the time. Many more were slated to arrive, to eventually tend to a mind-numbing backlog of nearly 62,000 wounded Americans.

The interior of the ancient structure was reminiscent of a scene from *Gone with the Wind*, a chaotic, disordered array of utter confusion. Army cots, soaked with blood and dirt from countless wounded soldiers were strewn haphazardly everywhere, totally out of any semblance of order. It was so unlike the military. From day one soldiers were taught order. Everything in military life was performed in a carefully prescribed manner, down to the precise manner in which uniforms were hung in wall lockers. The hospital could only be described as confused bedlam.

Medical staff and walking wounded had to weave in and out and around the cots, arrayed like an obstacle course that clearly inhibited efficiency of treatment. Litter bearers were obliged to lift stretchers high enough to avoid other patients and staff, as they methodically threaded their way through the disparate mob and narrow passages to locate an empty cot for newly arriving wounded. There was a pervasive sense that there was no time to set up operations to maximize efficiency because of the overpowering flood of seriously wounded.

---

[21] U.N. convoys continued to be fired on; individual soldiers were sometimes killed. The troop and hospital trains running between Pusan and Taegu - in spite of frequent rail side patrols, security posts and flatcars filled with infantry on each train - were fired on almost daily, sometimes with casualties.

A favorite trick of the insurgents was to slip close to the rails by night, set up a machine gun, and wait until a well-lighted hospital train–its passengers strapped helplessly in berths - puffed by. Then, in a matter of seconds the train could be sprayed with bullets, the gun dismantled and the guerrillas, in white peasant garb, gone into the night. Fehrenbach, p. 389.

Medical staff members were clearly overwhelmed by the lack of professional assistance to deal with the vast, constant overload of critically maimed soldiers. Doctors were exhaustively overburdened, and one could perceive the unmistakable weariness in the eyes of dedicated doctors and gallant nurses who unselfishly toiled nearly around the clock.

~~

Someone pointed out one of the cots for me to occupy. I meandered through the maze of the disorganized crowd, keeping my eye on the assigned stretcher, lest I lose sight of it in the surrounding pandemonium. The cot was saturated with fresh wet blood, and covered with the usual abhorrent flies. I wondered if the last occupier survived his terrible trauma. The excessive amount of spilled blood did not portend well for the patient, and I felt embarrassed in the knowledge that my flesh wound was more of a nuisance than of a serious nature.

I was directed to sit until a doctor was available to treat me, so I had the time to glance about and witness utter disarray, interwoven with moans of teenagers dying. The wait was lengthy as others were far more seriously wounded. Filthy bandages were discarded on the floor. The bindings placed on soldiers when they were initially wounded remained unchanged, and by the time they were able to reach this terminal medical facility, the dressings were foul, blood-caked, tattered rags.

Viscous blood mixed with body fluids seeped everywhere, on the floor, on the cots, and on the pathetic victims. Upon death, muscles relaxed and the corpses urinated. The gagging fumes permeated the entire complex. The absence of flush toilets in the country only heightened the awful stench that drifted in from the surrounding country and clashed head-on with the repulsive stink of the dead and the dying.

It was an awful wait for medical attention, as I gazed hypnotized around the huge, unsanitary room, viewing the plight of teenagers who gave their all in obedience to their country's leaders. Perhaps if those same leaders could view this terrible, demonic scene, other alternatives to war could be possible.

By now, my through-and-through bullet wound had essentially healed on its own. The physically exhausted doctor approached and inquired, "What happened to you, soldier?"

"I was shot about a week ago, sir, but it seems OK now."

"Let me be the judge of that. Where were you hit?"

Clearly the overworked military doctor had lost his forbearance, though he tried to mask it with his aloof demeanor. My shirt was already removed on the advice of the one who directed me to this particular blood-saturated cot.

I pointed to the entry hole of my gunshot near my left rear rib cage.

"I'm sorry, sir, I can't tell exactly where it came out. Somewhere out the side of my left back, I think."

"I see it," he replied curtly.

"Does this hurt?" he asked as he pressed his thumb or finger firmly in the exit hole.

"No sir," I lied.

"Well, I need to make sure that the bullet cleared your body."

With his stated goal to determine if the bullet clearly exited my body, he picked up a steel rod and without any hesitation or anesthesia, the doctor forced the rod into the now-healed entry bullet hole, tearing and ripping soft, supple flesh that had regenerated earlier. He continued to forcefully probe and drive the metal rod completely though, following the path of the initial enemy projectile until the rigid rod, now visible, was vigorously extruded from the exit wound. A massive amount of spurting blood sluiced the unique tool of torture, as the inflexible rod reopened what was once an earlier healed body wound.

It took everything I could possibly muster to keep from screaming from the God-awful pain that was more severe than the enemy round that initially tore through my body. I wasn't even provided with a lead bullet to bite down on to stifle the cry of pain as was routinely furnished in similar medical episodes during the Civil War. And this venue was clearly reminiscent of a scene from the Civil War.

Medical records attest that I was shot on 3 August, the day of the carnage at Chinju Pass, when in fact I was wounded at Anui, eight days earlier. That may have been the reason that the doctor forced the steel rod through my healed wound, believing it to be a recent gunshot injury only two days old.

In my view, the hospital was consecrated as sacred, hallowed ground as I observed the dead and the dying in these somber surroundings. An outcry of pain by me would be all but sacrilegious, given the severity of horrendous wounds of many young men who were brave enough to accept and stifle their extreme pain.

The school window was void of glass, similar to the schoolhouse at Anui as well as the train. Huge Sikorsky helicopters flown by Marine Squadron VMO-6 brought in the majority of critical cases of battlefield wounded. Despite the large carrying capacity, including wire stretchers bolted firmly to the skids of the aircraft, many young soldiers died en route to the hospital. This was the first systematic use of helicopters to evacuate the wounded, and it was a blessing. Transportation by any other means was slow, primitive and subject to frequent insurgent guerrilla attacks.

As the mammoth helicopters began their initial landing maneuver, the huge, horizontal blades whipped the heavy playground dust into a frenzied, squalid cyclone. The earth the landing threw up far surpassed what any convoy of trucks could muster, as the man-made wind spawned a hurricane of foul air difficult to inhale. The unbelievably violent backwash from the blades of these elephantine flying monsters spewed grit into the bowels of the building, and any pretense of sterilization was impossible under such adverse conditions.

The odious stench of fresh blood seemed to attract every filthy fly in the port city of Pusan. Added to that was the offensive, nauseating smell of unwashed uniforms and bodies, combined with the overpowering smell of antiseptic blending with foul odors drifting from the primitive city.

One could recognize immediately those young soldiers who recently died. The adolescent victims predictably died with mouths agape, permitting loathsome flies to crawl in and out of the orifice at will, seeking shelter to lay their fertile eggs. They perpetuated this vicious life cycle to propagate and nourish their enormous population. Other wounded, too incapacitated to move, lay motionless and helpless as myriad swarms of flies, lacking restrictions, crawled freely over faces and festering wounds.

Through it all, doctors and nurses carried on, performing the impossible in this dreadful makeshift environment. Those producers in the entertainment industry should have visited this facility before they embarked on their sitcom, M*A*S*H. It really wasn't humorous to watch young boys die by the score in the most awful, degrading manner. If the gravely wounded arrived at this terminus, they were seriously wounded, dying or dead. I was the exception.

The doctor applied new bandages to stop the fresh spurt of blood, as I bit my lower lip to stifle any outburst from pain. In an ineffectual attempt to appear nonchalant by gazing about, I noticed a cot situated in front of mine, placed in an irregular angle. The wounded soldier's boots were nearly facing me as he lay on his back. Unexpectedly, his treating doctor lifted him to a sitting position to examine his shirtless, wounded back. There was a huge bandage wrapped several times around his chest to staunch massive bleeding. Recent blood seepage soaked through the gauze bandage over the area of the heart, the soldier's *Red Badge of Courage*. I wondered how anyone could possibly survive a calamitous wound in such a critical region of the body.

I was startled beyond words. It was Stevens, presumed to have been slain at Chinju Pass and who later was unceremoniously thrown on the truck filled with the dead. When I glanced at Stevens, it was such a bittersweet feeling to see my good friend alive, even though, at the same time, he was borderline dead, eyes closed. I called his name softly, but he could not comprehend. He was in deep shock from loss of blood and the near-fatal wound.

Stevens was apparently shot in the back, the projectile ricocheting though his upper body, exiting the front chest cavity in close proximity to his heart. The exit wound tore a massive amount of tissue from the area of the left chest. It was understandable for Captain Hughes and his assistant to judge Stevens dead and throw him on the death truck. For all practicable purposes, Stevens was indeed, dead. His pulse was barely perceivable as he slipped into a dying coma. To this day I do not know if Stevens survived, though I would wager that anyone who could master the guitar as well as he, coupled with his perseverance and his love of life, could triumph over this tragedy as well. I am the only one alive today that knows of the circumstances of the ill-fated death ride that Stevens underwent before he was discovered to be alive, and off-loaded to the hospital. I have attempted many times to locate him so that I could share with him the legend of his near fatal ordeal of which even he is unaware. Alas, with a common name of Stevens and my inability to recall his given name, I have been in a lifetime quandary as how to locate him. My plaintive hope is that he will hear of the biannual reunion of the 29th Infantry Regiment at Fort Benning and respond.

I believe that I earned my first of three Purple Heart Medals when the doctor reopened my healed wound, rather than when I was originally shot at Anui. The Department of the Army posted the following information relative to my gunshot wound in this exact fashion, and again, this is perhaps why the doctor elected to reopen what he believed to be a fresh wound.

PETREDIS PAUL G JR *Rank=***PV2** *Serial Number=***RA19358907** *State of Record=***CA** *County of Record=***LOS ANGELES** *Race=*1 *Year of Birth=Branch* **INFANTRY** *Military Occupation Specialty* **(4745) Light Weapons Infantryman** *Assigned Unit* **29th Inf Regt**

RCT *Place of casualty*_**S Korea** *Date of Casualty (Year/Mo/Day)* **1950/08/03** *Casualty Description=***Seriously WIA by missile- Returned to Duty (FECOM)** *Dispositions of Evacuations*

The official Army record reproduced above noted 3 August as the date I was wounded in action the first time, when in actuality it was 27 July. Although the wound was not serious, one ought to factor in the psychological import of being shot at 18 years of age, just one month after the first American ground forces were committed to The Forgotten War.

I wasn't even provided with a clean uniform as I was unceremoniously dispatched from the hospital to my unit, then to the front, wherever that was.

THE GRAVEYARD

> High above all other cults and customs stands Ancestor Worship. It is the keystone of Korea's gateway to the happy lands of prosperity and success. To neglect it blocks the whole highway toward life and hope. A good ancestor worshiper may consult the Buddha, ... but to forget the ancestors and to resort to these only would be to pray to the shadow without the essence. Ancestor worship possesses completely the heart and soul of Korea. Gale, p. 69.

Because of my emotional confusion at the time, I do not remember boarding the same rickety train for the return trip north, or for that matter, whether I was even armed. I most likely was transported back to the train by way of the same military ambulance that carried me to the hospital. I do recall that I still wore the same filthy, dirt-encrusted uniform. I didn't realize it until much later, but the American Army committed to this conflict without the capabilities of logistical supply, particularly of ammunition.

Once the train was underway, I discovered the life-threatening, bone-breaking ride back was a reincarnation of the original excursion south. The return journey was also notable because of one of the wounded returnees. The soldier's head wound was so obvious that it could not be avoided. Whatever happened, happened to his head, because he had a head cast on that completely surrounded his head. The surgical white-colored dressing was at least two inches thick. He could not possibly don a helmet, relegating the young soldier to being a live moving target. There marched another classic example of the frenetic desperation of the American Army in the first bloody days after American ground forces were committed to The Forgotten War. The soldier should have been medevaced to a military hospital in Japan. Instead he was on his way back to battle. I was wondering about the reason as I recalled the words of a friend.

He queried me on why governments send boys to fight their wars instead of men, and I theorized it was because young men were physically fit, possessing strong stamina, particularly in order to scale the precipitous mountains of Korea while burdened with heavy implements of war.

"Wrong," he said. "They send boys to fight, because boys obey orders without question. Would you do the same things at 35 that they told you to do at age 18?"

My friend had a point.

After disembarking and walking for miles, attempting to pay attention to the military unit identification signs, I somehow wandered into the wrong regimental headquarters. It was the 27th *Wolf Hound* Infantry Regiment, one of three component regiments that made up the 25th Infantry Division. Colonel Michaelis, *Iron Mike,* American Army legend, with whom everyone wanted to serve, commanded the regiment.[22] He was tough, combat experienced and he single handedly melded his troops into a unified, formidable combat unit. When I first saw Colonel Michaelis, I was staring at an icon, handsome, well built, professional and charismatic. That was the Colonel.

When I first saw them together, the colonel seemed to be absorbed with Marguerite *Maggie* Higgens, reporter for the New York *Herald Tribune*.[23] She won the Pulitzer Prize for her dynamic, close up coverage of the Korean War, primarily by appearing suddenly at battle sites where angels feared to tread.

I was envious of the colonel. Higgens was tall, slim, leggy and gorgeous. I was a private.

Higgens arrived at Michael's regimental center of operations to draft a story about the colonel and his legendary *Wolf Hound* Regiment, when the Command Post came under unexpected, heavy attack by infiltrated NKPA soldiers.[24] Following a lengthy, concentrated running gun battle, the enemy ultimately was repulsed by regimental cadre, under the personal direction of Colonel Michaelis, but not before the foe inflicted heavy damage. The antagonists' use of heavy machine gun fire against personnel of regimental headquarters resulted in Higgens' narrow escape from death. She had had the foresight to dive under a table for protection during the surprise attack. The event was one of many documented close encounters during her war correspondent days near hostile action.

It was sweltering hot as usual, with sky-high humidity that drained all my energy during my search for Baker Company. I finally located my company after hiking in the direct sun for hours, arriving in a sopping, perspiration-dripping uniform which merely provided additional rank fumes to my filthy, heavy uniform shirt. Baker Company was widely dispersed, most likely to minimize casualties, should the enemy deploy artillery in the area. Lieutenant Hughes bivouacked the company in a small,

---

[22] Dwight Eisenhower… singled out Michaelis as one of four lieutenant colonels in the Army "of Extraordinary Ability." Blair, p.145.

[23] Aware that some of her colleagues disliked her for being pushy, she felt that she was the equal of any man and had proved herself in Europe. For her Korea was more than a story. It was a crusade. Toland, p. 50.

[24] Spurr, p. 26.

abandoned orchard that afforded no shelter from the searing heat.

There were more soldiers now assigned to the company than the 21 survivors who escaped from Anui. None of the survivors in the company knew from where they came, and we surmised the Army depleted other units of personnel, and then summarily erased those units from military history books. There were no new replacements to augment our ranks until late September when the draft was reactivated. I didn't know many Baker Company personnel who had been assigned to the unit in Okinawa just two months prior to the outbreak of The Forgotten War. I knew even less of the new conscripts assigned to B Company.

After I reported to company commander John C. Hughes, still a below grade 1st lieutenant, I was assigned to the 3rd Platoon. I wandered over to introduce myself only to recognize but one person—Jim Reed.

Later, we met often socially, subsequent to mutual discharges from service, and a great deal of lighthearted banter generally ensued.

~~

Baker Company formed in a single column and moved out a few hours later in the afternoon. I can't recall where I obtained another rifle, gun belt and helmet. They may have been issued to me at the hospital, before I boarded the same foul-smelling train in Pusan for the return trip to the company. There was no such thing as a front line during the first stage of the war. ROKs and Americans were fleeing to avoid further entrapment and wholesale massacre by the NKPA.

Only Hughes knew our objective and direction. We didn't know if we were advancing or retreating, but the survivors were sure the North Korean People's Army would pulverize them when they were next engaged. The single file column, with the usual five-yard interval between each soldier, snaked lengthily and silently through the hot and steamy, wide, fertile valley as we hiked the silt-laden roads of South Korea.

The humid, late afternoon slowly transformed to dusk, and then quickly evolved into night, as the arduous march continued on the ancient footpaths to God knows where. Hughes made a decision to seize the high ground, so the company veered from the road, crossed the wide, ever-present fields of sour-smelling rice paddies, walked the dikes to avoid the putrid water, and then began a slow, grueling ascent into the mountains.

Hughes forged a new, difficult trail, as we battled scrub brush that tore at uniforms, slipped back on virgin grasses, recovered to forge laboriously forward until we at last conquered the majestic summit. It was at high elevation, and a relatively level area, as opposed to the typical sharp crest of a mountain. Baker Company unknowingly entered the sanctuary of a Korean burial ground, a necropolis, a cemetery, whose consecrated soil is considered inviolate to the Korean people. The company approached and entered from the wrong way.

~~

Korean tradition dictates that the deceased be buried on the highest of peaks after due preparation. To that end, the Koreans sculpt the highest peak of a mountain range to bury their beloved dead for eternity and with utmost dignity. Hundreds of people gather to prepare the grounds by hacking, shoveling and tilling the soil until the crest of a mountain has been decapitated, leveled, widened and transformed into a grassy plain that only then is consecrated as a cemetery. The dead are buried overlooking panoramic vistas, and access is provided by use of a footpath from the base of the mountain to the gravesite. Hughes didn't know that. The company invaded via the scenic route.

The tortuous climb evolved into a slow paced struggle because of the precipitous, near vertical rise. After successfully scaling the towering mountain, company troops collapsed in absolute exhaustion on top of the mountain, gasping for air from the rigors of the arduous climb. The terrain was dry, awaiting the belated monsoon rains to cleanse the lands. The steaming, muggy humidity hung as a curtain in the motionless air and depleted exhausted soldiers of any last energy. They reposed in a park-like setting, as opposed to having been greeted by native shrub growth at the apex of a mountain. The area was seeded in meticulous lawn and appeared to have been recently tended. [25]

The night plodded wearily on, joined by the hot, sticky weather, as the troops who conquered the nearly sheer mountain lay exhausted. A glistening moon and stars shined brightly, and serenity descended softly and gently on the grassy park. Were it not for the intense heat, humidity and maddening swarms of mosquitoes, it would have been pleasant.

The mountains of South Korea were denuded of forests over hundreds of years by over-timbering for construction of homes that mimicked Japa-

---

[25] A professional "earth master" (Chi-sa) ground doctor, tomb inspector or what ever you may call him, is summoned by a chief of a house and asked to find a grave site for the family. He is father-confessor but instead of pointing upward he points down. He requires money too and the more the better, if the family would be redeemed by his lucky findings. He seeks out a quiet spur of a hill that looks off toward enclosing peaks. There must be no oozy waters, no noisy people, no nerve-wearing winds, but the gentle breeze, the quiet of the hills, and the full blessings of the sun-shine. Gale, p. 70.

nese residences, as well as for firewood. This cleared, consecrated area was ideal territory for a Korean cemetery, or if need be, to fight a war.

Westerners surmise the dead are buried in a sitting position based on the burial mounds' height of three to four feet. In fact the dead are entombed in the standing position. First, a two to three foot hole is dug. The deceased is covered with some type of shroud that protects the cadaver from soil, and, at the same time, allows dirt to adhere to the shroud. The result is a tent-like device that shields the deceased. The earth covering the shroud is seeded with grass to preserve the exterior mound of earth, as well as the immediate grounds. The loftier the peak, the higher the status of the deceased—and these were indeed, astounding heights.

In defiance of the ongoing brutal war, which now was approaching what soldiers naively believed to be the zenith of the conflict in only the second month, someone had taken painful steps to preserve this hallowed sanctuary meticulously. The company discovered later that had we traversed the east ridge, we would have found a long, gradual slope, with a well-worn footpath, that was almost arrow straight to the cemetery. The western ridge that we ascended afforded a near-impossible approach to gain entry into the sanctuary. We inadvertently violated consecrated grounds.

"Incoming mail! Incoming mail!" The number one feared words in the vernacular of an infantryman. There is no defense, except to hunker down and pray to God.

"Enemy artillery! Dig in! Dig in! Dig! Dig!" screamed a nearby platoon sergeant. Troops instantaneously removed entrenching tools and frantically started the collective defensive labor. The enemy hadn't quite zeroed in on the company completely as yet, the initial rounds were falling short and then long in the basic process of artillery fire to determine accurate location to emplace saturation fire.

They were getting close. How the enemy detected the company in the night will never be known. The smoking lamp was out. No one dare light up in such hostile territory. No one had to be given an order to that effect, as the consequences were understood. It may have been an enemy forward observer who was situated not far from us who signaled to the enemy artillery, advising our position, or it may have been an enemy agent, secreted in a village that observed our route and then reported us.

In the blink of an eye, I dove for shelter behind one of the burial mounds under the erroneous assumption that the mound would absorb most of the impact from any deadly rounds now screaming in. It is the most fearful sound in the world and one from which there is no protection.

I frantically dug, or rather hacked from a kneeling position to lower myself as a target, my body stretched beyond the point of balance, my entrenching tool set in the hoe position. I burrowed furiously in an area just behind a forward burial mound, rapidly digging for safety. A positive work ethic was refined, courtesy of the enemy. Dig or die. I was like a hurricane, shoveling huge clods of earth without letup. I had to make shelter from the lethal shrapnel that was the by-product of a high explosive artillery round.

Perspiration poured from my face, swamping me in a noiseless conspiracy with the elevated humidity, as I continued my demanding efforts. Sweat washed into my eyes causing salty liquid to burn to the point that I could not see. I attempted to wipe the briny secretion away with the back of my shirtsleeve, only to suffer grief from the disturbed soil from my uniform as I inadvertently smeared it into burning eyes.

The entrenching tool discovered earlier-disturbed soil from the initial excavation of the tomb, even though the grass-covered grave appeared to be eons old. Unexpectedly, the ground gave away, and in a split second, I plunged headfirst into the bottom of the crypt some two to three feet below ground level.

As an 18-year-old adolescent, I was naïve, immature, and absolutely terrified. My body weight was distributed so far forward that my upper body was trapped in this hideous hole from which there was no escape. My helmet dropped from my head and rolled next to me at the bottom of the abyss leaving me defenseless from falling debris. The bones of the dead, once poised in eternal reverie, now collapsed angrily, striking me again and again in the back of the head and shoulders, co-mingling with silt of the grave that spilled forth over my head and neck. By each and every means I futilely attempted to free myself from this grisly, jet-black chasm. It was impossible to release myself because of my death grip on the Army shovel. I dare not release it as the implement and rifle were the only objects that would permit me to survive. I needed both hands to work myself out, and I risked all by not releasing my grasp on the entrenching tool.

I could not cry out, for my shouts would go unheeded because of the horrific clamor of the enemy artillery roaring in. Heavy perspiration saturated my uniform, soaking my flesh and drawing every dirt particle like a magnet.

I continued to flinch in abject horror, my hand recoiling from the touch of the defiled, dank bones. It was as if I had touched a high voltage wire, forcing me in panic to retract my hand. I slid back again into the unfathomable abyss, my heart racing, adrenaline pumping and erasing any conceivable gains that I might have made. The onerous smell of death filled the chamber, magnified by the trapped stale air that was interred with the corpse. I struggled again with all of my might to exit the tomb, only to touch the contaminated, human bones again and again as I drew back in absolute terror. My head was pounding unmercifully from the blood rushing forward since I had pitched forward in a near upside-down position.

During this continuing nightmare, enemy artillery found its mark. The mountain was zeroed in, and enemy was pouring round after round into the company position. Everyone was dug in but me. Violent, earth-shaking explosions, followed by the shrill scream of razor-sharp shrapnel filled the blistering night, as cannon ripped through man and earth. At least the upper part of my body was safe. Or was it? Each time I attempted to escape, my tension and fright would build to a crescendo, as I slid back again in this vile chamber of horror. It was my forward weight that would not release me. The center of gravity acted as a ball and chain that continued my imprisonment. I was a captive of the worst nightmare that an 18-year-old could possibly endure, and I could not escape.

I reprised this futile escape exercise time after time, and after what seemed to be an eternity, and by some unknown miracle, I gained freedom by somehow backing out of this dark, damp chamber of horror.

When finally I broke free, I collapsed on my back, totally depleted, physically and emotionally. I panted and gasped for air as I lay in the cool grass, oblivious to the enemy rounds that wedded with the endless swarms of mosquitoes, now sapping my face of blood. I could not move. But I realized that I still had an unyielding grip on my entrenching tool. Even if it meant I was to die then and there from enemy artillery, I knew that I did not possess the capacity to move, let alone to dig again in an effort to save my life.

When first I pitched forward into this macabre *Alice in Wonderland* nightmare of the bottomless abyss, I recalled how my helmet fell from my head where it coupled with skeleton. *My helmet. I have to retrieve my helmet. No way.* I knew that I would be held accountable, not only because of the loss of my helmet. Because of the absence of one, I would expose my face to shine, the reflection of which might be observed by enemy. That was the primary reason we were taught in basic infantry training to not gaze skyward at low-flying observation airplanes.

There was not one thing or one person in the universe who could persuade me to retrieve my helmet where it lay. I would not go back in that horrific, bone-laden chasm for anything on earth. Even though I could have left my entrenching tool inside, which would have freed both hands to promote swifter escape, I would not do so. I would surely have to answer to someone for my loss, but it could never be as harsh as the first option. Someone would have to shoot me first.

There was a lull in the artillery barrage and then someone whispered hoarsely, "Move out!"

It was the platoon sergeant that grunted the command. Company personnel staggered piecemeal from makeshift shelters, as I struggled to lift myself from the grassy field. One followed another, quick time, bent over, single file, in absolute silence. Smoking was *verboten* as Baker Company rapidly fled east, away from the malignant artillery barrage. Hughes located relief from the deadly artillery less than half mile away, on the same mountain ridge. The enemy was unaware of the swift departure. They were left to kill everyone in the cemetery. Fortunately, they were wasting artillery shells on victims already dead.

"Dig in!" the NCO commanded in the same grating whisper to two men nearest him. The platoon sergeant led, the rest followed in silence, as he pointed to two soldiers at a time, on where to dig emplacements to form a cohesive defensive perimeter. As always, it was below the ridge to avoid a silhouette, particularly during the day. Foxholes dug below the crest of a mountain or skyline, were always standard operating procedure for the infantry. I didn't know the replacement soldier that was digging with me but it didn't matter as we hastily and silently eked out a hole large enough to accommodate the two of us.

Once the platoon secured a viable defensive perimeter, and the NCO confirmed that everyone was dug in at acceptable intervals, he returned to our position:

"Where's your helmet, soldier?" the sergeant asked in the same gruff whisper, because he didn't know me. We were both new to the restructured company.

"I don't know, Sarge. I think I lost it when the artillery was coming in on us," I lied.

"Well, rub a little dirt on your face then."

"OK, Sarge."

He apparently didn't notice the film of grit covering my face and head that resulted from falling in the burial pit. The sergeant also failed to detect the awful smell of death that I believed must permeate my soggy uniform. I couldn't escape the stench or the grime, as I tried to wipe the loathsome filth from my face, in the vain hope that I could wipe away the nightmare along with it.

And that was that.

During the night, I wondered how I would react when I was about to become involved in a third major attack in just a short period of approximately two weeks. I questioned just how much more of this intensive, fearful action could I endure before I either became a seasoned combat soldier or just cracked up completely in the effort?

It was my first exposure to enemy artillery, and the frightening occurrence plumbs to the very soul in the fear department among foot soldiers. It is so because there is no defense. It is not possible to fight back with bullets against an unseen enemy armed with an armada of cannon.

During basic training, recruits should have been exposed to controlled live action explosions and live machine gun fire overhead, which was the norm for infantry training during World War II. But this was the peacetime Army. There was no time for that. Soldiers were required to polish brass, clean equipment and rifles for the incessant inspections. That was it. None had fired an M-1 Rifle since they left the rifle range during basic training at Fort Ord. It seemed to be a thousand years ago.

We were on one hundred percent alert that night in anxious anticipation of enemy attack. No one slept. The mosquitoes were seemingly delegated to guarantee that no one so much as dozed. They fulfilled their task well, acting as a constant reminder to remain awake and alert.

During the very late and silent night, a single, deafening, ear-splitting explosion occurred on the top, level segment of our ridge. My foxhole buddy and I were dug in on the side of the hill in front of the blast, and we witnessed the brief flash of the explosion mirrored against the black sky. Curiously, we did not detect the awful scream of the incoming projectile, nor the whirling, buzz-saw clamor of deadly shrapnel that follows.

"God damn it, here it comes again!"

We braced fearfully for more of the same terrifying saturation explosions that would follow as sure as night follows day. They had our number. The enemy projectile was dead on, right in the center of our perimeter. Aim on that first shell and we were all dead. They located our position, and there would be no way for us to survive. They were going to pour it on, and on, and on, until a follow-up enemy infantry attack had a minimum of opponents to contend with. But something didn't figure. There was an absence of the terrifying whine of incoming mail, of the cannon fire and the awesome, fear-inspiring scream of body-ripping shrapnel.

"I don't believe it," I said to myself after about ten minutes.

There was no artillery bombardment. The enemy had us accurately in their sights, and they did not commence an artillery barrage. They fired one round and then ceased fire for whatever reason. Was it a signal to attack with overwhelming hordes of ground troops made aware of our position by the sole, location-seeking missile?

Logically, they should have saturated the area with artillery fire.

I don't get it, I thought again, but we didn't have to be told to stay alert. Most expected a swarm of enemy to attack our out-manned perimeter momentarily. Otherwise, what would be the object of pinpointing our location and then not proceed with saturation fire? I thought that I would never fathom this enigma. The answer came sooner than expected.

The next morning, just as dawn exploded in our faces, the reason and the source of the mammoth explosion were discovered. One of our soldiers dug in on the level center of the ridge by himself. No one noticed him, as all others were frantically preoccupied with digging respective defensive positions. The trauma of this night, and perhaps because he was a survivor of the Anui butchery, became too much for him. After his foxhole was dug, the lone soldier dropped into his hole, somehow procured a fragmentation hand grenade, held it to his stomach and pulled the pin. It was suicide by grenade.

When he died, his body slumped to the bottom of the hole, cross-legged similar to how an Indian sits. Encouraged by the sweltering hot night, *rigor mortis* rapidly came to pass. The next morning, Lieutenant Hughes and another man dragged the body from the hand-made burial chamber, still cross-legged, a frozen, immovable object. Both men jumped on the dead soldier's legs in an unsuccessful attempt to break them in hope of forcing the dead soldier to lie prostrate. He refused to cooperate in death just as he refused to believe in any possible life after our ordeal. Failing in that extreme effort, Hughes covered him with a poncho to screen it from view. It was a morale thing. When soldiers see one of their own cut down, it forces them to acknowledge that they are not immortal, and then morale takes a blistering nosedive.

The dead soldier was unceremoniously abandoned on the hill.

Lieutenant Hughes moved his company out at quick time to a new location. I, along with everyone else, never knew what was happening or where we were going this time.

We weren't paid to know, just to follow orders. Our monthly allotment was $74.00 per month with an additional $45.00 a month for hazardous duty. The pay was so great, we couldn't turn it down. There surely was not enough money in the world to compensate for the rigors and horrors of combat. But troops did get free postage. No one seemed to carry postage stamps in the infantry.

I got the soldier's helmet.

ASSAULT OF THE HILL

> On the last day of July, the North Koreans could look back on a spectacular triumph in their enveloping maneuver through southwest Korea. Chinju had fallen. Their troops were ready to march on Masan and, once past that place, to drive directly on Pusan. Appleman, p. 234.

The blacked-out convoy of deuce-and-a-half transport trucks slowly rolled to a silent stop about a mile away from the primitive rural outskirts west of the port city of Masan. It was around 2 a.m., 1 September 1950. Baker Company withdrew from east of the graveyard after dawn, leaving the suicide soldier abandoned to the elements. The raging, one-sided war at this early stage called for the lack of protocol in respect to corpse recovery. It was unimaginable that anyone would go back for him, and we couldn't take him with us. The company was still on the run, trying to elude the fatal net of the invading North Korean People's Army dedicated to destroying what was left of few survivors.[26]

It wasn't until later that the tide of this awful war shifted in favor of the embattled ROKs and American soldiers at The Perimeter. They rapidly transformed from besieged defensive fighters to offensive, taking the fight directly to the swiftly retreating NKPA, who were fleeing north. Graves Registration was able to return to the blood-soaked battlefields of Anui and Hadong to claim the bodies of hundreds of brutally slain teenage would-be warriors.

That was later. For now, embattled Allied troops were in full retreat, one step ahead of the surging North Korean People's Army.

Lieutenant Hughes marched his battle-exhausted Baker Company due east under broiling, cloudless skies for several hours, then dispersed the company on a treeless, abandoned farmer's field to wait the early morning. Sleep was impossible. The unbearably stifling heat of the day worked in concert with the flies to be adversaries. Despite not sleeping during the artillery barrage of the night before, it was impossible to do so now. The

---

[26] On the morning of 31 July, the 1st Battalion, 29th Infantry, was at Sanch'ong. It was unaware that Chinju, twenty air miles to the southeast had fallen and that the 19th Infantry Regiment had withdrawn eastward.

The mess trucks that went to Chinju the day before from the battalion had not returned. During the morning local villagers suddenly disappeared, a sure sign of that enemy forces were approaching. Colonel Wilson drove south to Tansong, ten air miles from Chinju, where he had a roadblock. While he talked with lieutenant Griffin, ... about 700 refugees streamed through the roadblock. All agreed that enemy troops were behind them. Appleman, p. 233.

blistering humid heat, drenching bodies in perspiration, was inexorably unforgiving. There was no place to hide.

The company was ordered to start a major counter-attack early the following morning. The Battle of Chinju Pass was supposed to represent a formidable counter-offensive against the NKPA. But the company abandoned the Pass to the enemy and put in motion another retreat further south.

Troops were uncertain if this was a planned advance or another withdrawal—a softer word for *retreat*. From the way that the war was disintegrating in those early days, there were murky suspicions. Following every major assault, more men were lost and precious ground was relinquished to the enemy, as American and ROK forces reeled in response to the massive NKPA attacks and continued a forced retreat south.

Baker Company learned after the fact that the objective was to attack a strategic hill somewhere in the proximity of Masan. The mountains of Korea are designated by numeral for military purposes according to one military historian; the author has been able to confirm that premise only once. Specific infamous battle sites often acquire a nickname, such as "Bloody Ridge", or "Hamburger Hill," but for military confirmation logistics, a numeral is supposedly assigned to preclude military error. It has been alleged that the elevation of the designated mountain is the determinant to identify each mountain accordingly; hence the higher the elevation of the mountain in relation to sea level, the higher the numeral. This mountain that Baker Company was assigned to attack was purported to be numeral 803. While Masan represented an important defensive link on the western front near the southern coast for the Army, the outskirts were merely barren, worthless, enemy-held territory. Despite the overt lack of strategic value of the immediate terrain, Baker Company was ordered to capture an enemy-held fortification.[27] An American infantry unit had held the position earlier, but they were apparently forced to retreat in the face of overwhelming enemy forces. It made this imminent assault an advance for all practical purposes.

The stated objective required the establishment of a defensive line around the west side of Masan, in order to strengthen The Perimeter. Once Baker Company secured its objective, it was to become one of the

---

[27] Even though our objective was purportedly numeral 803, I have never located evidence despite intensive research of historical archives. Therefore, I have relied on the information documented in Sergeant Harold Gamble's book, *Korea, I Was There*. Author

important links in the Pusan Perimeter—a chain of units being linked for the defense of the only land and port left to the besieged ROK and American Armies. The Perimeter came to be accepted as a tattered, beleaguered defensive line made up of the few survivors of initial bloody battles between the NKPA and the ROK and the United States 8th Army. The Allies were pitted in a bloody, last-ditch struggle to block the marauding NKPA, in a do-or-die effort to prevent an American Dunkirk, which would have resulted in the total collapse of American influence in Asia.

It was the critical defense of the last vestige of Allied-held territory situated at the very southeast corridor of South Korea where the Americans and ROK still reigned supreme. Anything less than total commitment would be fatal. There was nowhere to retreat, the forces having surrendered the rest of the country of the Republic of Korea to the lightning swift, barbaric invaders.

Allied defenders huddled anxiously in quickly-dug, shallow foxholes awaiting the next arrival of the massive, inexorable North Korean People's Army, whose final objective was to shatter the line, flood through and claim the port of Pusan as their ultimate trophy.

But not quite yet. First, the company had to capture the objective hill and hold.

There was not one iota of information during basic training on techniques for what was about to be demanded of exhausted soldiers. The assault unit was composed of the survivors of Anui and the Chinju Pass as well as new American replacements conscripted from other units of the 8th Army.

The 3rd Platoon, Baker Company, occupied the first two trucks in the convoy, so they got far less mucky than those that followed. Wheels of trucks agitated the ever-present dust into an enveloping fog, clouding the immediate area. Transports that followed closely were subjected to the foul powder from preceding transports. The unfortunate troops in the last transport truck were to inhale almost semi-solid dust on this trip. It didn't take long to learn that it was a definite asset to be in the lead truck, which became the least dust contaminated. However, it was the first truck to be fired upon or its riders the first troops to be deployed in a vital and dangerous situation. It was a trade off. The majority of the time troops were transported in platoon-size units that attacked as a single, independent unit. With a platoon complement of 43 men only two transporters would be needed.

Hughes ordered total silence when we stopped. Transport drivers were given strict directives to not slam tailgates, not rev engines, and that there be no lights or talking. Company troops silently formed two single-file columns on each side of the usual powdered dirt road. It was a relief to empty quietly from the trucks, clasping as much combat equipment to the body as possible to minimize noise, and to escape the storm of dust that roiled from transporters. Generally, soldiers could sweep some of the grit from uniforms, but not now. Absolute silence was essential.

Officers set the pace and steadfast troops followed, not having the least idea of what was to transpire, yet judging it not worthy of loss of life. Nothing was positive during the early stage of this bloody, erratic war. It was a terrible war of attrition with every battle lessening the odds of survival for each individual.

An eerie sort of walk commenced in the dark, with troops barely able to distinguish the person in front. The company marched approximately two miles, heading directly west through a heavy fog of disturbed road dust, until they came to a crossroad. Third Platoon was near the middle of the column, where they were able to see the ghost outlines of soldiers preceding in the dark, before they abruptly turned north. Soldiers accented by the murky night appeared to be phantom aliens from outer space.

After about 500 feet, Lieutenant Hughes, leading the company, halted, as the rest of the company continued deployment north for about 40 yards. The second in command, the Executive Officer, in hushed tones directed each soldier to separate from each other, whispering in each ear, *keep five*, a well-worn cliché used in the parlance of infantry that meant keep five yards apart from one another. The Exec moved down the line and whispered his admonition to every soldier until all company personnel were made aware and complied.

The only discernable sight in this darkened night was the faint glow of shimmering water in the serene rice paddies west of the road. The fresh, unusually clear water captured the reflection of the moon in the water, as a faint waft of breeze caused the reflection to glisten.

Troops thought the attack would commence west, based on the direction they were positioned on the road. If the attack began now, the likelihood of friendly fire by a brother soldier loomed high. Prior to the lineup, officers softy ordered the company to *fix bayonets*, to attach bayonets to the rifle silently, preparatory to the anticipated attack.

The action stopped. Only the swarms of mosquitoes were active, but no one dared slap at them given the possibility of causing noise. Soldiers silently rubbed exposed faces and hands in the hope that many mosquitoes would be killed as they clung to flesh, fanatical in the search for human blood.

It was fatiguing to stand for so long, so in time troops dropped to a kneeling position, and from there they moved to squatting, and thence to sitting on the ground. The faint glimmer of sunrise slowly appeared from the east, to the rear of the would-be attackers. Now it would be a daylight attack, since the American Army generally never took the offensive at night. What a way to learn an up-to-the-minute Army maneuver—by live action. There would be no whistle blown to stop the attack for a critique of the exercise. This operation will not be reviewed, nor executed more than once. This was penciled in as a one-time exercise with the number of dead bodies determining the outcome. Not one of the attackers knew what to do.

Does one stop and kneel? Do they charge to the summit without slowing? Some would never know how to assault a hill properly. Some, it was believed, would die.

The faint rays of sunlight slowly gained altitude, clearly disclosing the position to enemy, whom we presumed to be heavily fortified, holding the summit of the unnamed hill, patiently waiting for the offense to begin.

Stranded on the road without shelter, spread five yards apart from each other, the troops were analogous to ducks in a county fair arcade game, framed in a shooting gallery set up to allow the enemy to shoot them down once they took the first step towards the now-visible low, elongated hill.

Homer's epic saga of the Trojan War, chronicled in *The Iliad,* a historical masterpiece of ancient Greek literature, spoke to this war maneuver. The ancient Greek warriors lined up facing west as the first rays of dawn emerged. The Trojans, in defense of their fortress, were forced to face the rising sun, causing them to squint, to their disadvantage. The Greeks attacked from the east. Ever since, military strategists throughout the ages have emulated the strategic war plans of the Grecian warriors, utilizing an easterly advance attack whenever feasible.

It was now broad daylight. Soldiers lit up without asking. Everyone smoked. If you were a nonsmoker before you hit the ground running in Korea, you became a smoker. Smoking was prevalent, as the practice was utilized to ease tension, reduce boredom, and elevate one to manhood. Each C-ration box contained packs of cigarettes and matches for the users, a furtherance of tobacco addiction. *Smoke 'em if you got 'em* was the order of the day.

The first priority was to take the hill. *If that's what is expected, why doesn't someone start the operation?* was the thought of many. The unit had been in an exposed position for over six hours, and no one initiated an order. The ever-present flies harassed the hapless troops mercilessly. The continuous stench of human waste was so powerful it nearly burned nostrils, while backs ached from standing and sitting on the hard, dirt road for so long. But it was mostly the flies. There was no end and no protection from the masses of vermin. If one was able to swat one successfully, it was as if an enemy soldier had been slain.

A whistle blew suddenly, alerting troops along the skirmish line. They looked to the source of the sound and the 3rd Platoon lieutenant gave the hand signal to assemble, holding his right hand straight in the air, forefinger extended, as the hand waved rapidly in a small circle. We trotted to his position and gathered around.

"We just got a message from 8th Army Commander, General Walker: 'Stand or die!' There will be no retreat from Korea, period! Now, get back to your positions and get ready to take this Goddamn hill!"

The message date of delivery? September 1950. Just a little more than one month after our unit was decimated at Anui. It was an order sent from General Walton Walker down through the chain of command to Lieutenant Hughes insisting that the objective would be achieved.

Ironically, the message, *Stand or Die!* was initially issued to 25th Infantry Division Army ground troops on 26 July, just one day prior to the massacre at Anui. By then the company, indeed both battalions, were effectively destroyed by the savagery of the North Korean Army. Then there was no need for a statement.[28]

Why was this crucial message not explained earlier, when by now it was September? The obvious answer was that the company had been on the run ever since the bloody night of 27 July, attempting to outdistance the NKPA.

General Walker never quite said that. The order in essence came from General MacArthur, which of course MacArthur denied, along with a litany of other repudiations. The press crucified Walker for the statement. He was quoted and maligned as being the author of Stand AND Die in

---

[28] In his memoirs MacArthur does not mention this crucial meeting with Walker. However circumspect his language, MacArthur gave Walker a message. The Eighth Army was expendable: Regardless of how many men perished, and under what circumstances, it must stand or die-or STAND AND DIE. Old army man Walker understood. Golden, p. 174.

every newspaper in the United States, much to his chagrin. General Walker never said Stand *AND* Die. The print and radio media exaggerated his message to convey to the people of the United States that the besieged American 8th Army was being systematically dismantled in Korea.

The order, directed to the 25th Infantry Division, soon to incorporate Baker Company into the division, was belatedly conveyed to the company, prior to the imminent assault of this hill. The order applied to the entire 8th Army, but it was generally assumed by us that the order pertained only to Baker Company. Troops trotted back to their respective positions, feeling more dejected than ever.

The platoon leaders could bluster, demand and command all they wished. The simple truth was the enemy wouldn't be handing free passes when the attack commenced. Our leaders would be right alongside of the troops, dropping and dying with the rest.

On the far right, just west of the road, on a shallow rise, lay a dead North Korean soldier, in the most unusual stage of death. His stomach was violently ripped open, exposing the thin membrane of a stomach lining, which contained a huge gas pocket.

Pink in color, the stomach lining resembled a gigantic balloon protruding from his abdomen. None had ever viewed a body with a configuration like that before, eliciting some interest although tensions were high.

Et Voilà, Messieurs! Foie Gras!

"Hey! You don't have any balls if you don't stick that gook!" a soldier on the line, out of boredom, shouted to the trooper posted to the extreme north of the attack line, the one soldier posted directly opposite the corpse.

"Yeah, stick him and see what happens! Don't be a square!" chimed another.

Several others picked up the cadence, chanting for the soldier to stick the bloated stomach with his fixed bayonet, just to see what would occur.

The soldier dutifully complied and after the gaseous lining was penetrated, a hideous, repugnant stink was released. It was as if someone had thrown a tear gas grenade containing the most revolting and putrid stench in the world. The horrible, ghastly odor permeated the entire attack line, and the former encouraging chides now turned to spurious condemnation of the person who bayoneted the stomach of the corrupt corpse. Everyone was on edge because of the pending attack, and they took the brunt of their anxiety out on the unfortunate individual who, in fact, had been urged on by all.

Now it was at least midmorning, as a quad-fifty half-track roared up, closely shadowed by the usual cloud of road dust. A behemoth of a weapons carrier, it was powered by an immense engine that propelled two huge front pneumatic rubber tires, working in conjunction with the rear left and right tank track. Heavily armor plated, the conveyance was outfitted with four 50-caliber machine guns locked into fixed position, which when fired, spewed lethal rounds covering a given area with precision, devastating, firepower. No enemy could survive. The concentrated firepower spit fire and steel from four barrels at one time, at the configured firing rate of 400 to 550 rounds per minute. With a comfortable range of 2,500 yards, it was an awesome support weapon. It was the first time the company ever observed a deadly weapon of such magnitude of firepower. Originally designed in World War II as an anti-aircraft weapon, it carried such awesome fire power that it came in general use as support for the infantry, primarily because the enemy in this godforsaken country opted to fight in huge masses. Unfortunately, the quad-fifties could not traverse high mountains where the fiercest fighting took place.

Lieutenant Hughes, just as did General MacArthur, believed himself immortal. Lieutenant Hughes was standing in the center of the recently water-filled rice paddy, shouting, waving his M-2 Carbine wildly in the air, stirring his company to action, urging the nervous troops to follow his lead. Hughes was going in first.

One could barely hear him over the thunderous clamor of the quad's 50-caliber machine guns firing in unison, now sweeping the hill from side to side, just over Lieutenant Hughes' head. The mass of 50-caliber rounds was so devastating that the foliage was falling as if a gigantic thresher was mowing the bushes in a vertical manner. Nothing or no one could possibly survive that annihilating, methodical display of heavy rounds. Literally every inch of the hill was saturated by mind-numbing heavy firepower. Troops winced in recoil at the unending stream of rounds blasting fire from the barrels of the four machine guns, as many thought, *Man, I'm glad that I'm not on the receiving end of that incredible fire.*

"Come on men, we're gonna take this goddamn hill and not stop till we get to the top! We've got cover and nobody is going to stop us! Follow me! Let's go! Let's go!" Hughes was visibly worked up, whipping his company into frenzy, continuously waving his carbine high in the air. None could believe their eyes. Heavy 50-caliber rounds continued to streak death over Hughes' head onto the foliaged covered hill, destroying the hill, and everything in front. When the commander waved his light carbine high in the air, a wayward round from one of the machine guns accidentally shattered the stock on his carbine. Soldiers stood dumbfounded, mouths agape as the wood stock shattered, flinging shards of the stock in all directions.

Lieutenant Hughes didn't miss a beat. He shouted, "Let's get up that hill where it's safe!"

He turned his back and started running for the hill, sloshing through foot-high water held captive in the paddies. The company broke into a quick run, following in a wide, sweeping line.

Man, that guy is going to get his first, we thought, *so we're with him.*

Everyone had the same thought as we surged forward, one solid line of fanatically-screaming, committed soldiers. The dread of Anui, Hadong and Chinju were left behind on the road as the company quickly advanced.

It was rumored that as Lieutenant Hughes led the assault on the hill, he flushed a North Korean soldier hidden in the rice paddy. The commander purportedly grabbed the alleged soldier by the hair of his head and forced the enemy soldier to march in front of him as a living shield, forcing the way and covering the lieutenant during the attack. I believe this incident to be highly implausible, simply because a solitary soldier would be unlikely to be there unless he was badly wounded and abandoned. And if that were true, the wounded enemy soldier would most likely be unable to walk. Moreover, enemy soldiers always had heads near shaven, unless they were guerrillas. Corroboration of this alleged incident was never made. Yet there was no question as to the legendary courage of Lieutenant Hughes.

In the midst of the attack a couple of soldiers opted to use rice paddy dikes to traverse the sector, until they had to wade through the water at the last moment, a lesson learned in the escape of Anui. Wet boots and soaking wool socks have a propensity to raise blisters. Running at full speed with the company, but on the dikes with my rifle at the ready, I managed to keep in the same formation as the others, until something in the water caught my eye. I stopped momentarily as it registered on me. A most bizarre sight. A body. Not an ordinary dead soldier, but a civilian man lying face up, nearly submerged in the clear water. He was hidden from the road by the rice paddy dikes, and no one saw him until I stopped my rapid run in awed shock.

His eyes were closed as if he were sleeping. I felt he was ready to awaken in his own time to overpower us. He had a long flowing white mustache that matched his long, thin chin beard. This new, well-preserved corpse resembled a long-departed member of the tenth-century Manchu Dynasty of China. He looked as ominously threatening as did a Manchu.

I was so startled that I was lagging in the line by a couple of yards, so I had to race to catch up. I didn't have a chance to notice his clothing, but in reflection, he must have been an unfortunate elderly native Korean farmer who was caught in the crossfire. The Korean culture was deeply influenced by the Chinese, and this pitiful victim had more than likely copied the mustache and beard of his ancient Chinese conquerors.

Charge the hill, rifle held at high port, ready to kill or suffer the consequences of hesitation!

The hill was eventually conquered without a shot fired. The front of the prominence was so sheer as troops charged forward, that it was impossible to scale. The company broke off in somewhat equal ranks and headed for two ancient footpaths situated on the north and south ends of the clifflike knoll. Once on top, we were gasping ferociously for air to revitalize us while awaiting the expected counter-attack. Breaths recovered and sensing that an imminent counter-attack was forthcoming, one of the lieutenants screamed, "Dig in!"

They never came. The enemy abandoned the hill for reasons unknown. We were soon to learn why.

I spied an abandoned foxhole partially back-filled with dirt and facing west, just below the skyline, and it came to me. This had to have been an Allied-held position prior to our company taking it back. The North Korean Army had no need to dig emplacements at this stage of the war because of their unceasing offensive. Moreover, the enemy would have no reason to dig in facing west since their surging assaults were spawned from east and north, heading west and south.

The foxhole was half done. Remove the soft, pliable, loose soil from the once-functioning foxhole and I would save at least an hour's worth of digging.

Clank.

My entrenching tool used as a hoe hit something metal. I had no idea what was occurring. I swung the tool mightily as if it was an ax, and once again I heard the distinct clank of heavy metal. This time somehow I caught the object on my entrenching tool, and I pulled ever so slightly, fearing a possible booby trap. I heard the unmistakable soft sound of a sizzle. A white phosphorus rocket, upon exposure to air, burst into a blazing conflagration. I leaped back just in time to avoid spitting embers that would burn through flesh in an instant. I watched in astonishment as my foxhole was consumed in raging fire.

"Oh my God, what's going on?" The now out of control inferno attracted curious soldiers to the scene.

Eventually, the fire began to ebb, and I gently pulled on the object again. The smoldering mass was a William Peter, a white phosphorous five-inch rocket fired from an attack fighter plane that buried itself in the disturbed soil of the foxhole causing it to extinguish immediately. It was my ill fortune to resurrect it from the dead by digging, which allowed oxygen to breathe life into the lungs of the spent rocket. It was poor judgment on my part, moving the missile, even though, at the time I could see the rear guiding fins of the bomb. It was a very close call.

My new foxhole buddy showed up and we readied the once fiery pit for habitation. I wondered what Allied unit was forced from this defensive position. It had to be Americans or ROKs because the emplacements were dug in below the crest of the hill, facing west. Lieutenant Suddaby anchored his 2nd Platoon to the far northwest position on the hill and he reported that there was American barbed wire fencing placed at the bottom of the hill, in front of his position. I discovered a discarded American steel barbed wire pole a few days later.

The probability that Allied units were dug in with enough time to string the ineffectual wire was beyond comprehension. The ROK Army, assisted by the Americans, was in no position to even attempt to stop the gigantic rupture of a surging, overflowing dam. No one knew of any American or ROK unit that was able to hold back the tremendous tidal wave of enemy from their intended goal, particularly with this pittance of barbed wire. During this early phase of the Korean War, because of the enemy's superior equipment, arms, and numbers, Americans were either forced into full retreat or they were surrounded and destroyed.

Baker Company dug in rapidly and fortified the hill the best they could, waiting in anticipation for the enemy. They would not disappoint us. They were en route. Defensive obstacles such as mines and barbed wire meant to impede or slow the fanatical enemy were unavailable. The threadbare American 8th Army simply did not possess such equipment for defense in a major battle, let alone to implement a rolling offensive. Even sufficient ammunition was lacking. This terrible war was a surreal drain of vital resources.

Armageddon was two nights away.

REVENGE

There is no one but yourself to keep your back door open. You can live without food, but you cannot last long without ammunition. Lt. Gen. Walton H. Walker, July 1950

They tried to psyche us. They came on us with every noise imaginable, except the proverbial brass band, unlike the mood of silent stealth preferred in American infantry tactics. They were here to kill us and then drive on to Pusan to finish their conquest of South Korea. The NKPA didn't know about our orders to "Stand or die! There will be no retreat from South Korea!"

Moreover, the 6th North Korean Infantry Division apparently did not realize American 8th Army's latest order superseded all others. There would be no retreat again. But even more significant was the score to settle with the North Korean Army.

If the NKPA wanted the hill so much, they were going to pay dearly in blood and body for it. Since this forthcoming battle was the enemy's initiative, Baker Company defenders waited silently with little fear, but some uneasiness, to collectively deliver as many of the North Korean soldiers to their ancestors as possible. For that matter, send them COD.

The unit didn't know it at the time, but when this hill was captured unopposed two days earlier, Baker Company became a crucial link in the official chain defending the last vestige of South Korea—the Pusan Perimeter. Baker Company was positioned west of the port city of Masan, charged with holding the defensive line at all cost.

The best defense is a good offense!

A tiresome cliché, but not in all cases, and certainly not now. Baker Company held the high ground and there would be no retreat if we were overrun. The haunting "Stand or Die" edict ruled.

So, if we were to die on this fly, mosquito and rat-infested, night-soil saturated, terraced hill, we would give them a run for their money. Baker Company was ready even though ammunition was light and none but the 2nd Platoon apparently possessed a few fragmentation hand grenades. Company personnel could have used a case of hand grenades each, and if they had been available, we could have possibly held the enemy at bay.

This was the first opportunity to be in a position to fight back. The few survivors of Anui and Chinju were no longer afraid and they were ready, even though it portended to be a massive battle. The imported new personnel sent to augment the ranks were unaware of the strength of the NKPA, and of course, everyone questioned the pittance of ammunition doled out—about 80 trifling rounds per person.

Throughout these ferocious battles, I developed an irrational sensation of hanging at the periphery of the earth, just as ancient mariners believed the world was flat. If I progressed forward from my defensive emplacement, I would fall from this fictitious precipice into a bottomless abyss. Moreover, in my mind, there was no one to my rear who could save me. I was on my own, and I had to hang on tenaciously and defend myself to keep on the safe side of the earth. Though this sensation was not a particularly frightening sensation, it emanated, I believe, from the will to survive.

They were laughing, drinking and shouting curses at us from the bottom of the hill.

"Hey Yankee! Tonight you die!" strong voices screamed in unison.

Someone from our hill shouted back, "Screw you! Come and get us, yellow bellied bastards!"

My money was on Lt. Reed Suddaby.

Then in retort, another chorus of coordinated shouts from enemy:

"Banzai! Banzai! Banzai!"

The words were Japanese; the Korean word was "Manzai!" The enemy, milling about at the base of the hill evidently chose "Banzai!" as a method to unnerve the defenders, knowing young troops were familiar with the expression from World War II. All Koreans spoke fluent Japanese at the time, because of strict demands placed on them by the Japanese during their 40-year occupation of the peninsula.[29]

So the enemy screamed "Banzai", as a psychological term to unnerve. What does the word Banzai represent in English? Freely interpreted, it means *hurrah or hooray*.

The NKPA were making a thunderous racket at the base of the hill all associated with preparations for a massive attack. Atypical sounds came of tinkling glass from liquor bottles, rattling of ammunition boxes, shouting obvious profanities, singing interspersed with laughing, along with a cacophony of sundry sounds related to combat, such as the loading of weapons. The *rack* or engagement of a round into a firing chamber is an unforgettable hair-raising sound.

---

[29] Members of the North Korean People's Army never spoke Korean to American prisoners of war. Instead they reverted to the Japanese language. When they decided to kill prisoners, they spoke their native Korean tongue in order that captured Americans would not comprehend. It made it easier to cut down unsuspecting prisoners. Author.

The United States Army does not fight in the fashion of the NKPA. American infantry strategy prescribes *fire and maneuver* by stealth, engaging in combat offensively during the day, and never in massed concentrations. Not so for the enemy before us, readying an attack, massing by the thousands below Baker Company's defensive positions.

The eerie, squeaking wheels of many Soviet SG-43 Sokolov Pulemyot Maxima water-cooled, heavy machine guns sounded as they were being pushed forward into firing positions. With a firing rate of 520 to 580 rounds per minute of 7.62-caliber ammunition, they were not as lethal as American 50-caliber machine guns, and the enemy weaponry lacked the knock down power of the rounds. When the company seized this hill, the backup of quad fifties, preceded the attack; however, because American armored vehicles could not maneuver in mountain ranges, they remained road-bound.

The tortured sounds of grunting and cursing demonstrated that the North Korean 6th Division was putting into play tremendous laborious efforts to push the enormous guns partially uphill in order to position them suitable for attack. It would soon be a fusillade of death when they began to saturate the hill, concentrating deadly fire on defenders as they huddled anxiously in foxholes. Upon implementation of a designated signal, enemy foot soldiers would immediately charge the hill when machine gun fire ceased, and bayonet or shoot any who survived.

I hope somebody puts those gook guns out before they get started!

All heard the ominous sounds of the awesome guns being emplaced for battle, but most couldn't get a fix on their location. It was an experience fraught with apprehension. After the bloody battle concluded, it was ascertained that the enemy penetrated the defensive field of fire range near the north side, moved laterally in front of the position and then lined up by the hundreds in order to implement a protracted frontal attack.

"Hey, Yankees! Tonight you die!"

"Screw you, gooks! Come and get us!" someone from Baker Company side shouted in retort.

Defending troops believed it was Lieutenant Suddaby again. Suddaby, only 20 years old, knew how to inspire, and his thunderous, hoarse bellow in defiance of the enemy was meant to instill confidence, not only for his platoon, but also for the entire company. Never mind that his answer might have given his position away.

Enemy bugles screamed loud, off-pitch, eerie blares, raising the hair on the back of heads because of the ominous resound of the confounding instrument. Yet it did not generate panic among the company. Indeed, the enemy noise elevated adrenaline levels to the maximum. Young American defenders were at the pinnacle of alertness. They did not waver. They had no options. They waited in silent anticipation. The pandemonium continued until it gradually spilled over into an ear-splitting din, as enemy became more and more brazen, inspired by the false sense of courage borne of heavy consumption of alcohol, interwoven with authoritative shouts of encouragement by their commanders.

Survivors of Anui and Chinju were beat up emotionally from never-ending attacks by the NKPA shredding machine. But this night was different. Troops were dug in and prepared. Alertness was at the highest level. Pupils of eyes dilated to take in as much as possible. Heartbeats raced in anticipation of the monumental struggle lying ahead. Nerves were honed to the ultimate. There was a crucial priority—do or die.

It was probably ten at night, yet the temperature still hovered over 100 degrees. We were steaming and sweating, as dank humidity made uniforms drenching wet. Perspiration poured from our faces, limbs and bodies. Hands sweaty and slick became liabilities for preparing to fire when the enemy swept in as a Tsunami—a tidal wave of killers clad in mustard green uniforms. The future killing hill would soon transform into a virtual human sea, surging relentlessly forward, determined to breach the thin defensive line. Once that occurrence became a reality, blood-thirsty enemy would transform into swarming ants, crawling insatiably over the terraced battlefield, slaying anything alive before them.

One matured in a hurry because one had to, or died trying, making one come of age before whiskers were acquired.

The awful, uncoordinated noise at the base of the hill was developing into a screeching crescendo interweaving sounds of off-key shouts and screams, accompanied by bugles, whistles and horns blaring.

Abruptly absolute silence pervaded the night. No one moved. The universe or at least this part—this god-forsaken hill— became frozen in time and place, in anticipation of what was sure to follow. The enemy was silent as well; the sounds of bravado were substituted with eerie, nervous silence. It was the silence of death.

Time stood still. Hearts stood still. The oxymoron *the silence was deafening* ruled this night. Minds began to cry out for sounds, any sounds to reassure that this night was not a night of bizarre imagination, but one of certainty. There must be some way to break this soundless barrier. To instill life back into this noiseless, audacious occurrence was paramount, or near insanity would prevail. Breaths were collectively gasped and sealed in motionless bodies, sealed by white-hued lips locked in nervous anticipation of what was soon to transpire.

Waiting, impatiently, you matured because you donated all of your time to it.

Loud, shrill noises screamed from a military whistle that penetrated the quiet night, shattering the awful silence, and then the world suddenly became alive again. It was the signal to attack. The first human wave was lined up ready to strike.

I'm as ready as I can be. I hope we all feel the same.

Each soldier sensed the same defensive reaction to what was coming. It was a knee jerk reaction of *kill or be killed*. My hands and face were perspiring profusely, and I quickly wiped the sweat from my face with my right hand, then on to my trouser leg. I needed dry hands to be prepared to reload the eight-round clips of ammunition without hesitation. Yet it wasn't fear, as when I was nearly overcome with that debilitating affliction at Anui. Rather, it was more of a sensation of uneasy realization that soldiers would collide with adversaries very soon, as they huddled in sweltering heat on this sweaty, muggy night.

For the first time, the ever-present maddening swarms of mosquitoes evacuated this killing arena, or else no one paid heed to them. This was to be Baker Company's arena now. Troops knew the hill and the outlying fields far beyond. Daily combat and reconnaissance patrols jabbing and feinting at enemy positions provided us profound knowledge of the terrain. During those earlier daily patrols, as soldiers penetrated deep into enemy territory, the communications man strung commo wire by the mile from a huge spool, to stay in touch with the company by use of the SCR 300 radio borne on the back of the radio operator. The wire was severed upon return from patrol in an area far from the perimeter, so enemy could not trace the wire to defensive positions. There was enough wire out there for North Korean sadists to tie every captured American soldier's hands behind their backs before torture was set in motion.

Powerful deep screams harmonizing by the thousands shattered the otherwise still night from where the enormous horde of enemy troops was massing.

"Banzai! Banzai! Banzai! Hey Yankees, you die tonight! Banzai! Banzai! Banzai!"

They were fanatic in their attack waves, defined correctly by military historians as *The Human Sea*.

North Korean Army General Kim Chaek ordered roiling, successive attacks in wave after wave. Defenders were aware of the enemy's practice of butchery, although none spoke to it. All understood the fundamental results of surrender, and none were buying into it. As absurd as it sounded, it would be a *fight to the death,* simply because there were no other options. The company was formed of amateurs when professionals were needed. And none were eager to die.

Some company personnel determined the exact location of the North Korean command post. The enemy honchos huddled under huge trees beyond this terraced garden hill, beyond sight now limited by blackness of night. The silhouette of tree foliage gently merged into a mock stage set backdrop of inky sky, aiding the foe in concealment.

"Somebody fire off a flare!" I whispered, more to myself than to my fellow occupant in our foxhole. He didn't answer, and I was getting uneasy over this crucial omission. The NKPA *always* attacked at night, with ferocious battles lasting until daylight or sooner depending upon the success of the invaders. If they overran a defensive position; they would keep attacking until they confronted the next obstacle.

Pitch-black sky lit up like daylight by flares could stop them in their tracks. Anxious soldiers were waiting in uneasy anticipation to hear that peculiar thunking explosion of the flare gun, followed by the rapid accent of the flare.

A pyrotechnic burst would reach its zenith, adhered to by a blazing comet tail, until it burst, transforming the black night sky into daylight. Its mission accomplished, the smoldering star would very slowly waft down, inhibited from precipitous descent by way of two diminutive attached parachutes. The company would have about five minutes of glory, slaughtering foes as they milled aimlessly around in helpless confusion. I recalled vividly the fear of the illuminating flare during my experience at Anui, and it would be so poetic that I was able to survive that terrible night, only to return the favor by striking back tonight with the aid of the same *night into day pyrotechnic display*. It was not outside of the bounds of reality to believe that the very same enemy standing below was in fact the same confidant killers of Anui.

A flare would light up the sky and turn night into broad daylight. Then the forthcoming onslaught would revert strongly to defenders advantage. The North Koreans never operated in the daylight, unless they were in the course of slaughtering units as they did at Anui. This attack was not quite in their hands as yet. They would be caught unprepared, and so much murderous rifle and machine gun fire would be poured on that they would be killed by the hundreds before they could organize their first wave. We had to do without most of the other implements of war, but the flare was crucial to the defense.[30]

No anti-personnel land mines were placed to drive the stake of terror into the hearts of enemy. No trip flares (flares designed to ignite when a stretched wire is disturbed by a foot) to announce the arrival of enemy troops. No *William Peter* (white phosphorous) hand grenades to terrorize them. No barbed wire fences to slow their assault. Just a few 30-caliber light machine guns and about 200 rifles with a meager allotment of ammunition per man. The American Army was warring on the cheap.

Furthermore, B Company's 60-millimeter mortar squad was, for all purposes, out of action. The enemy was too close. To discharge mortars at such close range from the rear, behind the defensive line, would entail firing almost straight up in the air, allowing for the raining death to be not more than 20 feet away from defensive positions. It would have been an impossible effort that would likely have killed as many defenders as enemy. The military had the logistical and supply knowledge to expedite forces and supplies, but this ground war was in its infancy, and the war machine needed to be oiled. Ammunition and supply deliveries were imminent. We just had to hold on long enough, we were told. Our mettle was about to be tested.

Still Baker Company held the upper hand. Defenders were dug in and ready. Below, the enemy were milling about, getting orders to line up for the first wave of attack. The tap of the funeral drum would soon come at shorter intervals.

Even though I was situated on the right side of the foxhole, my partner to my left did not notice the movement. Right in front of our position was an enemy scout, naked except for skimpy shorts, barefoot, bareheaded and carrying a rifle in his right hand. He never saw us. He crept quickly, bent over as he passed right in front of our emplacement! He was no farther than five to seven feet from us.

I did all of the right things taught at basic training, instantly shouldering, aiming my rifle directly at the scout, my right arm automatically at a level 45-degree angle holding the rifle properly, with my left arm tucked directly under the piece (weapon) for stability.

---

[30] This failure to fire a flare that fateful night caused me consternation for years, until I reconnected with Lieutenant, now Colonel (Retired) Suddaby at a reunion of our unit from Okinawa in Fort Benning, Georgia. When I broached the subject, he replied matter-of-factly. "Very simple," he solemnly replied. "We had no flares." Author.

Instinctively, I pushed the butt of the rifle into the small of the shoulder tightly as I squeezed off a round. I did all of the right things, except one. When I attempted to fire, I realized that my *safety lever* was on. In all of the excitement, I failed to do the most important combat preparation. In basic training, training officers drilled into recruits time and again to ensure the safety position was always on, and I reacted to my basic training character rather than to this now unfolding actual combat situation.

Infantry instructors never taught the practical side of warfare during basic training. To this day I am hard on myself remembering this incident. Had I remembered to unlock the *safety* I would have eliminated one enemy, but more importantly, I would have been the one to alert the company that the attack was officially underway. I would have dropped the starting flag that could have officially launched this event.

Then the attack began. Enemy machine gunners fired directional machine gun fire into our positions, dispensing searing, certain death from Soviet guns. Baker Company weapons platoon was the more accurate as they counter-fired, slaughtering enemy gunners time and again. As fresh enemy crews wielded their weapons, they met certain death from American machine gun fire crashing into Asian bodies, leaving sprawled, bleeding and dead soldiers at their guns. Enemy replacement gunners had to drag bodies of comrades away to make room to operate their own guns. They too would be shot down, and summarily dragged away themselves. And so it went. Now the insurgent infantry was primed to attack.

Here they come! The wave, the Human Sea! Shoulder to shoulder, screaming, charging our positions. Screaming and firing. Firing and screaming.

For us it was like fighting during the Revolutionary War when the first line would fire, kneel down to reload, while the line standing behind fired, then knelt to reload. Close order formations, shoulder to shoulder, along with bright uniforms, became passé upon the invention of automatic weaponry. No one advised the belligerent NKPA, much to their loss.

They were crumpling dead, mostly face first in front of foxholes, killed in action, just as another band of warriors lined up to take the place of the their fallen brethren. Anxious defenders fired almost in unison, as wave after human wave attempted to overrun the hill. Time was not measured by a ticking watch, but rather by the methodical roar of gunfire. If death had an odor, its foulness permeated this hill tonight. We could sniff fresh, odious fatality deep down in our lungs. We found ourselves touching our bodies periodically to ensure we were still alive.

The NKPA 6th Division pitched Soviet-made fragmentation and concussion grenades as they charged positions time after time. Deadly explosions were going off all over the assaulted hill, but it was one-sided. The grenades were all owned and dispensed by the North Korean People's Army.

The Grim Reaper had his hands full this night, this night when I lost a distinct portion of my innocence. This was the night I was to kill my first human being. There would be no remorse. This was the quintessence of survival of the fittest, or rather, who had the most firepower. This was the night to avenge the slaughter of kids left at Anui and at Hadong and to save asses at the same time.

Nemesis, the Greek Goddess of Retribution, was gazing down from the heavens on us this night!

"Banzai! Banzai! Banzai!! Tonight you die!"

Shouts of conquest from enemy soldiers screaming with pseudo bravado meshed with gruesome conflicting shrieks of the mortally wounded. Rounds thudded mercilessly, spinning into collapsing bodies lurching forward to die unprotected by the shroud of dark night. Still they came, bugles blowing, whistles shrilling, gongs clanging.

NKPA charges flooded on and on nonstop, seemingly boiling from the earth as a tide of lava. But, rather than the surging fiery hue of molten magma, the infidels, clad in the mustard green of enemy, roiled forward to our defensive positions. The foes had but one goal, and young defenders knew what those intransigent adversaries had in mind, as well as what was expected of us. The absolute urgency required the resolve of life or death to stop them before they could charge with bayonets fixed.

Kill the yellow-bellied bastards!

Screams. God-awful screams when a bullet crashed into an enemy body, extracting life even before the corpse collapsed to the ground. The bitter smell of gunfire wafted down the hill. Not enough by far to conceal the enemy, but enough to let them know what was in store for them. Not a word from our side now. Quiet, save the almost spontaneous shatter of unified rifle fire when the enemy lunged in unison toward the foxholes. And so it went—a crescendo of firepower.

Die, you sons of bitches! Scream and let us know that you aren't so goddamn invincible when it's a matched game! Keep coming, you yellow-bellied bastards. Tonight is pay back! That was the tape being played over and over in every head of every soldier on line. Defenders were in a subdued but unified mind-set. There was not a man who confessed to being afraid, and we were afraid many, many times earlier. The task at hand precluded any time for concern. For the first time, this was an even match, and the combatants were much too engaged to dwell on fear.[31]

The terraced hill was their undoing. Defenders could not get a clear, unobstructed shot at attackers, because of the partial shelter of the terraces. Conversely, when attackers made their final burst of attack on the top terrace, they could not take precise aim until the last second. By then, it was too late. Before foes could raise their weapons to fire with any accuracy, they were shot down at point blank range. Still, the enemy tried to substitute volume for accuracy. Burp guns fired back in retaliation on the killing hill, enemy bodies stacking up, one on another immediately in front of each foxhole, and still they unhesitatingly advanced.

"Hey, help! Don't shoot," a softly whimpered cry emanated from the left.

"GI! I need to get with you guys!"

"Password?" my partner on the left hissed. Perhaps it was an over cautious demand on our part. Still, the voice was not one we recognized, so no chances would be taken. The enemy used the remark *GI* much more than did Americans, and it was thought to be an enemy ruse, so my buddy wheeled and leveled his rifle at the source, as I was watching and waiting for the next frontal charge to commence. There was a long delay, and finally the voice muttered softly in nervous response:

"Shit, I can't think of the fuckin password!"

Despite the overwhelming attack in progress, with our nerves frayed and on edge, and instincts honed to the infinite, we both smiled a nervous reaction, knowing that the anxious response was more authentic than any password that could ever have been devised.

"Crawl over quick as you can!" my cohort hoarsely whispered.

Neither of us knew him. For that matter, my foxhole partner and I were strangers to each other as well. The soldier sited in the foxhole to the left was also a replacement. We learned from him that his foxhole buddy was just shot dead from a single round. The overpowering velocity of the projectile crashed into the forehead of the unfortunate soldier, just

---

[31] The fighting in the four main sectors went on day after endless day. As the battles violently surged back and forth, hills changed hands with maddening monotony. The early September heat was dreadful. No one dared sleep. Very few men got a decent meal; even drinking water was scarce. The American casualties were ghastly: By September 15 total Eighth Army casualties had climbed to 18,165: 4,599 killed or mortally wounded; 12,377 wounded; the rest missing. Truly it was a "savage sacrifice" of "beef" cattle in the slaughter-house. Worse, there were few or no replacements. Beginning on August 23, MacArthur had diverted 390 officers and 5,400 enlisted men to build up the 7th Division for Inchon. Blair, p. 262.

below the line of the helmet. The force of the impact snapped the victim's head, obviously breaking his neck, but that was of little consequence. He died instantly, slithering awkwardly to the bottom of his hole, crumpled in death, as his spirit drained from his gory defiled face and drifted lazily skyward to meet his Maker.

The surviving soldier was new, and paralyzed with fear. There was no way that he was going to stay alone to face the North Korean onslaught. His absence would leave a gaping break in the perimeter defense, but he would be no good by himself. He was as terrified as I was at Anui. The first battle brings out uncompromising fear in everyone. I understood his unspoken terror, empathizing with him from when I was finally able to confront my devastating horror at Anui. Still, he hesitated.

"Come on, we're covering you! Crawl over!"

During a short lull in the enemy line up, the new recruit scrambled rapidly on his stomach to our position. Our foxhole was wide and deep. Now we were three.[32]

"Here they come again. Shoot the bastards!" my comrade next to me muttered matter-of-fact in response to the continuous bugle calls, gongs and whistles. All fired a unified volley. It was hard to miss. Enemy infantrymen collapsed by the score at point blank range. The defensive rate of fire corresponded to their wave after wave attack. Their leaders sent an assault line forward. They were shot down. They dispatched another line and they were killed as well. The same scenario over and over.

"Banzai! Banzai! Banzai!" the strident screams continued unabated in disharmonious chords from thousands of enemy.

The off-key choral group lacked a competent choir director.

They leaped forward yet again in another unbroken line. Defenders fired and enemy collapsed. More bugles, whistles and gongs, followed by shouts, screams and coordinated rifle fire synchronized to the waves of attacks. The body-strewn hill was alive with gunfire and smoke, while the air rocked in pandemonium and reeked with the dank smell of blood-stained bodies. One could smell the stench that permeated the hill from so many hundreds of slain and maimed barbarian soldiers.

"Son of a bitch, if we only had grenades! We could kill hundreds

---

[32] I picked up a lot of survival tips on my own from World War II veterans who augmented our ranks before the draft was re-initiated. The army went through the records to determine those who had earned the Combat Infantry Badge during the war. Those who had were rushed to Korea, and shoved on front lines as light weapons infantrymen, MOS 04745 (Military Occupation Specialty- the number designates a light weapons infantryman). Author

more. And not just in front of foxholes, but at the bottom of the hill, where they were lining up to attack!"

The North Korean savages soon discovered the gap in the line to the left, the foxhole now abandoned, the surviving occupant now with us. Apparently, the enemy could sense that there was no defensive gunfire emanating from the abandoned foxhole.

"Cover the left side on the next wave! Make sure they don't go through that hole, or we are dead meat!" my partner whispered to the new confederate.

Movement was discerned to the left.

Psst, "Watch the left side," my buddy whispered again to the soldier who joined us. The new occupant fired a burst at a hurdling adversary soldier to the left and dropped him stone dead.

"Good shot!" my partner whispered.

The young recruit turned and barely nodded. He was concentrating too hard to feel terror now that he again was among living beings.

The lack of fear instinctively transposed into calculated reflection. None seemed to be afraid because for the first time they were capable of striking back. There was no time to develop a sense of fear. Defenders were too busy killing lest they be killed.

"Braaap!" A Soviet AK-47. An enemy soldier fired a burst from the second terrace down, protected by the backstop of the next lower terrace. He was right in front of our foxhole. We simultaneously fell to knees, to the bottom of the hole, ears ringing from deafening enemy gunfire.

"I'm not hit. How about you?" I whispered softly to the guy next to me, not hearing my words because of the clamorous ringing in my ears.

"I'm OK," the new guy whispered.

"Me too."

"Braaap!"

Another burst of sub machine gun fire apparently was initiated by the same enemy, just a moment after we rose from the bottom of the hole to face them again. We drew back instinctively in painful reaction to the second burst from the submachine gun. We fell abruptly to our knees again with the most agonizing ringing in our ears that one can imagine. Both ears had the most excruciating pain from the near hits to our heads. Those that espouse the theory that bullets *whiz* or *sing by* ears have never encountered close range rounds near the ears. It is, in fact, a violent explosion that is deafening.

We three went through the same ritual of confirming that none were wounded as we rose the third time to face the enemy. This time the new guy on the left was shot through his right ear, sustaining a clean hole through the outer middle ridge near the ear lobe. He was shaken, and though minor, the slight wound would qualify for a Purple Heart Medal. But more importantly, he would be hearing impaired for life, if he lived through this terrible night.

None could hear at any rate. All suffered debilitating deafness from the near proximity of enemy rounds to our ears.

Time out! There is a lesson here in war. It is called on-the-job training, and if a lab course is required, one better not cut classes or ditch school. Passing this course is de rigueur, and one cannot repeat the curriculum.

"I gotta piss!"

"Me too!"

The new occupant removed the liner from his head armor, urinated in the helmet and passed it to my partner who performed likewise. The helmet was passed to me, and after all answered nature's call, I leaned forward from our emplacement during a brief lull, and dumped it on the next lower level, about three feet lower, where several enemy lay dead directly in front of our foxhole.

"Here's to you," I said to myself, as the sour, warm yellow liquid splashed on one of the dead.

God shared our dingy foxhole that night. Since each of us suffered severe incessant ringing in our ears, it can only be presumed each round from the sub-machine gun had to pass directly between us. One or two inches to the left or right and the attacker surely could have chalked up three kills.

"I'm going to kill that son of a bitch," I whispered softly and firmly to the guy next to me.

"Cover me when he fires again, and I'll be waiting."

I knew from observing the muzzle blast of the AK-47 exactly from where the sub-machine gunfire emanated, a distance of no more than 12 feet from our emplacement. I intended to crawl from the hole, lie approximately ten feet to my right, and fix my aim barely to the right of his fire. Assuming he was right handed, I estimated where his body presumably had to be. Eight quick rounds and I was sure to get him. I was relatively calm and steady of purpose. When he fired for the fourth time, I intended to dispatch him, post haste, to his ancestors.

"Psst. Hey! It's Pete. Don't shoot. I'm coming over," I whispered to the guys in the foxhole to my right. No answer. I repeated the words, turning directly to their direction, holding my hand cupped to my mouth to direct my voice to them over the din of the rifle fire. This time they acknowledged me with an *OK,* because one apparently recognized my voice. I crawled from the foxhole about ten feet north of the emplacement and lay among some small vegetables in the heat and the height of this mother of all battles. The soldier with the AK-47 would not suspect the change in my position. My rifle steadied as I planned to fire eight rapid rounds into him as soon as he fired again.

"Grenade!"

An enemy attacker from a lower terrace threw it. I saw it coming—a Soviet Army fragmentation hand grenade. The bomb landed several feet behind the guys in the foxhole to whom I had earlier called and perhaps 15 feet from me.

They ducked. I couldn't. I pressed my body as far to the earth as I possibly could and quickly turned my face away from the lethal bomb, as I simultaneously pushed my helmet as far as it would fit on my head. I opened my mouth wide to ease the concussion that was sure to follow. The explosion was brain shattering.

I was struck with numerous superficial shrapnel wounds generally to the right side of my body, suffering more from the explosive sound of the grenade than from the shrapnel, as the blast seemed to lift me from the ground. I crawled back in my hole. I never had the chance to annihilate the shooter of the AK-47. He either crawled away or was killed by someone else.

Ammunition was running dangerously low. All knew the consequences of running out, and every shot counted from then on. To ensure they died, when enemy charged in response to the bugles, our troops were compelled to hold fire until the enemy was nearly upon them. Then we fired only a short burst. Without hesitation, some unsheathed bayonets ready to fix, in case of depletion of ammunition.

No one ordered *fix bayonets,* but troops were ready for any eventuality. There wasn't a mad dog among the company who would surrender, as troops rallied for the last stand.

Baker Company had both good and bad advantages.

The bad: None were trained in bayonet warfare.

The good: Baker Company held the high ground. Our opponents would either shoot us down when our ammunition was exhausted or take us on in the last duel, by bayonet.

The result if the NKPA won the coin toss of this battle was carnage.

This battle was no different than at the Alamo when brave forefathers knew the surrender order from General Antonio Lopez De Santa Anna meant *take no prisoners*. Presumably, there was some anxiousness about hand-to-hand combat, given the lack of training, but it was one additional method of fighting. All knew that none would be taken alive, so it came down to a matter of do or die, pure and simple.

The machine gunner from 2nd Platoon, Al Norris, set up a field of fire in a slight draw, elevated just above the defensive line of the concave, terraced hill. Norris was trained extensively in the light machine gun. He understood his weapon as riflemen knew the M-1 Rifle. Norris fired constantly and relentlessly and everyone had a clear view of his glorious stream of fire. Troops stared mesmerized as tracer rounds screamed down on adversaries— the staccato bullets clearly hitting their marks, followed by blood curdling screams from wounded and dying enemy soldiers below. Some, no doubt, questioned if the machine gunner's constant rate of fire would burn the barrel of the machine gun, but Norris obviously knew better. Suddenly, the machine gun stopped.

Malfunction! Holy shit! It just gotta get shooting again! There are too many gooks to stop by rifle fire!

A defective cartridge expanded and froze in the firing chamber, and although the gunner was able to quickly break down the automatic weapon to repair it, it was of no use. The machine gun required a special tool, a ruptured cartridge extractor, and Norris had none. That left only one other machine gun in the entire company to hold off at least a regiment of fanatics. Soon, troops would be down to throwing rocks at the assault waves, but there were no rocks to throw.

First Platoon, commanded by Lieutenant DeLashment, anchored the northern-most position of Baker Company. Their platoon machine gun was emplaced at a lower level because of the natural descent in elevation of the hill, even though the firing position still presented an excellent and formidable field of fire. The range of the automatic weapon traversed from the north, lower level of the hill, to directly south, annihilating enemy by the score as they surged west to the defensive perimeter. The enemy never knew what hit them, until they discovered the source of the fire, and some of them reversed course to assault and eliminate the last machine gun and the crew.

The machine gun crew of DeLashment's platoon ceased fire in response to a newly-formed, frontal attack against their position by the North Korean Army. The NKPA soldiers were determined to knock out the emplacement gun that killed so many of their comrades—by using counter enemy machine gun fire the defensive position would have been annihilated.

The 1st Platoon machine gun crew resorted to hand grenade defense, in an effort to replace the machine gun fire from their position. Somehow this platoon came into possession of hand grenades. Dressler, the gunner, attempted to arm a fragmentation grenade by removing the attached pull ring without success. Someone earlier had bent the cotter pin of the ring on the grenade over so hard to safely secure the lethal implement of war, that it became impossible to remove. With that, Dressler passed the grenade to Cagle to try his luck at removal of the safety pin.

Now, a brief word about Cagle. A small, thin, wiry young man, with a ready smile and heavy facial hair given his young age of 18, he had a reputation in Okinawa as the person who always had the proverbial black cloud hovering over his head. Cagle always meant well, but somehow everything he attempted ended up as a fiasco. This abrupt war was merely an extension of his ongoing tribulations. He was to be commended for his ability to free the grenade of the safety pin by forcefully extracting it. The next logical step was to watch for enemy soldiers charging forward together and then to toss the lethal projectile at them to inflict maximum fatalities.

But, that was not Cagle. Instead, he passed the now live grenade, holding the safety spoon firmly against the grenade, back to Dressler, who apparently was so shocked by Cagle's action, he dropped the grenade in the bottom of the foxhole. During this transaction, the safety spoon automatically flew off, arming the lethal bomb. In about 4.8 seconds, any segment of life remaining would be forfeited. The inevitable violent explosion would ring down the final curtain on this ill-fated machine gun crew. There was apparently a mad scramble for the out-of- control, active grenade, about to explode at the bottom of the foxhole. It ended in tragedy with the loss of one hand, severe and multiple shrapnel wounds to two of the occupants, while the last of the gun crew remained relatively unscathed, having jumped clear at the last moment.

As the years have passed, no one could recall exactly who received what injuries. The last of the machine guns was now out of action. Now, it was up to the riflemen to face the swarming horde of lunging enemy before them.

Still they came. It was imperative to hold until daylight. The enemy night-fighters would fade as blood-bloated vampires back to their cave at the first ray of sunlight. If Baker Company possessed the hill at the break of dawn, it was theirs to keep, to have and to hold, from this night forward, at least for this battle. There was no question. One side or the other would claim the prominence in the morning, and it better not be the North Koreans. Each knew the consequences of surrender, and we were going to do exactly as General Walker proclaimed, forever branded in every mind of every soldier:

"Stand or Die. There will be no retreat!"

The battle raged all through the night, and just before dawn, it was sensed the North Koreans might fall back and withdraw to secondary positions. They were taking devastating losses. In between the tremendous charges the company discerned in the dim night the outlines of dead enemy soldiers by the hundreds, most piled upon each other in front of American defensive positions. The most dedicated enemy were taken out on the last upper terrace, slain just in front of foxholes. Those enemy who lunged fanatically forward so near to defensive positions died from point-blank rifle shots to the chest as they thrust on, driven by drunken passion and misplaced political ideology. They were determined to kill or be killed. They were accommodated. Regretfully, there was no one around to award them a medal for their heroic determination. They were slain for their resolute and unbridled efforts instead, and in the end, no one cared.

Have another round of drinks, gentlemen. Baker Company is picking up the tab.

The savage attacks continued in knee jerk reaction to their bugles, whistles and gongs, but there appeared to be a sense the pace of attacking enemy was now more measured. The attack lines were no longer shoulder-to-shoulder, nor were their unnerving battle cries as strident.

And so, finally, a diminuendo of retaliatory fire. It was estimated that Baker Company had been massacring the NKPA 6th Division for over seven hours. Now, if dawn was truly approaching, the foe would be in the process of dragging their dead from this disastrous killing hill. There was this thing about the brutal North Korean Army—they needed to be victorious in every battle, so by carrying away their dead, it was a shallow attempt to minimize the actual death count that would surely be taken at sunrise.

Oh my God! Let there be light!

Dawn crept in at long last, peeking ever so cautiously and slowly over the eastern horizon, as if the sun itself was afraid of enemy fire, and then it suddenly exploded into flaming light of day. Sunshine poured into defensive positions and flushed survivors from foxholes as company troops stared in astonished awe at hundreds and hundreds of bodies slouched haphazardly on all levels of the terraces. Corpses lay in every conceivable position, strewn about the hill in grotesque, contorted positions of death. The stench of killing and the utter desolation of a stricken, blood-soaked battlefield consecrated the land as a living testament of brave, young, untrained, American soldiers.

We won! We won! We are kings of the hill! We turned those sons of bitches back!

Lieutenant Suddaby ran to the ridgeline, exposing his silhouette, the pale sky as a backdrop, cupped his hands to his mouth, and screamed to the vanished enemy, "Count your soldiers, Joe!"

One North Korean soldier feigning death among a group of his dead comrades, suddenly leaped up and bolted for his life, his face contorted with abject fear. No one fired. We let him go. He had a free pass to tell his buddies. Tell them for us:

"Our days of retreat are over. You have met your match. Shoot your best shot. We'll be ready. Tell them."

The shooting gallery at the State Fair closed early. All of the prizes, Kewpie dolls and Teddy bears were awarded early for outstanding marksmanship!

The battle was best described as a phenomenal, one-sided slaughter.

Someone started it, and it didn't end for three or four minutes, maybe five or six. It was much too emotional to track.

"Rah! Rah! Rah!"

The unrestrained shouting of young soldiers melded into a rampage of staccato noise, not at all orchestrated. The blaring chant wedded into one, unified, triumphant scream.

The choir of victorious soldiers sang at its best this blessed morning. All was calm, all was bright. Exuberant soldiers were standing near foxholes, pumping rifles skyward, screaming at the top of lungs, some screaming from utter relief, others hurling epithets at vanquished enemy. It was not the typical high school type of cheer perhaps heard at a local football game, but rather it was the deep-throated shrieks of exhilarated young boys who fought because they had to and won because they had to.

In stark contrast, the battered bodies of North Korean soldiers lay awkwardly reposed in death. It was unknown how many enemy dead had been dragged away. The count of enemy dead that morning confirmed over a thousand killed. By extrapolation, it was estimated to be at a minimum of five wounded for each enemy dead soldier. Baker Company was attacked by at least 5,000 North Korean soldiers, a full enemy regiment.

There were about 200 of us, and for the most part, all were basic riflemen.

Sayonara, 6th Infantry Division, North Korean People's Army.

Baker Company lost about 14 killed and 21 wounded during this major battle, including minor wounds to me, others and the soldier in our foxhole who was shot through the ear. A small matter, for now, it was all quiet on the western front.

THE DAY AFTER

> In the early days of August the NKPA closed on the Pusan Perimeter with ten divisions. It mounted strong pressure on all fronts, but its main effort was directed in the southwest - the flanking attack of the 4th and 6th divisions designed to capture Masan and Pusan. Blair, p. 179.

The dog days of summer continued to nip at troop heels unaccustomed to the unbearable heat. Even before mid-morning it was hot and steamy and the corpses continued the natural process of decomposing. Flies, typically out in strength, compelled troops to constantly brush them from profusely-sweating faces, while armies of mosquitoes were abed, waiting to feast that night. What a god-awful place to hold a war.

The word was out that the North Korean People's Army was coming back again tonight to finish the job—break through this time, once and for all, and drive into the last vestige of UN real estate, the strategic port of Pusan.[33] There they would kill everyone, except those who could escape by boat. The NKPA were going to inflict the fatal stab to what the enemy perceived as the soft underbelly of Allied defenses. Americans were barely holding to the last vestige of land west of Masan, where the enemy was destroyed the night before. This night they would trip over their rotting comrades to get to Baker Company first.

The distinct, low rumble of an American deuce-and-a-half, six-by-six truck growled hoarsely as it pulled up and screeched to a stop on the road behind the entrenched company where the attack was launched to seize this hill three days earlier. The truck was laden with precious cargo—ammunition. The delivery by the merchants of death was one day too late. The defenders could have used the arms and ammunition before the NKPD knocked on the door utilizing heavy weapons, in the hope of gaining admittance to the hill.

The hotshot truck driver must have been new to the wretched roads of Korea, or he would have slowed to a crawl before stopping, mindful to avoid churning up the mountainous cloud of filthy dust. Poetic justice. He had to stand by and breathe the noxious cloud of grit he caused. His part-

---

[33] With time running against it, the North Korean high Command prepared a massive co-ordinated offensive all along the Pusan Perimeter for the first of September. As the North Korean's Peoples Army prepared for its great effort, it brought 13 infantry divisions, 1 armored division, 2 armored brigades, and miscellaneous security forces into the line. Appleman, p. 394.

ner, riding shotgun because of frequent guerrilla sniper action behind the lines, was sheeted ghostlike in the same onerous powder, though he never said a word. After the dust settled, about half of the company sauntered off the hill, to stand in line for whatever ammunition was available. The other half of the company stood watch, but for the most part the hill was secure from enemy until night.

"Where were you guys yesterday; we could have used this ammo last night, instead of having to hold back until the last minute!" grumbled one member of the company.

There was no doubt that another major attack was imminent.[34] But this pending battle was hopefully to be a turnaround of the previous night, when defenders had to judiciously guard against the complete expenditure of ammunition during the all night battle. Company personnel vaguely heard of the Pusan Perimeter earlier and the massive assault against the unit last night was apparently a component of it. It was learned much later that the battle became a historic and integral phase of the Korean War, although we had little knowledge at the time.

I grabbed a full case of fragmentation hand grenades, Mark IIIA-1—fourteen ounces of fatal fury, with a timed fuse of 4 to 4.8 seconds. Twenty-four in all and two bandoleers of 30-caliber M-1 ammo completed my allotment. The grenades, packed in a wood crate, had removable straps. Whoever was in charge of this particular weaponry had the unusual foresight to plan ahead knowing a combat soldier is generally short on pry bars and nail pullers. It was exciting to realize my good fortune to seize a vast treasure of these potent implements of war. The two bandoliers of M-1 ammunition were secured around my neck, the crate of grenades hoisted to my shoulder. I returned to my position.

During the process of removing each grenade from the heavy cardboard container, my platoon leader, Sergeant Miller, approached and said, "Pete, would you take a couple of guys to help you set up a couple of dead gooks and put them at the bottom of the hill to look like an OP?"[35]

---

[34] Thousands of NKPA troops swarmed at Fisher's positions. In an awesome display of courage, tenacity and battlefield skill, the 1/35 under Bernard Teeters, the 2/35 under John Wilkin, and Woolfolk's 3/35 held steady on their positions, inflicting an appalling slaughter on the NKPA. However, when an attached ROK element gave way, 3,000 of the enemy went around Fisher's flanks and isolated the 35th. Blair, p. 246.

[35] An Observation Post is generally a two man position situated far ahead of the MLR, [the main line of resistance], which is in contact with the commander by radio when enemy forces approach—a very dangerous job, with an extraordinarily high fatality rate. Author.

"Sure Sarge," I replied, "we'll start with the ripe ones off the hill."

"Maybe you can find some rice bags to put up a make-shift shelter, so they will be spotted easier." And then Miller added, "Be sure to remove the bolts from the rifles so they can't be used again."

"OK Ben, will do."

Third Platoon members were at ease around Miller, especially when he called everyone by their nickname. I was *Pete*. It was a trend in those days to answer to a nickname. Combat draws an unspoken emotional closeness between leaders and grunts.

It was to be a revolting job, but Miller trusted me to do it right, most likely because I was one of the very few fortunate to survive both Anui and Chinju Pass. And I obeyed orders, even when put in request form. Sergeant Miller never ordered. He didn't have to, what with his brand of charisma. Miller's directions were always put in question form, yet everyone accepted them as a directive. He was our new platoon leader, apparently assigned to the company since Chinju Pass. We didn't know where Sergeant Miller came from or much else about him. He was a low-key nom-com who earned respect from all.

Miller let his platoon know that he was a grunt once just like us. All anyone knew of Miller was that he fought in the China-Burma Campaign with Merrill's Marauders, a legendary commando unit in the Asia Theater of Operations during World War II. He should have been a lieutenant, because the position of a platoon leader called for a commissioned officer's ranking. We had it better. Sergeant Miller was heads above any lieutenant, given his style of leadership and his extensive combat experience.[36]

"Hey, guys, will you give me a hand?" I inquired as I approached two nearby soldiers talking softly and smoking together.

"I'm not sure. What's going on?" asked one.

"Sergeant Miller wants us to take a couple of gooks and set them up at the bottom of the hill to look like an OP"

---

[36] On 2 September, immediately prior to the major defensive battle the very next night, Lieutenant John C. Hughes was officially promoted to the rank of captain, in accordance to 8th Army Special Orders number 40.

Consequently, the three other 2nd lieutenants were elevated to 1st lieutenant at the same time. There appeared to be an absence of fairness. Sergeant Miller had more combat experience than all of the officers combined. While the other lieutenants fairly earned their elevated commissioned rank, it did not equate to real-life application, in that Sergeant Miller was limited by his non-com rank. The three other platoon leaders obtained their rank through university ROTC programs or OCS (officer's candidate school). Miller earned his stripes though blistering combat. Author

"OK. Might as well. Can't dance. Let's go," he cheerfully replied. He was new and glad to be alive after the night before. Everyone was. I led them in front of my position first (I knew what I was doing) and we positioned the bodies to drag them away. We grabbed one cadaver with each hand by the bottom of each enemy trouser leg, preparatory to dragging them from battle positions as so much undesirable debris.

It was necessary for bodies to be transported far enough away from the line to hopefully minimize the nearness of the fly population and at the same time, keep the deplorable smell away. The six corpses were dragged unceremoniously to the bottom of the hill in one load, two per each man. At the edge of each terrace, we had to jump to the next terrace about three feet below, while still maintaining a grip on the trouser legs of the dearly departed. When we stepped forward again, the dragged bodies struck the ground forcefully and gracelessly. We continued until we reached the bottom of the fortification.

What they didn't know didn't hurt them.

Meanwhile, the wretched, humid day began to have its customary oppressive way. Heavy field shirts were soaking wet, as if one was engaged in jungle warfare somewhere on a remote, tropical island. Perspiration irritatingly dripped from of the tip of my nose, but I was reluctant to release my hold on my cadavers, so I endured the aggravation until the bodies were unceremoniously dragged and subsequently abandoned. The bounteous rats would feast tonight and counter the corpses' traditional expectation to pass on to ancestor land. They deserved what they got, and then some.

Once back on the top terrace, the three of us spotted two really dead North Koreans sprawled in front of the foxhole to the left, where one of 14 Americans was slain. I hoped the dead enemy was shot by the new occupant of our position last night. *Really dead* was mentioned for a reason. Both dead soldiers carried small arms ammunition bandoleers crisscrossed across their chests, apparently in imitation of a Pancho Villa-type insurgent, and both bodies were slowly smoldering. They died face down, fatally shot in the chest, which in time ignited individual rounds of ammunition. Every minute or two, the creeping, slow-burning flesh of the smoldering bodies would ignite a round from the ammo bandoleers on each body, and the corpses would shudder slightly as a result of the exploded round. They were lucky to be dead.

The back of every cadaver we saw was saturated with sticky, gooey blood, swarming with feasting flies, continuously seeping and refusing to coagulate because of the blistering, steamy day. These two enemy soldiers had huge gaping holes in each chest cavity, as a result of the ongoing bursts of rounds that fed the fires, allowing the bodies to persistently burn. Each explosion caused the entry hole to widen and smolder further. There was no end to this unique cycle of burning bodies and exploding ammunition.

During, and especially following, the all-night battle, one could actually smell the distinctive odor of blood as it oozed from a thousand corpses. It was a repulsive stink which continued to corrupt the battle zone. Smoldering human bodies emit the quintessence of gagging stench. There is no other odor in the world that can equal the abhorrent smell of burning human flesh.

Despite the repugnant reek we decided not to move the two burning cadavers, for fear of exposure to the frequently exploding rounds. Each ignited round was potentially deadly shrapnel, but now they were being safely absorbed by the smoldering bodies. What is the saying? *He died a thousand deaths.*

The *noir* humor of infantryman increases in proportion to the imminent possibility of death, and causes one to derisively ridicule enemy dead. Each time one of the bodies recoiled from the explosion of a round, soldiers chuckled. It is considered a release of emotion and tension that softens reality. It is the unadulterated relief that we are glad that it was them rather than us who died. They were sardonically named *The Bobbsy Twins*.

Everyone wanted the dead as far from defensive positions as possible, primarily to avoid the awful smell of death with the ever-present accompaniment of swarming flies, but we three were only accountable to the 3rd Platoon. The two other rifle platoons were performing the Lord's work as well, while the fourth, the weapons platoon, positioned to the back of the hill, had it best of all, having had no enemy penetrate to their rear position.

The three of us moved down the line to the next North Korean corpse—another one dead, flat on his face. I rolled the body over onto his back, my fingers tacky from his blood as we watched his slimy stomach slide to the ground as it evacuated his body. Very small white matter gushed from the stomach along with the usual intestinal parts.

The slain enemy soldier released his putrid stench of stomach gases from his body in retaliation. It was a foul miasma that replicated the whiff that reeked from the corpse on the road the day we assaulted and held this hill. We gagged. It was as if the corpse attacked us one last time to seek revenge. I gasped both from the wretched stink and the sight of the viscera that slid to the ground.

Fortunately, my comrades didn't notice my reaction of shock, as I quickly reverted to an air of nonchalant indifference. I was a survivor of Anui and Chinju Pass, and I wasn't going to let these new replacements believe that I was the least repulsed by this revolting scene. After all, I was an experienced combat infantryman.

Some had witnessed many dead from both sides, but I don't believe they ever saw the inside of a body up close and personal before. This was a real-life lesson in anatomy. A serious three-way discussion ensued between us as to the make-up of the small white matter that was the primary contents of the stomach. One of the soldiers believed it to be maggots, but two of us reasoned it was rice, opining that it was too soon for the inevitable maggots—larvae spawned by flies. Rationally, flies would have nested in the blown-out back of the corpse, where the bloody access was readily available rather than crawl under the body to lay fertile eggs. The cadaver did not offer a comment either way.

The body was not worthy to stand in as one of two decoys, but we had to dispose of him down the terraces at any rate. When dragged down the hill, the body left a trail of minute white rice or maggots, depending on whose viewpoint one embraced, along with pieces of his entrails that similarly dribbled in the wake. The cadaver was deposited among a large group of similarly dead enemy soldiers at the bottom of the hill, now scattered about the ground near the trees.

Eventually, two suitable cadavers were found that seemed to work, except for one problem. Because of the steaming, humid summer night, coupled with the soaring heat continuing through the day, rigor mortis rapidly set in. Rigor mortis is the process of becoming rigid and unable to bend following death and is affected by a host of variables, including temperature. The dead invariably initiated their final death repose face down.

No funeral rites for the NKPA 6th Division were forthcoming.

Once two bodies were dragged down the hill in a position to set them up as decoys, the three of us took turns jumping on the lower extremities of the bodies, hoping to break the legs in order to prop them up in a sitting position. The femur bone, largest in the body, connecting the hip to the knee, was the one to break, but it was impossible to fracture. The bones were too pliable and elastic, because of the young ages of the enemy, coupled with their recent demise. Our company commander had tried the same futile exercise of jumping on the upper legs of the pathetic soldier in our unit who took his own life near the cemetery about two weeks previously. Hughes was unsuccessful. So were we.

All the while, ferocious flies were constantly interfering with our unique task. They compelled me to resort to swinging my arms erratically, wildly, in a vain attempt to intimidate the swarms attacking my face and hands. I tried to wipe flowing perspiration from my face with the back of my filthy and now bloody hands. The salty perspiration burned my eyes, and blended together with the dirt on my face, which I had been unable to wash for the month since I left the hospital.

Now, they had focused on the blood on my hands, and I thought it would be a reprieve from my face, but they were there massing voraciously, covering every part of exposed flesh. My blood ran cold at the feeling of the insatiable multitudes swarming on us, knowing they had just feasted on the dead.

Surprisingly, an American barbed wire stanchion was discovered, a heavy steel rod with a corkscrew end, made to twist into the ground, with three loops forged in the shaft to accommodate and secure barbed wire. The pole was apparently abandoned by the American or ROK infantry unit that briefly held this emplacement before relinquishing it to overwhelming enemy. The two dead NKPA soldiers from the south side of the perimeter were emplaced in an OP. The inability to break the legs of the cadavers, allowing us to position them in a somewhat sitting position, posed a dilemma. I remarked to my friends, "You guys hold him, and I'll stick him in the back, and we'll prop him up on the rod."

The others thought that stabbing one body in the back and propping it was as good idea as any, so they both held the corpse under each arm, as I ran from about ten feet from the rear, lunging at the cadaver with all of the strength I possessed, thrusting the sharp, corkscrew end of the shaft into his lower back. When I speared him, the rod bounced from his body. I felt the sickening tremor of death evacuate the body, resonate through the nucleus of the shaft and flood into my hands. It was similar to striking a hard object with a steel rod that causes a vibrating shock-like effect to the holder. However, instead of shock, I experienced the subtle, grisly sensation of death permeate through my hands and invade my body. I dropped the pole and vomited.

After recovering, we propped two outdated, abandoned Russian rifles near the bodies after one of us removed the firing bolts and cast them far from the corpses. One of the group collected two field caps from nearby dead comrades, and they were respectfully placed on the heads of our dead observers. They still lay in more of a lying position than sitting, but it was the best that we could do. At least they were face up now.

Thank you for your contribution to the war effort, gentlemen.

It was hoped the returning enemy force, in their eagerness, would fire on these decoy soldiers and expose their position prematurely to us.

We did the best that we could to comply with Sergeant Miller's directive, trying to place the bodies, but I will never forget the impact on my emotions during that grisly operation. I needed to wash my hands after handling the bodies, but there was never any spare water available, and barely enough to drink. The boiling heat was stifling as I continually spat on my contaminated, filthy hands in an abortive effort to wash away the blood and the emotional sensation. And I thought I was mature.

The flies developed addictive behavior in their lust for enemy blood on my hands. I dragged my fingers in the dirt to cleanse the blood that never seemed to leave my hands. Ever since that appalling episode, I have suffered the obsessive behavior of constantly washing my hands for no conscious reason.

Upon returning to my defensive position, I turned to my task at hand, readying the hand grenades for the forthcoming night battle. My fear of battle since Chinju Pass was now displaced by a powerful sense of vengeance, and I was ready. I believed I performed well the night before, and I eagerly looked forward to the coming struggle. In fact, I literally prayed for the return of the enemy, because now I was armed with numerous portable bombs, I was confident of slaying them as they broached the hill. Finally, I had the weapons to strike back.

I wanted to avenge my lost buddies, but more than anything else in the entire world, I wanted to prove to myself, once and for all, that I was not a coward.

The cardboard canisters containing the fragmentation hand grenades were sealed with wide, heavy, bright yellow tape that seemed to scream, *Handle with caution!* One could imagine if just one grenade exploded in a case lot, what the result would be for an entire ammunition cache.

I filled each empty can with dirt to replicate the weight of the actual explosive device. Although they were not grenade shaped, they would suffice. I took note of where the majority of the bodies lay, which was somewhat widespread, given that there were a thousand dead scattered below.

The containers were ideal for hand grenade practice. From my foxhole, I sighted a target, a large group of fallen enemy, and threw each simulated grenade container in the typical, correct overhand throw that was taught in basic training. Satisfied with the results of practice, tossing them where I expected the enemy, I developed confidence for the night's forthcoming battle.

While engrossed in the task of unpacking grenades, a thought had occurred to me in respect to the two smoldering enemy bodies left near our positions. Despite the danger in moving them, I knew that the horrible stench, particularly in the still of the night, would be too overwhelming to tolerate. My friends had returned to their respective positions, so I dragged the cadavers one at a time down the terraces myself.

~~

Several squad members were sitting around, waiting for the night to unfold. I borrowed the tooth brush stub from one of the three of us who shared it, brushed my teeth without tooth paste or powder, just to scrape the filth from my mouth, rinsed with a swig of polluted water from the canteen, and then cleaned my rifle with the same tooth brush.

The M-1 Rifle is an extension of an infantryman's life. They were cleaned to avoid the disaster of having a jammed weapon, leaving one to the mercy of the enemy who had no mercy to render. No one had to remind soldiers to complete this task. It was left to the individual to maintain a functioning weapon or to die with one that failed to operate. It was Ernie Pyle, beloved war correspondent of World War II, killed during the Battle for Okinawa, who succinctly remarked, "Young soldiers with dirty faces but clean rifles."

~~

Infantrymen undergo a startling metamorphosis in the adjustment to crude, primitive living conditions. One couldn't sleep because of the heat of the oppressive sun, coupled with the ever-present armies of flies, while the debilitating effects of sleep deprivation is the biggest negative effect in the life of a foot soldier. In due time the effects of the battleground permeate the very soul of the infantryman. One develops the deep-set, hollowed-eyed, unfocussed stare known as the *1000 yard stare.* Infantrymen in time gaze without seeing.

One hour on, one hour off of sentry duty, waiting for the enemy, was every bit as devastating as a deadly disease. None could ever get sufficient sleep. The awful, decayed stench of the last of the organized North Korean 6th Division continued to haunt us, though carcasses made a royal feast for the flies during the day and for the voracious rats at night.

When the company took control of the hill three days earlier, on 1 September, the mosquitoes became our enemy at night on a parallel with the NKPA.

We looked for ways to acquire some semblance of protection from the marauding flood of parasitic mosquitoes when performing sentry duty. I used my heavy field shirt. I would pull the shirt, more of a light jacket, over my head and button the top button over the top of my head, and then carefully set my helmet on the top of my head. After many failed attempts, by very slow and deliberate movement, I was able to tuck just the bottom edge of the shirt into the top of my field trousers. With that accomplished, I sat on the edge of the foxhole, pulled both hands into the sleeves of my shirt before grabbing the edge of each sleeve. By holding on, I was as mosquito proof as I could possibly be. I sat rigid, without any movement for an hour, on the lookout for enemy soldiers, peeking out through a fold in the shirt, between the buttonholes.

When my hour was up, my foxhole buddy began to stand his one-hour watch. Every sentry relieved of duty for a brief hour would collapse, and fall deep asleep by the time their movement to the bottom of the hole ceased. Then the mosquitoes would take their revenge, attack and swarm uncontrollably over hands and faces without mercy, feasting on young American-brand blood. The second hour of watch was worse. Mosquitoes sensed the smell of blood from earlier wounds, driving them into frenzied attacks, drawn to bleeding faces as if blood was a magnet.

Almost everyone contracted malaria to some degree or another, and it was years before the malaria devil relinquished his ruthless grip on us after we matriculated to civilian life. Later in the conflict, I had the misfortune of contracting severe hepatitis, leaving me persistently exhausted during my adult life. I will never know if it was the lack of sleep or the hepatitis that plagued me.

In times of peace, fireflies seem to epitomize an aura of serenity and tranquility, of laid-back southern charm and hospitality. Catfish fishing, sleeping in a hammock on a sunny, lazy day, carefree days and nights with the smell of fresh-mowed lawns and iced tea on the veranda. Fireflies were not the same in Korea.

To defenders, fireflies portended danger, and here on the hill, soldiers were mesmerized by them, for in collective minds they were seen as if they were far off enemy soldiers carrying lanterns. The fireflies were our enemy, as were the scrub pines that seemed to move ever so slowly, while we were on watch for the enemy. Brush, small trees, and vegetation were summarily cut down, but fireflies floated aimlessly in the black night sky, resembling enemy coming for us. We couldn't get rid of them, any more than the tormenting flies and mosquitoes, so we lived with them; but the flies and mosquitoes did not raise the hair on the back of necks as did fireflies. The fireflies, and there were always so many, caused adrenaline to remain at the highest level while we were on sentry duty. The North Korean People's Army never came back that night. For me and many others it was actually a disappointment. We defenders were ready and confidant. It was not realized then but the back of the NKPA was broken. Despite continuous, fanatical charges by the well-armed, well-trained enemy, the Perimeter continued to hold.

Baker Company, as well as all other soldiers positioned on the Pusan Perimeter staved off the enemy and defeated a mighty army. An enormous loss of life, overextended supply lines and the inability to break through were their downfall. More than any factor was the strategic error to attack the entire Pusan Perimeter at the same time, rather than marshalling sufficient manpower at tactical locations. The Americans and the ROKs at the Perimeter held on long enough for the United States military forces to provide adequate ammunition, supplies, and reinforcements. The North Korean Army had lost a golden opportunity to push the American Army and the ROKs into the Strait of Tsushima (Strait of Korea). American commanders never told us. We had to read it later in history books.

~~

It was now around ten days since the foes were slain and, compounded by the hot, humid weather, bodies rotting in this jungle-like, steamy climate made the area intolerable. There was no souvenir hunting or weapons retrieval among the rotting corpses. By then the multitude of rats had infiltrated and nested in their treasure of untold amounts of decayed food. The trash heap. The smell was worse than ever, and something had to be done to prevent an epidemic.

One morning, a large group of South Korean rural farmers, comprised mainly of old men, women and children, appeared in the area. They dragged the horrendous bodies away. I recently learned from Suddaby that someone paid the farmers to drag the cadavers away and bury them. I never thought of the effect that this task would have played on them emotionally, particularly the children, until later in life when I realized the debilitating effect of Post Traumatic Stress Disorder. The children had to be emotionally torn for life because of the horrors of this brutal war to which they were ruthlessly exposed. I have come to realize that if my life were rewound with the knowledge that I have today, I would not have permitted those innocent children to even view those grotesque bodies, let alone to bury them.

Colonel Wong Lichan, representing the People's Republic of China, was posted to Korea in early August 1950, as a special envoy of the new Chinese Communist Government for the purpose of monitoring the war. Wong was assigned to the 6th Division of The North Korea People's Army, commanded by General Kim Chaek, whom Wong admired as a friend and a competent field leader. Wong noted that General Kim was thoroughly trained in combat in China against the Japanese and later, the Chinese Nationalist Army of Chiang Kai-shek.

Colonel Wong, born and raised in Manchuria, spoke fluent Korean as well, so General Kim invited him (Wong) to a scheduled staff conference in early September. Wong expected to learn the triumphant news of the fall of Pusan to the NKPA. Instead the colonel heard from Kim of the destruction of the NKPA 6th Division:

> Our 6th Division's offensive has failed. For this I take full responsibility. Our soldiers did their utmost. No, more than that... they did better than any commander. They captured Chinju. They fought their way to the outskirts of Masan....But their efforts came too late. The enemy was reinforced and determined. Battles are not won with hindsight. Yet I must freely admit it would have been better if our gallant comrades had driven sooner toward Pusan instead of first mopping up the southwestern coastal areas. That is my mistake. It is now history. But, let me emphasize, the setback is not irretrievable. Spurr, p. 19.

Our company held the fortification until late afternoon of 18 September 1950, the longest deployment of the company in one location. Because of the unremitting attacks by the die-hard NKPA, the units of the 8th Army at The Perimeter were unable to break out to implement the southern pincer movement until three days subsequent to the Inchon landing. The company had a date with destiny and a rendezvous with the Allies advancing south—the ROK Army, the American 7th Infantry Division and the 1st Marine Division.

Now, it was the Allies' turn.

REMINISCENCES OF THE HILL, PART I
Patrol to the South

> While the great majority of South Koreans were loyal to the Syngman Rhee government, elements in the South continued in armed opposition, with the support of some of the peasantry. Because of this support and the broken terrain, where each valley remained almost a world to itself the survivors of the NKPA and the guerrillas melted into the population. They were seemingly peaceful agriculturists by day, becoming armed marauders at night. Fehrenbach, pp. 388-9.

Oily, dark smoke wafted from the makeshift cook stove. It was constructed by bending four sides on the top of an empty C-ration can, to allow air to invade when gasoline was poured among sand and rocks in the can. The can contained the small fire and prevented an all-out conflagration. C-rations were vile and became unpalatable to us after we had subsisted on them for months. That is, if troopers could ever get them. It seemed about half of the time they did without, having none available.

Charring C-rations was the only way to make them edible, so I placed a can of hamburger patties and gravy on the stove to scorch. Now it was late in the afternoon and the enemy had identified our position, so the heavily-drifting smoke was little more then a taunt and a challenge to them to return to do battle again. As yet it appeared that they had no stomach for another round.

C-rations were so unpopular that a democratic method of serving was implemented. The top cover of the cardboard ration box was cut by the squad leader without revealing the name of the contents printed on the top of each can. Then the box was deftly turned over so the name rested unseen on the ground, and the cardboard was lifted off. Each soldier selected an anonymous can. A loud groan inevitably followed when contents were identified. If anyone couldn't make a trade with another, the unopened can was cast to the corpses. It was just easier to go without eating.

"Hi Pete," said Sergeant Miller with his usual pleasant smile, as he ambled to my position where I was cremating the infamous food.

"That looks damn near fit to eat," he remarked with an understanding smile. After passing pleasantries about the stench of the North Korean remains, comparing it to the similarity of the odor of the C-rations, he said, "I'm going for the 1st and 2nd squad leaders and will be right back. OK?"

Shortly thereafter, Miller, my friend Sgt. Jim Reed, and another person who later was killed, strolled up. Miller nonchalantly said, "We are moving out at 0500 hours sharp tomorrow to shake down a village south of us that has been identified as a center for anyone that hasn't already been grabbed by the ROK Army to serve. Third and 4th squads will stay behind, and 1st and 2nd squads will take the village. Any questions?"

Jim Reed matter of factly asked, "What kind of equipment do we carry?"

Sergeant Miller replied, "Minimal. This will probably be an easy patrol, so a belt of ammo for each guy, and, oh yeah, we won't be needing no grenades, and every man bring one can of rations for themselves. We don't expect any trouble, and even if we do find some, the village is too tight for grenades. Be sure to eat before we get on the truck at 0500 hours sharp. We should be back by late afternoon at the latest."

Both squad leaders acknowledged Sergeant Miller's instructions and wandered off to brief other squad members. Platoon members were glad to be going to this village, wherever it lay. Most were getting mountain fever, after about eight days deployed in one place, and they looked forward to a break in a monotonous routine. I silently marveled how the Army could have intelligence on a suspect village when the entire course of the war to date was caught up in total chaos.

Could this be a turning point in the war? True, the company had managed to repel the enemy, avoid another retreat, and maul an enemy force severely.

~~

It was a pleasant, late afternoon. The flies had disappeared for the most part. Dusk was settling in ever so slowly, while the wide expanse of blue sky dappled with billowing, cumulus clouds offered a clear panoramic view from the top of the hill.

It wouldn't be long before the mosquitoes would return and make the 50-percent alert watches nearly impossible. Some wondered why the Army couldn't have thought enough to stock mosquito repellent along with other supplies, until they reflected on all-night battles during which ammunition was nearly exhausted. But by now, the company had been issued what they hoped was sufficient small arms ammunition to repel enemy again. Perhaps the Army in their infinite wisdom would have acquired and dispensed some type of fly repellent. Sure.

Members of the company used to compete to ride shotgun beside the company jeep driver until a tragic event unfolded. Every man in the company was allowed to ride one time when the company jeep driver made a scheduled daily run to division headquarters situated in the rear. Secret orders, mail and other necessities to run a war were the responsibility of the company driver. Everyday the company needed one man to ride shotgun against possible guerrilla attacks.

Early in the conflict, the Women's Christian Temperance Society made a big uproar to the effect, "Our boys are getting drunk on the front lines."

The Society must have had tremendous political influence, because the one can of beer a day allotment, put in effect a mere few days earlier, was abruptly cancelled as suddenly as it began.

"Give them candy instead," was the suggested substitution. Even more depraved however, was the ludicrous suggestion to provide a can of cola, always warm, for every soldier on the front line. The company jeep driver developed many friends in the rear echelon because of his daily journeys, for whoever accompanied him was sure to locate a beer or two from the driver's sources. To be assigned to the rear echelon was heaven on earth

Major field commanders generally laid claim to a schoolhouse or other large building as headquarters. Everyone assigned to the rear slept in cots with mosquito-proof netting and had all of the beer they wanted. Hot food was served three times a day, and it wasn't C-rations. Soldiers on the line were fighting a war. The rear echelon was on a carefully scripted campout.

One particular usual hot and humid day, traveling on the road back from division headquarters, a guerrilla sniper lay in wait as the company jeep came into his gun sight around a bend in the road. One shot rang out The driver was slain instantly from a high-powered rifle bullet to the neck, and the jeep continued erratically on, then careened off the road at a high rate of speed before the conveyance nose-dived into a watery rice paddy. The sniper's round tore the jeep driver's neck almost out, as his head gyrated in uncontrolled spasms. The body pitched forward upon impact of the jeep. There the dead driver hung prostrate across the folded-down windshield, his head facing to the left. The inescapable flow of blood poured onto the glass of the windshield, where it was held captive by the frame of the destroyed vehicle. Massive, gooey blood erupted as if some one had cut the driver's throat from ear to ear.

The passenger leaped from the vehicle after it lurched to an abrupt stop as a second shot rang out nearly striking the surviving soldier. Because of the survivor's instant movement, the sniper missed and the projectile shot through his canteen attached to the left rear of his gun belt. He lost his rifle in the surprise attack, but the soldier, though seriously injured as a result of the crash, managed to crawl through the mucky rice paddy to the raised embankment of the pond. There he was afforded protection from further sniper attack. The survivor was forced to crawl through the foul rice paddy for over a mile to get out of vision of the renegade sniper.

Soaked in feces and suffering from deep lacerations, contusions, and severe shock, he eventually made it back to the company, where he swore he would never again ride in a jeep during his stay in Korea. He never did. He was killed two months later, when the Chinese Volunteers entered the war.

An infantry squad, reinforced with an armored escort, was dispatched immediately to the area of the incident to recover crucial documents relating to the conflict, the body, and the jeep, which was a total loss. The sniper had by then withdrawn only to move to another area to inflict physical and psychological damage on Allied forces.

~~

Slightly before five in the morning, 3rd Platoon was on the footpath behind the hill heading for the patiently-waiting deuce-and-a-half truck requisitioned for the day's operation. The transport easily held 20 soldiers, approximately half of the platoon, all sitting down. I was finishing the last of my can of C-rations. I threw the empty can into the rice paddy, wiped my steel spoon on my filthy trouser leg and returned the spoon to my right hand shirt pocket before I climbed onto the truck.

With only one truck, the normally suffocating dust was not as bad as usual. Sergeant Miller rode in the cab with the driver. The driver would not dare play his clever game of intentionally hitting potholes to agitate passengers. The ride was smooth enough that the passengers fell fast sleep in the dark, in spite of being in a sitting position during the trip. It didn't take long to sleep anywhere for a few guarded moments, and the brief interlude revived the platoon. This was one of those special moments arranged by Sergeant Miller.

The sun began to rise, ushering in another scorching summer day. None could get accustomed to the life-sapping humidity. As daylight infected the sullen sky, we started to stir from our brief, appreciated sleep. No one spoke because of the short interlude of tranquility between sleep and wakefulness. The men were exhausted from weeks without uninterrupted sleep, and they could have slept through the day had they have been allowed to do so. Not a soul stirred. The troops were still in a distracted mode of semi sleep, and the mere act of sitting without the need of concentrating was a crude method to revive senses and refortify emotional energy.

The truck lurched to a stop near a typical rural village.

"OK. Let's go! Spread out and let's sweep the area. Watch your asses, shoot first and ask questions later. This is supposed to be a high-powered group. Let's go!" said Sergeant Miller in his hard Texas accent. The platoon had finally arrived and they sprang out of the deuce-and-a-half eager for something different to do.

"Fan out! Don't bunch up. Search everyone, man or woman, if they look or act suspicious!"

Sergeant Miller knew his stuff. His teenage years in the China-Burma campaign as a part of Merrill's Marauders made him a top soldier, imbued with all of the knowledge to stay alive and to watch over us.

The best prospect of finding enemy would be if they fled from the rear of the village into the nearby hills west of this village. One who was not enemy would not flee, I reasoned, as I picked up the pace to get to the rear. I was just at the outskirts of this large village, when someone from the hills fired a burst from an automatic at me.

"Braaap!"

The distinct report from a Soviet AK-47 submachine gun went whizzing around me, and I was alone. Leaping instinctively headfirst into a fallow rice field just to the left of the footpath, my survival instincts took control. I was no longer the terrified teenager that I was at Anui.

While airborne I swiftly slid my right hand from the small of the stock to the butt of my M-1 Rifle. During basic training, we learned that when falling, one should not grasp the small of the stock, as it will cause the stock of the rifle to shatter upon impact. That specific area is where the shooter holds the rifle in firing position with the right index finger on the trigger.

I landed hard on dry solid ground that had not been irrigated for months because of the war. The instant I landed, I turned my head skyward to see that the dense growth of dry rice plant had resumed its natural position. I was hidden.

Good, I thought. The sniper saw me leap into the rice field, but he didn't know where I landed and most likely he would be hesitant to shoot again in fear that he would expose his position.

I had come a long way since those terrifying days at Anui and Chinju Pass. Here I had just been shot at, and now I was nearly falling asleep in this serene, dry, rice field. No flies, no intense heat, no humidity—just tranquil shade. I had to fight against falling asleep. What if I didn't hear them at the conclusion of this objective, and they moved out without me, thinking I was dead? I'd be stuck in the middle of an enemy-saturated village. Now boredom began to set in. I couldn't stay here for long, as other enemy might be coming. I recalled the area before I leaped into the field, and I had remembered an ochre-colored, adobe-style wall to the right of the footpath.

I leaped up quickly, bounded from the rice paddy, and raced across the footpath to find shelter behind the ancient wall. I removed my helmet after I found a spot between some thick branches of a tree and the wall. I was camouflaged so well that I had ample opportunity to search for the sniper that shot at me. It was a personal thing now. He tried to kill me, and I wanted to kill him in return. It was basic depraved war conduct.

Some call it survival of the fittest.

Two soldiers, clad in unusual uniforms, strolled up, and from the sanctuary of the wall, I cautioned them that I had just been fired upon.

"Hey guys! Watch your asses; I was just shot at by an AK-47!"

The soldiers hurriedly joined me behind the wall for protection. Their accents were decidedly British, and they mentioned that they landed in Korea on 29 August 1950 as a contingent of the British 27th Commonwealth Brigade. The two soldiers watched for the sniper beside where I had posted myself, so I moved further down the wall, closer to the rice paddy, where a section of the ancient wall had crumbled. I stationed myself inside of the large opening near the left side, so I was less a target. The sniper could obviously observe us, while his location remained unknown, and I strained to discover him. A slight movement in the foliage, a hint of a different color, the shape of an object that was not similar to the surroundings, or possibly the minute gleam of metal. Anything to expose his position so I could respond in kind.

My attention was engrossed in locating the sniper, as I knelt near the opening of the wall with the barrel of my rifle extended, open to view. Scanning the densely-covered hill from where the burst of firepower emanated, at the last second I sensed movement out of the corner of my left eye. Impossible, I thought. My entire body was inside of the wall, yet for some inexplicable reason, I sensed a form approaching me rapidly, running parallel to the wall on the outside. I peered out the wall just in time to see what I believed at the time to be a South Korean farmer leap toward me, in what I thought was a slip caused by being off balance. As he touched my rifle, I instinctively jerked it inside and at the same time I motioned to the farmer for his safety.

"Papa-san, Get in here! You're going to get killed out there!"

He was frantically waved inside to the safety of the village. Once he was safe within the confines of the village, he smiled and bowed graciously, and I returned the gesture by nodding my head to him. Although it was clear he did not understand my words, he did comprehend the hand signals. The farmer walked about ten paces, as I watched him impassively, when he turned and faced me again, flashing a wide smile displaying clean white teeth. I believed he was about to enter the sanctuary of the village where he would be out of danger. The farmer turned back again and continued his walk into the main area of the village.

I returned to my mission of seeking the sniper. It was my fantasy that he was the same enemy who killed our jeep driver, which afforded me the impetus to attempt to even the score, although the odds of the sniper being the killer of the company driver were remote indeed. My eyes began to water from the stifling heat, as I wiped constant perspiration from my forehead. My helmet was under the tree where the young British soldiers were stationed.

"Brappp!"

The sound of a sub-machine gun in the center of the village! Not the indescribable meld of rounds of the infamous Soviet AK-47, but instead, the deep, powerful rumble of a burst of rounds from a United States Browning Automatic Rifle, known far and wide as the *BAR*. Who had the BAR, and what is happening, I fearfully wondered, my heart pounding, as I raced back to the source of the shots.

It was Gilliam, a tall lanky easy-going Midwestern Afro-American, with a quick smile—a member of one of our four squads.

"Gilliam, what the fuck happened?" I implored, panting, nearly out of breath!

"That motha fucka tried to grab my BAR." That's all that Gillian said in his routine, unexcitable monotone.

On the ground, lay the same person that I thought was the innocent Korean farmer caught up in the middle of this terrible civil war.

"That's the same son of a bitch who was trying to take my rifle and kill me with my own weapon!" I impulsively shouted aloud.

My brow broke out in perspiration of what might have been. My knees felt weak. My anger was rising. I was the good guy. No, I was the *patsy*.

Killed in the line of duty, my mother would read in the telegram from the Department of Defense. I would hope that out of courtesy to her, they would omit any passage that would refer to:

Slain by stupidity.

I could not believe that I had been so asinine, particularly since I knew what to expect.

Despite having at least six rounds at point-blank range fired into his chest and stomach, the guerilla was crawling slowly on the ground. His female consort was trying to treat his wounds, but the enemy kept up the same, slow crawl. Blood was oozing on the ground, coagulating into the dirt he was dragging his body through.

"Crawl, you bastard," I said to myself. I was angry, but not at the dying would-be killer. I was mentally flagellating myself.

The guerrilla carried his wallet in a rear pocket that was exposed from the rural Korean white jacket as he crawled. I removed his wallet, as he continued to crawl, and there he was. He was a commissioned officer in the North Korea People's Army. A small, school-sized, sepia-colored full-faced photograph, complete with Sam Browne Belt across his right shoulder and attached to his heavy leather Army belt. He sported a rigid, high neck collar with his rank displayed on each collar side, and the same small trim mustache common to officers of the NKPA.

I reflected on what Sergeant Miller intoned at the briefing:

"Village loaded with guerrillas . . . Watch your asses. . . shoot first and ask questions later..."

I felt like a complete fool. The man shot down was a North Korean officer in every sense. Short cropped haircut, neatly shaven, thin-trimmed mustache, not that old in age after I viewed him in depth. He lacked the deeply lined permanently-bronzed face of the farmer who toiled in the fields all his life.

For good measure, I grinned as he continued to crawl on his stomach, his face wrenched in pain, even though he did not interrupt his steadfast crawl in the least. Had Gilliam shot him in the face or head, he would have died right then, rather than later from his many chest and stomach wounds. I could not bring myself to shoot him in the head, and I didn't know why. Then it came to me. I was angrier at myself than at the North Korean officer. Moreover, there is a wide gap between ground warfare and murder. I was not a North Korean soldier in any sense, and he was already in his death throes.

These villagers got off easy. Had the circumstances been reversed and this operation was conducted by North Korean Forces, they would have slaughtered every man, woman, and child, and particularly the young woman who tried to aid the spy. We left her alone, and I never heard if they found other enemy infiltrators. Certainly it was a major operation to have included British forces as well.

I showed the photograph of the dying enemy officer to Sgt. Miller, and he kept it.

"Hey, Sarge, that's my souvenir!"

"Sorry Pete, we turn it over to G-2 (intelligence unit) for identification."

That made sense, coupled with the fact that an American would suffer instant death if captured with a photo of one of the enemy.

Much later in life I learned through extensive studies that American society is generally steeped in revulsion of the killing of other humans. Interviews conducted with veterans disclosed that our infantrymen for the most part subconsciously fired over the heads of enemy, rather than at their bodies, in order not to slay them. Perhaps this may have been the case with me, but in Gilliam's case it was a matter of quick thinking to avoid having the BAR turned on him. Gilliam should have received a medal of valor for his extraordinary swift thinking during this action, but those types of medals always seemed to be reserved for officers. Enlisted men receive the Military Order of the Purple Heart in lieu of medals of valor.

Yet in reflection, during our recent all-night battle with the entire North Korean 6th Infantry Division, we all fired to kill. Perhaps the extreme closeness in distance to each other, compounded with an acute shortage of ammunition, and, especially the *take no prisoners* philosophy of the enemy altered the equation.

Gilliam did receive some notable recognition however. During the village sweep, he momentarily removed his helmet to mop perspiration from his head, and a bird flying overhead co-incidentally made a direct hit on the top of his head. We made sure that he never forgot that part. Good natured as he was, he accepted it in fun. From then on, Gilliam was dubbed with a new nickname, and was now known far and wide as *shit head*.

If any other infiltrators were found, they must have been turned over to the ROK Army for interrogation, a fate as horrendous as what the North Korean Army could muster.

Sergeant Miller was right on all counts. We arrived back to our hill that afternoon. If he were alive today, I believe that I could share with him how I erred so seriously that very fateful day. I am sure that Miller would have laughed. I never told anyone, other than my initial spontaneous outburst, that the spy tried to kill me in the same manner.

The operation was over and we reloaded on the trucks for the ride back in the sweltering heat. No one spoke as we sat lifeless, the ever-present dust caking on our bodies.

REMINISCENCES OF THE HILL, PART II
Patrol to the North

> The art of warfare is this: It is best to keep one's own state intact; to crush the enemy's state is only a second best. It is best to keep one's own army, battalion, company or five man squad intact; to crush the enemy's army, battalion, company, or five man squad is only a second best. So to win a hundred victories in a hundred battles is not the highest excellence; the highest excellence is to subdue the enemy's army without fighting at all. The Art of Warfare, Sun Tzu

The Monsoons roared in with a vengeance making up for lost time by imposing non-stop, flooding rain for five days. No let up, just warm, heavy, tropical sheets of unrelenting rain. It was as if God compressed His earlier 40 days of rain into a five-day event. It is said that the Monsoon season starts here in *The Land of the Morning Calm* the first part of June. But it was approximately 7 September when Heaven's doors were stuck open for five days.

Everything was beyond soaking wet, except the rifles. Carefully wrapped in each man's poncho, they were the most important item on the list of what to keep dry.[37] No cigarettes, no matches, no fires to heat C-rations, no mail and no enemy, but clean, dry, ready-to-immediately-operate M-1 Rifles.

The war was called because of rain. Fingers transformed into wrinkled, prune-like, uncoordinated digits from the awesome, brutal rain. Feet were as sodden and wrinkled as fingers and bodies were water-logged and saturated.

Patrols, both combat and reconnaissance, were aborted. The enemy couldn't possibly function either, so it devolved into a tie game.

Now the company was confident enough to hold this position no matter the odds. Sufficient ammunition, grenades, land mines, and especially flares, could hold and repel any enemy units who were audacious enough to assault. Troops developed somewhat of a poignant attachment to the defensive position, reflecting on earlier days of massive losses of men, unprecedented retreat, and arduous forced marches. Each day soldiers completed minor improvements to make life more tolerable on the fortifica-

---

[37] In respect to ponchos—The Korean War memorial in Washington D.C. displays 19 larger than life sculpted statutes depicting American soldiers on a combat patrol. All of the figures are clad in rectangular plastic type ponchos. In no case was the poncho ever worn on a patrol mission given the extreme shiny reflection and the unacceptable swishing noise generated when walking. Soldiers on patrol accepted inclement weather as one component of the duty of an infantryman. Author.

tion. Some cut in dirt steps on the two paths leading to the rice paddies, to avoid slipping while hauling heavy loads. During the day, others hacked to death enemy, which were actually scrub pines. At night the bushes transmogrified into enemy, and appeared to move slowly about in front of the perimeter. Those standing sentry duty were mesmerized by the shadowy figures. They would blink furiously to determine if they saw dangerous enemy or innocent bushes.

Corpses were long buried, even though hours were used up holding my hands into the purifying rain in an attempt to wash the imaginary blood away that was ingrained when dragging away and setting up slain bodies the day after the major battle. The rain didn't work. Try as I might, the *blood* remained. The insufferable flies, mosquitoes and life-sapping humidity went on a five-day furlough from the war. It was impossible to sleep during the day in pre-monsoon times, and it was nearly unfeasible to sleep in the pouring rain, but brief dozing during the deluge was indeed achievable. Troops sat at the edge of the highest terrace where defensive positions were emplaced. With legs hanging down, individuals fell on their backs, and with a section of soggy cardboard from ration cartons for a pillow, (more to keep the mud out), they covered their faces with the helmet and fell fast, dead asleep. None had slept for days and now this was a golden opportunity. It was amazing to all how a brief respite or two of deep sleep could revitalize one's very being.

Furthermore, the earlier stench of the now buried, rotting bodies intermingled with the awful odor of night soil from rural agriculture fields was temporarily dissipated.

Uniforms washed naturally, simply because we remained outside without protection from rain, unless one could describe a helmet as some category of rain gear. Bodies were clean for the first time since the unit departed from the decrepit dock at Okinawa 20 July. This was the first shower, albeit through our uniforms, since the unit's arrival, but it was considered successful, instilling a positive mood in soldiers. Six weeks without a shower was severe, even though the inability to maintain any degree of hygiene steadily worsened as the war wore tediously on.

On 6 September, the Company was apprised that they were no longer Baker Company, 29th Infantry Regiment, but now they were ordained as King Company, 35th Infantry Regiment, 25th Infantry Division. The 29th Regiment lost such a disproportionate number of soldiers from both battalions during the initial enemy encounters, that the unit was written off in a paper change, and survivors were assimilated into the 25th Infantry Division. Normally with such extraordinary losses as the 29th Regiment sustained, the unit would be erased from the T, O & E (Table of Organization and Equipment) of the Army. In this immediate case, the Army dispatched men and weapons to Korea, while the headquarters of the 29th Regiment remained in Okinawa. Headquarters considered the deployment of personnel and equipment to the war zone as replacements. In the Army's opinion, the 29th Infantry Regiment was still considered a viable regiment. The survivors were not.

Floods eventually abated and the sun was summarily ejected from hibernation, taking its usual place in the eastern sky. It took days for everything to get back to normal. Walking was nearly impossible because of ponderous mud caking to bottoms of boots. A few steps and it was as if one was transporting 20 pounds on the bottom of each foot. Take one step, shake the foot to dislodge the muck, but it would stick as if the mud were a magnet.

Fingers dried enough to manipulate them once again. Lighting a cigarette after a week's hiatus was a very pleasant experience.

The life of a light weapons infantryman is arduous indeed.

A new replacement and I were discussing various aspects of his new assignment when he remarked in essence, how flavorsome C-rations tasted.

"Give it a week," I replied scornfully, as I noted Sergeant Bruner strolling to my position.

Bruner said, "Pete, the skipper asked me to take out a special patrol tomorrow morning. You want to come along?"

"Sure," I enthusiastically replied.

It was bewildering, as Riley was assigned to another platoon, and by nature a rifle company tends to emplace positions on a platoon level, resulting in *de facto* isolation between the four platoons. Infantry companies have a complement in excess of 200 soldiers, yet it is common to not be acquainted with the majority of the unit. In fact, I cannot recall having seen Sergeant Bruner since our return from Anui over a month earlier.

Riley and I never discussed getting out of Anui alive that night, and I recalled how he and the two others flattened on the ground when the North Koreans fired the flare. He apparently didn't see how I went by the book and froze during the episode with the flare while they were lying face down. Presumably, though, he had to appreciate that I executed correctly after I slid up to the three of them safely at the edge of the rice paddies in Anui when the flare extinguished. The thought of that night brought goose bumps back to my flesh.

Whatever, he apparently put his faith in me, and I was grateful that he understood and forgave my experience of terror on the first day of combat. He had seen it all before in World War II, I suppose.

"We're heading east to the mountain range and then north in the morning to check about some infiltrators slipping in," he said sort of matter of fact. "The natives have reported the sighting of North Koreans in uniform around the area. I'm taking a squad with one mortar and rifles only. It's too far to carry anything heavy, considering our mission."

"OK Sarge, I'll be up, whenever you are ready in the morning."

Riley strolled off. No one needed an alarm clock, as troops would be performing one-hour on, one hour-off sentry duty. All would all be awake before daybreak because the countless flies made sleep impossible during the day.

Dawn emerged from hiding behind the last of monsoon storm clouds and the sun brought the heat of day along. It was destined to be another killer humid day, as Sergeant Bruner stopped by. I fell in line silently with the others, marching with weapons platoon. The mortar operator apparently had a trick no one was aware of or questioned, being riflemen by trade. The operator left the heavy mortar base plate with bipods at his position on the hill, carrying only the 60-millimeter mortar tube, tied by rope on the placement knob at the bottom and then secured near the top, slung over his shoulder. It was presumed he knew what he was doing. He had the mortar training—others did not.

Riley stepped off quickly leading the column over the well-traveled south footpath off of the hill and onto the road beyond the rice paddies. The dead North Korean soldier with the punctured stomach had disappeared, in all probability buried unceremoniously due to the reeking stench of death.

Sergeant Bruner carried the M-2 Carbine, a semi or automatic 30-caliber firearm dependent on the need, with a banana clip taped upside down to an additional banana clip. When one clip was exhausted, the shooter would be able to quickly push the magazine retention button and the empty clip would fall free, allowing the shooter to quickly reinsert the opposite end in order to continue firing.

Clip is a misnomer, although everyone seemed to refer to the carbine magazine as such. The difference being, a magazine is a permanent segment of the carbine that necessitates the hand reloading of each magazine. The cartridges are shorter and lighter than M-1 Ammo. A clip, as used in the M-1 Rifle, holds eight rounds of 30-caliber ammunition together, and when the last shot is fired, the action automatically ejects the clip as well as the last spent cartridge. The rifleman reloads with another expendable clip, which, again, holds the regular eight rounds.

Riley was additionally armed with the officer-issued M1911-A1 semi-automatic 45-caliber pistol sheathed in the standard black shoulder holster. Sergeant Bruner considered the pistol his pride, although to date he apparently had not the opportunity to fire it.

The dirt road was pleasant for the first time that anyone recalled. It was still damp from the monsoons, but packed firm, with no soggy mud to tramp through. And, for the first time, there was no gagging dust to inhale. The patrol made good time marching due east on the same road used on the morning the unit assaulted the hill.

The patrol marched for several hours, single file, engaging in small talk and smoking as we walked, which was rather unusual.

Sergeant Bruner led us off of the main road onto a secondary road that eventually passed small native villages. The residents were genuinely supportive of our presence and waved to the patrol as we passed, the squad returning waves in return. Their gratitude for American assistance validated our presence.

The Pusan Perimeter was still holding and residents were safe as long as the North Korean Army could not breach the lines.

Some time later the squad halted at the base of the foothills which transformed into a stately mountain range, running basically north-south. The sheer height would make it a likely entry for infiltrators, given the inability to defend such a precarious site with adequate firepower to seal the route. For the enemy, the mountain offered a place to create a small trickle through a mighty dam—but one of many during the early phase of the conflict.

Sitting off of the road on a rest break at the direction of Sergeant Bruner, the patrol was smoking quietly, but not talking. Riley proceeded alone with carbine and binoculars and he established a discreet spot to survey the range for enemy personnel without being seen.

About 20 minutes later he trotted back and conferred with the mortar operator. Riley pointed to a given area in the low foothills and the mortar man placed the base of the mortar on the damp footpath. He held it steady by hand, the tube wrapped in cloth because of the heat that would generate from firing.

The mortar man kept adjusting his weapon by hand, in what is known as *Kentucky windage*, a slang infantry term for the rough adjustment of sights on a weapon, the origin possibly from the frontier days of Daniel Boone. Once satisfied with the coordinates of the mortar, the mortar man called for his loader to drop the mortar down the tube, where it would strike the firing pin, which in turn, would explode and speed the deadly missile on its way. It was a beautiful shot. The mortar man placed it very near the objective pointed out by Sergeant Riley.

There was one slight flaw in this otherwise superlative operation. The heavy base plate, which not only steadied and adjusted the coordinates to fire accurately, was missing. The purpose of the base plate, we riflemen learned, was to absorb the heavy recoil of the tube when the mortar is fired. In this case, the first thing that was noticed was when the first projectile was fired, the tube recoiled and shot itself directly into the soft ground, out of sight. The mortar just disappeared into the earth. The two mortar men started digging nonchalantly on each side of the ground where the mortar tube once stood so menacingly, and they eventually extricated it.

Everyone broke out in uproarious laughter, violating the noise rule, but it couldn't be helped. Riley sported a big grin, indicating tacit approval of our outburst.

That was the biggest tension breaker for us, given the trauma to which we had been exposed since our arrival in this god-forsaken country. None of us could stop laughing to the consternation of the mortar man, who apparently never anticipated the consequences of firing the weapon without the base plate. And we riflemen always thought that the heavy weapons troops had undergone a lot of specialized training.

After cleaning the muck from the tube, he tried again. This time the operator elected to place his steel helmet on the ground and place the tube inside of the helmet to be used as a makeshift base plate. This result was even worse. After the next firing, the tube did not burrow itself in the ground as before. This time the recoil of the fired mortar punched through his steel helmet, which caused it to *flower* out at the top. The recoil spread the metal apart and outward, as if it were a significant part of plant growth. It resembled the stalk of a pineapple. It was hard to contain our laughter—not a prudent way to conduct ourselves, presuming the enemy was near.

By now the sun had risen to its zenith, the flies returned to harass, the humidity was peaking and the fertilized fields were emitting their usual foul, reeking stink.

Sergeant Bruner led us up from the foothills into the high mountain range, by way of an ancient footpath. There was no talking as we quietly and swiftly moved single file through the thin brush that grew to the edge of the foot path. We carried our rifles at the ready, noticing that the path had been recently used because some of the foliage on each side of the path was freshly disturbed and broken.

After a mile or so, Sergeant Bruner abruptly stopped and quickly raised his left hand to indicate to us to also stop and remain as silent as possible. We froze in place. Riley silently signaled to us to remain as he moved ahead stealthily. He disappeared out of sight and a matter of minutes we heard the staccato burst from an automatic weapon. A second "brappp" followed almost immediately.

Rushing forward, we found five dead North Korean soldiers. Riley killed them all with his automatic carbine! They had been taking a rest break, sitting down, smoking and talking when Sergeant Bruner sent them to meet their maker. This was a lesson on how not to conduct a patrol. They never had a chance to use their weapons. Sergeant Bruner fired 60 rounds on full automatic, firing 30 rounds from the inserted magazine and then deftly extracting it to reinsert the other taped-on magazine. The pungent smell of gun smoke hung heavily in the stifling humid air and blood was splashed all over the trail. It was an outdoor slaughterhouse.

Riley was as calm as if he did this routinely everyday. He directed us to search the bodies for possible intelligence, while he continued on ahead to scout for more enemy. We went through wallets, without contrition, finding family photographs of spouses, children and of them. The North Koreans started this mess and they were ruthlessly brutal when they were on the winning side. Now, we were getting even. I hoped that later their comrades would initiate a search party for them and see them where they lay. We threw the family photos on the ground among the bodies as a further act of contempt and kept the other personal army photos for Riley to submit to Intelligence.

Sergeant Burner arrived back at the area about the time that one of our guys found a small leather pouch hanging from the belt of one of the slain soldiers. The searching soldier opened the drawstring, peeked in, shuddered, and poured the contents on the ground.

Fingers! Obviously fingers from dead GIs. Most likely they were the forefingers, the trigger fingers of each American soldier that this vicious beast personally killed—bizarre and grotesque souvenirs of his days of combat. He was fortunate to be dead. That killer had stepped over the line of decency and if he were alive, there is no telling what would have happened to him under our angry charge.

The dead soldier had been sitting on a rock with his back to Sergeant Bruner when Riley shot him and the other four. He never knew what hit him when the force of many rounds pitched him forward on his face.

"Turn him over," commanded Sergeant Burner.

The soldier who found the fingers stood over the corpse and rolled the dead North Korean over to reveal his face. Sergeant Bruner removed his 45-caliber pistol from the holster and with his right arm extended straight he shot both eyes out of the dead soldier with two successive rounds. Eardrums ached from the resonance of the two 45-caliber rounds in such a close area. Riley calmly holstered his weapon and said softly, "My granddad said that if an Indian ever lost his eyes, he would never be able to find his way to the happy hunting grounds, or, in the case of the white man, heaven. I hope that works for this son of a bitch."

I was glad that Sergeant Burner didn't ask us to roll the corpse over again. Besides no eyes, he would have had no back of the head, given the impact of the 45-caliber rounds. Then I thought of the next group of North Korean soldiers to infiltrate our lines. They would come across this carnage, complete with family photographs scattered on the ground in contempt and succumb to a real morale buster.

"Let's go." He turned and we all fell into single file for the long march back. There was no other intelligence information found. They were most likely on patrol themselves in order to find a means to break through the now well-fortified Pusan Perimeter. I wondered what their unit would think when the North Korean soldiers never returned? It no doubt would give some consternation to their leaders. Would they send a party out to try to locate them? I hoped so.

I had earlier learned a good lesson from Sergeant Bruner, about talking in the wilderness. It was too late for the five dead enemy to learn that same important rule.

We erased that macabre incident of the fingers from our minds. To dwell on such an atrocity would only affect our morale. Besides, the unfortunate GIs were more than likely already dead when their fingers were unceremoniously removed, we hoped. Our respect went to valiant Sergeant Bruner, who killed five of them at one time. That act should warrant a medal of valor, even if he was not a commissioned officer. Five against one, and they would have gone for their weapons when they first saw Riley.

The mortar man was a good sport, because he was able to laugh at himself. He wore his coveted steel crown complete with a flourishing steel flower top with pride and distinction all the way back to our base camp, while we grinned with him.

It was about 3 p.m. when we ended up on the road again, heading back in the direction of our hill before dark. Talking and smoking was allowed as we were now back in our own territory.

It was a very good day.

We returned to the hill, to learn our unit had mail call earlier, and I had several letters waiting for me from family and friends. There were sufficient C-rations to go around, so we were all able to choose what we wanted for a change. Coincidentally, we all chose pork and beans.

We sat around cross-legged talking and joking, with our food and our mail. Our rifles as always were nearby. We were clean, washed from the monsoons, and it was the twilight between the flies and the mosquitoes. And it was cooling slightly. What could be better?

Sergeant Bruner reported to the captain on the events of the patrol, and we suspected that he would minimize his role in the killing of five enemy soldiers. We vowed that we would spread the word about his one-man siege to others, so that Captain Hughes would get the straight story.

"Hey Pete! You better get a haircut, before the old man sees you!" one in the group laughingly said to me.

"OK," I replied, smiling. "I don't need any problems. Break out the bayonet. By the way, who's got the toothbrush? It's time for my weekly cleaning."

"I got it," said the soldier, as he fished it from his front pocket, bringing out his spoon for C-rations along with the brush. He tossed the brush to me, and I grabbed it while pulling out my canteen that was attached to the left rear part of my gun belt. The handle of the brush was broken off to make it less likely to be lost in the deep pocket of our heavy field shirts. It was the only toothbrush among the three of us.

The same toothbrush had the auxiliary use of cleaning our rifles. We had to keep the human feces in the dirt from jamming our weapons.

I took a swig of water, brushed around for a while, shook off the brush and spit out the now foul water.

"I'm next," said one of the three, and I tossed it to him. He duplicated the ritual, and then threw it back to the official keeper of the toothbrush.

I happened to glance at the bottom of my canteen cup where the canteen slides into it. It was filthy, with a heavy layer of muck in the bottom.

Each of us had slipped a sock over the canteen to minimize noise and to keep the utensil from shining. The sock turned out to be a dirt magnet because of the moisture of the canteen sweating. I wiped the bottom of my large filthy metal cup with my equally filthy hand, and I was back in business.

We always carried our spoon in the right pocket of our heavy shirts, because the pocket-sized Gideon Bible, with the red cover, was always carried in the left pocket as protection to the heart. We had heard about how a GI had his life saved when a round from an enemy sniper struck, and embedded in the Bible, saving the man's life.

I tried to always read the Lord's Prayer just before being committed to battle, but one had to be careful not to be seen. Nothing is sacred in the infantry. We laughed at everything, especially dead NKPA soldiers. It was a facade to deflect concern for our own lives during these overwhelming battles.

We were the only company around that was required to shave every day, but because all of us were so young, it was more like a weekly chore. We were still boys, and we knew that it was a morale thing and our morale was sky-high under the command of Captain Hughes. He believed in that, as well as in digging in at every overnight stop. His strong discipline saved King Company later in the war.

Yeah, it really turned out to be a very good day.

INCHON

> The Inch'on landing put the United States X Corp in the enemy's rear. Concurrently, Eighth Army was to launch a general attack all along its front to fix and hold the enemy's combat strength and prevent movement of units from the Pusan Perimeter to reinforce the threatened area in its rear. This attack would also strive to break the cordon that had for six weeks held Eighth Army within a shrinking Pusan Perimeter. Appleman, p. 542.

MacArthur intended to destroy the enemy supply lines and the NKPA offensive against the Pusan Perimeter by landing troops at Inchon, behind enemy lines.[38] The assault at Inchon scheduled for 15 September 1950 was intended to relieve the siege in the south, and then to recapture the South Korean capitol. It was but a matter of time before an American amphibious landing would take place, but the North Korean enemy knew not where. Kim Il-sung believed the fall of Pusan, and thus the entire peninsula, was imminent, and would render any landing a moot point.

The Dear Leader's obsession was to break through the fractured, reeling line of the Pusan Perimeter, then forge on to Pusan proper, where his troops would by-pass the surviving beleaguered defenders.[39] Once the major port was secured and in control of the NKPA, military stratagem would have placed the ill-fated American and ROK troops in an inescapable vise, to be slaughtered to the last man.

~~

King Company kicked off the hill late in the afternoon of 18 September, three days late because of never-ending attacks by the NKPA. The company headed back to the road whence we came 18 days earlier, in columns of two on each side of the road. The direction was due west, confirmed by the irritating glare of the sun in our eyes. Helmets were lowered as far down on the front of heads as possible to ward off the blinding, scorching sun. The ever-present road silt was churning once again but because we were marching rather than riding in trucks and tanks, the dusty grit was tolerable.

The route turned north before sunset and we were blessed by having eyes diverted from the blinding sun as we continued the relentless pace set by Captain Hughes. Dusk cooled the scorching hot day somewhat, as we marched onward in the same column of twos on each side of the road. We

---

[38] Blair, p. 232.

[39] Dear Leader is a title currently given the head of government in North Korea. Editor.

were on the first leg of a long, forced march. With nightfall, orders were passed down the line that the smoking lamp was out.

After several hours of continuous marching through the night, a gradual steepness to the road began as we came upon Chinju Pass, that horrifying battle site where Tex ambled along the road, uniform burned completely off, and died along with hundreds more young American soldiers. That was the awful day of 3 August 1950.

Troops began to grumble because of the lengthy march without a break, while a silent few held an opposite view. The company was now as far north as it had ever ventured, other than Anui, and now the North Koreans were obviously in headlong retreat. I was one of few soldiers of B Company who was a fortunate survivor of both battles, so I had a different mindset than others in respect to this forced march, particularly as we were passing through Chinju Pass. The vast majority of company personnel were new replacements, so they could not relate to this terrible location. The few surviving veterans didn't want to speak of it, so it was an even trade.

No one was informed of the Inchon landing, but it was sensed that there had to be a purpose for this offensive. Perhaps had they told us of our mission, which was to engage the enemy in a giant pincer movement, it might have been more readily accepted. The grumbling accelerated in direct proportion to the distance traveled, as the march continued at least ten hours more without respite.

Traversing the Notch, or Pass—that elongated, excavated, level spot at the summit—evoked an intensive restless feeling in me. Awful memories of Anui and this Pass came flooding back.

Now I was tramping through this appalling place again, the location and the source of what became a lifetime of nightmares. My eyes were focused on the dense shrubbery in the hills to the west of Chinju Pass where the dreaded North Korean 6th Division had moved to a lower draw to engage the American 19th Infantry Regiment, 3 August 1950.

I was subconsciously looking for the thousands of cigarette glows that I saw at Anui that terrible night, and I wondered apprehensively if this was one more imaginative ambush set by the enemy. I had a sickening feeling in my stomach at the Pass, and I would be relieved when we marched through.

It was silent and serene as we marched to the summit. I avoided glancing at the runoff ditch on the right side where the first squad, including me, cowered in absolute terror on that dreadful day, and where later, slain North Korean soldiers by the score were unceremoniously bulldozed into eternity.

Gone was the convoy of North Korean armaments of tanks and trucks, as we methodically descended the north side of the Pass. Could it have been a figment of my imagination? The memory of this appalling disaster seemed so long ago. Yet, this was 18 September, and Chinju was our second initiation into battle during the very first part of August, the 3rd to be exact. There was no evidence that wholesale butchery ever occurred. I wondered where the destroyed American tanks and trucks were. This was enemy territory until we arrived this second time, and I couldn't imagine the NKPA removing the destroyed conveyances while they were so dedicated to breaking through the Perimeter.

At the break of dawn came a first ten-minute break. We had marched from afternoon through the night without respite, and now soldiers crumpled to the ground without a word. A World War II infantryman gave me a suggestion long ago and I put it to use. I lay on the ground on my back and propped my legs high against a mature tree growing along the dirt road. During the brief break, the pulsating cramps in my legs seem to subside, albeit just for a few minutes.

The nauseating smell was everywhere, and the flies found and clung to us as usual. With the sun rising rapidly it became too hot to wear the field jacket, and to carry it was cumbersome. It was better to wear the jacket and perspire. To throw it away was out of the question. The coat was bound to be needed later. My sweat-soaked field jacket was coated with loathsome filthy dirt from lying positioned on my back, attempting to ease the ache in my legs.

OK, off your asses,
And on your feet,
Outa the shade,
And in the heat

Saddle Up! one of the sergeants bellowed, scarcely ten minutes later.

Troops came to hate those words as they groaned, raised aching bodies, staggered back on the filthy road, and commenced the northward crusade again. Soldiers were so fatigued that no one talked. Some opened cans of vile C-rations and ate during the march. Others lit up because it was well into the morning. For the most part, the main body was just barely able to put one foot in front of the other. A quip about the infantry came back to haunt me—*I joined the Army to see the world, but I didn't know I had to march to see it.*

The parody rang true. Many had the sensation that they could actually sleep while marching during this unbelievably taxing, forced 20-hour march, sporadically intermingled with very brief rests. In later years, when I described the sense of sleep deprivation to the few other veterans of this protracted march, they acknowledged the same—that indeed, one could literally sleep while feet continued to march. The consciousness of the mind seems to shut down while motor nerves continue to function. Blisters formed on feet unaccustomed to marching for such a long duration, but the pain was disregarded. As long as Captain Hughes set the pace, everyone followed.

My mind wandered to when I was a child at the Saturday afternoon matinee, viewing glorious, victorious, World War II American fighting in-fantrymen—*That's what I am going to be when I grow up. A soldier! Not just any ordinary soldier, but an infantry soldier!*

I was regretful that I didn't know the whole story at the time, because of another axiom relating to the infantry: When one is shot (as I was at Anui), it was said, *That bullet had your name on it.*

Then the absurdity was carried one step further.

I don't worry about the bullet with my name on it as much; it's the bullet that says To whom it may concern *that bothers me.*

We were heading to Taejon.

On 6 July 1950 Smith's battalion, Task Force Smith, was dug in along the main highway between Osan and Suwon, near the center of South Korea. The battalion was dispatched from the occupation of Japan with little notice, and no information in respect to holding against the attacking NKPA.[40]

It was no contest. Major General Dean was ordered to commit his entire command, earlier spread throughout six installations in Japan, to Korea. It was an impossible task. Task Force Smith was flown in to try to slow the flow of the tank-led North Korea armies, while the remainder of the 24th Division followed by ship to reinforce the Task Force when transportation was finally arranged.

The siege at Taejon is a history unto itself, and much too lengthy to chronicle here. Suffice to say that the commander of the 24th Division, General Dean, by the time the rest of the division arrived, was captured days later in an unsuccessful attempt to locate American lines. Surprisingly,

---

[40] When you get to Pusan, head for Taejon. We want to stop the North Koreans as far from Pusan as we can. Block the main road as far north as possible. Make contact with General Church. If you can't find him, go to Taejon and beyond if you can. Sorry I can't give you more information - That's all I've got. Good luck and God bless you and your men." Gen. William Dean.

he was not murdered by his captors at the time of capture, the foe not realizing who he was. General Dean was imprisoned as a prisoner of war for 35 months—held in solitary confinement the entire time.

The General had personally destroyed many T-34 Russian tanks during that awful battle of Taejon. He was criticized by various Army strategists who opined that the General failed to command his division by abandoning his leadership role in favor of personally participating in infantry actions. Those critics should have walked in the General's boots, because those at the higher echelon saw the general's actions in a far different light.

Major General William Frishe Dean was awarded the nation's highest award for valor, the Medal of Honor.

A drastic modification of military planning has resulted from the initial debacle at Taejon. Among military strategists in various war colleges and the Pentagon today, there is an axiom considered throughout scheduling of military exercises and deployments—*No more Task Force Smiths.*

The meaning is clear. It is futile to try to slow or stop a near invincible military force with an under strength, out-gunned defensive unit.

King Company was placed in the second assault wave to attack. The NKPA deployed a large unit of hardened, suicidal, rear-guard soldiers to stop the rumbling offensive of the 8th Army, much to their regret.

Every North Korean soldier we found in his single-man foxhole had been slain by the first assault wave. It was the first of many times that I noticed that each man had his own individual defensive hole. No doubt to discourage a conspiracy to defect.

Two soldiers emplaced together would talk.

It was of further interest to note that each enemy soldier died with his rifle in his right hand and with a crumpled *safe conduct* leaflet tightly grasped in his left hand. The leaflet was printed on one side in Korean, and on the opposite side, English. The English version ordered all UN soldiers to treat surrendering enemy with dignity and humane treatment and was signed by General MacArthur. No American would violate that directive, for fear of consequences. The Korean translation assured the surrendering North Korean soldier that he would be treated with dignity and respect upon surrendering to American Forces. The NKPA had no such pamphlets, nor would they abide by them, even if they printed and dispensed them.

It was standing procedure for any commander of the North Korean People's Army to shoot any NKPA soldiers found in possession of a safe conduct leaflet. Captured enemy confided that many memorized the leaflet words to avoid being caught with one.

The enemy was so overwhelmed by American firepower that they dared not rise from the confines of their shelters to surrender. They were slain in their trenches, slightly late in presenting the leaflets.

King Company and other units followed up the advance attackers and swept through the city of Taejon. Objective: to kill or capture enemy hold-outs. Numerous destroyed Russian T-34 tanks were pushed from the road like so much road kill. No one paid attention to the demolished armor, concentrating instead on pursuing entrenched, rear guard, suicide enemy, as Allied units swept through the city before nightfall to eliminate any danger from by-passed enemy.

Defensive positions were emplaced in the hills surrounding the city, and after the company dug in for the night, soldiers collapsed wearily in foxholes. No one ordered one hour off one hour on, sentry duty. It would have been impossible to implement. The company was forced marched sixteen to eighteen hours a day, every day. There was no let up or any explanations. There never were.

The Perimeter was broken once and for all, although by then, costly tactical errors by the NKPA, coupled with massive, critical imports of American soldiers, arms and material through the port of Pusan made the Perimeter, while still problematic to hold, in much better position than it was at the onset of the conflict.

Very early next morning we were directed to return to the main highway to move north again. We were astonished to see the same five destroyed enemy T-34 tanks with the sides freshly painted—*This tank destroyed by Gen Dean.* Someone had a great marketing technique. We could have used the painter on line with us.

King Company was en route to Seoul.

YALU OR BUST

> Initially America had entered the Korean War with the aim of evicting the NKPA from South Korea and restoring the status quo ante bellum. By the time of Inchon President Truman had made the decision to enlarge the war. American forces would cross the 38th Parallel, wipe out whatever was left of the NKPA, dispose the Communist regime of Kim Il Sung, and unify Korea under a single, popularly elected government. Blair, p. 325.

The first step of the first GI boot to cross over the line on 9 October 1950 portended the beginning of the end for the UN forces in North Korea. The politically-charged border, more familiarly known as the 38th Parallel, was the narrow arena housing the march to unanticipated nearly total defeat. The heady, sweet victory of the Inchon landing, coupled with the recapture of the South Korean capitol Seoul, on 25 September, was like a cocaine rush—wild, disorienting, unreal, carrying minds beyond the boundaries of common sense.

It was a crazy time. Roads were choked with thousands of tanks and trucks filled with grinning, laughing soldiers, towing heavy artillery, crossing the 38th Parallel. It was a pell-mell race without caution, everyone shouting gleefully, waving newly-issued pile caps, throwing essential clothing and equipment away. The end was near for the remaining North Korean Army. Presuming they would reach the Yalu River, the border between North Korea and Manchuria, the UN forces expected to triumph, then head home. Tanks and trucks had *Yalu or bust!* painted on the sides. The phrase echoed the 30's dust bowl Oklahoman's migration to the west, *California or bust!* No, by god! Now, it was *the Yalu or bust!*

Yea! The war was over and by the grace of God, we lived through it! Now we are going home!

But first there was unfinished business. The principal attention was focused on a vital objective. American prisoners of war were the primary concern, and to that end, the 187th Airborne Regiment made a parachute combat assault approximately 35 miles north of the capitol of North Korea, Pyongyang, on 20 October 1950. The stated goal was to rescue two trains comprised of young UN prisoners of war that were being taken north, ostensibly to be used as pawns during a latter phase of the war.

One hundred thirteen planes took part in the ferrying of 2,800 soldiers armed with M-1 rifles or M-2 carbines, in addition to a 45-caliber pistol per man.

The parachute drop zone was scheduled to be 30 air miles north of

Pyongyang in the valley between the two towns that had not yet fallen to the surging American and ROK armies. The wide valley between Sunchon to Sukchon was identified as what was believed at the time to be north of the slow-moving prison trains; hence, the aforementioned drop zone was targeted to make optimal use of the fertile, wide valley in order to simultaneously capture both prison trains.

The 187th Airborne Regiment jumped too late. Horrible weather delayed the assault jump by five precious hours. Were it not for the weather, there would have been an excellent chance to rescue UN prisoners. And if not, at least the Allies would have apprehended and meted the same punishment to those lawless, brutal captors.

The Communist railroad line ran more or less northwest from Pyongyang situated directly west of Sunchon, approximately 17 miles away.

Extensive records as to the Sunchon Tunnel Massacre are available. I find no information as to the fate of the Sukchon train since documentation is lacking other than that it departed the train station at Pyongyang, on 17 October, concurrently with the Sunchon-bound prison train. The Capitol was captured and secured on 20 October by Allied Forces, just three days too late.

Appalling evidence, later pieced together, tragically verified what many had dreaded. Traveling only at night and hiding in railroad tunnels through the day in order to escape the wrath of the American Air Force, the trains were decidedly slow. The tracks headed due north on the east side led toward the town of Sunchon, and from there on through to Manchuria, through very difficult mountainous passage.

The fate of the prison train at Sunchon illustrates the brutality of the NKPA. Approximately 150 American prisoners disembarked the prison train, while hidden from Air Force observation in a tunnel near Sunchon. North Korean guards, under the pretext of feeding the captives, some from the 29th Infantry Regiment, were ordered from the train. From there they were marched south to a small ravine behind the train and across from the main dirt road.

Survivor James Yeager remembers:

> The fifth day they broke the train up because of air strikes during the day. That evening we were told that they were going to feed us. The gooks marched us back south down the tracks and turned us up a small ravine. Setting us down in a column of three, Toney and I were setting (sic) together in the third rank. Up on the bank in front of us stood a burp gunner (a Russian machine gun) and he turned to his right and started firing. Toney and I rolled to our right, my head

in the armpit of the man on my right, I could feel his body jerk and respond to the number of rounds he received, his reaction was so violent that he kicked my shin so hard that I thought I had been hit. His blood ran over my head, shoulder and back. The gooks started to bayonet and shoot the men who had not been killed in the firing, many of them were crying out for their mothers in their last moments of agony.

Toney and I played dead. Toney was hit, the bullet going through both his thighs after the gooks went back to get some more men it turned dark and I helped Toney up and we crawled up the ditch.

Here we found five other men and hid in a millet field for the rest of the night. The next day we went of (sic) on a ridge and that afternoon General Almond with the 187th airborne and 3rd ROK's found us. The jump had been delayed by bad weather for 5 hours. Toney and I were two of the twenty one survivors of the Suchon Tunnel Massacre as the press called it. James Yeager, L Company, Survivor, captured at Hadong, 27 July 1950.

They were methodically machine gunned and slaughtered, as they sat in a rough ravine on orders of their captors. A few survivors feigned death until the train, carrying prominent North Korean officials, chugged north toward Kanggye, the palatial mansion of Kim Il-sung 30 miles from Manchuria.

As to the train heading northwest toward Sukchon, there appears to be no data relative to the fate of those soldiers, other than innuendo and hearsay. Rumors were heard to the effect that the train, bearing approximately 150 prisoners, pulled into a tunnel, out of view of the searching American Air Force and was set afire with gasoline. As the prisoners reportedly fled the fire, they were methodically shot down by remnants of the NKPA brandishing Russian-made machine guns.

The 25th Infantry Division was deployed to North Korea once the first body of American troops surged across the 38th Parallel, on 9 October. The division was moving north in a wide sweep of the valleys with the objective to kill or capture stragglers of the North Korean Army.

Those in the infantry, particularly individuals who suffered the agonies of the war from its outset, crossed the Parallel with trepidation. The war was over. No one cared about a few hundred, or even a few thousand enemy soldiers who eluded the pincer movement between Inchon and the Pusan Perimeter. The South Korean Army could and should finish the mop up. Everyone would have been better off had that happened.

The company objective was to recapture the town of Kaesong, lying on the northwest part of South Korea near to the 38th Parallel. Prior to the

World War II Armistice, Kaesong was a part of South Korea as well as the former headquarters of KMAG (Korean Military Advisory Group). American advisors were stationed just south of the volatile border separating the two Koreas, ostensibly to prevent the opposing sides from clashing.

After the signing of the armistice, Kaesong became an official component of North Korea. Armistice negotiations were initially held at Kaesong, prior to the transfer of permanent quarters at Pan Mun Jom for the continuance of discussions related to the armistice.

~~

It was poetic revenge for King Company. KMAG in Kaesong was the first sector to fall to the iron fist of the NKPA on 25 June 1950. When American and ROKs retreated, they abandoned a row of American Quonset huts—military half-round, corrugated steel buildings prevalent in the Far East and utilized primarily for temporary military housing.

Following the unopposed recapture of Kaesong, the company was billeted in the original Quonset huts and issued, of all items, blankets—one to lie on and one to cover ourselves. Filthy uniforms reeking with every stench in the world were gratefully removed. Uniforms had blood, human feces from the fields, body odor and so on. Just to sleep in a horizontal position, not sitting staring numbly for enemy approach among a mass of mosquitoes, was ecstasy beyond description.

K Company was notified that they were in reserve, since the war was considered ended for all realistic purposes. It was the first time that the unit was pulled from the arena of battle since their inauspicious arrival in Korea, and it was heaven on earth to sleep indoors for the first time. Exhausted troops were permitted to sleep through the night, the first time that anyone could recall having that blessed luxury.

The cooks opened all the C-rations and mixed them together and heated them. The hot food for the first time was a culinary delight, even though the concoction was abominable.

"What's for dinner tonight, cookie?" asked one of the old-timers of one of the cooks, as we waited in the cold, in a long single line, the two-part mess kits balanced precariously in the left hand, while grasping a filthy canteen cup in the right hand.

"Owl shit!" replied the cook in a loud, sarcastic voice, so that everyone could overhear, believing it to be a clever, quick-witted answer.

"Oh, I thought it was something we couldn't eat," came the testy reply from the one who asked. Everyone cracked up. Tensions from the insufferable rigors of combat were easing.

As one moved through the chow line, servers would slam a portion of food from a large spoon, and it was the recipient's duty to balance the mess kit enough to avoid spilling. On occasion a canned peach half or fruit cocktail was served for dessert, the same abominable bilious fare that was a part of the lackluster C-Rations.

Coffee, situated at the end of the chow line, was another matter. For some unknown reason, the mess sergeant was never able to field someone to serve the sugar or *cream* (reconstituted dry milk). Soldiers would extend the canteen cup to a server who would ladle a cup of coffee (also reconstituted) into the metal cup, hoping the offensive liquid would not scald a grimy hand.

Now came the delicate part. In order to procure sugar and/or cream, the person, upon reaching the far end of the chow line, would have to gingerly bend to place his canteen of coffee on a low box, in order to free his right hand to partake of the sugar and/or cream. In an attempt to perform this sensitive movement, the M-1 Rifle, always carried slung over the right shoulder, would invariably slip from the shoulder, due to the man lowering the right side of his body. In an instant, the out-of-control rifle would strike the helmet, dislodging it from the head, which in a domino effect, would simultaneously strike the food carried in the two-part mess kit held in the left hand, ultimately spilling the entire botched mess to the ground. Enraged, the soldier was obliged to return to the end of the chow line to try again. It took on the average of two incidents for one to learn the lesson and just drink black coffee. It was a lifetime custom, learned courtesy the United States Army. I know of no ex-infantrymen who use cream and/or sugar in their coffee.

The American Army must have entered into a conspiracy with Theodore Geisel, who composed many children's books under the name *Dr. Seuss*. Among his stories was *Green Eggs and Ham*. The unit never had ham, but green eggs were served every morning for breakfast.

The war was over and we were getting supplies of every item imaginable, provided that it was reconstituted. The tasteless, rubber-like, light green block of reconstituted scrambled eggs was a diversion from C-Rations and even welcomed for a while. It was the first time that anyone saw scrambled eggs sliced. The eggs were formed into a quivering block, the server slicing a portion off as if it were meat loaf.

Occasionally, they would serve sausage. While perhaps not reconstituted, it was in a unique category. Short, very thick, greasy, with a jacket made of plastic. Once penetrated, the sausage would collapse, as air trapped inside escaped.

The genie released from the bottle!

What remained was a tough, inedible, but readily-chewable piece of plastic that after being masticated for a time would be expectorated, leaving the taste of mystery meat on one's palate.

No toast. Bread, or what was to pass for bread, a cellulose tile of sponge, topped with a dab of lard which never went anywhere. After pushing it around the tile for ages with the spoon, the only eating utensil, one would surrender to the inevitable, and discard the blob of white fat.

~~

One slow, cool morning, Sergeant Miller put his platoon through an exercise program; his version of the child's game of *drop the hankie*. This was no child's game. Instead of the innocuous and safe *hankie,* Sergeant Miller donated his belt. The 40-plus soldiers of the 3rd Platoon were directed to form a wide circle, facing in. The one with the belt would casually stroll the outer perimeter and drop the belt behind an unsuspecting soldier, who would pick the belt up and chase the person around the outer perimeter striking him with the heavy metal buckle. The pursued would receive wounds ranging from lacerations to contusions to bruises as he rapidly fled for the sanctuary of the pursuer's empty position in the circle. The *game* continued until virtually everyone in the platoon was injured, except for the fleetest of our group. Miller's theory was play hard, fight hard. Most just wanted to catch up on sleep.

~~

The company fell out early one morning. It was sensed by watching leaders that this— whatever we were called upon to do— would be a no-brainer. Everyone was laid back. *Hell, the war was over! Let's go home to Okinawa, where the living is easy!*

"What's going on this morning?"

"Shit who knows? At least we won't get our asses shot off again, I hope," said one soldier.

We were smoking and joking in formation and life was really lax. Soon, the skipper, Captain Hughes, ambled up and stood in front of his company and breezily barked, "At ease!"

"Men, we are being honored today with the presence of Regimental Commander Henry Fisher who will present King Company with the very first Presidential Unit Citation ever awarded to a company level unit in the history of the Army. I want you to know that I am very proud of every one of you! You held firm on September 3rd and performed gallantly for the last mission of B Company. Since then, as you know, we have reverted to the 25th!"

"Platoon leaders, by platoon, column of fours!" bellowed Hughes to platoon leaders.

Troops fell in line four abreast starting with the 1st Platoon and the company began marching through the fair-sized town. Now, it was for sure that the war was over. They were awarding citations.

"Hot damn, we are heroes now," someone quipped.

The troops felt pretty good about what the skipper said and they picked up the tempo as they marched erect, proud, soldierly, with that sharp garrison cadence. Helmets were on straight; rifles, while not at right shoulder arms, were slung facing straight up in a professional manner. Everything was smart except the filthy, stinking bodies and uniforms that matched the odor of bodies. It was over three months since anyone showered. The last time was in Okinawa and these were original uniforms, still unwashed except for a rinse by the monsoon rains that allowed for a brief cleansing of a sort.

The entire 3rd Battalion would be there and Baker Company was the one being commended. Company members were aware of what was accomplished on 3 September to the regret of the *late* NKPA 6th Division, but no one knew the significance of the determined defensive stand. The Company held their position against a full regiment, thus preventing an enemy breakthrough. Of course, there were no other options but to hold the enemy at bay or otherwise be killed if they overran the unit.

The actual tribute to the Company lay in the fact that from this day forward, anyone serving in Baker Company of the 29th Infantry Regiment in the future would proudly wear an award that only about 200 young soldiers earned, the coveted second award, Presidential Unit Citation.

As the unit marched briskly through the town of Kaesong, citizens were out, waving white cloths and ROK flags as King Company soldiers stared stone faced straight ahead. Many soldiers were glancing from corners of eyes noticing inhabitants smiling, pleased that the American Army was here. It was subtle, but it was there. Not a hostile stare from anyone.

The formal march led to a large school with high walls and a wide-open entrance, just like the schoolhouse at Anui. King Company marched smartly into the grounds where they were directed to sit in a pre-designated area. As other troops filed in, they were directed to other specific positions. Someone spent a lot of time and effort to plan this ceremony well. There is a job for everyone in the Army.

We dropped in place and sat cross legged, with M-1 Rifles to each person's right, the barrel of the weapon leaning against the right shoulder. I asked the soldier next to me, "I gotta take a leak, where's the latrine?"

"How the fuck do I know, we came in together, remember?"

I jumped up to see where I thought a school restroom would be, ignoring my buddy's remark. I did ask a dumb question, so I deserved his answer. In fact, he made me laugh with his rejoinder. I headed to the northwest corner of the school ground, and by following my nose I found the alleged toilet. Again, I was confronted with the stomach wrenching, vomiting stench of raw sewage. I could never get used to it.

There was no door, no floor other than dirt, and no urinal. It was a long ditch dug god knows how long ago, filled with the vilest, most putrid, substance on earth. Flies were swarming all around, first on the mess and then on my flesh. I clasped my filthy left palm over my mouth and nose to blot out the gagging stink, as I held a death grip on the leather sling of my rifle. There was a fleeting, instantaneous moment of a fantasy that my rifle, as it sometimes did, would slip from my shoulder. I could imagine it sliding from my shoulder, falling in that horrible, raw sewage. This was a co-ed toilet without privacy. One either faced the wood wall or would reverse and squat with the back to the same wall, depending on nature's calling. Both sexes used the same open facility at the same time. There was no toilet paper. There was no washbasin. Gazing rigidly straight ahead, I could feel the filthy flies crawling over my neck, face and hands, while I continued my white-knuckle grip on the leather sling of my rifle with my right hand, my left hand covering my mouth and nose. It was then that I noticed printed on the wall at eye level, with pencil, small letters in English,

Kilroy was here.

I was shocked, believing that I had to be the first American visiting this appalling dungeon trying its best to pass as a school toilet. It had to be an American POW on stopover on their forced march northward. Prisoners were housed in schools such as this, because of the high, surrounding walls. The unfortunate prisoner would have been better served if he had used his own name and the date for intelligence and tracking purposes.

Returning to my platoon, I spied a major coming by, and I nodded respectfully and said, "Mornin', Major."

"Morning to you, soldier," he echoed with a slight smile.

I reflected on how much different the Army was in combat than during garrison life. Still relatively new to the Army, I would normally have been quaking at the sight of such a high-ranking illustrious officer, saluting him smartly. Now a simple nod to the officer would do. No one wanted to be saluted in a war zone.

My sitting spot was still open as I sat next to my buddy, noticing that nothing unusual seemed to have occurred.

"Anything exciting happened when I was in the shit house?"

"Nope. Same-o, same-o."

The Army band arrived and the first thought was, *We don't have enough replacements and all these guys have to do is sit around and polish their instruments. We could have used some help a hundred times over and these guys weren't available. They should be lucky that the god-damned war was over.*

That's what jealousy does. Secretly, everyone would have changed places in a minute with any of them.

Piccolo player Pete. Why not?

It must have been around 10 a.m. when the boring speeches started. The sun was shining, the flies were out as usual, but it was just about a perfect day. Not torridly hot as summer, and we didn't know or care about the winter weather, because we would be heading back to Okinawa any day now.

I was getting drowsy along with the rest of the guys, and I knew it wouldn't be very appropriate to fall asleep when our former B Company was here to be honored. Then I started to nod and as I drifted off, I remembered that all of us qualified for the *Combat Infantry Badge*, a very coveted award that commands respect from every member of the Army.

The fact of the matter is, the CIB is awarded in recognition of not finding a more suitable and safer job in the Army. With my one (at that time) Purple Heart, it made it all the more compelling that there were other safer and more secure venues available. Still, our combat leaders were famous for their individual heroism during major battles in World War II and now, Korea, so it seems that a few were enthralled with the *Infantry*. I certainly was.

Absent-mindedly, and in an effort to stay awake, I removed one of my fragmentary hand grenades from my gun belt suspenders and began to toy with it. I had taken many grenades apart because it was really easy and safe to do. One merely unscrewed it as if it were a cap on a jar. Then it became two parts—one, the body, filled with flaked TNT, and the other, composed of a fuse of solid TNT. The *spoon*, or safety handle, was held in place and secured by the retaining ring, preventing the spring with firing pin from striking the primer cap, which in turn would have activated the grenade. Very simple. To reassemble the grenade, one merely screwed it back together into the original configuration.

In this instance, a very curious thing happened. After I unscrewed the grenade, I noticed that for the first time, the fuse did not exit as it should. It remained in the body, along with the explosive charge, rather than being coupled to the other component. It didn't strike me as particularly serious, unless the firing pin should somehow strike the percussion cap, and the pin was already secured in the other half. Still, it was very unusual, so I nudged my buddy to the right and I started to say,

"Hey look at th. . .

He looked at the grenade and screamed at the top of his very being:

"LIVE GRENADE!"

I never witnessed such pandemonium in my life. People were shouting, screaming, falling and running for their lives. I looked up to see the entire band fall backwards from their chairs. It seemed that everyone picked up the chant:

LIVE GRENADE! LIVE GRENADE!

Soldiers were jousting, bumping, crashing into one another attempting to escape from this schoolyard with their lives No one knew what or where this so-called grenade was. Everyone was running amok, confused, panicked, and not knowing what was going on. It devolved into mass hysteria. In about ten seconds, or so it seemed, I was the only one left in the entire schoolyard. I was alone. There was going to be hell to pay for this, I just knew. At the beginning of this event I didn't think much of it, because I thought that the grenade was safe until my friend just had to scream. Now I became nervous, as I slowly arose and gingerly walked to the closest point, the tall wall at the south side of the schoolyard, all the while having fantasies of the drum roll that would accompany me as I was marched up gallows steps.

I discovered that the nefarious sewage system was not confined to the hideous area I first visited. The ditch continued on, snake like, creating a path of raw sewage entirely around the school ground as it slowly, over the years, edged filthily forward. That is where I gently placed the dismantled hand grenade. The offensive, sickening, human sludge would devour the grenade in no time.

Much to my relief, nothing was said to me. The program must have been nearly over, or else everyone lost interest. The agenda was not resumed. We moved out the next morning heading north.

~~

It was now autumn and the ground would soon become soaked and the annual freeze would begin. The colorful leaves of deciduous trees were falling, and there was a slight nip in the crisp air. Wood smoke emitting from native hooches filled the air covering the nauseous odor of human waste with sweet, musky scent. The dreadful sounds of war were absent as were the grisly remnants of conflict.

As a result of the rapid change of weather, we had to eat standing up, balancing our precarious mess kits in the left hand, eating with the right, while occasionally having to perform a deep knee bend to retrieve the coffee in the canteen cup placed on the ground. Life was getting cold and miserable, and none could comprehend why we were being herded north, when the war was clearly over.

An unusual phenomenon was beginning to occur. We were loosening up and getting to know each other personally, just as it was in Okinawa. This terrible war was another matter, and there was a reason. Because loss of life so personally affected us, we tended not to be on familiar terms with one another. The loss of a buddy was a traumatic incident that deeply affected all, sometimes for life. That was the way it was at Anui and Chinju Pass when we lost close friends from Okinawa whom we knew so well. It just hurt so much to lose a close friend. So, everyone kept their personal thoughts to themselves and conversed in general, rather than in close, personal, terms.

After two days at Kaesong, the Company had been reactivated from reserve status and sent back to the so-called front, wherever that was. Our Company K was transported by truck to catch up with the foot marching, spirited, charging 8th Army. We traveled all day in the trucks, jammed together, standing up, until we eventually stopped for the night. Customary foxholes were automatically dug, and it was noticed that the ground was becoming harder to dig because of the early hoarfrost. There were no more rumors of a return to Okinawa.

We had no food again for the entire day and as the cold night air emerged, hunger pangs began again. Smoking was permitted on this night, probably as a diversion from the lack of food. Smoking seemed to warm and prevent the cold night air from penetrating until cigarettes were extinguished. Besides, while now reactivated to combat level, our unit was not yet the vanguard of the 8th Army. The bedding so appreciated at Kaesong was now a distant memory. The company loaded on trucks before dawn the next morning, still without any food, and the grumbling began early. We couldn't live on cigarettes alone, and we knew that rear echelon personnel were living the life of Riley, while essential supplies to those on the front lines were either ignored or diverted. Resentment was mounting, because of the inequity of the military continually putting us in harm's way, while depriving us of the necessities of life. Some wondered just how far these inequities were carried, and how higher ranking commanders fared.[41]

After traveling several hours, the trucks suddenly slowed and then stopped abruptly at the side of the road. Two soldiers carrying a large cardboard box secured by a black steel strap walked behind the truck and heaved the box into our soldier-crammed truck. The container was boldly marked *50 to 1 rations*. That was new to all of us. We didn't know the contents, nor did we care. It was food. That is what was needed.

A bayonet was brought out that made quick work of the black steel band. The case was ferociously torn into and all the occupants fought like savages to grab something, anything to eat. It was pathetic to see this highly disciplined team regress to that level, but the consistent lack of food pushed each to his limit.

I was no exception, as I fought like a savage with the rest of them to get a can, any can of food. I reached in the box along with many other hands inside and I felt a large heavy can. I scored. I forced the can out, feeling fingernails clawing at my hand in a savage attempt to compel me to release my hold on the can. Once free, I secured the can close to my stomach, as if I were carrying a football through the line. In reality, I was securing my prize, to prevent anyone from wresting it away. This primitive behavior was the epitome of the Law of the Jungle! I peeked at the label stamped on the top of the olive-drab can when it was safe to do so. *Uncooked bacon*. In complete disgust, I cocked my arm, ready to throw the can in the adjoining rice paddy.

What in the fuck am I going to do with a can of raw bacon? I wondered. Swearing was cool. It demonstrated that you were a man, even at 18 years.

"Hold on Pete! Whacha got there?"

"A fuckin goddamn can of raw fuckin bacon, that's what!" I growled as

---

[41] Keeping in step with their commander, O.P. Smith, the senior Marines viewed Almond and the X corps staff with mounting contempt. They ridiculed Almond's "luxurious" field living quarters – a van rigged with a refrigerator, a hot-water shower and a flush toilet. They made jokes about the X Corps mess, which was provided with fine china, linen and silverware, even silver napkin rings and which FEAF supplied daily with fresh fruit, vegetables, and meat. Blair, p. 288.

I angrily readied myself to propel the missile in the field.

"Hey man! Don't do that. Toss it to me!" implored Sergeant Perry, standing on the ground at the rear of the truck. I tossed the can to the sergeant. If he liked raw bacon, more power to him.

"Piss call!" someone screamed in concert with the tailgate dropping heavily with a profound thud. Troops leaped off, some smiling with their treasure, most, like me, considerably disgusted. We never saw bulk rations like that before or since, and we wondered if it was for the officers in the rear, who always ate better, and a lot more regularly than foot soldiers.

This is appropriate, I thought as I was relieving myself along with many others, at the edge of the road.

Piss call from someone pissed off, I thought to myself.

"On the trucks! Let's go! Move it!"

Troops scrambled on board. We moved sullenly up north again. The grumbling became heated and loud. It was almost mutiny from an outspoken few. Despite my outraged feelings, I elected not to speak out. I was an old timer, and I believed it best to set an example of some kind of military bearing. Besides it was well drilled into us at basic training.

Do as you are ordered without questioning.

Other occupants who had joined the company later united in the chorus of the discouraged, bewailing the lack of food. After a few minutes everyone got it out of their systems, and occupants fell into deep silence.

A few miles up the road we noticed the troops in the truck ahead of us laughing and pointing to the right side of the road. As we neared the area, we noticed the source of their merriment. It was the corpse of a North Korean soldier, struck by napalm from Allied warplanes. It was a hideous sight but provoked laughter, probably to ease the psychological tension of death that was so tightly concealed within us. Our laughter brought notice to the truck following us and, as they approached they all looked to the right to see the source of the outburst and then duplicated our snickers.

It was about three in the afternoon when the trucks pulled off the road, separating to park individually among various trees for partial camouflage. Captain Hughes, in his lead jeep, decided that this was enough troop movement for the day. We were to be blessed in digging our trench during daylight for a change.

After we disembarked, Sergeant Perry, shouted, "First squad, 3rd Platoon follow me!"

Perry led us some distance from the unit, over a rise in the land, where we were out of eyesight, isolated from the rest of the company. Perry stopped, and when we gathered around him, he said solemnly, "You men hit that village (pointing to an abandoned village about a quarter mile away.) Scrounge up anything you can find that we can eat. Corn, sweet potatoes, anything. And don't come back until you have something!"

"Shit. A new fuckin sergeant and this is what I have to put up with. It's bad enough to fight this fuckin war, now I am in the grocery business," I murmured.

We spread into a wide sweep out of habit and mindful of possible enemy before we converged on the abandoned village. The inhabitants had a type of root cellar, a nondescript hut built under the shade of a tree. The hut was used to maintain various vegetables in a cool environment to preserve the food through the cold, bleak winter until the farmers would replant in the spring. This was an indigenous, continuous life cycle, interrupted only for war.

A treasure-trove of some type of yam or sweet potato native to Korea was found that none had seen before. We knew them to be edible, or else they would not have been stored. Stuffing every pocket with the wealth, we looked around for anything else. There was no corn to be found but we did notice the large pickling jars containing the Korean basic winter vegetable, kim-chi, a fermented cabbage. One could smell the offensive fumes from a mile away, and it was not at all appealing.

Later on, while moving further north, I had an opportunity to try kim-chi and it was decidedly spicy but OK. Most of us developed a taste for spice due to the bland make-up of C-Rations, and we didn't realize what we had been missing all of this time.

After about an hour, we headed back to 1st Squad's bivouac which had been designated by Sergeant Perry, who believed in dispersing broadly in case of artillery attack. Upon approaching the camp area, olfactory senses kicked into high gear. The smell of fresh-cooked bacon. It was the same can that I was in the midst of throwing away but had been salvaged by Sergeant Perry.

The afternoon became even better. Sergeant Perry, after building a small, hot fire, shrewdly opened the can of bacon in a unique manner. He ignored each end of the large can (the top and bottom) and instead, split the can open with a sharp knife length-wise. Once opened, he peeled both of the sides back to expose the bacon where it lay in each half of the container, similar to a homemade barbeque fashioned from the long half of a 55-gallon steel drum.

The cooked bacon was removed and separated into even portions for each on a bed of dried leaves, leaving the grease from the bacon remaining in the can. Sergeant Perry, grinning and joking wildly, commenced to slice the unwashed yams into french-fry cuts and then he dumped them into the boiling grease. It took no time at all for our pillaged items to cook in the hot can. No C-rations for us that night, as the odor wafted throughout the main body of our company. Several troops wandered over to see what was up, but it was too late. By then the food was gone.

One of the squad said, feigning sincerity, "Gosh guys, if we thought you wanted some we certainly would have saved some for you."

They walked away grumbling.

Each day, the battalion made a continuous wide sweep of the valley ostensibly to flush North Korean soldiers from hiding. The enemy was easy to spot because of their youth and near shaved heads. Unfortunately, they were not to be found, having fled north much earlier.

Our platoon of white, black and South Korean soldiers flushed inhabitants from shelters as we proceeded north, on foot.

One particular day, deep in North Korea, we sensed that inhabitants were hiding in their make-shift bomb shelter, a deep hole dug in the ground, then hollowed out horizontally to protect the natives from Air Force attack. The squad must have looked straggly and certainly menacing to the natives. They could have smelled us coming.

"Kim, order them out," I voiced firmly, pointing to the hole at the same time, and Kim knew just what was needed. Sergeant Perry was with Miller backing up another unit. Kim was one of our Republic of Korea Soldiers (ROKS) who didn't really understand our language, but he was perceptive, and he seemed to have a sixth sense as to what was needed. Kim shouted into the shelter, apparently for everyone to come out with hands up.

In this incident, a young Korean mother became hysterical with terror, screaming and crying, believing that she and her family would be slaughtered by the Americans and the soldiers of South Korea. Her children were screaming and crying along with the mother, while an elderly Korean man managed to remain relatively calm and stoic. Obviously there was no enemy so I slung my M-1 Garand rifle over my right shoulder demonstrating a less menacing stance. The rest of the squad followed suit.

The young woman continued to shriek and tremble, terrified by our presence, so I pulled two cigarettes from my pack, lit them and passed one to the screaming Korean mother. She continued screaming and crying and during her wrought-up behavior, she would frequently inhale lightly and immediately exhale the smoke in an emotional, high-strung manner. She was absolutely horrified, even though we meant no harm.

"Kim, tell her we are friends; that we will not hurt them."

Kim could tell by my voice, as I used what I hoped was a gentle tone, what to say, and after a time they calmed down in response to whatever Kim said to them. I told Kim to tell them that I was going to throw a hand grenade in the shelter to make sure there were no enemy soldiers hiding there, as I held a fragmentation hand grenade in my hand. Kim grasped the meaning immediately and instructed the family. They didn't seem to mind, so I presumed the shelter to be unoccupied, as I returned the grenade to my pouch. I gave a cigarette to the elderly gentleman and I was rewarded with a huge smile and a deep bow followed by the Korean word *kamsahapnida* (thank you).

The children were small, afraid, and still screaming, so the squad removed their helmets and knelt, hopefully becoming less threatening to them. There were about five of us in a half circle, kneeling before these crying children. I offered them a piece of the round, hard as nails, chocolate from my C-Rations. They put it in their mouths and immediately spit it out in disgust. Everyone laughed and the ice was broken.

~~

Thanksgiving Day, 23 November was like any other day in North Korea. Freezing cold, wet and miserable, but there were two events that stood out from the ordinary. Lieutenant Miller grabbed the first squad for a special patrol. We were to pick up an enemy soldier, wounded by aircraft, who had been informed on by a native North Korean farmer. The patrol took a medic and somehow someone found another Korean farmer with an A frame, a primitive wood backpack used to carry heavy burdens. It was just another routine assignment, but it turned out to be very significant. We made the history books of the Korean War once again.

> Thanksgiving Day had perhaps special omens for K Company, 35th Infantry. One of its patrols that day found a wounded Chinese soldier, the 25th Division's first Chinese Prisoner in the war. Appleman, p. 41.

Doc Harold Gamble, 1st Battalion medic, who accompanied the patrol, put a patch on the Chinese soldier's grisly upper leg wound and hoisted him onto the A frame, and the North Korean native carried him back to the company perimeter.

A rumor started to the effect that the wounded prisoner asked Miller in English, "Sergeant Miller, give me a cigarette."

The tale started because it was believed that Sergeant Miller had been training Chinese soldiers for combat while he was in Burma, which was untrue. Sergeant Miller was fighting in Burma to save his ass. During World War II, Miller was assigned to Merrill's Marauders, the first force to engage the enemy on the continent of Asia. An 80-percent casualty rate caused the team to be disbanded 10 August 1944.

When we returned from our patrol, the second unusual event happened. We had a Thanksgiving Day meal. It was the first deviation from C-Rations since we arrived in Korea. Because our squad was the only one to go on patrol that day we were allowed to buck the line and be served first. A glorious day. All of a sudden the weather seemed more tolerable. Still, there was no word on our return to peaceful, warm, Okinawa.

The next day, 24 November, General MacArthur was flown in to Sinanju, a small hamlet on the south bank of the dreaded, soon to run with blood, infamous Chonchon River. The general signaled that the kick-off for the *Final Offensive* in Korea would begin at 10 a.m. that morning.

We in the infantry didn't like it. We found those same freshly dug enemy foxholes each night when we halted. The enemy had been withdrawing every night for about a week. That was fine. They were running for the sanctuary of Manchuria. The problem was, why did they take the time and effort to dig in every night if they were fleeing north? [42]

The high command ignored the evidence and continued to push troops north to comply with MacArthur's fiat. The mechanized units were road-bound and didn't have the remotest concept as to what ground troops discovered in the desolate mountains off of the roads. We wondered why command failed to consider the possibility of a trap in the making.

Words cannot possibly describe the bitter cold at night in North Korea. After a protracted march without respite, when we did stop for a few moments, perspiration generated by the forced march began to freeze. If one was fortunate enough to be in the vicinity of an abandoned farmhouse on the road, a soldier would toss a white phosphorous hand grenade into the house. In a scant moment the once placid house erupted into a raging inferno. Near-frozen troops gathered around in an attempt to soak as

---

[42] On the night of November 25 Eighth Army was almost casually disposed. The men had two successful days of combat under their belts; the task lying ahead did not appear to hold great danger. Few men took the precaution of digging foxholes in the frozen ground....At about 8:00 p.m. the Chinese attacked in massive force....The total surprise of this awesome ground attack shocked and paralyzed most Americans and panicked not a few. Blair, p. 440.

much heat as possible to sustain them as they pushed north again.

There was no hint of a stabilized Allied front, only an out-of-control, pell-mell race to the Yalu border. The company was unaware of what other 8th Army units were up against, but we knew that Chinese units were pulling back from the fighting front directly north of King Company.

"Something is rotten in the State of Denmark," quipped someone who obviously knew Shakespeare's Hamlet.

Moreover, company personnel were not apprised that FECOM G-2 (Far East Command, Intelligence) Tokyo, was fudging estimates, downplaying the numerical strength of the Chinese Volunteer Army. Instead of 30 to 40 thousand disorganized, demoralized enemy troops, as intelligence claimed, there were in fact 300,000 well trained and combat-tested Chinese Communists soldiers on line, patiently waiting to slaughter the overconfident American Army.

We were the *Paper Tiger*.

THE CALM BEFORE THE STORM

> Chinese forces were already moving across the Yalu into Korea. No codes had to be broken to interpret Mao's policy. On September 25 in Beijing, Ambassador K. M. Panikkar had been told by Nieh Yen-jung, acting chief of the people's Liberation Army, that the Chinese would not "sit back with folded hands and let the Americans come up to the border." Weintraub, p. 176.

"Piss call! Piss call! Everybody up! Hey men, the world's on fire. Everybody rise, but do not shine. Get up and piss!" growled Sergeant Perry.

The world wasn't on fire. It was simply the hooch, slang in Japanese for a Korean house. But Perry was right, up to a point. It was not the world ablaze; it was the squad's temporary sleeping quarters.

First Squad, 3rd Platoon, comprised of nine inseparable troops, dead to the world, grumbled when aroused from deep sleep, to arise, congregate in a corner of the wooden floored house and urinate. The floor, smoldering brightly, was about to break out in a roar of fire. One half of the squad at a time formed a semi-circle, and, in unison, urinated on the smoldering wood. Members still more asleep than awake did not utter a word.

The fire brigade returned to respective sleeping areas and collapsed back on the tatami mats, instantaneously resuming sleep, as the other half of the nine-man squad completed the fire drill. Sergeant Perry, the new replacement platoon sergeant, who sounded the alarm, finished his call of nature, and the remainder of the squad was back to sleep, as if nothing had transpired. It was no different than naturally arousing at night to relieve oneself and then falling back to slumber immediately thereafter.

Steam sputtering from urine splattering on glowing embers emitted a sour odor. In retrospect, it is a wonder that squad members did not perish from carbon monoxide poisoning from the smoldering wood or fall ill from the toxic smell of burning urine.

Korean homes are constructed in the ancient Japanese tradition. The houses are built of rough-hewn wood, with opaque waxed paper windows and a similarly covered sliding shoji door. Roofs are thatched. The floor, also wood, is raised about two feet from ground level.

The typical Korean house has a primitive but amazingly practical heating system. An attached small hut comprises the kitchen. There the woman of the house builds a small fire under the hearth, a hand-molded device with a black iron kettle embedded in the semi-hardened clay which cannot be removed without breaking the adobe hearth. As the fire intensifies, the food in the kettle cooks; excess smoke evacuates through a rough chimney, and corresponding heat is vacuumed naturally into six-inch clay pipes secured under the wood floor and attached to the make-shift stove. Heat emits from the pipes, and is dispersed under the floor, maintaining uniform low heat to warm the floor.

That is, until American soldiers occupied these abandoned houses. Soldiers tended to construct fires too large and too hot, generally resulting in fires in the floors and ultimately through the entire house, unless the fire was arrested in time. Conversely, a Korean woman of the house knows how to fire the clay oven precisely and at what temperature to heat the house and cook the food simultaneously.

Swarms of lice are attracted to this warm temperature and propagate in the tatami mats, to the consternation of inhabitants. Even so, the majority of infantrymen preferred to cohabitate with lice as opposed to the opposite extreme—outside cold buffeted by harsh winds and biting frost.

"Everybody up! Let's go! Let's go!"

Sergeant Perry was once again rousing 1st Squad for a combat patrol to some unknown objective. It seemed that we had just fallen back to sleep following the impromptu fire drill, as Perry was heard shouting into adjacent houses, rousting the three other squads. Those squad members were blessed with uninterrupted sleep during the frigid night. Third Platoon was advised that the objective would entail mountaineering in the early morning, a definite sign of an arduous mission, and certainly fraught with biting cold rain or sleet, if nothing else.

Infantrymen lead a fireman's life. Dead asleep one moment, and wide awake the next. The squad stumbled from the warm confines of the hooch where the crisp, wintry morning air stimulated soldiers and shocked them into instant awareness. Platoon members felt pampered by having the privilege of sleeping in abandoned houses for the past two nights.

Meanwhile, autumn had been rationed to two weeks, quickly replaced by an appalling winter. The extraordinary blistering hot, humid, summer seemed now to be a distant memory, as the weather rapidly spun into winter. The American Army was way into the territory of North Korea, forging north to Manchuria, unknowingly to face its destiny. The 3rd Platoon, consisting of 42 soldiers, departed on foot at about 4 a.m. It was as dark as midnight when the platoon moved east of the company position across a wide valley to the mountains. None wore field jackets, despite the chilly morning, knowing the platoon would spend most of the day hiking and crawling up a treacherous slope, perspiring all of the way. It was better to be cold and miserable than sweating and miserable.

By now the war was victoriously concluded for all practical purposes. The American 8th Army was in a mopping-up phase, digging out stubborn pockets of bypassed NKPA soldiers—resisters who preferred to die rather than surrender. UN forces accommodated rear-guard enemy when they would rather fight than surrender. Because of their past atrocities to the civilian population and young American soldiers who were unfortunate enough to become prisoners, there was unquestionably a lack of empathy for die-hard enemy holdouts.

Third Platoon's mission was to march into the eastern North Korean mountains on a search and destroy mission, seeking stray North Korean Army units who had eluded the Inchon Landing pincer movement.

The platoon was to traverse the wide valley before dawn in order to be in position at the base of the mountains by sunrise. An incredibly thick blanket of moist fog hung heavily in the wide, fertile valley, preventing platoon members from glimpsing just how steep and formidable was the mountain.

Throughout this mopping-up phase of the conflict, subsequent to the American 8th Army wheeling to the offensive, platoon leader Sergeant Miller bivouacked with company commander Hughes and the other three platoon leaders, all of whom were 1st Lieutenants. The purpose, ostensibly, was to keep informed and coordinated on King Company's tactical concerns during this new phase of the war. Sergeant Miller was the only sergeant in the group of platoon leaders, in nonconformance of the T /O & E (Table of Organization and Equipment). According to Army regulations, a rifle platoon was to be commanded by someone of the rank of 1st lieutenant. Captain Hughes preferred Sergeant Miller to lead the 3rd Platoon as an acting lieutenant rather than to fill the position with a so-called ninety-day wonder, replacement lieutenant. Members of the 3rd Platoon were more than content with Sergeant Miller, he being the only combat experienced soldier, other than the Captain. He had displayed his ability to lead and inspire his men.

More than 50 years later, I learned from Colonel Hughes how low-key and irreverent Sergeant Miller really was. Naturally, basic infantry troops were oblivious of dark infantry humor bantered on a command level, but Hughes told me a story about Miller that went something like this:

Lieutenant Suddaby might casually say, "Hey, Miller, the old man says you are taking your platoon on patrol early tomorrow morning. That's a great wristwatch you have. Why don't you just leave it here, because chances are, you won't be coming back, and you don't want some gook to take it off your cold, cold wrist, do you? Honestly, I'll be sure to mail it on to your wife."

Sergeant Miller, defying military courtesy toward a commissioned officer, would generally testily respond, "Why you snotty nosed punk! I was fighting alongside of Merrill's Marauders, risking my ass, while you were still nursing on your mother's tit!"

Colonel Hughes related how he frequently had to bite hard on his pipe stem to keep from laughing at the kibitzing of the two, very close friends. Young, inexperienced soldiers would have been aghast had they have been privy to those conversations. Miller was our sergeant and friend, and collectively we considered him immortal, but we could not imagine such a discourse between two such divergent leadership positions.

Sergeant Miller led the force across the wet, foggy, valley. Filthy but dry uniforms soon devolved into soggy waterlogged messes, as troops sloughed across rice paddy dikes during the vast valley crossing. For at least three miles, the unit attempted to walk the dikes, struggling to maintain balance in a zigzag direction, dependent on the course of the rice paddy. When one would slip from solid ground, a boot would careen from the bank, break through the thin layer of ice, and submerge one's leg up to mid knee in ice-cold water. Climbing back on the bank, the victim would leave a slippery, soggy trail so that it became harder for the next soldier to navigate.

Heading the march by the 1st Squad was a blessing during this foray. Being third behind Sergeant Miller, our group was able to walk the banks of the rice paddies, which remained fairly dry. Platoon members had a great relationship with Sergeant Miller, even though he was relatively unknown, having joined the unit much later as a replacement, along with newly-drafted soldiers who were untrained. But Miller was not of the untrained. His exploits from fighting in the jungles of Burma bode well for all.

Sergeant Perry was last in the column; picking up the rear in infantry parlance, and at six feet plus, it had to be a struggle for him. By the time the 40 or so tramped over wet, crumbly dikes of rice paddies the banks lay in ruin.

Each man was deep in personal thoughts, silent. Conversation was permitted, but the arduous hike in total darkness took profound concentration to maintain balance on that very cold, gloomy morning. Specific leg muscles seldom used were called into play in an attempt to maintain footing on slippery dikes, soon causing cramps and aches to nearly all.

Fortunately, the patrol was traveling light. No machine guns or extra hand grenades. The only heavy weapon was the 3.5-inch rocket launcher, actually an anti-tank weapon, manned by Bob Jones, who rejoined the squad after he recovered from three shots to his lower body at Chinju Pass. Ammo bearer, Pierce, a huge man, carried two rounds of projectiles for the bazooka, in addition to his M-1 rifle.

A strident boast from a rooster crowing haughtily pierced the still of the ebony morning, as troops slogged quietly past a small North Korean village of sleeping inhabitants. The rooster obviously assumed the role of the town crier for the benefit of villagers. Possessed by a North Korean farmer, the rooster was considered the enemy as well, according to our thinking.

Icy rice paddy dikes surrendered to the sound of marching boots breaking the crusty frozen road. The dark, silent column of soldiers, including many ROK soldiers integrated into American ranks, steadily pushed forward. These dedicated ROK soldiers did their best to learn the English language while the majority of Americans were generally too lazy to try to comprehend basic Korean.

The blanket of fog soaked us in moisture, and hung as a veiled back drop as Sergeant Miller led his platoon up the back-side of a precipitous mountain, utilizing what seemed an ancient footpath. Despite the steep altitude of the mountain, one could distinguish that the trail was not overgrown despite the recent conclusion of the monsoon season. Our shapes clad in olive-drab uniforms were absorbed by the dense fog, as soldiers silently ascended the steep, narrow mountain. An arduous task lay ahead, given the sheerness of the ascent, even though the path was not heavily soaked and provided a manageable way for us to climb without slipping. The sun, if ever it was to rise, would be wreathed in somber gray.

Troops compensated for the steepness of the trek by leaning sharply forward, due to the steep incline, as condensation on breaths blended surreptitiously with fog. The platoon began ascending, accompanied with short, frequent gasps of air that gained in volume in direct proportion to the incline. Visibility was restricted to less than two feet, requiring each soldier to follow another at close proximity, marching in route step. Gone was the traditional five-yard minimum interval between individuals, but no one would be lost.

Both sides of the mountain gradually narrowed to an apex as the unit climbed relentlessly on. After scaling the tapered ridge for over three hours without a point of reference, the sensation was as if the ascension of the path led directly from the planet on into the heavens—the wet, dense fog creating an illusion of a blissful, cloudy atmosphere.

During a very brief rest stop, and then as we continued onward and upward, the fog thinned slightly, exposing the north side of the mountain. It was developing into an extremely dangerous, razor back, jagged cliff. From these astounding heights, viewing straight downward, we saw a small valley approximately 200 feet loom into view below. The south edge of the narrow footpath was less abrupt in nature, but yet quite steep. If one would plunge from the left side of the path, it would mean instant death, while one might survive a misstep on the right, if it was possible to seize a tree or other substantial growth in order to arrest a fall.

The elevation was in excess of over 4,000 feet by now. We plodded on for another 20 minutes or so when Ben Miller stopped the platoon for another rest break. The air was thin and soldiers were weary from the tremendous exertion.

The fog now allowed visibility of about 20 yards when we observed the severity of the cliff on the north side. The troopers sat in silence, not talking or smoking, because of absolute fatigue. It was to be a saving grace, as one could not possibly imagine what anyone would be doing on this isolated, god-forbidden mountain, but someone must have known more than they told us.

Voices!

All at once the muffled sound of voices sifted through the air! Someone was to the rear of the patrol, obviously unaware of our presence and actually following the platoon. Sergeant Miller immediately crossed his arms once, rapidly in front of his face, the sign for silence. Something was not right. The voices remained at the same level of tone but now they were clearly more numerous. Whoever they were, they obviously were taking a rest below the platoon on the path we had climbed. Luckily no one smoked during the rest breaks because of weariness, which would have left tale-tell evidence of a freshly-discarded cigarette butt.

I was standing next to Ben Miller, when he motioned for one of our ROK soldiers to come up to him. When the ROK soldier trotted up, Ben said just above a whisper, "Sneak down and see who they are!"

Our Korean comrade knew enough English to understand the meaning of Sergeant Miller's order. He unslung his rifle, stooped over and cautiously proceeded down the footpath we ascended earlier. About five minutes later the soldier reappeared and approached Miller where he whispered, "OK, OK, ROK solders."

With that, Miller whispered softly, more to himself than to anyone, "Bull shit! Nobody's supposed to be up here but us!"

He waved the approach here sign to Sergeant Perry to confer. Miller silently pulled out his Army topographical map from his breast pocket and was studying it when Sergeant Perry quietly approached.

"Perry," he whispered, "go down and see who they are. Nobody should be up here but us."

Sergeant Perry positioned his rifle at port arms ready to fire, and he proceeded quickly and silently down the footpath in the direction of the muffled voices. In the interim, the rest of the unit spread out the best they could.

Engage the enemy and destroy them by fire and movement. That was straight out of the Army infantry manual referencing infantry operations.

The platoon was set to destroy them, ready to set up the mother lode of all ambushes. Remember Anui!

The problem was, there was nowhere to maneuver. If one were to select the worse possible site to stage an ambush, this was it. The platoon had the high ground and the footpath and that was it.

Perry trotted softly back. He quietly whispered to Sergeant Miller, whom I was standing next to, "If those suckers are ROKs, they're all wearing red stars on their caps!"

Miller tried his best to point out areas to take cover, but there was just so little room to spread out for realistic deployment. Had the unit had a wider area, they could have spread out in a quarter circle and slaughtered them when they entered the lethal field of cross fire.

A huge boulder blocked the exact center of the summit of the mountain causing the footpath to veer to the north side of the ridge. Miller assumed a firing position behind the boulder and I lay down in the middle of the path, in a prone shooting position next to him. Soldiers dispersed as best they could due to limited space. One soldier never found a location while others in the platoon seized defensive positions.

The fog, now rapidly burning away, was scattered by the now heated sun looking curiously down on these unfolding events. The enemy finished their rest and continued onward and upward, talking softly, unaware of our presence until they unknowingly walked into Miller's trap. All knew to withhold fire until Sergeant Miller fired the first round. That was a given.

The enemy leaders were leading the way, plodding innocently on, and they never knew what hit them.

Sergeant Miller, armed with the M-2 Carbine, put it on full automatic. Braap! And the leader collapsed, mortally wounded, then rolled off the cliff. Miller had officially sprung the trap.

Sayonara, sons of bitches!

The killing mountain spun into a penny-shooting arcade. The platoon opened up with a rain of bullets relentlessly inundating the downward slope. The enemy fled in absolute disarray and panic as some fled for their lives back down the path. Many successfully escaped momentarily down the less steep cliff into an abrupt, narrow valley where enemy separated and commenced to hysterically claw their way up the next steep mountain, fleeing for their lives.

Platoon soldiers raced to where the enemy had stopped to rest, hoping to slay as many as possible, but they were confined to a single file, so most of the enemy eluded the ambush.

This attack yielded more enemy arms at one time than the entire battalion ever witnessed. A large, hemp woven rice sack containing Soviet manufactured fragmentary hand grenades had been carried by two men, slung on a stout bamboo pole resting on their shoulders. The grenades were dropped in panic as enemy fled. I grabbed the heavy sack and dragged it rapidly uphill, where Miller's attack originated. It was estimated that the bag and contents weighed in excess of 200 pounds.

Recovering to the starting point with the sack of grenades, I noticed Jones preparing to fire the 3.5-inch rocket launcher. Bill Pierce, his ammo bearer, inserted the anti-tank projectile, looked quickly around to confirm that no one was standing to the rear of the weapon to be killed by the back blast, as Jones lined up his target. Pierce tapped Jones' helmet, signaling that it was safe to fire and then Pierce backed away from the weapon as well.

Jones spotted four or five enemy soldiers congregating together, frantically scrambling up the opposite mountain. There were two tremendous explosions, both from the rocket launcher—one from the front of weapon, followed simultaneously by a thunderous blast of fire roaring from the rear tube of the launcher. The projectile went true to the target, but with few enemy hit. The projectile is manufactured with a hollow tip, so that when it strikes an armored vehicle, the tip collapses in a nanosecond. The projectile is designed to penetrate heavy armor plating as the full charge of the projectile burns through armor plate, rather than bouncing off.

The 3.5-inch rocket launchers, designed near the conclusion of World War II, were rushed to the war zone too late to replace the flimsy 2.36-inch rocket launcher, which had no effect on the monstrous Soviet T-34 tanks so prevalent during the first phase of this war. It was just another classic example of the draconian budget slashes to the military following World War II.

Jones fired a second deafening explosive round with the same general results; however, the psychological damage was incalculable. The monstrous explosions clearly scared the hell out of the enemy.

Moments later, I peered over the cliff, discovering a clear view of a grove of trees nestled in the narrow valley floor directly below. It was imperative to destroy the huge cache of recovered weapons and this appeared to be as good a place as any to dispose of the grenades.

No one was up to carrying the heavy load back, so once the container was dragged into position, I began grasping grenades, pulling safety pins and tossing the grenades into the trees below, one after the other. I hoped enemy would be hiding among the trees. By the time the fragmentary grenades reached the ground they burst into deafening explosions. Over 200 grenades were exploded until the supply was eventually exhausted.

As we moved down the hill, Jones and Pierce and I spotted at least five two-wheeled, water cooled, heavy machine guns, provided to the NKPA by the Soviets. It was unimaginable how anyone could possibly cart such weighty arms up this steep grade, as the two-wheeled chariots of death could not be rolled in this harsh terrain. They had to be carried aloft by dedicated enemy soldiers.

Sergeant Miller inspected the machine guns, determining one crucial component of the machine guns which, upon removal, rendered each gun inoperable. He removed the same part from each weapon and randomly handed them out. The wheeled guns were then rolled from the precipitous cliff, crashing far below, shattering beyond use upon impact. The armor-plated shields, weighing over 100 pounds, were scuttled along with the heavy, water-cooled machine guns.

Now late in the afternoon, Miller directed platoon members to carry as many enemy rifles back as possible; but with such a huge weapons cache, few could be carried. Consequently, firing bolts from each Soviet rifle were removed and carried a reasonable distance and thrown randomly into the valley below, along with key components of the machine guns. Many threw the bulk of rifles off of both sides of the cliffs at the killing site.

Sergeant Miller led his platoon on the arduous journey back, discovering that descending was every bit as fatiguing as climbing. All were impeded by the sheer descent, and similarly hindered by additional arms being brought out. The fog began to thicken once again as the unit moved down the precipitous mountain to the abyss of the cold valley.

Dusk collapsed into pitch black night, accompanied by impenetrable fog. Another day passed without food and this particular patrol had lasted at least 16 hours by the time troops worked their way down to the valley floor.

The platoon traversed the same rice paddy dikes on the return hike, where about two miles from the company base, a curious sight was noted. Captain Hughes lined up about eight vehicles in a semi-circle and had them turn on headlights as a beacon to guide the platoon back. It was a nice, but futile gesture. The headlights blinded the platoon as the light refracted from the icy rice paddies directly at eye level. The platoon was long overdue, because of the disruption on the top of the mountain.

It seemed as if an eternity passed by the time the platoon returned to base camp, where troops collapsed on floors of confiscated houses that were now cold. No one cared. Soldiers were too exhausted to start another fire. Each selected a can of C-Rations, ate, smoked a cigarette in silence, and then collapsed into state of unconsciousness. No one would be aroused to urinate on a smoldering floor this night.

Several positives resulted from the patrol. The next day one of the enemy surrendered to King Company, believing he would be killed if he continued to flee. Johnny, a Korean orphan of about 14 years, who had quickly mastered elementary English, did the interpreting for Hughes. Questioning the prisoner, Captain Hughes learned the enemy force was considering reorganizing to counterattack, knowing that they vastly outnumbered the platoon. That was until Jones fired the bazooka. The enemy soldier believed that artillery was emplaced on top of the mountain, which dissuaded them from any plan. Also learned was the number of enemy troops, their organization, and their plan of escape.

Many wondered from where the enemy materialized. There was no possible way to scale that glacier-like mountain except by trudging the same path as did the patrol earlier. Based upon information gleaned from the surrendered enemy soldier, there were approximately 400 enemy attempting to escape to Manchuria. So many questions arose as a consequence of the incident: Where could they have been hiding? Why didn't they move at night, while the company was on minimum alert?

Another question which could have been resolved at the time had anyone thought to ask. Why was the platoon ordered to check out the steep mountain? Did they have intelligence on enemy troop movement? Now, inquisitiveness is moot, but at the time it demonstrated that the Allies were taking the offensive to the NKPA, and the Allies were winning. But then, this was the calm before the storm.

Miller led us up the mountain as a sergeant and he descended the mountain as a lieutenant. Lieutenant Benjamin Miller. A battlefield commission! His was a promotion based on accomplishment and leadership, the most glorious and honorable way to promote from non-commissioned officer status to the heady rank of a commissioned officer. And Miller skipped the rank of 2nd lieutenant, Hughes promoting him to 1st lieutenant, on par with 1st Lieutenants Suddaby, DeLashment, and two others. Lieutenant Miller was a much-heralded infantryman and the entire company was excited about his battlefield promotion and none more so than Lieutenant Suddaby, who also was a superb infantry combat platoon leader.

Despite being commanded by a sergeant for so long, the 3rd Platoon had the highest morale and was blessed with an outstanding leader, who was always called on for important missions such the one just concluded. The result of the combat patrol rated a column in Stars and Stripes, the official newspaper of the Armed Forces, which wrote to the incident on that foggy wet, miserable, day:

DRY GULCHED
By PFC Will Burns
25th INF DIV IN KOREA

Here's the story of how a 42-man platoon routed 700 North Koreans with a neat bit of Texas strategy called "dry gulch." Sgt. Benjamin H. Miller of Galveston, Texas, earned himself a battlefield commission to 2nd lieutenant for his heroic leadership during the fray. He set the trap and led his small group of men in a daring ambush of an entire Red battalion.

It happened Oct. 18 during a heavy late-afternoon fog on Hill 830 near Hamchang. Miller's platoon, ordered to move west, was halfway down the hill when they bumped into the Red battalion. Backed by his 42 men, Miller boldly ordered the 700 Communists to surrender. They declined, so the American platoon opened fire and the Reds scurried away. Shortly afterward, the Red battalion was heard coming up behind the American platoon so Miller quickly deployed his men for an ambush in the dense fog. The Reds were within 50 yards of the trap when Miller again called for them to surrender. They refused, so the Texan "dry gulched 'em," in his native state's fashion.

When the smoke cleared away, 70 Communists lay dead and many others wounded. The rest had run out of the hills. Not one of Miller's men was hurt. Intelligence reports revealed the Reds were part of a coast guard battalion moving to a rendezvous from where they would make a run to the north.

The reporter was in error, relying on hearsay information. It was impossible for the platoon to kill 70 of the enemy due to the dense fog, coupled with their panicky dispersion from their long line once the volley began. Some believe that exaggerated enemy body count was a product of the Vietnam War, but apparently the practice is germane to war itself.

I had a conversation with Mrs. Miller, Ben's wife, many years later, when I first learned that Ben was called by the Lord only three months before I finally located Miller's family. Mrs. Miller recounted how Ben retired from the Army as a 1st lieutenant, but he was unable to adapt to the role of a commissioned officer. Ben raged at officers at the Officer's Club for the least trivial reason, and either initiated a fight or stormed out. She didn't know why, but I did. Ben was no different than any other combat soldier. Over time, the horror of war grips a person's psyche for life. No one is immune.

As Ben Miller's wife said to me: "Ben was a soldier's soldier."

Amen to that Mrs. Miller.

THE CHINESE CARD

>...in order to draw an enemy into a fight unfavorable to him but favorable to us, we should often engage him when he is on the move and should look for conditions favorable to ourselves in the advantageousness of the terrain...and fatigue and advertence on the part of the enemy. This means that we should allow the enemy... to penetrate deep. Mao Tse-tung

"Pssst, they're here," I whispered to Bill Pierce, the BAR man with whom I shared the foxhole.

"Goddamn it! Don't you think that I can hear?" he hissed in irritation.

His response sounded as if he wanted to fault me for the approaching enemy.

"Don't blame me; I didn't invite them." I retorted in the same whisper. I was angry but it was realized that we were exhausted, freezing, unfed, and nerves were frayed. Besides, the Chinese didn't arrive with a brass band preceding them, announcing their arrival, as did the NKPA. These new fighters, those now in front of our line, arrived silently and only their sheer numbers gave their presence away. This night would not be a cake walk.

The weather was so god-awful cold that I wanted to crawl into my pile cap and hibernate!

King Company was unaware another major assault was pending, though they were ready for any eventuality. They had seen many signs as they marched through North Korea to the Manchurian border.

~~

During a week of sighting recently-abandoned enemy defensive emplacements, the question arose why they did not flee to the sanctuary of Manchuria when Chinese territory was considered inviolate soil to the American Army and its Allies? Instead, the Chinese combatants voluntarily withdrew north about 20 miles each night, dug in, lit campfires, and then just as suddenly, vacated the defensive line only to withdraw the next night.

Surely the intent was more than a desire to camp out. Enemy strategy was to avoid Allied confrontation, continue to withdraw north out of range, until the entire cadre of Chinese Volunteer troops were stabilized into one enormous, unified front. The enemy drew the lucky straw to select the arena of battle.

As enemy continued to pull back in an organized withdrawal in concert with adjacent Chinese infantry, UN troops were baffled, but their high command was not.

The higher echelon, in unwavering, blind obedience to General MacArthur, executed his order to forge to the border in total disregard of sound military principles. Troops were underfed, ill-equipped, and exhausted, but they were ordered to scramble to reach the Yalu River. The regimental field staff had a premonition of a disaster, but they were overruled by MacArthur's obsession to drive to the border at any cost.

The American 8th Army was arrayed on line with Allies, including ROK, British and the fearless Turkish Brigade. Company K of the 35th Regiment was staged in north central North Korea, approximately 30 short air miles south of the Yalu River, and north of the Chongchon River, near a diminutive town known as Ipstok. History was to record this area in the vicinity of the Chongchon as the most significant and bloody battle area of the entire Korean War.

Tenth Corps, consisting of the 1st Marine Division, the 3rd and 7th Infantry Divisions and many ROK Divisions, was situated at and east of the Chosin Reservoir, near the center of the peninsula, where enormous Chinese Communist Forces from all points of the compass grouped in anticipation of a massive attack against the overwhelmed the X Corps.

On 25 and 26 November 1950, the Chinese Volunteers unleashed 300,000 combat soldiers against two unsuspecting American infantry divisions, the 2nd and the 25th; like every other infantry unit hunkered down on the main line of resistance, the disorganized units crumbled and disintegrated before the oncoming human tide of the Chinese Red Army. By the time the enemy concluded this bloody assault, only remnants of UN units survived. The CCF isolated the 35th Infantry Cacti Regiment, one of three regiments of the historic 25th Infantry Tropic Lightning Division.

For reasons soon to be known, the troops of the stranded 35th Infantry Regiment were bypassed.[43] Following the rout of the 8th Army, General Peng, Commander in Chief of all Communist Forces in Korea, after inflicting unsustainable losses against the American 2nd Division, pivoted his armies west and drove them in a frontal attack position against the unsuspecting 35th Regiment.

---

[43] The immunity of the 35th Infantry on the night of 25-26 November and the day of 26 November from Chinese attack, when it was general elsewhere across the Eighth Army front, seems to have been intentional....with their attack forces advancing south of the 35th Infantry on both its left and right flanks and with the 35th having no contact with friendly forces on either flank, the enemy envisioned a perfect trap for the unit as it advanced into the heart of their assembly areas.... Fortunately, the 25th Division CP realized the danger facing the regiment and stopped it on the morning of 26 November." Appleman, p.150.

That the Chinese warriors bypassed the entire 35th Infantry Regiment was especially serious for King and Love Companies. The regiment was stranded more than 24 hours north of the retreating Americans and in CCF-controlled land. The enemy cut off the Regiment so they could engage it before it could break through to unite with retreating Allied forces.[44] The Regiment was an isolated island surrounded in a sea of shifting sands of enemy infantry. Propelled like mighty tectonic shifting plates from the bottomless abyss of the earth, enemy seemed to possess the underwater force and turbulence of a tsunami.[45]

~~

Around King Company, surrounding units quickly rekindled coals to reinvigorate life-saving fires in the dim hope of repelling the bitterly-cold subzero Arctic temperature. Campfires on the front lines in any war are dangerous and unthinkable, but the extreme Manchurian cold mandated it. Given that Allied forces were not as yet engaged with the enemy, commanders turned a blind eye, tacitly permitting this unusual breach of security.

The only other option was to freeze to death. Soldiers reflected how the company was issued cold weather gear approximately six weeks earlier, including heavy woolen overcoats, which were immediately discarded. The first rain had convinced us of their uselessness. They soaked up the rain like a sponge and emitted an odor like a sweated horse blanket. The weight and bulk of the coats, particularly when wet, hindered our ability to move rapidly through these formidable mountains. Moreover, we believed the enemy could clearly smell the foul odor of stagnant, wet wool from a significant distance. We wished we had them now.

---

[44] Military analysts and line commanders at the time of this military debacle discovered that initial mass attacks by the CCF would isolate small groups of American infantry and then brutally destroy them. The slightest hint a soldier was alive would result in an immediate bullet to the back of the head.

Victors removed American boots to replace the inadequate, canvas covered, rubber soled footwear of the CCF.

The discovery of stragglers returning to Allied safety within two or three days led some commanders to hold defensive positions against great odds in the hope that enough stragglers would find their way back thorough enemy territory. Author.

[45] The Chinese attacks against the 35th were particularly persistent because that is where the Chinese command intended to open a penetration. More than a division of enemy troops, about 10,000, according to prisoner information, stood ready behind assault teams to pour through the penetration into the rear of the 35th Infantry lines if K Company had broken Despite the heavy fighting during the night, the casualties of L and K companies were not heavy - a tribute to good leadership, discipline, and professional use of weapons. Appleman, p.151.

Fortunately for us on this late night of 27 November, Captain Hughes ordered the company to dig in as usual, but that there be no bonfires in King Company's sector. Only Hughes could implement such harsh orders. Company troops readily accepted that he was the unqualified leader, always knowing what was best for the company, and what was best to keep us alive. The skipper suffered the bitter cold along with the rest of the company.

This night, as on previous nights, we ignored the foxholes of the Chinese forces, primarily because they were emplaced on the south side of the hill, while King Company's goal was to defend the north side—the direction of attack. Any of these lines of abandoned enemy emplacements could have been the jumping-off point for a CCF offensive drive if Chinese soldiers had been given the signal.

King Company knew to dig in, but the arduous task was nearly impossible. Terrain was frozen solid to below a foot, and the native shale joined in a conspiracy to thwart all efforts. Troops were exhausted as a result of plus 20-mile forced marches through formidable mountains, hindered by nearly unconquerable terrain, lack of food and sleep deprivation.

Subzero air seared lungs as exhausted soldiers gasped desperately for life-needed oxygen. Legs ached and cramped from tramping through dense, frozen, mountainous forests. The hostile environment, unfit for man or beast, was forced upon unsophisticated, adolescent warriors, who were illogically driven to achieve a nebulous objective.

Following hours of tedious painstaking labor, my partner and I managed to dig an approximately 18-inch deep hole, barely wide enough for two. Company personnel had no concept this was to be the night that would spin out of control into a crucial disaster or they would have dug deeper for additional protection. It was later learned many units in the 8th Army line failed to dig because of the frozen ground. We dug and the company dug, because we were disciplined. We had to dig. Other units lay on the frozen ground without the benefit of cover. This night of all nights was the night to dig! Dig, as if your life depended on it. Dig! For your life does depend on it! Dig!

On the frozen terrain, shale and rock were strewn about as if ice-age glaciers had wrought their havoc centuries past. But, in this instance, these redoubtable mountains were fashioned eons ago when vast continents collided. The sparse outcroppings of small pines afforded no one the luxury of concealment or protection, nor were they an obstacle to the fanatical charges of the Chinese People's Volunteer Army, now flooding into the sector in determined preparation for attack.

Pierce and I dug in on the high ground, weapons aimed down a natural draw, a break in the mountainous terrain. The company defensive line was haphazard, predicated more on the geography of the area rather than the main line of resistance (MLA). Some of the hastily-dug emplacements were higher or lower rather than in a relatively straight line necessary for maximum security. No one gave much thought as to where to dig, because this was originally thought to be simply another uneventful night like so many others in these rugged, desolate, unforgiving mountains.

King Company was spread more than thin, out of sight of each other, barely dug in due to frozen terrain on this craggy, icy mountain, somewhere in the steep, hostile Chokyong Range. We were uninvited guests of the almost impenetrable mountains of North Korea near the Chongchon River. This unholy unconsecrated ground was another badland, that hostile terra firma of wasteland, unfit for cultivation or any other domestic purpose except to die upon. Soldiers of the company waited in lingering anticipation, in eerie silence, for the approach of the enemy.

The dark humor of an infantryman shows in one of Murphy's Military Laws, stated succinctly: "If the advance is going well, there is an ambush ahead!" Many obvious signs discovered by advancing Allied ground troops led them to believe a new phase of the war was either here right now, or, about to storm down.

A wind-swept front chilled defenders to the bone on this crystal clear night with temperatures plunging to subzero—too cold to snow. Despite these hardships, Allies were blessed with a full moon that washed the hills with an ominous, grotesque hue resembling the sickening pallor of a corpse.

That moon was like a pale night-lighting pyrotechnic flare hoisted to the heavens and allowed to remain frozen, dangling and illuminating. It was easier to look down and focus on the gathering storm than it was for the enemy to raise their heads in an attempt to locate company positions. Defenders had a clear view of the enemy lining up in battle formation for their first assault wave. They, no doubt, wished that someone would douse the glaring light of the post-harvest moon.

Now psychological forces held sway. The CCF knew them as signals. Opposing forces believed them to be a demonic orchestration of fearful sights and sounds. Vivid, colorful, flares were activated in an eerie sort of recital, accompanied by an off-key, disharmonious symphony.

Fanatical opponents bolted from the gates of Hell and surged forward by the hundreds, aiming for sparsely-emplaced foxholes. Without an iota of fear, our foes swept forward to be cut down from murderous fire spewing from defending machine gun, BAR and rifle. The first wave was cut to pieces and another one formed to attack. They met the same fate and still they came. Troops waited for the enemy to regroup to form another charge. Playing their bugles, whistles gongs and sheep horns fanatically, the enemy again swept forward in a unified charge.[46]

Every weapon was brought to bear against the attackers in a go-for-broke five-minute fusillade, except for the heavy weapons platoon. Where were the mortars? It was an ideal situation to employ the 60-millimeter mortars, because of the huge density of enemy. It would have been a rain of death because of the enormous concentration of enemy troops.

Allies were so disorganized by the earlier relentless but haphazard drive to the north that there was no telling where the mortars were placed. The catastrophic answer came later. The light 60-mm mortar positions were overrun by CCF attacking from the rear, killing the crews and confiscating the weaponry. The next afternoon enemy turned these same captured mortars against surrounded, isolated King Company.

The defensive perimeter was so severely extended defenders could neither see nor contact one another. In one enormous skirmish line they attacked again and again, from every conceivable direction, swarming, overrunning company positions. Strategists at division headquarters who pointlessly ordered the regiment to withdraw were a breath too late.

The encircled 35th Regiment was on the Chinese short-list to be annihilated. Survivors of those horrific battles were wounded, captured or

---

[46]After the Unsan campaign, the CCF 66th Army, which at first stood in reserve behind the 39th Army, published a summary of battle conclusions reached as a result of their experiences in that campaign.... A few of the conclusions stated in it may help explain their method of fighting and of using to advantage what they thought were fatal weaknesses of the American Forces:

Their infantrymen are weak, afraid to die and haven't the courage to attack or defend. They depend on their planes, tanks, and artillery. At the same time, they are afraid of our firepower.... They must have proper terrain and good weather to transport the great amount of equipment. They can operate rapidly along good highway and flat country; not in hill country . . . They specialize in day fighting. They are not familiar with night fighting or hand to hand combat. They are afraid of our big knives and grenades; of our courageous attack, regular combat, infiltration. If defeated, they have no orderly formation. Without the use of their mortars, they become completely lost, and, as in the operation at Unsan in October 1950, are killed off. They become dazed and completely demoralized.

They are not good in a fight. At Unsan, they were surrounded for several days and did nothing. They are afraid when the rear is cut off. When transportation comes to a standstill, the infantry loses the will to fight . . . Those surrounded by us will think we are well organized and equipped with weapons, In this case, they will surrender rather than fight. Appleman, p. 113.

forced to shoot their way out of the emplaced Chinese bamboo net. No one got a free pass. A few eventually were able to drive through a wall of fire to return to friendly lines. Those valiant company defenders who managed to discern the soft underbelly of the surrounding Chinese, blasted a hole in the human Asian wall to escape, but they did so with irreparable damage to themselves—victimized by gunshot, shrapnel and/or severe frostbite. Only about one platoon survived.

During the savage night assault the enemy was able to penetrate King Company's defensive perimeter, breaching the line through the rear, where protective positions are generally the weakest.

Captain Hughes drove forward with several King Company soldiers in a dangerous but essential attempt to plug the break in the lines and kill the intruding enemy, resulting in the Captain being struck and severely wounded by enemy hand grenade shrapnel. Bleeding profusely, Captain Hughes lost consciousness, but other soldiers killed the attacking marauders and the defensive line was reinforced. Had the effort not have been put in play and the rupture of the line not sealed, the entire complement of King Company would have been slain from within by enemy troops.

There were three DSC's, the second-highest tribute available, awarded for this action. One was given to Colonel Hughes.

> The DSC (Distinguished Service Cross) was awarded for Ung-Pong, Korea on November 27th, 1950. Capt. Hughes led a small force up a slope through mortar, grenade and small arms fire. Although wounded, he refused medical aid, gained the crest of the ridge and recaptured a portion of lost ground. Subsequently, when enemy machine-gun fire raked his unit, he led a daring charge on the emplacement, which annihilated the hostile crew with grenade and rifle fire, and routed the remaining enemy from the ridge. Capt. Hughes remained on the ridge and exposed himself to heavy fire to direct the defense until daylight when the enemy attack was defiantly repulsed. *Quoted from the DSC award.*

A rumor swept the company like a hurricane wind that the new acting captain was so frightened during this battle that he refused to leave the sanctuary of his foxhole. I could empathize with his fear, predicated on my initial baptism of combat during the terrible ordeal at Anui closely followed by the carnage of Chinju Pass. But this was different. I was an insignificant rifleman, while the acting commander was expected to take command of the company. The company was leaderless, and we were isolated from each other, ignorant of the battle situation of the other defenders.

Quiet seeped softly into the battlefield. Acrid smoke from many guns hovered heavy in the valley while Chinese troops reorganized for yet another attack. Driven by blind obedience, the CCF believed American imperialists would invade Chinese soil with their armies. Whatever the reason, the enemy went to their deaths with their philosophy. The frozen shale-like ground offered no comfort to the dead and dying assailants. The blood of the victims was immediately staunched by the bitter Manchurian winter. Incredibly, hundreds of mortally wounded enemy lay with little blood. There was no gory show of blood to display their final commitment to their leaders.

There also was no shortage of enemy soldiers to cut down as they charged. The cliff-like terrain in front of the riflemen prevented the enemy from sweeping the immediate line in front. Two King Company riflemen concentrated their firepower to the left, as the enemy was pouring through the draw. Troops witnessed the faint glow of muzzle blasts from M-1 rifles to the left, but the distance between defensive positions precluded them from discerning their positions. The draw was alive with the choking smell of gunfire, punctuated by the flash of staccato rounds of tracer ammunition from both sides. Without a doubt, based upon the sounds of war, the warriors were assaulting our positions with a plethora of American weaponry acquired from the Chinese Civil War.

"Medic...Medic," wailed a voice mournfully.

Cries for help went unheard by deafened ears, or the plaintive pleas were ignored. No one dared to respond. Whoever called, it was not believed by defenders to be the cry of a wounded American, nor could any friendly wounded be helped even if the sorrowful cry for emergency first-aid did indeed emanate from the dying lips of a fallen comrade. Defenders had learned the hard way, Chinese Forces had a high ratio of English-speaking fighters, and every strategy was employed to deceive Americans. There was no one who would risk vacating a defensive position in the middle of a major battle for a rescue attempt. If he was indeed American, he must die alone.

Pierce took care of the multitudes charging our position from the right. Between the firepower of the riflemen and the automatic gunfire from the BAR, the foe didn't have a chance in this sector. The lofty elevation was too severe for the opponents to overcome as enemy soldiers crumpled mortally wounded. Hundreds and hundreds of fanatical soldiers tried to break through defensive lines. The responding firepower was so concentrated we worried we would deplete our ammunition, or worse yet, burn or freeze the barrel of the BAR.

The draw was akin to a funnel, where enemy massed together because they couldn't overcome the steep fronts of some of the other positions. Once out of the narrow draw, the enemy quickly spread to widen ranks and sweep frontally before the company. Those who tried failed, but they kept coming and coming without end. The mass of humanity headed for the BAR position because it appeared to be the easiest to overrun, but they made fatal mistakes, which allowed us to live and them to not. The fire from the BAR was withering and murderous, as bodies collapsed upon one another. Still they surged forward, sidestepping fallen comrades, preparing to take up the cause with a vengeance and kill or be killed.

Defensive firepower was dead-on, and the sweep of automatic fire caught the Chinese unaware, ripping their assault line from one end to the other. They were once a long, frontal line of sacrificial troops. Now, the attackers were having simultaneous violent seizures as bullets ripped into crumpling bodies that died as they collapsed to the frozen ground.

It was approximately 20 degrees below zero, and still they came. I frantically tore off my clumsy mittens in order to reload magazines for the BAR shooter. I began to rip 30-caliber rounds from M-1 Rifle clips that held eight rounds. The mere act of touching my fingers to bare metal was excruciatingly painful. It was difficult enough to force rounds into sharp-cornered BAR magazines and even hold the spring-loaded, 20-round magazine, but it was even more devastatingly painful to have to force needed rounds from M-1 clips in order to reload the BAR magazines.

The BAR expends between 300 and 600 rounds per minute and there wasn't enough time to reload the magazines. The shooter had problems as well. The bipod in front, which normally held the weight and steadied the weapon, was of no use when the weapon was pointed downgrade; hence the operator had to hold the 16-pound automatic rifle in his arms all night, as he aimed and fired from the shoulder.

In spite of the appalling, bitter weather, and the charge of the CCF, the body of defenders remained calm. We had a job to do, which placed the uncontrollable fear of battle on hold. The constant exposure to close combat had melded King Company personnel into seasoned, combat-hardened soldiers. Both protagonists and antagonists sensed that when the advantage of battle dominantly shifts to the adversary, there is not much left other than fear and death for the defenders.

The will dies first, followed by pride, and then the body picks up the rear.

"Damn it, Bill, slow down, I can't keep up!" I spat in frustrated anger.

"Tell it to them!" he hissed in return, continuing his rapid, lethal firepower, sweeping the front before us.

And still they came. The CCF exhibited the same ferocious determination as the North Koreans, but with one notable exception. The Chinese kept coming. When one fell, it seemed as if two would take his place. The North Koreans assaulted in wave after wave, but once repelled, they would regroup and reassemble in another wave to resume the attack. There was a very brief interlude between attacks by the North Koreans, but not so for the Chinese Volunteers. There simply was no end to their manpower, their fanatical determination. They marched on the company, firing automatic weapons from the hip, some with fixed bayonets ready to thrust if soldiers dropped into foxholes to avoid heavy small arms fire.

The Chinese bayoneting technique was quite simple. Go for the throat, that soft tissue area, to sever the jugular vein. A stab to the face or to the chest would not penetrate deeply. They didn't want to waste an extra shot to the victim to dislodge the bayonet by recoil from the skeletal portion of the body.

The enemy's fatal mistake was not to evaluate the source of the defensive fire from our position. Had they taken the time to observe the superiority of automatic firepower, they would have taken specific steps to put the BAR out of action. I was too busy to contemplate that issue, as the urgency to reload magazines was paramount. The enemy kept on the attack without respite.

All night long the Chinese so-called Volunteers sprang forward in response to the sounds of their mobile symphony, charging positions again and again and again with concentrated small arms fire. It is a given that an automatic weapons man is one of the first to be killed in close, relentless combat. The enemy is quick to dispatch any opponent who has the capability to slay their troops by automatic fire. Communist commanders sent their single-minded forces to certain death, as they fell by the hundreds mortally wounded in front of smoking, bullet ridden defensive positions.

The attackers continued to charge with guns and guts. The initial massive sorties along the 8th Army main line of resistance were unparalleled in modern warfare. The Chinese Communist volunteers were truly on a one-way mission. They had every intention of driving the Allies from every square inch of North Korea, and that is exactly what they did. This was not a reprise of The Hill, when, during the first part of September, the NKPA had the protection of a terraced hill to afford them some cover before they were massacred directly in front of company foxholes.

Attempting to traverse the clear, upward slope illuminated by full moon placed Chinese combatants at a disadvantage, and none were able to gain any ground within 30 feet of our positions because of the enormous quantity of defensive fire. The Chinese grenadiers, daringly preceding infantry, were renowned for their assaults with stick grenades, both of the concussion as well as the fragmentary type. But the two styles of grenade were equally ineffective in our immediate front during this all-night siege.

Stick grenades, made of a bamboo body, housing a heavy steel projectile on one end with an aluminum cap screwed to the other, were deadly and numerous. Removal of the cap would expose a string, that when pulled, would activate the timer. The grenade would explode with such force that they were lethal within a 30-yard radius.

Now, it was my turn. I had two aces in the hole, and my poker cards were rifle grenades. I carried them stuck in my field jacket for over a month without finding a suitable target. While these rifle grenades were ostensibly manufactured as anti-tank weapons, they were in reality unsuitable against heavy armor. Even a direct hit by these projectiles would merely irritate a tank crew. They felt angered someone would have the temerity to attempt to stop a mighty, mobile fortress with an instrument having the strength of a fly. Even so, the recoil was so great that it had to be fired from the ground, the rifle butt absorbing the recoil.

A particular style of grenade launcher was affixed to the muzzle of the M-1 Rifle, and the gray, round-nosed, and finned projectile was mounted to the launcher. An expressly-manufactured blank round to fire the grenade was loaded in the chamber. It is common to break the clavicle when this grenade is fired from the shoulder. Accuracy is sacrificed when it is discharged from the ground because the weapon reverts to a very crude mortar, without any semblance of precision.

Possible broken clavicle or not, I was going to make the most of these rifle grenades and there was no better time than now. Once loaded and ready to fire, I leaned forward as far as possible without pitching forward. It was imperative to neutralize the mammoth recoil as much as possible. The secret to success is in the placement of the rifle to the body. One must push the butt of the rifle as firmly as possible into the hollow of the shoulder just as if the rifle were an extension of one's body.

Hold on firmly with all of the might that one could possibly possess, and murmur a silent prayer. With that, I aimed down the draw, and fired.

The blast and the dynamic force of the follow-up recoil threw me violently back against the hole. Like a pro football quarterback who has just been forcibly sacked, though he instantly rebounds to watch the aerial descent of his Hail Mary pass, so it was with me. I leaped forward to ascertain the result. The projectile went swift as an arrow, right where the Chinese were massing for the next attack wave. A burst of yellow-orange flame erupted, coinciding with a thunderous explosion. The grenade must have struck a boulder, which presumably showered the area with deadly shrapnel. I was amply rewarded, hearing at least two different agonizing screams near my target. I quickly reloaded as before and fired again. The second time was much easier, as I knew what to expect. The recoil had the kick of a mule, but by eliminating slack, I harnessed the backlash.

The next day my shoulder throbbed and heavy black and blue welts covered my upper right shoulder area, but nothing was broken. Firing the grenades was worth the effort. I heard no sounds from the enemy after the second explosion and I wondered if they believed that we had some type of artillery on the hill. And, I was no longer bogged down with having to carry the grenades.

"OK, Bill, it's your turn," I whispered, as I went back to the cursed task of reloading of BAR magazines with my still exposed right hand.

Dawn was slowly breaking when enemy bugles sounded recall. The surviving Chinese soldiers withdrew as silently as they came, dragging dead and wounded with them in order to treat wounds and assess losses of comrades. That was not the case for other Allied units who attempted in vain to hold back the flood of the Volunteer Golden Horde.

There was not the exhilarating, great to be alive, we stopped them cold sentiment after this ferocious battle. The unit was beat, physically, mentally and emotionally. We were just plain worn out.

That morning, some had the strength to descend the hill to assess enemy losses and confiscate weapons. Hundreds and hundreds of dead soldiers armed with rifles and automatic weapons were strewn about the battlefield. Any notion to carry away this enormous cache of weapons was abandoned, as the huge quantity was too much to take at the time. Except for one. I spotted a beautiful American-made Thompson sub-machine gun—the exact type American gangsters of the 20's and 30's utilized. The automatic was equipped with a round drum magazine attached to the front, which fired huge, stub-nosed 45-caliber rounds.

I carried the treasure back up the slippery shale hill to show fellow soldiers. Everyone wanted it until it was discovered that the Chinese soldier who was the previous owner must have been killed after an M-1 round first shot off the magazine retention clip. Likewise, I realized that it was too heavy and cumbersome to carry long distances and that the magazine would have to be held in place to fire. The weapon was discarded.

To everyone's surprise, it was discovered all of the arms were Made in the USA. It was years later we learned this booty was courtesy of Generalissimo Chiang Kai-shek, leader of the dishonored Kuomintang Nationalist Army who fled to the island of Formosa, now Taiwan, with their treasury and their lives. They left hundreds of thousands of arms, courtesy of the Treasury of the United States of America as well as over two million Nationalist soldiers who switched sides to join the Chinese Communist cause.

The next day, late in the morning as the company was moving rapidly to the rear, an American observation plane dropped a note to battalion commanders to report there were now so many Chinese troops advancing, that it appeared that the ground was moving. Now, they were moving ahead in broad daylight, so many and now so brazen that the invincible US Air Force was helpless to contain them. Gone were the days when Chinese troops would clandestinely and stealthily cross the border during the night. Now the many Volunteers had no fear. It would not be the last time for me to encounter this overwhelming horde of dedicated, fighting men.

Sergeant Perry was among the many killed by Chinese soldiers the night of the 27 November 1950 attack against King Company.

THE WITHDRAWAL

> Enemy reactions developed in the course of our assault operations of the past four days disclose that a major segment of the Chinese continental forces in army, corps and divisional organization of an aggregate strength of over 200,000 men is now arrayed against the United Nations forces in North Korea. ... Consequently, we face an entirely new war. General Douglas MacArthur, 28 November 1950

A few from the company who survived the awful night were sitting on the frozen hill following the all-night battle against Chinese Communist Forces. All were chilled and totally exhausted, physically and emotionally. The UN forces earlier stormed through snow-bound mountains and valleys with no reprieve, responding in knee-jerk reaction to General MacArthur's 24 November fiat to attack to the Manchurian border. Now surviving defenders were deep in discussion, pondering how the company survived yet another awful massacre, and particularly why they were now locked in mortal combat against Chinese soldiers. The conversation was interrupted by a brusque shout. "Let's go you men! Haul ass! We're moving out!"

King Company still held the hill the Chinese so furiously attacked. Though the CCF paid an enormous price in human life, they didn't gain an inch. Now, the company was apparently relinquishing the temporary fortification to them, gratis.

The new adversaries, Chinese Forces, silently ceased attack just before the break of dawn, and instigated an orderly withdrawal, which permitted me the luxury of thawing my right hand near a campfire started immediately in the below-zero cold. It was a given the enemy was somewhere north starting bonfires as well. To not be embraced by flame in this atrociously frigid environment was to die from freezing.

The CCF emulated the North Korean Army in their shared interest to attack only at night. As a consequence of the battle, my right hand, so long exposed to the elements, continued to plague me.

When the few stragglers glanced up, they saw groups were moving out so rapidly, those hanging back had to run to catch up to the single line of soldiers marching swiftly south. Apparently, the high command was now in the process of serious retreat without any notification or concern to company members. Platoon leader Lieutenant Benjamin Miller was not to be found. Because defensive positions were positioned so far apart the night of the appalling attack, communication was lost, which added to the utter chaos. There was so much confusion and pandemonium this morning, that no one knew who was killed, wounded, captured or if the enemy successfully breached the defensive perimeter. The dead and seriously wounded who couldn't escape with Captain Hughes were abandoned to the enemy.

Word passed down the line through the grapevine that the acting company commander was heading the column. He shall remain anonymous because of his obvious serious breaches of command, fraught with misinformation and indecision. He caused the company to wander over a great portion of the combat sector of North Korea without reason. No one knew him, and he was heading this vacillating withdrawal. Some wondered aloud why regular lieutenants were missing from the company. No one responded, being out of breath from the below-zero weather and the blistering pace of the retreat. The missing lieutenants were presumed to be dead following the last night's assault by Chinese Forces. One wondered why, if the company remained for all purposes, one integral unit, were the slain or seriously wounded abandoned after the attack? Very few survivors ever knew for over a half of a century.

Everyone fell into single file as company personnel blended into an amalgamation of one disorganized mass. Some recognized each other from brief associations before, being assigned to other platoons. Others were strangers to other members. Infantry companies tend to stay semi-isolated by platoon, so it was generally rare that troops from one platoon knew others in the company.

A small number seemed to know what was transpiring, but the majority knew nothing. It probably was for the best. Unknown to us, the survivors of the initial attack were literally surrounded by a sea of newly-deployed Chinese infantry.

A few soldiers catching up to the rear of the racing company were forced into double-time mode, just to maintain the pace set by the head of the column. Fortunately for all, the customary, unbearably heavy load of C-rations and ammunition was greatly lightened.

What in the hell is the damned hurry? troops naively wondered. They were soon to discover the awful reason.

It was late morning 28 November, below zero degrees and there were no rations left, troops having last eaten the day before. Ammunition was reduced to dangerously low levels because of unremitting fire during the enormous attack the night before. Chinese forces were nearly as unstoppable as the North Korean assault troops. Baker Company's debut of counterassault on 3 September, when the now-destroyed NKPA 6th Division was ground up, bode the company well for future combat in this apparent continuance of war.

Unknown to company personnel, the 8th Army line collapsed one day earlier from the monumental force of the all-out attack by hundreds of thousands of Chinese Communist infantrymen. King Company, as well as Love Company, managed to hold despite numerically superior enemy attacking them, and they were unaware the UN forces were retreating.

How come we didn't destroy the weapons of the Chinese? some questioned as they ran to catch up. Other than burning some captured American-issued dynamite in the campfire, the other implements of war were abandoned to be recycled for the CCF.

Because of the frantically swift pace, no one spoke or even attempted to light up, for attempting to do so would entail the loss of a brief precious moment. All collective energy was expended on this half-running, forced march. The *smoke 'em if you got 'em* tenet was unsuitable at this pace.

Many tried to recall when they were ever on such a fast-paced evacuation and nothing came to mind. Hughes was miraculously evacuated at sunrise, after the enemy withdrew, and now it seemed to be just a couple of hours since then. No enemy could move that quickly to surround us, many naively believed. Troops felt leaderless without the skipper. Similar abiding faith was held in our four platoon leaders as well, and many were concerned by the absence of platoon leaders Miller and Suddaby.

It was conjecture, but many believed Captain Hughes had led his company so far into enemy territory that an order had been given to pull back to consolidate the MLR (main line of resistance). Now King Company was isolated and apparently abandoned, which added to the consternation. Additionally, no one had knowledge of the new acting captain.[47]

Replacement personnel had not come under enemy fire excepting the 3rd Platoon, led by Lieutenant Miller, when they ambushed and dispersed a North Korean Coast Guard Battalion on 17 October near the hamlet of Hamchang, North Korea. The majority of members of King Company had

---

[47] Company members discovered much later the replacement captain had been commissioned as a second lieutenant at the termination of World War II, mustered from the service and then enrolled in the Army Reserve Corps, where he eventually was promoted to captain. He, along with 19 others, was activated and shipped out to the 35th Infantry Regiment four months into the war. The regimental commander, Colonel Hank Fisher, having no need for additional officers, arbitrarily assigned them to various infantry companies. Colonel Fisher needed masses of combat soldiers instead of officers. The new officers proved to be more of a nuisance than assistance. Regrettably, not one of them had any infantry combat experience. Author.

not been baptized into the horror of war until the previous night's encounter with the CCF.

There had been some incidental, minor confrontations such as when one or two enemy guerrillas fired a burst of rounds at the unit and then fled for their lives over a hill. On a few occasions, friendly North Korean farmers notified the UN forces about seriously wounded foes abandoned by enemy forces. American units advanced to villages, accompanied by ROK comrades and Korean laborers, equipped with ancient A frames, to carry wounded to Allied lines for treatment and interrogation.

That had been back in October. Rumors early on were these wounded enemy soldiers were in fact Chinese Communist troops, not members of the scattered and decimated North Korean People's Army.

"No sweat," troops were told. "Just a few Chinese volunteers trying to make a show for their defeated North Korean brothers." Sure.

After several miles of swift semi-running using ancient footpaths, the person leading the company suddenly and unexpectedly veered from the path and headed hurriedly across virgin countryside, knee-high in brush and deep snow. Being one of the last in the column now turned to a distinct advantage because brush and snow was well trampled by those who preceded. At last, the rear of the column found the going easier.

Eventually troops started a steep climb, as surrounding frozen foothills, white with glistening snow, gradually mutated into lofty mountains heavy with tremendous drifts of white powder. Laboriously, troops tried to navigate the steep incline, hampered by the absence of a path between the walls of deep, deep snow. To be a trail blazer in the lofty and bitterly cold mountains of North Korea was a formidable task in itself. Added to that, the burden of heavy weapons made it all the more difficult to ascend. Despite the intense cold, everyone perspired freely from the protracted and furiously-paced march, and by the time the summit was attained, troops collapsed in utter fatigue. Extreme perspiration flowed, immediately hardening into ice. Throats burned from bitter cold air as soldiers struggled to breathe, desperately in need of oxygen.

Concurrently, the adversary began firing captured American heavy mortars onto the mountain where the remaining members of King Company were positioned.

A carnival of chaos and pandemonium spread over the mountain top.

One moment troops were at rest on top of the mountain gasping for air and sensing the sweat freezing on faces and bodies, and in the very next instant, the conflict erupted violently again, shattering bodies, minds and morale.

"Incoming Mail!"[48]

Heavy mortar fire was dead on in the sector of the hapless, disorganized company. What was once a well-trained, skillful cadre of troops, recognized throughout the regiment as the preeminent company because of the leadership of Captain Hughes, now degenerated into a rabble of bewildered soldiers.

Cohesiveness was evacuated with Captain Hughes.

Chinese forces zeroed in the coordinates of the area prior to the company approach of the summit. Missiles plummeted rapidly and silently in, exploding methodically among confused soldiers. The first projectile displayed the usual fire, smoke, and deafening noise, but the terrifying scream of shrapnel was lacking even though the enormous blast caved in an area forming a large crater in the heavy snow.

That was no dud. This is real, some thought, *but what happened to the shrapnel?*

I don't believe this, many reflected to themselves.

Absence of shrapnel was what one would expect in a training exercise or a war movie. Could it have been a dud? The real thing would have spewed deadly debris all over, and the explosion would have taken out the troops milling nervously about. Yet, all of the components of a live mortar attack were there, *sans* the shrapnel. But that was just the first missile, and the preamble to hell in the snow was about to be put into play.

The enemy had our coordinates, and they made deadly use of them. Mortars began raining in, and there was no protection. No one knew from whence they were coming. Tree limbs and heavy layers of snow were falling everywhere, severed by white hot, lethal shrapnel. Some mortars exploded when they hit trees, fatal shrapnel tearing the mountaintop apart. Snow and dirt were exploding in large clumps as the whistling death of soaring steel shrapnel came screaming in, unabated. Anxiety and bewilderment set in. We couldn't stay here much longer without losing every man. Despite the below-zero temperature, blood seeped on the snow from those who collapsed to the ground, dead.

The mortar attack was a prelude to a massive enemy encirclement of

---

[48] Mortars have a lofty trajectory when dispatched on their deadly mission and explode as if hell rained death from heaven. Artillery fire is as lethal, but because of its relatively flat trajectory one sometimes can seek shelter. The difference is that mortar fire often is soundless as it hones in on target. One moment everything seems to be in order, the next instant anyone near is catapulted in the air, only to land dead or dismembered. Author.

our position by the Chinese Army, and we remaining survivors lacked sufficient firepower to repel the enemy or to staunch the human tide. Company personnel were nearly out of ammunition and soon the foe would advance, rout and kill survivors. Only the highest echelon of command was aware of the near destruction of every unit on line in the 8th Army. Headquarters was overwhelmed with a flood of radio communications frantically pouring in, pleading for reinforcements to counter the massive CCF attacks.

The new captain suddenly screamed an irrational order. "Every man for himself!" he shrieked in panic.

The Army has a strict, ironclad structure of a chain of command. No one had the right to usurp the orders of the temporary commander, but in this case someone should have taken command. They call it *mutiny* in the maritime service, but some action was needed in our present predicament, to prevent total collapse and the ultimate disintegration of King Company.

The acting commander, by coincidence, had been in his first battle just the night before when the Chinese struck in force. We heard rumors this captain had remained frozen in terror, huddled at the bottom of his foxhole. First-time battle is a mind-numbing terror never erased from one's memory. Nevertheless, the acting commander was responsible for, and in command of, King Company. Had Lieutenants Miller and Suddaby, along with a number of stray soldiers, not have been cut off and isolated by enemy, subsequent to the formidable Chinese suicide attack, this would have been a much different situation.[49] Any one of the four very capable lieutenants could have taken control of the company and kept the remainder of the unit together as a cohesive team without the consent of the acting

---

[49] At the first reunion after a 50-year hiatus, I commented to Colonel Hughes about the disintegration of the company, among many other long conversations as to the war. "Skipper, if you weren't hit so badly the night of the Chinese attack, we could have shot our way out and got back to the lines if you were there, and the whole company probably could have made it out. When the replacement captain said, 'Every man for himself,' I knew the store was closed, and we (King Company) just disintegrated."

He pondered on that for several moments, slowly drawing on his sweet smelling pipe smoke—his pipe seeming to be forever a part of him. He removed it and slowly replied, "Yes, the acting captain was court martialed for that. I knew he wasn't going to make it as a company commander and I was going to recommend to the battalion commander that he (acting commander) not take over the company, but the Chinese attack happened before I could arrange anything."

Captain Hughes was up for promotion to Major which would have taken him from the direct combat zone, to the relative safety of the rear, raised his pay, and elevated his up-and-coming military career. He turned the promotion down because he believed the acting company commander was not qualified. Author.

commander. Remnants of the company were in a chaotic situation while the Chinese Volunteer Army was in the process of taking apart the entire 35th Regiment, now completely isolated from all units in the 8th Army. King Company was now down to approximately three-platoon strength, both from the original attack and the devastating mortar blitzkrieg.

Chinese forces utilized the skills of captured American soldiers to great advantage. American soldiers were forced to either load ammunition, or they were pushed ahead of attacking Chinese infantry, as human shields. The precise accuracy of the heavy mortar barrage was most likely executed by captured Americans, forced to fire on fellow comrades, under threat of death.

This was new enemy, with new tactics, no longer restricting combat exclusively to night time. Here, boldly, in broad daylight, they threw away any semblance of caution, swarming everywhere like frenzied, ravenous locusts.

~~

The company broke apart. Lieutenant Suddaby and my platoon leader, Lieutenant Miller, were presumed to have been killed in action the night before. The remaining rifle platoons were in a confused state because of the absence of our platoon leaders. We lost contact with our usual squads, platoons, and even close friends.

Lieutenant DeLashment and a couple of sergeants stepped forward to rescue what was left of a disintegrating situation. They began hastily to organize a withdrawal, and so the surviving members of the company formed into three separate groups. My friends, Bob Jones and Rodney Scott, and I each ended up in different groups, even though we had served in the same nine-man squad together since our survival at Anui.

Lieutenant DeLashment said, "1st Platoon, follow me." His battle-hardened platoon automatically fell in behind him, as I silently applauded his leadership abilities. Lieutenant DeLashment's group quickly headed down the west side of the mountain, forging a new trail through heavy snow drifts.

A sergeant stepped forward and shouted, "Those going out with me, fall in, and let's move out!" and he and about 40 soldiers followed DeLashment's platoon to the west.

Shortly thereafter a sergeant we didn't recognize, who was possibly from the weapons platoon, shouted, "Follow me and let's go!" I threw my lot in with this third and last group of about 40 soldiers who fled via the west side, able to follow a path forged by the two preceding trail-blazer groups.

~~

At the same time, around 20 survivors of Suddaby's platoon attempted to escape down the east side of the mountain, where a primitive road lay, not realizing that the enemy was forming assault lines.

Chinese soldiers concealed in the fields east of the road had King Company under surveillance from the beginning. The section of King Company who fled east toward the main road attempted to seek shelter in a culvert beneath a small, rural bridge. Instead they were brought under concentrated machine gun and rifle fire. Without respite, fire was ripping into confused, disoriented young American soldiers, generally from the east. The small-arms fire, torrential, immediate, and severe, was pouring unrelentingly on hapless soldiers. The enemy knew the company's location but King Company survivors could not return defensive fire because of the well-camouflaged Chinese forces, numbering in the thousands. The Chinese dragon was everywhere.

CCF small arms fire continued unabated. The area was saturated with ferocious CCF infantry; they began a rush and came out of concealment, boldly exposing themselves, forming frontal assault lines, vastly outnumbering American soldiers by more than 20 to one.

Arthur W. Buckley, a corporal assigned to Suddaby's 2nd Platoon, was in the group that fled to the road, and he is now possibly the last survivor of that specific debacle. Mr. Buckley related his appalling experience in written correspondence to the author:

> I thought that I would relate a few lines to your book with respect to about the time that you were captured.
>
> Actually, the only unit that came down that hill with me (when we met the tanks) was the remnants of the second platoon led by our platoon Sgt. Edgar "Pappy" Pappert. We had stayed on the hill to cover that part of the company that was led out by Lt. Suddaby and some other platoon leader. Lt. Suddaby tells me that he had with him the 1st and 3rd platoons (At least initially). I have no idea where the fourth platoon was, maybe mixed in with other groups. He apparently got separated from them a few hours later (I'm not sure how long that few hours were). Suddaby seems to have gotten separated from that group at some time. The platoon that you were in was, at least initially, with him and another platoon leader. In any case he came out about 5 or 6 days later, I think, by him. Suddaby said at some point when crossing a road, he and a Sgt. got separated from the main group. He said that when they tried to go back to get that group (your platoon??) they found that, that group had been captured.

When Pappert's group came down the hill on the north side there were only about 20 of us including 4 or 5 wounded. We initially came down to the MSR where we started to take a lot of fire. We ducked into a culvert (small bridge) under the road to return fire. I still had my BAR and we had a machine gun (without tripod) presumably from the fourth squad (I was in the 2nd squad). Shortly after this we heard the tanks coming, we thought initially they might be gook tanks, but they were from the 89th Tank BN (Charlie co. I think). Someone ran back to contact them and they started to give us support and cover while we ran back to them. I will never forget how happy I was to climb up on that tank!! The name on the side of that tank was "The Lemon". It's funny but I had not thought about the name of that tank in 50 years!

For whatever reason the 3 tanks decided not to go down the road (Thank God, we heard later that the Chinks had several road blocks between where we were and our lines, where ever they were) The tanks went cross country before turning South to our lines (It could have been several hours or a couple of days). It was a few days after we got back to our lines that I got hit by shrapnel (around the 2nd or 3rd of Dec). I was back in Japan warm and safe when Suddaby (and yourself) got back to "safety".

In any case that is my recollection as far as it goes. I do remember that when we were coming down the hill Pappert sent a few guys out to check out a couple of huts that were on our left on our way down, the guys never came back (I'm sure glad that he wanted to keep the BAR with him!!)"

Another American soldier situated further north related that when he saw American tanks approach into view, he observed Chinese soldiers swarming over them by the score, each trying desperately, in a suicidal manner, to be the one to have the honor of disabling and destroying a tank by bare hands. The multitude of enemy soldiers appeared as if they were insects, so many seeking a position on the beleaguered tanks in an attempt to stop them. It was indescribable, deadly combat. I know of no other campaigns where armor of any nation was literally attacked by swarms of unarmed soldiers. While continuing their methodical, lumbering retreat southward, the tanks, apparently acting on radio communication, rotated the turrets of their armored conveyances mounted with 30-caliber machine guns, and commenced firing at each others' tanks, shooting barbarians off of opposing tanks as if they were multitudes of ants being brushed from a picnic table.

Those Chinese soldiers who attempted to force entry into a tank's hatch by blocking the driver's view window, fell forward and were crushed under the wide, plodding steel tracks of the massive Sherman tanks. Blood, flesh and pulverized bone was splattered and ground into the frozen dirt road by the icy and muddy tank tracks. Now those dedicated armor attackers were transformed from humans to nothing more than cheap, shoddy veneer on the path.

The armored armada followed up by turning on torrents of ear-splitting 76-millimeter cannon accompanied by corresponding machine gun fire, blazing east in an ineffective endeavor to hold the fanatically charging enemy at bay. Enemy responded with coordinated firepower on the tanks and the stranded American infantry soldiers. The bold defensive action of the tanks eventually allowed isolated, pin-downed survivors to race from the culvert to the sanctuary of escaping tanks. Some managed to climb aboard the Sherman tanks as the enormous vehicles forged relentlessly ahead, with the determination to break out. Those who were unable to mount the methodically plodding armored destroyers positioned themselves between the sides of the skillfully driven tanks and the road in order to avoid the concentration of small arms fire.

Heroic tank crews risked their lives to protect that group from King Company. Those survivors escaped relatively unscathed. The tanks continuously shielded the struggling soldiers until they ultimately reached the safety of Allied lines, several days later.

~~

The enemy was east. To head west away from the mortars and firepower of the enemy seemed the logical course of action to our three groups. We hoped to navigate our way south in a risky attempt to escape capture and ultimately regroup with the decimated American 8th Army.

Lieutenant DeLashment's group, the first to break out, had moved swiftly and silently down the west side of the frigid mountain. The time was anybody's guess, probably around late morning. After a two-hour struggle along a southwest corridor near the ridgeline, they heard someone call, "Hey! We are down here! Down here! Come on down, we need help!" The shouts reverberated from the valley floor. Some stray unit appeared to be in dire trouble.

Lieutenant DeLashment quickly led the way down the mountain in the belief it was another American unit similarly isolated by the tremendous incursion of Chinese forces. Good. If they had sufficient ammunition, with two units melded together they would present a formidable fighting force to shoot their way to freedom. Certainly they would constitute more forces than those left on the mountain.

A strong odor of garlic permeated the still, chilled air as they approached the group. Garlic was chewed and consumed by the clove by

Chinese soldiers in the belief that the contents warded off the common cold and other ailments. By then, Lieutenant DeLashment knew it was over. He had unwittingly led his group into an enemy encampment.

This Chinese Army unit made the easiest capture of their command. They bluffed the Americans into approaching them. Fortunately, this group of captives, including Rodney Scott of the 3rd Platoon, was treated relatively humanely. The captives were fed and photographed, posed as what they were—captured American prisoners of war— for the benefit of the ecstatic Asian home front. The Chinese captors returned unloaded M-1 rifles to the American prisoners to grasp for the photographer, who attentively posed and snapped photos of the prisoners. The rifles were taken back and then the interrogations began. The niceties evaporated.

Most likely the Chinese commanding officer was the one who spoke fluent English, and who deceived DeLashment's unit into leaving the hill. This leader must have been in close contact for years with westerners, generally Christian missionaries, and he may have harbored some relatively positive feelings toward Americans.

The captors permitted the prisoners to sleep under the trees until night when they were roughly awakened and herded together, force-marched on the road all night and then held in houses in abandoned villages during the day. The guards assumed positions around the perimeter of the village, primarily for one reason. American fighter planes were known to routinely strafe villages to see if enemy soldiers would flee. Had a captive panicked and attempted to bolt from a house under air attack, enemy sentries hiding among trees would immediately shoot down the fleeing prisoner. That order was made very clear to all captured prisoners, because the Chinese did not desire to be on the receiving end of a continuous massive sortie by the Air Force.

During the second day of captivity, as Lieutenant DeLashment's 1st Platoon was routinely housed in a village following their second all-night march, an air strike occurred. The fighter planes made their usual strafe of the village with 50-caliber machine gun rounds. One projectile struck Frederick Worrill, a member of Lieutenant DeLashment's platoon who was packed tightly together with other prisoners in one of the houses. Many were killed instantly. Unbelievably, Worrill was struck by a round and survived. He was the first person I ever heard of who survived a wound from a 50-caliber bullet. The round entered his left lower back, and ricocheted from his hipbone and lodged in his lower back. The element that saved Worrill's life was that the copper projectile apparently disengaged from the lead insert, and the lead insert is what struck him. Worrill believes that the sortie was aborted when an American prisoner with red hair fell dead out the door onto the ground outside. He might have been observed by the attacking Air Force, which noted they were obviously American prisoners.

Worrill was trucked that night by Chinese captors to an underground North Korean hospital where a North Korean doctor, at the request of the Chinese captors, operated on him. Had this situation occurred under the jurisdiction of North Korean soldiers, he would have been shot at the scene. Worrill's wound left him with a hole in his back one could place a thumb into, and a lifetime respect for the Chinese.

~~

The last two bands who made the dangerous journey down the west side of the mountain each met a different destiny. At separate times during their attempt to escape from behind enemy lines, each group was captured.

I was in one of them.

CAPTURE!

In the first six months of Korea, American arms faltered on the battlefield because of a lack of American material and psychological preparation for bloodletting, and in those first six months almost all the American POW's were taken . . . . A human being in a prison camp, in the hands of his enemies, is flesh and shuddering vulnerable... In a POW cage, he is flesh, no matter how strong the spirit. He has no gun, he has no leader, and his comrades are flesh, too. Fehrenbach, p.316.

We need to get the hell out of here, like right now, I was thinking. The other two columns had moved out immediately after our captured mortars zeroed in on us. Fortunately for now, the dense, snow-packed trees were taking the brunt of the first explosions, but troops sensed the immediate danger of remaining in this zeroed-in, one-sided battleground. The screaming, white-hot shrapnel was right on target and King Company was the unfortunate recipient.[50]

The third group assembled quickly and followed the same path down the mountain on the make-shift trail that the first two groups before had forged, moving down and dead ahead through snow-bound, virgin terrain. The hastily-drafted plan was to separate at the bottom of the mountain where each column would proceed independent of the others, each group going generally west, then swinging south in an attempt to locate American lines. There was little snow on the valley floor but the glacial Manchurian winter cold chilled soldiers to the bone as they anxiously moved out. It was well below freezing and our inadequate clothing was little barrier against the unbelievable temperature. I had mislaid my mittens earlier, last recalling having them when I had to remove them during the major assault by the Chinese Volunteer Army to reload BAR magazines for the shooter.

Members of the company who opted to escape via the east, were no doubt moving rapidly out as well, putting a quickly drawn escape plan in action. Anyone who lingered on that god-forsaken hill would never survive the deadly saturation mortar barrage.

The morning slipped into late afternoon, while the ungodly below-zero temperature stood still. If there was a temperature gauge, surely it would have shattered from the unbearable cold. Nothing could move eas-

---

[50] *Shrapnel* was invented in 1784 by British Artillery Officer Lieutenant Henry Shrapnel, who devised an anti-personnel projectile filled with musket balls that were timed to release over the heads of enemy infantry, inflicting lethal damage. Now it is the projectile itself that explodes, scattering the deadly shrapnel as we know it. *Shrapnel* in the strict sense is now considered passé. Author.

ily in the wind and snow sweeping out of Siberia. My sense was that our group was heading somewhat northwest. It wasn't logical to be heading back into obvious enemy territory, but the leader of this group apparently knew more than others. Whoever was leading us had to be better qualified than the acting captain whom we last noticed back on the hill.

It was an easy march; we were traveling light. Having consumed the last of the wretched food the evening before the attack, we were carrying no heavy C-ration cans. The bulk of our ammunition was nearly depleted during the attack. During the intensive firefight I had the golden opportunity to finally fire the two rifle grenades; though they were not heavy, they had been awkward to carry.[51]

Following an ancient footpath, we marched silently, single file off the mountain, still relatively unconcerned. We believed the Chinese were withdrawing further north, as they had been before they suddenly turned on us and engaged us in that bloody battle. We thought their losses probably depleted their forces just as when we wiped out a regiment of the infamous North Korean 6th Division on 3 September. Now the North Korean Army was destroyed, we had been told. Of course, that was incorrect, as Communist Volunteers replaced their Asian contemporaries as a more numerous though less well-armed foe. But we didn't know that then.

~~

We were sure we heard them before they saw us, as our leader motioned us by hand signal into the brush-covered dry creek bed adjacent to the native footpath that had been our route of escape. The group collectively and silently slipped into the temporary sanctuary even though we were a reasonably large group of about 40 troops.

Breaths were held and bodies froze. Condensed air emanated from breathing and it was wondered if the foe could discern that. A careless movement by any of us—stepping on a dry twig or branch—would sound like a rifle shot in this isolated, rural land. We could hear them talking rapidly, and by the tone of their voices they seemed overly excited. The brush was dense enough to conceal us, we believed.

Then we realized that they were aware of us. The dense foliage was

---

[51] The weather continued to remain below freezing, but it was nothing to equal the night of the awful, initial, massive Chinese attack. Much later I learned through history and tales from other survivors, that extreme subzero weather froze weapons of soldiers, disabling arms, causing them to become inoperative. Many tales of soldiers having to urinate on weapons in order to operate them certainly has credence, given the need to urinate that is common to traumatic crisis. Author.

similar to a rough-hewn tunnel, made up of heavy leaves, impervious to the Manchurian winter; even so, it was clear that we were detected. Now it was the enemy's time for revenge. A solitary Chinese or North Korean soldier stepped forward from a shallow rise in the land screaming an incomprehensible order to the group in hiding. The brazen enemy soldier materialized boldly into view, cradling an automatic rifle in his right arm, and extending his left arm in a horizontal fashion as he waved his hand up and down from the wrist, the peculiar signal of Asians meaning, *come here!*

He was wearing the mustard green-colored uniform of the enemy, but at this point no one knew whether he was North Korean or Chinese. There was no question as to what to expect if they were North Korean, but no one knew the Chinese Army philosophy of treatment of prisoners of war.

There was no question as to which side he represented, evidenced by the bright red star above the bill of his combat cap. He repeatedly shouted the same unintelligible orders, and in unison with the hand gesture, the meaning was quite clear—*come here!* The surly glare etched on his grim face portended a *take no prisoners* look, and it was believed he would kill the group in a minute if no one submitted to his order. His nationality was soon discovered. He had to be North Korean.

"It's over. Drop your weapons and follow me," the sergeant sighed flatly in a feeble attempt to mask deep resignation in his voice.

I didn't recognize the sergeant, so he obviously was from one of the other platoons, most likely the weapons platoon whose unit was generally isolated from the three rifle platoons. The weapons platoon was always to the company rear with the mortars. All presumed the sergeant knew best, and all other options were null and void, but I wasn't excited about the decision to surrender, reflecting on past experiences with surrendering to the brutal enemy.

The sergeant dropped his rifle carelessly to the ground, probably to emphasize by demonstration the futility of further action. He bent over to clear the over-hanging foliage, moved forward from the brush onto the meadow with arms held high in the air, the internationally recognized sign of surrender.

The others similarly discarded their weapons as they exited the sanctuary, raising arms in surrender, following the sergeant. I was on the left side of the group, nearest the path and I realized later that I did a very curious thing, given that we were directed to abandon our rifles. Instead of dropping my weapon to the ground, for some irrational reason, I carefully leaned my M-1 Rifle against the dry creek bank, more out of habit and perhaps subconsciously in the belief that it might be needed again, ready to fire. Really a ridiculous idea, given that the M-1 held only eight rounds and reloading would be impossible under these dire circumstances of obviously being surrounded. At any rate, I wasn't sure if I had more than the minimum amount of ammunition in my weapon. Not that it mattered. A semi-automatic rifle is no contest against the brutal automatic burst of an AK-47.

The platoon-sized group strode from the brush-covered creek onto the peaceful lea, single file, being somewhat hampered by restrictive growth at the egress, raising arms automatically as they exited. I looked at each one in our group as they passed me, and the thought struck me: I was the sole soldier in this particular group that was one of the 21 survivors in our first battle at Anui on 27 July.[52] My anxiousness to avoid surrender was compounded by that fact, and I was the only one out of all of the others who personally knew of the unspeakable atrocities committed by the North Korean People's Army. It didn't matter if one was an untrained teenage soldier or an innocent Korean citizen.

We had no concept about the combat ethics of the Chinese Volunteers and whether our lives would be spared upon surrender. For that matter, apparently no one had a thought until a brief moment later whether they were Chinese or Korean soldiers.

I estimate it was 1600 hours, 28 November, Korea time, when I was the last person to reluctantly abandon my hiding place and move onto the meadow, arms raised in surrender. I held to the left side and rear of the widely dispersed, disorganized group. My eyes were furtively glancing about, as I tried to grasp as much of this complicated situation as possible.

Pandemonium was instantaneous. Gunfire erupted from the far right! I couldn't get a fix on where the gunfire was coming from, but in a matter of a split second, I recognized the rate of fire as being distinctly from a Soviet burp gun, the infamous AK-47.

My comrades were collapsing like rag dolls, one spinning as if he were a grotesque ballerina pirouetting to the fatal roar of the Russian burp gun. The clearing seemed to erupt like a mighty volcano, screaming bullets recasting the peaceful meadow into a bizarre killing field. Agonized

---

[52] That terrible engagement not only had decimated our ranks, it also erased the regiment from the annals of the history books pertaining to the Korean War. The majority of military historians of the Korean War never knew of the 29th Infantry Regiment from Okinawa. Surrender now called our survival into question. Author.

screams of pain from dying soldiers pierced the bitterly cold air, now garbled with fierce shouting in a foreign tongue. Confused soldiers were bolting powerlessly for their lives, only to drop mortally wounded from blazing guns. The stench of residue gunpowder smoke collided with the frozen afternoon temperature, and the smell lingered heavily in the still, frosty air.

Honed by months of combat experience and coupled with the incredible good fortune that I was the last person in line, I instantaneously froze in a split second to assess the source of the firing. I immediately realized I was the farthest away from the source of the lethal gunfire. I grabbed the soldier one pace ahead of me by his left arm, pulling to let him know that there was possibly a way out of this unprovoked slaughter. We spun and ran for our lives back along the same ancient footpath whence we came.

Without any signal or word to my friend, I leaped feet first into a ditch that ran parallel to the right side of the path, and landed on my back, followed closely by my companion who apparently noted my actions and intuitively duplicated the movement.

There lay an abundance of dead, dry plant growth, a collateral victim of the severest Korean winter in 30 years, and we quickly covered our bodies with foliage and lay silent. I knew that I had not totally covered my entire body by weeds to camouflage myself. I didn't know the condition of my buddy, but I hoped that he was alert enough to comply, given the disastrous consequences. Lying in the late afternoon in the cold ditch motionless, my thoughts crazily returned to that awful night of the escape from the schoolhouse. Perhaps by reliving my action of freezing in response to that dreadful, unexpected flare, I somehow, unconsciously, communicated the solution to this current crisis to my companion. I prayed that he covered himself and remained motionless as well.

The shooting stopped as suddenly as it started, though the guttural shouting in the foreign tongue continued unabated. Shouts and screams seemed to be everywhere. My heart was pounding to the point that I thought it would be overheard by the enemy, but we didn't move, as we lay paralyzed with fear in the frozen ditch, flat on our backs. Moreover, we didn't dare attempt to cover ourselves further lest the enemy notice movement.

God was good to us that fateful late afternoon. No enemy soldiers walked near the path where we were hiding, although we could hear them talking, searching the heavy brush covering the dry creek bed for possible stragglers. Incredibly, we were hiding just across the footpath from where they were searching, not more than ten feet away. The simple truth, I think, is the enemy simply didn't believe that anyone escaped.

We would have been numb with shock to know that our valiant Army was currently engaged in the longest retreat in the history of the United States Army—over 250 miles to what the Army believed to be the sanctuary of South Korea. The Chinese Volunteer Army would not dare to cross the politically charged border into South Korea, or so the Americans fervently prayed.

Nightfall comes early in the dead of winter on the Korean Peninsula, especially when one is so far north as was our unit. Dusk won over by smothering the light of day. With the darkness came the body-numbing, paralyzing, sub-freezing cold, which is beyond description. I thought that I would die of the cold, but we continued to lie, silent and still. Eventually we stirred slowly and stiffly from hiding, keenly alert, but nearly frozen from the icy temperature. Our bodies ached from the stillness we endured in the freezing cold. The enemy apparently departed earlier, but we were afraid to move until dark. Now we were desperate to find our way back to American lines, wherever they lay.

We were totally lost. Not having the slightest concept of where we were or in which direction to head, we began our forced flight. It seemed as if some gargantuan monster picked us up and placed us in the middle of nowhere, testing our ability to extricate ourselves from an impossible maze.[53] We had dim light, courtesy of a full moon as we forged two abreast through a barren frozen field, unaware we had gradually drifted from the weathered path,

We didn't talk and perhaps we should have. To risk being heard by the enemy was a remote concern, but in reflection, by mutually agreeing to a plan of escape might have proved to be more effective. Still, what plan could possibly be formulated? We needed a start and we had no conception of where to begin. We were equally ignorant of the topographical surroundings and the absence of civilization or of any roads. We were lost souls and we were devastated.

I recalled the days of my escape from Anui. While behind enemy lines for six days we didn't talk at all, and in fact, that is how we heard the two

---

[53] Here ridges trend mostly north-south but valleys extend in all directions. The region is rugged, partly forested, and well drained but unfavorable for cross-country movement. Hills and ridges are generally 1,500 to 5,000 feet high and are steep....Existing roads are narrow and winding and cross steep passes 2,000 to 3,600 feet high. JANIS, study of Korea, 1945.

stragglers we met on the road during my first escape. We heard them talking, and they would have been shot dead as a result, were they enemy instead of misplaced stragglers like ourselves.

I was in absolute despair, yet so very grateful to be alive. I was burdened with the fear of the unknown. Words cannot describe the terrible trepidation that washed over me. The futility of being just isolated soldiers in the middle of the avenging Chinese Army in enemy territory, freezing because of inadequate clothing, was so depressingly overwhelming. Frustrated, anxious, wandering hopelessly and aimlessly, not having an inkling as to which way to head. Knowing now that we were deep in enemy controlled land and knowing they would kill us on sight.[54]

Hunger pangs began gnawing at our stomachs. It seemed to be about two days since we had eaten. Those awful C-rations that tasted so bad in fair or frigid weather and weighed us down during our forced marches would be an epicurean delight at this point. No cigarettes between us, though we knew better than to even think of smoking at night in enemy territory.

We wandered hopelessly lost for hours on end, becoming more discouraged with every step. My hands were throbbing with pain as a consequence of losing my mittens. Our march was on a frozen field and the noise of our boots striking the frozen ground sounded like firecrackers exploding.

Following the initial attack of the Chinese I made an error in judgment. I should have paid attention to the shade of the uniforms of the slain enemy. The thought never occurred to me that we had encountered North Korean assault units still viable as cohesive fighting units. I had a sense that they were in fact Chinese troops simply by the manner in which they attacked. While the Chinese were swarming to our positions with sheer manpower, they were swift, silent, steadfast warriors, unlike the screaming, human sea attacks by the NKPA. The CCF employed an array of signaling devices, not so much to unnerve the opponents, as it was to coordinate attack procedures. Now, I will never be sure to which army our

---

[54] The North Korean People's Army did not sign the Geneva Convention, or abide by its provisions. Conversely, it was later learned Chinese Communist Forces set examples of humane treatment toward American prisoners of war, particularly in prisoner camps. The camps under the NKPA killed almost half of the prison population, which provoked an international outcry against their brutality. Once the Chinese Communists Forces assumed authority for Allied prisoners, deaths and inhumane treatment plummeted. That is not to say that there were not exceptions to violations of the Convention on both sides of the barbed wire. Some South Korean Army soldiers were equally inhumane. Author.

group surrendered, though it is a moot point.

I believe that in the total history of our country, encompassing all of our armed conflicts both here and abroad, I had won a first prize. The fact is I was indeed, captured, even though only momentarily. I must hold the dubious distinction of being the shortest-held prisoner of war in United States history. While the Army allowed me *one day* as an official American prisoner of war, I was to later endure another unique distinction pertaining to the Korean War.

I was the only American on record to escape from North Korea during the UN's total and permanent retreat from that country.

MY BUDDY AND ME

> When we let freedom ring, when we let it ring from every village and every hamlet, from every state and every city, we will be able to speed up that day when all of God's children, black men and white men, Jews and Gentiles, Protestants and Catholics, will be able to join hands and sing in the words of that old Negro spiritual "Free at last! Free at last! Thank God Almighty, we are free at last!" Martin Luther King, Jr.

Somehow we ended up in those awful, titanic, snow-bound Chokyuryong Mountains without a beginning or an end. One time we supposed we were on the valley floor that gradually gave rise to low foothills. Our purpose was to maintain a straight line to avoid getting disoriented during the night. What we thought was sensible reasoning caused us somehow to become completely disoriented in the lofty heights without realizing it.

The idea to maintain a somewhat straight line heading south to locate American lines failed. The lofty, snowed-in mountains twisted and turned, rendering our decision invalid. The approximately 30-degree below zero temperature kept us moving for fear of freezing to death. We were totally spent, having marched ever since our pullback, capture and escape. We hadn't eaten in three or four days and the pangs of hunger were ever so slowly ebbing from our systems. The need for food was gradually diminishing. Moreover, we were without weapons, water, cigarettes, or canteens and no mittens, extra woolen socks, or replacement felt insoles for our sno-pacs, caustically referred to as *Mickey Mouse* boots.

Our bearings were skewed as we struggled in the jet-black night, slipping, and collapsing precariously down one draw, only to struggle, crawling on knees and ungloved hands back to firm ground only to plummet down the opposite slope. No words were spoken between us, not because of possible enemy activity, but to preserve every ounce of energy required to forge on. The absence of any rudimentary paths indicated that no one, at least in modern times, had ever entered these Goliath heights of the earth.

In any other country in the world we would have detected lights from vehicles or houses. Not here. It was if the bowels of the earth swallowed us whole, only to spit us out in the middle of the most isolated spot on earth, where no one had gone before. There was no trail to follow, no light to find our way—just bitter, bitter, god-awful cold. It seemed that initially, despite the towering elevation, there were only patches of snow with which to contend. The below zero temperature had to be much lower than if it were snowing. The snow was to come later as we continued to climb.[55]

A brief rest was mandated on rare occasions, but the bitter cold would not allow us any respite. Occasionally we whispered to each other, more for morale then for advice because neither of us had the slightest idea of what to do. One thing we did know. There was no fear that the enemy would be around. Only fools and forlorn lost soldiers would be found in this unforgiving mountain chain. The Chokyuryongs separated us from the valley from whence the Chonchong River flowed, and the jagged west coast of North Korea. The infamous Chonchong River was the initial site of the push of overwhelming Chinese Communist Forces against 8th Army.

The Battle of the Chongchon was the most critical and bloody battle of the entire Korean War with the greatest loss of life at any one time to the American Army. The 2nd Infantry Division sustained by far the greatest ratio of casualties when fresh Chinese Forces poured through crumbling defensive lines en masse, to inflict the fatal *coup de main* on American and ROK forces.

We were but two further casualties of that infamous mêlée of the Chongchon, but our confrontation with the *Golden Horde* was not until two days later—27 November 1950.

We barely struggled on. The cold, the exhaustion, the forlorn feeling of abandonment sapped us of our last iota of strength. The two of us finally collapsed into a small indentation in the earth; immediately, without a word spoken, we grasped each other, wrapping arms around one another, melding our faint body heat together, permitting each to survive. Had we not, we both would have perished of hypothermia immediately on that bitter arctic night. We were able to doze only fitfully for brief moments, which alleviated a minute portion of our exhausted state. I accepted the notion that if either of us were able to grasp the substance of sleep, he should not stir, lest he rouse the other. It had to be that way so that we two could survive.

Dawn rolled in slowly because the fog in the still sky acted as a barrier. It seemed even more frigid than ever as we continued our usual

---

[55] "The sight of this terrain" he (Ridgway) wrote, "was of little comfort to a soldier commanding a mechanized army. The granite peaks rose to 6,000 feet, the ridges were knife-edged, the slopes steep, and the narrow valleys twisted and turned like snakes. The roads were trails and the lower hills were covered with scrub oak and stunted pines, fine cover for a single soldier who knew how to conceal himself. It was guerrilla country, an ideal battleground for the walking Chinese rifleman, but a miserable place for our road-bound troops who rode on wheels." Toland, p. 377.

stumbling, wandering lost through the snowbound mountains again. We stopped for no more than moments and yet it seemed an eternity.

The obscured sun was trying to punch through the gloomy sky without success, but it was enough for us. We now knew where east was by the faint light and we took advantage of the brief information for direction. Our mountain range disagreed. While we were trying to maintain a southerly direction, the mountains refused to accommodate us. To head south would mean to crawl down one steep mountain slope only to climb back up yet another perilous mountain cliff in order to maintain our direction. It was impossible.

Staying on the topographical crest, more familiarly called the skyline in Army vernacular, rerouted us in the craziest directions, which accounted for our becoming hopelessly lost again and again.

Oh, for a compass!

I reached into the pocket of my fatigue trousers and retrieved the pocket watch that I had taken from the body of a dead Chinese soldier following our 27 November baptism of fire with the Chinese—the all night battle. The watch worked only intermittently, which turned out to be worse than no watch at all. We were taught in basic training how to utilize a timepiece as a compass.[56] But one had to first know the time of day. I would look at the watch periodically, and find that it had stopped movement! We were frustrated from being lost in such serpentine and unforgiving land without any reasonable direction. We stopped, rested and hid in the lofty mountains until we estimated when the sun was at its zenith. We reset the watch when it appeared to be about noon, so we reoriented ourselves once more and started off again in what we believed to be a somewhat southerly direction.

After about two hours of further struggle through the massive snowdrifts of the mountain range, slipping and stumbling through virgin territory, we decided to check our bearings. The watch indicated 20 minutes past noon! In frustration, I threw the watch into the canyon below. To be in possession of a watch of Chinese origin was the kiss of death anyway, if we were to be recaptured, and the watch working only sporadically made it that much more of a liability.

The days were short at this latitude at this time of year but we pressed

---

[56] Point the hour hand to the sun. Look to the space between the hour hand and the 12. Halfway between is due south in the morning. In the afternoon do the reverse. Look at the hour hand pointed to the sun, find the 12, and halfway back toward the 12 is south. Editor

on until well after nightfall. The bitter cold became more pronounced once the hazy sun faded from the horizon, so we continued our self-imposed forced march just to keep from freezing to death. We were once again confused as to what direction to go, but we had to do something to stay alive. An ever-so-brief rest would end in our freezing to death.

Again the frigid cloudy day evolved into another moonless, starless night, with the heavens as black as coal. It became even more difficult to keep track of one another as we forged a new trail. Now we were caught up in heavy snow again, as we trailed, one behind the other.

The black night caused us to become separated somehow and anxiety set in. We called to each other in quiet tones to no avail. We both had the sense to stop where we were, to avoid a further drift from our locations.

Pete, Pete where are you? The voice was so faint that I could barely hear.
Over here!
Where?
Over here!
Where is here?
Over here!

We gradually increased the level of tone to a shout. The forest would muffle our voices, and no one else would be so insane as to be where we were in the first place.

Where are you?
Over here!
Keep yelling, so I can find you!
Over here! Over here! Over here!

We found each other at last, and it was as if two long-lost friends, separated for years, united again. We said nothing more, but deep in our hearts we were so gratified to find that we were no longer alone. To be on one's own in those artic, treacherous mountains would mean death. The sub-zero cold would extinguish the life out of each of us individually, but as we embraced each other again, it would provide an extension of life. So when we could no long continue because of complete exhaustion and sleep deprivation, we once more provided life-saving heat to each other during precious minutes in the frigid night. Sleep was but momentary, but each second of collapsed stupor allowed us to become revitalized in order to force ourselves forward. Under these horrific circumstances, we could imagine that we could not have survived independently, so we had an unspoken affirmation that we would endure cooperatively.

It was not yet quite dawn, but we could see the sky grudgingly allowing a hint of light from one small part of the heavens at the horizon, and we knew that it was east. It was folly to remain here to freeze to death, so we struggled on to ward off the cold and attempt to escape from these treacherous mountains.

Somehow, a miracle occurred! We had worked our way down a dangerously sheer cliff-like precipice in the mountains and stared into what was the outer rim of a huge valley.

"A house! Look, there's a house!"

"Let's go!"

It was about mid-morning and we were about to discover a way clear of these appalling mountains that had impeded us for two days. We headed east in the direction of the house. It appeared to be five or seven miles away, but we made good time. We never let the house out of our view as we worked our way onto the valley floor, as by now, the decline was gentle so that it mercifully eased the physical torture that we had endured for the past two days.

"What do you think?"

"I dunno."

"Might as well try it. I'm not all that hungry, but when will we get a chance eat again?" I asked.

We were staring at a bowl of rice that was placed on the ground just outside of the shoji door of the abandoned house—food meant to appease Buddha. The owners left everything they owned as they fled south to freedom. We had quickly closed on the small village, once we spotted it from the apex of the mountain.

The bitter cold was left behind in the Chokyuryong Mountains, as we contemplated having our first meal in many days. Our hunger pangs had subsided, but we didn't know when we would eat again, if ever. We decided that to eat would be fuel to sustain us, even though our systems were shut down to hunger. With that, I scraped off the outer crust of the rice where the beetles and flies had crawled, and broke the hardened mass into two parts. We didn't wolf it down, as our appetites had diminished some time ago, but still we ate. It was rancid. No, it was rotten! We had no idea how long the food had been there.

We gradually forced our share of the putrid food down, ignoring the sour, rancid, taste, and we were on our way. We could have slept in the house, even for a few hours, but our senses ordained that we keep moving. We had to find American lines.

As we headed down the first of somewhat level land since our days on the offensive, we were able to step up our pace. The main road that separated the valley seemed equally divided between two chains of mountains on each side of the valley. The dirt road ranged in a general north-south azimuth from where we were. We stayed to the base of our mountain, the one that previously held us captive. We headed south in the very gentle foothills where there were a few abandoned houses scattered about. We realized that we were now in an inhabited part of the country, which caused us immense relief. And even better, the sun had conquered the earlier foreboding dark sky. Yes, the sun was shining.

It must have been about noon, as we continued our southern flight, aided by the sun's orientation. Shortly, we came upon a house that was occupied. The owner, a friendly, middle-aged farmer with a weathered and wrinkled face, wore the traditional white-padded clothing of the rural Korean. He was taking his chances by staying at his house, rather than fleeing with the majority of the people.

The sun was out; the snow laid only in infrequent patches here in this wide valley though the frozen ground still refused to surrender to the sun's warmth. We sat on the front porch and absorbed every ray of sun we could to help drive away the ogre of cold that captured us in the mountains until we escaped from its clutches this very morning. Through pantomime, the farmer described how two soldiers, North Korean or Chinese, had been wounded or killed by the Air Force. His gestures were so vivid, that it was as if we could communicate through a common language. With that, he bowed politely, apparently to excuse himself and he re-entered his house. He returned shortly holding two ancient Russian rifles that seemed to be as tall as he, along with a foreign army backpack, unopened and covered with an immense amount of dried blood.

We wanted to stay mainly because of the pleasantness of the day. It was like dropping in on an old friend to sit in the sun, and exchange small talk. He did not offer us any food, nor did we ask for any. The vile poison that we forced down earlier that morning diminished any desire for anything else. Moreover, we knew that there was not enough food to sustain the populace. Then, as now, it is open knowledge that starvation is prevalent among the Korean civilians. Their two-million-man well-fed army is the exception, of course.

Our Korean friend insisted that we take the rifles and backpack with us and we agreed so as not to offend him. In truth, he did not want to be involved in a war that he did not comprehend. His ambition and his aim were to work his farm, and live peaceably without the outside interference of warring nations. I supposed that he was a bit confused as to why two alien nations chose his country to engage in the ungentlemanly act of war. We slung the rifles over our shoulders, waved goodbye as he waved in return, while he sustained the same pleasant smile. We wondered if his friendliness to us would be the same as for Chinese troops, and we decided that it would.

Survival of the fittest. Go along to get along.

About a mile away we threw the backpack in a frozen rice paddy without opening it, and we stopped to examine our newly-acquired weapons. They were vintage Russian—The Degtyarev Antitank, PTRD-1941, 14.5 mm. Used as a long-range sniper rifle, they were long—so drawn-out that they almost threw us off balance when we carried them at sling-arm position. The GIs referred to them to as elephant guns. The rifles had to be six feet in length, and with a bayonet affixed, which was missing, almost eight feet in length. I didn't notice a date of manufacture or if they were loaded. We were afraid to try to operate them as we thought that we might accidentally discharge a round. That would be all we needed at this point and place. We should have thrown the rifles away. Two bolt-action rifles against thousands of Chinese soldiers were ridiculous. Additionally, the enemy would want to know where we acquired them, but we carried them anyway, with the honest thought of throwing them away later.

We made good time on the main road, which now was lined with utility poles that aided us in direction. Unknown to us at the time, electricity generated by huge hydroelectric generators was supplied to large towns and cities. The Japanese built the electrical system during their harsh 40-year occupation. The utility poles would serve us well as guides.

Night dropped like a black curtain pinned to the sky by the few visible stars framed in the ink-black night by the monstrous mountains that had been our captors. The black night turned blacker, unaided by moon or stars. The still-frozen ground was the last of the intense cold we suffered in the mammoth mountain chain from which we escaped. The cold night, the level ground, and our confidence inspired us to walk down the main road. Not only would we not become lost again, but by looking back north at the reverse side of the utility poles, our direction would be reaffirmed. The Army had a proclivity to erect signs, hundreds of signs, to indicate locations for northbound units. That was all that we needed for a compass, and we were dead sure that we had outrun the vanguard of the Golden Horde. We surely would meet up with American units at any time.

Now we felt better. Those precious moments of deep slumber, even for a brief minute or two in the enormous Chokyuryongs, were enough to press on. We had not slept well for so long during this offensive action that it seemed that a tolerance was built up allowing us to survive with less sleep than normal. Those nights of 50-percent alert, one person in each foxhole standing with rotation each hour had conditioned us. Knowing that it would be a matter of just hours before we would be out of harm's way invigorated us and we became animated again.

"What will we say when we hit American lines? Hey, don't shoot! We are Americans?" my friend asked.

"Good question," I replied. After a moment, I said, "No, that won't work." I remembered the terrible attacks during the Pusan Perimeter when the NKPA nearly pushed the American 8th Army off the peninsula. The North Koreans screamed the words *American* and *Yankee* frequently to frighten young Americans just before a monumental attack.

After I mentioned those battles fought before my buddy even arrived in Korea, I said, "You missed that action, so trust me, that won't work. Some goddamned trigger happy new replacement will snuff us for sure."

We walked on for about half an hour without saying anything. I was mulling it over and over because the thought hadn't occurred to me until my friend brought it up.

"I heard that two GIs were killed by their own troops during The Perimeter when they didn't know the password," my buddy said.

"Jesus, what if they ask us, we don't know, and they blast us?"

More protracted silence. I finally said, "Let's say this: *Don't shoot! Wounded Americans from K Company of the 35th.*"

The Chinese would never come up with a real unit like ours, and the idea of being wounded would subconsciously ease their fingers off the triggers. I liked my idea at first, but I was still mulling over a better response for when we would soon be confronted by Americans. We were so positive that they were dead ahead, and we hoped that it would be daylight when we found them.

The night turned blacker yet, and we fell into silence again as we marched south on the main road. Every once and a while, as we approached a pole off to the east side of the road we would look for any posted signs that indicated American military units, and there were many. Our confidence soared, knowing that we were ahead of the Chinese forces. Clearly, we were in *no man's land,* even if there was no evidence of Allied forces at this point. More importantly, we were heading in the right direction for the first time since our escape. We were going to succeed.

We continued to walk in silence as I mulled over my comrade's inquiry as to what to do on approach to friendly lines. If we were fired upon, it would be referred to as *Friendly Fire*. That inane statement has to be the epitome of an oxymoron. When one is killed or maimed by his respective forces, it certainly isn't *friendly* by any stretch of the imagination. *Disaster* would be a more compelling word, given real-life circumstances. One thing for sure, we would discard these primitive weapons long before we get back. That would be a dead giveaway to friendly troops if they saw these behemoth rifles.

"Wait! I got it!" I remarked loudly, as I became ecstatic with what I perceived as the correct and obvious solution. "When we get near enough, we can remove our white thermal underwear tops, tie them to our Soviet rifles so they will be raised high, and just march into the Allied lines!"

Not in one instance had I ever read in history that the symbolic gesture of waving a white flag had ever been violated, since it is one of the sacred warfare traditions. I'm not sure why it is, though. Then I recalled that several villages, albeit abandoned, had placed white sheets on thatched roofs. I assumed the purpose was while abandoning them during the war, they signaled that they wanted their homes to be saved from burning.

Everything was just great. I thought, W*e were almost back, we escaped the Chinese, the weather was cold, but not frigid, and we were not wounded. Hallelujah!*

We must have walked in silence for another hour or so, though the quiet seemed a little awkward, except for our boots crunching on the icy road. We walked side by side.

Despite the ebony night, I could see on the horizon in front of us, a finger of land that had from time immemorial jutted out from west to east, and partially blocked the arrow-straight north-south road. Primitive engineers, or more correctly, laborers, had simply excavated that part of the mound down to grade where the roadway was to traverse. That allowed the remaining part of the natural small knoll east of the road to remain undisturbed, because it was no impediment to the road.

Within an hour we advanced near to this ancient road cut out, and I whispered softly to my companion, "I smell gas."

Just then the entire world exploded in our faces! There was an immediate forceful, threatening shout right in front of us from someone who stepped from shadows of the knoll on the east side of the road, and in an infinitesimal moment, the scream was followed by three loud explosions from a high powered rifle at point blank range. *Bam! Bam! Bam!* Simultaneously, or rather in more of a split-second reaction, we bolted from the road, dropping our primitive rifles. I recalled later the clatter of weapons when the rifles met the road as we fled for our lives. I remembered the feel of my buddy's left shoulder against my right shoulder as we fled in unconditional terror.

All of a sudden his touch was not there. I kept running until the frigid night air seemed to burst my lungs, and then I had to stop. The loathsome, repulsive food we had consumed earlier that morning began to come up. I bent over, hands on knees, opened my mouth, and evacuated that vile, dreadful poison totally from my system in one brief moment. It was if I had consumed gasoline because of the abhorrent after-taste. Obnoxious steam erupted from the disgusting mess when the cold air collided with the putrid mass. I ran once again further west, in case they would initiate a chase for me. The evidence of fresh, steaming vomit would be a good sign for them to track me.

Finally, I stopped, turned and faced them. All the while my heart was beating loudly, out of synchronization and intermingled with involuntary gasps as I struggled desperately for air. I was just sure that enemy could hear my heart beating as well as my frantic gasps for air. I was prepared to flee again, at the slightest provocation of the soldiers.

Flashlights began playing in the dark, dancing off the ebony-black sky, wildly searching horizontally, presumably for me, then dipping, canvassing the icy ground. They were conducting a methodical search. The various lights melded together as one bright beam and then the waltzing beams abruptly froze, focused on the body of my buddy, sprawled, obviously dead, on the ground.

When the darting, searching lights came to rest on his supine body, spontaneous laughter erupted.

You dirty bastards. You sons of bitches, I thought furiously as the flashlights led the way for the soldiers returning to their positions at the apparent petroleum cache on the road. They never fired into his body again, so they and I realized that he was dead. I wanted to crawl back, drag my buddy to safety and breathe life into him, so that we could continue our escape together, but the reality was there. I was now demoted to a party of one.

Good-bye, my brother.

So many thoughts entered my mind that terrible night as I stood in the field out of sight of the sentries. The first order, of course, would be to report him *KIA,* the acronym for Killed in Action. At least his family would not have to pray for a safe return from his current status as *MIA*—Missing in Action. But, at that precise moment I forgot his name, and ever since then, it has eluded me. This mental and emotional block has haunted me all my life. The daily, intense and terrible guilt of being the survivor, while my closest companion was killed, knows no bounds. Each and every day of my life I try to recall his name without success. In the past, I went so far as to obtain a copy of the company roster from the archives of the military, during that stage of the war. Even with that, I had developed a mental impasse because of tremendous guilt associated with being a survivor, while a very decent and honorable soldier died in a most terrible manner.

And, namelessly...

~~

He was my buddy. He was my friend. He was my brother and he was African American. He was my age, 18 years old, with a pleasant smile, and he hailed from the farmland of the Midwest—Nebraska. We were very close, even though we joined the service at separate times and separate places and never met until he joined our company in early autumn. We tacitly knew that we would remain friends for life, simply because we sensed that if ever we escaped safely to American lines, we would share a unique, albeit horrifying experience that no others could possibly comprehend.

I wanted to contact his family. I wanted to visit with them to extend my condolences and to share with them our experiences and how he died. This would have been unheard of in 1951, because of insane, regressive racial barriers; but that illogical tenet did not apply to me, then or now. For you see, he was my brother.

Today, his family likely has passed on, save perhaps for siblings, now elderly like me. I search military magazines and the Internet for names of next of kin attempting to locate information on lost loved ones in the vain hope of somehow recalling his name but it is still to no avail. I probe the deepest ocean of my consciousness with failure. Yet, when I think of him, I can recall the exact image of his pleasant, smiling face, deposited into my memory bank forever.

~~

More than 50 years later, preparatory to a revisit of South Korea, I purchased a map of the Koreas from a local map store. My interest lay in a return to the sites of the bloody battles we endured so many years ago. I was searching for catharsis. Out of curiosity, I reversed the map to scan the country of North Korea.

The name of a town stood out and I froze in absolute terror. Anju! Something very terrible, something very hideous, happened in *Anju!* But what? It haunted me day and night for months on end. I was consumed with the name of *Anju!* Why *Anju?* There were so many other towns and villages that came to my mind without evoking such emotion. Little by little, bit-by-bit, the pain and terror that I endured and then excised from my mind for over 50 years reentered my awareness.

Anju was the town where we were headed. The outskirts of *Anju* was where my buddy was slain and that is where his remains lie, no doubt, even today. Yes, of course! We were on the northern outskirts of *Anju!* Throughout my years, I have not only subconsciously manacled my brain from recall of my friend's name, but I had emotionally blocked the entire incident as well.

While the name *Anju* has restored my memory somewhat piecemeal relative to the events that transpired that awful night, my acute guilt continues to prevail and that factor suppresses my ability to recall my friend's name. Guilt, along with anger, is a major component of Post Traumatic Stress Disorder or Syndrome. It always will be.

I learned something from this tragedy, however.

~~

Rule number one: never walk on a road, but parallel the road about 50 yards to the east or west to stay oriented. It was a relatively easy task, given that rural Korean roads are generally constructed approximately two feet higher than normal ground level, to account for surrounding rice paddies.

~~

Recent disclosures reveal the innumerable facets of President Truman's Police Action. We now glean facts from the enemy's perspective, and one little known detail is that Chinese Forces, early in the conflict, moved vehicles at night. To accommodate the various motor conveyances, the enemy secreted caches of fuel along their supply lines that were effectively camouflaged during the day from observation by the United States Air Force. The gap on both sides of the road near where my friend's body lies unidentified and untended was an ideal camouflage site. The vast, open plains of the valley would have been ill suited to conceal similar supplies.

Additionally, the horrendous, explosive report of the killing rifle must have been one of our very own. It likely was confiscated from one of the thousands of slain GIs when hundreds of thousands of the Golden Horde slammed through every seam of Allied lines in North Korea and precipitated the humiliating 250-mile retreat of the Allied Army.

The sentries, because of the volatile nature of the supplies they guarded, were no doubt given strict orders in regard to smoking. Young soldiers throughout the world seem to have a propensity to smoke, and the Chinese soldiers were no different. Had they have been allowed to smoke cigarettes that awful night, we could have discerned the light from miles away and acted accordingly. There is no doubt in my mind that if not but for this tragic night both of us would have been alive to endure the entire horrific ordeal that was to follow.

I turned slowly and started my walk south again. The sound of boots crunching ice was noticeably subdued, for now I was alone.

THE LONG MARCH

> The veterans of the Long March had traveled more than 6,000 miles; they crossed 18 mountain ranges, 24 rivers, 12 different provinces, and had averaged nearly 24 miles a day for the 235 days and the 18 nights of actual travel. Appleman, p. 750.

Precious time was lost as I drifted in crazy, disoriented circles attempting to contact our forces. I found not a sign of the American Army, whom I prayed would soon sustain a defensive position.

My state following the death of my companion left me in such emotional shock that for the life of me, I cannot recall how or where I spent the night. It had to be outside, marching through the below-freezing mountains, trying to ward off sleep.

A bank of ebony clouds hung low over the mountains. Snow, more deep snow was imminent. Daylight arose without notice, because I was in such a paralyzed state of exhaustion and trepidation. Any ability to analyze the weather, terrain or any other facet of my now one-man exodus to safety eluded me. After our earlier passage down a main road heading south when those three lethal shots rang out that extinguished the life of my young companion, I had to continue.

I was still staggering in a circuitous route which eventually led to nowhere, stumbling through what I think of as *Unland,* oblivious of my location. I was traumatized, and I didn't know what to do. The recollection of those earlier shocking days of the ground war haunted me, when the North Korean Army took such savage reprisals on captured, teenage American soldiers. Upon reflection I decided our captors must have been remnants of the North Korean Army.

My friend was killed instantly or they would have put a finishing round to his head. His nightmare was over. My nightmare, being alone in below-zero weather, was now in progress. I calculated that it was about four days from the time of our capture and escape, and about two days since my buddy died on the northern outskirts of Anju.

Somehow I had again worked my way out of those formidable mountains onto an immense valley floor, though it had taken over a day of exhaustive effort. These two days by myself were so very trying indeed. I felt an immense emotional loss, but I persisted—my only option left was to move forward, or I would die. The thought of my scattered company was but a distant memory.

The entire valley area was draped with deep snow, cloaking everything in purity, masking the true harshness of life in this awful place. The beautiful white carpet was as striking as ever a landscape scene could be. The sun, brazenly exposed, shone in all of its glory, but striking off of the brilliant snow cover, it did not disperse the unbearable subzero cold.

Nevertheless, the blanket of white did cover the filth and destruction of wanton havoc caused by the war. Corpses by the hundreds, if not thousands, lay soaked in frozen raw sewage, scattered among burned, destroyed houses. It was the first time there was not the gut-wrenching stench of night soil caused by spreading human excrement upon the crops. The odor was vanquished by the snow blanket. It was serene now, but when the spring thaw arrived, the flies would lust for the dead and the countless mosquitoes would harvest the living.

I remained hopelessly lost.

The normal components of communication to help guide me in this isolated part of the world were nonexistent. There were no utility poles because there was no electricity and no telephone lines for the same reason. The ancient main road was buried by heavy snow. The adjacent rice paddies that once formed a crazy quilt patchwork defining the rural scene were now transformed into a unified white blanket. I had no way to orient myself out of this grotesque nightmare.

As I was struggling forward, I had a fantasy. I imagined that I could view a group of American prisoners of war, mercilessly force-marched northward on the main road, ruthlessly driven by their Chinese captors. [57] I watched from afar, and I realized that the Chinese forces could have shot them, rather than expending time and energy to restrain them. I acquiesced to my horrendous dilemma, approached with arms raised in surrender and I was at once absorbed as an integral part the hapless crowd. It was more than fantasy. It was wishful thinking.

I wondered if I would ever get back to American lines alive, for if I surrendered again as a lone, isolated soldier, I would be killed in the most

---

[57] No aspect of the Korean Conflict caused more bitterness - bordering on hysteria in the United States - than postwar revelations of the treatment of United Nations prisoners by their Communist captors. The bald figures speak more eloquently than any other narrative. Of 7,140 American prisoners to fall into enemy hands, 2,701 died in captivity. Some fifty of the 1,188 Commonwealth officers and other ranks posted as missing or prisoners died in enemy hands. The west was appalled to hear of the discovery in a railroad tunnel, during the 1950 advance into North Korea, of the bodies of a hundred prisoners massacred by the retreating Communists. From the outbreak of war, Kim Il Sung's army made it plain that it killed Americans whenever it suited its convenience to do so. Hastings, p.287.

terrible way. But, if they were taking prisoners, and I was to be one of them, I would have a better chance of survival than in my present predicament. At the very least, I would not be alone in this treacherous wasteland.

I might be tortured, starved to death, frozen or any other fate inflicted upon American prisoners, but I would be among soldiers who suffered equally, and I was sure that I could hold my own. The North Korean People's Army was in charge of the prison camps that were strategically located along the south side of the Yalu River bordering Chinese-governed Manchuria. The prisons were purposely sited there to prevent rescue efforts of Allied prisoners. The enemy's plan was to hastily force prisoners across the Yalu River into Manchuria, where for political reasons prisoners would be ensconced in sacrosanct territory. Manchuria was a safe house forbidden to enter, in accordance with the edicts set forth by the Truman Administration, with the advice and consent of the Allies. They had good reason. No one, including the CCF, wanted to expand the war beyond the periphery of the Korean Peninsula.

Despite the deaths of more than a quarter of American prisoners of war during the earliest stage of the war, I was an active, dues-paying member of a combat organization, as opposed to being an incarcerated individual. Once recaptured, I believed that I would place in the upper 50-percentile group of survivors, given my experience and my very good fortune of survival during this present calamity. Little did I realize that the toxic food left for Buddha that I reluctantly consumed would cause such debilitation and near death in the immediate future. I could never have survived imprisonment. My membership in life would have been revoked.

A curious village spread into view. While I had not paid due attention before, there must have been other quite similar ones. This small village, more of a cluster of ancient houses constructed at the foot of a steep mountain, was protected by a wood stockade erected around the perimeter. Tall tree trunks were embedded in the ground abutting each other to form a wall, quite similar to early American frontier forts. I did not notice if the tops of the posts were hewed to a point for further defensive protection, simply because I was soon to be distracted.

Without a thought, I entered through the wide opening in the front of this small village and I noticed other houses situated left and right of a house in the center. As I walked into the courtyard, I was perhaps 30 feet from the middle house, when the shoji-type opaque waxed-paper door slid open and an enemy soldier appeared in the doorway. Both of us were shocked as we momentarily stared motionlessly at each other, frozen in awkward surprise. This was no Chinese trooper, but a North Korean soldier, and from his lackadaisical demeanor this was obviously his residence.

My only recourse was to surrender again, because of the short distance between us. He couldn't miss from such a point-blank range. The soldier leaped from the porch at the same time that I raised my arms in surrender. When his foot touched he ground, he dropped to his right knee, placed the butt of his rifle on the ground, and injected a round into the chamber of his weapon by lever action. He carried some type of carbine. This was no Daisy Red Ryder BB Carbine from days of carefree childhood.

Son of a bitch! The son of a bitch is going to kill me!

My instantaneous reaction was to run for my life, and that is just what I did. I spun on my right foot, fled out of the gate, raced to the left, and ran right up the steep mountain situated behind the village as fast as my feet would propel me. I was frightened, but survival logic kicked in. If I were going to be killed, I would be shot on the run, rather than with hands tied behind, waiting for the inevitable shot to the head. My head was down as I ran for my life because it allowed more speed, and at the same time, I could see and avoid patches of snow that would leave evidence of my boot prints as I sprinted forward while weaving from side to side. Not realizing it at the time, my swift, erratic movements must have made a more elusive target for the enemy soldier, as I counted the shots he was firing. I was banking on the fact that he was so excited that he failed to take accurate aim, and I was right. I never once heard the sound of rounds pass by my head that had been so deafening in the horrific battles at the Pusan Perimeter some months before.

As I was making the horrifying dash for my life, heart racing, simultaneously gasping for air, I had instant recall of my childhood at the Saturday afternoon double feature cowboy movies. As inane as it seemed, I was a willing victim of subconscious response, spawned from early childhood. During the film, we children would count the rounds fired from the six guns of cowboy adversaries. Six rounds were all that revolvers held; yet once we counted 21 shots fired without reloading from one pistol. Shouts of derision and jeers came from everywhere in the audience, filling the theater with scornful laughter. Habits are hard to break, because that is exactly what I was doing here

Three, four, five, six!

I made it, I thought!

He is out of ammo! He is out of ammo! Hallelujah! I outran that son of a

bitch! Hallelujah!

Seven, eight! Oh my God, how many more rounds will he fire at me?

The seeming lifetime of rapid, but erratic shooting came to an eerie silent end, ceasing as abruptly as it started. I was gratified.

Now, a new and dire threat loomed on the horizon of my awareness. The hunter would be doggedly tracking me with an insatiable lust to finish me off. Why not? I was unarmed, lost and easy prey for *The Deer Hunter*. I might be capable of outrunning the enemy, but not of outrunning his bullets. I had headed for the mountain. Once the hunter ascended the summit, I would have no choice but to flee down the opposite side of the mountain. The hunter would have the luxury of assuming a prone position, taking careful aim, and shooting me dead with but one round. I would be an easy target, as deep snow completely shrouded the other side of the mountain. My olive-drab uniform would stand out in stark contrast to the surrounding landscape. That was obviously why the hostile enemy village was sited where it was—to gain the maximum warmth from the sun, and the least snow during the winter.

Upon ascending the crest, I discovered an outcropping of boulders in which to hide. I was now ensconced in a natural fort, safe for the time being. I had but to watch for the hunter coming for me, and then make a move accordingly.

Incredibly, a military action was occurring on the opposite side of my hiding position in a narrow valley at the bottom of this steep outcropping. I made a crucial decision that I was to regret for the rest of my life. I judged the time to be early afternoon, as I witnessed a squadron of American F-86 fighter jet planes engaged in a sortie against the enemy. Because the jet fighter planes flew so fast, they relied on a two-man helicopter/spotter team to locate and direct fire to the enemy. One of the helicopter team was the pilot, the other, the spotter, whose sole responsibility was to search the sector for enemy, and communicate his findings to the marauding F-86's.

The helicopter was hovering east of me, yet not that much higher than my position, because of the height of my mountain. I judged the aircraft to be less than a mile away from my position. This was only the second time I had been fired upon by the enemy since my escape, and I was convinced that the North Korean soldier was climbing the mountain to kill me. I reasoned that the night my buddy was killed and I was not pursued, was simply because of the black night in which I could evade the enemy. This situation was different. It was daylight, my pursuer knew my location, and he had nothing to do other than to track me and finish me off.

Not realizing that I was not being chased, I hid among the boulders, cursing myself for the lack of a mirror to signal the helicopter crew. They were not that far away, and while searching for enemy, they would have continuously scanned this broad area. In retrospect, I should have dropped to the opposite side of the mountain a few feet, out of sight of my would-be assassin, removed my white thermal underwear top, and flagged the crew.

I was so sure they would see me from above, and fly over to investigate. They would determine that I was American, and they would drop enough to allow me to grab one of the skids and hold on for dear life. This long, almost eternal, nightmare would be over, and I might never have been so physically and emotionally affected.

The squadron concluded their mission and flew away leaving me in a state of deep despair. So close and yet so far. I had to continue in spite the stressful melancholy that haunted me. Were there more of us out there, running like terrified deer from a horde of hunters? I never had such a golden opportunity to escape as this one, and I allowed it to slip through my fingers. Had I known what the future held for me, I would have risked my life to be rescued.

To return to the side of the mountain whence I started was not a consideration, so I descended the opposite side toward where the planes were attacking. I was impaled on the horns of a dilemma, having no choice but to map out a plan of escape. The enemy was all around me. I was clearly in the middle of a massive Chinese Communist Army, surrounded, with no means of escape. I was in their midst, and I couldn't do anything about it. The attack by the fighter planes obviously meant that enemy was here, and in enormous numbers. By the grace of God I evaded the enemy, but the price to pay was exorbitantly high. I was still in the dreadful mountains.

Now, I moved on, lost as usual, because there was no way for me to determine direction. I staggered through areas of patchy snow, areas of deep snow, and yet other areas with nearly no snow at all, though the temperature seemed to be equal, still far below zero. I came to the realization that I was once again captured by the snows of this forbidden area.

When my friend was alive, just two days earlier, we were destined to roam around aimlessly in a hopeless attempt to locate Allied forces. The same deep layer of snow that saturated the mountains where we were hopelessly floundering essentially entombed us. The incredibly heavy drifts of snow obscured any chance of orientating ourselves. There were no visible paths, roads or trails to follow. We might as well have been completely stranded in the vicious, life threatening, glacier-bound clutches of the North Pole.

Now that I was alone, this, the second day, was very trying indeed, as I endeavored to keep from freezing. I slept fitfully under an evergreen tree for a brief time, as I dug deep through snow with bare hands to find pine needles to cover me to ward off the frost. After a few minutes, I felt myself plummeting into freeze mode again, so I arose and reeled forward. My hands were throbbing from digging in the snow and exposure to the air without hand protection.

I was still hopelessly off course. The snow in those formidable mountains had been at least 18 inches deep, forcing me to exert the greatest of efforts to thwart the frigid, overpowering elements. Had I possessed snowshoes, I could have trod reasonably well on top of the powdery snow. Having none caused my legs to plunge to the solid ground below, and as I struggled to extricate one leg in order to place the opposite limb forward, it caused me to stagger, reel and fall so frequently that I felt I would, in due time, perish. With no path to guide me, I again and again inadvertently drifted from solid terrain and rolled partially down the mountain, which forced me to crawl back on frozen hands to my former position.

Staggering and stumbling for hours on end with no relief in sight, I was totally spent of energy. Perspiration from this abnormal, stressful exertion turned to frost in the sub-zero temperature. I lurched on, hopelessly lost, yet somehow I miraculously, but unknowingly worked my way out of the sheer mountain range to low-lying foothills.

In due course and by the grace of God, I found my way to an area where the snow scarcely covered the ground and in some places only ice was present. In these foothills I came across the epitome of Asian determination. I have never beheld such an awe-inspiring sight before or since.

It was a pyramid. It was the largest, most colossal pyramid I ever witnessed in my life, constructed entirely of stacked rice sacks made from tightly-woven hemp rope and each of the hundreds of thousands of sacks were filled with sand. The base of the edifice was beyond measurement .It seemed to be a least a mile square at the base alone. From there the pyramid worked its way into the heavens, thousands of feet high, maintaining symmetrical beauty on all four sides as the incredible structure consistently gained altitude. When I attempted to view the apex of this magnificent, unbelievable work of labor, I tilted my head back so far that my pile cap fell from my head. My eyes were directed at twelve o'clock on a clock dial, as I gazed open mouthed skyward in search of the purpose for this behemoth, man-made composition.

My fixated stare directed me to the apex of the pyramid, where I noticed two mountainous peaks situated very close together. There lay two tunnels, one on each side of the gigantic mountains just below each peak. What once was a mighty trestle bridge constructed to span a rail line from tunnel to tunnel across this mile-high chasm with attendant railroad tracks, was now supported permanently on this gargantuan pyramid. The original trestle bridge and tracks had been blown completely away by precision Air Force bombing with results more effective than I have ever witnessed. American bombers had to figuratively thread the needle to successfully blast that bridge between these two closely-situated mountain peaks. All for naught. Asian coolies assembled this mighty pyramid that soared to the heavens and negated the artistry of bombardment by the Air Force.

The muddy color of the rice bags aided in the camouflage of the pyramid, but even so, there was not a bomb built big enough at the time to destroy this solid, sand-bagged edifice. It was as if ancient Egyptians were transported by a time machine to this site to replicate construction of the pyramids, except with the use of dissimilar materials.

An eerie feeling engulfed me, standing right where sometime earlier, hundreds, perhaps thousands of coolies toiled feverishly, erecting this support for the railroad bridge in what the Air Force would have believed to be an impossible task. Surely, they had heard legends of the tenacity of Chinese workers who hacked airfields out of mountains and conquered roads from deep gorges during World War II.

From the foothills I spotted a road in this dense, snow-covered valley. I was mystified that the roads bore no snow, while the valley was replete with the white powder. I was on my way again and I made a pact to myself that, come what may, I would stay within sight of a road, any road for that matter.

Rule number one was strictly abided by after the death of my friend. Never walk down a road, but parallel the road to keep oriented as to direction.

After many miles, I discovered a road, as I was walking south, approximately 50 yards to the west of the north-south road and I observed a most incredible sight. I was staring at hundreds upon hundreds of abandoned American vehicles; mostly infantry personnel carriers—deuce-and-a-halfs. There were no signs of battle on the multitude of these troop carriers. They sat there idle as if they were ready to move out once a cargo of troops was laden. There was an absence of any living thing in this eerie, ghost-like setting. No dead soldiers of any nationality, no scars to the landscape. No stench of battle in the air, no blood soaked snow. There was only the serenity of recently-fallen snow that transposed this terrible area into a pseudo-perfect photo.

My curiosity overrode my common sense, and I walked to examine this million-dollar plus gift to the Chinese Communist Volunteer Army. Once on the road, I could see as far as my eyes would view south in this huge desolate valley. I could barely discern the American tank miles ahead that must have led this solemn procession. The tank appeared to have slid in the snow, careened and blocked the road. With that, these hundreds upon hundreds of trucks apparently disgorged their passengers. The vehicles were left as a gift to the new owners. Every vehicle was devoid of equipment, save 30-caliber machine guns still ready to fire which were mounted in the front of the cargo space, over the cab of every truck. Miles upon miles of abandoned trucks.

I was astounded to view the tremendous loss of this equipment that lay abandoned without any obvious efforts to destroy them. A white phosphorous hand grenade thrown in the bed, or better yet into the cab of each vehicle, would make short work of these precious transportation necessities, depriving the enemy of their use.

And what of the passengers? There must have been thousands of soldiers who fled this debacle. How far behind was I? Were they a day's march from me? Perhaps even less? I could have postulated a thousand guesses but I had no answers. There was not so much as a cigarette butt on the snow to suggest a clue as to the last moments of this haunting, colossal mystery.

Returning to the field, I continued west for about 50 yards, and again turned to a southward march through the frozen rice paddies and fields. As I walked, my mind again wandered to the convoy, searching for the least clue as to what occurred perhaps just a day before my arrival, but I lacked any answers. It was a hope, albeit, a slim one that these American soldiers lay just ahead. I continued my struggle all day, staggering on from lack of sleep and physical exhaustion. The weather forbade me to stop for even the briefest of moments.

Suddenly my reserve tank of energy just sputtered empty. I couldn't take another step, I believed, unless I had sleep. This was perhaps my second day since my buddy was shot, and we were together two days without sleep, excepting fleeting moments when we clutched each other at night to keep from freezing. And before that, it was two days of all night, stay awake and alert for battle, defending against the first massive CCF attack. Both armed forces moved rapidly south, the pursued and the pursuers. I was in between and on foot. Though I was physically exhausted, the absolute first imperative was to sleep. But where? I was in the middle of a cleared corn field, staggering parallel to the road. The weather remained tolerable, provided I didn't cease motion.

My once steady march cadence of strong, sustained movement evolved into an uncontrolled stagger of imbalance and disorientation. I blinked frequently to stay awake as I sensed my body was on auto-pilot while my reasoning powers were shutting down.

Gazing ahead, I spied in the far distance a dark object clashing against the pure white snow background. My initial response was that it was an enemy soldier lying in wait to shoot me as I neared. Nonsensical behavior considering the very late hour, the isolated area and the freezing temperature. As I came upon the object, I discovered it to be a solitary stack of frozen corn stalks, bundled together, now resembling a small Indian teepee, and centered in this vast, barren field.

Recalling grade school lessons about Eskimos living in ice dwellings, I prayed for a similar relationship with this object, as I kicked in the bottom of the frozen stalks to crawl in. In doing so, I evicted a family of rodents—rats and mice who were now compelled to take my place in the open.

No sooner did I crawl inside this makeshift shelter, assuming a fetal position, than I fell instantly into deep slumber. In an instant, vivid dream sequences emerged, so real that I believed them to be reality. Rather than drifting off in a fantasy of being safely home with family and friends, my reverie took another form.

General MacArthur issued his unequivocal order to sweep to the Manchurian border on 24 November, the day following Thanksgiving Day. Prior to that, troops began receiving holiday packages from home, and so that is the tack my dreams swept me on.

"Hey Pete! Look at this. My mom smuggled a bottle of hooch in this Quaker Oats carton. Take a swig," said one of the Afro-American soldiers in our squad, brandishing his usual warm grin.

Stevens was there and my best friend, Gene Putzier, whom I met at the recruitment station in Los Angeles, was there as well.

"Hey Gene. What's in the box from your family, *escargot?*" Gene, ferociously proud of his French ancestry, replied, "Nope, cookies from Mom, and if you don't watch your mouth, you are cut off!"

"OK, OK, far be it from me to ruin a good thing," I jokingly replied.

Never mind that Gene was captured at Anui during the lopsided catastrophe of 27 July 1950, and later ruthlessly murdered by his NKPA captors.

The banter went on and on and I could hear the sounds of packages being opened, smell the foodstuffs, taste the delicacies, and it was all so real. Then I awoke having no concept of how long I slept, a few minutes, perhaps an hour, I will never know.

It was still dark when I backed out on hands and knees from my frozen corn-stalk igloo to face the same surroundings as before, but with one noticeable difference. Once on my feet again, I plunged into an ocean of despair so deeply that I was literally immobile. I had to garner all of the emotional residue left in me as bottomless depression submerged me so intensely that tears welled in my eyes. This so realistic reverie cut deep into my soul, leaving me with the realization that yes, it was but a dream and life goes on. I went on, hopefully on a southern heading.

I had somehow bypassed the city of Anju that lay south of where the gasoline cache was stored, yet later I had no recollection of the place. I was not to learn of the name of the settlement until nearly a half-century later and revive memories of the horrific circumstances of the murder of my slain partner.

In later years, I was also to learn that this road that I walked beside was the primary escape route of the American 8th Army and their Allies. Sections of units successfully breached the series of murderous roadblocks placed by the Chinese Forces, which had been emplaced to annihilate the American Army. If one roadblock was broken through, there were many more emplacements down the road to stop those in retreat. Survivors obviously fled the vehicles to retreat swiftly on foot through the mountains in order to slip back through enemy lines. The awesome firepower of the Chinese forces killed everyone on the roads.

The sensations affiliated with hunger had long subsided. I regularly consumed snow to ward off dehydration and to excise the foul taste in my mouth, but the most precious need of all for me was not to be had. . . sleep—deep, deep sleep.

Around mid-morning, I became engulfed in an area of fresh, powdery snow, about knee high. The effort to pull one leg out of the snow pack, and extend it forward to complete a step, followed by the other, called on me to expend the maximum exhaustive effort that I was able to muster. This was precisely when my fantasy companions entered my life.

Two imaginary American soldiers, also unarmed, appeared, one on each side of me, and they began to argue between each other as to which way to get back to American lines. My abnormal hallucinations were real; the soldiers were not. The argument was always the same and it centered on how to get back to the American side of the fence.

Goddamn it quit arguing and let's work this out, I muttered to myself, an irrational acknowledgment of their presence and of my delusions.

That was the constant theme of my trauma. The imagined soldiers continued a verbal barrage of argument between each other, as they ignored me in the middle. I was nonexistent to my mythical companions. Despite my pleas for mutual cooperation, they refused to listen. Much later in life, I was to discover that hallucinations are a common reaction to starvation, exhaustion, stress, sleep deprivation and a host of other variables that affect one's psyche. I qualified for all.

Still in the snowdrifts, my illusory companions were in overtime mode in argument as to what to do next. For myself, I had not the slightest idea of a solution.

Keep walking Paul; we have got to get out of this mess somehow.

The bickering continued between them and in my hallucinating mind, I growled at them, *Shut up and let's work together. We have made it this far and there aren't any other options and you guys know it damn well, just the same as me!*

The thought of surrender was not an option. Who knows what they would do, but to take me, a stray soldier, prisoner again was out of the question.

Hey you guys, all of us know what would happen in that case, so just forget it!

By responding to my hallucinations I acknowledged, without realizing it at the time, that I stepped beyond the stage of normalcy. I was delirious.

By the grace of God, I eventually found my way out of the knee-deep snow, where it was possible to walk with less effort, which enabled me to increase my pace. The snow mass blanketed every object on the ground and countryside and left a sort of serenity that seduced me into a lull of complacency. Meanwhile, I noticed that my fantasy companions abandoned me as my stride became easier.

Then I slipped into abnormal, obsessive-compulsive deliriums. A ditty, an old drinking-type song, kept playing through my head over and over again.

> *Show me the way to go home,*
> *I'm tired and I want to go to bed.*

Oh, I had a little drink about an hour ago,
and it's gone right to my head.
Wherever I may roam, on land or sea or foam.
You will always hear me singing this song
Show me the way to go home.

The song continued non-stop until my hallucinations of the two soldiers reappeared, at which time they regained control of my mind.

The sun was my constant companion this day and as it shined, my morale was bolstered. To find that the sun still existed pleased me, but the reflection upon the white carpet affected my eyes. I judged the time to be early afternoon. Squinting was the only means to walk without sunglasses in the vast, frozen wasteland. I tried to protect my eyes from the sun by shading with my right hand to the forehead, but I shortly dispensed of the futile exercise, which took more effort than I could spare. I was soon to realize just how severely the homogenization of snow and sun was to affect my sight.

It was in the early afternoon, I suppose, when I noticed a small village, apparently abandoned, to my left, (east) across the road, huddled among a large stand of evergreen trees. In hope of finding food or clothing, I decided to enter.

I was mindful of rule number two: Do not enter a village without a diligent search for enemy activity. With that in mind, I crept up behind the village from the north side, the rear, hidden among the shelter of the pine trees. The low-hanging branches forced me to stoop in order to clear the snow-laden pine boughs. There was one last tree to clear and I would be in the open, subject to view. As I looked up, I was startled and shocked to view an incredible sight. There stood the most magnificent horse that I have ever seen. The reins were tied to a bough of the tree, and the steed stood there stately, proudly, adorned with a beautiful English-style, leather saddle. The horse was dark brown with the shiniest coat, obviously a result of recent grooming. Small of ear and rump, he was in perfect proportion in every way.

Gentle wafts of steamed air emanated from the creature's nostrils as his warm breath clashed with the bitter Manchurian wind-blown cold. I was astounded, but what brought my adrenaline to a rush was the saddle blanket. Olive green cloth trimmed with about a two inch red border, superimposed with a large red star on the rear center.

Jesus Christ! I nearly walked into the headquarters of the commanding general of the entire Chinese Volunteer Force!

The owner of that magnificent animal had to be of a very high stature in the CCF hierarchy. I stealthily, silently backed out the same way that I had entered. I was ready to run for my life once again if the rider spied me when he came back for his mount. The horse owner was obviously using an abandoned house for rest, yet I saw no sign of other enemy. The sight of the splendid mount gave me pause. It was clear that the equine was associated with a high-ranking military commander; ergo there must be an army to command.

Once across the road again, I hurriedly made my way west before pivoting to head south. Sheer willpower forced me on my way as mind-altering physical exhaustion took control of my emaciated body. I staggered on for hours on hours. Daylight gently blended into night in an incomprehensible conspiracy with the forbidding mountains, which darkened in unison with the collapse of day. I continued my exodus. Where was the Promised Land that I sought so desperately? The snow in the valley floor was but a pittance in relation to the covered mountains, which were as foreboding as ever.

"It's three o'clock in the . . .

I believed that I was in *no man's land,* that unpredictable void between two opposing armies. But then, what about that magnificent horse? Surely the officer-owner had to be a high-ranking officer, but why would he be so far in front of his army? The Americans might be only five to ten miles away. I firmly believed that I had left the main body of enemy troops and I was, at last, ahead of and in front of the Chinese Communist armies. I was near to finding the American 8th Army. My Army.

The position of the sun before it slowly descended behind the mountains allowed time for me to surmise that my direction was still roughly on a southern tack, and I was relieved. I must have made over 20 miles that day, judging from experience. This day, utilizing the road for orientation aligned me squarely with American forces, most likely dead ahead. Surely by now the Allies had stopped their retreat, and they *must* have established a defensive position. I was bound to find them soon.

Later on, when it became so dark that I could barely find my way, I heard the noise of heavy vehicular traffic to my left, again east of the road. I would have supposed that it was in the foothills from the immediate nature of the surrounding area, but that couldn't be. There had to be a road, yet I was so sure that I was the sole occupant of the road. Perhaps it was a staging area, the conveyances parked and camouflaged during the day, and put in motion during the night. I climbed a gentle slope toward the direction of the noise, the clamor seeming to rise from a small knoll directly to my front. I differentiated the distinct noise of many trucks, mixed with the roar of tanks. I quickly crested the knoll, bent over to lower my silhouette while I sought to view the enemy activity below. I found shelter under a large evergreen tree, clear of snow on the ground, believing that my uniform of olive drab would blend in nicely with the bare ground under the tree. My discombobulated thought was that since I could not see my hand in front of me, it had to be just as dark to everyone else. I would remain totally immobile until my eyes became accustomed to the pitch-black night, so I could view the activity of the Chinese forces.

As I sat, waiting for my eyes to adjust to the night, my fantasy began:

When I get back to my side, I will have a wealth of information for the intelligence people.

I had gained much knowledge about enemy tactics, and G-2 (Intelligence) would be getting solid information, which would turn the tide of battle in favor of the UN. I had the depth of information so desperately needed to counteract the enemy. I knew where they bivouacked, how they implemented procedures to foil the Air Force, and when they moved. The more earnestly I thought of it, the more I realized that the Americans could really turn the tide of the war with the knowledge I had gained. [58]

I could offer solid advice. Shoot up large villages during the day because the enemy is billeted there, hiding and sleeping during the day. Residents had abandoned the villages to the combatants, as they all headed south in search of peace for their shattered lives. What remains is pure enemy. Bomb military vehicles that drive displaying the iridescent colors that are placed on the horizontal, lowered windshields, utilized for the benefit of American fighter planes. The panels distinguish friend from foe, even though the enemy changed panels daily in accordance with Allied maneuvers to confound the Air Force. Obviously, enemy agents behind Allied lines communicated with their comrades in the north daily as to what color was ordered for the day. Initially, the Volunteers used quilts color-matched to imitate the American iridescent panels, but it was no

---

[58] There is little doubt that in the first six months of the war, thousands of the interdiction missions flown by the Air Force were valueless because of inadequate targeting. "The Air Force bombed all the main routes during the winter retreat of 1950," said Major John Sloane, an officer on the ground with the Argyll & Sutherland Highlanders, "but they achieved very little because they didn't understand Chinese techniques. The Communists simply weren't on the main routes." Attempts to identify and bomb Communist troops on the move, especially during the first weeks of the war when target intelligence was almost nonexistent, caused substantial casualties among friendly forces and refugee columns fleeing desperately from the battle field. Hastings, p. 255.

time at all before they captured entire convoys of American tanks, trucks and jeeps, abandoned as Allied forces fled south.

Witness the forsaken convoy that I observed earlier. The CCF had all of the iridescent panels they needed and then some. I watched from hiding as they drove captured American vehicles brazenly in the open, because no one knew where the enemy lay. For that matter, no one knew the precise location of Allied Forces, given the disorganized, harried retreat now under way.

My reverie was shattered by a harsh shout from someone very near, and in the same unintelligible language.

That couldn't be about me, I thought. The shrill command instantly repeated!

My God, it is about me! I realized, as I quickly crawled from under the tree, leaped up and fled back over the knoll and quickly disappeared in the ink black night.

How could anyone possibly see me when it was so dark out, when I couldn't see anything in front of me?

The answer came to me later.

I was snow blind.

The days of walking through covered fields of snow had taken a toll on my eyes. How stupid of me not to realize the same darkness prevailed on both sides of the small knoll. I was very fortunate that the sentry didn't fire on me first, and ask questions later. I suppose because I was so far behind enemy lines the Chinese would think it incomprehensible for an American to be practicing the spy game.

The sentry's challenging shout forced me to seek the shelter of the foothills situated of the west side of this valley. It would be easy for the Chinese forces to search the valley for me by following my footprints in the snow. Once across this small valley, I considered a climb just in the foothills. But a reprise of my earlier lost days in the mountains flooded back. With a vow to stay at the edge of the valley, where the foothills began, I was determined not to re-enter the forbidden mountains. I was disoriented and delirious, but there was no other choice than to press on.

I missed my friend more than words can say.

It was very late at night. I mentally kicked myself for not knowing how to orient myself via interpretation of the stars. I had not paid attention to that phase of training in the Boy Scouts, and the Army didn't dwell on such a difficult subject in the peacetime military. But what does a teenage soldier know?

Actually, when I enlisted, I was so entranced with the Army and the infantry in particular, that I paid strict attention during basic infantry training. Had they presented astronomy as a subject, I am sure that I would have mastered the course. Classes on map reading put almost everyone to sleep, but I grasped it because I wanted to.

Ironically, a map would be of little value now. I needed to know my precise location in order to work with a chart. If I had a compass, it would be the second most valuable find. The first? Discovering the American Army.

I'm tired and I want to. . .

THE CAMPGROUND

Yea, though I walk through the valley of the shadow of death, I will feel no evil: For thou art with me: Thy rod and thy staff, they comfort me. Psalm 23:4.

The starry night, eerily black and tranquil, was much too cold for snow. The temperature was taking a toll on my hands. I could not walk and protect my hands from the elements at the same time. The American Army field uniform was not configured to have pockets to accommodate hands. Army tradition forbade hands in pockets at all times, and whoever designed the uniform lacked the foresight of aiding an individual in such a perilous situation as I now found myself.

My sno-pacs, made for cold weather, were perfect to walk in, as the rubber boots captured and retained heat from the feet, to keep them warm. It was much too cold to perspire, and given the circumstances, I was doing well. I had the elevated, dirt road in my sight to act as a compass, and my pace was rapid and strong. The sound of crunching ice resounding from marching on the icy veneer of the field was reassuring, and I was making excellent time. The enemy was behind me, I was sure, and it was just a matter of time until I located Allied forces. Even the lack of sleep was not a factor on this night, nor was the lack of food. My desire above all else, aside from returning to Allied military control, was to be warm. This frigid weather took such an arduous toll that I had to move to keep from freezing, and my usually destructive sleep deficit declined into a minimal issue for now.

But there was one curious item that I could not comprehend. The southern sky was painted a light hue, contrasting sharply with the otherwise black night. I was miles from the source, and as the distance closed, I had a premonition, and it wasn't good.

If that's what I think it is, I'm in trouble. I thought. No, it's even worse than that; I'm a dead man walking, in spite of being successful so far. There isn't any other way I can go much farther than a couple of more miles and then it's goodbye, Paul, unless I can think of way a way through the vast, unexpected maze of light.

After my buddy was killed, I was sure that I had outrun the CCF, and I initially believed I was in the vicinity of the American Army. Now reality jolted me. Enemy was swarming over the entirety of North Korea. Now, I perceived they were dead ahead. At the time I could not comprehend the enormous numbers of Communist Chinese enemy who bolted from their political sanctuary in Manchuria to aid their crushed NKPA brethren.

Campfires! Enemy campfires! Oh, my God, I just knew they were enemy campfires!

I didn't want to believe it when I saw the sky lit up and discernable for miles north. And not just a few insignificant fires here and there. There were hundreds upon hundreds of enemy bonfires to warm bodies and souls of thousands and thousands of enemy troops. The blazes seemed to be a fiery band dividing the ebony night from the tangled, black countryside. An enormous belt of fire was cascading down from the western mountain, roiling as molten lava into the valley below, and then forging east to splash to the other side of the foothills. On the west side, just off the dirt road, the body of camp fires was partially sheltered by a sparse forest of pine trees that offered little protection against a possible sortie by Air Force fighter planes.

Only the road was spared from illumination. But, the road held a more sinister fate for me than did the enemy bivouac and I knew well the peril of the former. I would not violate rule number one again. There would be sentries on the road, just as alert and ready to kill as the ones north of Anju, who shot my buddy and then laughed about it.

I continued my march south, trudging through frozen, barren fields, always keeping the raised road in view. No enemy could see me at this distance, though my uniform had to be in stark contrast to the snow-covered surroundings. I could run for my life when necessary. It was forebodingly pitch black, and I estimated the time to be before midnight from the point where I was walking. The bright lights would cast another aspect on a new, dangerous challenge.

I could barely make out the cut in the road from this distance, but I knew it would be trouble. It was an exact version of the one that portended disaster at Anju when enemy sentries stepped from deep shadows to shoot at my friend and me. To traverse this ominous road would be a certain route to death. There just had to be another way through.

My two hallucinatory companions returned. They were the same two soldiers on each side of me as before, and still engaged in constant argument. The argument was always the same, centering on how to overcome a new, dangerous obstacle.

Goddamn it. Quit arguing and let's work this out together.

Still moving south, my imaginary companions were in overtime mode arguing over what to do next. For myself, I had not the slightest indication as to a solution. Then, one of the illusionary soldiers said to me, *Hey Paul, They own the road!*

I was startled beyond reason; *they* never had spoken directly to me before.

Keep walking Paul, we've got to get out of this somehow, I thought to myself.

The hallucinatory advice and bickering continued, and finally in my unreliable mind, I whispered to them,

Shut up and let's work together. We have made it this far and there aren't any other options and you guys know it damn well. Surrender again would be as bad as the last time, so just cool it, you guys. You know damn well what would happen, so forget it.

Keep up the pace, Paul. You still have a long way to go before the big decision has to be made. Until then, just keep up the march. You don't even have to be cautious of the sound of your boots on the iced over, frozen fields at this point. That was a smart move, Paul. Walk off the road about fifty yards and parallel it, but don't lose sight of it, I reassured myself silently, but irrationally.

That's the only compass you have to keep oriented to your way south. There just isn't any other way to go. Follow the road. Follow the road.

My illusory partners continued to keep up the steady barrage of arguments until I whispered aloud, "Shut up!"

All of a sudden the capricious pair became silent. I frightened myself by speaking aloud; then I realized it was symptomatic of amplified, delusional behavior. Talking aloud was of deep concern to me, because I learned months ago about the hidden dangers of talking, particularly at night in an inappropriate environment. But more importantly, I sensed that my mind was being affected by this disturbing nightmare, of which I had apparently lost control, even if it was but for a moment.

My oral outburst brought me back to reality, as I concentrated on the resonance of my boots on the ice. It became the focus of my attention, and it recharged my thinking. In a way, it was a comforting sound, given the circumstance, the sound echoing a strong march cadence; it centered my thinking process. That strong march cadence had a threefold objective: Find the US Army. Avoid another run in with the marauding Chinese Volunteers. Keep from freezing to death in the cold night air.

To circumvent the enemy, at least a full division in my estimation, was out of the question. The fires were multitudinous, extending beyond belief for miles, snaking into mountains, precluding me from detouring to avoid the enemy. A whole damn division at the least. Ten thousand enemy troops to one unarmed stray soldier. Not very good odds. Still, I would be involved with just a fraction of the multitude of combatants, which improved the odds significantly. Even so, it would take only one shot to cut me down, as they did my friend.

My very life and my plight were reduced to three basic possibilities. I could try to sneak down the road and be shot to certain death by sentries. To walk around the bivouac perimeter was an impossible task. The time frame would entail so many hours that the enemy would be on their way again before I could ever begin to reach the east or west perimeter. And even if I could possibly circumvent the enemy, they would gain on me by the time I could return to my off-road hike south again.

The last and only real option, dreadful as it seemed, was to infiltrate their perimeter and walk through them. Though this rather erratic decision appeared to be a sign of *bravado*, the simple truth was that there was no other alternative. I pondered the odds of this forthcoming venture, as I waited impatiently for hours for blazing campfires to subside and ebb into embers. My silent approach was near enough to monitor the soldiers mingling on the small hill above and west of the road. The Chinese congregated around the countless fires, casually talking, squatting, hands extended to the fire to harness the heat in an attempt to keep from freezing. They were oblivious of my presence. I searched the black night for standing soldiers. They would be the sentries. There were none that I could detect. Still, past experiences reminded me that I had to consider the obvious threat of watchful, alert sentries. I nearly died by not considering the terrible event that resulted in the death of my buddy and when I attempted to walk around the enemy unit sleeping in the village.

It seemed to be an eternity before troops began to turn in one by one. I walked back north out of earshot of the bivouac, where my idea was pondered again. I was stomping my boots to keep from freezing, knowing it was safe to do so. I realized it would take but one Chinese soldier to notice me and then all efforts would have been in vain. Again, I vacillated, pondering other solutions, but no other plan came to mind. There were no other options.

The American combat uniform was similar in color to the Chinese Army field uniform, that is, a similar shade of green. I presumed they would not be readily differentiated in the dark.

The opposing armies wore pile caps in lieu of helmets, in consideration of the bitter winter cold. Both armies had closely similar earflaps on their pile caps, but with a minor distinction—the Chinese Volunteers generally wore their earflaps down as a protection from frostbite. For some reason, I never saw an American soldier with earflaps down, no matter the temperature. American troops tied their earflaps to the top of the cap, out of the way. Comfort was sacrificed for a clearer, unimpeded view of the constantly shifting battle-tested enemy horde, enabling Allied soldiers to fire weapons with an unrestricted view.

The truth was, earflaps were a nuisance because of the frequent slaps to the face the ear protectors gave in response to rapid head movement. American pile caps had a wide brim that folded up in the front of the cap, while the Chinese combat cap had a narrow front brim. Other than that, given the similarities and the circumstances, I believed my scheme was so audacious that it might work. Sergeant Bruner proved that a daring maneuver would succeed when four of us slipped through enemy positions following the escape from the schoolhouse in Anui. Bruner's plan worked then. My plan might work now.

Who in the world would expect an American enemy soldier to meander through an opposing forces unit? Especially when the stray soldier was obviously scores of miles deep in enemy territory. It was an astonishing implausibility.

With the notion ultimately settled, I untied my earflaps. I was going to try it. Nothing ventured, nothing gained. I opted for the west side, because I thought the sparse forest would give me some sort of cover, even though that idea was groundless. It was not like infiltrating the level valley, east of the road where I could be observed an extended distance away. There they would just wait for me if I were noticed. Moreover, if I were to attempt entry into the enemy perimeter on the east side, I would have to backtrack a great distance, in order to cross the road without being detected by well armed, lurking guards.

Meander. Yes, that was the key. In order to pull this bold scheme off, I had to saunter casually through the bivouac, as if I was one of them. Anything else would be as a deer bounding through their territory, bringing out the hunter in them. I mulled it over and over until I psyched myself into the belief that, yes, it just might work. Then I backed off of the campsite area again since I had hours to wait before campfires diminished sufficiently to attempt my feat.

I needed to maintain movement to avoid freezing to death. Other concerns arose. What if I had the inability to stifle a cough, or perhaps I were to slip and fall on ice?

Hours seemed like days before the fires began to dim as I continuously walked in an enormous circle to avoid freezing to death. I wanted to stomp my feet to warm them, but I had again ventured within hearing range of the occupants. I wanted so much to stand by the ever-so-inviting fires, attempting to recall the last time that I was warm, away from this horrific frozenness. I walked north again out of view of the camp. There was ample time to approach again, as they slept. I wondered why they were sleeping at night, when usually they always appeared to move forward during the night, sleeping during the day to escape the fervent wrath of the United States Air Force.

Without consistent reasoning, I developed an illogical impression that this bastion of Chinese troops bivouacked in front of me was in fact the vanguard of the entire Chinese Volunteer Army. It was my confused conviction that these soldiers at rest were soon to become active cadre in yet another major assault against the American and Allied forces. I prayed silently that friendly forces had ceased their protracted retreat and stabilized some semblance of a defensive front by now.

Similarly, it was my distorted sense that if I successfully passed through these slumbering soldiers, I would enter a void between the two forces; a *no man's land*. I became fallaciously elated to the point that I was almost overcome with relief that this horrendous nightmare might soon be over. If I succeeded, I would soon be back to American lines. The fantasies began:

I would be led to a warm fire, fed a piping hot meal, not of C-Ration variety, but grilled steak, before I climbed in a down sleeping bag, inside of a warm tent. In the morning I would be fed a fresh, hot breakfast, and then driven to the rear echelon to be debriefed by G-2. The invaluable information that I provided would turn the tide of the war, and I would be recognized for my priceless contribution. Then I re-entered reality. I had to pass through this enemy encampment.

Before I considered the ascent, I carefully scrutinized the area for sentries among the sleepers, and I saw none. My heart seemed to be working overtime, and yet I was surprisingly composed, except for the surge of adrenaline pumping through my system. I had a purpose and the focus on this objective erased any thoughts of caution. There was no turning back.

This is it. It's now or never. Thankfully my phantom companions deserted me as I was now in deep concentration for the task at hand. I silently ascended the short foothill, probably 50 yards west of where the road was surely posted with alert sentries. I stepped forward, hunched over, mindful of where I would take the next step. I was fortunate that while the ground was frozen on the hill, it was not iced over as were the level, barren fields. I would not have to worry about the abnormal sounds of ice cracking.

Bent over to lower my profile, I continued upward, feeling the ground before me for dry brush, a twig, anything that would disrupt the natural harmony of the surroundings. I was blessed. The parched, iced-over abandoned fields where I was walking had been laden with ice. The slope leading to the summit was not. The grade was frozen, but it was free of ice, a distinct advantage in terms of the lack of atypical noise. If I stepped on a dry stick for example, while scaling this low hill, it would be an unnatural sound that would awaken a hyper-vigilant foe. There, as I scaled cautiously, stealthily to the zenith, I sensed the adrenalin rise, my heart starting to pound, even though I rigidly forced myself to maintain my composure.

As soon as I conquered the hill, and stepped to the apex, I noticed by campfire light a rather wide area relatively level, and then I drew back startled, as I glimpsed the first enemy soldier, asleep in his shallow trench. I was so close to him that I looked directly down on him. The Chinese soldier was lying on his back and his hole, though quite shallow, was dug long enough to accommodate his supine body. I had never seen a foxhole of that configuration before, but I was more intrigued by his face. He appeared to be a young teenager, no older than me, and he appeared to be docile in sleep, even though he had his combat cap on. Both of us, I opined, were thrown into this chaotic blood bath, expected to kill as many humans as possible.

Then I realized what a fool I was. What if he stirred and awakened and saw my face? How stupid of me. I was one of the round eyes in this vast, barren country of slant eyes, and I would have given myself away. I quickly removed my eyes from the young sleeping soldier, and instead, I gazed straight ahead, shuffling softly in a measured, deliberate manner. I decided to squint which gave me more confidence, even though I really didn't know if it would be a plausible impersonation. I allowed my arms to hang loosely in as a natural position as possible. Clearly, I did not want to appear like an American soldier in any way.

Blessedly, the now dim coals emitted just enough light for me to find my way. Was I, in effect, walking down the aisle of a darkened movie theater, guided securely by dim passageway lights? I forced myself to harness my pace to a careless amble, as I navigated around oceans of enemy sleepers in foxholes, my eyes now directed straight ahead. I kept my head straight, with an ever so slight movement from side to side on rare occasion. I needed to saunter as naturally as possible. My heart was beating ferociously, and I felt lighted-headed from this eerie experience, as I skirted one foxhole after another; yet I was extraordinarily composed and confident. Not so for my eyes. They were focused as if they were two searchlights, piercing the black night, squinting, probing for any and every point of danger. Despite the narrowing of my vision, I mentally took note of the surroundings.

The canopy of a million stars was partially obliterated by the overhanging tree limbs, interlaced to arrest the earlier smoke of the campfires. A very strong, pungent, odor of garlic, body odor, tobacco, and fermented cabbage intermingled with the sweet, smoky fumes of burning embers, saturated the tranquil night air. I sensed that I was an intruder in some kind of opium den, the enemy in the arms of slumber, enhanced with strong odors, faint light and eerie silence.

Time stood still, and I perceived that somehow I was a figure in a bizarre reverie. I felt as if I was projected outside of and independent of my body, peering from above, indifferently viewing this bizarre setting, as I walked the enemy gauntlet.

My adrenaline was pumping at full throttle, but for some crazy reason I remained calm. A new tape recording was playing over and over in my head operating at fast forward:

I'm doing it! I'm doing it! I'm pulling it off!

A soldier rose abruptly about 20 feet away from me, apparently to urinate. He noticed me, and uttered some unintelligible words to me. From his slow, indifferent pronouncement, I sensed that it did not call for a response. I reasoned he made a statement to no one in particular. Nevertheless, as I slowly turned away from him and wandered in the opposite direction, I grunted an *Uh*, mindful to maintain my nonchalant pace.[59]

It seemed to take an eternity to accomplish my mission, as I restrained myself from any deviation of my plan. I wanted to break into a full speed run now that I had traversed the major part of the campground, but I vigilantly contained myself. My audacious strategy was working, just as I

---

[59] Many years later, I viewed a film, which although unrelated to my present dire circumstance, had a similar problematic theme. *The High and the Mighty*. The essence of the plot involved a commercial airliner, en route to the US from Hawaii, which developed engine trouble after the airliner exceeded the halfway point, the point of no return. It was impossible to turn back, as the departure point was now farther away than was the destination. Despite the wide incongruity in both situations, I had a flashback. I recalled as I meandered through the enemy camp, I noticed a halfway point in this frightful journey that made such a startlingly impact on my mind. Both the film characters and I were put in a no win situation, although by the grace of God both parties prevailed. Author.

prayed.

Thank you, Sergeant Bruner. I owe you one.

Now, approximately three quarters of the way across the terrain, I allowed myself to take a deep breath. The sleeping enemy became less and less concentrated; the vast majority seemed to be drawn like moths to the comfort of the fires. Few of them settled for exposure to the wrath of the bitter winter outside of their select inner circle.

In time, I saw the abrupt termination of the somewhat level terrain, as I slipped slowly and silently down the hill, careful to maintain the same, steady cadence just as I did on my ascent, when it suddenly hit me. I realized I was now out of harm's way. I was elated. I did it. I congratulated myself and I wanted to congratulate my hallucinatory comrades, but they were nowhere to be found.

Once again I was on familiar terrain, but now I was south of and gratefully out of range of enemy.

Let them tarry in their dungeon abode of raw opium. I set my direction for what I perceived to be due south, verified by the same arrow-straight road, believing that the United States Army was not far away. I stopped to tie my earflaps to the top of my pile cap and I once again manifested as an American soldier. Shoulders back, stomach in, I began the foot soldiers' cadence of 120 steps per minute, arms swinging six inches to the front, three inches to the rear. Forward March. Hup, two, three, four. Hup, two, three, four. Duty, Honor, Country.

I marched steadily the remainder of the night, despite the absence of food, water, and most importantly, sleep. I didn't mind. I was finally free of the marauding, fleet-footed enemy and I was for the very first time, ahead of them.

I would find the American Army in the morning.

THE ICEMAN COMETH

> But October became November; the evenings grew chilly, the mornings misty, the blue sky changed to gray, and the first snow the marines were to know in Korea whitened the surrounding mountains. The north wind from Siberia blew more blustering and searching. It grew steadily colder…The air had rapidly grown colder, the days shorter. One of North Korea's most bitter winters lay around the corner, just how bitter no one can even imagine. Knox, p. 434.

Absent from my memory is how or where I walked the day following my successful infiltration through the enemy bivouac. Staggering deliriously on, I somehow became lost in the frigid mountains for the greater part of the night.

How I ended up there again I will never know. It was now December 1950, and I was lost in time, distance and location. The only saving grace was that I was away from the armed enemy for now, though the harsh elements now assumed the role of adversary. I was hopelessly disoriented, perhaps 30 air miles from the infamous Yalu River, the agreed border shared equally between the two vast, Asian Communist countries.

My eyebrows, eyelids and stubble of a beard were crusted with ice. My hands, lacking mittens, were red in color and in mind-searing, unbearable pain. It was impossible to attempt to put frozen hands into frozen pockets. Lacking needed shelter from the wind blowing, snow blasting, glacial weather, I had no choice but to continually move my fingers to keep them from freezing as I lurched on, impeded by deep, hostile snowdrifts.

God, I could never imagine any weather so terribly cold in my life.

I was expending precious energy needed elsewhere for survival. Up to this point, it was only my hands that suffered the rigors of sub-arctic weather.

"I'll make it," I said to myself.

"I made it this far. I can make it back. I owe it to my buddy, so his family can be informed of his tragic, violent death in order to put the immense sorrow to rest."

The heavy, snow-covered terrain, coupled with my hallucinatory thoughts, disrupted my ability to configure a logical destination. Each step forward took me further and further from my vision of finding my unit. I was falling farther behind, because of the Great Retreat of the American

Army.[60] The absence of the thunderous roar of artillery fire and other vociferous sounds of warfare was maddeningly perplexing. It had to mean there was no enemy to fire at, and even more to the point, no American or ROK units near enough to retaliate with defensive counter fire.

A compass to orient me would be a blessing, for I was completely at the mercy of the terribly black, snowing sky that adamantly refused to share the location of moon and stars with me. I was on my own as to what direction to head.

Now as I rounded a wide-sweeping protracted bend in the mountain, absolute silence inexplicably replaced the menacing roaring sounds of the Manchurian storm. The mountain apparently sheltered the area in which I just found myself.

The old oxymoron, the silence was deafening, was the case. The only sound now was that of the unsteady crunch of my boots striking the ice-crusted snow. When I stopped because I thought I heard or sensed something out of the ordinary, it was as if Mother Nature turned off all sounds. I stood rigidly silent, listening for haunting sounds that did not come, stared for figures that did not materialize, prayed for colleagues who were dead. That left only the very placid, almost silent wisp of snow now softly sifting through pine boughs to escort me on my perilous journey. On so many fearful occasions, I would stop nervously and peer behind me as if someone were following. It was nonsensical behavior, given the terrible Manchurian wind and snow forced every living creature to shelter, except for the pursued—and my pursuers were only so many unknown steps to my front and to rear.

My self-imposed forced exodus in what I anxiously hoped was a southern heading, was one of constant falling, collapsing, struggling to rise, only to repeat this torturous movement over and over again. Tears ripped from eyes by icy, howling wind froze to my cheeks, with no respite. I had never been encased in the frigid abyss of sub-arctic weather before and I

---

[60] When Colonel Freeman's 23rd RCT (Regimental Combat Team) hastily mounted trucks and tanks for a quick departure on the road west of Anju they joined the tide of soldiers and transports that had preceded them on the coastal road west and then south. Only the 5th RCT, still manning the roadblock five miles east of Anju, remained to follow them. The next morning before daylight a small, enemy plane strafed Sukchong, Maj. Sam Radlow of the 23rd Infantry said later that, at Sukchong, everyone seemed to be blowing ammunition and running wildly about making preparations to move further south. Rumors were rife, he said, that the army was going to evacuate Korea and orders were to get on the road and move south - and to keep going. This view was generally prevalent among Eighth Army personnel as the big retreat began. As it progressed, the idea of getting out of Korea seemed to become a settled issue. Appleman, p. 354.

lacked knowledge of what to do. Heavy, nearly impassable North Korean snow was my captor.[61]

I was keenly aware that I once again could feel myself beginning to freeze to death if I stopped for the briefest moment. Were it not for the bitter cold that felt like a knife stabbing my lower back through my flimsy field jacket, I would have surrendered to the reverie of death. It would be so easy to just stop and die on the spot.

My entire body was wracked with agonizing pain. I batted my eyelids to knock the ice off to no avail. My nose was so frozen that I couldn't breathe through it. My lungs were tortured raw by the frozen glacial air because of the constant need to gasp through my mouth in desperation for precious oxygen. My throat was seared and burned from the intake of frozen air.

Each minute was an hour, each day, an eternity. *Oh, God please help me!*

Gradually, I sensed a slight change in the sound of the crunch of snow beneath my boots. I couldn't see. It was a black and white world. The sky was jet black and it appeared to be very late at night. I crudely estimated it to be perhaps two or three hours before dawn. I was blinded by the snow positioned everywhere, and saw icy white grotesque figures, lacking form or shape. I didn't know if I was on a road, foot path or in a field. The trees seemed to have melted away some time past and I felt naked in the middle of territory completely dominated by surging enemy. I was disoriented, in shock and unable to grasp in which direction to move. I was a lost soul in a lost world.

---

[61] "There's hundreds like this, maybe thousands," his Korean driver said laconically. "Some of them coolies, most of them soldiers."

The two men crouched beneath white camouflage netting while American aircraft rumbled through the overcast sky. The cruel Siberian wind hissed about their ears, stirring up a mist of powered snow that coated the rigid figures with further, merciful concealment. Colonel Wong hunched deeper inside his padded clothing, feeling distinctly sick and trying to silence his ever-chattering teeth.

"What do you expect with this weather?" the driver grumbled. "There'll be an awful stink round here next spring." He walked over to one of the figures and tapped irreverently with his foot. The corpse had frozen while kneeling beside a tree, as if sheltering from the cold.

"Like rock, see?" said the driver. With another tap the mask of snow slid off the face to reveal a gaunt, unshaven man with gaping mouth. The snowmen grew more numerous as Wong and his driver headed south. Whole platoons seemed to have perished, squatting in squad order, rifles on shoulders, kitbags on backs, and all snow sheathed, terrible. Gangs of coolies had frozen to death, pressed down by their heavy A-frames, and there were scattering of North Korean refugees, women and children mostly, heaped hopelessly together in search of warmth. A few old men in tall Korean hats had chosen to meet their end sitting bolt upright, hands folded in laps like Buddha's frosted by the snow. Spurr, pp. 265-6, 267.

Struggling forward and then, all of a sudden without warning and in the briefest of a moment, I suddenly sensed myself plunging. But this time it was no loss of balance. I didn't fall off of a typical concealed snow-covered ledge, only to wearily struggle to crawl back on hands and knees to eventually regain my footing. This was a different, peculiar, frightening fall. The ground simply surrendered to my weight, willingly yielding to the initial false impression of solid terrain. With the last bit of ebbing strength that I possessed, I tried to straighten my body as I simultaneously crashed through ice into icy water, up to my armpits.

Oh my God! Oh my God!

My breath escaped me as I struggled to gain some understanding of this new menace and a sense of balance during my fall into ice water. I became surrounded by life-menacing solid ice, beginning to envelop me in a frozen cocoon.

I was entombed as in an ancient Egyptian sarcophagus, an eternal frozen crypt for the dead. Yet, miraculously, I was still alive. Unbearable, glacially-frigid water began to solidify and wrap a liquid blanket of unyielding, rapidly-forming ice, destined to kill. It would kill me. It was god-awful, relentless, freezing water. My ill-fated plunge came to pass so quickly that through the many decades, I have been unable to express my emotional response to this worst of all disasters that could possibly have befallen me. My reasoning was muted because of the absolutely indescribable rapidity of this catastrophic event.

Yet, I was not afraid. I was deeply concerned. I was angry. Angry at myself, even though I should have realized that my disastrous plunge could not have been anticipated, given the deep snow blanketing this vast, worthless wasteland. It was my silent fury, and I dare not cry out.

I felt I would have been much better off to have been shot dead rather than to suffer this absolutely calamitous turning point of my life. After enduring so many sufferings and unbelievable catastrophes, only to have my life end here clearly was a tragic anticlimax to my perilous journey.

Anyone would have died as a result of this catastrophic accident, and I was no exception. The risk of death from my earlier gunshot wound paled in comparison to what I now faced. This foreboding disaster of epic proportions was the closest to death that anyone could possibly fathom without crossing over that intimidating threshold to the uncomprehending, silent, permanent sleep. Perhaps it would have been better to have merely sat down earlier and ceded to death. I had merely to stop and allow the unforgiving winter blanket of death to fall over me and claim me as it did so many thousands of others.

The blackness of the night compounded my suffering. It was so implausible to believe that I must be at the terminus of my very last chance of survival. Just as the remains of my friend will never be returned, nor his sorrowful death elucidated to his family, so would my remains and the account of my death be lost for all time. Both of us would be left to rot unclaimed in this unholy, primitive land.

~~

Recollections of those days of November before the CCF entered the war came back to me in a rush. We were issued winter clothing and shown a propaganda training film on the devastating results of exposure to frost bite. The horrific training film, shown outdoors on a white sheet draped on a stretched wire, depicted treatment of frostbite victims. A doctor, with the use of pliers, walking down a row of frost bite victims would nonchalantly snap the toes off of Battle of the Bulge victims, as though the toes were so many dead twigs.

It was a loathsome display of suffering—an orgy of fright. Those were cold injuries from exposure to the elements. What would mine be like as a direct result of a fall through ice into near-frozen water?

I will never remember how I extricated myself from this confining tomb of water into which I plummeted. I will never know. In the pitch-black night I floundered into one of the most terrifying situations of my life, and there was no one to help me. Now this was to be the ultimate test of my resolve.

I had no idea what this body of water was. It was much too deep for irrigation and too deep for the bank of a river, unless I unknowingly walked on solid ice until it became too thin to support me. An unimportant point if ever there was. No matter. I had a life-threatening disaster to consider. How to save my body and my feet when I was so far behind enemy lines was my only thought. I knew the past. Infantrymen move on their feet, and if those are lost, everything is lost. My feet were lost, I believed. My battle seemed over.

I managed to crawl to safety. My entire uniform up to the armpits had frozen when the water collided with the below zero freezing air. I swung my arms rapidly and forcefully in front of me in a cross pattern and the ice broke off in shards as if it had never cloaked me. I followed this with a deep knee bend, which similarly broke the ice as it did to my upper torso.

With these many years of reflection, I wondered how the freezing water did not penetrate completely through my sparse clothing. The field jacket may have been water repellent to a degree, but certainly field trousers were not. Yet, after I extracted myself from my would-be watery tomb and followed up with these movements, it was if this catastrophe was a fiction of my mind. My uniform resumed a dry condition, as if I had never endured this ghastly experience, except for water that flooded into my boots up to the top and then instantly froze. The ice in my boots brought me to reality. Each foot was literally encased in a block of ice. I almost lost my will to continue because of this final devastating occurrence. No, I had to forge on.

One instant it was pitch black, and the next moment it was daylight. Never in my life had I witnessed such a rapid transition from dark to light. God rolled up the window shade of night to allow the daylight to flow in. Was it some kind of omen to help me or was it yet another hindrance to my goal? It was impossible to tell the location of the rising sun because of the chalk gray sky that cast a depressing pall over the heavens and this forsaken land. The invisible sun refused to budge. It was stuck in the leaden sky and stubbornly refused to move.

I had to get my boots off as soon as possible!

My sense was that I was heading north contrary to heading south as I should, but I didn't know what to do. I realized that it was imperative that I find shelter to remove my boots. In fact, if I were recaptured and by the sheer grace of God, eventually placed in a prison camp, I would never have survived the effects of gangrened feet, which was sure to follow. It would be a slow and painful death indeed.

I had to remove my boots!

Miracle of miracles. As I trudged forward, I found myself struggling across a wide, barren field with a bombed-out hut in the distance abutting the typical Korean dirt road.

That's where I can remove my boots!

Now, I noticed that despite the dense blanket of snow, I had entered an area that I may have bypassed during my journey at night. There was much less snow covering the area. I was, at long last, out of the treacherous mountains.

There were two roads visible, which prevented the snow from adhering, while the surrounding countryside continued to bear a veil of pure white. The dirt road nearest me appeared to run in a general north-south direction intersecting the other road at a more northeast to southwest azimuth. It was that Korean laissez faire road building. The hut adjacent to the road loomed in front of me about 50 yards away, and that is where I would remove my boots.

I was off the road to the west, exposed to unobstructed view, standing in a snow covered frozen corn field gleaned clear of the stalks, where my olive-drab field uniform stood in stark contrast to nature's white virgin surroundings. I was approximately halfway to the hut situated on the near side where the road ran directly in front. From out of my right eye I spied movement at the extreme northeast of the crossroads.

Enemy soldiers! Son of a bitch. What now!

They were fast approaching in one body, and I was in the middle of this snow-covered field right where they were heading. What was I to do? I tried to move quickly to the sanctuary of the shack, as I picked up my pace. Then I noticed they were closing so fast that I had no chance to reach the hovel in time, so I slowed my pace and then I stopped. We were about to collide with each other. I pretended to pick some object up to examine, in a feigned, futile effort to justify my presence, praying that I would appear to be Chinese, as I watched them anxiously out of the corner of my eye. In the excitement, I had forgotten to lower my earflaps, as I did during my earlier ruse with the enemy.

They were no more than 40 yards away and then they passed me running right in front of me. I was directly in their view, yet, they ignored me. They had to have seen me. It was impossible not to have.

Now, I was a spectator of one of the most amazing feats of military drill I have ever witnessed. I stood there, mouth agape, as I scrutinized their eyes. Not one of the platoon of 40 soldiers ever glanced at me. Each enemy eye was focused on the man in front. It was as if I never existed. They just absolutely ignored me. They saw me, but their exercise drill took precedence.

They were huge Chinese soldiers, none of whom were below six feet, four inches, and clad in uniforms unlike I had ever seen before.[62] Their uniforms were more of a blue-green hue as opposed to the regular enemy field-combat uniforms. Their jackets were of the winter-lined type, with vertical stitching about four inches apart sewn in vertical panels. They wore pile caps, adorned with bright red stars, the symbol of Communism, with the earflaps tied up, and they carried no weapons or other accoutrements of war. They had to be a very elite military unit, who lacked the time or the interest to stop to kill a surviving, lone American soldier.

---

[62] Most Americans expected Chinamen to be dwarves, but they found themselves to be assaulted by units, which included men six feet and over. Hastings, p. 170.

The amazing part was their precision drill, which I have never witnessed in any other military unit. They quick-stepped in double time, but using a far more rapid movement than usual even for that punishing cadence. Further, each man perfectly lined behind the other was almost touching. As they marched, or rather ran, they brought each leg to a 45-degree angle, coinciding with the unmoving position of their forearms, also held at 45 degrees, pressed tightly to their sides. It was if they were a unified body of one, each dependent on the other to retain this unbelievable coordination. One misstep by just one soldier would cause the entire formation to crumble. I was awestruck by their ability to run so close to each other in such complete harmony, and run for miles, as I just witnessed, without a misstep. The sheer physical aspects were mind-boggling. One person running alone would be fatigued, let alone this body of troops running so closely in unison.

La crème de la crème!

This was a special force, if ever there was, but I had no idea of their role in this new disaster being administrated to the US Army by these Chinese combatants. I nearly felt an emotional tie, or at the least, a deep respect for them, given their outstanding competence, enemy or not. They passed first me, then the hovel, and continued their precision drill as I turned in awe to watch them until they faded from sight around a bend in the road. They never looked back.

As I contemplated the close order drill, I thought of the contrast; the American Army command for double-time march is at a much slower pace. The distance between columns is one arm's length, while legs are raised about 22 degrees during the run. Even at that comfortable distance between each other, it is not uncommon to manage to step on another's heel. The American Army had not developed the discipline of this elite group.

Once again I focused on the shanty. A fighter aircraft rocket apparently blew a large opening to the rear of the building earlier, allowing me to enter. Once inside, I realized my very good fortune in not arriving prior to the enemy as they doubled-timed by. There was no shelter. There was no inside. The entire front had been blown away, leaving the structure with only two sides standing, while the rear of the hovel, where I entered, had taken a secondary impact from another rocket. I saw an aluminum cooking pot and a pan, strewn on the floor among other debris. A cloud of filthy dust erupted when I gave the cooking utensils a sharp kick to find room to remove my frozen boots as quickly as possible. There was no place to sit. For all reasonable purposes, I was still outside.

The shack stood alone on a corner of the somewhat intersecting roads, and it was quite old. It may have been erected for some purpose having to do with the crossroads, many years ago. The questionable location of the shack must have aroused the interest of an American fighter pilot who apparently dispatched rockets into the building, converting it into one massive piece of rubble.

Because I elected to not sit, I forced myself to bend over to remove my boots. I had to get them off as soon as possible, and I was freezing. The condensation of warm breath from deep in my lungs spewed forth as mist, clouding my view, and slowing my effort to get out of my boots.

The training film of the snapped-off toes kept replaying in my mind. It was as if I were brain dead except for my one obsession. Each second that my ice-encased feet remained in those frozen rubber tombs called sno-pacs brought me closer to destruction. The sno-pacs were composed of rubber to about ankle high. From there leather was added to complete the boot to calf high. Bootlaces held the rubber portion together through metal eyelets, and from there up steel hooks were embedded in the leather portion of the boots to provide for the final lacing process.

The knots that held the laces together were frozen. Try as I might, they would not release. I beat on the frozen knots of both boots with the sides of my fists, and still they would not yield. It seemed a lifetime as I continuously beat on the knots, until the pain of my frozen hands forced me into capitulation.

After gently rubbing my frozen hands together to ease the acute pain, I once again beat on the knots of my boots, until again the pain forced me to desist. I sat on my hands in a desperate attempt to warm them momentarily without success. The frozen ground only accentuated the pain of my frozen hands. I looked around for some tool to assist me and there was none. Even if I found a cutting instrument to sever the bootlaces, I had to consider the aftermath. I needed laces to hold my boots together once they were put back on. I returned to beating on the knots.

As I continued beating on my laces with the side of my fists, I noticed that my fingernails were turning a bright blue. Frozen fingers. I placed my hands in my trouser pockets in order to thaw them. No use.

Finally, the knotted laces of my left boot responded to my beating, and with frozen fingers that I could barely manipulate, I very slowly was able to untie the laces. The laces were razor sharp, and as I desperately wound them around my fingers and palm, the laces cut deep, severing the outer layer of heavy skin. Yet I did not bleed. A quick examination of my hands displayed numerous lacerations that defied nature's process of bleeding. It was just too frigid. The pain was excruciating but I had no option but to continue.

As I tugged forcefully on the left bootlace, the ice gradually released its hold on the steel hooks and surrendered to my efforts. Little by little, I was able to free each lace that had been held captive by the ice that welded the laces to the steel hooks, until I came to the eyelets. There was just no way I would be able to unthread my laces on the rubber portion of the boots. Ice filled every crevice of the eyelets and held the laces prisoner.

In desperation, I turned to focus on my right boot. The steel hooks in the leather part of my right boot finally released their deadly hold on my laces. The same excruciating pain permeated through my fingers as I broke each section of the frozen bootlace from the steel hook that was its captor. Minute pieces of ice flew like shrapnel, and I was eventually able to eject a portion of the lace from the lacing hooks.

I felt I must die. It just became colder and colder. My now lobster-red hands were throbbing in excruciating pain. I could have just as well remained in the field behind me for all that this two-sided wall did to contain heat.

Eventually, I was able to untie the laces, little by little, bit by bit, from eyelets that at last relinquished their persistent hold on my left boot. My back developed severe pain from the protracted standing and bending over, and I could feel the pain of ice permeating the back of my field jacket as if it were snowing on my back from having bent over so long.

Ultimately to my great relief, I was able now to sit on the frozen earth, while I attempted to extract my foot from the left boot. With a mighty effort I grasped my left boot with both hands and pulled with every ounce of my remaining strength. The boot finally came off my foot and I was momentarily elated, only to find yet another obstacle. My woolen sock was frozen to my skin, and the felt insole was frozen to my sock.

Removal of my felt insole from my left sock presented no problem, but the sock itself turned into a gargantuan problem. I had to peel the sock slowly from my foot in order to avoid tearing flesh. I began a very slow, painful, methodical process lest I damage my feet further.

Eventually, I was able to remove my right boot by the same effort, and I stared at both of my feet, unprotected and exposed to the below zero weather. My toes were bright lobster red; the right foot exhibited a deeper hue of red because of my inability to remove both boots at the same time.

I unbuttoned and removed my field jacket, raised my buttocks off the floor and slid the jacket from under me and wrapped it around my feet. The cold went through me like a knife, and the field jacket provided absolutely no solace or warmth to my now severely damaged red-flushed toes.

In the training film regarding frozen feet, we were instructed to remove socks and felt insoles each day, replace them with alternate dry ones, and place the recently removed socks and felt insoles under our armpits to dry them. My dilemma was that I had no other pair to rotate.

The sno-pacs caused feet to perspire because the rubber cannot breathe; hence, the necessity of rotating socks and felt insoles daily. In my case, the sub-arctic weather was beyond the point that my feet would perspire, and as long as I kept moving that danger was minimal.

During this running retreat, the feet of thousands of American soldiers would perspire. Then the soldiers would be pinned down by deadly enemy roadblocks for so long that the sweat in the boots would freeze, and that is why the toll in frostbite was more severe for Army troops where the main thrust of the Chinese assaults took place.

But the frost was neutral. Thousands, perhaps hundreds of thousands of hapless Chinese warriors fell victim to this vilest of all evils. Canvas shoes worn by the enemy were an invitation to frostbite.

Years later I read historical accounts where poorly-equipped Chinese infantrymen would surrender, having no feet. The indescribable cold literally froze feet off, leaving them to negotiate their way on stumps of legs. They lacked mittens and their rubber-soled canvas-bodied were unfit for this deplorable, bitter cold.

I was able to somewhat rejuvenate the frozen items—boots, socks and insoles into a cold, wet, clammy mass. Lacking any other options, I delicately put my soggy socks back on, returned the ice cold watery felt insoles to the bottom of the boots, and forced my boots back on. With that, I laced my combat footwear, stood up and continued on my journey.

I would eventually catch up to the Americans, if only I knew in what direction to proceed.

SLEEPING WITH THE ENEMY

> When the 35th Regiment of the 25th Division was withdrawing south from the front, Col. Henry Fisher, its commander, said, "I saw a warehouse burning. It had trench coats in it – enough for a division of 15,000 men. I was told." The building and its contents were being burned to prevent capture by the enemy... As a result of these orders much winter clothing for American troops, not yet issued was burned in division dumps. In some cases the winter clothing was not issued earlier because of fear that the troops would throw it away before cold weather. Most of the winter clothing, however, was late getting to the front because the quartermaster organization in the United States had not foreseen or been informed that it would have to provide Eighth Army for a winter campaign in North Korea. Appleman, p. 358.

Even though by a determined struggle, I managed to put my boots on and retie them, I knew that my toes were still frozen. They were rigid and unresponsive to movement. My fingers were almost as frozen, but I did have some mobility of my fingers.

I had to get out of here. Clearly, the entire area was swarming with enemy soldiers.

Surprisingly, my depression and extreme fatigue after plummeting through the ice had lessened a bit. I had to keep moving. It was my hope that by continuing my forced march, circulation in my feet would be restored, and eventually my boots and feet would dry from body heat.

The outside temperature matched the temperature of my feet, so the discomfort seemed to be equal, except for the chafing of my wet socks against my feet. My concern now was that erosion of my skin caused by wetness inside would affect my ability to walk. Despite that, I made a vow that I would not remove my boots again to examine my feet because I couldn't do anything about it in any case.

All of these thoughts were set aside as I continued my journey in what I hoped was a southerly direction. The snow had mainly disappeared from this sector, but the cold did not. It seemed to be much colder in this drier area than when I was locked into deep snow. I continued my journey off of the main road, still about 50 yards away, and parallel, so as not to lose orientation, even though I was unsure as to my direction. The huge outcroppings of the Korean mountains rose from the depths of hell in an awkward manner without any semblance of order.

I did not permit myself the luxury of feeling sorry for myself, because I was so very fortunate just to be alive up to this point, and I just believed that I would find the Army soon.

Not only that, but I realized that my feet were that much sought after, but highly-elusive million dollar wound! Those who have served in the infantry will appreciate the term. Each one of us had prayed at one time or another for the same situation, even in a fleeting, guarded moment. It was an honorable way to leave the arena of death. If ever I got back to friendly lines, I would cash in my reward to the doctors at once. It was my lottery ticket.

Among the parlance of an infantryman, and there are many terms, *a million dollar wound* is ranked as the highest order. Simply defined, it is a wound or injury that takes an infantryman out of harm's way via hospitalization. There are many cases wherein a soldier *accidentally* shoots himself, generally in the foot, while hypothetically *cleaning* his rifle. That unconstructive action has connotations that may or may not involve military jurisprudence, while the former case is an honorable way out. Enemy action, or the elements causing the injury, justifies the wound. The term is derived because the recipient would not take a million dollars in trade for the wound. At the same time, the wound or injury is not life-threatening enough nor of a permanent nature that would seriously impair an individual for life.

It goes without saying, given my present circumstances, that I was in that category of refusing a million dollars. I put that dream on hold and out of my mind as I concentrated all of my efforts in getting back alive.

Somehow, I drifted back into the mountains without realizing it. It was as if a magnet pulled me. Low lying foothills were so gradual in elevation. It seemed that scaling a minor hill would eventually terminate with a view of a valley floor. Coupled with inimitable twists and turns of footpaths one is lost again. The only thing that could possibly save me would be a compass.

I lost my bearings rapidly. Before I knew it, I was on an ancient footpath barely three feet wide at the crest, with a straight down incline on each side. The higher I climbed on the footpath the steeper the slope became on each side of the precipitous mountain. It was like one was situated on the cutting edge of a gigantic razor blade, a *razorback* in the vernacular of an infantryman,

My sense was that I was heading in a westerly direction, because the deciduous trees on the north side were void of leaves while the sun was shining on the south side. The path was overgrown with tall wispy grass that I parted as I continued my forced march. It appeared natives had not used this path in a year, probably because of the war. The tall grass was likely a result of the late monsoon season, followed with the scorching summer. The foliage was not so dense as to offer concealment and that eventually became my undoing.

The mountain path grew steeper with each step, and before long I spied a small village huddled against the south side, at the base of and abutting the mountain, obviously to achieve the maximum amount of protection from the harsh weather. My path was so high, that I literally could look down on the village, as if I were sky borne.

Chinese soldiers! The shoji sliding door was open and I could see them sleeping in the house, on the porch and in the yard. Hundreds of them!

I judged the time to be about noon, as I saw them asleep. I didn't perceive them to be a threat, because I would simply continue on my journey and bypass them.

Quietly, I continued walking the now-level razorback, intending to sneak around the force. I continued parting the tall, thin high grass, using a breast stroke type of movement, my arms extended in front of me. I was nearly in alignment with the village, but much higher, almost three stories higher than the small village below. I would pass the village shortly and be well away from here by the time they rose at sundown to begin their crusade southward.

A deep guttural ear-piercing scream! Someone no farther than ten feet from me caused me to instantly and instinctively dive head first off of the cliff to the left. My momentum coincided with three of the loudest rounds I ever heard fired from a high-powered rifle shot at point-blank range.

Scores of years of fallen leaves had broken my fall, as I rolled over and over in an almost freefall motion down a nearly straight down cliff. I curled myself into a ball as I plummeted swiftly downward and away from the hostile sentry. The barren trees that would be an impregnable forest in the spring still allowed me some protection from the direct sight of the enemy sentry.

When I hit the bottom, I quickly scooped up an armful of leaves to finish hiding that part of me that had not already been covered by the dense layer of leaves. Once again, I lay there, gasping for breath, my heart pounding, adrenaline flowing and absolutely petrified by my once-again near death episode. And it was not over. I could just sense the sentry staring down the mountain, searching for my body. He had to believe that he shot me at such close distance.

It seemed that I passed hours lying motionless, fearful, gasping, as I considered my next move. I had to think one step ahead of them. I knew that should they initiate a search for me, they could not descend that precipitous cliff without holding on to the barren trees. That would preclude them from being able to fire on me again, while the sound of footsteps on the dry, brittle leaves would alert me to run for my life. The only immediate danger I could think of would be the chance the soldiers would line up on the path ready to fire at me, once I was flushed from the pile of leaves at the bottom of the cliff.

An eternity seemed to roll by and my anxiousness began to heighten. I had no sense as to what direction to flee, but I knew that I must. With that I bolted from my hiding place and ran as fast as my legs would carry me. I headed for shelter I knew would block me from the view of the enemy, but today I cannot recall if it was another forest, village or a land rise.

Today, in retrospect, I realize they would not expend needless energy to track a lone, stray soldier. Still, the duration between the sentry's shout, and the instantaneous firing of three rounds at point blank range did not allow any option for surrender. The sentry intended to kill me on the spot and only the nanosecond between his premature shout and my instantaneous reaction prevented my immediate death once again. It was just another episode that led to lifelong panic attacks.[63]

My adrenaline level gradually lessened, and I put fear out of my mind as so much excess baggage at this point of my life, because I had to be able to run for my life. My feet were as wet as when I fell through the ice and I was concerned with the loss of my feet.

My journey brought me to some inhabited houses just off of the main road, but I still couldn't discern a correct direction.

Daylight began to fail, and I knew I had a serious problem with the weather. The temperature continuously dropped to below freezing at night as the year approached its end, and this was my first night out since I fell through the ice. I knew that my feet would freeze again, even if I stopped for a moment or two. I had to get out of the weather, now more than ever because of my wet feet. To stop now in this sub-zero temperature would instantly refreeze the soggy, wet socks and insoles.

Realization of this danger mandated that I must find an occupied house to warm up in briefly, whatever the danger, and then leave as soon as pos-

---

[63] Aside from the near fatal diseases of trichinosis, hepatitis, ascaris, frost bite and hypothermia when they all arose to the surface at one time, the silent and severe, lifelong affliction of emotional trauma, now diagnosed as Post Traumatic Stress Disorder (or Syndrome) remained submerged in the subconscious. My years of ongoing panic attacks are directly attributed to the close encounters with death that I was exposed to on a daily basis. Author.

sible to avoid the oncoming enemy. I could not brave the cold night air again.

So, the decision was made. I could not afford to fall asleep outdoors. Hopelessly looking for shelter, I couldn't find any houses as I trudged on for hours, praying the direction was south. The unbearable fatigue set in to the point where I was becoming delirious again.

You will always hear me singing this song.

It seemed as if I had walked for hours and hours without respite, and somehow I again found my way into an area of deep snow. It seemed that I was again in the mountains, but in truth, I had remained in the mountains since being confronted by the enemy sentry.

Show me the way to go home.

When the sentry shot at me, there was an absence of snow. Recalling the event, it occurred to me later that there was no snow when I saw the Chinese soldiers asleep, or I could not have escaped. The north side, where I presumed I leapt from the cliff, would have been the last place for snow to melt because of the position of the sun. While it no doubt would have cushioned my fall, it would have covered the life saving dry leaves that allowed me to conceal myself and I would have left my footprints tracks to follow. I was so deeply perplexed by how the snow seemed to be deep and everywhere at once and just as suddenly absent.

The night was playing tricks on my eyes, aided by my now once again, delirious state. I kept slipping and falling, putting my hands out to break the fall, only to feel the coarse icy snow dig in to the palms of my hands.

A house! I saw the first house in my many hours of struggling and falling through mammoth snowdrifts in these tortuous mountains. But I was disoriented. A house in the confines of these formidable mountains was an impossibility. Perhaps I had walked out of the treacherous mountains unaware, just as when I entered them unknowingly. No matter. I had to find shelter.

Light emanated from the house, dim, most likely a reflection from the common hibachi. As I approached the house from the side, I spied movement at the outside rear of the house. It appeared to be an adult man, just one individual, a civilian, as I scrutinized him and the immediate surroundings from deep shadows. Could he be the possessor of this small but hopefully warm house? What in the world was he doing outside at this late hour and in this sub-zero air? I had to get inside.

I made my move.

It's now or never. There was no other house, abandoned or not, and even if I found an abandoned house, the temperature inside would be the same as the outside. I had to find a heated house or I would die.

He was startled when I approached, but he did not cry out. He was too busy loading some possessions on a medieval handcart, and I thought that very strange, given the very late hour, which may perhaps have been around midnight.

"Papasan," I whispered so softly, slang in Japanese for a male elder, as I made a gesture to sleep by putting my two hands together as in prayer, and resting my leaning head on my coupled hands. He whispered to me in the quietest of tone, but it was of course, in the Korean language. Thinking that he did not understand, I whispered near his ear, again, followed with the same gesture. He returned the conversation in a whisper and added his own gesture by pointing to his house as he whispered in his native language.

Then I got it! Holy Shit!

The enemy was inside and they just evicted him! I was one adobe wall from eternity. I was outside freezing. The enemy was inside, very warm. God, how I wished I could change places. I patted the man on the back in a gesture of thanks, so very grateful that he didn't give me away.

I silently and quickly backed from the area. When I was at last out of sight of the house, I turned and continued plodding on, wandering aimlessly, in hope that I was heading south.

Despondency streaked over me in a rush. For all I knew, I was heading north to Manchuria, and that was as likely a direction as any. My death was imminent from exposure.

I simply had to find an inhabited house. I would take my chances with any inhabitants, but I had to get warm, if only briefly. My problem became twofold. It was too frigid for the enemy to remain outside, so if by chance I did find a house, I had the choice of being slain by the enemy, or possibly slain by the occupants. After all, this area was deep in the interior, the guts of North Korea, and the population had been propagandized against *Imperialist Americans* for years.

It must have been an hour later, perhaps 1 or 2 a.m., when I detected another small village, constructed with high wood pole palisade walls like those I encountered the day after my friend was mortally wounded. My mind, still disoriented, continued to believe that I was still trapped in the mountains, yet here lay another dwelling.

I'd long since lost the road, but I must have escaped once again from the tenacious grip of the precarious mountains; it just didn't seem so. The odds of finding an inhabited dwelling were extraordinary, given that the residents, almost to a person, were fleeing for their lives.

When I approached the opening in the protective wall, I moved quickly and silently, taking a position inside the perimeter, lurking in dark shadows to scrutinize any activity. My advantageous position was sufficient to reconnoiter what I viewed as five darkened houses, with one abode emitting precious light and fumes of burning wood, signifying that someone was inside.

Now, the next item on the agenda was to determine if enemy soldiers were billeted there. If Chinese military were inside, they no doubt would be officers and it would be unthinkable for them to show any mercy on a stray enemy soldier.

Time stood still. After what seemed to be hours, a shoji door slid open quickly and then slammed shut just as rapidly against the extreme outside weather. I missed a golden opportunity to observe any activity in the hooch during this brief interlude.

While the yard was flooded with precious light, it took every ounce of force to restrain myself from bolting for the life saving, warm house. Instead, I melded further back into shadows, warily viewing and evaluating this very precarious venture.

The intoxicating aroma of wood smoke beckoning from the hibachi was insanely magnetic. A soft, alluring enticement, the smoke summoned me to bask in the serene comfort of a warm, inviting home.

An elderly Korean farmer, clad in the traditional white, heavy cotton garb of the peasant toiler, had exited the house, and commenced urinating on the barren, frozen yard, very near to the wood porch of his hooch.

Now, on this very freezing cold and dark night I contemplated what my next step would be, as I gathered the courage to approach him. I was thankful that I was able to watch him exit his house so I could distinguish what I was up against. It would have been difficult to walk to the door, knock and invite myself in. Now we two were about to meet on neutral turf; yet, I envisioned all sorts of dire and fatal scenarios.

As I neared him, he startled in surprise and fear. I whispered to him and made the same gesture of hands held together as a pillow for sleep, as I had with my other would-be landlord. He nodded solemnly, his long, thin white flowing beard clinging to his stomach. The elder turned and walked the few steps to his house preceding me, and stepped onto the porch. Then he turned to me and slowly waved with his left arm, palm up, simultaneously sliding the door open. I followed him in and he rapidly slid the door closed behind us. For a desperate moment I felt trapped, and then I realized that the extreme cold required the door to be closed as rapidly as possible.

It was warm. For the first time in about two months, I was inside and I was warm. My elderly rural friend gestured to me to lie near the rear of the dwelling, about ten feet away from his glowingly warm hibachi, in use by two male friends or relatives of about the same elderly age. It would be three against one if I made an error. I noticed that the hibachi was located near the sliding door, and I wondered if caution of carbon monoxide poisoning had anything to do with its location near a door that could be left ajar to allow fresh air to enter. There were no other inhabitants. No women or children. Could my luck have finally turned for the better?

The customary hibachi in North Korea was situated in a hole cut in the wooden floor, with a large, low table over the top, which when covered with a quilt, allowed the heat to be confined under the quilt to cover cross-legged sitters, their feet and laps. The elderly man returned to his friends, and I watched them carefully to see if I could discern any suspicious movements. They conversed in very low tones, as if they thought that I could understand them, but they didn't look at me, and I felt that to be a good sign. All three were smoking the hand-fashioned cigarette secured in a small upturned metal bowl of a long, slender wooden smoking pipe.

My plan was established in my mind. If any of them left the house, I would flee in a flash. I knew that I didn't have to worry about radios or telephones, so I could escape in the pitch-black night, should any of them attempt to go for help. There was no question I was the enemy and in my mind they would try to gain the upper hand any way they could. My presumption was that they did not possess weapons, or they would have shot me. As a last resort, I could kick my way out if needed, provided I left my boots on.

More than anything, I needed to take my boots off, and dry the insides, but I was so concerned I would have to flee for my life again, I dared not take the chance of being bare footed. I watched them warily, as I lay on my right side, my head propped in my cupped right hand, my elbow bent, supported by the floor. I was reclined on the traditional woven, fibrous, lice infested, tatami mats. My hands began a tortuous tingling and burning, a clear indication of frostbite damage to the nerve endings.

As long as my head remained tilted upward, I was sure not to sleep, and I could react to any movements by these North Koreans in an instant.

I had no intention of having my throat cut while I was sleeping with the enemy. The slightest movement by any of them, and I would be back in the wilderness, swallowed by the elusive darkness. I would warm up and be on my way. I dare not fall asleep.

It was daylight. I had collapsed into deep sleep. My heart was racing erratically, my adrenaline peaking to the maximum level again. One moment I was in an unconscious stupor, the next instant I readied myself for flight or fight, senses honed to high alert, as I suddenly awoke, heart pounding.

While I slept, my Korean landlord touched my field trousers with his fingers near the ankle, ostensibly to determine the thickness. The Army's theory of layered clothing as opposed to one heavy item is much more efficient for warmth, and it is now common practice in the private sector as well. The caveat was that American soldiers should have been better clothed for fighting in this type of arctic climate, and my quantity of summer clothing was far below minimal to survive. My Korean savior was unaware that I was also wearing thermal underwear, allowing air space to exist between layered items. Although I was cold beyond description during my ordeal, it was my extremities that actually froze.

The Korean rural population is clad in one-piece white cotton, heavily padded trousers and a coat that does little to protect against frigid Manchurian winds and snows. Whatever, that Good Samaritan would always believe that American infantry soldiers were woefully unprotected in this most bitter, cold climate.

The Korean farmer was as startled as me at my instant reflex when he touched my trousers. He leaped back in alarm, but then he quickly composed himself, enough to let me know that it was now daylight, and I was no longer welcome. If the Chinese or North Korean military should happen by, and discover his charitable deed to me, he would have been shot on the spot.

I smiled and gave a short wave to him. He nodded gravely and unsmiling, so I supposed that he didn't want to display partiality to an American. He, as well as all North Korean citizens that I encountered extended a hand of assistance to me during this tortuous ordeal. I cannot think of a country in the world that extended such benevolent assistance to a member of what they were led to believe was the enemy.

~~

There were so many times that I would ask for directions from the various inhabitants as the miles rolled by that I began to notice a pattern as

I spoke with the friendly farmers. First, there seemed to be an absence of women for whatever reason. There were generally elderly men and numerous small children occupying the villages at the time, while by far, the majority of the villages were abandoned to the Chinese blitz. I suspected all of the able-bodied men were conscripts or volunteers in the North Korean Army that by now was seriously depleted of manpower.

By use of a stick, I would draw a rough outline of the peninsula of Korea, and hand the pointer to the elder, while at the same time I would ask "Seoul, Seoul?" Most times they did not understand and now in retrospect I realize that it was my error of judgment. I forgot to factor in the bamboo wall that separated the two countries for the past five years. While my orientation was to Seoul, it would have been better to refer to Pyongyang, capitol of North Korea, when asking for directions. I also noticed that because of the language barrier, the elderly would tend to shout, apparently in belief that I would comprehend clearer by them elevating their voices. Conversely, I noted the young children tended to understand more readily, as children seem to do, and I began to turn to them for directions. They were unafraid and they seemed to like me, as I noted their smiles. The feeling was certainly mutual.

~~

As I continued my journey I recall observing an apparently abandoned village at dusk, after invoking rule number two: Always look for enemy before entering any deserted village.

Not observing any foe, I entered close to the village outer perimeter, keeping mindful to remain away from the proximity of the center of the ancient village, in case I was forced to flee. If I walked toward the middle of the village, I would be exposed to view from every house, drastically lessening my chances for escape and survival.

I approached the first house situated on the left, near the extreme south end of this village, whose houses were constructed in a half circle style. It was an advantage that permitted me to pass from house to house with minimum exposure to view.

Each house, at least in this village, possessed a commonality. Every house contained a beautiful, shiny, black-lacquered wooden bureau consisting of many drawers, the top and sides embedded with mother of pearl, inset in various beautiful patterns. As they fled for their lives, the inhabitants abandoned them.

Artfully and expertly Japanese hand-made, they would command a handsome price on today's antique market. Some bureaus were locked, and I saw no purpose to break into them, not only because of the noise that might attract attention, but because the Korean populace owned little if anything of value save this beautiful furniture. While I could not imagine the owner returning, I would not consider destroying these stunning heirlooms for little purpose.

In the third house I investigated, I saw the same type of bureau as in the others, but this dresser was unlocked. I rummaged through the top drawer. Clothing and such of no useful value was thrown to the floor. I hoped to find some type of hand wear for my frozen hands.

As I scoured through the second drawer, I found what had to be the most important treasure of my life during these terrible, arduous times—a compass. An honest to God, authentic American military compass. This was the implement to guide me safely south to security.

The compass was relatively new, made for the American military with a wrist strap to wear as one would wear a wristwatch, complete with a luminous dial that would guide me through the night. That compass must have had the most uncanny history ever. It boggled my mind to deduce how it ended in a beautiful drawer in a small house in a little village in largely abandoned North Korea. This village seemed to be so far away from where the Army was deployed that there was no logical explanation as to how the instrument arrived in this village in this part of enemy country. The only sure fact was that the residents did flee for their lives.

Perhaps the inhabitants of this particular house took flight during the American retreat and left the compass behind. Were a Korean refugee found in possession of a compass by either side of the conflict, it would have no doubt prompted extensive questioning. Prior to the CCF incursion, Allied casualties during the frenzied race north for the Yalu border were relatively light and any slain American soldiers would had been removed by Graves Registration personnel as quickly as possible. I often wondered about this incident, and I never could determine a valid reason.

My odds of survival improved. No matter what the future bode for me, I would never be lost again. Whatever the needle on the compass read, I would comply. A mountain in my path? I knew at the time how to *shoot a back azimuth,* and then how to reorient myself again to the desired direction. The obstreperous, clutching mountains would never ever take advantage of me again, by their constant twisting and turning without reason.

~~

I recall that in late October, the Army outran the supply chain as they raced for the North Korean border. Although troops obeyed without question, morale was in the trenches. None understood why they were called upon to exert the maximum effort, yet the American Army failed to provide sufficient food, ammunition, clothing and equipment.

Company Commander John Hughes performed a miracle that was unforgettable, though it was believed to be our much-respected Korean friend Johnny, who did the trick.

Over a month earlier, we were ordered to fall out on a main road going north where a fair-sized village was located. We had no inkling of what was to transpire, only that we were exhausted and hungry as usual. The company hadn't eaten in over a day.

After some time a large group of smiling villagers approached the company, carrying a huge quantity of native Korean food on trays to serve to more than 200 King Company soldiers. It was a veritable feast, consisting mainly of steamed rice, their staple, along with exotic Korean dishes. The main side dish was kim-chi, odorous but very pleasurable to eat. It would be difficult to return to the bland C-rations.

The collective smiles of the farmers did not go without notice, as it was clear to all that these North Korean inhabitants were providing their food to the company from the goodness of their hearts. Food was in very short supply throughout the peninsula, because of the ravages of war. Rice and other vital foodstuffs were not planted because of the on-going armed conflict. Moreover, the north was predominately an industrially- oriented country that did not do well with the agrarian use of the land.

It was a heartfelt relief to discover that the North Korean rural population was friendly and they would not sell me out. Every frigid night for days after, I was able to share their homes at night with the unspoken proviso that I would get out at the first sign of daylight. Any fear of retribution while I slept was never a consideration, after that first encounter, when I spent the night with the three elderly Koreans.

~~

Better things were yet to come, but I didn't know it at the time.

HELLO MR. KIM

> The horrors of that civilian march southward are indescribable...Unlike the flight of six months ago, the ground was frozen, the nights bitterly cold, the trails nearly impassable over the mountains. Every train that we can divert from military needs were used for the civilians. And they swarmed [aboard] until the flat cars, the box cars, the gondolas were alive with near frozen bits of humanity. . . . Jammed on top of the cars, many were crushed in the mountain tunnels. Others froze to death, or half-freezing, lost their holds and fell off....Vastly complicating all these military preparations was the growing flood of South Korean refugees, who were fleeing the CCF. They were already clogging the roads and bridges by the tens of thousands. The abandonment of Seoul was certain to add tens of thousands, perhaps hundreds of thousands more. Since their presence was already interfering with military movements, Ridgeway ordered Eighth Army engineer Pat Strong to expedite their evacuation southward, using the military trains returning to Pusan. Blair, p. 598.

It was about a week since my companion was shot dead. I was encapsulated by the stress that goes with being alone in hostile country. Each time I was shot at, I learned a new lesson, and I wondered how many more lessons I would be subjected to until I ultimately flunked.

It seemed to be about early afternoon when I was confronted with rule number two: Never walk into a village without reconnoitering for the enemy. Opposed to the small and abandoned villages that I entered before, the one I now came upon was teeming with more than the usual aggregate of inhabitants. Clearly, they could not all be residents. It seemed more like a staging area, an area for a jump-off point to God knows where, rather than the usual sparse village population.

Moreover, this area was directly in the middle of my route of escape, and for me to avoid the village would entail many additional hours and many miles to navigate. I could not afford to squander either time or energy, both of which were priceless items. Any trek near the road to the east was out of the question, given that now the possessors of the road were refugees in flight, interlaced with enemy troops, and hostile to the American invaders from the south, or so I believed. To the west of this teeming village lay the dreadful Taebaek Mountains and I would not dare to venture near there again to be lured back by some exotic, unseen siren to my certain, frozen death. It was instant replay of the situation I found myself in when I infiltrated the enemy encampment days before. But this scenario was different. This was daylight, and none were asleep.

As part of my strategy to determine the relative safety of this crowded village, I secreted myself behind a boulder, assessing the mannerisms of the people in order to decide whether to walk through, or if absolutely necessary, to walk around the village. There were obviously more people than the village could possibly contain, and I was baffled and concerned by their numbers and their obvious uneasiness. It appeared as if they were a multitude of caged animals, pacing about without any clear purpose. Perhaps they were nervous and feeling some impending sense of doom. It was a different mood than I had encountered when we searched villages during the offensive in Korea. I couldn't understand why there were so many people milling about in this village, given that almost every community had been abandoned. In time, the vast majority of inhabitants were to head south in one long, twisted line of hundreds of thousands of itinerant souls, each seeking to reach the safety of South Korea.

A barely audible voice sounded an *uh* and in a split second response, honed by subconscious and instantaneous reactions from the times I was shot at, I whirled around. I saw and instantly mentally processed the source of the sound. There stood a handsome boy of about 14, dressed in a neat, clean student uniform of gray trimmed in dark blue. From his approximate age, I hazarded him to be a high school student.

His hair was very close cropped, nearly shaven as if he were a soldier of the North Korean Army, but clearly he was no soldier, evidenced by his youth and the look of terror on his face. He ran past me into the village I had under observation. The boy began screaming at the top of his voice, as he ran for his life. There was no question why he was shouting. He had just inadvertently bumped into the enemy.

Son of A bitch! I'm a dead man! I thought. What choices do I have? Run for my life again, and be hunted down for the kill? Try to hide where was no place to hide?

Damn! If they shot down 40 of us, think of the fun they would have with me, as one individual.

I had no choice.

The sole option left was to walk into the village brazenly, yet humbly and pray to God that there were no enemy soldiers. For that matter, pray also there was no one there who hated Americans.

When I entered the town square, in the midst of many people there was a male appearing to be about 30 or so, wearing the traditional white cotton clothing of the rural Korean people and armed with a rifle slung over his right shoulder. He approached me with a big smile. Both he and his clothing were filthy, understandable given these trying circumstances, and I discerned the strong odor of garlic and kim-chi on his breath. The man was well built, about the same size as me and unshaven. He may have been a displaced South Korean soldier. There was an armband on his left upper sleeve, which depicted the flag of South Korea, unthinkable in this far north, hostile country, and what did I do? I pushed him away from me.

"Get away from me!" I shouted as I physically pushed him in the chest. I must have been insane!

We clearly had a language barrier, and obviously I hurt him deeply. In my craziness, I perceived him to be the enemy, and I pushed him away as if he did not have the means to step back and shoot me between the eyes. I could see the hurt and confusion in his eyes as he shrugged and wandered away. The many villagers were staring at me with mouths agape in stunned silence, as I wondered how this situation would end. I thought of running for my life, but at this point no one had made any threatening gestures.

Then it struck me. In my twisted thinking, this was a subconscious replay of the same situation when the *friendly* farmer tried to grab my rifle to shoot me during the first part of September, when we conducted a raid on a village of suspected North Korean agents deep in South Korea. That friendly farmer turned out to be a North Korean officer.

After the man, head drooping, disappointedly wandered off, I quickly glanced around to assess my next step, when I was approached by another man. He was muscularly thin and wiry and very clean, sporting a neatly trimmed small mustache. He was taller than me and lithe of movement.

A queasy feeling came over me, and I didn't know if I should attempt to bluff the natives with bravado. The young schoolboy gave me some indication of the hostility I might encounter when he fled into this village and screamed to everyone that the enemy (me) was here. I wasn't the enemy. I just wanted to get back safely to American lines. I did not perceive me to be a threat to anyone.

"Hello, my name is Kim," he said in perfect English. The man displayed a broad smile that revealed teeth white and perfectly aligned against the backdrop of a smooth, well-tanned face. Yet his facial appearance did not have the deep, ruddy furrowed lines of one who toiled in the fields for a livelihood. His pure white cotton pants and jacket were immaculate. Kim stood and walked tall and he imbued confidence by his very presence.

"Hello, my name is Paul, and I am happy to meet you."

And I really was, even though I was astonished and responded with some anxiousness. I was amazed someone could communicate with me in this hostile environment. How could it be possible for anyone to know the English language in this suppressive, dictatorial land? Was he an enemy agent, and would he kill me on the spot or interrogate me? Where did he learn English? I had a million questions.

What was his purpose, and what was he doing in this village? I wondered.

After talking with him for a few minutes, I was put at ease by Mr. Kim. Here was a person who might possibly help me and who spoke perfect English as well. Never mind that he was North Korean, because I sensed that Mr. Kim was as lost as me.

Mr. Kim related his story to me in brief. He had been a political prisoner of the regime of Kim Il-sung. Mr. Kim heard through the grapevine that the North Korean Army was slaughtering political prisoners just before the Army fled north to the political sanctuary of Manchuria in their attempt to evade the swift charging American and Allied Armies.

Mr. Kim's description of imprisonment brought back an appalling remembrance to me. While advancing north with my unit, near the South Korean city of Taejon we came across the epitome of man's inhumanity to man. There had been a hastily-carved ditch, apparently created by bulldozer, filled with several hundred men, women and children slaughtered by the uncivilized brutality of their North Korean captors. Every victim had their hands bound behind them and all were methodically shot in the back of the head. The corpses pitched head long into the ditch, as some fell on each other in a grisly semblance of trying to embrace each other even though their hands were tied behind them. Their inability to embrace each other in their death was accomplished vicariously by the flow of blood intermingling with each other.

In their haste to retreat, the North Korean murderers failed to cover the bodies in order to conceal their insidious crimes or out of disrespect to the victims.

That was not to be the fate for Mr. Kim and his fellow escaped prisoners.

In their urgency to escape the hastily-planned entrapment net cast by an American parachute assault north of the retreating enemy, the NKPA murdered hundreds of American and Allied prisoners who were an impediment to their frantic retreat. The higher echelon of the NKPA, including the villainous Kim Il-sung and his entourage of assassins, managed to escape the web of containment. When the end was near for the fleeing NKPA, they ran out of time to continue their slaughter of the North Korean political prisoners, and by trying to save their own skins, the North Korean Communists abandoned the remaining prisoners to their destinies.

Mr. Kim was imprisoned for many years. Now he was a free man, if only recently. It seemed that half of the population had been imprisoned while the other half of the insidious regime murdered or imprisoned the innocent ones. One on one.

By the grace of God we met. Mr. Kim had a predicament equal to mine. It would only be a matter of time before the North Korean Army would return and the enemy would surely not take the time to imprison him again. A bullet to the back of the head would simplify matters quickly, and I secretly wondered if Mr. Kim realized that fact. Moreover, despite an incredible refugee grapevine, he and the others believed that the notorious 38th Parallel was closed to North Korean refugees in order to prevent clandestine enemy guerrilla fighters from infiltrating into South Korea.

I understood current military policy was to allow all refugees safe passage into South Korea, and that only suspicious-appearing individuals were searched for weapons. Discretion being necessary in order to gain Mr. Kim's assistance, I thought it unwise to share that information with him. This was to be the glue that cemented our relationship. We, in essence, were saving each other's lives. We needed each other, and to express it succinctly, it was clearly our *quid pro quo*.

We made an agreement to the effect that he would try to bring me out to American military control and I, in turn, would vouch for the honesty of him and his fellow escapees. In retrospect, gained over many years of reflection, I have pondered the unbelievable odds of two people uniting to the degree that we did. We needed each other in order to survive and formulated a mutual life-saving purpose. Our initial agreement to assist each other became a friendship that developed deeper and deeper. He was my savior and I was grateful for his help. I began to feel a powerful friendship for him and appreciation for the bond developing between us.

After my escape and many years later, I happened to watch the best film of 1943, *Casablanca*, and in a notable scene Rick shouts aloud to himself in a drunken rage about the irreclaimable Ilsa:

Of all the gin joints in all the towns, in the world, she has to walk into mine.

I thought back to Mr. Kim and my flashback was somewhat similar:

Of all the shacks in all the villages in North Korea, how did I manage to stumble into the one person who might save my life?

Mr. Kim was my guiding light and my deliverance.

"Put these on Mr. Paul. It will help to get you back to the Americans."

He held open a typical Korean heavy, white cotton, baggy coat, and I easily slipped it over my Army field jacket. It had a hood sewn into the garment, and was devoid of buttons. The coat was held in place by means of a sewn on cotton belt of the same material, used to tie the jacket together after one side was folded over the other in double-breasted style.

It was a bizarre scene, as I fantasized I was trying on formal attire at some expensive men's store—a haberdashery—being assisted by the salesman. The trousers of the same heavy, cotton material slipped over my Army fatigue trousers just as easily, eliminating the need to remove my boots. One size fits all. The baggy trousers were held up by a heavy cotton draw belt sewn onto the garment waist seam. Both of them were very comfortable, and it added another layer of protection against the cold.

Certainly, I was in violation of the Geneva Convention by covering my uniform with civilian attire. They could shoot me as a spy. But they would shoot me under any circumstance, so it really didn't matter. After shaking hands to solidify and validate our agreement, Mr. Kim immediately led us off. We walked a few miles to the main road, teeming with masses of refugees. This would be my baptism into a unique experience that has profoundly influenced me for life. This is not only because of the severe subsequent traumas, but also because of the sheer exultation and joy of surviving against all odds made possible only through the daring efforts of Kim and company.

Mr. Kim's followers were, on and off, a group of eight, not counting me. All were young and all desperate to break out. Some refugees entered the group and others left for reasons I never knew. There were two rifles distributed among the men—really boys like me—though I did not know if they were soldiers separated from their ROK units, or if they were escaped political prisoners.

It seems that in my 50-plus years of banked memories, there was another male somewhat older than us, but not quite the age of Mr. Kim. I recalled that he seemed to exercise some authority in the group as well, and he was always armed. I sensed from his bearing he may have been a military man.

The language barrier precluded any communication between me and the group, except when Mr. Kim would interpret among us. The unspoken assurance of a smile between us was as deeply meaningful as was comprehensible conversation.

When this first day eventually evolved into frigid night, Mr. Kim stopped in a village just to the west of the road, peered around briefly and then headed to an abandoned house facing and abutting the road. We were on the outskirts of a small town—more of a large village—still far to the north of the infamous capitol of Pyongyang. When I entered the house I immediately noticed that it was heated. Someone ahead of us had thoughtfully built a fire to accommodate us. I will never know how this happened, because I was too immature to solicit that type of information from Mr. Kim.

This was to be the night I removed my boots for the first time since my calamitous collapse through the ice so many days ago, except of course, for when the mishap first occurred. I left my socks on, glued to my toes by toxic pus. I had no interest in examining the condition of my feet at this point. I was embarrassed by the horrible odor emanating from the infection, so I removed my field jacket and wrapped my socked feet in a bundle to keep the deplorable stench confined. And I apologized to Mr. Kim for it, and I implored him to explain to the others. He did, with a smile to alert me that it was just fine.

My socks, insoles and the interior of my boots dried over night, noticeably speeded and aided by the heat in the house. It was the only time that I removed my footwear until the end. Ignorance is bliss. Meanwhile I caught up on sleep. As soon as the candle was snuffed for the night, I instantly spiraled into deep sleep that revived my physical and mental senses.

We arose every morning before dawn, lacking food or drink, and immediately melded with other hundreds of thousands of equally starving and pitiful refugees all heading south to escape the wrath of the oncoming North Korean and Chinese armies. No one was walking north.

The sun made an extraordinary effort to gleam through the dim sky one particular morning. It was an omen. The awful snowstorms sweeping down from the desolate plains of Siberia had long ago erased my memory of the god-awful torrid, humid summer and replaced those memories instead with the current nightmare of unforgiving artic winter.

Another enigma I have thought of over the years was how the refugees could possibly sleep at night, because of the intense frigid night that dropped below zero. Could they actually sleep? We do know that we were all wanting for food, though there was none to be had. Every night we billeted in some abandoned house, but there were not enough shelters to accommodate the hundreds of thousands of other freezing refugees. Additionally, the empty houses required heat or they were as cold inside as out and it appeared there was no firewood available, but for our group, the hooches were always warm. Again, I never had the presence of mind at the time to ask Mr. Kim.

Now, as I wind down in my years, I often contemplate how the misery and horror of those tortured people allowed them the courage to continue their journey. And this is not propaganda that I am espousing. Those unfortunate people had absolutely no political agenda. Nor did I. They were trying desperately to get out to save themselves from starvation and to escape the brutal horrors of war in which they were entwined. So was I.

One very early morning, we were walking down the main road, which traditionally is approximately two to three feet higher than the abutting rice paddies, presumably to serve as a levee to contain the water in the paddies. When the road made an inexplicable curve to the left, I spied movement in the frozen rice paddy, just off of the east side of the road. Because of the density of the refugees, coupled with the protracted distance, we could not make out what was occurring.

Eventually, we approached the area and discovered to our horror the movement was of an adult male, victim of an American Air Force sortie that attacked the columns of refugees earlier. His body had been rolled from the road, and the cold water in the paddy eventually turned to solid ice, entombing him, with the exception of his right arm, which was above the ice, exposing the cadaver's arm to the harsh elements. Both the victim's arm and sleeve jacket were the same sallow gray. The source of the movement was that of a starving dog who was tearing viciously at the heavy cotton sleeve of the coat of the victim to get to the frozen flesh of the arm. It was my hope that someone would come along hungry enough to slay, butcher, cook the beast, and then feast on it to stave off starvation.

All who passed this way, while stoically staring straight ahead, allowed the scene a sideward, fleeting perfunctory glance, dismissed it, and went about their business of survival for themselves. I did the same.

I sensed that many people knew, recognized, or at least heard of Mr. Kim. His very presence seemed to inspire a sense of confidence, enhanced by the manner in which he carried himself and by the way he spoke. Soft toned, yet with an unspoken air of command. A born leader.

Mr. Kim had a brother who lived in Boston, Massachusetts, but it must have been more than that to have had him imprisoned. Mr. Kim shared with me that he had been an engineer in the mighty hydroelectric plants of the Chosin (now Chanjin) Reservoir, and owing to his fluent command of English, he certainly would have been an asset to the Communist regime. Clearly, his aura of honesty and integrity was his undoing.

No matter how unique and positive the qualities one possessed, if one spoke against the State, he would be imprisoned or murdered. Mr. Kim apparently qualified for both categories.

Hundreds of thousands of frigid refugees huddled in grievous misery in the bitter cold night outside on the road where they collectively stopped en masse for the night to rest. There were no fires to protect the innocents, for there was a lack of wood for fuel. Our journey took us through the vast, open valleys of North Korea, where iced over and abandoned rice paddies abounded for miles and miles, separated only by the main road of escape. Each family had only what possessions they carried with them, and not one ounce more. I marveled how everyone integrated, although I was sure that the bulk of them were strangers to one another. Hundreds of thousands of refugees snaked along the road like one meandering, monstrous serpent. After each nightly stop, before the break of dawn, the refugees commenced the journey south again, rising as one body.

The refugee problem was like a gigantic snowball rolling down a mountain, gathering speed and magnitude, swelling out of control, in a monstrous and ever-growing pitiful mass of souls. By the time the refugees moved south following the retreat of the United States 8th Army, the refugee situation became uncontrollable.

During our southbound exodus, even the occasional primitive outdoor hole-in-the-ground farm toilet was not used by the horde of refugees. Men, women and children would simply step from the road onto the frozen rice paddy, lift their dresses to hip level, or drop trousers, as the case might be, squat to relieve themselves, wipe with their hand. No one in this vast, unending mass of people paid the least attention.

It was very late at night as we followed Mr. Kim into our new abode, again heated when we arrived. I will never know who prepared the myriad houses for us or how Mr. Kim knew which abandoned house was reserved for us. No matter, I fell to the floor immediately and collapsed into a state of intense sleep.

Tomorrow was another day for marching south. We would soon come upon the Americans.

THE INNOCENTS

> It had been a long and terrible war, the cost of which could never be accurately reckoned. The Pentagon estimated that military casualties on both sides came close to 2.4 million. Other sources estimated that North and South Korean civilian casualties were about 2 million. If these figures are approximately accurate, then about 4.4 million men, women, and children were killed wounded or otherwise incapacitated in the war. Both North Korea and South Korea were utterly ravaged. It would take decades for each nation to rise from the rubble. Blair, p. 975.

Another bitterly frigid day was beginning under the usual dreary skies. Dawn was positioned to open its curtain to yield the precious light essential for us to forge on with our intrepid mission—the unremitting quest to seek a safe haven. Even now we were blessed. The ominous gray-colored sky grew more morose as it tried to constrain the deluge that might pour misery down on the endless horde of refugees at any time. None of the hundreds of thousands of refugees or I were equipped for the devastating imminent storms of rain. The road would transform into a quagmire, for the ice holding this wretched road together would have surrendered to the floods spilling from the heavens, off-setting the rhythm of the untold multitude of shuffling feet.

When our group joined the twisting rope of humanity plodding south on the road I was met by a curious sight. This was yet another instance when the road to freedom made a very odd wide bend to the southeast for some unknown reason in this vast, malodorous valley. No natural impediments caused the road to be redirected so it resembled a meandering stream, liberated to wander where it might.

Closer observation of the infrastructure representative of the free-spirited Koreans demonstrated that roads are not usually locked into rigid Occidental modes of tradition. The primitive roads of Korea do not generally bisect at right angles but rather roam illogically, disrespecting government mandates. These roads, as the inhabitants, tended to exhibit a sense of laissez faire until the North Korean bamboo curtain slammed defiantly down.

Among the eight of us with Mr. Kim were two young, beautiful Korean girls about my age. Two of the younger males from the group instigated a rivalry for the attention of the young ladies. I longed to be a contender as well, for my post-puberty-driven glands were peaking despite my current calamitous situation.

Fortunately, the language barrier and common sense forbade me to even display a hint of such a thought. I was on the road to deliverance and I wouldn't jeopardize that for anything on earth. I had only one life.

My *Mickey Mouse* boots and socks were at last dry since that first night with Mr. Kim and his group. The pain of gangrene was more pronounced, but I would not allow that to be an impediment to my mission. I was confident I would be back in military control by the time the inability to walk became a factor to consider.

Pondering my frightful circumstances, delicious images of these young, attractive North Korean ladies swept me away in reveries that presented me with an additional imperative to survive. I wondered if they were sisters. Perhaps they were my age, and they were so very lovely. During my abysmal ordeal, I became consumed not only with the less than trite obsession of escaping, but in fleeting moments, I reflected on the absence of a normal, typical childhood.

My tortured mind cried out for some sanity in respect to the life-threatening dilemma in which I found myself hopelessly mired. It was nearly too much for an inexperienced, naïve 18-year old to comprehend. My extraordinary predicament was far beyond the scope a high school student could process.

During the quiet evenings when catching a rushed sight of these beautiful girls, I fantasized about how my life should have been, rather than what I was enduring during this terrible, protracted flight for life. The joy and comfort of having a girl friend and sharing interludes of happiness and pleasure was alien to me. Attending high school and being among friends and social groups was foreign to me. I could only relate to the stark reality of barracks life.

Having never attended high school left a painful void in my life. I missed the formative years—years of uncertainties and years of joy, years of maturing and years of carefree youth, years of social integration and years of building lifetime friendships. They all eluded me.

I wondered how high school days were. I wanted to relive my life vicariously through the eyes of rhapsodic, carefree youth. I wanted to learn of prom nights and football games, Saturday-night dances, social gatherings and working together on homework assignments. I wondered about my first date. Would we kiss and embrace passionately in a car on a small town lover's lane? I missed all of those blissful, adolescent growing experiences. Most importantly, I missed the development of social graces that are formed for life through trial and error by high school experiences.

I missed them all.

My mind would go on a drifting voyage. As a teenager, I wanted to see the world in all its splendor, never dreaming that I would be cast upon some filthy, forbidding country to assume a dynamic role in the unmitigated horror of war. In retrospect, I pondered so many times as to what destiny held for me. A young man, beholding youthful pleasures as one matriculates though joyful, adolescent adventures, is a far cry from one marching and soldiering into potential death, being thrown into and fighting to survive the horrific repugnance of war.

Consequently, it is difficult to share wartime experiences. Those who have never been exposed to the dread of *in your face combat* cannot, nor are expected to be able to relate to those experiences. My fearful times in Korea are too painful to comprehend. No one, without the experience of intimate, wartime encounters, can possibly fathom how they affected for life those so-few survivors.

Battle-weary infantry soldiers know what it is like, and we understand the brotherhood that binds us without the need for words. We accept it as it is. We share with no one, because no one could possibly comprehend the trepidation of close up war when it slaps you smartly across the face. Someone will say, meaning well of course: *It must have been terrible.* Those are mere words, albeit sincere, but still words without comprehension.

No one, unless they experience the reality of infantry combat first hand, could ever possibly conceive the depth of the terrible, the fear, the horror, crashing headlong into the psyche forever. The quintessence of combat is death, and the battlefield never leaves one's mind. Loud sudden explosions with or without provocation cause one to recoil in horrified automatic reaction for the remainder of one's life. The Pavlov effect. Post Traumatic Stress Disorder. I know it as *The Gray Badge of Courage.*

Still, I asked for it. My aptitude test indicated that there were other career venues for me, particularly in foreign language science. But, after being propagandized as a child by World War II war movies, I opted for the infantry. I had it coming. It would serve no purpose to flagellate myself as to my lot in life. I chose it; I would live with it. Or, I would perish from it.

My thoughts would turn to the two young ladies of North Korea, in an effort to stave off appalling images of massive, unchecked bloodshed in this awful country. I had never had the luxury in my life of a kiss from an innocent young lady. I was ignorant of the anatomy of a woman. I was virgin. I killed enemy in defense and I was awarded the *Military Order of the Purple*

Heart in return when they tried to kill me, and yet, a normal childhood eluded me. I longed to be with these lovely North Korean lasses, just to be in the company of someone morally immaculate and decent and beautiful.

And, I wondered what the two young ladies pondered about me, as I fantasized? Could they have secretly thought of me in their deep, forbidden secret thoughts? They had an array of young handsome admirers, and they could select whomever they wished. Yet, could there have been some magic to view me as a type of *Lieutenant Pinkerton* from Puccini's magic opera, *Madame Butterfly*? They might have had such thoughts. I will never know.

~~

One particularly very cold evening, gathered together in the snug, heated hooch, I managed to sneak a forbidden, secret, momentary glance at them. This particular night I set myself apart from the others, excusing myself to Mr. Kim, using the language barrier as a ruse. I positioned myself strategically as I lay on the floor, in order to glance at everyone as they spoke in their native tongue. I used this subterfuge in order to gaze at the girls without being obvious as they spoke.

Once, as one of the girls began to speak, she turned to me, and our eyes met for a fraction of a moment. For a brief faint interlude, a knowing whisper of a smile formed on her lovely face. In that rapturous instant as our eyes met, and as we riveted on each other, I felt the rush of two young people caught up in a precarious and grisly struggle for survival that only we two could fathom. I wondered how life would be if we were together alone without this appalling carnage that melded us as one.

Her magical image, enhanced by subtle candlelight dancing from rough wood walls, embodied everything that was right for two young people who were pointlessly placed in harm's way. During the days we would glance momentarily at each other and for a moment nod, and oh so fleetingly exchange a brief smile before we merged for the daily migration southward. We were strangers in a vast sea of strangers, and we were on an impersonal journey to fulfill our respective missions of the sum and substance of escape.

But it was the nights that prevailed. There was something about the evenings that made things seem so serene, so tranquil. It may have been the soft glow from the candle. It may have been the sweet, intoxicating aroma of the fire, producing the life-saving heat to allow us to survive. Perhaps it was the commonality that drew us inexplicably closer and closer together, just as a magnet lures the metal to its bosom, to its very being.

Did I imagine the hint of a beguiling smile from the maiden or did I misconstrue? Had I have been articulate in the Korean language I would have known from when our eyes first met the answer to that seemingly unspoken attraction.

When first we met, both maidens were clad in the white cotton clothing of the rural farmer, as was I.

My untamed, uncontrollable imagination ascended as I fantasized the lasses alone with me, they untying the cotton belt that would release the last sole vestige of clothing between their lithe, firm, but supple cream white bodies and me. Erotic images of diminutive, well-defined, firm, white breasts characteristic of youth danced in my head, as I crazily contemplated how my virginity would be swept away with purity. When they occasionally leaned forward while sitting on the tatami mats in our nightly hooches, I wondered what the loose fitting garments had hidden from me. The maidens were lacking under apparel that would restrict the melding of two passionate bodies uniting as one. In my near-deranged mind, I was just one cotton belt away from undiminished, unmitigated sensual ecstasy.

The petite, exhilarating and sumptuous hint of cleavage between their firm and lithesome breasts exposed them as women to be desired, while I imagined that the ruddy triangle of their lower bodies defined them as undeniably sensual women. Sweet and delicious and non-threatening and giving with all of the bittersweet, succulent mystification they could spawn.

"Mr. Paul, do you have something to say to us? You are so quiet. I can tell them for you if you wish," Mr. Kim inquired. Everyone was smiling at me, apparently awaiting a response.

I was shocked into instantaneous recovery from my reverie.

Oh my God! Did Mr. Kim read my mind or were my covert mannerisms such that it was so painfully obvious? Was what I had just fantasized now so apparent to all? My God, did I offend anyone?

I was so very unsure of how I should respond, as I struggled for meaningful words to respond to Mr. Kim's query. "I just want to say that I am so happy to be here with you," I meekly stammered uncertainly. "And now I must sleep. Thank you, Mr. Kim, and good night to everybody," as I turned my head away from the group, awash in total, silent embarrassment.

I was deep in sleep before the candle was snuffed for the night.

~~

The next day as we halted for a few minutes off of the icy road, I briefly considered enlisting the assistance of Mr. Kim as an interpreter. Could he act as a liaison between the ladies and me? Surely there was no harm in just conversing softly together, with an interpreter serving as a proper chaperone.

It was as if a diminutive guardian angel was sitting on my shoulder whispering softly in my ear: "Remember your classes during basic training in regard to courtesy abroad. Respect the culture and mores of people of other lands. Paul, could your actions be an affront to others? Perhaps in this culture your deeds would be misconstrued. What may seem innocent to you could be a social affront to others. What is the most important issue in your life now?"

East is East, and West is West, and never the twain shall meet.

I was Walter Mitty, the consummate dreamer. Mr. Kim's words shattered my latest thoughts and brought me sharply back to reality. "Mr. Paul. We must go." I put my thoughts of the Korean maidens back into the pocket of my mind, as we stiffly arose to continue the struggle forthwith on our fateful mission.

By 10 a.m. we must have walked between ten and 15 more miles south on the massively crowded road. We had been marching for some time, and as I walked, my mind drifted back, mired in thoughts of my terrifying days alone before I was salvaged by Mr. Kim.

The memories didn't come in chronological order. They just came. Continuing on and on, one painful step after the other, the constant rhythm of the pace induced a trancelike state of mind, bringing freely-wandering memories of past days.

There is an old, old saying among infantry soldiers:

There are no atheists in foxholes.

Acquiring my compass was fate unto itself.

Being one of 21 to survive Anui, my several narrow escapes from enemy killers, the finding of the compass in such an unlikely place—all gave me pause to reflect. The amazing meeting with Mr. Kim, who was bringing me out from Hell, was no coincidence. These events could not have happened, I firmly believe, to anyone else in this manner in a hundred years, and I was the rarefied beneficiary of these astonishing events.

These marvelous, God-sanctified protections transformed me into a true believer. A Supreme Being had something else in store for me other than being shot to death alone, behind hostile lines, terminating with my flesh rotting from bone, my skeleton left to scatter to the four winds, never to be claimed by family.

"Mr. Paul, your legs are going wrong. Please ride the bicycle again."

My philosophical thoughts were interrupted by Mr. Kim. His words jolted me to the present. He must have noticed my limp. Although it was painful, I was determined to walk as much as possible. I was determined to get back, even if by the absolute necessity of crawling. Riding on the bicycle for an extended period would soften me and might perhaps lull me with a false sense of protection. What if, for instance, we somehow became separated? It was a logical possibility given the multitude of refugees. I would have to press on alone, although with my precious compass, coupled with the nearness of the Americans and the obvious absence of the CCF, I believed I might succeed. Provided of course, I maintained the same determination I developed since my capture, even though I wavered in the face of adversity many times. I owed that much and more to my buddy.

My feet had to hang down when I rode as a passenger on the bicycle, accentuating the pulsating pain caused by gangrene. It seemed inadequate circulation caused blood to settle to my infected feet. Frost-damaged arteries affecting my lower extremities was the likely culprit. When I walked and limped, it was less painful than riding on the bicycle. Moreover, the operator of the bicycle had to pedal far faster than did a walker in order to maintain balance. As a consequence, we distanced ourselves from Mr. Kim and his associates by several miles. I was reluctant to lose sight of my guide for fear of missing him among the horde of refugees as they, too, pursued the freedom road south.

"OK," I suddenly said, and my Korean friend seemed to understand. He stopped and I slipped off of the bicycle rack mounted over the rear wheel while he pulled the bicycle to the edge of the road where we sat waiting for Mr. Kim. I was ill at ease because of our language barrier—my North Korean friend no doubt feeling the same. We had no cigarettes to share and no means for small talk. We had so much to impart, to talk about, but it was as if we were from two different planets, at this moment thrown together for mutual survival. Both of us sat silently, absorbed in our own personal worlds. This late morning the sun was trying frantically to punch through the dense overcast without success, though it was now pleasant enough. I noted our breath no longer condensed in the air. In truth, any weather was tolerable compared to the ominous and depressing exposure to the frigid mountains of northern Korea and frozen winds blowing in from desolate Manchuria.

Wandering recollections materialized again as I ruminated on the days when I was alone before the fateful encounter with Mr. Kim. I reflected on the surreal experience of sighting the pyramid and the resolve of the Chinese to do the impossible.

~~

I learned later that during this phase of my escape, once Mao realized the Americans and her allies conceded North Korea to the Chinese, he ordered multiple armies to eject Allied enemy from Korea. By attempting to drive the Allies into the Strait of Tsushima (The Strait of Korea), Mao misread the tenacity of UN forces, under the new command of General Matthew B. Ridgway. That became the fatal downfall for the Chinese— their private Waterloo. That ill-conceived enemy objective cost an estimated one million *additional* deaths to the Chinese Volunteers, the flower of the youth of Communist China. They too, should have stopped at the border, the 38th Parallel, and returned their young men to China to tend the neglected rice fields.

More bombs were dropped on the Korean Peninsula during this three-year conflict than all of the bombs combined during the entire global phase of World War II; yet, in this venue it was largely ineffective. Pyongyang and other cities and towns simply went underground with their government and their essential services.

Coolies dismantled large lengths of train track just before dawn and laid the track askew, deceiving Allied Air forces into believing railroad tracks had been destroyed. Once the marauding Air Force abandoned the area, the track was hurriedly placed back in operation each evening, while pilots were relaxing at the officer's club making note of their successes.

Enemy trains rolled all night bringing troops and war materiel to the front, unobserved and unencumbered. Munitions were scattered in and around villages and petrol was camouflaged. Whenever a rail line was severed by the Air Force, Chinese workers were dispatched to bomb sites to repair any ruptures to the crude transportation system within minutes to no more than a few hours. The northwestern-most city of North Korea, Sinuiju, whose bridge spans the Yalu River, and connects with the border city of Antong (now called Andong) in Manchuria, was severed by the Air Force many times, because it was the nearest entry point for Chinese forces from China proper, just east of the bridge. Yet, the bridge was cleverly refurbished for maximum use following each bombing.

There was a terrible toll to pay for this strategic bombing operation. A little-known fact of the war was that Russian-made MiG-15's, flown by Russian pilots, managed to down five B-29 Super Fortresses in just one week earlier the next year. The American public was led to believe the American Air Force ruled the skies unopposed during the conflict, but the gigantic American bombers were relegated to bombing missions at night for safety purposes.

What Allied military leaders were unaware of at the time was that the frozen condition of the Yalu River during this extremely harsh winter allowed for heavy enemy vehicular traffic to maneuver across the iced-over river under the protective cover of night. Moreover, the destroyed bridge decks themselves were temporarily sheeted with heavy lumber during the night to accommodate trucks, artillery and tanks. Just before dawn, male laborers dismantled reinforcement boards from the bridge that had accommodated vehicles during night-transportation operations, and then peasant women using primitive brooms swept vehicle tracks from the frozen Yalu River. When daylight cast light on the war zone, everything appeared to be the same to the raiding Allied Air Force as it was the day before.

A motion picture filmed in 1954 was based upon the best-selling book *The Bridges of Toko-Ri* by James Michener. It is a vivid chronicle of a very dangerous, but strategically necessary attack on the enemy bridges. For years I wondered if that colossal pyramid I witnessed was *The Bridge*. It was not. Research indicated the *Bridges of Toko-Ri* were located on the eastern part of the peninsula, and I was clearly stranded in the west. Yet, to be hopelessly lost in this crucial area where no apparent warfare occurred, makes me believe I am the sole American to view this mammoth pyramid.

It would be of notable interest if North Korea would engage the west diplomatically again to the point that both nations would exchange military information relative to the war, and as one example, provide information and location relative to this gargantuan, 20th century wonder of the world.

Surely, by virtue of its enormity, the pyramid must continue to rule the mountains even after 50-plus years. There is no doubt in my mind that the pyramid still stands. Time may have taken its toll and the edifice may have settled slightly over the years. No doubt the trestles holding the weight of the tracks were replaced many years ago in order to accommodate a more dynamic rail service, but there would be no purpose to expend needless effort to dismantle this titanic monument to Chinese determination.

∼∼

"Mr. Paul, how do you feel? You are stopped."

My contemplation about the pyramid was jolted from me by the arrival of Mr. Kim, who met us as we sat at the edge of the road. I was completely lost, ruminating on my unusual experiences when Mr. Kim spoke.

"Fine, Mr. Kim, I feel very good. I was waiting for you. Can I walk with you for a while? I want to give your friend a rest."

"Please, we shall go," said Mr. Kim, sporting his usual friendly smile.

We walked together, observing the once-bustling capital, Pyongyang, rising decrepitly in the distance.

The urgency of circumstances called for us to rest but briefly. It was imperative to elude the pursuing hot breath of the dragon—the surging, always threatening Chinese forces.

"Thank you very much," I said with as big a smile as I could muster to a woman who came up to me. She had singled me out, obviously because I was an American, and she sidled up to me from the left side of the road. Then she handed me a small object. At the time, Mr. Kim walked near the right outside edge of the dirt road, and I walked next to him to his left.

I bowed to the thoughtful lady refugee as deeply as I could without pitching forward as we both continued our plodding march south. She beamed in return, bowing in response to me as she smilingly eased her way back to the left side of the road, whence she came. The Good Samaritan blended easily with the southbound throng.

I judged her to be perhaps 30, an elderly woman to me at the time, but attractive given the profoundly arduous life she led. She must have endured years of hard labor toiling in the harshest of climates, yet the woman was able to maintain her national pride and dignity and bearing.

"What is this, Mr. Kim?"

"It is Korean candy. It is made from rice and it is good. You will like it. It is, how do you say, Caffy?"

"Taffy?"

"Ah so, yes. Taffy."

"I want to give you some, Mr. Kim."

"No thank you, Mr. Paul. It is for you, and you will like it I am sure."

I glanced at my gift once more. I held an approximately six-inch long maize-colored hard substance, perhaps three inches wide, and when I bit down on it, I immediately broke a molar from the lower right segment of my teeth.

Son of a bitch! That's all I need now. A broken tooth, while I am exposed to the elements, and without any means of treatment.

Could it possibly get any worse? A toothache without relief ranks high in the pain threshold. I would have to live with it.

Mr. Kim was right. It was the best tasting candy I ever had. I savored every bite, having this piece of goodwill presented to me by a total stranger, in the presence of thousands of refuges more worthy and needy. It was one more positive exposure to refugees that gave me the will to press on along with them.

Most likely it was the candy that did me in, infecting me with a disease that would cause me great misery. Korean taffy is kneaded by hand. The lack of toilet tissue and clean water to wash was the culprit. The candy was literally teeming with infectious *ascaris lumbricoides*, borne in the ever-present human feces. And that is what I ingested along with the candy.[64]

The *Honey Bucket* agent was noticeably absent during this trek. At least the tools of his trade were missing. Usually equipped with two large, approximate three-foot high, wide brimmed terracotta urns, balanced and carried on a stout pole across his strong shoulders, he was shunned by all. His arduous career consisted of traveling from farm to farm, ladling the putrid semi-aqueous human excrement from out-holes and carrying them to neighborhood fields for fertilization. One could smell his repulsive and revolting presence for great distances.

Where were the elders? Certainly many of them were killed early in the war when they darted unexpectedly in front of high-speeding deuce-and-a-half transport trucks driven rapidly by young, spirited American soldiers. It was a guarded mystery as to why the elders, appearing as if they were attempting suicide without provocation, would run directly in front of the path of a mammoth, speeding Army vehicle.

Credit the demons. Rural citizens came to believe they were plagued by demons. They reasoned that every tree, spring, ravine and mountain was possessed by demons. The monsters arise from sour rice paddies to make malignant sport of humans by delivering havoc and affecting their destinies. Nor are the demons confined to natural habitats. The devils infest roofs, fireplaces, walls, and ceilings. The demons haunt the believers day and night, making life nearly impossible to tolerate. They are over-

---

[64] The use of human excrement as fertilizer produced a never ending cycle of intestinal parasites. Ascaris lumbricoiees is a sometimes fatal round worm. In Korea the infestation rate hovered near 100 percent. The infected host carries the parasites unsuspectingly for approximately two weeks as the nematodes hatch in the small intestine. It is there each of the female adult nematodes spews 200,000 eggs each per day. In the interim, the juvenile worms penetrate the intestinal wall and migrate into the lungs. Edema of the lungs causes blood vessels to hemorrhage, causing a type of pneumonia. Female parasites reach 18 inches in length, causing blockage of the gastrointestinal tract, and sometimes evacuate the body through the mouth or nose. Author.

flowing in the villages, so hideous and grotesque carved wood posts are strategically placed at the village entries to ward off these evil spirits.

What better way to eradicate the troublesome devils than to dart suddenly across the path of a speeding truck, hopeful of barely escaping death, while the ever-pursuing demon is crushed by the mammoth motor vehicle. Many Korean elders were one step too slow.

It was easy to spot those elders, all looking alike, clad in their traditional white Korean clothes, sporting long white mustaches that cascaded into flowing beards of the Fu Man-chu style. Their attire was unique as well. First, they donned a black cloth scull cap, over which a high-top hat was placed, composed of braided horsehair, fashioned as netting and held together by varnish emitting a most peculiar odor. Korean elders traditionally wore a long, outer robe over the light, white summer cotton shirt and pantaloons complete with leggings, and were shod with rubber, canoe-shaped footwear. Each senior seemed to wear glasses and all smoked cigarettes, inserted in a small metal pipe bowl with about a 13-inch wood stem, affixed with a metal mouthpiece. The elders resembled life-size replicas of Asian chess set pieces.

My friendship with Mr. Kim was developing deeper every day, and I admired his ability to control the situation at all times. One evening after dark when we all settled into our quarters for the night, there was a commotion. Someone screamed loudly and frantically outside, followed by three loud, distinct reports from a high velocity rifle! Instantly thereafter, the door slid open swiftly and someone shouted to the group within. Two of the young men armed with rifles, along with Mr. Kim, bolted rapidly from the house in response to the scream.

My adrenaline elevated to the zenith, and I started to shake, wondering what was happening; I had no idea what had occurred outside. Were there Chinese troops out there? Panic set in again.

After what seemed an eternity, they returned and Mr. Kim calmly said, "Someone said a man was a spy, but he is not a spy. He is on our side, so he is free."

My adrenaline ebbed in direct proportion to the news. I was relieved knowing the situation. I never asked Mr. Kim for an explanation of the shots fired or of the panic shout outside of the door of our temporary hovel. The incident was closed, though I pondered how refugees could differentiate between the two clashing opponents. In retrospect, I could not imagine a spy in the midst of us outcasts, since the Chinese and restructured North Korean Armies were hard on the heels of the fleeing Allies to carry out Mao's military stratagem: *Drive the imperialist Yankees from all of Korea.*

We were on the road again just before the rise of the ever-elusive sun and we were cold, shaking from the contrasting temperature change between the warm hooch and the frigid outdoors. But in time the brooding sun began to betray a glimmer of morning; the sky overcast as usual, near frigid cold, but tolerable.

I was walking beside Mr. Kim, when a boy of about ten approached me from the rear, accelerating his pace to catch up with me as I tramped among the evacuees. He was a refugee as well, but he was dressed in a very dashing school uniform, as opposed to the norm of the male Koreans, who were generally clad in their heavy, white cotton clothing. The youngster sported a very short haircut, suggestive of a North Korean soldier, and his school uniform of gray with dark blue trim was neat and immaculate. It appeared all male students had the same close-cropped, near shaven haircut.

In contrast, I was filthy. I had at least a two week old adolescent stubble of a beard. I was unwashed, with a uniform that had been worn since October, exposed to dirt, mud, and blood. My hands, face and body were grimy, my hair had matted from the lack of washing, and I smelled offensive. Multitudes of body lice whose parasitic need for blood was prime were swarming. I was sorry that the boy and I hadn't met in October when I had my first and only shower and clean change of uniform since boarding the Japanese troop transport ship, the *Tagasaka Maru.*

"Good morning sir. My name is Roh, and I am a Christian."

"Well, good for you. I am a Christian, too, and my name is Paul."

"May I show you a photograph of my uncle?"

"Yes, of course. I would like very much to see his picture."

We continued our normal pace of walking as the boy simultaneously pulled out his wallet and fished for his photograph. His English was so impeccable he lacked an accent. I was dumfounded to learn that a young boy from North Korea could speak English and profess to be a Christian, residing in such a suppressive, intolerant and totalitarian country.

The lad quickly produced a photograph and passed the school size, small, sepia-tinted photo to me. At the same time he brandished a bright and knowing smile to attest he was very proud of his uncle, now in military service. The photograph depicted a scowling North Korean Army officer in full uniform, replete with Sam Browne belt that crossed from his right shoulder to the left waist.

"My uncle is a major in the army."

"My, he is a handsome man. You must be very proud of him. But, please excuse me for I must catch up with my friends." With that, I left the youngster, sped my cadence and caught up with Mr. Kim, saying nothing to him. I was made terribly uneasy by this encounter, and I scarcely believed that it actually happened. This incident was impossible I thought, and should I ever get out alive, I would never repeat this story to anyone, simply because of the sheer implausibility of the event. This experience, coupled with the finding of my compass became two incidents I rated the highest on the unimaginable scale. I dare not tell a soul.

I have always regretted my inability to have the confidence that I needed that day. I could have engaged the lad in conversation and learned so much from him, because it was clear that he wanted to converse. He was proud of his ability to speak English, and I rudely deprived him of using his skills. Now I wonder who and where his benefactors were? Was he a part of a religious mission, an orphan? Where was his family, if he had one? His uncle was accounted for, but where were the rest of them? I was mystified.

At 18 I lacked the social skills needed to engage in interaction even though it was with a person who, with their friendship and language abilities, may have helped me. At times I questioned myself as to the reality of this event, given it was not that long before I had been hallucinating while fleeing from the Chinese.

The boy Roh was too young to appreciate the upheaval of his country and the reasons for the awful conflict. The devotion to his uncle was certainly expected. In retrospect, I regret so much I avoided him. He is no doubt alive somewhere today, and I would like to meet him again and to talk with him. It must be a given that of the hundreds of thousands, indeed, millions of fleeing refugees, I had to be the only American among them, and only because of my incredible liaison with Mr. Kim. Moreover, the lad's ability to speak English, coupled with his young age, would put him in a position to recall past events of this nature whether he resides in Korea, America or elsewhere.

Roh's incomprehension of this war speaks to the diligence and character of the missionaries.[65] They obviously had no interest in a political

---

[65] Elders at the West Gate Presbyterian Church reverently removed the black wooden cross from above the altar. Others packed prayer books and Bibles. Christianity had been permitted in the north until the UN forces crossed the 38th Parallel-as long as priests and pastors did not take an anti-Communist stance. But those who professed the faith now feared repression. Spurr, p. 223.

agenda, given that their sole purpose was to spread the gospel of their individual religious persuasion.

Early morning the next day Mr. Kim led us from our rough wooden sanctuary to the road to merge with the masses heading south as usual before daybreak. By then the road was already strangled with massive foot traffic. The southward torrent of refugees continued smooth, deliberate and nonstop. No one dared cease movement, for just as a powerful slow moving, unstoppable freight train, they would have been trampled by those who followed.

I felt comfortable with the refugees; I was part of them. Wearing civilian clothing over my distinctive uniform classified me as a spy, rather than what I was in reality—a hapless refugee. Regardless, I would have been shot if recaptured, no matter the circumstances. I was concerned for my benefactors, who would suffer the same punishment.

We were nearing the outskirts of Pyongyang, where the Americans would surely be diligently defending the North Korean capitol from recapture by the enemy. Deliverance was near at hand. Would I be able to find the Americans today, I wondered? Surely they would be defending the capitol to prevent the surging CCF from recapturing this magnificent trophy of the peninsula. There was much too much at stake, politically or strategically to do otherwise. The credibility of the Allies in the eyes of the world rested upon the holding of Pyongyang.

My link-up was imminent.

THE DAY OF THE PLANES

American studies after the war argued very persuasively that strategic bombing of enemy cities, factories and overland communications networks was not only ineffective but actually counter productive - as in England during the blitz or in Germany late in the war - it galvanized the nation, encouraged defiant and resourceful improvisation, and strengthened the will to resist. Whelan, p. 171.

This was no nine-to-five escape. We were on the road from dark to dark. The American 8th Army had the luxury of fleeing by motorized convoy to escape the clutches of the pursuing Chinese Communist Forces. The Chinese Volunteers had the tenacity to pursue the retreating Americans non-stop on foot to renew battle with the Americans.

My North Korean friends and I were lost in between the two armies and among hundreds of thousands of refugees desperately fleeing one step ahead of the surging Chinese armies. It would do no good to try to get out faster, because human endurance would have been taxed beyond limit. The only way out was to join with the refugees and abide their schedule.

The usual dirt road was void of most ice except for the outer edges. By the grace of God, I at last did not have to deal with sleep deprivation. My two hallucinatory companions were left back in the snow far south of Anju. The audiotape in my head—*It's Three O'clock in the Morning*—rewound and no longer played.

Dawn had not quite arrived as yet, though the refugees had started their exodus much earlier, judging by the smooth flow of human traffic. It was too cold for them to linger, and there was no other recourse but to forge ahead. From my experience of being lost and disoriented in the treacherous, frozen Taebak Mountains it seemed to become even more deadly frigid just before daylight, and the refugees knew this unusual phenomena as well.

Our group quickly blended with the horde as we continued the journey among them. The agricultural fields normally covered with raw human sewage were layered with partial drifts of snow, and where there was a lack of snow, the fields were sealed with a heavy film of ice, depriving the legions of flies from reproducing until the spring thaw. Everything seemed so tranquil and serene as the sounds of war were left behind. The ice-concealed effluvium was in hibernation, except where the migrants answered nature's call.

Mr. Kim mentioned that there were reports of sighting American Indian soldiers the past two days. He was referring to Afro-American soldiers, who apparently were seen just 20 miles to the south the previous day. My heart leaped at the thought that I might be so near to deliverance. Surely in just one more day, I would have made it. I would finally be back in American hands and safety.

When we marched well in excess of those 20 miles, Mr. Kim was again informed that American soldiers were spotted approximately an additional 20 miles further south, having been observed the day before. My heart sank

I marveled at the incredible grapevine of the Korean refugees. Despite the absence of modern methods of communications, we were consistently informed by word of mouth as to what was transpiring during the exodus.

There was no beginning or end to the refugee line. The outcasts were generally silent until a critical calamity struck that mandated information be quickly dispensed up and down the endless lines. Information on methods to outwit the American Air Force, their routine schedule of attack (which was like clock work), the awareness of Chinese forces, enemy agents and other pertinent information was quickly spread throughout the chain of humanity.

We were in the middle of a vast valley, trudging on a two-foot high dirt road held captive by miles and miles of frozen, abandoned rice paddies. The dirt road was pock marked for reasons I would soon learn, much to my dismay.

I recall we were approaching a town called Sunan, north of Pyongyang, the capitol of North Korea, where this road would ultimately terminate into the recently-destroyed capitol. Surely that was where the American Army would be, defending the capitol at all cost against the aggressive, invading Golden Horde.

My one and only meal since before the 27 November Chinese attack—the rancid, rotten offering to Buddha—was vomited on the night my companion was slain, yet I was not hungry. By now, it had been about nine days since I had last eaten.[66] None in our North Korean group had provisions since we met, and it appeared that there was no concern relative to the acquisition of food. But if there was one deep and overriding aspiration, it was our craving, not for food, but the all-consuming hunger to escape with our lives.

---

[66] The present brutal regime has no use for the rural population. Considering them a liability, they dole a minimum amount of food to sustain them. That food would better serve Dictator Kim to feed the vast army, the second largest in the world. Author.

There was little noise, save the creaking of oxen-drawn carts, intermingled with the subdued clattering sounds of hand-pulled rudimentary barrows, blending with the soft, melodious sounds of thousands of the native shoes shuffling softly in irregular harmony along the road.

In the direction of freedom, perhaps five miles or more, I noticed scores of refugees leaving the road on both sides in what seemed to be an orderly, methodical manner.

What the hell is going on here? I thought to myself.

Suddenly, someone screamed harshly in the Korean language something that apparently meant, "Planes! Planes!" A squadron of American combat fighter planes poured over the horizon, but not just fighter planes—jet-powered Air Force couriers of death.

Specifically, we spotted four North American-produced F-86 Saber fighter/bombers—one-man aircraft, powered by a single General Electric J-47 jet engine. Armed with six 50-caliber machine guns, eight to 24 five-inch rockets, or up to two thousand pounds of other weapons of death, including the most feared of all—napalm. They flew so fast that they often fired on American troops in error. No chance of slaughtering American soldiers now. Except for me. [67]

American ground forces feared the planes when they flew in support in the early days of combat, because they were so fast that they frequently overshot their targets and fired on Allied units. It would not be easy to discover one combat soldier who was not a victim of a deadly, erroneous strafing attack by American jet fighter planes—a horrifying experience. The planes were held in terror as well by this struggling mass of freedom-seeking refugees, wondering if they would survive the forthcoming horror.

I knew the lethal carnage that would spit from their deadly arsenal. Still, there was a glimmer of hope. The length of this massive caravan stretched for untold miles, as far as the eye could see, both north and south. There might be a faint chance that we would escape the fusillade that would bring us into deadly harm's way.

Those who left the road obviously were survivors of other perilous

---

[67] Then, when the Chinese came and the retreat began, Moon and his family began walking. "There were too many people," he said. We could not keep together. When the American fighters came, machine-gunning the roads, everyone scattered like bean shoots." He never saw his family again. For eighteen days he walked towards Seoul, scavenging scraps of food from abandoned houses, pathetically waving a South Koran flag when the F-86s strafed the refugee columns, as he saw them do repeatedly. Hastings, p. 168.

raids, and now they cowered in trepidation behind what little shelter the frozen dikes of the rice paddies afforded. Those who were physically able to flee from the road, to take a chance on the dangerously slick rice paddies, knew to get as far as possible from the mass of road-bound refugees.

The aircraft swooped in from the south, low and angry, giving the appearance of silver bullets shining against the backdrop of the drab, southern line of the Chokyuryong Mountain range. The fighter planes banked suddenly, left and up, turned south and leveled off, appearing now more as if they were silver salmon shooting the falls than the deadly aircraft they were. In spite of the excruciating pain from the gangrene of my feet, I ran from the road to the east and stood upright, facing the deadly aircraft, mesmerized.

I was about to meet my baptism of fire by air attack administered by the United States Air Force.

Just then the first aircraft pushed off into a shallow dive, banked low, where I could clearly see the grim face of the pilot as he stabilized the wings, flying about 30 feet over the innocents, disgorging his deadly arsenal of 50-caliber rounds from six machine guns firing in unison. The planes spat deadly bursts of death, intermixed with the mortally feared, earsplitting explosions of five-inch rockets.

Glancing up again, I saw the second jet fighter maneuver into the same path as the lead aircraft that by now had peeled off and raced to the east. The second plane was a few miles to the north when it banked sharply, reversed course to south, leveled off on a southern azimuth, aligned the aircraft to the road, and then came in screaming fast and low. I was hypnotized by the horror that was unfolding before my eyes.

Standing there clad in my bulky, rural Korean white cotton clothing covering my Army field uniform, I became momentarily oblivious to the death raining down on the helpless, defenseless civilians. The unfortunates were now to be sacrificed—paying the supreme price for their determined quest for freedom. I was powerless to repulse the attack.

"Dear God! Please make them go away!" I whispered softly to myself. I was dumbfounded at the thousands of innocent lives taken in vain, not to mention the sheer waste of resources on such an innocent group of people. Hundreds of thousands of enemy troops lay peacefully asleep in shallow hills and abandoned villages, while these pathetic souls were needlessly being ripped to shreds by American pilots.

The Chinese forces had a better warning system than the helpless, unorganized refugees. When American aircraft approached a given area, a

Chinese sentry simply chanted, *Fei-Ji! Fei-Ji!* (Airplane! Airplane!), simultaneously firing one rifle shot in the air. The resonance was picked up by the next sentry who would repeat the same cadence, where it was ultimately passed to the north almost as rapidly as radio transmission.

"Can't they see the women and children, the ox carts, the young and the old and the infirm?" I spat in fear and disgust.

I again noticed the pilot's uncompromising faces through the Plexiglas canopy of their aircraft. Where was the helicopter spotter that I hungered to flag down a week or so ago? If a helicopter was here, I could have signaled them, because they could hover slowly enough to verify that I was an American soldier. That would have put an end to this needless massacre instantly, showing the jet aircraft they were just slaughtering masses of innocent people caught in the middle of undeclared mortal combat.

Thousands of blameless people would be spared untimely, cruel deaths and more importantly, the ill-fated, unfounded and false belief that enemy soldiers intermingled with the citizenry would finally be put to rest. I was the single person in this vast arena of war who absolutely knew that no enemy mixed with the refugees, and I knew it first hand, from the refugee side of the fence. The so-called intelligence apparatus could say what they wished—I could contradict unfounded intelligence dogma.

I watched in horror as the innocents were shot dead, the bright rounds first appearing to fire slowly, and then speeding up as they hunted their prey. Every machine gun ammunition belt had an incendiary round inserted at every fifth shot, described as a *tracer* because it allows the attacker to zero in on his target, by observing the trajectory of the red-hot rounds. I became sick to my stomach as I witnessed this appalling carnage unfold in front of me. I had enough.

I began running back to the road as fast as possible. I compare it to running across a freeway during rush hour, only instead of high-speed autos it was treetop-level death. To this day I will never comprehend why I chose to return to the arena of slaughter, when I had been relatively safe from air attack when on the rice paddy dike.

Because of the inexorable sorties of the F-86's, one following another, I had to tread around or leap over new corpses that a moment ago were living human beings, as the determined pilots continued the slaughter unabated, relentless in their efforts to massacre as many innocents as possible.

The unending caravan of oxen, carts, and refugees had stopped dead in its tracks, slaughtered by the ferocious, indifferent attack of the fighter planes. I couldn't find my North Korean friends because of the catastrophic hell unfolding around us. The F-86's continued to come in swift and low, with a roar that revolved into a high pitched scream, far beyond the range that the human ear can tolerate.

Funnels of black smoke from the incessant rocket fire streamed upward in wispy columns, as lethal rockets left hundreds of slain bodies of innocents in their wake, along with dismembered oxen, carts and parcels. The orange-red violent rocket explosions were followed by falling debris and bodies both human and animal marked by the telltale plume of thick smoke. The very viscera of the earth seemed to spew forth to bare the hell surrounding us.

An abandoned adobe shack with the traditional tule roof lay just west of the roadway partially blocked from my view by an ox-cart laden with all the household items that an innocent family could carry.

The cart was piled high with everything these wretched souls possessed, covered with a tarp like fabric and tied with heavy rope. At the rear of the cart, a small child of about two years of age was strapped to the cart in an upright position. She was clad in the traditional heavy clothing, complete with hood. The child resembled a doll or a little Indian girl tied in her papoose board. Her petite arms and feet were spread eagle, her body secured by the ropes though she seemed to be in comfort. It was a very practical solution given that she was in the midst of untold thousands of refugees, where becoming lost in this unending wave of humanity would be a permanent and tragic toll. I gave the child a fleeting, cursory look as I fled for my life into the hovel.

Once inside the shack, I initially believed it to be a sanctuary from the carnage crashing around me. I was like an ostrich, my head in a hole. I couldn't see the airplanes, ergo, they couldn't see me. My determination to seek shelter in this dilapidated shack was the worst possible decision to make. I was in the awful situation of being the black center ring of a giant target.

The attacking planes were determined to reduce the structure to rubble, and I had nowhere to flee. The concentrated, non-stop firepower stormed downward as I cowered against the west wall in unequivocal terror and in the false illusion that I could escape death by disappearing. Heavy automatic gunfire ripped through the thatched roof as if the roof did not exist, while I watched in speechless horror as I saw the tracer rounds inch closer and closer to me. My ears were ringing from the unbearable clamor of roaring guns and screaming jet fighter planes. I was momentarily deaf. I was paralyzed with fear.

The force of the huge caliber rounds tore through the mud floor, ripping large clods of dirt from the smooth earthen mass. The dust strangled my throat, my eyes watered from the gagging man-made haze. My alarm was as great as at Anui. And that same frigid block of ice formulated by sheer terror reentered my stomach, just as it did at Anui.

I stretched my body into an elongated position in the false belief that I could to make myself a smaller target for what I genuinely believed was to be my forthcoming, violent death. I trembled in response to the terror to which I was subjected. I had been in a hopeless situation since my capture, with so many close calls, constantly being shot at by Chinese forces. This new horror was much more intense. I was not armed. I could not fight back. I could not escape. I cowered in unmitigated panic.

There was no chance to flee. I was feeling as a helpless deer caught in the cross hairs of a hunter's high-powered rifle or frozen in front of a speeding auto encountered at night with headlights bright. There is a term for this devastating reaction: *Flight or Fight*. Since this encounter I added the word *Freeze* for incidents such as this. I could not fight because I had no means to defend myself. The flight or the panic took control of my emotions. I was *frozen* with fear. The persistent, non-stop firepower from heavy machine gun rounds continued to sweep down, the bullets nearly rupturing the remainder of the thatched roof off, setting it afire from lethal incendiaries. I glanced fearfully toward the once-covered roof for a moment and I saw the now-exposed leaden sky, crudely framed by smoldering embers and smoke from the tule reeds.

"Mr. Paul!" Mr. Kim screamed hoarsely at the top of his lungs, as he rushed into the now nearly-destroyed shanty.

"You must come with me and take off your white suit and show them your Army suit, and then they will go away! Come with me to show them!"

"I can't! I can't! Mr. Kim! They are coming too fast! They will think that I am Chinese!" I screamed.

"You must help us!"

"Mr. Kim, they won't believe me! They will know that I am Chinese, for sure. They are flying too fast to see I am American!"

Just then the shack violently shuddered as before and nearly collapsed from yet another nearby rocket that must have had our names on it. Mr. Kim was thrown violently on me by the deadly concussion from the nearby rocket. We both gripped each other in utter terror believing that we were to die together in each other's arms.

We lay prone, squeezing each other in wretched terror, watching in horror as the ever-present machine gun rounds continued to rip the remaining thatched roof as the tracers ran hot and true. A giant sewing machine of rounds was stitching a deadly pattern of death for anyone in their path. Every tracer round appeared to be about five or six inches apart which meant that the unseen, explosive rounds were one inch apart. To be struck by just one white-hot round would kill a person instantly, or at the very least, rip a limb from the body. There was no chance of survival when the rounds came that close together in their quest to claim victims. I was perspiring in the frigid cold. The filth on my face turned to muck from the heavy sweat of fear that overwhelmed and consumed me.

It was a lifetime of mind-numbing terror that refused to go away. Wave after hideous wave of crashing death was expended on us without reprieve. Roar after roar that continuously extinguished precious life from those whose only crime was to seek a better and more peaceful existence. It was bad enough to uproot a lifetime of tradition of family, friends and ancestors, but to die in the most horrible way on some isolated road, only to be shoved off the path, becoming a nameless, abandoned corpse in order to make way for the surviving was too grisly an end.

An eternity passed before the squadron ultimately terminated their sortie and left the area, no doubt pleased with their successful mission.

Mr. Kim and I gathered ourselves together and staggered back to the road to survey the carnage left by the Air Force. I couldn't hear and that queasy, icy feeling of terror in the pit of my stomach would not go away. In my heart I knew that I was incapable of absorbing any further horrific punishment. My emotional system could not take any more. I was shattered.

The first thing I saw after we staggered back on the road was the diminutive child. She took a 50-caliber hit in the exact center of her little chest, as if she was the quintessence of a living target. The ropes that held her still maintained her spread-eagle position, but her little head now drooped low in acknowledgment of her ghastly death.

I was ashamed. My body still quivered in fear, but the anger soon supplanted the fear. I was cautious. I wondered if, since I was a member of the same side, the multitudes would turn on me to exact their pound of flesh? Perhaps hang me, or tie me up and stone me to death? Anything was possible.

Our stunned, fragmented informal group, once comprised of eight, eventually located each other. As we gathered around momentarily to check to see if any were missing, wounded, or killed, two from the group were noticeably absent and presumed to have been slain. For us survivors, there were barely distinguishable faint smiles all around, an ever so inconspicuous nod. No words were spoken—but it was not out of deference or lack of comprehension of the Korean language. It was clearly because the majority managed to survive this man-induced catastrophe, and words in any language could not convey the nearness to death we just endured. It was beyond sharing, notwithstanding the guilt that follows as surely as night follows day. Because survivors are so grateful to live, we instinctively and subconsciously believe it to be through the supreme sacrifice by the dead. They took our places.

There was no sweet, intoxicating euphoric fever of survival of this awful ordeal. There was numbness, shock and disbelief. The eternal question *is there life after death* was answered that fateful morning as we rose from the ashes of mortality to again stagger on. We had metamorphosed from the dead back into the world of the living.

Collectively and not speaking, we again began our exodus south. I noticed that my gift from the Lord, my unbelievably found compass was missing. It must have detached from where I had it strapped to my left wrist, as Mr. Kim and I clutched each other in mortal fear. I would not likely find the compass, surely now covered by debris. No matter. To hell with the compass that I had prayed for during all of those anguishing days and nights when I was on the run by myself. Mr. Kim was my friend and my compass now.

I was trembling as I marched silently next to Mr. Kim. We were zombies, moving silently through the rubble of war, real honest to God war. We moved in silent unison automatically, subconsciously skirting bodies of man and beast as if Mr. Kim and I were joined as one. I stole a glimpse of Mr. Kim, and I saw the raw, expressionless stare on his face, just as was displayed on the fixed faces of the other refugees. I had to possess the same vacant stare as everyone else. It was a death mask for the living.

The corpses strewn about the road were but one small part of the estimated over two million innocent people slaughtered in this senseless war. None of the dead wore a death mask. They didn't have to.

Just ahead, I spied an overturned wagon tethered to a dead ox. When the creature was slain, he rolled on his right side, head on the ground, with eyes wide open. As we approached the animal from some distance away, I sensed that the exposed eye was staring at me. Totally mesmerized, I was fixated on the eye that appeared to watch me approach. We drew abreast of the brute, and he continued his forlorn, fixated gaze at me. I said nothing to Mr. Kim, but as we passed the beast, I could not help but to turn to peer back again at the forsaken, emaciated, slaughtered ox. His eye continued to follow me, as if he were pleading for someone to help him. The ox must have believed that I could breathe life back into him, or was it me, in fact, that wanted to revive him from death? If that were true, and I had gained such omnipotent power, I would have had a higher priority—the defenseless slain infant strapped to the wagon.

One of the young men with the bicycle pulled up and motioned to me to mount the bicycle on the back passenger railing. I pulled the attached hood of my Korean jacket over my head and wrapped my arms tightly around his thin, muscular body as he skillfully maneuvered around the dead, dying, and debris. The disorganized mob of people had automatically united as one and started off again, as if this was one insignificant incident and one price to pay for their continuous southbound quest for freedom. I turned my head to the rear and looked at the movement of survivors, while my hood covered my head.[68]

Aside from my boots, I could have passed as just one of thousands of living North Koreans, but I didn't feel that way. As I surveyed the horrific slaughter from my backward view, I sensed that the living were glaring at me. I was sure that if they could catch up with the bicycle, it would be my death. But later, after so many additional days with the innocents, I realized that they, like me, while exhibiting a stoic bearing, were numb from the terror of this, and other unspeakable ordeals. We continued on.

Smoldering and burning flesh. Innocents fell to uncontrolled vomiting induced by the wretched and unforgettable stink commingled with the sight of pitiful, torn bodies from this catastrophe. Bodies burned not only

---

[68] Mr. Kim and I never discussed the subject further of trying to ward the jet aircraft off by exposing the uniform kept concealed by my Korean farm clothing. While I cannot revisit this ordeal except in the context of today, I absolutely believe that I did the right thing at the time by doing nothing. The military genuinely believed that the enemy infiltrated the refugee lines in order to move their attack units forward. To expose me in my uniform would convince the Air Force that their erroneous military information was indeed correct, and that I was merely attempting some kind of barbaric ruse.

Who in their right mind would believe that an American soldier would be among this mass of itinerant humanity? Moreover, the concept of direct Soviet involvement in the war was always considered a factor, and I might have been mistaken for a Russian soldier or some uniformed advisor, given any possibility that the aircraft could slow enough to recognize a Caucasian in the midst of oceans of Asians. Author.

beyond description, but burned beyond the shape of a human. Napalm.[69] The cruelest way to die. The hideous stench of human smoldering flesh was so stomach-turning, I wanted to vomit, but because there was nothing in me, I could only gag and retch in revulsion. Each jet plane carried 75 gallons of insidious death in two fuel tanks for a total of 150 gallons of lethal jellied gasoline.[70]

Those who would survive the inferno would die of suffocation as the oxygen in the air was sucked from their lungs. Those who died as a direct result of the searing, withering flames would be as if they had immolated themselves, but, without a cause. They were martyrs all, not by choice.

Bodies after bodies for mile upon mile. I was repulsed by this willful and unnecessary carnage. Napalm victims die a horrible death. After seeing hundreds of victims of napalm, I have never seen one body that died face up. The immediate contraction of the muscles in their arms forces the body to turn as it twists in post-death convulsions and withers like dying leaves on campfire logs. It appears that in death they choose to lie on their sides or most generally on their front. Muscles of the inner elbows contract when the flesh burns, as do muscles of the hands, which results in fists formed in death. The victims assume a convoluted position similar to that of a boxer, with fists and defensive, contracted arms. I call it simply *the napalm boxer's pose.*

I could not look anymore. I grasped the middle of my fellow escapee even tighter as he continuously and expertly weaved in and out of the conflagration on the road. I pressed my face to his back to shield my eyes from this butchery. I was no stranger to bodies. I reflected on when our company killed a thousand North Korean soldiers that stormed our defensive position during the Pusan Perimeter and none had remorse. This was dif-

---

[69] Mao Tse-tung's eldest son, Mao Anying was slain in a napalm attack on October 25th, somewhere near Pyongyang, the capitol of North Korea, where he was planning for the Chinese intervention. Mao added the loss of his beloved eldest son to his list to even the score with the Americans. He was off to a very good start. Author.

[70] By mistake the lead plane dropped its napalm short. It crashed down near the A/A vehicle at the head of the column. Its billowing, searing flames engulfed about a dozen Americans. These included two 1/32 platoon leaders, George E. Foster (West Point 1950) and Henry M. Moore, both badly burned, Foster fatally. Private first Class James Ransome Jr., remembered that the napalm "hit and exploded in the middle" of his squad. He continued: "I don't know how in the world the flames missed me. In my lifetime, I'll never know. Men all around me were burned. They lay rolling in the snow. Men I knew, marched and fought with begged me to shoot them … I couldn't . . It was terrible. Where the napalm had burned the skin to a crisp, it would be peeled back from the face, arms, and legs . . . Like fried potato chips. JSC record, p. 2.

ferent. This was unnecessary.[71] This was the same as when we viewed 1500 innocent Korean victims, first imprisoned and then shot dead by soldiers of the North Korean Army. That was murder. This was murder. I retched at the sight.

If there could be one positive note, it was that the weather hovered below freezing. The cold weather coagulated the blood of the victims, both human and animal, preventing a massive glut of blood from saturating the dirt road, where other victims would literally slip and fall into a sanguineous, gooey mass. The brutal dead of winter prevented that awful slippage.

Ancestor worship possesses the very heart and soul of the Koreans. Above all other religions, that of honor and worship to the ancestors appears to be the highest order. It is taught from generation to generation that those who ignore or neglect the ritual of ancestor worship bar the way to eternal happiness for themselves. Now, on this filthy blood-soaked, pock-marked road, there was an absence of altars, shrines, priests, prayers and graves. The bodies were abandoned to the elements because ancestor worship now, by necessity, took a back seat to the intractable determination to live.

Life goes on. We went on. We were sure to find the Americans by tomorrow. The nightmare would soon be over.

---

[71] The Geneva Convention has since prohibited the use of napalm, that most appalling of all weapons, and our country willingly signed the accord. Yet napalm was used against insurgents during the Vietnam War. Napalm was a product invented by the United States, first used by General Chennault's Flying Tigers. Since then United States purportedly has developed firebombs far more lethal than napalm. Author.

PYONGYANG AND BEYOND

> We went through Pyongyang at night and the whole city looked like it was burning. In one place the engineers burned a rations dump about the size of a football field. God, it was a shame to see in a land of hunger all the food going up in smoke. There was U.S. military equipment everywhere. I don't know how much was destroyed. It looked like we were going to pursue a scorched-earth policy. I believe we set on fire most of the villages we passed through. We weren't going to give the Chinese too many places to shelter in during the rest of the winter. Cpl. Leonard Korgie, HQ Co. 21st Infantry.

The once majestic oldest city of the Koreas, and the capitol of North Korea since 15 August 1945, was no more. From 25 June 1950 on, Pyongyang was blown from the face of the earth in retaliation for the invasion by the North Korean People's Army into defenseless South Korea. The United States Air Force punished the northern invaders by reducing their jewel-like capitol to rubble. Anything of value left standing was blown to bits by US demolition squads before they evacuated the capitol on 3 December.[72]

An inadvertent exception was a huge portrait of *Dear Leader* Kim Il Sung, left behind in the wake of the frantic retreat of the North Korean Army, the Russian and Chinese advisors and their concubines.

Several thousand North Korean Army soldiers earlier escaped the pincer movement employed by the United States 10th Corps who successfully landed at Inchon, and moved rapidly south, following the capture of the Republic of Korea's capitol city of Seoul. At the same time, the American 8th Army was poised to break out of the Pusan Perimeter, with the objective of attacking northward, to close the trap on the enemy in concert with the 10th Corps.

General Walton Walker, Commander of the United States 8th Army, confiscated Kim Il-Sung's presidential palace as his headquarters during the brief stay of his army when the Allied armies pushed north, across the 38th Parallel into North Korean territory. Walker's Army was advancing north

---

[72] The greatest concentration of demolition targets was in Pyongyang. Just about every bridge along the withdrawal route was destroyed. In Pyongyang the most important demolition targets were the Taedong River bridges. The rear-guard commander authorized the time of their destruction. The Rail Transportation Office (RTO) north of the Taedong was also authorized to order execution of the demolitions. There were several large buildings in the heart of Pyongyang that were marked for demolition. Appleman, p.370.

to the Yalu River from Pyŏngyang. American commanders and staff ignored the huge portrait hanging in the bedroom of the soon to be abandoned presidential palace, leaving it for the North Koreans to reclaim.

The entry of the Chinese Communist Army into the war as early as October 1950 forever altered the future of the conflict in North Korea. Walker's Army hastily evacuated the Capitol in the face of the oncoming red tide, but not until incalculable millions of dollars of American war materiel went up in smoke, intentionally torched by frantically-retreating American forces to avoid supplies falling into CCF hands.[73]

Meanwhile, the horde of refugees unexpectedly coalesced into a much denser throng than the usual masses, with no beginning, no end, just one twisted gathering of humanity, shoulder to shoulder, seeking to escape the war with a minimum of emotional and physical scars.[74]

Mr. Kim and I didn't know those facts at the time. We entered the Capitol, perhaps 9 or 10 December, at about midmorning, and it appeared that the capitol was a lost soul, in search of a government, any government, legitimate or not. I didn't know if it was by chance or by design, but Mr. Kim elected to take the far west road, barely skirting the Capitol. Later verification confirmed that had we entered the heart of the Capitol via the main road, we would have been blocked and isolated by blown bridges.

Nothing much had changed except the condition of my feet and the weather. The poisonous fluid seeping from my toes and saturating my wool socks became more pronounced as time went by. I had no means to alleviate the infection other than amputation. I wasn't ready for that until I could escape this catastrophic nightmare.[75]

The weather turned noticeably milder, though the dreary skies persisted. Approaching the west part of the capitol, I sensed a not-so-subtle change in the quantity of the refugee population. The number of pathetic refugees soared. Now a solid mass of plodding humanity clogged roads.

---

[73] Hastings, p. 167.

[74] Often enemy agents infiltrated the refugees, dressing like them and then gathering intelligence or creating chaos whenever an opportunity arose. Appleman, pp. 361-362

[75] American captives suffering gangrenous wounds were treated by American doctors, who were themselves prisoners, by a primitive therapy. The lack of medical tools did not dissuade the doctors from their Hippocratic Oath. They simply improvised. The prisoner was invited to talk outside on a pretext. There, flies would congregate on the wounds to lay their eggs, which would hatch into larvae, called maggots. The maggots fed on the dead, diseased flesh, and consumed the entire afflicted area. Then the fly larvae expired. Maggots are unable to survive on living tissue. The patient might not recover, but the gangrene was arrested. Author.

There was a reason for the tremendous influx of the refugees, as hundreds of thousands of additional victims were streaming out of the Capitol, joining the masses on the road, fleeing in panic in front of a storm of advancing Chinese forces. The spawned refugees of the city seemed to instinctively form irregular patterns of migration, jockeying for breathing space on the road, but in due course, blending with countrymen in this massed exodus. Danger also joined the multitudes, for if one unfortunate victim was to stumble and fall, the surging lava flow of mankind, unable to slow, stop or veer from the area, would trample the fallen ones.

Mr. Kim urged me back on the bicycle due to the worsening condition of my feet, even though the pulsating pain from having my legs hanging down was more excruciating than it was from walking. The throbbing pain concerned me, making me wonder when blood poisoning and other complications would strike, rendering me unable to continue. No, I would persevere, even if it meant crawling to get back.

The bloated headwaters of the Taedong are born east of the ancient capitol, nourished by many smaller tributaries until the stream amalgamates into one mighty body of water near the central part of the city. From there the river surges generally east to southwest, abruptly altering course near the town of Kangson. The Taedong continues flowing almost directly south, slowly transforming into a subdued, shallow, meandering stream.

The wide bridges formerly spanning the commanding Taedong River in the central part of Pyongyang had been enormous, erected to carry large amounts of pedestrian and vehicular traffic to and from the viscera of the Capitol.[76]

The immense steel trestle bridges were destroyed either by Air Force bombers or by ground-based demolition experts, as Allied armies anxiously fled the capitol. What remained of the overpasses was reduced to shattered steel skeletons, resting and rusting for eternity at the bottom of

---

[76] Off to the right and left of the bridges was being enacted one of the great human tragedies of our time . . . a sight to remember as long as those of us who witnessed it shall live… In a zero wind that seared the face like a blowtorch, hundreds of thousands of Koreans were running, stumbling, falling, as they fled across the ice. Women with tiny babies in their arms, men bearing their old, sick, crippled fathers and mothers on their backs, others bent under great bundles of household gear flowed down the northern bank and across the ice toward the frozen plain on the southern shore. Some pushed little two-wheeled carts piled high with goods and little children. Others prodded burdened oxen… there was no weeping, no crying. Without a sound, except the dry whisper of their slippers on the snow, and the deep pant of their hard-drawn breath, they moved in utter silence. Ridgway, p. 96.

the powerful Taedong River. Those twisted, torn metal girders lingering above the frigid waterline exhibited, in mute testimony, the awesome, agonizing power of bombs and high explosives.

The rationale for destroying the spans was clearly to put in place some method to slow the potent, advancing Chinese forces. The operation was merely one more futile means to impede the foe from continuing the relentless, lightning assault against retreating Allies. To that end, Allied forces burned every vessel in the immediate vicinity of the Taedong capable of transporting troops, in hope of depriving enemy forces from the means of crossing the huge waterway.

It didn't work. Nothing worked.

Mr. Kim knew something of the relationship of the Taedong in respect to the capitol that I didn't know, and that knowledge was to later save our lives. Any notion of crossing to the south side of Pyongyang would have necessitated the perilous feat of scaling slippery, precipitous heights of exposed, twisted steel carcasses. Mr. Kim obviously had information that the Taedong River slowed and developed into a neutered, shallow stream as it coursed westward.[77]

He knew we should take caution, avoid the infrastructure of Pyongyang, and take the correct detour, which began at the right fork. From there, we took the secondary trail, which drifted lazily somewhat southwest. The Taedong River, also wandering, then coupled with the road and they meandered side by side, paralleling one another. As a result, none of us had to scale the broken bridges of Pyongyang.

An old Chinese saying is, *A picture is worth a thousand words.* A photographer named Max Desfor won the Pulitzer Prize for photography in 1950 for his exceptional photograph depicting the plight of the determined refugees. One of the wrecked bridges in Pyongyang, swarming with hundreds, perhaps thousands of wretched refugees, was captured for eternity on film.[78] Some victims were revealed to be burdened with all of their worldly belongings, strapped to their backs, some with only the clothes they wore. Each and every one attempted to maintain a handhold, desperately trying to traverse and survive this obstacle, this epitome of a nearly-insurmountable impediment. The unfortunates who slipped and plunged

---

[77] Years later I confirmed that fact. At the time of the Great Allied Retreat, there was much ado about the bridges in the Capitol being razed by Allied units in an effort to slow the charge of the Chinese Communist forces. Nothing was mentioned about the tame Taedong rivulet on the western outskirts of the capitol. Author.

[78] Reproduced on p. 342.

into icy depths perished in a matter of moments. It was impossible to rescue fallen victims swept away by churning, near-frozen waters. Another lost soul would stand, eager to take the place of the fallen.

We arrived where the prodigious, turbulent waters of the Taedong River became a mere rivulet and rendered unnecessary any need to confront the destroyed spans. The direction wisely chosen by Mr. Kim carried us unimpeded southwest, on a meandering course away from the perils of Pyongyang. Instead we were gently nudged towards the major, historical sea port city of Chinnampo. There, another, similar challenge was standing to greet and test our mettle.

I wondered if I would have been physically capable of crossing the broken, jagged spans of Pyongyang. My feet were clumsy and sensitive because of the gangrene, and both hands, now with limited mobility, and lacking strength, were nearly as frozen. For now though, we were comparatively safe. Our daily rate of travel averaged approximately 25 miles, as we trekked from night to day and back into night.

There was not an army in the world that could possibly keep up with the motorized retreat of UN forces. We were ahead of the Communist advance and we would prevail in due course. Our group would soon stumble into friendly lines, we believed.

While still on the western outskirts of the capitol heading south, we crossed into a densely-populated area comprised primarily of archaic, rickety residences. There were no shops, factories or commercial developments. This particular road within the city was unusually lined with houses on both sides of the avenue.

I was riding on the back of the bicycle when from out of nowhere someone again shouted, "American!"

The shout was about me. The flawless grapevine of the refugees struck once again. The word was out. Here was an American soldier in the Capitol City of Pyongyang, and it was me. How in the world could they possibly know, as I was still disguised in white Korean peasant garb? Over 50 young Korean males, all about my age, swarmed out of all parts of this area of the city and surrounded me. All were strangers, yet they grinned, shouted, danced about and clapped me on the back and shoulders as a sign of friendship.

Laughing and shouting, their clamor caused the horde of refugee civilians to yield to the mob. They were a newly formed militia and moved to form an informal double line, falling in behind the bicycle, without a prompt or cue. I was elated. If they could march, so could I. I slid from the rear frame of the bicycle, said OK to my bicyclist friend, and Mr. Kim and I led this small army south on one of the main throughways of Pyongyang. Occasionally, we would turn and wave to the makeshift army, who responded with waves and screams of joy.

I can't believe this, I thought.

Not only am I most likely the last American to escape from North Korea, thanks to the courage and resoluteness of Mr. Kim, I am bringing potential, friendly troops with me. An unbelievable incident. The continuous, tumultuous hullabaloo emanating from the rabble was so boisterous that it caused the southbound mass of walking humanity ahead of us to turn once more in response to the cacophony. The horde of refugees graciously stepped aside and yielded the road to the noisy mob.

Struggling on, I noted the contrast between the new-found, potential young inductees and the sorrowful, ever-present mask of bleakness on the faces of the refugees.

Mr. Kim joined me and together with the bicyclist wheeling his bike, we walked three abreast, south on our way to freedom, followed doggedly by the enthusiastic group of rowdy young men.

Food continued to be at the bottom of the list of priorities. We drank well water to stave off dehydration, while the cold continued to be our uninvited, persistent escort. Mr. Kim was constantly getting assurances from other refugees that the American Army was just ahead. We were well ahead of the marauding Chinese forces. If we had cigarettes, life would be almost perfect. And, we were bringing a crowd of willing, volunteer cadre to bolster the beleaguered ROK Army.

The pain in my feet disappeared. It may have been the psychological boost in my spirits, because of the newfound, friendly *army*. It was midmorning when we left the capitol. Mr. Kim led us, walking on the main southwest unpaved highway accompanied by an off-key orchestra composed of creaking hand carts, crying babies slung on backs of young mothers, elderly men and women, and young children, all shuffling along on the icy dirt road.

The thought struck me that I had not seen the young ladies of our group for some days now. I last saw them alive perhaps several days prior. No matter. We were finally getting close to the end of this journey of narrow escapes after all of these tortuous days, and they would be ones that would manage to escape as well.

Now beyond the mutilated capitol, we passed through a large town, name unknown, probably seven or ten miles south. The road was tree lined on the west, absent summer leaves, which normally seize and hold thick clouds of road dust. Off from the east side of the road were row upon row of shanties nearly abutting each other. The rear of the houses faced the grimy road, and ingress to the houses was accomplished by walking between structures, and entering from the opposite side.

Planes!

I looked to the southern sky and I spotted a flight of four single engine, gull winged, gray Marine Corsair fighter bombers soaring loftily in deadly circles—vultures circling, searching for prey, spurting unremitting, staccato death from 50-caliber machine guns.

Oh my God! What is going on? They are killing refugees again! Oh, my God!

All of a sudden a shrill ear-piercing, shriek permeated the still air in a calamitous, unknown language. In the briefest of moments, the road appeared to swallow the people. I blinked and I was standing on this major dirt road alone. I was abandoned. The hordes of untold refugees simply evaporated. I turned around and the militia had disappeared as well. I was by myself on the road and I was in complete shock.

Oh, my God wha . . . . .

The interlude was broken by my bicyclist friend, who had fled with the other refugees. Then, by the grace of God, he risked his life to return for me. My friend grabbed me powerfully and forcefully, yanking me through a narrow opening between two shacks situated on the east side. He was nearly breathless. There was no question as to the extreme urgency, but not a word would be uttered between us. He continually jerked and pulled me with ferocious intensity rapidly around to the front of house, opposite from the road.

Oh, my God, what in the hell is happening?

My adrenaline crested instantly again from this very sudden, traumatic outbreak, an instant, horrific disruption of our earlier routine.

What is happening? Jesus Christ! What is going on? For God's sake, what is going on?

Panic raged through me. My friend rapidly slid the shoji door of the house open and forcefully pushed me in, and I fell to the floor from his push, but I swiftly recovered, and leaped up. In his mind there was no time to waste. I glimpsed into his eyes as he forcefully pushed me down into the southwest corner of the house. His eyes said it all. He was terrified as well. But he apparently realized the obvious danger and I did not.

My friend grabbed a quilt from the tatami mat, left in the unoccupied house, threw it above me, and as the quilt was descending on my head, he made a gesture by putting his right hand to the center of his face that obviously meant to stay quiet. We occidentals place our forefinger in the same vertical manner to closed lips. There was no time to lose. He ran out the door, slammed the sliding door shut and fled for his life.

I noticed rapid, blurred shadows right outside of the opaque windows. Shouting Chinese troops, fleeing northbound, and I was one waxed-paper, opaque window away from them. Terror rumbled through my system as if it was a freight train. How could this be? We were so close to freedom and now the Chinese were here. *This is impossible!* I lamented to myself.

I couldn't stand the horrific suspense. I leaped up, not thinking coherently as to what to do. A million thoughts flashed through my mind. I huddled into a ball on the floor again and covered myself with the quilt. All the while I heard the screams and shouts and curses of men pushing and hauling heavy equipment as they continued fleeing north. I threw the quilt off and I jumped up again and started to pace the floor.

Oh my God! What if one of the troops discerns my shadow through the opaque window and is curious enough to investigate? What if the planes break formation, head north and attack the CCF where we are? Could I muster the courage to withstand yet another air attack without falling to pieces? What if napalm was dropped? That would be a horrible way to die, if the planes did attack!

I would have to run for my life from the shack and possibly into direct contact of a Chinese soldier, who would as soon shoot me down, to retaliate for the attacking Marine marauders. Still if I must die, it would be a fate better than death by napalm.

Should I take my chances and flee through this town? Where would I go? What if the Chinese infiltrate the town and seek shelter in this very house? A million *what ifs*. No answers. I lay down again in a ball on the floor and again covered myself. I could visualize a Chinese soldier, fleeing from the planes, running into this house. He was sure to fire at me, knowing that someone was hiding who didn't belong here. I would be blasted at point blank range by 20 rounds or more from his Russian AK-47. Not one chance in hell to survive.

I sprang to my feet once more and repeatedly and reflexively paced the floor before I reminded myself the frenzy of my actions could arouse the enemy. I was sure that I was going to have a heart attack. My breathing was clipped, I was gasping for air in short staccato breaths and I felt faint. I was in the flight mode again. Once more I hid under the quilt as the nonstop screaming and cursing rumbled on in harsh, unharmonious concert with the sound of squeaky, droning wheels of hand carts, motor conveyances, and foot power, not more than three feet from my window.

What are you doing to me God? I can't take much more of this. I have maxed to the limit on adrenaline, and surely the enemy must hear my heart pounding and come to investigate.

What are my options? What are my odds? This morbid thought spun over and over in my head. What can I do? I just can't get myself to concentrate.

Paul, you must think! Pull yourself together and think! It's no use.

I was once more at the mercy of a mélange of terrors.

All those events of the past ghastly nightmarish days melded together; I lost my perspective on how to survive. A deer constantly shot at until it panics at the slightest sound or movement—that was me.

If only the horrendous shouting would stop.

Please, Dear God send them away. Send the planes away. Don't have them machine gun us again or dispatch death dealing rockets on their mission of death. Don't allow the planes to drop the hideous excruciating torturous death of napalm. I prayed for my life and I prayed for the safety of my friends. I was worn out. My sense of survival was washed from my system. Kill me if you will, but I just can't take another day of horror like this.

The insane commotion began a feeble effort to fade, but I didn't realize it because I was like the proverbial cornered rat.

A dark looming shadow appeared at the door, and suddenly the door slid open with a loud bang that I thought to be a gunshot. I nearly fainted in response. I expected to be cut down like some gangster in a B movie, but instead, it was my bicyclist friend. He was grim-faced and shaken. My friend took me gently by the arm and silently led me out of the chamber of horrors. We went stumbling, reeling and shaking back to the road together. We were twins—both in deep shock, subdued, anesthetized.

The exodus continued. The roadside that swallowed the untold mass refugees earlier, spit them right back out on the road, and now, everything was the same. Well, not quite. The volunteer militia disappeared. They were never seen again.

Mr. Kim, my bicycle friend, now walking his bicycle, and I resumed our march three abreast, without words spoken, and, as I glanced at their eyes, I realized that I was the same as they. Gone was any animation in faces. Now, the eyes of my friends betrayed what I had come to know. I realized the brutal transformation we endured. The disasters and terrors we were subjected to over these days had taken their ultimate toll.

We all looked alike. No one could separate us from other refugees who also endured this life of terror to the point that they, like us, became saturated, deadened. We were now all official refugees in the strongest sense. We were branded in the brain, so as never to forget. Mindless creatures poking on in a zombie-like trance. Brains so scrambled with trauma that we could no long function as normal beings.

Would we recover? I never did.

Refugees, I am of you.

Ever so slowly, my thoughts became rational and I began questioning again. From where could this Chinese Army possibly have originated? It was impossible, I kept repeating to myself. We were on this road from the time that I met Mr. Kim, so far north of here, well over 100 miles at the very least. We were on this road every day, all day, until the darkness of night. When our group, now down to six, slept together in abandoned houses during the night, the million-plus mass of refugees huddled together for warmth defying the sub-zero weather, just outside our door.

No one could have possibly passed, especially such a huge unit of enemy troops. How could they possibly get so far, so fast? Where could they have come from? They couldn't have vehicles, because they couldn't negotiate any of the roads flooded with refugees. Yet, I heard the din of moving vehicles from the waxed paper window.

~~

In my mature years I poured over maps of this area many times in the vain hope of some how deciphering how the Chinese Forces could have possibly bypassed us to end ahead of us. There were no other roads available for them to traverse this area so rapidly.[79]

As the Americans and their Allies were in full retreat, it was understandable that a wide gap between two opposing forces would occur. That was a given. How the enemy could stay on the heels of their enemy, as if they were running dogs nipping at speeding auto tires, is beyond comprehension. The attacking Chinese soldiers, at this point, were invincible, determined and fearless.

I remained dumbfounded for answers to this cloudiest of enigmas until I read Roy Appleman's book, *Disaster in Korea*. I had wondered, not know-

---

[79] About the same time enemy troops entered Pyongyang, other enemy units reached the port of Chinnampo, at the mouth of the Taedong river, and began crossing to the south side. Aerial observation confirmed that enemy troops were crossing the river by ferry near Chinnampo on 6 December, but did not confirm that enemy troops were yet in the city. Large numbers of Korean refugees fled in front of the Chinese, about 10,000 of them being reported in the Chinnampo area. Appleman, p.415.

ing how this movement of the enemy was possible. The memory seemed it could have been another terrible nightmare, but it was all too vivid. I continue to proclaim that no army could possibly deploy as rapidly as did these persistent enemy. Yet there they were, right in front of us again.

~~

We continued our struggle forward and eventually we approached the area where the Marine Corsairs were sighted in engagement against the enemy. I searched for evidence of this recent aircraft attack against the Chinese Army. Surely there would be bodies of freshly-slain Chinese soldiers, along with newly-disabled vehicles, motorized and hand pulled, when the planes had them in their gun-sights. There was none.

Perhaps it was a bad dream after all.

~~

Communist China, the sleeping dragon, stirred from slumber on 9 October 1950, to the clamor of the heavy thud of Allied boots cracking ice on squalid, abandoned rice paddies and to the clatter of armored conveyances, defiantly clanking weighty steel treads on icy, stinking roads. They were in harmony with massive convoys filled with exuberant young ROKs, Americans, British, Turks, and others. The Allies were on their way north, but the Chinese would soon have something to say about that.

Now, our group, along with the incalculable mass of other innocent refugees was caught in the middle, fleeing from the dragon to escape its fiery breath, the enemy hotly pursuing the evading UN forces in a determined attempt to engage them once again in mortal combat. No, I was not running from the dragon. Rather, *I was running with the Dragon.*[80]

In retrospect, I appreciate the plight of those disfranchised young men who joined our refugee group in Pyongyang. The hunger for survival is so powerful that they were willing to serve any cause, though yearning to be on the winning side. They owed no allegiance to either government. They just wanted to live.

Well known among historians was the fact that the *Democratic* leader of South Korea, Syngman Rhee, was sadistic in the tyrannical control of his regime, while enjoying the blessings and the treasure of the United States.

Fellow former American prisoners of war relate that many of their guards spoke basic English, as many were South Koreans who fled to

---

[80] I hope to never again to read in some uninformed source in regard to this awful conflict that the Allied Army was victorious in this northern war. I witnessed the results from the other side. The United Nations lost in North Korea. The People's Liberation Army (People's Republic of China) won in North Korea and tied in South Korea. Author.

North Korea because of the brutality of the Rhee regime. Thousands went to their deaths under the auspices of the Republic of Korea, founded 15 August 1948, and ruled tyrannically by President Syngman Rhee.[81]

Nor is this an apologia for the systematic brutality of the Democratic People's Republic of Korea, under the abominable regime of Kim Il-Sung, whose army and secret police murdered, starved and imprisoned hundreds of thousands of citizens. The Communist North was by far worse in the race for first place in the category of evil. In a matter of just five years, the border was blasted open by war to allow two sides to kill each other while millions of innocent North and South Korean citizens, starving and repressed, accepted the challenge of escape.

Now, it is some 50-odd years later and nothing has changed, except in China. The dragon has evolved into the world's super-power in trade.

---

[81] There were atrocities on both sides, and Kim Il-sung became so concerned by those committed on American and ROK prisoners that he issued this order: "Some of us are still slaughtering enemy troops that come to surrender. Therefore, the responsibility of teaching the soldiers to take prisoners of war and to treat them kindly rests on the political section of each unit." No similar order was issued by President Rhee. Toland, p.129.

CHINNAMPO

> In order to mount large-scale military maneuvers in both sectors of North Korea, it was necessary early in the operation to seize two large seaports, one on the east coast, one on the west coast. The likeliest targets were Chinnampo, serving the North Korea capitol of Pyongyang (as Inchon served Seoul) on the west coast, and opposite, Wonson, a large, protected bay on the east coast. Blair, p. 330.

We were too late. Our refugee group arrived in the west coast major port city of Chinnampo, around the second week of December. The American Army evacuated the port on 5 December, as part of Task Force 90. One thousand, eight hundred United States Army and Navy personnel, along with 5,900 ROK soldiers steamed to liberty. They were gone before we could catch up with them. My fervent hope for freedom steamed with them.

The city was in shambles. Not a building was standing. Once a thriving major port and rail center for supply to Pyongyang, and other large cities, it now lay in ruin. It had been completely cleared of lethal Russian sea mines by 20 November, after Navy under-water experts spent considerable time and energy in mine-sweeping operations to clear the harbor. Chinnampo, more an inlet than a harbor, replaced the Port of Inchon for supplying the rapidly moving 8th Army in their northward assault. Five thousand tons of supplies were off-loaded daily, but it was a short-lived operation. The invading Chinese Communist Army was now attacking as fast as the Allied armies could retreat. After the time and expense of establishing the port to supply the once bold, advancing Allied armies, it was surrendered in a brief moment.

The inlet was fed by two rivers far to the east—the Taedong flowing from the north, and from the south, the Chaeryong. The confluence of the two rivers then coursed westward, effectively cutting off any means of escape for refugees, including me.[82] At least the Chinese Forces would be stopped by this unconquerable barrier as well, and that would hopefully allow us time to locate the Allied lines. None of us in the untold masses of refugees realized that the enemy infiltration succeeded.

---

[82] About the same time enemy troops entered Pyongyang, other enemy units reached the port of Chinnampo, at the mouth of the Taedong River, and began crossing to the south side.... Korean civilian reports said the enemy were screening large masses of refugees for conscription of young men to fill depleted North Korean units. Other agents reported a small group of Chinese soldiers.... Appleman, p.415.

The enormous trestle bridge that once spanned the sea inlet was demolished by explosives, either by Army demolition experts or by the Air Force. Perhaps it was a combination of the two. Similar to the destroyed bridges in the Capitol, skeletal remains protruded above the water and provided bare handholds to the desperate, fleeing refugees. The main portion of the structure was sunk, effectively blocking passage to the entrance of the harbor. The handhold escape route spanning nearly the entire waterway could only be scaled by the desperate refugees after unburdening themselves of personal property. The below-freezing temperature of the exposed steel must have been unbearable to the bare hands of escapees. Additionally, it would be too cumbersome for enemy troops with weapons and supplies to attempt any type of mass crossing.

Desperate refugees ascended the barren and abandoned structure with extreme care, then had to cross the last segment of the river by fording the icy water. To fall into the frigid water near the middle of the harbor meant near-instant death and so many of the pitiful refugees died in this appalling manner. The south end of the shattered trestle lacked enough above-water steel to permit the grasp needed to complete the crossing clear of the near-freezing water.

Someone ingeniously had tied a heavy line from the last handhold of the exposed bridge to a large tree on the south side of the land. The escapees could complete the crossing using the cord, as a handhold, although they were immersed in the now shallow, icy water for brief moments. Because of that, refugees had to seek immediate shelter in the abandoned village just to the south of the inlet to avoid freezing to death.

There they removed and exchanged wet clothing for dried clothes left by previous refugees who earlier crossed this tremendous obstacle. It was the Good Samaritan concept. They would exchange the clothes of the refugees who went before, and leave their own soaked, cold apparel which would in time dry, for the ones to follow.

Personal property was haphazardly discarded everywhere. With much physical effort, these homeless souls had carried their few paltry possessions over 200 miles, only to abandon them. They crossed the inlet with only the clothes they wore. The abandonment of personal possessions had but one exception. Bundles and boxes formerly carried as backpacks were forsaken, but babies had to be taken by their mothers. The infants were sturdily lashed to the backs of their young mothers, perilously placed in harm's way. Mothers braved the treacherous current with additional cargo too precious to leave.

This sunken bridge was more dangerous to scale than the submerged bridges at Pyongyang. The steel carcass of this bridge at Chinnampo was much more formidable and dangerous because of limited hand holds.

The massive rail yard matched the bridge in destruction. The honor for that monstrous wide-spread demolition was credited to the Air Force during their relentless bombing crusade. There were fewer bodies lying in this area of the city compared to that awful day of the plane attack north of this junction. Still, the relentless determination of the vast horde of refugees had not wavered. It was safer for them to hide among the debris of former buildings, than to be exposed on the open road.

I noticed a native rubber shoe lying off of the road. There was a foot in it. I had no idea where the rest of the remains were. Perhaps the extreme cold cauterized and stanched the flow of blood, allowing the victim to survive. Bodies dead for some time were covered in heavy grit from the highways.

The city had been pulverized daily by the Air Force, and I could only envision, by using the strongest of imagination, that a city once actually stood there. It was flattened. The strong odor of human urine and feces and decomposing bodies hung in the air. It was putrid evidence of the over three million total refugees.

The wide and relatively level banks of the inlet afforded space for ancient villages. The buildings were set back in consideration of the natural ebb and flow of the tides, which left wide but forlorn sandy beaches on each side. The villages on both sides were spared by the Air Force, who apparently believed that civilians resided there. Moreover, the Chinese had not continued their blitzkrieg assault this far south as yet, or so I believed. We presumed villages were spared wanton destruction by the Air Force because of the absence of invading Chinese warriors.

I noticed a large dory-type boat stranded or beached on the north bank of this wide, treacherous inlet, but, for the moment, I didn't give it a second thought. I was oblivious to almost everything except for watching for Chinese troops, having put my trust and my life in the hands of Mr. Kim for all other matters.

The charisma of Mr. Kim continued to prevail, because as we entered the village, our group was invited into a large house on the bank of the inlet. When we entered, there were between 20 and 30 people inside, now including us, all squatting on tatami mats. The standard hibachi was noticeably missing. The lady of the house may have cooked the meager meal outside, in a mud nook built adjacent to the house.

As I looked around, I spied the same individual that I so rudely and crazily brushed aside when I first entered the village of Mr. Kim. The militiaman still carried his rifle and even now wore the armband of the Republic of Korea on his upper arm. We avoided each other's glance. Then at one point our eyes riveted on each other. I was so sorry for my behavior when we first met. I wanted to apologize, but I lacked the finesse, language and social manners to bring myself to do that, so I averted my eyes from his. I wondered how he arrived at the house before we arrived, and I was glad that he escaped the carnage on the road, for it was clear that he was a true patriot. I can think of no other who would have the courage to brandish that South Korean armband in the middle of North Korea, even among refugees.

The room appeared hazy or smoky, even though I did not see anyone smoking. Even though the room was crowded, no one paid attention to me. When they did look at me, I saw the same stoic glances as I did after the air strike, as I rode on the back of the bicycle. Now, I realized that they were glancing at me impersonally. I was just one more individual longing for safety. Even though the language barrier precluded us from conversation, I was one of them.[83]

"Mr. Paul, drink this, it is good for you, and it is boiled." Mr. Kim handed me a lacquered, terra cotta-colored wood small soup bowl.

"Thank you very much. What is it, Mr. Kim?"

"It is water, and you must drink it. It is boiled and it is good to drink."

I looked in the bowl to view the vilest potion I ever saw. It was slime. Warm slime, with white blobs of gelatin resembling jellyfish. It reeked of night soil. I recalled my very young days when my mother made starch, preparatory to ironing; it resembled that slimy concoction exactly. I was not thirsty, nor did I want to drink that putrid mess. I gazed around, and no one was paying attention to me. I knew full well that Mr. Kim was my protector, and that he would never do anything to harm me. I was not going to insult him or hurt his feelings, so I accepted the bowl with both

---

[83] Many years later, while viewing the World War II film drama, *Thirty Seconds over Tokyo* I saw a scene where American pilots and crews crash-landed near China. Survivors were brought to a native house where their injuries were tended by many Chinese villagers. I had a terrible panicked flashback because of the circumstances and surroundings of the film. The scenes were so similar to this house I had occupied. This hut, as was the one depicted in the film, was dark, crowded with Asians with similar attire and the dwelling was constructed similarly. But our hut had an additional item that no one could possibly capture or duplicate on film, and that was the odious stench. There is nowhere on earth that could equal the horrendous smell of this place. And my seriously gangrened feet were a very large contributor to this stench. Author.

hands outstretched.

"Thank you, Mr. Kim."

I put the bowl to my lips and allowed the vile, very warm fluid to pass down my throat while I held my lips tightly together in an effort to prevent the gelatine-like substance from slithering in.

"Thank you very much, Mr. Kim. It was very good," I lied, after consuming most of it. I wiped the excess fluid from my filthy face and lips with the back of my even filthier hand.

During this episode, as everyone began to doze from exhaustion, I discovered another minor problem. I was infested with lice. Sleeping with the enemy had its good points and its bad. This was the bad. The lice apparently joined me the night that the three elders allowed me to share their dwelling. The cold weather probably did not allow the residents to air and sun the tatami mats, where lice nested and propagated. Once they located me, the lice continued to breed and lay eggs in the seams of my uniform, my hair, and every fold of my skin, and propagated and feasted on my blood. A very minor discomfort, given my present situation, and one from which apparently everyone in Korea universally suffered.

Gradually everyone awoke to share a bare minimum of something to eat—watery stew, lacking much substance, and I wondered how in the world any food at all was available in this land of starvation, let alone enough to share with strangers. Mr. Kim explained that the resident housewife was a Good Samaritan who opened her home to refugees, and while they were resting, she cooked for everyone. I learned later that the food was the very barest to survive. Not rice, meat or vegetables, but weeds, grass, tree bark and the like were made into a soupy mixture. It was scarcely enough to sustain life. The war put a crippling halt to the harvesting of rice, as well as the growing of other food so vital to sustain life for inhabitants of both sides of the 38th Parallel.

I had not eaten in about 10 or 11 days. I was not hungry. I weighed less than 100 pounds by now, but still the hunger pangs had subsided long ago.

"Here, Mr. Paul, this is for you." Mr. Kim, with a bold, proud smile handed me a bowl of soup-like mixture with a large piece of meat steaming inside.

"You are our guest, and so it is for you." I smiled in return and thanked him.

When I glanced at the face of the *Good Samaritan* lady, I was rewarded with the warmest of smiles. I smiled in return and bowed my head to her, and I said, "Thank you for your kindness."

Mr. Kim interpreted my message to her. She beamed, and every one in the room smiled with her. Then it hit me. This was the only time, Mr. Kim being the exception, that I saw refugees smile.

"Thank you, Mr. Kim. What is it?" I peered into the bowl curiously.

"It is a rat. I am sorry that we have no other meat, but it is good for you." Mr. Kim's eyes said it all. I was the guest of honor, and this delicacy was indeed, reserved for a special guest. And that was me, and while I was hesitant, I was also truly honored. The graveness of this occasion shouted to the world the fervent message, *We really don't have to kill one another. Let the world be friends.*

"Thank you very much Mr. Kim. This is very kind of you, and please say thank you to the lady for me again."

Mr. Kim interpreted and conveyed my message in Korean to her again and she smiled again while she so very politely bowed deeply as she backed from the house.

I stared at my treasure, as I scrutinized the piece of meat more closely. I saw that it was headless and tailless. The feet had been removed and the animal had been skinned. I didn't hesitate a moment because I realized that in this ongoing, dreadful episode of my life, there were others in North Korea, then, as now, who would do anything in the world to share this luxury. It would have been deeply offensive to them had I refused to eat, and I knew that it truly was an honor, given that the populace was starving. My only problem was the fact that I was not hungry at all. Had it been a sirloin steak, I still lacked the appetite or the imagination to eat, in spite of my emaciated condition.

I was handed *hashii* (chopsticks) with which to eat, and I was glad that I was not quite a complete novice.[84] We had practiced when we first arrived in Okinawa with soldiers who had served in Japan earlier. No one paid attention to me and I noticed that they were all speaking in hushed tones, so as not to disturb others. I started on my meal. It was difficult to even try to eat because the chopsticks made it difficult to remove the flesh from the bone.

---

[84] Hashii—Japanese for chopsticks—were handier than our solitary issued spoon. Those who served in Japan during the Occupation became quite adept at the use of hashii. They taught the rest of us. We from the regiment in Okinawa were generally not permitted to mingle with the citizens, so we learned little of their colorful history and culture. The Okinawans seemed to be more distant than the very friendly Japanese. Perhaps the Okinawans felt that they were not part of the Emperor of Japan's edict of non-resistance to the occupiers. I called it the Velvet Occupation when I later served in Japan. Author.

I kept at it and I gradually consumed enough to believe I would not offend anyone. I thanked Mr. Kim for his generosity and suggested that someone else finish it as I was now completely full. He said something in Korean, and the lady of the house took the remnants and the bowl, radiating her continuous sincere and glowing smile.

"Thank you. It was very good," I said as I wiped the soupy liquid from my mouth.

After we had sat idling in the room for about an hour, a loud, shrill whistle sounded.

"Come, Mr. Paul, it is time. We must go!" Mr. Kim quickly arose. I sensed an air of extraordinary urgency, and I became anxious again.

A few people rushed from several other houses in response to the whistle, including some from our group. When I stepped outside, Mr. Kim and my bicyclist friend grabbed me under each arm and hurriedly half-carried, half-walked me to the same boat I noticed beached earlier. They picked me up under my arms and swung me into the boat, where several women already were seated. I smiled briefly to the ladies, but I got no response except wooden expressions.

Upon a shrill, loud command, several male refugees pushed the heavy, clumsy boat into the water and leaped in at the last moment, to avoid the icy inlet, as the boat became water borne. The bicycle was thrown in the aft of the boat at the last moment. The patriot militia man was aboard as well, and when I managed to catch his eye, I smiled at him. I was relieved when he returned the smile. We never saw each other again. I hoped that he made it out alive, and I believe he could escape if he had the good sense to remove his arm band and throw away his rifle. Refugees did not carry weapons. All they want is to be left alone to live a peaceful life.

In the meantime, men, apparently local inhabitants, were busy rowing in unison as intensely as possible, propelling the ark-like boat swiftly forward, parallel to the sunken bridge. I gazed in awe at the determined, anxious refugees trying frantically to scale the destroyed trestle. The inlet from the Yellow Sea was incredibly wide and rough. I was unsure if it was the delta of the river that flowed into the ocean or if it was high tide in the inlet rushing in from the sea. Whatever the source, the water was roiling as the oarsmen rowed silently and swiftly together. The air of urgency continued to prevail, but I didn't know why.

After a protracted interval, we completed our voyage as the bow of the boat plowed forcefully onto the sand and beached itself on the south shore. Mr. Kim and my bicycle friend lifted me from the boat while others pulled the boat farther from the near-frozen inlet. Mr. Kim and my other friend again half-carried me, half-walked me at a rapid pace. I noticed that the others were running alongside, apparently to seek shelter.

When the three of us approached the nearest of the houses, the numerous boat passengers poured anxiously inside other archaic huts. Our house, as most of the others, was abandoned, sparse in nature, and lacked furniture. Our group of refugees huddled on the tatami mats again, just we did as in the Good Samaritan's home. Normally, in these homes, as in Japan, it was customary to remove one's shoes before entering a dwelling. These were not normal times.

Two or three inhabitants rushed from one of the occupied houses on the south side, to the boat, and reversing direction by walking rapidly backwards, swept the footprints from the sand, using rough, hand-made brooms. All at once the atmosphere seemed to be a little lighter, as approximately 20 of the group of about 40 from the boat conversed softly. Crossing the water was a major obstacle, and from the expressions on the refugees' faces, and their very gentle speech tones, it was apparent that they were relieved to complete this major hurdle. I wondered the criteria as to who was allowed to proceed by boat and who must take their chances on traversing the dangerous trestle.

Planes! Suddenly the planes were back! They buzzed frightfully low exactly over our position, as we collectively froze in absolute terror. I thought that this time I would bolt from the shanty and run for my life if we were to be attacked again. Even though I could barely walk by then, I knew that I could muster the determination to run.

For some reason, the aircraft held fire. They almost always fired a burst of 50-caliber rounds into houses to see if anyone fled into the open. During the dreadful, prolonged silence, everyone, especially me, held their panicked breaths as we anxiously and fearfully peered upward. The inhabitants, including me, were cowering nervously inside, where of course the planes were not visible—but it just seemed to be a natural tendency to gaze in apprehension skyward. It was if the warring marauders could hear us if we spoke, so dead silence prevailed, more out of fear than of logic. We waited fearfully for the planes to spurt red-hot rounds and the infamous rockets again on us and on this village. Instead, in time, they soared away to seek other targets, or to return to their base of operations. I sighed in unspoken relief, as did others.

I learned many things from Mr. Kim in respect to this adventure. He told me that according to the refugee grapevine, the people on the north side, the Good Samaritans, identified and compiled the timetable of regularly-scheduled flights of the Air Force, combined with the added knowledge as to how long it would normally take to cross the water. The Good Samaritans coordinated the water passage by counting exactly enough refugees to fill the boat and advised them when to take flight as fast as they could for the boat, on command of the whistle. Meanwhile, the Samaritan group followed the fleeing boat passengers as they boarded the boat, sweeping away the remaining many telltale footprints on the beach.

What Mr. Kim did not tell me, and what I discerned, was that we were among the first to make the dangerous voyage. It appeared Mr. Kim continued to be given preference. Perhaps he was awarded some status because I was along, and if that was true, I was pleased for all. More likely, because he was an outspoken critic of the Communist regime, his political stand called for his imprisonment, and as a result, Mr. Kim grew to be a living martyr to the masses of refugees.

As dusk settled in, the evening began to cool rapidly. Strangers all, except for Mr. Kim's group, lay in silence and camaraderie next to each other. The group huddled together for warmth and then fell into deep, fretful sleep as one body. We would begin our journey again south at daybreak, or perhaps even before.[85]

"Mr. Paul, I have news for you that you will like."

I immediately perked at his words. "What is it Mr. Kim?"

"The Americans are now a little ways away, and tomorrow we shall find them, I am sure."

"Oh, Mr. Kim, I hope that is real. I want to tell the Americans how you helped me, and I could not return except for you."

"Will they allow me to go to South Korea with my friends?" Mr. Kim asked earnestly.

"Mr. Kim, you saved my life, and I will tell the Americans that. They will let us all in, I know."

---

[85] As I now view a North Korean map and focus on the city of Chinnampo or "Nampo", as it is now known, I can understand how the sheer vastness of the waterway would have prevented me from crossing without the indispensable help of Mr. Kim. Author.

DAY FOURTEEN

By the end of November and the first day of December, the Chinese 2nd phase offensive had decisively defeated the Eighth Army, and the latter was gathering speed in a headlong retreat southward. The days and nights from the evening of 25 November to 1 December 1950 are crowded with a churning, hectic, often bizarre, series of battles, large and small, clear across the Eighth Army front. Appleman, p. 80.

He didn't have to say anything because as Mr. Kim whispered, "Wake up, Mr. Paul, we must go," I subconsciously sensed Mr. Kim's approaching presence. With his gentle touch but sound of urgency, I leaped from deep sleep to total awareness, alert, heart racing and adrenaline pumping at the maximum. By now, my instinct for survival was honed to its peak. Each time I awoke, I would react in the same frightful manner—silent alarm bells crashing through my body. It had to be devastating to my internal system.

It was impossible not to sleep, given the exhaustive forced journey tortuously endured by all. Foreign sounds of warfare, no matter how subtle, would have alerted me from sleep. The sound of a vehicle, the muffled sounds of harsh foreign masculine tongues, even the sound of an unusual occurrence, such as footsteps shuffling in a unified tempo, would awaken instant vigilance in me. It was that Pavlov thing again.

The air was foul as usual when I awoke, and the house, unheated, was cold although not frozen. The body heat emitting from this mass of desolate refugees jammed together like a room full of stuffed rag dolls was adequate. It was impossible to move. Bodies were intertwined with neighbors, mostly strangers all. Breathing was laborious and heavy, no doubt due to the continuous and exhausting forced march without sustenance or respite. Children were quiet, counseled by parents, while infants wailed uncontrollably. The room was awash with heavy, odious foul stenches from myriad sources—body odor, feces, the sour stench of newborn vomit. I was not without sin, for I was responsible for a preponderance of the sickening, gagging reek. I had to have been the one that had not bathed in the longest period among us. The vomit-inducing reek of my acutely infected gangrened feet added to the deplorable stench. Pus, draining from infected, rotting tissue, could not be staunched.

The collective exhaustive and debilitating migration drained all of any remaining strength. Everyone slept through the bawling of infants, many born during this forced march. It was amazing to see young mothers breastfeeding the newborn when the mothers themselves were nothing more than emaciated living skeletons. The lack of nourishment, and the unsanitary conditions of life on the run allowed only basic care for newborns.

"OK Mr. Kim. Thank you, I am ready."

We were ready to start another day in search of the Allied Army, and the estimation we were at least three days behind them continued to prevail. It was still dark, a new day, and this was the 14th day since my capture, and escape. I seemed to be the equivalent of an escaped felon from a southern chain gang—a target painted on the back of my grimy, prison uniform, a dead or alive bounty on my head. In fact, if I were a chain gang escapee, I could go underground and be absorbed into society. Not so here, as I was the only non-Asian fugitive in this oriental warring land of brotherly hate.

"Another day, another dollar," I muttered. God, I wished that it were.

There was no way to estimate the ill-fated miles I covered ever since my journey began with my capture and until I connected with my North Korean saviors.

In adult years, scrutinizing a map of North Korea, I plotted my journey from the site of King Company's defense against the Chinese Communist forces somewhere near a village or small town called *Ipstok*. The total distance traveled equated to over 200 excruciating miles.

It gave me comfort to be with friends. Our relationships became so deep and intertwined because the universal will to break out melded us as one. Other than the language barrier, it seemed that I had been living with the fleeing immigrants in perpetuity.

For the last two days, Mr. Kim had been informed by local residents that they recently observed American soldiers. I was elated. Then we traveled that distance, and the American Army apparently retreated another 20 miles south. My mind was at low ebb. I was crushed and demoralized.

Somehow though, this early morning for the very first time, once we began marching, something seemed different. It wasn't the weather because it was as frigid as ever. I could almost sense something in the air when I first stepped from the dirty little hut in the dirty little village.

The horde of refugees had thinned considerably. I had no idea why, unless it was that dreadful obstacle that almost all refugees but us few had to cross—the sunken bridge that once spanned the mighty inlet at Chinnampo.

Now, there seemed to be serenity in this valley. Yes, that was it. Serenity. No mass activity of refugees. The absence of wagon and cart. The missing thunderous roar of overhead fighter jet aircraft bursting through leaden skies seeking to slaughter. No bodies, artillery fire, clanking roar of tanks or screams of peasants in terror. Just peace. An expansive, quiet, open valley laden with calm.

The faint, delectable smell of burning wood wafted through the cold air, and the source could only emanate from the kitchen of a native dwelling. There were only two explanations for the farmhouse to be occupied. We were now either in *no man's land*, ahead of the massive Chinese Army, or the occupants within were but a few of hundreds who stood in absolute defiance of the Chinese onslaught. Whatever the reason, the pungent aroma of the fire replaced the ugly stench of war materiel and memories of cordite, gunpowder, the vapors from artillery or tank, the unforgettable stench of rotting bodies.

The towering Taebaek Mountains to the west were voraciously devouring enormous drifts of new snowfall, storing it in vast bellies of underground cavities, only to unleash and nurture, in gentle streams, the agrarian valley when the spring thaw would follow.

The Chinese and the newly-restructured North Korean armies had to be right behind us, or ahead of us, or among us, for all we knew. For reasons known only to the enemy, the Chinese veered inland from Pyonyang, crossing Chinnampo at the confluence of the rivers Taedong and Chaeryong. Despite that, we made better time owing to the meager ranks of the remaining refugee population.[86]

The sudden absence of the mass of the civilian population concerned me. Was this some sinister omen? Perhaps hundreds of thousands of refugees were diverted when the CCF pursued the Americans south, near the source of the Taedong River. No—Mr. Kim would surely have known the reason for the disappearance of the multitude.

I was just so very lucky to be alive, and so indebted to my North Korean compatriots. I am able to chronicle these extraordinary events solely because of their efforts to save a young, confused soldier thrown into a man's world of bloody conflict. Thousands of emaciated, decent, starving people numbed by the terrors of war, were willing to accept *the enemy*

---

[86] Much later in life I wondered how this carnage and near destruction of the American army came about. The brass knew the enemy was coming, because captured prisoners forthrightly disclosed being assigned to a plethora of various enemy armies. Someone should have read the war tactics of Mao Tse-tung to the American decision makers—"Enemy advances, we retreat; Enemy halts, we harass; Enemy tires; we pursue." Author.

among them—me.

Thank you, Mr. Kim. Thank you, Lord.

Moreover, living, if it could be called that, among the refugees for so long, was an indelible faith-inspiring life experience. In subsequent undeclared wars involving our nation, my heart was to cry out first and foremost for the innocents, the innocents, the innocents. I knew. No one else cared. To them the appalling number of blameless civilians slain, numbering over two million, was merely a statistic.

My gangrened feet were causing pulsating pain, and I started to limp, although I hoped it wasn't obvious. I had not the least intention of being a burden to my group in any manner.

Once again as I rode on the bicycle, the pain in my feet continued, unrelenting. Now a harsh throb developed, rumbled through my legs down to my feet where the sensation was that my feet would literally explode from pounding tremors. I realized that were I to be recaptured and not shot, infectious poison would result in my death in just a matter of days.

My friend the bicycle driver, unencumbered by the earlier horde of evacuees, peddled rapidly enough to keep a steady balance. He would stop whenever our distance became so great that we had to wait for the others.

Mr. Kim shortly strolled up in his usual quick step to where we awaited him beside the road, the bicycle lying nearby. He too had a determined mission, and by his unfaltering pace, Mr. Kim demonstrated that he was intent on evading his previous captors as well. There was absolutely no chance that Mr. Kim would survive if he were re-captured.

During the wait, I reflected on how long ago it was since I had eaten. It had to have been at least 16 days. I didn't consider that vile and toxic rancid rice left for Buddha as food. The boiled rat that I ate in the refugee hut in Chinnampo really couldn't count for much either. I was struck by how long a person could go without food. I felt as strong as ever.

Still, eventually one would have to have some nourishment or perish. My system was not at that point as yet. As long as water was available from snow on the ground or native village wells, I would survive. Moreover, while my weight plunged from over 140 to under 100 pounds, I still had the fortitude and the will to continue.

Judging from the position of the opaque sun, it was late morning or early afternoon by the time we completed about a 15-mile journey to the south. Unimpeded by the enemy, we still carried the habit of looking over shoulders for them. We never knew when they might spring up again.[87]

Our group was still in North Korean territory, and still most likely within the confines of enemy presence, although perhaps by this time the area may have been construed as *no man's land*. I will never know.

We stopped at a rare, rural crossroads where I saw numerous civilians in their typical rural clothing, milling aimlessly about. I sensed something out of place because prior refugees never wandered. They had, as a semi-unified body, massed in one enormous throng, all heading south. This group was reminiscent of the crowded village where I first met Mr. Kim. No one present seemed to have a purpose.

All of a sudden I saw it. An American jeep. The canvas top was down, and it was parked near a typical country intersection of two dirt roads. Relatively clean, and clearly not a bombed-out hulk, it seemed to be a readily-drivable vehicle.

When we approached the conveyance, I was lifted and gently carried by Mr. Kim and my other friend, the bicyclist, who placed me across the rear seat of the uncovered jeep. I noticed the South Korean driver and his armed escort, both clad in American uniforms, standing by. They saluted me and greeted me with wide, sincere smiles. I was dumbfounded about how they had materialized. Moreover I didn't detect a sense of urgency at this time and place, as I had experienced for these last frenzied 14 days of my life on the run.

The lead-hued sky continued to restrain the deluge that was close to bursting from heavy, rain filled clouds. This oncoming storm would not dare to rain on my parade this day. But, even if the heavy rains or snows did arrive, I was used to it. I survived the monsoons and the unbelievable bitterness of snows in the insidious mountains of North Korea.

The jeep was most likely equipped with the usual canvas top for an emergency, but I could have cared less. I scarcely dared to believe I was at long last near freedom. This terrible nightmare might be nearly over. In my heart I just knew that I could not absorb another disappointment.

More than anything, I was in mild shock. The feeling was not like the distress of being shot at, which causes severe trauma—this sensation was rather one of incredible disbelief. This was the nearest that I had come to a

---

[87] The Chinese Communist Forces were in great haste to re-engage the United Nation Forces before the shattered 8th Army could stop to deploy defensive positions. The Chinese knew Mao's tactic—the Americans learned the hard way. Mao ordered his Korean War field commander, General Peng, to continue the relentless attack against the swiftly retreating United Nations Forces, despite the intense fatigue of the CCF. Author.

successful end to my perilous journey. This was even closer to evading the enemy than when I was so near to the American helicopter on that fateful day when I was so in fear of exposing my position by making a futile attempt to signal for assistance.

This was now my 14th day behind enemy lines, and as I gaze in hindsight, it seemed then to have been a lifetime of fear.

Someone, most likely Mr. Kim, unlaced my boots and slowly and skillfully removed them while I was lying on the jeep. Now, I felt no pain. The same person was delicately removing my woolen socks, separating the pus-laden socks from toes that were glued to the bottom of the socks by gelled poison.

"Here is the doctor," Mr. Kim said softly as he glanced to the east.

I followed his gaze, and I observed the doctor approach. He was clad in a very formal morning suit consisting of black and gray striped trousers, white shirt with a wide black tie slightly hidden by a wool, gray, buttoned vest. The doctor had on a black formal long swallow-tailed suit jacket, buttoned smartly at the waist, and patent leather shoes. The physician was sporting a black top hat to complete the ensemble. He carried a very large satchel in his right hand. Though the bag appeared to be very cumbersome and heavy, the doctor carried it, not along the right side of his body, but away from his body. He was a doctor, and he wanted everyone, especially me, to know that he was a qualified medical professional.

The North Korean grapevine continued to thrive. Someone must have alerted the doctor to the effect that an injured American soldier needed emergency medical treatment. Of course it would be an honor for him to assist an American soldier who sacrificed life and limb to help free the North Korean people from the tyranny and the yoke of oppression of the brutal North Korean regime. And then I ruined it.

The doctor was about 20 yards away, when I happened to glance at my now exposed feet. I was horrified. Every one of the digits was ebony black and brittle and as hard as walnut shells. Flesh had rotted so they resembled small dead twigs. And, just like a dead tree shoot, my toes had turned as hard and lifeless. Exposed to the air, the severely infected toes emitted putrid, onerous stench. I became light-headed at the ghastly sight.

My memory instantly flashed back to the ghastly training film relating to frostbite prevention shown to the company during a lull in the war in early November.

By then the Korean doctor was at my side grinning a wide, toothy greeting. His crinkling, friendly eyes were framed behind thick, black, horn-rimmed glasses. I sensed the faint scent of mothballs and antiseptic emanating from the thick wool suit worn by the doctor. He must not have donned the suit in years. The doctor set his medical valise next to me at the rear of the jeep, and opened it. My flashback to that dreadful film haunted me. I said the cruelest thing that one could possibly say, believing that this wonderful doctor would amputate my toes with pliers.

"Mr. Kim, please tell the doctor that the American Army will not allow anyone except the Army to take care of me."

I was frightened of any treatment by the doctor, but even worse, I was unkind and rude.

"Mr. Paul, please let the doctor to look at you. He is here to help you," Mr. Kim said quietly, plaintively and firmly.

I should have let it go at that. Who cared if I lost my toes? Mr. Kim saved my life, and there was nothing more significant. If I were shot dead by the enemy, frozen toes would not matter.

"Mr. Kim, I am so sorry that the Army has such orders, but I must obey the Army."

I could sense the distress in Mr. Kim's eyes and voice when he softly interpreted my message in Korean to the doctor. I looked into the eyes of the doctor, and I saw the terrible hurt and disappointment in his crestfallen face. I felt terrible, but at that time my concern was that the doctor would just snap my toes off as I saw in the film.

Whenever I revisit my painful display of such utter ignorance and disrespect, I feel so very deeply ashamed. The doctor was entitled to his day in the sun, and I selfishly deprived him of one the most glorious moments of his entire life. That is why he dressed as he did. He wanted me to be assured that it was an absolute honor for him to tend to me, that he was well qualified, and I shamefully rebuffed him. And yet I should have known better. When the considerate Good Samaritan in Chinnampo offered me the only meat available—the rat—I knew better than to have refused her kindness.

Each time I think of my self-centeredness during this tragic event in my life, I want to engage in self-flagellation for my unkindness to all of these very genuine people who were bringing me to freedom at the risk of their own lives. The little things: Sending someone ahead to alert the doctor, providing me with the only food available, making sure that I slept in a warm house almost every night, hiding me from the enemy at the very risks of their lives. And this is how I demonstrated my gratitude.

Paul, the ugly American.

If I could relive this one day of deep shame, I would gladly allow the doctor to practice his medical skills on me. He would certainly have discerned that there was living tissue beneath the gangrenous outer shell, and he would not have amputated. More than likely, he would have sprinkled or dressed my toes with some herbal medication to slow the festering infection and gangrene. As I learned later, the Orient is awash with many natural herbal medications that can perform miracles.

It is much too late now, because by now the doctor and my friends may have passed on, but I would just like to say to all of them in brief, wherever you are, that I am so deeply ashamed of myself, and I ask for your forgiveness.

Someone had obviously ordered the two South Korean soldiers to stand by to pick me up, but for the life of me, to this day I could never understand how they would know about me. It remains one of the enigmas that haunt me to this day.

The South Korean jeep driver now nervously indicated by words and gestures to Mr. Kim that it was time to go. My boots were off so I donated them to one in Mr. Kim's entourage. We smiled at each other, and Mr. Kim and I, along with my bicyclist friend, embraced and shook hands.

"Goodbye, Mr. Paul. Good luck to you."

That is all that Mr. Kim said.

"Thank you, Mr. Kim, the same to you."

A very unfitting farewell to those who saved my life, and to the many days of terror that we suffered together.

Thank you Mr. Kim, for saving my life.[88]

~~

The jeep sped off in a cloud of the same obnoxious road dust that gagged me since the day I arrived in Korea. This time the recipients of the silt were my North Korean friends who were waving goodbye to me as the jeep sped down the isolated, desolate road. I waved in return, my eyes welling with tears.

During the race down the road, I wondered if there was such an ur-

---

[88] It would have been prudent at the time to somehow exchange names and addresses to keep connected through the years. But, as a thoughtless 18-year-old, at the time I lacked the foresight and Mr. Kim lacked an address. I have returned to South Korea twice in these past 50 years to visit, and I often wondered if it would be possible to find Mr. Kim alive and well. But Kim, the surname, like Jones or Smith in the United States, is so common, that it would be impossible to trace. Furthermore, over one million North Korean refugees marched to freedom into South Korea, to escape the tyranny and starvation of the north. It would not be possible for the Republic of Korea to keep records of the refugees, as they were assimilated into South Korean societies. Author.

gency to get where we were going, or if the young driver was just enthralled with the sense of speed. No matter, for now I realistically believed that rescue was possible. I now believed so fervently in my ultimate rescue, that giving my boots to one of my North Korean friends was of no consequence.

The driver seemed to be heading west, based upon the position of the obscured sun and I wondered why the direction chosen was not south. The answer came soon enough. An entire infantry division of South Korean soldiers, also stranded behind enemy lines, loomed into view. My morale soared. Even though we were still behind enemy lines, there was strength in numbers—10,000 of them more or less. Even if we were captured, the enemy would not annihilate an entire division unless of course, the adversaries were reconstructed North Korean Army units. Still the foe would have an immense battle against these fully armed and trained South Korean soldiers.

Awestruck at the line of deuce-and-a-half trucks, I stared in disbelief, attempting to comprehend the reality of this new situation. Hundreds of them, all covered with dark brown tarpaulins. In my entire Army career, I had never seen a covered transport truck. The bellies of the mobile beasts were filled with fighting soldiers, armed to the teeth. This unit was no out-of-control infantry division. Each truck was spaced equidistant from the vehicle ahead. No clamorous noise emanated from within the conveyances. Each driver sat upright, silent and motionless at the wheel, but the most amazing part of it all, was the absolute cleanliness of every vehicle. Possibly it was a new division put together and sent to the front, far too late to attack the charging Chinese Communist armies.

I marveled at how they maintained this precise coordination when the Chinese Forces were overwhelmingly slaughtering Allied units. It revealed the professionalism of their division commander. This was obviously a well-disciplined South Korean infantry division with high morale, pride in unit and unwavering esprit de corps.

Our driver drove up to the only other jeep in the convoy, which seemed to be the vehicle that headed this division. The driver exited and marched stiffly to a tall, erect officer, who appeared to be the commanding general of the division. Military salutes were exchanged and soft words spoken between the two. Then the jeep driver again smartly saluted the commanding general, effected a soldierly about face, and marched back to his jeep.

When he returned, he and his armed escort gently picked me up and carried me to the general's jeep, which was covered. I crawled into the back seat because it was difficult for them assist me because of the obstruction of the cover. They smiled, waved and returned to their jeep. I returned their smiles and waved. I was slowly beginning to allow myself to relax, perhaps accepting that this might finally be the day of deliverance, if this experience was truly real. I sensed the physical and emotional tension that had sustained me for 14 days gradually begin to ebb from my system.

We waited for several minutes. I sat directly behind the driver in one of the two rear seats. We didn't speak because of the language difference, but it was hard for me to contain my emotions. I wanted to touch the driver, to confirm this was truly not a fantasy. During those horrendous nightmare days and nights, I could never imagine, and I dared not dream, of the relief that I now found. I thought back to my fallen buddy and how we could have shared this glorious moment together, had the Lord not taken him from me and from his family.

Now, the commanding general arrived at the passenger side of the jeep. As he entered, he gave me a very brief smile and a slight nod of his head. I grinned widely in return, not daring to allow myself the disappointment of another setback.

I understood the situation. The general was the one in charge, and he very subtly assured me of that, and that he was competent to lead his ROK division. I certainly was pleased with that. I just wanted to get the hell out of this terrible nightmare. He carried an awesome responsibility to get his division out, and I was merely one lost soldier in the whole vast scheme.

Around noon, the general nodded to his driver. That's all. Just a nod. With that, the driver put the vehicle in gear and slowly and smoothly drove in a westerly direction, accelerating to a medium speed to accommodate the convoy. I noticed a lack of radio contact with the convoy, and, as we continued the drive, I sensed that this well-disciplined and highly motivated assemblage apparently had implemented prearranged signals.

After several miles, the trucks behind us gradually slowed and then stopped at an isolated dirt road tee-section as if by magic. The jeep driver turned left and headed south. I thought perhaps some sort of mix-up occurred, and I wondered if I should tap the shoulder of the general and point to the rear, where the stopped trucks were now fading from sight. I thought better of my idea, and I was thankful that I didn't try to interfere. We had traveled, I suppose, two or three miles when the driver made an abrupt stop.

Where once stood a stupendous cement bridge that spanned a wide but shallow river, only rubble remained. The former stately bridge had collapsed into a massive pile of broken cement, blown by Army engineers to slow the encroaching enemy. The steep embankments forbade any vehicles to cross. The general calmly climbed from his seat and once outside, unfolded a large map and spread it on the flat hood of the jeep. I noted that no other officers were present for him to consult. This was his unit and he alone commanded it. Shortly, the general folded the map and reentered the vehicle. A few words were softly spoken to his driver, followed by a nod of understanding from the driver, and we were moving again.

The general was one of the calmest persons I ever met. The driver swung wide right off of the hardened road to initiate a U-turn and gradually accelerated to the same even speed until he approached the intersection where the trucks were parked.

With a slowing at the intersection, the driver turned left again in a westerly direction while the convoy drivers cranked up engines and followed. I was thunderstruck at the coordination of this marvelous South Korean Division. Had they originally followed the jeep as I thought they might, they would have created the most colossal traffic snarl imaginable. Hundreds of trucks would have had to back in reverse for miles or attempt to initiate U-turns on a narrow one-lane dirt road. This coordination was accomplished without any signals or radio contact. I was more than impressed. The American Army could learn something from this exercise.

The jeep continued west for perhaps 20 miles at a smooth, moderate speed. The sun lay sullenly low in the west as if it were resisting the normal ritual of setting, when the driver initiated an exact duplication of his earlier movement. Without a word or nod from the general, the driver turned left again on a southern azimuth, while the convoy again halted on the north side, facing west at an isolated, barren, rural intersection. Again the same circumstances prevailed. We were greeted by another blown bridge, and my concerns began to rise, but obviously the general's did not.

I scrutinized his mannerisms in an attempt to decipher the situation. Not a clue. He calmly duplicated his actions just as before. Stepping from the jeep, map in hand on the hood of the jeep, he scanned the chart, reentered the vehicle, and again spoke softly to his driver who responded with his customary nod. Then the driver turned the jeep around and headed north until he met the intersection, where he again turned west. The convoy followed.

By now the sun had abruptly lurched behind the mountain and we were instantly pitched into the abyss of night without warning. The high latitude of this pathetic, war-torn country made for short days in the winter. The ROK Division eventually evacuated this vast valley floor and again, with trepidation, I was heading back into those dreadfully deceitful western mountains of North Korea. The driver turned on his headlights after a murmur from the general, and the convoy followed suit, blazing headlights displaying from the hundreds of trucks following. We now resembled a huge, illuminated, snaking dragon.

I wouldn't do that if I were you, I thought anxiously to myself.

Never in all the time when we served in Korea did we ever run with headlights. It just wasn't done. We would be fair game for an enemy machine gunner who might set up an automatic weapon, slay scores of soldiers, and then fade into the ebony night before retaliatory action could be taken.

The general obviously knew what he was doing. The jeep toiled earnestly on its way up these horrible mountains; trucks were creaking, groaning, lurching and swaying, as they slowly and laboriously maneuvered up and around treacherous hairpin curves. We were back into snow country as the trucks arduously trekked up and up and strained forward, grinding into the primitive mountains as if they were being swallowed by an unseen gargantuan monster. I glanced out of the driver's side plastic window to view the magnificent southwestern sky lit almost in imitation of many, many flares fired in unison as the headlights cast beams at the clouds in the night sky. The sheer upward angle of this immense convoy climbing higher and steeper in these precipitous, forbidden mountains caused headlights to reflect against the high overcast. I imagined that the glow from these lights at this altitude could be seen for well over a hundred miles.

The descent was dangerously abrupt and sharply curved, but with the additional hazard of scorching brakes against red-hot brake drums. If a truck burned out its brakes entirely, the machine would metamorphose into a runaway mechanical demon. There was no place to go, other than off the precipitous cliff to hurtle into the steep canyon below, where everyone would perish, never to be found. Or the driver could unavoidably strike the vehicle ahead, which in turn, would strike the preceding motor vehicle until the convoy devolved into a maniac, unstoppable, runaway train that would rapidly careen straight from the cliff into a bottomless abyss. I shuddered.

It seemed until the end of time before the general's jeep began to gradually level near the bottom of this precipitous mountain. I turned and peered out of the rear clear plastic window at the convoy, ever so slow, creeping and winding its way down and around steep roads cut into sheer cliffs. Cautiously and methodically, drivers continuously harnessed their giant monsters as they deliberately negotiated the ongoing precipitous decline of the road. I sighed in complete relief to see that the convoy escaped.

After some length, the road regained some semblance of being level, and perhaps after approximately 500 yards, the dirt road terminated onto a concrete bridge. The bridge was still standing, and it was because of the keen judgment of the South Korean general. Had the drivers not turned on their headlights, the bridge would surely have been blown before our arrival and it would have cut off the last means of escape.

If this last standing bridge was destroyed, the American Army would have again implemented their swift withdrawal by motorized convoy, and the stranded ROK division could never have caught up with them. I did not know it at the time, but Allied commanders rapidly revised tactical plans as they fled south of the 38th Parallel in hope that the pursuing Chinese Communist Forces would halt at that infamous, political line. The complete capture and unification of North Korea by the Allies was now but a shattered dream.

Demolition teams apparently saw the headlights, and a senior officer, no doubt realizing that the convoy could only be a stranded Allied unit, rather than the enemy, ordered the bridge to be held intact until the convoy crossed into friendly territory.

The general's jeep slowly approached the bridge area and ground to a stop in response to a young, nervous American sentry posted just on the north side of the soon to be destroyed bridge.

It was now late night 12 December 1950, exactly 14 eternities after I was captured and escaped.

"Halt! Who goes there?" the guard cried out, remembering his formal military phrase from basic training. It was an order, not a question he posed. The nervous sentry poked his M-1 rile through the driver's side flap into the rear of the jeep pointing directly at me.

"Don't shoot! I'm American!" I screamed frantically.

And then I cried.

PHOTOS

Taejon, September 1950—South Korean civilians killed by retreating North Korean People's Army
From http://www.rt66.com/~korteng/SmallArms/mrdrciv.htm

Yalu River, Andong, October 1950. Fifteenth Chinese Field Army crosses the Yalu.
From http://www.rt66.com/~korteng/SmallArms/yalu1.htm

Iconic Korean War photo
From http://history.amedd.army.mil/art/korea_files/

Civilians fleeing south over Taedong River, using destroyed bridge at Pyongyang, Dec. 1950. Pulitzer Prize-winning photo by Max Desfor
http://www.trumanlibrary.org/korea/koreawar.htm

Chinese Communist Forces casualties resulting from a major battle
From *National Archives*

The author dressed in typical Korean clothes, and joined refugees fleeing to South Korea in a line similar to the one shown here
US Army photo

Chinese Communist Forces napalm victims
From *National Archives*

Author's display of campaign ribbons and medals
Photo by Allen Davis

PART II

Red China is not the powerful nation seeking to dominate the world. Frankly, in the opinion of the Joint Chiefs of Staff, this strategy would involve us in the wrong war, at the wrong place, at the wrong time, and with the wrong enemy.
General Omar Bradley
Testimony before the Senate Committees
On Armed Services and Foreign Relations,
15th May, 1951

THE BATTLE RAGES

> General MacArthur told everyone there would be one more push and that we would be home by Christmas. In our bull sessions we concluded that Russia and China would not sit idly around while one of their friends was replaced by one of its enemies. They would just not permit South Korea to gain control over the north. The Communists were not that dumb. However, we all felt that General MacArthur knew something we did not know and, in fact, we would be home for Christmas. Word was out: The Chinese had withdrawn back north of the Yalu. It was some surprise then, that our Ida Company on patrol one day had a fire fight with a Chinese unit mounted on horses. Cpl. Barnett, Med Co. 3rd Batt., 19th Inf.

MacArthur was aware of the shifting tides of enemy movement, but he ignored the grim reality of the situation. His absolute denial of Chinese enemy troop strength, now realistically estimated to be between 250,000 and 300,000, was unpardonable. As detailed in the header quotation, Ida Company engaged Chinese Communists forces prior to the official, massive entry of Communist forces. Other infantry units also observed concrete evidence of recent enemy troop movement, including newly-dug enemy foxholes, and smoldering fires, abandoned as Allied forces poured north.[89]

Prior to the conflict which drew the CCF into the fray, the Chinese Communist government cranked its public propaganda machine into overtime mode to saturate the world with their political position on America's invasion of North Korea. The Chinese provocateurs were prepared to enforce their words with deeds.[90]

Unquestionably, Communist China's intent was to vigorously, and militarily, bar an enemy state from existing adjacent to their border. That theme time and again was voiced to the world, echoed by Chinese Prime Minister Chou En-lai, prior to the CCF incursion into North Korea. It goes without saying that *no* nation would tolerate such a threat to its na-

---

[89] The Chinese People's Volunteers crossed the Yalu River gingerly at first, its leaders uncertain whether the Americans would resort to the use of the atomic bomb – a weapon still looked on by some as simply a more powerful instrument of destruction, and as a viable option even in limited warfare. Moreover, the Chinese were not only cautious, but deliberately pulled their first punches, hoping the barbarians would get their message and evacuate North Korea. When that failed, they forced the longest, most disgraceful retreat in U.S. history. Spurr, p. 5.

[90] According to the new Chinese Government, the dispute between the two Koreas is an internal matter for both sides (the divided Koreas) to resolve between themselves, without foreign influence or assistance. Furthermore, the Chinese People's Liberation Army had no quarrel with the government of South Korea in her attempt to resolve those matters. Author.

tional borders.

The sounds of sabers were not only rattling, they were being unsheathed. The CCF was deadly serious in respect to ejecting any foreign government with such contrary political ideology, and bar them from camping next to their border.[91]

The United States 8th Army was positioned on the west side of the peninsula. In the in east, the US X Corps comprised of the 1st Marine Division, Army 3rd and 7th Divisions, augmented by ROK infantry divisions, were on the CCF *list of things to do*—to be annihilated.

Many people remember the oft-used idiom *paper tiger,* the Chinese Communist government's expression of their perception of the vulnerability of the American Army as a fighting force. The phrase generally implies a *facade, lacking strength.*

Chinese military also felt the South Korean soldiers violated the political and geographical sanctuary of North Korea.

Now let us dissect the CCF's intent and plan of attack. The ROK 6th Division was the crack division of the ROK Army, but they had an innate fear of Chinese forces, induced by accounts of the overwhelming Communist victories over Chiang Kai-shek forces in southern China. By attacking and destroying the most outstanding unit, the CCF's intent was to strike terror in the hearts of the ROK Armies.

The cadre of the 6th ROK Division, a component of the ROK 11 Corps, was cobbled together, trained, inspired and led by Major General Paik Sun-yup, the most fearless, respected officer in the entire ROK Army. General *Whitey* Paik survived the horrific war and eventually retired as the country's first four-star general and Chief of Staff.[92]

On a typical dreary, frosty day in late autumn, 25 October, Republic of Korea Army General Paik was temporarily in command of the ROK 11 Corps. Learning of the recent capture of many Chinese-speaking prisoners of war, he instructed that they be brought to him for interrogation. Gen-

---

[91] To set up Mao's trap, the Volunteers in the east had suddenly withdrawn on November 7 from their attack on the Marines heading up to the Chosin Reservoir. Two days later the Volunteers on the west had also withdrawn as if beaten.

On November 10, Walker and Almond, following MacArthur's order, continued pushing north. By the end of a week, both were approaching the area Peng was preparing for the crucial battles. Unfortunately, Eighth Army and X Corps intelligence sections had grossly underestimated Peng's strength-in fact they were still under the illusion that Lin Piao (sic) was in charge of the Volunteers and failed to identify the whereabouts of the invisible enemy that was secretly preparing for their annihilation. Toland, p.275.

[92] Paik in the Korean language translates to the English word *white.* Author.

eral Paik, who spoke fluent Chinese as well as English, determined that they were not only Chinese Communist warriors, but soldiers from *Southern China*, far distant from Manchuria. Piecing together the enormity of the CCF commitment, Paik immediately sounded the alarm to 8th Army Intelligence. The black clouds of a gathering storm of enormous armed conflict were about to rain down. In lackadaisical response, 8th Army Intelligence turned a deaf ear to the alarms that General Paik was sending.

Several historians claim that it was merely divine fate for the Chinese Communist Forces to succeed as they did. They sense the resultant victorious conclusion of the first of three offensives was a mere aberration, impelling the CCF to consider further the possibility of driving the Americans and Allies from the peninsula. That the CCF expanded the conflict was believed to be an afterthought. Chinese prisoners of war, captured with telling documents, revealed the Chinese Communist Forces dubbed their operations *Phase One Chinese Offensive*, *Phase Two Chinese Offensive*, to be followed by a final *Phase Three Chinese Offensive*. The ultimate objective was to drive the Allies from Korea and into the Tsushima (Korea Strait) Strait. By analyzing the wide-ranging unit assignments of Chinese prisoners, it was clear that those captured individually attested to the commitment of the largest contingent of enemy troops arrayed against a modern army. The information should have given the Allies pause to consider its imminent disastrous ramifications.

Other analysts went even further by suggesting that Chinese Communist Forces had not accomplished their objective and they would drive forward with their mission to expel the intruders from the peninsula, the 38th Parallel be damned. The rout of the Allied Army was so successful that the CCF allegedly became so intoxicated with the sweet taste of victory that they prematurely implemented prearranged plans to continue their triumphant offensive against the Allies. The CCF referred to this as *Phase Three Chinese Offensive.*

~~

The date of 25 October is significant, as it was little more than one month later when the CCF launched their *Phase Two Chinese Offensive*. Approximately 300,000 Chinese warriors stormed the entire Allied battlefront.

The next day, 26 October, the 2nd Regiment of the famed ROK 6th Division was overwhelmed in the vicinity of Onjong, near the approximate center of northern Korea. The regiment was cut to pieces with scattered remnants forced to flee through the hills, dispersing in the face of smothering, overwhelming, grenade-tossing, Chinese Communist infantry.

Then the CCF turned on the famed ROK 6th Division and a segment of the ROK 8th Division, both of which were put to rout, and nearly destroyed. Captured Chinese soldiers claimed that they had lain in wait since 17 October to ambush the ROK units.[93] The 15th Regiment of the ROK 6th Division was damaged so badly that they ceased to exist as a fighting unit.

By overwhelming the distinguished 6th ROK Division, Chinese forces demonstrated to the world that they could be invincible over all other armed forces in Korea. When the smoke of battle cleared, the mammoth attack against the elite ROK 6th Division all but destroyed the unit, even if they must sustain inordinate loss of manpower.[94]

The first attack against any ROK Division was meant as a decisive warning for the Americans and the UN allies to immediately withdraw from North Korea. The Chinese troops intended to set an example by completely destroying a selected unit, hoping that the Americans would withdraw.

Logistically, it was a radical decision on the part of the CCF to lay siege to an enemy division positioned so far away. The 6th ROK Division was assaulting north across the 38th Parallel in the central zone of the peninsula, a fair distance from the CCF. However, the Chinese chose to set an example by slaughtering the 6th ROK Infantry Division, planning to cause ROK defenses to more likely be the first to yield in succeeding battles. Chinese commanders believed ROK infantry units were less trained than their American counterparts. Paradoxically, at the time, American ground units were as inexperienced as the ROK Army, but no one alluded to that fact. Moreover, rumors were rampant to the effect that the ROK Army was prone to *bug out,* the colloquium for wholesale, unrestrained retreat. However, incidents investigated by KMAG (Korean Military Advisory Group) clearly established that the percentage of ROK units failing to hold

---

[93]What about the Chinese? Staff officers were unimpressed. Complacency paralyzed American thinking from Supreme Headquarters in Tokyo all the way to the fighting front. Everyone, including MacArthur, assumed that the Chinese would have intervened weeks ago if they had really meant business. Today it was just too late. Spurr, p. 134.

[94]More than three full weeks before the main Chinese onslaught was delivered with full force, Peking delivered a ferocious warning by fire: we are here, said the Chinese, in the unmistakable language of rifle and grenade, in the mountains of Korea that you cannot penetrate. We can strike at will against your forces, and they are ill equipped in mind and body - above all, in mind -to meet us. We are willing to accept heavy casualties in order to achieve tactical success. The armies of Syngman Rhee are entirely incapable of resisting our assaults. Hastings, p. 130.

defensive positions were equal to those of other Allied units. Moreover, in fairness to the gallant ROK infantry units, the Chinese massed a disproportionate ratio of troops against the ROK units to insure that any ROK front would, in fact, collapse.

Meanwhile, the 3rd and Capitol ROK Divisions were racing north across the North Korean border, where Chinese forces were absent, paralleling the east coast of the peninsula. Those divisions crossed into North Korea on 30 September 1950, the first and farthest distance away from the Communist Chinese enemy. President of South Korea Syngman Rhee ordered ROK division commanders to refuse to accept the notion that non-entry into North Korea was applicable to his ROK Army. He specifically ordered his ROK units to advance north to the Yalu. As a result, the ROK divisions deployed on the east coast sustained uncharacteristically heavy casualties, inflicted by dedicated North Korean Army rear-guard soldiers entrenched in elaborate, pre-war-built, defense bunkers.

As a consequence of the Allied intrusion, Chinese Commander Peng Te-huai vetoed any plans for Allied forces to entrench on the south side of the Yalu River border directly across from Chinese territory. The Chinese general needed elbow room to attack. Peng had no intention of commencing his prodigious offensive from Chinese territory on the north side of the slow moving, sometimes frozen border river. Peng Te-huai coveted depth of field in order to unleash his ready armies into dense attack mode. With that intent in mind, he launched a series of ferocious charges against now-doomed units who earlier managed to gain some semblance of a foothold on the south bank of the Yalu. The Allied units were sent reeling, staggering in bloody retreat from incessant CCF assaults.

As stated before, Chinese Communist Forces then proceeded to destroy the ROK 7th Regiment of the 6th Division with little effort, as the regiment unsuspectingly entered Chosan, situated on the south bank of the Yalu River. The 7th ROK Regiment and units of 17th Regiment of the US 7th Infantry Division were the sole units assigned to the 8th Army— indeed, to the entire Allied front—to reach the final objective, the Yalu River. Those Allied forces paid dearly for the distinction. The units were cut off, surrounded, and systematically destroyed by Chinese Volunteer Forces.

Despite the utter destruction of ROK divisions, Americans in authority failed to heed the message to leave North Korea. Failing to deter MacArthur, China realized that only by deployment of overwhelming manpower could they manage to neutralize the technological advantage held by the Allies.

The Americans were next in line. Once a gaping chasm in the solidified line was penetrated by the surging red tide, enemy back-up units, numbering in the thousands, would flood through.

They used well thought out tactics to counter the Americans' advantages. Thick blankets of smoke, billowing from dozens of brush fires were all the cover the CCF needed to obscure the landscape from the sight of Allied support aircraft. They had a plan and the intentionally-set blazes were but one small item used to thwart the efficiency of Allied air support.

Thousands of disciplined enemy infantry marched in orderly fashion, on a heading of southwest, approaching Unsan. The enemy objective was to emplace death-dealing road blocks to prevent any survivors from escaping.

On that day, 1 November 1950, the weather hovered just above zero and the Chinese Communist Forces had just arrived in force. They confidently knocked on the door of Unsan, a primitive, unpretentious market-town, invited themselves in, and then proceeded to tear apart the embattled 8th Cavalry Regiment. The UN forces were once again put on official notice by the near annihilation of the 8th Cavalry that no foreigners would be allowed to violate the Communist sanctuary of North Korea. This was the first arena of battle of organized CCF deployment against American troops in the Korean War.

Again venting their fury against the intrusion of the foreigners, the CCF swarmed over the unsuspecting US 1st Cavalry Division east of Unsan on 1 through 4 November 1950. A carefully-laid plan to trap American forces was initiated when the Communist Chinese Forces lay siege to the 3rd Battalion, 8th Cavalry Regiment, destroying them piece-meal, rendering the battalion utterly ineffective as a fighting unit. Six hundred young Americans combat soldiers were killed at the time.[95]

The unsuspecting American cavalry battalion was transported by truck to the Unsan area where they disembarked and were left to die in the fro-

---

[95] At about dusk the same day, November 1, the CCF fell on Unsan in full fury. It was later determined that two full CCF divisions (20,000 men) mounted the assault. It came simultaneously from the north, north-west, and west against the ROK 15th Regiment, Milliken's 1/8, and Walton's 2/8. Blowing bugles, horns, and whistles and firing signal flares, the Chinese infantry, supported solely by light mortars swarmed skillfully – and bravely – over the hills. To the ROKs and Americans, the oncoming waves of massed manpower were astonishing, terrifying, and, to those Americans who believed the war was over, utterly demoralizing. Blair, p. 382.

zen fields. During the battle, the 8th Cavalry Regiment was forced to abandon all motorized vehicles, and the few survivors fled into the hills and mountains, in hope of working their way back to friendly lines. The CCF later made good use of the abandoned American vehicles.

Heavily-defended positions were no match against the CCF, pouring into secondary locations, making flanking attacks both east and west, targeting and surrounding adjacent infantry units. The tactical maneuvers were certified Chinese Revolutionary guerilla warfare.

The casualty rate for the 8th Cavalry Regiment was incredibly appalling:

1st Battalion: 269 KIA, 100 POWs
2nd Battalion: 220 KIA, 110 POWs
3rd Battalion: 600 KIA, 140 POWs

It was street fighting at its rawest. Chinese commandos, clad in Allied uniforms, pilfered earlier from slaughtered ROK division soldiers, marched boldly into Unsan, having been instructed earlier on how to march like American or South Korean soldiers. American sentries of M Company, 3rd battalion carelessly allowed the enemy commando unit through, believing them to be ROK soldiers. Once inside the town, the elite squad of Chinese commandos, known as *The Sharp Swords*, went to work, meticulously implementing well-rehearsed plans, creating destruction and havoc as they executed their assigned tasks precisely. Courageous groups of intrepid, but disorganized Americans banded together, repelling infiltrated enemy fighters. American soldiers, decidedly outnumbered, backs to the walls, fought heroically but generally ineffectively because of the enormous manpower thrown against them. The casualty rate was alarmingly extraordinary.[96]

Survivors, wounded or not, withdrew to a barren field where a small defensive perimeter was formed quickly, pitting every American survivor in a desperate attempt to repel the enemy. Tanks not destroyed by the suicide charges of enemy commandos were pressed into service to reinforce the beleaguered perimeter. Wounded and knowing they could not

---

[96]Late in the day General Milburn, the corps commander, met with General Gay, the 1st Cavalry Division commander, in a quiet hollow a few thousand yards behind the battlefront....Milburn talked with Gay and staff officers. Then he made the decision: any attempt to rescue the 3rd Battalion would probably be futile and endanger the entire corps. This is the most heartrending decision of my entire career, Milburn told Gay and other officers; abandoning these men runs contrary to the traditions of the U. S. Army. I do not like the decision; I do not expect you to like the decision. But the decision is now made. Goulden, p. 293.

survive or escape, the Allied soldiers chose to fight until they were slain. Heavy mortars fired continuously in the vain hope of stopping the wave after crushing wave of CCF. Dead Chinese troops lay by the hundreds, hindering their brethren from a direct frontal running attack because of the enormous numbers of dead blocking the way.

All efforts to rescue them ended in failure, with the would-be saviors from the remnants of the 5th Cavalry regiment suffering massive losses during fruitless attempts to free the embattled 8th Regiment

The besieged 3rd Battalion, 8th Cavalry Regiment was informed by radio that their unit was abandoned, scratched from the list of active units, and left to the CCF. Still, surrender was not on the list of options for the besieged battalion. They chose rather, to fight to the death. [97]

The Chinese 347th Regiment unexpectedly, but temporarily, withdrew at dawn, allowing American survivors to find a small dry ravine in which to escape. Approximately 200 able bodied were able to traverse the area. Heartbreakingly, wounded had to be left behind. Rescue efforts were stymied by the Chinese, and only a few manage to escape.

Master Sergeant Frank C. Plass, 1st Sergeant, Love Company (Heavy Weapons Company), 8th Cavalry Regiment, was one of the very few survivors who managed to escape. Trapped in Unsan, severely wounded in the back by shrapnel, Sergeant Plass continued to return fire. Master Sergeant Frank Plass was an infantryman holding the rare distinction of fighting in three separate wars—World War II, the Korean War, and lastly, the Vietnam War, in each case serving in the dangerous profession of *infantry*. He also accumulated two Purple hearts and the Silver Star, the nation's third-highest medal for bravery, in the course of his illustrious military career.

The *Phase One Chinese Offensive* succeeded beyond the wildest expectations of Mao, General Peng and the CCF. Executed between 25 October and 8 November 1950, the offensive was accomplished without a flaw

In accordance with their plan and before that fateful two-day interval, the CCF made an orderly withdrawal north, evading the Allied armies. It was a trap—one of the oldest ruses of warfare, and one that MacArthur

---

[97] The command post – a dugout in the side of the hill – became the final American refuge, with defenders beating back the Chinese with what Major Veale F. Moriarty, the battalion executive office, called "cowboy and Indian" tactics – close range pistol fire, fistfights, a strategically tossed grenade. Through strength of command Moriarty kept the battalion alive. During a brief dawn respite in the fighting he and others managed to bring more than 170 wounded troops back into the perimeter. There was no time to count the dead. Goulden, p. 292.

sent his unknowing troops into. By their organized pull back, the CCF was to draw the entire Allied Army off guard. The strategy of the CCF turned into a blood bath against the ripped-apart ROK 6th Division and American 1st Calvary Division. The ensuing battles were marathon disasters, with the eye of the storm now focused on the town of Kunu-ri.

Thirty-fifth Infantry Regiment soldiers were unaware of the Goliath battles which transpired earlier, and did not anticipate the immense forces the regiment would face in the immediate future.[98] The war was over as far as units were told. No one spoke of the recently-dug Chinese foxholes troops were discovering.

The *Phase Two Chinese Offensive* was right on schedule, 26 November 1950, with even more devastating results awaiting MacArthur's disorganized units, who were for the most part unable to get a fix on these immense attacks. Chinese infantrymen were flooding the vast valleys of North Korea with hundreds of thousands of combatant Volunteers. This was put in action by the CCF, just two days after MacArthur's order to thrust to the Manchurian border, when he confidently asserted, "Tell the boys for me, when they get to the Yalu, they are going home."

Much to the astonishment of military analysts who discounted the phases of the Chinese Communist plans, the US subsequently discovered that China indeed intended to drive the American Army into the sea, à la Dunkirk, after the Americans ignored Chinese warnings in respect to crossing into North Korea. This future enemy operation, though ending in failure, came to be known as *Phase Three Chinese Offensive*.

In the interim, Lieutenant General Ned Almond, MacArthur's protégé and Chief of Staff, was driving the X Corps to the Yalu from the east coast of North Korea, despite overwhelming enemy resistance. Almond's first loyalty was to MacArthur, and his last priority was to the troops.

The Chinese Volunteer Army was after the big prize—the 1st Marine Division, a component of X Corps, under the direct command of General Almond. If that august unit was annihilated, the American public would be outraged.

To ensure the eradication of the 1st Marine Division, General Peng placed the CCF IX Army under the command of General Sung Shin-lun, a

---

[98] The most noteworthy event of its advance (the 35th Regt.) was coming upon the place south of Unsan where the CCF had surprised and overrun large numbers of the 3rd Battalion, 8th Cavalry, three weeks earlier, in the CCF 1st Phase Offensive. There members of the 2nd Battalion, 35th Infantry, found a shambles of 31 dead men, most of them still in their sleeping bags, and about 30 vehicles burned. Appleman, p.149.

graduate of the prestigious Whampoa Military Academy and a veteran of the Long March. Sung deployed the CCF 58th, 59th, and 60th Divisions south from Manchuria to the Yudam area where they were to seal the eastern sector of the net, entrapping the American Marine Division. From there, the enemy was to wheel east, attack and destroy the American 7th Division. This tactical maneuver was accomplished in an adroit manner. The 7th Division was all but destroyed.

Immediately prior to the entry of the CCF into Korea, and before deployment of the CCF IX Army to the Yudam, MacArthur's assault plan called for an amphibious landing behind enemy lines at Wonson. He intended to reprise the maneuver for which he became so famous during World War II.

However, a protracted mine-clearing project of Russian sea mines in Wonson Harbor threw the carefully-planned operation askew. The Navy assignment delayed the proposed landing by several days, leaving 71 amphibious assault transports bobbing and drifting back and forth just outside of the enemy harbor. The unexpected hindrance was satirically dubbed *Operation Yo-Yo*. Eventually, the 1st Marine Division landed at the harbor, and South Korean troops of the 3rd ROK Division, moving rapidly north on the eastern seaboard, were waiting to greet embarrassed Marines, storming ashore with no enemy to confront. They called it *an administrative landing*.

The 1st Marine Division, commanded by Marine Major General Oliver P. Smith, an astute strategist, chafed under the overbearing orders of Lieutenant General Almond, and later in the war it was quoted that Smith vowed never to be subordinate to Almond again. Smith and Almond clashed earlier over deployment tactics at the Inchon Landing of 15 September, causing a bitterness to fester. This was the first time a Marine division was placed under the direct authority of an Army commander.

Army X Corps commander Almond ordered Marine General Smith to redeploy the westbound Marine division directly north to the Yalu border on the east side of North Korea, near the Russian frontier, pursuant to MacArthur's wish. Smith thought otherwise.

General Smith refused to be rushed, setting armed base camps as he moved his regiment west. When the two other regiments of his division, the 5th and 7th, reassembled under Smith's direct command, along with Colonel *Chesty* Puller's 1st Regiment, the consolidated division then marched west in an orderly manner. The initial objective was to seal a controversial 60-to-80-mile gap in the lines between the Marines, 7th and

ROK Divisions on the east and the 8th Army anchored on the west side of the peninsula.

"What's the matter, Ollie, you afraid of a few Chinese laundrymen?" Almond taunted scornfully, which appropriately drew no response from General Smith or his staff.

During a temporary lull in the campaign, Smith wisely ordered ground dug and leveled near his headquarters and when Almond inquired as to the reason, Smith replied simply to Almond, "They will be landing sites to evacuate casualties."

Almond snorted, "What casualties?"

Little did Almond know what the CCF had in store for the Marines. By the time the last of the unit sailed from Hungnam Harbor, the casualty rate for the 1st Marine Division reached in excess of 11,000. There were 7,000 casualties from frostbite alone.

It was Smith's division and he was responsible. By then the Marine division was taking heavy fire near the approximate center of the peninsula from the IX Chinese Field Army, comprised of 12 divisions, 120,000 strong.

During the fighting on the peninsula, this so-called *gap* between Allied lines proved to be the biggest controversy in the sphere of tactics during the entire war. It was alleged that this huge, unprotected gap allowed the mass of enemy forces to flood into Allied lines unopposed. The Chinese then employed forceful, flanking attacks against the US 2nd and 25th Infantry Division in the west. Simultaneously, the CCF forced flanking attacks to the east, where the 1st Marine Division was surrounded in the vicinity of the Chosin Reservoir. The difference was that General Smiths' division was flanked from the north, and then eventually from the west. The enemy was dedicated to the destruction of the Marine division.

~~

Twenty-two years later the opening of China to the US, in response to signals from the Communists, became a reality with President Richard M. Nixon's historic visit to Communist China in 1972.

Detente between the former adversaries replaced decades of hostility. Eventually, copious information from the Chinese government was disseminated to historians about the military role China played in Korea.

Two of the most controversial subjects were the commander and the Gap. Who was the Chinese commanding officer who so successfully routed the Allied Forces? The second enigma had to do with the 60-to-80-mile gap between forces, and exactly how the Chinese armies exploited it.

An in-depth examination of the controversial *Gap* is necessary at this point of history.[99]

Chinese military authorities emphatically maintained that the so-called gap, that unoccupied territory separating the 8th Army from the X Corps, was never a consideration in the enemy's tactical movements, because of an insurmountable mountain range. The formidable Taeback mountain range that comprises a section of the gap precluded both the Chinese forces and the Allied forces from any meaningful opportunity to emplace either an offensive or a defensive line. It was simply physically impossible to establish a defensive foothold or to assault the precipitous mountainous zone.

General MacArthur used this gambit to establish two separate fighting forces independent of each other, having both units reporting directly and separately to him. This was an unprecedented maneuver in warfare. The American unified force was in actuality two separate armies, lacking any interdependence or liaison between one another. MacArthur directed his various units from his office in Tokyo charting them as if he played a game of chess. Chief commanders had no freedom at the front to be able to move units to counter enemy maneuvers. Field commanders were the *knights* and the soldiers were the *pawns*. MacArthur was highly criticized by the JCS for violating the principle of *unity of command*, although he was eventually exonerated as to this matter of enemy encroachment through the Senate Hearings of 1951:

> On the drive north of the 38th parallel, MacArthur had deliberately separated the Eighth Army, under Walker, from the operations of X Corps, under his own Chief of Staff, General Edward Almond. The two divisions of X Corps - 7th and 1st Marine - landed on the east coast and moved north, miles out of ground contact with the Eighth Army, Thus, it was that, when disaster struck, Almond's and Walker's formations endured entirely separate nightmares, divided by the central spine of North Korean mountains. All that they possessed in common were the horrors of weather, isolation, Chinese attack— and the threat of absolute disaster overtaking American arms. Hastings, p. 147.

Almond raced to the border without due diligence merely to satisfy MacArthur. Almond eventually fell from grace just as did MacArthur,

---

[99] When Secretary of Defense George C. Marshall in the National Security Council meeting of 9 November, spoke disapprovingly of the deposition of the X Corps in Korea, he was referring to the separate commands of Eighth Army in the west and of X Corps in the east and northeast. The two commands were not in physical contact with each other. They were separated by the so-called gap. Appleman, p. 29.

along with intelligence chief General Willoughby, who cooked the books on CCF strength.

Those leaders theorized that it would be an effortless operation, and their mindset led to the near-total destruction of America's fighting forces in the Korean Theater. Almond stated that a few Chinese were going to make a show for their North Korean brethren and then head home. The American military leadership in the Far East Command cast their lot and lost credibility with national and international leaders through the loss of thousands of Allied soldiers.

The beginning of the end for the Allies occurred on 26 November 1950, when it appeared that every Chinese soldier in the world came streaming out of the hills in a direct frontal attack. Most headed directly to the front, while numerous others intentionally skirted Allied lines.

The *Phase Two Chinese Offensive* was officially underway. Years later, it was learned that the thrust of the CCF attack was not the Gap at all, but a small key rail center described as Kunu-ri. The hamlet, a small mining community, lay north of the Chongchon River and west of the Chosin Reservoir. Besieged Americans and Allies retreated from Kunu-ri to the south side of the river. This area became notorious as The Battle of the Chongchon.[100] The Chinese, in well-executed maneuvers, smashed through disintegrating lines of the 2nd Division, massacring everyone who stood in opposition. Following up, enemy pursued pre-designated objectives, crashing through or by-passing crumbling Allied defenses, implanting road blocks one after the other in the hills overlooking the only road of escape. Some were assigned to flanking attacks against the exposed lines of Allied units, killing those in the rear of the main Chinese thrust.

Walter Winchell reported on these events, opening with his famous "Good evening, Mr. and Mrs. America, and all the ships at sea. Flash!" He went on, saying, "If you have a son overseas, write to him. If you have a son in the 2nd Division, pray for him."

Untold numbers of disoriented Americans defenders were killed when

---

[100] Some men were not so fortunate. The tanks they had been riding pulled out without them. The tank crews were safe, but scared. Forsaken soldiers chased down the road, heedless of the shooting, screaming to the drivers to wait. Trucks and jeeps bursting free of the shambles charged madly after the fast-disappearing armor.

Five frightful miles from the departure line the column entered the gully on the highest point of the Suchon Road. Americans called it the "Gauntlet." Those who entered and lived to tell the tale never forgot what followed. The men riding the lead tank got off easy. They shot past lines of wrecked Turkish trucks, emptying clip after clip of ammunition at occasional Chinese. Spurr, p. 201.

the CCF overran American positions. Some were killed in their foxholes. Others, attempting to withdraw, were shot down as they fled.

Through their efforts, the CCF gained thousands of weapons, ammunition, rations and other combat supplies.

To have an infantry division command post (Headquarters, or CP) struck and overrun was unimaginable. Headquarters is situated far to the rear of the main body of troops, out of jeopardy behind battle lines. Battle plans, strategic maps and personnel were prey to enemy who could gain a wealth of intelligence from such a seizure; such intelligence would contribute to a disastrous rout. The 2nd Division Headquarters was overwhelmed by thousands of Chinese soldiers.[101]

Kunu-ri does not appear on a topical map of North Korea today; nonetheless, it has historical implications that mark that site as among the major contemporary military catastrophes of modern America. These include Pearl Harbor, Bataan and Corregidor, Bastogne and now Kunu-ri.[102]

While this episode was unfolding, the entire 35th Regiment was surrounded. The regiment, one of three comprising the 25th Infantry Division, was intentionally by-passed. The Chinese Communist Volunteers was saving the best for last. The 8th Army was the main course. The 35th Infantry Regiment was the dessert.

Enemy machine gun fire ripped up and down the only escape route of the 2nd Division, striking every vehicle. Military ambulances, clearly marked with *The Red Cross* insignia and filled with gravely wounded soldiers were blasted mercilessly from the road, set afire, as billowing flames

---

[101] This helped compound the fears of the 2nd Division, whose exposure was growing more dangerous hourly. The Chinese had been crossing the Chonchon in force bearing heavily on the exposed 23rd at Kujang-dong. "Still no word from IX Corps," General Keiser radioed in desperation to Major General Frank W. Milburn, commander of the nearby 1 Corps. Milburn asked: "How are things going?" Keiser replied: "Bad, right now. We're getting hit in my command post." Milburn then said: "Well, come out my way."

. . . Their newly acquired maps showed the Chinese their current location - three kilometers from the mountain road between Kunu-ri and Sunchon. It was that road, a vital communications vein, the Chinese were determined to sever. They had forced-marched the entire way, some 40 kilometers, simply to reach this narrow stretch. Weary as they were, Colonel Yang wanted his battalion to settle into blocking positions before dawn. There was no time to lose. The enemy had to be kept off balance. Roadblocks across the supply road would panic them out of Kunu-ri. The Chinese would be waiting in ambush. Spurr, pp. 193- 195.

[102] By December 2 the withdrawal of Eighth Army from the Chongchon River had been carried out. Three ROK divisions (6th; 7th; 8th) had disintegrated. The American 2nd Division had been wrecked: the Turkish Brigade had lost a fifth of its men (about 1,000) and was utterly disorganized. Bill Kean's 25th Division had suffered heavy losses in Corley's 24th and Michael's 27th Regiments and Dolvin's Tank Battalion. Blair, p. 501.

lapped at screaming, severely wounded adolescent occupants. They died agonizingly together in their smoldering, twisted, steel crypts. The thin metal flesh of unarmored trucks and jeeps was no match for the withering fire power of the Chinese soldiers hidden in the mountains overlooking the passes, pouring steel jacketed death into anything that moved through their gauntlet.

The adversary shrewdly allowed supporting American tanks to ram through the opening of the gauntlet, knowing that their comrades would confront the armored conveyances with another prepared road block a few miles down the road. By then, the first road block closed as if a steel curtain dropped. Chinese troops slew those who tried to escape. The Chinese controlled the roads. Weather unfit for flying prevented Allied air power from interdicting. Many tanks, trucks and other motorized conveyances were destroyed, along with occupants. Panicked drivers and occupants, attempting to escape, rammed vehicles together in their haste. Tires, radiators, fuel tanks and vehicles were blown by the score, then ignited and set on ablaze by tracer ammunition, leaving carcasses that once were vehicles. Soldiers, unable to escape, were cremated alive by gasoline.

Scores of displaced soldiers cowered in the freezing ditches along the road from massive firepower, and those soldiers too, were incinerated alive by gasoline from ruptured fuel tanks set ablaze. Smoke wafted upward obscured the Allies as well as the enemy from air support.

It was one of the most savage, ferocious attacks recorded in modern warfare.[103] It was The Battle of the Chongchon. Chinese forces asked for no quarter, nor did they give any. The few, fortunate Americans to break through these initial bloody roadblocks were destined to meet their fate at the next road block down the line. In subsequent attempts to break through these impediments, few escaped. Some American tanks were de-

---

[103] Beyond the Pass there were new problems. Keleher remembered:

"For the next five hundred yards the road was temporally impassible because of the numerous burning vehicles and the pile-up of dead men, coupled with the rush of the wounded from the ditches, struggling to get aboard anything that rolled. When we checked to make a turn-out, away from a blazing wreck, either there would be bodies in our way, or we would almost be borne down by wounded men who literally threw themselves upon us.

At one point I got out of the quarter- ton to remove a body from the road. Then I saw that the man was still moving. . . .I squeezed him into our trailer. But as I put him aboard, other wounded men piled on the trailer in such numbers that the jeep couldn't pull ahead. It was necessary to beat them off....I had to get off and wrestle off a dozen wounded who were trying to board us. There wasn't space for even one of them and I couldn't give them my place because I had to keep my battalion moving." Blair, p. 490.

stroyed by expert enemy anti-tank weapons. Other Chinese soldiers on suicide missions rushed American tanks and artillery, tossing satchels of high explosives at the heavy weapons and armored vehicles.

Supply vehicles racing north, filled with ammunition and fuel destined for beleaguered defenders, were encircled and similarly destroyed by Chinese, as motorized convoys trapped by fire attempted to crash through the barriers. It was a rout.

Entire artillery battalions abandoned cannon in place when they were overwhelmed by thousands of enemy, forcing gun-crews to flee for their lives. American soldiers, isolated, cut off from their units, fled in the face of this continuous offensive. The Chinese had limited arms, but American technology was no match for the massive numbers of peasant enemy foot soldiers. The Chinese swarmed over Allied positions, tossed grenades in front of them, followed by gunfire. Few survived.

Chinese soldiers, hardened on the hills, valleys and the Steppes of Asia possessed the stamina to march, fight, and march again without provisions or sleep for extensive hours. With the conviction that Americans would not halt at the North Korean border, the young Chinese soldiers gave their lives for their cause, believing that the Americans intended to invade China through Manchuria. In reality, it was only a solitary person who voiced a desire to invade China. The voice was MacArthur's.

In the interim, the 1st Marine Division, forging west to the Chosin Reservoir east of Kunu-ri, now found themselves cut off and surrounded. Withering machine gun and rifle fire stormed down on exposed marines, caught in the valleys where the roads ran level and offered no place to hide. The end looked near when the Chinese Communist IX Army severed the Marine supply line in several key sections along the line of retreat. Without replacement ammunition, food and other essential needs, the marines were doomed.

When informed that the Marines were surrounded by 100,000 Chinese troops bent on massacre, it was purported that Colonel Puller roared, "Good! They won't get away from us now!"[104]

At Udong-ni, near the Chosin Reservoir, the Marines were nearly overwhelmed by unremitting waves of suicide-bent Chinese soldiers. Enemy charged unflinchingly at Marines with the massacre of the corps at the

---

[104] Lewis Chesty Puller, the most decorated marine in the history of The Corps, awarded an unprecedented Five Navy Crosses for heroism, was eventually promoted to four star general and the Commandant of the United States Marine Corps. Born in 1898, Puller won two Navy Crosses, the first of five, for heroism during the Nicaragua Campaign of 1931. Author.

top of their lists. Chinese fired heavy mortars in a saturation pattern from the mountains north, as thousands of Chinese soldiers threw themselves at the Marines in wave after wave. A defensive perimeter was rapidly fixed and the Marines were eventually able to repulse the enemy, inflicting extreme losses on the CCF. All this transpired during the most severe winter storm in 30 years. Manchurian and Siberian winds and snows collided forcefully, rapidly veered south, dispensing sub-zero weather across the whole of North Korea.

When the Marines ultimately managed to break through, they were again surrounded at a site northeast called Hagaru, now a famous battle site recorded in the annals of Marine history. The battle at Hagaru consumed days and caused huge casualties. Artillery fired at point blank range. Chinese Volunteers numbering in the thousands attempted to overwhelm the 1st Marine Division time and again as Marines formed other perimeters of defense. The isolated, surrounded Marines faced complete annihilation, taking fire from every degree of the compass. Enemy, ordered to slay the Marine Corps to the last man, set upon the defenders in the face of heavy rifle fire, where they were cut down by the hundreds.

Blood froze before it could coagulate. Feet, soggy with sweat from incessant forced marches, froze instantly when besieged Marines were pinned down by incessant enemy firepower. Over 7,000 marine casualties resulted from frostbite alone.

At Koto-ri, X Corps 7th Division united with the Marines and on 6 December, both units shot their way out of the surrounding enemy trap, pushing south to Hungnam, the North Korean port of evacuation, and the terminus of a 78 mile journey.

The CCF, attempting to frustrate the Marine breakout, blew a key bridge on the escape route, leaving a 29-foot insurmountable chasm in the now-obstructed mountainous terrain. Marine engineers quickly huddled and came up with the concept of bolt together, eight-foot sections of a unique bridge, which was immediately ordered by radio. Within a matter hours, spans of bridge were air dropped by special parachute to the besieged, cut off Marines. Marine engineers quickly assembled the short spans together and within hours the bridge was assembled and in place to convoy beleaguered troops southeast again.

The toll from frost bite in itself was extreme on both sides, but even more so to the Chinese warriors, shod only in canvas rubber-sole shoes in this bitterly cold, unforgiving climate. That they were able to mount suicide attacks, forming attack ranks in below-zero weather, spoke to their dedication and ideology. Additionally, their heavy bulky, padded trousers and combat coats were not nearly as efficient for warmth as the layered clothing worn by ROKs and Americans. Warriors on both sides were near death from freezing cold, creating heavy casualties equal to those incurred from the fierce fighting itself.

Exhausted, starved and frozen, some soldiers of the CCF refused to fight any longer and surrendered to the Marines by the hundreds. Many had fingers blackened and welded together by gangrene, unable to release their hands from their rifles. Others surrendered on stumps, where once were feet. It was a brutal war, in a brutal country, in a brutal climate.

The three Marine regiments forged together into one mighty, cohesive unit and systematically blasted their way forward. Fanatically charging enemy were fired upon at point blank range by 105 and 155 howitzers, killing crowds of Chinese racing down mountains in suicidal waves. General Smith at the vanguard, breaking through the juggernaut of opposing enemy, began pushing southeast with his 1st Division toward the secondary port of Hungnam. Marines deployed artillery, firing point blank at masses of enemy in the mountains while Marine air support attempted to keep the enemy at bay. Unarmed, unguarded Chinese prisoners willingly joined the swelling horde of the self-imposed exodus; Marines were powering their way through heavy snow and below-zero temperatures, along with untold numbers of starving, freezing refugees, terrified by the oncoming rush of encroaching Chinese.

It was at night however, when the Marines were called upon to exert the maximum effort to survive. Air support, artillery and heavy mortar fire were either unavailable or useless at night. Fires lit to keep from freezing to death during the day were magnets to the Chinese. At night, life-saving fires were not lit, preventing enemy any advantage to lay siege to valiant marines. The CCF stormed defenses time after time, wave after murderous wave, until the light of dawn drove them back to defensive positions just before Allied air support could begin.

War correspondents were cut off and surrounded along with the Marines, but able to evacuate by light aircraft if necessary. They inquired if the Marines were not, in fact, retreating, to which General Smith roared that now famous retort, "Retreat hell! We are just advancing in a different direction!"

Noted *Life* photographer and former Marine, David Douglas Duncan, captured the gripping, graphic horrors of war on film that was immortalized both in *Life Magazine* and in a follow-up book titled *This is War*. During his photographic expedition, Duncan interviewed a young Marine, Richard Wiggs for an article.[105] He was said to have asked the youth, "If I were God and it was Christmas, what would you wish for?" The young Marine replied, "Just give me tomorrow."[106]

General Smith led his Marines out, despite the overwhelming concentration of enemy arrayed against them and entrenched in the mountains north and south of the division. The 1st Division succeeded in breaking out of the perilous situation and in the process, the entire IX Chinese Army of 100,000 (10 enemy divisions) was destroyed, as Marines hammered steadily southeast towards the port of Hungnam. Under heavy attack at all times, they repulsed repeated enemy suicide waves, suffering heavy losses, but inflicting huge losses on the enemy in return.

When the Marines reached the town of Udong-ni, the ordeal was about half over. They managed to outrace the Chinese Army and as a consequence, they were rewarded with the sight of relatively level terrain from there to the port of Hungnam. The mountains were outmarched. The Chinese failed in their mission and suffered the complete loss of a Chinese army in the process.

So ended the aspiration of Mao. Knowing the American public's admiration of the Marines, he hoped to slaughter the 1st Marine Division. The public was enamored with the saga of their bloody, heroic battles spanning the Pacific islands during World War II. Americans proudly revered the USMC for their heroic deeds.

Two distinct incidents interdicted to foil Chairman Mao's dream to succeed in the total destruction of the US Marine Corps. First, the logistics made it an unachievable undertaking to move sufficient numbers of enemy replacement troops on foot, across the vast, frozen steppes of Manchuria and then turn south through nearly impassable mountains on the peninsula. Second, Mao failed to comprehend the fighting spirit of the Marine Corps, particularly under the brilliant command of Major General Smith.

During this same time frame, 8th Army was similarly confronted by huge numbers of Chinese attackers. General Walker, however, possessed a professional regard for the safety of his 8th Army. Contrarily, General Almond ordered units including the 1st Marine Division to race irresponsibly to the Manchurian border in the face of blatant, heavy enemy opposi-

---

[105] Callaghan, p. B 01.
[106] Toland, p. 362.

tion.

In respect to his 8th Army, General Walker was heard to remark cautiously to his forward pursuing commanders that if they smelled Chinese food cooking, pull back.[107]

Walker did exactly that. He ordered the swiftly advancing 24th Infantry Division to withdraw to the south, bringing the forward-pushing division even with his main line of defense. In doing so, Walker narrowly avoided the loss of the 24th Division. MacArthur was infuriated, insisting that the 8th Army again go on the offensive, to complete MacArthur's objective—the conquest of all North Korea, inclusive of the border of Manchuria.

Media at the time were critical of units of 8th Army for what some correspondents perceived as disintegration and retreat in the face of the hard-charging enemy. They compared units of the 8th Army to the unified Marines and their Allies situated on the east coast of the northern sector of the peninsula. Doubts were raised in respect to the efforts of 8th Army units.

One should consider the geographical zone of the war in relation to the battle situation. Mainland China proper lies directly west of the province of Manchuria, bordering the western-most city of Anton (now Dandong) in Manchuria. Communist China's sister city Sinanju, also the most northwest city, rests directly south of the Yalu River in North Korea. The preponderance of enemy troops and materiel flowed directly from China into this western area of North Korea, and was precisely where the American 8th Army was positioned. Enemy supply lines were comparatively short at this juncture, allowing implements of war, particularly enormous concentrations of troops, to be quickly deployed against the advancing 8th Army. The enemy was additionally blessed by the politically-designated sanctuary of Manchuria, in which to mass men and materiel, then move them surreptitiously to the front during the dark of night.

Conversely, as the Marines broke out of the Chosin Reservoir trap, leaving the destruction of an entire Chinese Army as a reminder of the Marines' presence, enemy supply lines were now radically overextended. The CCF had to cross the entire breadth of the Korean peninsula on foot, and thereafter forge south in order to pursue the Marines. By then it was

---

[107] . . . .The visit was a brief one. He directed General Church to tell Dick Stephens, whose 21st Infantry was leading the western attack, that "if he smells Chinese chow, pull back immediately." By this one command he had taken it upon himself to change from that of an all-out attack to one of reconnaissance in force. Once done, a look of calmness returned to his face. Toland, p. 283.

too late. The Marines escaped, bringing their dead, wounded, and equipment with them.

This is not to be considered an apologia, nor is it criticism of any of the units that fought so courageously and suffered so very terribly in North Korea during this winter of discontent. Allied armies endured unmitigated horror, both from the cold as well as from the enemy, particularly the 2nd Infantry Division, who suffered by far the preponderance of casualties. The 9th, 23rd and the 38th Infantry Regiments constituting the 2nd Infantry Division suffered 33% casualties, with 4,930 young American soldiers massacred within the first few hours and days of battle—an enormous and needless loss of life.

Fingers of criticism pointed directly to commanders, particularly MacArthur, for failing to interpret Chinese intelligence. The general recognized the overwhelming strength of the Chinese assailants, but his egotistical need to win one last *big one* to cap his contentious career took precedence over sound military judgment.

A contemporary documentary film titled *War at the 38th Parallel*, in reference to the Korean War, stated succinctly, "MacArthur and his staff didn't see any Chinese soldiers, because they didn't want to see them."*[108]*

Late 29 November, following in the steps of the Chinese imposed debacle of Allied forces, General of the 8th Army, Walton Walker, under pressure from MacArthur, released what apparently was a public relations memorandum. Initially it appeared to be a hoax, given the rancor of the memo's content. When it was established as authentic, the preposterous message spread consternation, rage and anxiety through the rank and file soldiering in the frozen trenches of Korea:

> The assault launched by the Eighth Army five days ago probably saved our forces from a trap which might well have destroyed them. Had we waited passively in place, the 200,000 Chinese troops thrown against my lines would have increased within a short time to double that strength. From beyond the Yalu they undoubtedly would have brought the other 200,000 additional Chinese troops known to be assembled there. We naturally had hoped to find at least some semblance of truth in the public assurance of the Chinese Communist authorities that no formal military intervention had been perpetrated. However, only by assault tactics could the actualities have been fully developed. In my

---

[108] Finally, there was the "MacArthur factor." Almond's G-3, Jack Chiles, an alumnus of GHQ who had observed Willoughby at close hand, remembered: "MacArthur did not 'want' the Chinese to enter the war in Korea. Anything that MacArthur wanted, Willoughby produced intelligence for. . . . . In this case Willoughby falsified the intelligence reports. . . . He should have gone to jail." Blair, p. 377.

opinion this saved the army from possible destruction. The timing of our attack to develop the situation was, indeed, most fortunate. Spurr, p. 5.

Walker's message flew in the face of reality. It was none other than MacArthur himself who specifically ordered his forces to the Yalu River on 24 November with the unattainable objective of consolidating the Koreas. Commanders, consumed with self image, and a patronizing attitude toward MacArthur, caused them to stand by, dispatching thousands of soldiers to die, without the least remorse. As Joseph Stalin, the late leader of the *late* Soviet Union once pontificated, "One death is a tragedy; a million deaths is a statistic."

A month later to the day, the Joint Chiefs of Staff sent a dispatch with the opposite view of the acceptable losses after assessing those that resulted from attacks by the CCF. The Joint Chiefs' response message was precisely contrary to the flowery, condescending memorandum from General Walker. On 29 December 1950 the following cablegram was dispatched to General Douglas MacArthur, following routine reading by the President, staff and the Department of Defense. Undersecretary of Defense, Robert Lovett, aptly characterized the cable as a *jig is up message*.

> ....Since developments may force our withdrawal from Korea, it is important, particularly in view of the continued threat to Japan, to determine, in advance, our last reasonable opportunity for an orderly evacuation. It seems to us that if you are forced back to positions in the vicinity of the Kum River and a line generally east-ward there from, and if thereafter the Chinese Communists mass large forces against your positions with an evident capability of forcing us out of Korea, it would then be necessary, under these conditions, to direct you to commence a withdrawal to Japan...... Goulden, p. 430.

On 1 December 1950 The Far East Command issued an official directive to all Allied forces to *disengage from the enemy*—a command for deliberate, unqualified retreat.

Some historians place the fatality rate for Allied forces at 60,000 resulting from the incursion into North Korea. Given the tremendous losses suffered by the Republic of Korea Army alone, the figure appears to be more than plausible. Inasmuch as absolutely nothing was gained from this armed misadventure, the question arises as to why this debacle was permitted in the first place? The answer lies in the comprehensive works of many researchers.

The evidence is crystal clear as to who holds culpability. Clearly MacArthur, President Truman, the Joint Chiefs of Staff, Congress and the news media all played a significant role; consequently, all bear responsibility for this act of dereliction. The voices of reason were few, and they were muted. Allies all over the world expressed profound anxiety in respect to the obvious folly of entering into North Korea. The war was disadvantageous to the Allies for any purpose other than a minor role of *mopping up* renegade, disorganized stragglers, which could easily have been accomplished. Even if the Republic of Korea Army elected to avoid the disputed territory of North Korea, it would not have been a loss. Joseph Stalin, premier of the Soviet Union, would not re-supply or refurbish a beaten North Korean Army. He was gazing east to Europe, wanting no further part of the Korean debacle. The Russian Premier's blatant refusal to come to the military and/or economic aid of China was to cause a permanent rift between those two Communist countries.

Additionally, it is doubtful that the Communist Chinese government would supply military aid to North Korea. As long as a buffer continued to exist between Manchuria and North Korea, China would more than likely again revert to *ante bellum status quo*. The Communist country lacked fundamental resources to continue the conflict, to rearm the North Korean Army, or to provide continuing manpower or crucial supplies to the impoverished country. The primary thrust for China was to rebuild its country, given the traumatic chaos of World War II, which followed closely in the footsteps of the Chinese Civil War. Membership in the world body, the United Nations, still thwarted by the US, was an issue of paramount concern. China could no longer afford to return to the status of The Middle Kingdom. The planet was shrinking rapidly and China *had* to be a viable component of the world.

MACARTHUR

> It must be recognized that the historian is not likely to alter the profound convictions of men; such is not his intention. But the reader must understand that to both the protagonists in the dispute between General MacArthur and the Truman Administration and to their analysts, one's party's success constitutes the other's failure, one man's objectivity is necessarily another's bias. Higgins, p. vii.

No text on the history of the Korean War would be complete without considering the impact of the conflict between the war-time philosophies of General MacArthur and US President Harry S. Truman.

Not since the days of the Civil War when General George McClellan continuously challenged President Abraham Lincoln's authority has there been such controversy. Then and during the Korean War, there was systematic animosity and open rebellion, creating an ethical and political conflict between a sitting Commander-in-Chief and the commanding general, each in an ongoing struggle for power as their personalities clashed with one another.

The author recognizes this phase of history as a contentious subject with equal supporters and detractors on both sides of the issue. It appears that no one is at a loss for an opinion on the key role that the General played during this crucial episode of history that nearly drew the major world powers into World War III. Therefore, substantial documentation is presented which hopefully neither embellishes nor discounts documented facts relating to the commanding general and his disagreement over theory with Truman during the three-year period of the Korean War.

Additionally, the author frequently refers to both of the US major political parties, the *Democrats* and the *Republicans* in this chapter, because both parties played a significant role in the formation of policies, attitudes and events affecting the Korean Conflict.

The controversy arose publicly prior to the off-year congressional race of 1950. Following the election, the Democrats, led by Truman, barely held the majority in Congress. The election results were mainly influenced by the escalation of the Korean War, and the near destruction of their forces during that war. The Democratic Party became a mere shadow of its former self, reduced to a scant majority of two in the Senate, and a mere twelve in the House of Representatives.

This off-year election was a far cry from the national Presidential election of 1948, when Truman, unexpectedly, squeaked by with a narrow victory over the favored Thomas Dewy, and carried major gains in Congress for the Democratic Party.

Even more significant among Republican 1950 election gains were three ultra-conservative and pro-Nationalist China supporters—Richard Nixon of California, Everett Dirksen of Illinois, and John Butler of Maryland. The trio was identified as *The China Lobby*. Thereafter, because of divergent and radical political views, both parties clashed frequently over the divided ideology reflected in the Korean War stalemate.

General MacArthur's military philosophy was deeply influenced by the military strategies and successes of the Roman Empire, and in particular, Julius Caesar. To comprehend the tenets held by MacArthur, one must examine the lesson inherent in the phrase *Crossing the Rubicon*.

During the first century BC, the Rubicon was accepted as the boundary between Italy and the Roman province of Gaul, and it was here that Roman senators drew the line and forbade any army to enter, lest the government be usurped by force. It was the clear intent of the senate to uphold the civil charter separate from any military force that could overturn civil authority and its attendant laws.

After the triumphant defeat of Cisalpine Gaul, Julius Caesar led his Roman Legions across the Rubicon into Italy, intending to occupy Rome, despite strong protests from the Senate. The act was considered treason.

Because of the bellicose intentions of Caesar, the Senate was imperiled. Caesar was called on by the frightened Senate body to resign and disband his army, or be branded an enemy of the State. Caesar refused. Backed by his Legions, he defiantly entered Rome. Caesar became powerful enough to appoint himself dictator to serve in perpetuity.

Historian William Manchester titled his biography of General Douglas MacArthur *American Caesar*.

Political rather than military law is the unwavering foundation of democratic societies throughout the world. To further ensure an absolute delineation between civilian and military rule is maintained, the US Congress ordained a safety measure. The founders of our nation, knowledgeable about the history of rulers controlling subjects' destinies through military force, recognized grave, potential dangers from the military and they preemptively acted.

It was deemed essential to a democratic form of government that military power be subservient to freely elected officials and be held accountable to them. The military must have a clear delineation of limits of authority. Our founding ancestors deliberately intended that the military, though necessary, should not in any manner infringe on the *Constitutional Rights* of the people.

Much ado has been made that MacArthur was hamstrung, preventing him from exercising his duty as Commanding General of Allied Forces in the Korean Theater. The issue is not whether MacArthur was wrong or right in the tactical and strategic planning and execution of war. Rather it is whether he accidentally or intentionally navigated into the waters of civilian government policies in respect to governing the ship of the war.

Was MacArthur trying to pull Truman and the Democrats' chestnuts from the fire, or was the General attempting to clandestinely usurp civilian authority?[109] Regretfully, the onerous debate moved to the international center stage.

The principal intent here is to conduct a societal autopsy to determine reasons for the violent deaths of scores of thousands of American youth.

~~

As a point of interest to those who believe that the government of the US was obligated by treaty to militarily defend South Korea, the author emphasizes that not only was there no such treaty, but the administration by all measures, intentional or not, inadvertently and ultimately *invited* the North Korean People's Army to invade The Republic of Korea.

General Dwight D. Eisenhower, influential Republican Senator Robert A. Taft, and the then-majority Republican Congress assumed that the Democratic Truman Administration overtly convinced the Communists that the US would not defend South Korea or Formosa against armed aggression. The very spark that could ignite World War III hinged on the sensitive handling of the Korean issue.

History has established that Premier Kim Il-sung, *The Dear Leader of The Democratic People's Republic of North Korea,* sought the blessing and approval of both Premier Joseph Stalin of the USSR, and China's Mao Tse-tung for Kim's quest to place the entire peninsula under Communist domination.

---

[109] The problem can be stated simply. The Korean War was the most unpopular war in our history; and one reason lay in the fact that it was limited.... Not only was it a limited war; it was a most peculiar kind of limited war. It was an undeclared war against an unidentified enemy. Its aims were generally not comprehensive, possibly because they were never adequately explained by the Truman Administration. Higgins, p. viii

Higgins' book was published before the Vietnam War, which most certainly overshadowed the political and emotional effects of the Korean War. For purposes of this account, the author has limited the role of General MacArthur to his position as Supreme Commander, Far East Command, during the Korean Conflict. Author.

The fly in the ointment was President Truman. After the fact (and after the invasion started) he drew the proverbial line in the sand, and at the last moment the President decided to militarily defend South Korea. This was no idle transformation of heart. The President had what appeared to be valid reasons, given the international *Cold War* crisis.

The loss of Nationalist China to the Communists and the subsequent exile to Formosa (now Taiwan) of Generalissimo Chang Kai-shek in 1949 happened on Democratic President Truman's watch and he and his administration was, in due course, held exclusively responsible by a rancorous and alienated Congress. Appeasement was a well-worn accusation cast against all Democrats at the time.

At the time, President Truman believed that the more his administration labored to breach the wall of cultural and political mistrust between the Soviet Union and the free world, the more passion inflamed the *Cold War*. Truman recalled bitterly and with a great deal of antipathy the Munich Agreement signed on 29 September 1938. The signatures of Neville Chamberlain, (England) Edouard Daladier, (France) Adolph Hitler (Germany) and Benito Mussolini (Italy) attested to the claim the Agreement created *Peace in Our Time,* according to the naïve and hoodwinked Chamberlain. In exchange for granting Hitler the fortified area of German-speaking peoples, the *Sudetenland*, recognized then as Czechoslovakia, Hitler promised to curtail further belligerent military acts. *Der Fuehrer* had earlier annexed his native Austria to Germany. The pact was a notable public charade from the beginning, which in due course plunged Europe into World War II. On 1 September 1939, Hitler's Germanic Forces, without provocation, and in violation of the Munich Agreement, attacked and conquered Poland. The rest is history.

Truman sensed a similar parallel between the Munich Pact and the activities of Stalin of the USSR who threatened world peace following the aftermath of catastrophic World War II. Consequently, the President drew a firm line in the sand against further Communist aggression, though the Republicans continued to hold the conviction that the administration, from their viewpoint, was simply weak on political tactics.

The President abruptly and irrevocably reversed his foreign policy, believing to ignore and covertly condone the invasion of South Korea would be construed as the ultimate appeasement, by both the Republican Party and the Communist Bloc. That unequivocal belief at the time was to play a major role the Chinese Communist Forces' entry into Korea.

Truman had a well-honed axe to grind with the military. Early in his formative years, Truman dreamed of a commission as a cadet at West Point in the Army, or at the least, an appointment to the US Naval Academy at Annapolis. Truman was rejected by both academies for the reason of poor eyesight, medical doctors signifying *flat* eyes as the rationale. While Truman was aware of vision distortion since childhood, he turned rapaciously against the military, used the military academies as his *scapegoat*, and harbored an irrational, intense dislike for anyone of significant position within the military hierarchy.

When Truman was elected to the Senate, he feverishly aspired to, and was ultimately appointed to the Senate Military Affairs Committee. He diligently used the committee to expose waste and cronyism in the military. His Senatorial reputation soared with the public at large, and his committee concurrently vaulted to fame as advocates for taxpayers, through the elimination of excess and fraud within the military.

Truman's dogged perseverance propelled him into the Vice-Presidency slot. He was inaugurated President of the US on 12 April 1945 following the unexpected death of President Franklin Delano Roosevelt.

As President, he hastily formulated the decision to defend South Korea by military means despite the fact that the US was fundamentally unprepared to meet the challenges of armed conflict so soon after World War II. The majority view of the Joint Chiefs of Staff initially differed from that of the President. The Chiefs cited an acute shortage of materials needed to wage war, and in particular, a lack of sufficiently-trained fighting soldiers. On one hand, Truman was prepared to send American soldiers to war. On the other, he had instigated draconian budget cuts, slashing military budgets to lessen the deficit, which as a result, reduced the military to a second-class, impotent force. The newly-formed Chinese Communist Government referred to the American Army as *Paper Tigers*.

General MacArthur, then Supreme Commander of the Far East, was anointed to lead the US and her allies in defending the southern peninsula against the invading NKPA, despite vocal misgivings of General Dwight D. Eisenhower.[110]

---

[110] Few men knew MacArthur as well as Eisenhower, who had served directly under him twice - in the War Department from 1930 to 1932 and in Manila from 1935 to 1939. In a remarkable prescient and candid aside, Eisenhower warned that MacArthur was ill suited to run the Korean War. "In commenting upon General MacArthur," Ridgeway jotted in his desk journal, "Ice expressed the wish that he would like to see a younger general out there, rather than, as he expressed it, "an 'untouchable' whose actions you cannot predict, and who will decide what information he wants Washington to have and what he will withhold. Blair, pp. 78-9.

On 31 July 1950, a month after the Korean invasion, the administration was compelled to confer with Chiang Kai-shek in respect to refusing Chiang's offer of thousands of Nationalist troops to aid in the defense of South Korea. A further rejoinder was to caution Chiang against forays on the mainland for the purpose of provoking a Communist invasion. Truman was adamant that he did not want to alienate the new Chinese Communist regime in any manner.

Responsible administration officials specially requested that a senior officer on MacArthur's staff be designated as the administration representative, but the request left a vague void for MacArthur to use his own judgment, and the General seized on that opportunity to personally represent the US for the meeting with Chiang.

An assessment report by General MacArthur about Formosa and the Truman-Acheson hands-off Formosa policy strongly recommended a reversal of administration policy. MacArthur supposed that the massing of 200,000 Communist soldiers on the mainland, directly opposite Formosa, portended an assault on the island and that the NKPA invasion was a mere diversionary feint that could well be contained by the newly-augmented South Korean Army. MacArthur went public with his opinion that Formosa should be defended, contrary to administrative policy.

Public remarks by Chiang subsequent to the meeting also led international observers to believe that MacArthur's then-private undisclosed remarks to the Nationalist Leader were not only provocatively contrary to the policy of the US Administration, but there appeared to be a tacit, implied threat of leaning toward armed confrontation with Red China.

Secretary of Defense Louis Johnson forwarded MacArthur's assessment paper to Secretary of State Dean Acheson.[111]

Those delicate documents warned of an eminent strike against Chiang and his forces on Formosa by the Chinese Communist Government. Secretary Johnson concurred with, and supported MacArthur' official position. The administration's official assessment was quite the opposite. Truman believed that Chiang posed the greater risk and he (Chiang) would be the one to provoke the wrath of the mainland Chinese by implementing guerrilla raids against them.

The Truman administration ultimately came to the realization that millions upon millions of dollars poured down the rat hole of the so-called treasury of Chiang Kai-shek during World II was parceled to his war lords,

---

[111] Blair, p. 16.

a display of rampant corruption.

The Chinese Communist Government never forgot nor forgave President Franklin Roosevelt's sponsorship of Chiang throughout World War II and after, to the exclusion of the newly-established Communist government from the United Nations.

Secretary of Defense Johnson, by his endorsement of MacArthur's unbridled loyalty to the Formosa clan, caused the Truman Administration to believe that contrary to official policy, Johnson advocated a preventative war policy with Communist China, in agreement with, and as espoused by MacArthur. Johnson was in fact and in deed more allied to MacArthur's political position than to the President's. It logically followed that Johnson was eventually requested to resign. Johnson's position of Secretary of Defense went to General George C. Marshall. Marshall re-entered public service from retirement to serve at the behest of the President.[112]

Secretary of Defense Louis Johnson betrayed his office, the administration, and a lengthy friendship with President Truman which dated from World War I. There were worldwide concerns both by friend and foe over Johnson's and MacArthur's bellicose expressions.

The denunciation of General MacArthur by forces within the administration, in addition to foreign governments' antipathy, would have humbled and restrained the most vocal opponents, but this was not the style of MacArthur. He replied tersely on 5 August:

> It is extraordinarily difficult for me at times to exercise that degree of patience which is unquestionably demanded if the longtime policies which have been decreed are to be successfully accomplished without repercussions which would be detrimental to the well-being of the world, but I am restraining myself to the best of my ability and I am generally satisfied with the progress being made.

Averell Harriman, spokesman for the administration, was dispatched to Tokyo the very next day (6 August) to reinforce privately the harm from MacArthur's persistence in speaking on foreign affairs from a military posture. Mr. Harriman left the meeting believing that no inroads to the curtailment of MacArthur's public foreign policy statements could be made.

The Korean War was in utter chaos at the time. American units were

---

[112] General MacArthur and Defense Secretary Louis Johnson found themselves in agreement on the importance of Formosa Clearly the public diplomatic and private military policies of the United States had not be reconciled, which the Soviet Union could not be expected to know. Higgins, p. 14.

being ripped to shreds by the more numerous, experienced, trained and better-equipped NKPA. The Pusan Perimeter was not placed into effect until almost two weeks later. It was a desperate defensive measure to try to sustain a foothold and to prevent a collapse of the peninsula.

On 17 August, a little more than a week after Harriman's visit, the General received a request from The Veterans of Foreign Wars for a message from the General to be read at the forthcoming VFW national conclave. Conventional wisdom would suggest that any directive from MacArthur should be of such personal content that there could be no misconstruing of policy. The alternative solution for MacArthur would be to embrace the foreign policy of the administration as a matter of unity, since he, MacArthur, was a team member of the administration. Instead, MacArthur wrote defiantly in part:

> Nothing could be more fallacious than the threadbare argument by those who advocate appeasement and defeatism in the Pacific that if we defend Formosa we alienate Continental Asia. Those who speak thus do not understand the orient. They do not grasp that it is in the pattern of oriental psychology to respect and follow aggressive, resolute and dynamic leadership - to quickly turn from leadership characterized by timidity of vacillation, and they underestimate the oriental mentality.[113]

Truman was furious. He demanded that MacArthur retract the message to the VFW but the damage was done. MacArthur had underhandedly released copies of his message to the media prior to sending it on to the Veterans Convention.

Truman, decidedly angry, came to a decision to replace MacArthur with General Omar Bradley, then Chairman of the Joint Chiefs of Staff. However, the war was now at a critical stage so the President was reluctant to replace the General in the midst of the climatic phase of the war.

To neutralize the volatile situation in the Far East, Truman earlier had directed the US 7th Fleet to blockade the strait between Formosa and the mainland of China to forestall either Chiang or Mao from committing aggressive acts against each other. Even though it was contrary to the strong opposition of General MacArthur, Truman's decision to police the strait between Formosa (Taiwan) and the mainland was a neutral, preventative

---

[113] The "message" to the VFW was not only insubordinate and insulting to Truman but also arrogantly challenging to Peking. Peking was not likely to come to North Korea's aid merely as a response to MacArthur bombast. But the message coming so soon after MacArthur's provocative visit to Formosa, would no doubt cause further deep concern in Peking. Blair, pp.228-9.

maneuver.

The Chinese Communist Government interpreted the naval blockade as an intrusion into the personal affairs of their government.[114] It was the conviction of the Communists that the US intended to invade China, both from Formosa, as well as from North Korea.

That is precisely why the Communists entered the war on behalf of their North Korean brethren. Furthermore, the US policy to bar the new government of China from admission into United Nations was an affront to Asian governments, as well as various European nations. By now, most of the industrialized countries of the world recognized the Communist government as the legitimate government of China.

Moreover, this period was the shameful and politically embarrassing era of Senator Joseph R. McCarthy and the infamous *McCarthyites* who painted almost everyone in the current administration as *soft on Communism*. They alleged that the federal government, particularly the State Department, and other key agencies, were infiltrated and saturated with *card-carrying* Communist spies, *fellow travelers, pinkos* and *better red than dead* sympathizers.

To make matters even worse for the administration, there were recent bold-faced headlines that trumpeted the trials of people such as Judith Coplon, Alger Hiss, Claude Fuchs and especially the infamous Rosenbergs, executed for passing atomic bomb secrets to the Soviets. All of these incidents lent credence to the preposterous charges by the *McCarthyites*.

Truman had already painted himself into the political corner for losing Nationalist China to the Communists, as claimed by the China Lobby. Those three newly-elected conservative Republican senators were reinforced by the outcry in general by Congress. Truman had his plate full, yet there was more to come.

On 5 November 1950, MacArthur notified the Far East Air Force Commander, General Stratemeyer, that he (MacArthur) required Stratemeyer's Air Force to bomb the *Korean side* of the twelve crucial border bridges spanning the Yalu River.[115] He particularly wanted to target the three bridges situated at Sinuiju, where the largest amount of Chinese men

---

[114] Toland, p. 237.

[115] MacArthur's instruction to Stratemeyer ordering the destruction of the Yalu bridges was a clear violation of his JCS directive to stay "well clear" of the Manchurian border. Aware of that, and perhaps desiring to protect his rear politically, three hours before the scheduled takeoff of the bombers, Stratemeyer passed word of the impending operation to Air Force Chief of Staff Hoyt Vandenberg. Blair, p. 394.

and materiel was pouring into North Korea. MacArthur assumed destruction of these bridges would halt or significantly slow the entry of the enemy Chinese Forces massing into North Korea.

MacArthur failed to gain approval, or to even notify the JCS for this politically-sensitive operation, which was a fruitless attempt to alter the massive course of the CCF. In fact, he knew well beforehand that the destruction of the bridges would be an inconsequential loss to the enemy.

The North Koreans proved their dexterity at building submerged bridges in the Naktong River during the bloody days of the Pusan Perimeter. By fashioning a road of filled sandbags submerged in about a foot of water, the enemy could move men and vehicles at night. During the day, the underwater bridges were indiscernible to the target-seeking Air Force.

Moreover, the Yalu, though wide, is shallow and the river could be forded in the same manner as the Naktong. When the Yalu iced over, the surface was strong enough to move tanks and heavy weaponry at night undetected. Every morning before the American Air Force arrived, native women had swept away personnel and vehicle tracks from the iced-over river, and left no evidence of use. Many military strategists believe that blowing the bridges was a provocative war-like maneuver against the Red Chinese, since it was inconsequential to the current phase of the conflict.

President Truman intended to honor his pledge to the British that their government would be advised prior to the bombing of any targets in Manchuria including the bridges MacArthur considered Korean targets, even though precise bombing was problematic. The JCS ordered MacArthur to limit all bombings to five miles south of the Yalu

And just as Caesar, MacArthur made a controversial and uncompromising stand.

MacArthur in effect, blackmailed Truman into reversal of administration policy against bombing of the Yalu River bridges. The election was near and MacArthur unequivocally stated directly to Truman that "the blood of American troops would be on the President's hands for every hour of delay."[116]

---

[116] In Tokyo, from the first moment of the Chinese intervention, MacArthur issued a flood of bulletins and statements which drifted further and further from reality as each day went by. First, he declared that his own drive to the Yalu had forced the Chinese hand, interrupting plans for a grand Chinese offensive which would have been disastrous for the United Nations. He rejected utterly the suggestion that his forces were engaged in a retreat. He castigated "ignorant" correspondents for their inability to distinguish between a planned withdrawal and "a full flight." Hastings, p. 178.

The President blinked and then capitulated. Truman was leading a beleaguered government that was in the process of losing a foreign war (of his own making), alienating traditional allies in the UN, and facing increased public opposition. He dared not to go against the obtrusive threat from MacArthur.

On 6 November MacArthur directed two more messages to the JCS; one certainly seemed to contradict the substance of the other. On one hand MacArthur conceded that he might be forced to retreat, should the Chinese forces continue to be reinforced. In the other message, MacArthur requested permission to take the offensive for a "new American advance to take an accurate measure. . . .of the enemy strength."

Matters became even more convoluted when MacArthur, the next day, requested the right of *hot pursuit,* to pursue the enemy's fighter planes across into the political sanctuary of Manchuria.

When the Chinese intervened in the conflict, the USSR provided the Russian Air Force as ancillary support to the Chinese Communists. Russian-made MIG jet fighters challenged the US F-86. The MIG, a far superior aircraft to the F-86, was ultimately out-maneuvered and out-gunned by the superior flying skills of the American pilots, and because of that, at the time, it seemed to not be a real issue.

However, complete domination of the skies by the US Air Force was questionable. The enemy had the luxury of engaging in air combat with the American Air Force and then be allowed to break off the air maneuvers, and flee north of the Korean border into Manchurian sanctuary.

On the surface, *hot pursuit* appeared to be a reasonable request, but when the request was denied, a wider rift in our country erupted in respect to the administration of the war. The majority of the American public was outraged as they believed that MacArthur was prevented from doing his utmost to level the playing field.

Some historians claim that MacArthur, with malice aforethought, chose this date (7 November), to make his demand for hot pursuit in his quest to embarrass Truman and his fellow Democrats. It was Election Day and the Democrats, (albeit an off-year election) were suffering a resounding loss at the polls.

President Truman ordered that a special effort be made to determine the intentions of the Chinese Communists. Meanwhile, Chinese Communist forces were entering into North Korea in ever increasing numbers and newly-captured infantrymen revealed a huge marshalling of forces ready to contest the American intrusion, and nullify the American drive to the

Manchurian border.

G-2 (Intelligence) Chief, Major General Charles Willoughby, a protégé' of MacArthur, maintained a slight level of influence among General MacArthur's staff, principally because of his ability to *read* MacArthur. Consequently, Willoughby produced intelligence that MacArthur *wanted*. During this *Phase One Chinese Offensive*, there was strict, official denial emanating from Far East Intelligence of any organized Chinese intervention on the peninsula. The identity of the invaders, according to G-2, was that of reorganized North Korean Army units, when, in fact, the NKPA was in shambles, resulting in the inability to fight effectively as unified units. Salient tactical information from many captured Chinese who freely admitted to the number and location of their units was promptly discounted.

In the interim, in respect to the matter of bombing the south side of the Yalu bridges and the hot pursuit issue, Secretary of Defense Marshall directed a personal letter to MacArthur, in a lame attempt to placate the General. Marshall, speaking for the administration, and writing between the lines, allowed MacArthur to destroy the bridges on the Korean side if *American lives were in danger*. It was an election year and Truman was mired in a political dilemma.

On 16 November 1950, President Truman went public in an effort to placate the Chinese Communist government and at the same time, European Allies:

> Speaking for the United States Government and people, I can give assurances that we are supporting and are acting within the limits of United Nations policy in Korea, and that we have never entertained any intention to carry hostilities into China; so far as the United States is concerned, I wish to state unequivocally that because of our deep devotion to the cause of world peace, and our long-standing friendship for the people of China, we will take every honorable step to prevent any extension of the hostilities in the Far East. If the Chinese authorities or people believe otherwise, it can only be because they are deceived by those who whose advantage it is to prolong and extend hostilities in the Far East against the interest of all Far Eastern people.

Those reassuring public remarks by the President fell on deaf Chinese ears. Actions speak louder than words. The Yalu bridges were destroyed, and in the course of the bombing, the border city of Antong in Manchuria was also unintentionally bombed. Moreover, MacArthur was voicing clear, belligerent statements as to the US intent to invade the mainland of China, and at the same time, unleash Chiang's Nationalist Army forces in a secondary invasion of mainland China.

On 24 November, General MacArthur, in a special communiqué to the United Nations, directly contradicted President Truman's 16 November eloquent public speech relative to peace with the new China government.[117]

In truth, the UN did not have the stomach to pursue further north, fully realizing the CCF would not permit the conquest of North Korea by UN forces. While lacking in sophisticated weaponry, the Chinese Volunteers had demonstrated earlier that they possessed an endless manpower pool to pursue the war. It became a matter of *saving face* for both sides.

Moreover, the USSR would not permit American or South Korean Forces to reoccupy North Korea, confirmed by a secret Soviet document attesting to retaliation if US aircraft should violate the sanctuary of Manchurian skies. This could well have been the prelude of World War III; with both major adversaries now in possession of nuclear arms, it was not at all in doubt what dire circumstances would result.

Bowing to intense pressure of the UN allies involved in Korea, and to put a rein on MacArthur, the President, on 6 December, issued a blanket directive to all theater commanders ordering them to clear all important public statements with Washington, prior to release—an obviously specific directive to MacArthur.

On 24 March 1951, apprised of a planned presidential statement that would propose negotiations to end the war, MacArthur released his own declaration. The general proclaimed victory in South Korea, described Chinese military capabilities as hopelessly inferior, threatened an expansion of the war beyond Korea, and offered to meet with the enemy Commander-in-chief to arrange what amounted to unconditional surrender.

MacArthur said, "I stand ready at any time to confer in the field with the commander-in-chief of the enemy forces in the earnest effort to find any military means whereby realization of the political objectives of the UN in Korea to which no nation may justly take exception, might be accomplished without further bloodshed."

The proverbial straw that broke the camel's back happened on 5 April

---

[117] The gigantic U.N. pincers moved according to schedule today. The air forces, in full strength, completely interdicted the rear areas and an air reconnaissance beyond the enemy line, and along the entire length of the Yalu River border, showed little sign of hostile military activity. The left wing of envelopment advanced against stubborn and failing resistance. The right wing gallantly supported by naval, air and surface action, continued to exploit its commanding position. Our losses are extraordinarily light. The logistics situation is fully geared to sustain offensive action. The justice of our cause and promise of early completion of our mission is reflected in the morale of troops and commanders alike. MacArthur.

1951. House Minority Leader Republican Joe Martin read into the *Congressional Record* the General's answer to a letter from the Senator. MacArthur's letter was bombastic and against administration policy, calling for a "second Asiatic front" flowing from Nationalist forces on Formosa, and ending with, "There is no substitute for victory."

MacArthur talked out of both sides of his mouth. He stated in essence that he could not sustain Allied forces in Korea because of CCF aggression and that an evacuation was imminent unless the US declared war on China. A declaration of war on Communist China would widen the parameters of the hostilities to an international level. The essential thought was if the CCF could not be contained in North Korea, how could they be subdued in a world-wide conflict? This was important since the USSR publicly stated that they would support the Chinese Communist cause.

Chairman, Joint Chiefs of Staff, Omar Bradley wrote:

> MacArthur's reaction arose, I feel certain, at least in part from the fact that his legendary pride had been hurt. The Red Chinese had made a fool of the infallible "military genius,".... The only possible means left to MacArthur to regain his lost pride and military reputation was now to inflict an overwhelming defeat on those Red Chinese generals that made a fool of him. In order to do this he was now perfectly willing to propel us into all-out war with Red China and, possibly, with the Soviet Union, igniting World War III and a nuclear holocaust.

Secretary of Defense Marshall was treading lightly in putting forth his view of the insubordination of MacArthur and the events that led to the ultimate dismissal of the general.

President Truman scheduled an unusual hour to inform the American Public, indeed the whole world, with an unprecedented press conference held at 1 a.m., because it would be 3 p.m. on 10 April 1951, Tokyo time—enough time for MacArthur to be officially notified of his dismissal by Secretary of State Marshall:

> I have been directed to relay the following message to you from President Truman:
>
> I deeply regret that it has become my duty as President and Commander-in-Chief of the United States military forces to replace you as Supreme Commander, Allied Powers, Commander-in Chief, United Nations Command; Commander-in-Chief Far East; and Commanding General, US Army, Far East. You will turn over commands, effective at once, to Lt. Gen. Matthew B. Ridgway. You are authorized to have issued such orders as are necessary to complete desired travel to such place as you select. I have commands effective

at once to Lieutenant General Matthew B. Ridgway. You are authorized to have issued such orders as are necessary to complete desired travel to such place as you may select. My reasons for your replacement will be made concurrently with the delivery to you of the foregoing order, and are contained in the next following message. (Signed: Harry S. Truman)

The logical presumption was that General MacArthur was previously notified through official channels. He was not. The general read about his dismissal in the papers.

MacArthur had a multitude of admirers who believed in a sense of fair play and Manchester, the chief biographer of General Douglas MacArthur was among them. He wrote:

> Truman was asleep by then, but the event already bore his unmistakable stamp. Here, as so often in his feisty administration, he had done the right thing, in this case avoiding the hazards of a general war, in the wrong way. Because he insisted that MacArthur be fired, instead of permitting him to retire gracefully, millions questioned the President's motives. The deed seemed punitive, even indecent, and it violated all of the traditions which the General cherished. The unceremonious, preemptory dismissal denied him the right to deliver a farewell speech to his troops, to consult Ridgway, to speak to the Japanese people, or to discuss the forthcoming peace treaty with any Nipponese officials. Clark Lee wrote:

> "Nothing could alter the summary language of the order, nor the implication that after so many years of service, MacArthur had become a terrible threat to the security of the United States, so dangerous that he must at one instant stripped of all command and power; such a peril that he could not with ordinary decency and customary military protocol. "The Duke of Marlborough, boarding a plane in New York, said, "It's been done in a rather unceremonious way, don't you think?" Carlos Romero asked: "Was there a need to swing the axe in just that fashion?" Manchester, p. 644.

Frank Pace, Secretary of the Army, was to have personally delivered *the coup d'état* letter of dismissal to MacArthur, but Pace was nowhere to be found. The Secretary was touring the battlefields of Korea, oblivious of his role in this macabre scheme of intrigue.

Yet, MacArthur had his detractors. General Ridgway, MacArthur's replacement following the general's dismissal noted in his book: *The Korean War*:

> As far as I can recall, only once, prior to Korea, had the authority of the President of United States been in any way questioned by a military officer on active duty. That was during the Lincoln Administration, when General George B. McClellan openly flouted the orders of his Commander-in-Chief. Ridgway, p. 152.

General Dwight D. Eisenhower, the Supreme Commander of the North American Treaty Organization, when informed of the abrupt dismissal of MacArthur, addressed the matter from a military perspective. He said, "You know when you put on a uniform you impose restrictions on yourself what you can do and say."

Now, some 30 years after the fact, the primary reason for the dismissal of MacArthur was disclosed through the Freedom of Information Act.

During those times, as it is now, nations engage in the sordid business of spying on each other, friend or foe. While Secretary of State Stimson ruminated in the 20's to the effect *that gentlemen do not read one another's mail,* the practice was, and continues to be, widespread throughout the international diplomatic society.

In 1947, President Truman established the National Security Agency (NSA) and the Central Intelligence Agency (CIA) for the express purpose of spying and intelligence gathering. Coded messages from diplomats of Spain and Portugal, among others, were routinely intercepted and decoded. Although professing friendly diplomatic relations with the US, the countries suffered control by right-wing dictators. MacArthur leaned in principle towards those types of governments.

As a matter of diplomatic courtesy, world leaders adhere to an unspoken canon, and that is to never *admit* to the reading of another's mail.[118]

But: *Gentlemen do not read one another's mail.*

Two colossal gladiators met for mortal combat in the arena of international public opinion. Armed with enormous egos, each sought to slay the other. In the end, both opponents were bled of any respect and both of them lost the battle.

President Truman became despondent, took to drinking heavily, and by and large ignored his office. He declined to run for re-election in 1952,

---

[118] In mid-March 1951 President Truman was handed a sheaf of intercepted messages from Spanish and Portuguese diplomats in Tokyo in which they told superiors of conversations with General Mac-Arthur. The gist of the talks was that the general was confident that he could transform the Korean War into a major conflict in which he could dispose of the "Chinese Communist question" once and for all. MacArthur did not want Portugal or Spain to be alarmed if this happened. The Soviet Union would either keep out of the war or face destruction itself. . . .But the source of the information meant that neither Truman nor anyone else in the administration could use it publicly. The United States in 1951, was not about to admit that it snooped on friendly countries. The case for firing MacArthur would have to be built elsewhere, on his public utterances, of which there were many. The stricture handicapped Truman. Had he been able to reveal the Portuguese and Spanish conversations, MacArthur would have been destroyed over night. Goulden, p.478.

knowing that he was unelectable, because of the controversy over MacArthur and the failure of the Korean Police Action.

General MacArthur also spiraled into deep depression, although he put up his customary command facade while he sat out the remainder of his life at his luxury suite at the Waldorf-Astoria, New York. The General was largely discredited for his blunders when the Chinese Communists entered the war. Testimony against MacArthur during the Senate hearings of 1951, by Secretary of Defense Marshall, the Joint Chiefs of Staff and other credible witnesses contradicted testimony by MacArthur, and through the words of the military commanders, the needle of disrepute pointed to the General.

MacArthur died peacefully in his sleep and he was entombed on 11 April 1964. Prior to his death he rejected an offer for a burial plot at his beloved West Point, in favor of a grandiose memorial, the former splendid courthouse, dedicated in his honor at Norfolk, Virginia.

Norfolk is a Navy town.

Neither Presidents Truman nor Eisenhower attended his funeral.

While The General sought and basked in the sunshine of publicity during his entire life, his only child, Arthur, did not. Arthur named for his famous grandfather, who possessed the same traits as did his son, Douglas MacArthur. Both military MacArthurs were awarded the Medal of Honor. Both were sacked by presidents—Arthur by President Robert Taft, coincidentally in the Philippines, as was son Douglas, based in Japan, by President Harry Truman.

When Arthur attained adulthood, he changed his name and plunged into the deep waters of anonymity. Arthur lacked the drive, and the interest in pursuing international recognition or the adulation to which his father so ravenously aspired.

HISTORY AND OTHER CONTENTIOUS ISSUES

> The Korean soldier who used to stand guard by the Palace gates or drill out in the open square has been spirited away. He has gone, and now only the echo of his bugle-call remains to us. He was the nation's representative of power and glory, standing at present arms beautifully, or giving the general salute when the king went by. He is gone. The cicada-fly still sings, the tree-toad pipes, and the peasant (sic) quavers his old-fashioned throat notes of an evening, but "lights out" no longer greets the ear of the Korean soldier, and the reveille is silent. Gayle, pp 58-59.

When the bloodletting ceases and the choking smoke of armed hostilities dissipates to the four winds, ponderous questions arise that cry for explanation of cause and the effect of the conflict.

Errors were made on both sides of the *de facto,* infamous border, the 38th Parallel, which ultimately culminated in major unresolved issues on an international level. Is it possible to unravel these tragic events in the hope of clarifying exactly how these dreadful events in due course led to war?

Think of Korea as the *Poland of Asia.* Poland was annexed by the triple alliance of Prussia, Russia and Austria in 1772, 1793 and 1797. Korea likewise endured numerous invasions, principally by the empires of China, Japan and Russia through the years. Korea, like Poland, was similarly divided and annexed by conquering nations. The amiable Koreans were always the losers, just as were the intrepid Poles. There is a graphic adage among indigenous Koreans which speaks to that plight: *Korea is like a shrimp caught in the middle of a battle of whales.*

First, an examination of the geography of Korea is necessary for the precise reason that it is specifically this geographic setting that has continuously affected this embattled country over the ages. Korea is situated near the geographical site where three major empires thrive. These militaristic countries were drawn to the Korean peninsula as a magnet to the dependant country, primarily because of the strategic location and vast natural resources, even though the population remains in a state of poverty.

The Korean Peninsula projects outwardly southwest, as if it was a dagger pointed to the heart of the Japanese Empire. Meanwhile geographically, the peninsula lies approximately equidistant to China to the east, and shares a common border of 830 miles. The frozen, desolate plains of Siberia, a significant part of the Russian Empire, abut the extreme northeast border of North Korea. The Tumen River, flowing generally south for approximately 90 miles, is the recognized border between the two like-minded nations. The barren wasteland of Manchuria, a province of Communist China, is positioned directly north of the Peninsula. Korea lies in the same latitude as Boston, New York, Philadelphia, Baltimore and Washington, 35 to 43 degrees north latitude.

Korea, an elongated, narrow peninsula, is surrounded by many bodies of water—to the east, the Sea of Japan; and to the west—the Yellow Sea which also sweeps to the rocky coast of North China, washing on the reverse shore. Sprawling due south lies the turbulent China Sea, from which mighty Asian typhoons spawn.

From due north to south the peninsula is approximately 575-600 miles long and about 150 miles, on average, from east to west, encompassing approximately 80,000 square miles. The peninsula country of Korea is approximately one half the size of Japan, one third of Ontario and roughly equal to the area of Kansas. The climate is unbearably hot and humid in summer, contrasting sharply with below-freezing temperatures in winter. The monsoon season of torrential rains generally occurs from June through September; but during the initial phase of the war in Korea in June 1950, the rains were absent, failing to arrive until early September.

Three diverse countries played a significant role in the subjugation of the proud peoples of Korea; the historical transitions of the inhabitants were accomplished by invasion followed by forced occupation. The commanding empires of China, Russia and Japan conspired together and, conversely, competed against one another, politically and militaristically to subjugate and occupy the country. They impacted the folkways, mores, and culture of Korea. Frequent warfare between these principal bellicose states during the turbulent epochs of history was fought for the very soul of Korea.

The rich ethnicity and heritage of the Koreans was influenced to a large degree by various invading foreign countries, predominantly by Japan. But like Poland, Korea refused to surrender its language, religion and culture to the various conquerors. Koreans simply went underground, imbuing generation after generation with the Korean language, history and culture.

~~

Certain events resulted in hostilities that led to the Korean War.

Some who analyze the war insist that the United States of America had a treaty that specifically stated that the US guaranteed to intervene militarily in support of the Korean government upon military invasion by foreign belligerents. This is incorrect. In 1882, in an effort to constrain Japanese military aggression in Asia, China persuaded the Korean king to seek a treaty with the US in order to ensure protection for the destitute, frail government. The petition was recommended, more from China's fear of expansionist Japan, than for the welfare and future of Korea.

As a consequence of Chinese persuasion, a treaty was ratified in 1882 concerning Korea and the US, intended as nothing more than a *friendship pact*. Indeed, the extraordinarily broad language of the operative clause unmistakably affirmed:

> If other powers deal unjustly or oppressively with either government, the other will exert their good offices, on being informed of the case, to bring about an amicable agreement, thus showing their friendly feelings.

American diplomats negotiating the treaty at the time assumed that the gist of the agreement would conceivably encourage economic interests between both countries, perhaps in future years. The omission of reference to any American military assistance constrains the pact, limiting it to economic issues only on behalf the beleaguered country. The backward, diminutive country, helpless to defend herself, was exposed to the certainty of armed invasion by foreign belligerents.

The Japanese Empire seethed with rage that Korea dare seek support from a western dominion, through the auspices of enemy China, while China was in fact engaged in the cruel occupation of Korea, acting as the spoiler. Consequently, Japan rushed hordes of well-trained infantrymen to Seoul, intent to engage the Chinese military in battle, and in due course drove the pugnacious Chinese from Korea, expecting to regain absolute control of the country as well. Recognizing the immediate danger to him and his faithful followers, Korea's desperate king fled in panic to the sanctuary of the Russian Legation. The king issued orders to his followers to execute his pro-Japanese ministers, in retaliation for the invasion and their conspiratorial, abortive attempt to regain control of the Korean Empire.

America stood by, observing silently and impassively as for seven years, Russia and Japan quarreled over the empirical destiny of the Korean Peninsula. Ultimately, a formal treaty between the empires of Japan and Russia was struck in 1896, with an agreement to divide the Korean Peninsula into two discordant countries at, coincidentally, the 38th Parallel. The hapless Koreans had no say in the matter.

Notwithstanding the treaty, history chronicles that Japan and Russia continued to compete over the spoils of Korea, both claiming sovereignty over the powerless country for many years. In 1898, Russia intimidated China into a pact to lease the ice-free harbor of Port Arthur, situated on the north coast of China. The Russian Far East Feet required a warm water port to exercise control of the vast Pacific area. At the time, the Russians had power over only one other port in Asia, Vladivostok, situated northeast of the northern boundary of North Korea in the Sea of Japan, which is normally icebound on an average of three months a year.[119] The Russians manipulated a 99-year lease for Port Arthur from the defenseless Chinese government, at that time neutered by the destruction of the Boxers by the unified, great powers of Europe.[120]

Subsequent to the conclusion of the Boxer Rebellion in China in 1900, the US initiated an open door treaty, the *Anglo-Japanese Alliance of 1900*. On the surface, the treaty implied a guarantee of sovereignty for China, when it was essentially a subterfuge to permit European countries to loot China of her natural resources. It was a successful bid to abrogate China's rights. Rather than have one European government controlling a specific geographical zone of China, the US successfully argued for the suspension of self-imposed, individual borders, thereby permitting all to engage in the plunder of the Chinese empire.

The alliance, formulated to exclude the Empire of Russia, caused Russia anxiety about her holding, obliging her to post thousands of troops in Chinese Manchuria to protect Russian interests. Japan, believing that the Russian intrusion posed a threat to her empire, strongly objected, but to no avail. The overconfident Russians believed the Japanese Empire was a mere sub-culture, not worthy to bring to a negotiation table. At the same time, Moscow and Tokyo continued to compete for power and control over the Koreans.

By securing the warm-water port of Port Arthur, Russia embarked on even more expansionist adventures, to the deep consternation of the Japanese. Following the conclusion of the Boxer Rebellion, the Russians con-

---

[119] Russian translation: *Ruler of the east*. Author.

[120] Reform was effectively blocked by the empress dowager, Cu Xi, a former concubine whose fickle fingers held the threads of power. Alternately she courted, and incited rebellion against, the foreign devils, provoking still more encroachments on Chinese sovereignty. Plots to bring down the empress and her fellow Manchu's were formulated in southern and eastern China by republican patriots influenced both by missionaries and growing contact with the west. The conspirators were loosely led by Doctor Sun Yat Sen, a westernized physician who spent many years in exile lobbying for revolution. His moment came in 1911, some years after the death the empress dowager's death, when a military mutiny forced the abdication of the last of the Manchu rulers, the boy emperor Pu Yi. Spurr, p. 36.

structed a new segment of the Trans-Siberian Railroad, completely traversing the vast wasteland of Manchuria, terminating at Port Arthur, including a claim on Korea to complete the prize. Connecting spurs of the Trans-Siberian Railroad were constructed deep into North Korea to the trepidation of the Japanese, who actually controlled the country.

A compromise proposal from Japan to Russia was introduced in June 1903. If Russia officially recognized and honored Japan's interest in Korea, Japan in turn would recognize the rights of Russia in regard to the political and economic interests imposed by Russia in Manchuria, even though the territory was a province of China. At the same time, a cross agreement was added that specified both nations would respect the integrity of China and Korea. Russia refused. Russia was not about to withdraw their foothold from northern Korea. War was inevitable.

The Japanese, and all Asians, were held in unqualified contempt by the Monarchy of Russia, and indeed by all of the monarchies and governments of Europe, who considered their Christian kismet to be predicated upon the principle of *The Divine Right of Kings*. In regard to the Korean dispute, the European nations sided with Russia. It was Christianity versus the Infidels. The Christians would prevail, or so they believed.

Germany's Kaiser Wilhelm's exhortations had a striking success. Wilhelm hated Orientals, and raved of 'the Yellow Peril." In 1900, bidding farewell to a shipload of German Marines bound for China to help disperse the Boxer revolutionaries, the Kaiser shouted blood-curdling instructions:

> You must know, my men, that you are about to meet a crafty, well-armed, cruel foe! Meet him and beat him. Give no quarter. Take no prisoners. Kill him when he falls into your hands. Even as a thousand years ago, the Huns under king Attila made such a name for themselves as still resounds in terror through legend and fable, so may the name of Germany resound through Chinese a thousand years from now.

In writing to the *Star*, Wilhelm elevated his prejudice to a loftier level. Russia, he declared, had a Holy Mission in Asia:

> Clearly, it is the great task of the future for Russia to cultivate the Asian continent and to defend Europe from the inroads of the Great Yellow Race. In this you will always find me on your side, ready to help you as best I can. You have well understood the call of Providence. . . in the Defense of the Cross and the old Christian European culture against the inroads of the Mongols and Buddhism. . . I would let nobody try to interfere with you and attack from behind in Europe during the time that you were fulfilling the great mission which

Heaven has shaped for you.

The US had no interest or any capability at the time to expand eastward; consequently America abandoned Korea, notwithstanding the earlier treaty between the two countries.

The dubious treaty between the empires of Japan and Russia became the basis for future conflict which ultimately festered into the Russo-Japanese War of 1904/1905; hence, this phase will be the basis of chronicling the modern history of Korea, which ultimately led to the disastrous Korean War.

Deeds not words. The civilized world breathlessly beheld this drama unfolding as Russia ignored diplomatic courtesies expected of civilized countries. Russia treated the Japanese with disdain and scorn, believing that they, Russia, were in complete control. How could it be possible for a diminutive, upstart Asian country to challenge one of the mightiest empires on earth?[121] The world powers stood by watching the sights and sounds of the two countries girding for war.

War correspondents including *Call of the Wild* author Jack London, representing the newspaper giant William Randolph Hearst, sailed to the predestined battle front on the *SS Siberia*, 7 January 1904.

On a frigid night on 8 February 1904, (some historians put the date as the 6th) Japan steamed stealthily under a blanket of dense fog into Port Arthur, home of the Russian Far Eastern Fleet, and commenced to torpedo two unsuspecting Russian battleships and one destroyer. Sea mines dispersed by the Japanese navy blocked the mass of the Russian fleet from heaving to. If they dared to venture forth from the blockade, Japanese ships were there to harass the Russian fleet with pre-set mines and torpedoes from waiting Japanese gunboats. On 13 April, the Russian battle and flagship, *Petropavlovsk* attempted to sortie surreptitiously from the harbor of Port Arthur, thirsting to retaliate. The doomed ship struck a mine and quickly sunk with the appalling loss of 700 seamen, along with Russia's most distinguished Admiral, Markarov.

In a follow-up to the Port Arthur debacle, with seas secured, Japanese Expeditionary Forces landed troops at Inchon Harbor in March of 1904.

---

[121] The Russian advance into Korea made war with Japan inevitable. The Japanese would have preferred an agreement: Russia to keep Manchuria, leaving Japan a free hand in Korea. But the Mikado's ministers could not stand by and watch the Russian's swarm along the whole coast of Asia, planting the Tsar's double-headed eagle in every port and promontory facing their islands. Massie, p. 90.

Japan followed with a subsequent landing at Nampo (known also as Chinnampo) both on the west coast of the Korean Peninsula. Japanese ground troops overwhelmed five of Russia's elite Siberian regiments, then raced north to confront additional Russian forces, now off balance and reeling in the face of the coordinated, Japanese attack. Once north of the Yalu River, Japan triumphed over Russia in several key battles in Manchuria. The main forces of arms were conducted at Uiju, on the north side of the Yalu River, near the border of China. Losses were extraordinarily heavy on both sides, but the Japanese Army prevailed decisively. During May of the same year, Japanese troops landed on the Liaodong Peninsula, where they adroitly severed communication lines between Port Arthur and the Russian forces in Manchuria. The Russians, isolated and contained by the maneuver, were neutered. The besieged Russian forces were sent reeling in retreat, posing little threat to the attacking Japanese.

In the intervening time, Japanese ground forces, though extensively outnumbered, nonetheless managed to rout the Russian Far East Army, which fell back to defend Mukden, capitol of Manchuria (now known by the Chinese name of Shenyang). Japanese forces simultaneously lay siege to fortified Port Arthur on 5 December 1904, inflicting wanton destruction. The besieged fortress, surrounded with extensive, protective barbed wire and artillery, was no match for Japan's huge retaliatory artillery— monstrous 11-inch siege cannon.[122] The heavy artillery brought the fort to its knees, destroying fortified walls, trenches, and artillery emplacements. During the summer and fall of 1904, Japanese infantry stormed Russian fortifications time after time despite terrain laced with obstructing barbed-wire defenses, and finally Japanese forces were able to conquer battered Russian harbor defenses.

The brilliant operation resulted in the surrender of Port Arthur to the Japanese on 2 January 1905. The land battle was concluded, resulting in a disastrous, humiliating defeat for Russia. The loss of troops on both sides was appalling. Japan, while the clear victor, lost 57,780 troops to the vanquished Russians who listed 28,800 fatalities.

It was a matter of logistics as it is in every conflict. Supply lines of the Japanese were relatively short, only a few hundred sea miles, because of the proximity to the battle sites to the base of supply, Japan.

---

[122] Studying reports of the Russo-Japanese War, the world's most recent conflict between great powers, he (Krupp) noted that shellfire had led to protective entrenchments shielded by barbed wire. With frightful but flawless logic he foresaw that in any future hostilities barbed wire would be in great demand. Manchester, p. 254.

Russia, on the other hand, faced the daunting task of transporting soldiers, weapons and ancillary supplies over 4,000 miles from Moscow, by use of the single-track Trans-Siberian Railroad. It was even more laborious than one can imagine, because, at the time, the railroad was not complete. Lake Baikal created an insurmountable gap of over 100 miles. In summer, war materiel had to be ferried across the largest lake in the world. During winter, every individual soldier and each piece of armament had to be carried by sled across this vast frozen body of water. An alternative method was to skirt the immense lake, traveling south around the great body of water, which entailed an additional several hundred arduous miles.

Despite the horrific losses, Tsar Nicholas Romanoff II initiated a *go slow policy*, convinced that a retaliatory, declared war would inexorably draw other nations into the conflict, if Russia was the one to instigate further hostilities. The Tsar's fiat was met with indignation and derision by his ministers, prompting huge, screaming throngs of patriotic Russian citizens to flood the streets of Moscow and Saint Petersburg. Russian citizens demanded retribution for the loss of their Far East Fleet at Port Arthur and their destroyed armies in Manchuria. What could the Tsar be thinking? This was indeed war in the strongest sense, be it declared or not.

There was no turning back. Anxiety and anger were exerted by ministers, Russian citizens massing in the streets, and European empires demanding retaliatory measures by Russia. The Tsar reluctantly ordered the Russian Baltic Fleet to sea in October 1904, to steam half way around the planet with the intent to destroy the Japanese Fleet.

To the Tsar's dismay, the Russian Baltic Fleet, after sailing from the homeland and halfway around the world to avenge the loss of the Russian Far East Fleet, met the same catastrophic fate.

Admiral Heihachiro Togo, commander of the Japanese Navy, and hero of Japan, set an elaborate trap for the Russian Fleet in the Sea of Tsushima, (the strait between Korea and Japan). As the avenging Russians approached the Strait, Admiral Togo, from his flagship, ordered the yeoman to hoist various black, blue, red and yellow triangular communication flags. The message was clear. *On this one battle rests the fate of our nation. Let every man do his utmost!*

On 27 May 1905, at approximately 2 p.m., the Russian Fleet sped forth with eight battleships, into the Strait of Tsushima where Admiral Togo surreptitiously lay in wait. Togo situated his battleships 7000 yards across the strait in formation, and on command, the Japanese navy fired gigantic guns at one enemy ship after another. When the guns fell silent after a naval bombardment of only 45 minutes, Russia lost eight battleships, seven cruisers and six destroyers. Those mortally wounded ships were sent to the bottom by skilled torpedo boats that lashed at the stricken fleet, buzzing in and out and around the calm seas emulating enraged hornets, unleashing their deadly torpedoes one after the other.

The modern Russian fleet and army were annihilated and the entire world conceded that diminutive Japan had vaulted from feudalism into a modern-day industrial and military titan in little more than a generation. There were profound world-wide reverberations as a consequence of this small, irrelevant Asian county, being the first in modern history to bring one of the mightiest European nations to her knees.[123]

The Japanese, under tutelage of the British Navy, then the most powerful naval force in the world, had been taught well by the accommodating British. It wasn't until the prelude to World War I that Japanese naval personnel ceased using English as the language for Japanese naval commands.

Russia sued for peace, and President Theodore Roosevelt, with US personal interests in mind, offered to mediate a settlement and peace treaty between the two warring empires. Japan, the clear victor, agreed to the mediation, simply because the Japanese economy was destabilized as a result of the war. On 5 September 1905, the Treaty of Portsmouth (Maine) was drawn and signed by the two warring parties, effectively terminating hostilities.

Prominent ranking Japanese military personnel raged over what they perceived as a prejudicial agreement, believing the civilian democratic Japanese government incapable of negotiation in the interests of Japan. Military leaders seized power from the empire, eventually resulting in far more onerous acts of military aggression under military command.[124]

---

[123] Tsushima, the greatest sea battle since Trafalgar, had a powerful impact on naval thinking everywhere. It confronted Britain, whose whole existence depended on the Royal navy, with the appalling prospect of losing a war in one afternoon in a general fleet engagement. The Kaiser, who cherished his High Seas Fleet, became equally frightened. As a result, during the four years of the First World War the huge British and German navies collided only once, at Jutland. Massie, p. 95.

[124] By the middle of 1905 Japanese military successes against Russia had changed Roosevelt's thinking. His fear was now that Japan, intoxicated with confidence, might aspire to hegemony over a great Pacific empire. He was especially worried about the Philippines, over which the United States had recently established control in order to use the islands as a staging area for greatly expanded trade with China. Thus when Secretary of War William Howard Taft visited Tokyo in July 1905 to work out the preliminaries for Roosevelt's mediation of the Russo–Japanese War, he negotiated an agreement with Prime Minister Taro Katsura whereby the United States acknowledged the "suzerainty over" Korea in return for assurances that Japan would not challenge America's position in the Philippines. Whelan, p.15.

Japan received the short end of the arrangement. There was a tacit agreement between Japan and the US to the effect, that if Japan would not interfere with the American colonization of the Philippines, the US guaranteed Japan some of the spoils of war.

In the same characteristic mood of colonialism at the time, Britain was elated to accept Japan's official recognition of the British conquest and colonialism of India. The British reciprocated in kind, recognizing Japan's right to colonize and annex Korea and be the legitimate ruler of Korea and Manchuria. The subjugated countries overwhelmed by these new, great world powers had no say in the matter, but resentment and hostility gradually actualized, until the cry for independence became uncontrollable.

President Roosevelt was awarded the Nobel Prize for Peace in 1905 for brokering the pact at Portsmouth, but the seeds of discontent were sown throughout the Empire of Japan. Major riots broke out in large cities of Japan against the US. This indignity in the eyes of the Japanese evolved into a major contention which was one of the dominant factors as a prelude to World War II.[125]

~~

After having exercised control of Korea for so long, the Japanese formally annexed the peninsula of Korea in 1905. There began a 40-year brutal occupation of Korea. Japan made extensive improvements to the infrastructure of Korea, installing or constructing trains, roads, dams, bridges, and hydro-electric power. But at the same time, the Koreans were forbidden to speak their native tongue, could communicate only in Japanese, took Japanese names, had their land confiscated and their rice exported to Japan. Japanese troops suppressed an anti-Japanese uprising in Seoul on 1 March 1919 during which thousands of innocent Koreans were slain. Korean leaders fled to the haven of Shanghai, China and set up a provisional government. (Some historians place the provisional government at Chunking, China.)

The Japanese Empire continued to brood over the 1905 Treaty of Portsmouth, and felt it was lopsided and left them no alternative other than to even the score and invade certain islands in Southeast Asia to secure raw materials for their economic benefit. Thirty-five years later, Russia was concerned about the prospect of fighting on two fronts. At this time Russia faced Germany from the west and Japan from the east. Conse-

---

[125] Whelan p. 16.

quently, Russia enticed the Empire of Japan into the 1941 Neutrality Treaty of Non-Aggression.

Japan for many years secretively formulated elaborate plans for the destiny of their country, just as they had against the Russians at Port Arthur, China. Constrained by the Neutrality Treaty from attacking Russia, Japan changed course to attack southwest. They were about to put into play a scheme that Admiral Isoroku Yamamoto, commander of the Japanese Combined Fleet, planned in ultra secret for years. He deemed it essential to destroy the US Pacific fleet before Japan could implement tactical plans for the invasion of Southeast Asia.

The Japanese struck at a small harbor unknown to most Americans, other than military personnel and a few travelers. The pristine chain of islands, called Hawaii, was noted for a shallow water harbor and an American naval base named Pearl Harbor. Someone forgot to read the history of Japanese tactics. Japan attacked without giving the US prior notice of war. They had done the same at Port Arthur in 1904.

~~

Near the conclusion of World War II, Truman actually *invited* the USSR to attack Japan, believing that the Japanese in Manchuria maintained the Kwantung Army, a formidable, well-armed unit said to be independent of the governing powers in Tokyo. It was generally assumed that Japan would summon the Kwantung Army to the home islands for defensive measures before the US would launch the imminent invasion of Japan. It was for this reason that the US favored the USSR to engage the fierce Kwantung Army and to neutralize them, preventing the enemy army from slipping into Japan to aid in island defense.

But how could a Japanese army of that magnitude exist in Manchuria without international scrutiny? In 1931, militaristic Japan invaded and conquered Manchuria, designated the country as *Manchukuo,* and by the following February 1932, installed a Chinese puppet government. The Japanese military government appointed as ruler the last emperor of the Manchu Dynasty, Henry Pu-yi. The farce was no less than a shallow, political maneuver to claim legitimacy for the Japanese invaders, having the world believe that it was the Chinese who actually were the rulers of their own province. The mighty Japanese Kwantung Army was safely ensconced, originally created to ensure that the Japanese-inspired ersatz edicts of Pu-yi were followed. But, in reality, it was the Japanese who governed. The international community refused to recognize this blatant abuse of power by the Japanese and when Japan moved into China proper, installing similar puppet governments in Chinese provinces, the 1937 Sino-Japanese War was the consequence.[126]

Emperor Pu-yi had been the ghost leader, and the Kwantung Army was a ghost army when the USSR invaded. The protectorate army had been gradually siphoned off and deployed earlier to the various islands in the Pacific theater in defense of Japan. The US was unaware of the absence of this formidable Japanese Army when the proposal was first addressed to the Russians.

Two Atomic Bombs dropped August 6th and 9th on Hiroshima and Nagasaki, respectively, changed the equation of World War II the instant the bombs exploded. The Empire of Japan surrendered unconditionally on 14 August 1945, upon the proclamation of Japanese Emperor Hirohito, thus averting what would have surely have been the most savage campaign of World War II. Japan would have fought to the death for her home islands, were it not for the acquiescence of Emperor Hirohito. The Emperor's proclamation overrode any military design to convey the war forward.

At the conclusion of World War II, the US immediately flooded the island nation with US military to claim control, thus depriving the USSR of any interests in Japan. And that was precisely why the US offered an expeditious peace treaty to Japan, turning her from a belligerent government into a cooperator, allied with the US against the USSR in the Far East. Politics turn on a dime.[127]

Russia had declared war on Japan on 2 April 1945 when Prime Minister Molatov informed the Japanese Empire that Russia nullified the Neutrality Pact of Non-Aggression of 1941 during the waning days of World War II. The USSR had no compunction against violating the treaty, or in

---

[126] Protecting Japanese interests in Manchuria was the Kwantung Army, which had developed from the small force first stationed in southern Manchuria in 1906 to guard the ports and the railway lines that Japan had won in the war with Russia. The army became a much enlarged and quite independent command in 1919, in the wake of the concessions that Japan, one of the victorious Allied powers, extorted from China during World War I. From that time onward, the Kwantung Army's officers became more and more convinced that Japanese sovereignty over Manchuria was the key to Japan's future strength and prosperity. Whelan, pp. 18-19.

[127] By then, the administration had taken another major step toward the establishment of a liberal world order by negotiating a peace treaty with Japan. Concluded at a conference in San Francisco in September 1951, over clamorous Soviet opposition, the pact was a triumph on many counts. The participation of John Foster Dulles, and other Republicans symbolized the last major achievement of foreign policy bipartisanship under Truman. The practical result was to make a disarmed Japan a dependent ally of the United States and to provide for a continued, strategically vital American interest there. Thus was secured the position of the United States in the northwestern Pacific. Hamby, p. 571.

declaring war in the hope of achieving larger gains by the seizure of a large share of the spoils of war from Japan. The original purpose of the neutrality treaty was to negate Japan's militaristic goals of aggression, diverting them from attacking north, aiming at the jugular of Russia. By her signature, Japan agreed not to wage war with Russia, who likewise was bound by the same treaty.

To handle Japanese prisoners of war in Korea, prior to the conclusion of World War II, and pursuant to an agreement at Potsdam, Russian Premier Stalin and US President Truman agreed to an arbitrary line to be set at the 38th Parallel. Russia was to take charge of all Japanese prisoners north of the Korean parallel, while the US accepted Japanese prisoners south of the 38th. A *quid pro quo*.

That de facto line, the antithesis of a sovereign border, the 38th Parallel, was permanently closed by North Korea in retaliation when the US called for free elections throughout the peninsula in 1948. Russia rejected the bid and instead installed their own puppet government, headed by 33-year old Kim Il Sung, a former guerrilla fighter against the Japanese and later, the Nationalist Army of China.

Once the border was closed, sporadic raids developed in intensity on both sides, accompanied by guerrilla activity in the south by agents of North Korea, and discord among the citizenry was fomented by hundreds of secreted Communist agitators.

On 12 January 1950, Secretary of State Dean Acheson made a diplomatic speech before the International Press Club in Washington D.C. The essence of the speech was to delineate the countries of the Far East who were deemed essential to the security of the US. It was the outline of a political defensive wall in the Pacific. Any mention of South Korea or the island of Formosa (Taiwan) was designedly excluded.[128]

Secretary of State Acheson specifically omitted the names of the fledgling countries of South Korea and the Republic of China, exiled to the island of Formosa (now Taiwan). There was a reason. Formosa was the current bastion of Chiang Kai-shek along with his Chinese Nationalist Army who fled to the refugee island in 1949, just ahead of the victorious Chinese Communist People's Liberation Army (PLA). The US did not want to agitate Red China or the USSR, by giving support to the two contentious countries. However, the US, no matter the rhetoric, had an underlying fiduciary interest in the island.

---

[128] Higgens, p.52.

Acheson's policy of non-engagement in Korea (and Formosa) was reinforced by the Democratic Chairman of the Senate Foreign Relations Committee.[129] He admitted in May 1950 that Russia had the means to seize South Korea at its convenience and that the US would look the other way. That was an unequivocal, open invitation to invade South Korea, and the despotic North Korean Premier Kim Il Sung took full advantage. He flew to Moscow to have a private audience with Joseph Stalin, supreme leader of the USSR, seeking Stalin's consent to invade the south. Stalin knew the North Korean Army was fully capable of taking over the fledgling country known as the Republic of Korea. Stalin readily agreed, and he was quick to suggest to Kim that the newly-formed Communist government of China should now be invited to participate in any future military assistance of North Korea. Stalin had more important designs on eastern European countries and he wanted to avoid being mired in an Asian civil war not of his making. He did not want his fingerprints on the battle for South Korea, even though he armed North Korea with a bounty of massive and sophisticated weaponry.

North Korea was now a full-fledged puppet state, as were the communist-led countries of East Europe. Both geopolitical zones were solely dominated by the Soviet Union after World War II.

The Communist Democratic People's Republic of Korea soldiers were no rag-tag army. Members honed their combat skills on the battlefields of northern China and Korea against the once invincible army of the Japanese. Additionally, in their fanatical quest to unite under the banner of Communism throughout Asia, they joined forces with guerrilla leader, and future Chairman, Mao Tse-tung, in the civil war against the Kuomintang Government, the Nationalists in China.

The North Korean Army had developed significant fighting potential within three short years, when in 1948, the country was openly activated upon the official withdrawal of the Soviet Union. There was no public mention of the hundreds of Soviet cadre that remained to hone the NKPA into a precision fighting machine, which remained a shrouded secret to the

---

[129] Then came the worst bombshell of all: A published Q and A interview with Democratic Senator Tom Connally, who was a friend of the administration and who held the prestigious position of chairman of the Senate Committee on Foreign Relations. Asked by the editors of U.S. News & World Report if the United States would consider abandoning South Korea, Connally replied: "I am afraid that it is going to be seriously considered because I'm afraid it's gong to happen, whether we want it or not." In response to a follow-up question asking if Korea was not an "essential" part of America's defensive strategy, Connally replied: "No. . . I don't think it is very important." Blair, p. 54.

world. Moreover, there was no mention of the elements of the Chinese Liberation Army (PLA) that monitored the war from the first days of the invasion.

While surprisingly small by western military standards, the North Korean Army with over 135,000 soldiers was fully supplied by the generosity and largess of the Soviet Union. Hundreds of T-34 tanks, artillery, heavy mortars, rockets and aircraft were ancillary support for their well-trained army. Premier Stalin approved of the invasion of South Korea, believing that the Americans would not intercede. Secretary of State Dean Acheson's earlier speech said as much when he tacitly guaranteed the international community that the US would not meddle.

Thus, the NKPA savagely attacked across the 38th Parallel border on Sunday morning, 25 June 1950, at 4 a.m. (Korea time) following a massive pre-invasion artillery barrage.

American forces of all branches were sent as a counter, while the UN rushed to condemn North Korea for aggression and demanded the immediate withdrawal of the Communist forces to north of the Parallel, to no avail.

Then, General MacArthur enjoyed his victory of the well planned, well executed, but largely ineffective amphibious landing at the west port of Inchon in South Korea. He received tepid support from the Administration, military analysts, and, especially The Joint Chiefs of Staff.

After the victory in South Korea, General MacArthur, with the wide backing of America, looked north in anticipation of a speedy, comprehensive victory over the entire peninsula with the stated goal to finally unite the two divided countries.

Congress, urged by MacArthur's allies, was the catalyst to propel a wild rush to roll back the border and vanquish the remainder of the North Korean People's Army, once and for all. President Truman, having little choice because of Congressional influence, acceded to the General's request. Regretfully, there was a problem with this kind of convoluted and cavalier thinking. No one stood to oppose MacArthur.

On 3 October 1950, the People's Republic of China's Foreign Minister Chou En-lai informed the sympathetic Indian Ambassador to China, K.M. Pannikar, that the Chinese People's Army would intervene should any foreign armies cross into North Korea. The exception was given to the Republic of Korea, which they regarded as a belligerent in an internal matter that involved both countries.

> At one-thirty a.m., October 3, Pannikar (Indian Ambassador to China) telegraphed the gist of their conversation to New Delhi. Although MacArthur would not announce that the ROK 3rd Division had crossed the parallel until later in the day, Pannikar guessed it had been done; and he was sure the Chinese troops concentrated in Manchuria also moved across the Yalu. In the morning he shared this information with the British Minister.
>
> When the news was passed on to Acheson, the secretary of state did not take it seriously, because he distrusted Pannikar. "He was not a good reporter." Nor had Acheson taken seriously Chou's recent speech declaring that China would not stand aside if North Korea was invaded.
>
> Pannikar, nevertheless, was an accurate reporter. Chou En-lai's warning had not been mere rhetoric, and Chairman Mao had decided that very day to send troops to Korea to fight the Americans and South Koreans. Eighty percent of Chinese heavy industry lay in Manchuria; it had to be held. The Chinese troops, called the Volunteers Army, were to be led by their top field Officer, Lin piao, Commander in Chief of the Fourth Field Army. A wily man, Lin claimed to be sick, but many believe that he had no relish for fighting the Americans. Toland, pp.235-6

On the surface, it appeared be a magnanimous gesture when the Communists indicated that they had no quarrel with the Republic of Korea. In reality, China had absolutely no intention of allowing *puppet governments* of the US to control any area so close to the Chinese border. In the view of the newly formed People's Republic of China, America was viewed as the quintessence of evil capitalists. Consequently, the Republic of Korea Army (ROK) was the first to be savaged by the Chinese Volunteers as an unmistakable warning for all foreign forces to withdraw south of the 38th Parallel.

> Peking's position regarding North Korea was virtually identical to the American position regarding Formosa. The Chinese Communists were not out to impose their suzerainty on North Korea or even to establish military outposts there. They were simply determined that it not fall into enemy hands. Especially now that Japan was to be rearmed in alliance with the United States, it was absolutely vital, from Peking's point of view, that North Korea be Communist and friendly and that it continue to exist as a buffer between Manchuria and South Korea....
>
> Consider how the United States would feel if the situation were reversed. Whelan, p. 235.

There were other concerns—dissension in the ranks. Great Britain in particular was reluctant to join the trek northward.[130] The British were doing business with China through their China-leased outpost of Hong Kong. They, along with the majority of the UN, were strong advocates of the Chinese Communist government's right to exist and their entitlement to join the UN as the recognized representative of the largest country in the world. In hindsight, refusing them admittance was a momentous mistake by the US.

For it was the US that lobbied sufficient votes in the UN to deny a seat to Red China, despite the fact that the Communist government stood victorious over the soundly defeated Nationalist government, who fled in fear to the island of Formosa. The Nationalists lost the civil war despite the millions upon millions of unaccounted-for American dollars flowing endlessly into the insatiable coffers of Chiang. Truman eventually implemented a strategy to stop funding to the Nationalists, but it was too late. The Communists saw the US as an adulator of Chiang. To this day, the US continues to sell arms openly to the Taiwan government, over the vehement protests of Communist China. At the same time, the US has implemented a resolution in the UN to deny the exportation of weapons to the Chinese Communist government.

Perhaps the new government of China should have been invited to be seated in the UN at the time. Communist or not, they were the *bono fide, de facto* government of China. History most certainly would have taken a different course had Red China held a seat in the UN. At the very least, a dialogue could have been established and perhaps the Chinese Communist intervention in the Korean War might have been averted.

A pledge given by Truman to the British that the Allied advance would not pass north of the 40th Parallel (the parallel near Pyongyang) without prior consultation was violated. Further, Truman was trapped by a clever reporter into stating that the atomic bomb could be used in Korea as an alternative weapon. The British nearly pulled their combat contingency out of Korea over Truman's inadvertent statement.

Military analysts and historians should not have been shocked at the rout of the American Army at the hands of the Chinese Communist Forces. The invading Asian forces demonstrated a degree of tenacity un-

---

[130] The British had fought two massive and debilitating wars in the twentieth century. Once more they felt themselves sliding into a conflict, possibly a nuclear one, whose course they could not contain. Parliamentarians quoted some of the scarier statements by American senators who wanted to bomb Manchuria and mount a naval blockade of the China coast. Their one hope was that Britain still carried sufficient clout to urge restraint on Washington. Spurr, p. 246.

heralded in the annals of modern warfare. Accordingly, their exploits previous to the *Long March* and the historical rise of the Chinese Communists bears scrutiny.

The Chinese Communist forces recorded their first military skirmish during the Ranching Rebellion, 1 August 1927, when they were disenfranchised and ostracized from the Kuomintang Government, controlled by Chiang.

The resulting outfall degenerated into a 20-year civil war between the two opposing parties. The Communists, following a series of enormous battles, crashed through Nationalist forces lines on 21 October 1934 from Kiangsi Province, where Communist forces were surrounded.

The Communists were nearly defeated, primarily as the result of inferior tactical advice from a German officer named Otto Braun, a leftover from the German Legation during the Boxer Rebellion, and originally employed by the Russians. Braun's military advice resulted in the near annihilation of Communist forces.

The communist rout by the Chiang army resulted in *The Long March*, forcing Mao, Lin, Peng and thousands of other Communist loyalists to flee 6,000 miles to northeast China, barely escaping the net thrown by Chiang's Nationalist Army. With Mao as the undisputed leader, the rebels withdrew to reorganize their shattered forces. The Communists resurrected their beleaguered army to 600,000 strong in Shenshi Province, in Northeast China, where their base was established. Few of arms but powerful of determination, their armies struck again and again at Nationalist forces in hit and run guerrilla-type sorties, garnering weapons and demoralizing the Nationalists.

In 1947, The People's Liberation Army (PLA) under the leadership of Lin Paio, severed the Nationalist Army's communication to Manchuria and ultimately drove to southern China where they isolated and destroyed the Kuomintang military who were, at the time, resolutely supported by the government of the US.

The Chinese Communist government believed that the US was hostile to the new, legitimate government of China. If not, then why did they pursue an act of armed aggression against a defeated North Korean Army? From the Chinese point of view there was no need for the US to enter North Korea and to occupy foreign territory. The South Korean Government could easily have terminated the last resistance by the essentially destroyed North Korean Army.[131]

The Chinese Communists would never tolerate having a puppet government, friendly to the US, occupy territory so near to the Chinese Communist government domain of Manchuria. In the view of the Chinese, it was just a matter of time until the US would invade mainland China, in a two-pronged attack. The conviction among all Asians was that an attack in opposition to the Communist government would emanate from the island of Formosa, simultaneous with an attack though Manchuria. They believed the invaders would then march onto mainland China from the sanctuary of North Korea.

Even though the ROKs were situated in North Korea, the UN would have condemned, isolated and embargoed the Chinese Communist government for any aggression against South Korea, should the Communists have taken action there. It was matter for only the Koreans to resolve just as China initially purported. As it was, under prodding by the US, Communist China was condemned by the august body of the UN for invading North Korea.

One of the most important arguments of the Korean War was should UN forces (composed primarily of American soldiers) have entered the territory of North Korea in the face of threats of intervention by the People's Republic of China?

Veterans serving during that precarious phase of the Korean War generally believed that *to cross the line* (the 38th Parallel), given the threats of intervention by the Chinese Communist government, was nothing short of immoral. The war was over for all realistic reasons and to foolhardily enter the Communist lair would only stir the sleeping Chinese dragon.

Given the so-called rejection by the North Korean People's Army of the ultimatum to surrender, one must question the validity of MacArthur's expectation it would surrender. How was the enemy to surrender? By then the once elite and unbeatable NKPA was a scattered, disorganized muddle of men fleeing for their lives to the sacrosanct haven of Manchuria. There was no radio or other means to communicate with the van-

---

[131] By November 28 it must have been clear to Douglas MacArthur that he had blundered badly in Korea. The wine of victory had turned to vinegar. In a broad sense, Inchon had become another Anzio. He had been out smarted and out generaled by a "bunch of Chinese laundrymen" who had no close air support, no tanks, and very little artillery, modern communications, or logistical infrastructure. His reckless egotistical strategy after Inchon, undertaken in defiance of war warnings from Peking and a massive CCF build up in Manchuria, had been an arrogant, blind march to disaster. Blair, p. 464.

quished enemy. The once formidable government was nonexistent, and when last heard of, the remaining hierarchy of the Communist regime was on a slow train to China. The war was over.

MacArthur had the audacity to claim that the ROK Army was too weak to vanquish the pitiful remnants of what was once a mighty North Korean Army.

Thus, a new phase of the bloody conflict started, and to quote MacArthur after the initial disastrous results by the methodical invading Chinese forces: "This is an entirely new war."

THE COMMANDERS

> Was the Korean War worth fighting? It was a war of cruelty, stupidity, error, misjudgment, racism, prejudice and atrocities on both sides committed by people on high, middle, and low ranks. Only the numerous instances of humanity on all levels - heroism in battle, self-sacrifice, kindness and sympathy to an enemy - make writing about war bearable.
>
> Yet recent events in both Asia and Europe call a negative view of the Korean War into question. The forgotten war may eventually have turned out to have been the decisive conflict that started the collapse of communism. In any case, those who fought and died in that war did not fight and die in vain. Toland, p. 596.

General MacArthur's role in the Korean War has been addressed extensively earlier; consequently this compilation of information relates to the principal adversarial Chinese leader, Peng Te-huai. A discourse relating to other prominent commanders who were a major influence on the Korean War, 25 June 1950 to 27 July 1953, also is included.

Early western historians credited Chinese Communist General Lin Piao for the decisive defeat of the American Army in November/December, 1950 in North Korea. That presumption was incorrect. Lin (surnames are presented first in China) in fact never stepped foot in Korea; but, because Lin's elite 4th Field Army played an active, visible role in the conflict, it was assumed by early western sources that Lin indeed, personally directed his vast cadre against ROK's, Americans and allies.[132]

The 4th Field Army, the largest, most effective army of the Chinese Communist Forces, first factored in a decisive role in the downfall of the Nationalist Army, commanded by Chiang Kai-shek. An intimate friend and spokesman for the US, Chiang also served as the eyes and ears for America, monitoring the vast, turbulent Asian continent.

The beginning of the end for Chiang's Kuomintang Nationalist Army occurred when major components of Lin's elite, 4th Field Army completed a demanding, forced march beginning from the frozen waste lands of Manchuria, which in due course terminated at the shores of sweltering, humid South China. Lin's vast army consolidated with other dedicated Communist units, melding with the intent to capture or drive Chiang from power.

Nationalist Chiang and his out-fought, beleaguered army scarcely

---

[132] Peng Te-huai commanded the First Field Army, Lin Po-cheng the Second, Ch'en Yi the Third, and Lin Piao the Fourth. Peng Te-huai's First field Army normally was garrisoned in and responsible for northwest China, a critical area adjacent to the Soviet border. Appleman, p. 16.

evaded the Communist net by successfully fleeing to Formosa. General Lin, not to be deprived of the sweet taste of victory, urged his loyal forces to capture Hainan Island, a small strategic island in the Strait of Formosa (now Taiwan Strait). The successful capture of Hainan was to be the staging area for the Communist's final assault on Formosa, Chiang's fortified island of exile. The Communists believed then, as now, that the strategic island is the rightful possession of mainland China, and they had the right to invade (liberate?) Formosa, to rid the planet of Chiang and his warlord cronies.

Truman moved to checkmate Mao's intention by deploying the US 7th Fleet to patrol the strait, ostensibly to maintain a psychological peace between the Chinese Civil War combatants. Clearly, the American naval blockade was emplaced for the protection of Chiang. The view of the US was that the retention of the strategic island as well as the safety of Chiang and his followers was crucial to American influence in the Far East.

Victory denied and mission aborted, Lin relocated his gigantic 4th Field Army to Canton, China, where his forces entrained for the unit's movement back to Antung (or Antong), the major border city in Manchuria.[133]

Lin's reasoning for this strategic movement was to place his fighting units in a location where they could come to the aid of the NKPA in any eventuality, subsequent to the NKPA strike on South Korea 25 June 1950.

Historians, military intelligence and analysts, not to be faulted, did their best to ascertain the leader of enemy forces in Korea during this time when the foe was a dark, secret, closed society.

Two questions may be posed.

Number One—How was it possible for American intelligence services, particularly the staff of General MacArthur's Supreme Command, Far East, to be naively unconcerned over such an enormous enemy troop build up, particularly when the war was not progressing well for the NKPA? The armies of some 400,000 Chinese troops were observed arriving in Manchuria during the late spring, coinciding with the commencement of the Korean War. The Chinese enemy seemed unconcerned in their Manchurian bases while training in full view of American bombing and reconnaissance aircraft flying near the North Korean/Manchurian border. American military tacticians took little notice of this ticking time

---

[133] Following on the heels of the Fourth field Army, elements of the Third Field Army, which consisted of the 20th through the 37th Armies moved to Manchuria in the late summer and early autumn of 1950. By mid-October the Chinese forces of the Third and Fourth Field Armies had concentrated more than 400,000 troops in Manchuria close to Korea. Appleman, p.751.

bomb. The alarm should have sounded in Tokyo and elsewhere that there had to be a significant rationale for the mammoth escalation of Chinese forces.

More to the point, and unbelievably, no one paid attention to what the government of *new* China was saying.[134] The prevailing notion was if Chinese forces were to have intervened in the war, the most appropriate time would have been during the onset of hostilities when Allied forces were virtually crushed and nearly pushed into the sea, during the bloodletting siege of the Pusan Perimeter. Apparently, no one of authority considered that as long as there was a buffer between Manchuria and South Korea, the Chinese had no interest in the internal affairs between the two Koreas.

Truman branded his armed intervention in Korea a *Police Action*. In turn, Mao labeled the Chinese People's Liberation Army *Volunteers*. Both antagonists knew full well the dangers of escalating the conflict beyond the borders of Korea, which could ignite the fuse sparking World War III.

Number Two—who then, was the actual leader of Chinese forces in Korea, commanding all Communist forces, including defeated remnants of the North Korean People's Army, now under direct authority of the CCF, at Chinese insistence?

Transcribed military chronicles state Lin was the supreme commander of all Communists forces in Korea. Yet there is another hypothesis that he begged off command commitment due to illness, and that Mao had to replace Lin for that reason. The truth is far more intriguing.

Now comes Peng Teh-huai—the most important person, on the same level as General MacArthur, and the General's antagonist in the Korean War. Low keyed and little recognized outside of the vast Asian nations, General Peng embodied the spirit of Chairman Mao, as Mao's surrogate. Peng was in fact, the instrumental opponent who dared challenge and subsequently defeat, in North Korea, the mightiest army in the world—that of the US.

Peng, strong, brawny, large-boned and slightly bow legged, was born

---

[134] It was no coincidence that Premier Chou En-lai, in a speech that same day – the first anniversary of the Chinese Communist state – warned the West that the Chinese people "will not tolerate foreign aggression and will not stand aside should the imperialists wantonly invade the territory of neighbor." This clear threat to intervene in the Korean War if UN troops crossed the 38th Parallel was ignored in Washington. The Joint Chiefs cabled MacArthur: "We desire that you proceed with your operations without any further explanations or announcements and let action determine the outcome. Toland, p. 235.

of peasantry. Like legions of his similarly uneducated, poverty-stricken peers, he turned to banditry in his teens in Hunan Province where he was raised. Peng, realizing that his disruptive actions were creating even more turmoil among his peers, changed objectives. With that, the General channeled his efforts into forging a concentrated and loyal Anti-Nationalist guerrilla band, which he commanded.

Mainland China was in chaotic, political upheaval at the time, ruled by corrupt warlords who divided the country into subdivisions for profit, exacting punishing revenues from the destitute, uneducated proletariat. Chiang Kai-shek, dictator, administrator and coordinator of the many warlords, was richly indemnified for his part. *Let them eat cake,* so goes the parable. No one in the ruling hierarchy of China at the time took heed of the fate of luckless Marie Antoinette. Civil war was inevitable.[135]

Born with the courage of a lion, Peng was described by one scholar as *having the body of a bull, and the face of a bull dog.* Twice wounded in hand-to-hand combat fighting Chiang's Nationalist Army, he feared no one. He read haltingly, but excelled in physical endurance and aggressiveness, winning the loyalty of those who served with him. Peng was the epitome of a *soldier's general*, asking none to do what he would not himself do.

Mao addressed an emergency conference of the Communist Party of China's Central Committee on 4 October 1950, at Yi Nien Hall, Peking, in regard to the NKPA, which was being dismantled and destroyed by UN forces. He said, "When a neighbor is in mortal danger, it is hard to stand by and watch, no matter how logical such a course may be."

Attendees squirmed restlessly in seats. All remained awkwardly mute, except loyal and non-threatening Mao's chief aide, Prime Minister Chou En-lai, who fervently believed in, and vigorously endorsed Mao's agenda. General Lin, recognized as China's foremost military commander, expressed profound trepidation in respect to engaging the US in armed conflict. General Lin postulated that America's armed strength, coupled with sole possession of atomic weaponry, ordained America an invincible force. Other attendees gathered in the assembly hall, save Peng, concurred with and echoed Lin's passionate assessment. The fact that the new Chinese

---

[135] Nationalist catastrophes were amplified by the favoritism, corruption, and inflation that plagued Chiang Kai-sheck's regime. Greedy generals stole their troops pay and rations, padded the payrolls with nonexistent soldiers and peddled medical supplies and equipment on the black market. Government bureaucrats, eager to make up for the lean years in war time Chungking, lost no time squeezing contractors and disposing of relief shipments and anything else capable of turning a profit. Spurr. P. 45.

government lacked matching high-technological weaponry was of little concern to General Peng. In Peng's view, an overwhelming superiority of manpower, coupled with exacting tactics, would dictate the course of a war and lead to a decisive conclusion. General Peng perceived an armed confrontation against the US as being little more than an extension and continuation of the Chinese Civil War. Peng proved to be dead right on all counts.

Yet Peng remained mute during the conference until it reconvened the following day. The general mulled the matter over during the night, and he resolutely believed that indeed, the Americans and South Koreans could be defeated in Korea. Peng was reluctant to speak earlier because of an insufficiency of vocabulary, even though he did graduate from the prestigious military academy, Whampoa. He threw in his lot with Mao.[136] Other conferees strenuously and fervently spoke against warring with the US, and after listening quietly for several minutes as contrary views were bantered about, Peng rose and defiantly roared to the startled, assembled commanders:

> It is necessary to send troops to aid North Korea. If the father land suffers great destruction, it only means that our victory will be delayed by several years, as it was in the war of liberation. If the United States has troops stationed in Taiwan and on the banks of the Yalu River, it can always start some excuse to start an invasion.

Chairman Mao agreed and ordered the forthcoming CCF invasion into North Korea to be implemented at once, with the sole responsibility of guiding the war bequeathed to General Peng.[137] The course of modern history pertaining to the Far East was forever altered.

Mao respected the loyalty and ability of Peng. However, though the two were comrades and colleagues, and Peng commanded the Chinese 1st

---

[136] Whampoa Military Academy was established by Dr. Sun Yat-sen, The "father" of modern China, and founder of the Kuomintang, Nationalist government. The prestigious military school, where thousands of future military leaders of China were trained, opened 16 June 1924. The academy boasts graduates from the Communist mainland as well as Nationalists exiled on the island of Taiwan. The academy is situated on the small island of Huagpu (Whampoa) in south China, on the Pearl River. Author.

[137] Chou En-lai's warning had not been mere rhetoric, and Chairman Mao had decided that very day to send troops to Korea to fight the Americans and South Koreans. Eighty percent of Chinese heavy industry lay in Manchuria; it "had" to be held. The Chinese troops, called the Volunteers Army, were to be led by their top field officer, Lin Paio, commander in chief of the Fourth Field Army. A wily man, Lin claimed to be sick, but many believed he had no relish for fighting the Americans. Toland, pp.235-236.

Field Army, Mao was frequently at odds over Peng's military philosophy. Mao believed guerrilla tactics were superior to Peng's military doctrine, which Peng learned at the military academy and adhered to with passion. Though it was Mao who planned and guided the war from his war room in the palace, it was Peng who implemented the strategies and tactics.[138] Mao was involved in the analysis of tactics of the NKPA since that fateful day of invasion, 25 June 1950. Further, it was Mao who later alerted Kim Il-sung as to the imminent location of MacArthur's amphibious assault, exactly as to time and day. Mao was capable of reading tide charts as well as MacArthur. But he continued to have philosophical differences with Peng in regard to the war tactics of the Chinese Volunteers.

Author Toland corroborated the fact that *new* China was indeed reluctant to engage the US in armed hostilities. When the Mao Communists convened the conference, the Korean War for all practical purposes was successfully concluded. The NKPA was unequivocally defeated, reduced to shattered, disorganized remnants of a once mightily-armed, equipped and trained military complement. Now, the remaining embattled, stray North Korean soldiers could and should have been methodically hunted down and destroyed by ROK soldiers.

If, at the time, armed action against stray enemy soldiers was put in place solely by the ROK Army, Communist China would have been denied the excuse, indeed the right, to intercede, predicated upon the policy of non interference in internal affairs between the Koreas. Had Communist China invaded North Korea, the UN and the international community would have branded Communist China as an aggressor and in violation of international law. The UN had the authority to respond forcefully by all means available, including implementation of economic sanctions, i.e. embargoes and naval blockades of China's crucial ports.

Concurrently during this critical phase of history, Communist China was assiduously attempting to become the recognized, legitimate representative of China in the UN, seated in place of Nationalist China, who forfeited that right as an exiled, impotent government. The US was at-

---

[138] Yet Mao alone remained unconvinced of these lessons, and above all disputed Peng's downgrading of the importance of political officers, who in early stages of the Korean War constituted 10 percent of every formation's leadership down to sub-unit level. If the PLA was to be armed and organized like any other army, then it must depend on soviet weapons and equipment to an extent Mao found intolerable. When he purged Peng Te-huia and other senior PLA officers, he reversed their policies and preserved the PLA in much the way it was forged in the civil war. Hastings, p. 335.

tempting just as forcefully to block China from the coveted membership.

When ROK, American and Allied troops crossed the 38th Parallel into Communist North Korea, 9 October 1950, the equation immediately changed. It was new China that fervently believed that the Communist state was to be the next invasion targeted by the US. Certainly General MacArthur insolently vocalized that intent during numerous public forums. Under intense political pressure by the US, the UN branded China an armed aggressor for entering the Korean War. There was much disagreement throughout the international community as to who were the perpetrators and who were the victims. Was it the alleged provocative conduct of the UN of crossing into North Korea which subsequently opened the floodgates of Chinese intervention? Or rather was it Communist China who provoked armed aggression against members of the exalted body of international law, the UN? The UN postulated that the sole intent of the international body was to attempt to quench, or at the very least contain, the out of control fires of war in the besieged peninsula.

Peng was not reticent to challenge Mao about battle strategies.[139] They were comrades and collaborators since the onset of the Chinese Civil War, exchanging battle theories and concepts, with the ultimate objective of destroying Chiang's Nationalist Army.

Despite his unswerving loyalty to Mao, and regardless of his extraordinary victories on the battlefield, eventually the differences with Mao were to be General Peng's undoing,

General Peng's staff, quartered in the ancient capitol of Manchuria, Mukden, (now Shenyang) set up an operations base to conduct the new war from the political sanctuary of Manchuria. Commander Peng flew in a few days later and began at once to plan his military operation against UN forces. It was now the middle of October with autumn leaves falling, the odious scent of looming war hanging heavily in the crisp, fall air.

Peng ordered an enormous topographical model of the entire Korean Peninsula to be constructed, exact in every detail, where, in due course, it came to be the focal point of the war room. By use of the model as a

---

[139] The news of the crippling losses at Changjin so upset General Peng that he flew to Peking for a showdown with Mao Zedong. This much has been recorded in recent Chinese writings. Peng stormed into the Chairman's villa in Zhong Nan Hai one morning in late December, dragging him out of bed and creating an embarrassing fuss. Chinese troops in Korea were approaching exhaustion Peng loudly proclaimed; their equipment clothing, and logistics were entirely unsuited to a protracted, attritional campaign. The fiasco in northeast Korea showed that. The Third Phase offensive against Seoul would peter out disastrously, he predicted, unless the Soviets stopped applauding from the sidelines, got off their backsides, and poured in equipment and supplies. Spurr, pp. 266-7.

guide, Peng directed his battle commanders to traverse specific areas, shrewdly directing his mighty armies through the hills and mountains of North Korea.

There was no equivocation on Peng's part to engage the US and the Allies in this forthcoming mother of all battles. Peng and his assistants brimmed with confidence, confidently believing that the CCF could indeed, rout the Allies. All the while, MacArthur and his naive staff downplayed any CCF threat of intervention, certain it was tactically impossible for Chinese Communists to wage war against America and the Allies.

General Peng commanded a massive light-infantry force, but the ranks of the Volunteers had but few weapons of any consequence or conventionality. However, what the immeasurable peasant army lacked in bullets was made up by enormous numbers of troops. There was absolutely no end to the aggregate of loyal and dedicated common peasant soldiers. The manpower pool was a Chinese bottomless abyss that could field fresh, eager combatants forever.

Poorly armed and equipped, supplied with an illogical arsenal of Russian, Japanese and American small arms, the enemy also lacked vital basic infantry support units. The Chinese had no artillery, tanks, air power, rockets or rocket launchers. Instead they possessed loyalty and determination. The CCF, initially armed with few rifles, machine guns or mortars, amassed high-powered weapons through smothering infantry tactics, quickly overwhelming entire Allied units, and in the process, confiscating huge allotments of attendant arms and munitions.

The CCF lacked a sophisticated supply system, and relied exclusively on coolie labor that forged onward on foot, slightly to the rear of the attacking troops. Necessary to sustain a prolonged offensive, the itinerant cargo bearers were equipped with A-frames—crude, ancient, but efficient back packs. An average laborer carried 400 pounds of essential supplies to provide their aggressive, mobile army with needed equipment. Enemy supply lines were drastically overextended, from Peking to the fighting front. Motorized equipment was nearly nonexistent as a result of the protracted civil war against the Nationalists. The CCF was little more than a shoe-string, foot-oriented army.

Chinese soldiers were for the most part illiterate farmland peasants, lacking sophistication to operate high-tech weaponry, which fortunately for the Allies, was lacking as well. Troops were highly indoctrinated in Chinese Communist ideology, many having joined the insurgency earlier to overthrow the corrupt Nationalist government. Because of the lack of education, they were, as a rule, highly susceptible to leftist Communist propaganda, and they all avidly believed in their cause. Most were dedicated, fearless troops, possessing raw courage to perform to the maximum at the direction of commanders. Their abilities to sustain themselves on long, sometimes 20-hour marches, and then forcefully engage the enemy, were legendary. Rapid, mobile infantrymen survived on a basic ration of coarse grains carried with them allowing them to drive forward on foot, at lightning speeds and with courageous ferociousness.

Moreover, at the beginning of this armed revolution, and prior, during and following the exile of the Chinese Nationalist government, the military command of the CCF was one of benevolence. There was an absence of physical rank insignia between officers and soldiers. Communist soldiers knew their leaders by sight and fought alongside with them; consequently there was no need to distinguish officers with visible rank. And, unlike the Nationalist Army, for the most part there was an absence of corruption.

When the victorious Communists initially seized control of the mainland, the hierarchy immediately put into force anti-corruption measures which rippled through the population, almost immediately improving the quality of life of the peasantry. Even more importantly, it instilled fervor, passion and unquestionable loyalty among the soldiery. The militia would fight to the death in defense of these principles, reinforced by the governmental policy of equality to all.

Most substantially however, every person from Mao on down to the last pitiful soldier adamantly believed that the US was set on a collision course with China, with America's ultimate goal being the invasion and ultimate conquest of new China.

Electronic communications were nonexistent. Swift, young, unarmed couriers raced on foot carrying hand-written messages from one unit to another, the majority of the time under heavy artillery barrage. When a runner fell, another would take his place. Those dedicated couriers, once a message was delivered, stood by gasping for air, as commanders responded with written replies. Once again the youthful couriers were off, braving artillery fire, sprinting from one command to another, delivering vital messages in an archaic manner.

Concomitant with the primitive message system, surging infantry units attacking Allied lines relied on basic signaling devices to coordinate the ferocious attacks. Whistles, bugles, gongs, pyrotechnic devices such as flares, even shepherd's horns were employed to direct the peasant soldiers. Those signals, primarily implemented for CCF tactical movements, had a dual purpose, for they likewise unnerved the typical American fighting soldier. None ever had to cope with such a bewildering, frightening array of signals in a modern, technological army. It was a psychological nightmare to American soldiers, inducing a Pavlovian, subconscious reaction to signals which invariably portended massive infantry attack by the CCF.

Attack at night was the CCF mandate. Survivors of the Pusan Perimeter and other armed skirmishes were aware of these dreadful night assaults but they quickly adapted to them or they died. Deplorably however, the vast majority of American youth committed to battle against the Chinese infantry were inexperienced, raw replacements who faced, for the very first time, as MacArthur so aptly uttered, an entirely new enemy.

All of these maneuvers ordered by General Peng were to aggravate and eventually break the Allied forces in North Korea.

> In the period from 24 November to 25 December 1950 - one month - a series of disasters unequalled in our country's history overwhelmed American arms. The events seemed to spell utter and total defeat. When the Chinese troops entered the Korean War and confronted Americans, it marked the first time the United States found itself in military conflict with a communist force. Appleman, p. 4.

The war limped hopelessly on, stymied by intractable demands made during acrimonious negotiations with the Communists. The overriding demand of mandatory repatriation of all prisoners proved to be an unacceptable stipulation to the Allies, who, in turn, demanded voluntary repatriations supervised by UN agencies. Negotiations broke down and the war abruptly escalated and continued for yet another two years. Both adversaries elevated the conflict to an unsustainable level as tens of thousands of Chinese assault troops were slain in what reverted into a political war of attrition. Communist China proved to be the clear loser in terms of numbers of battle casualties, exhausting hundreds of thousands of young lives who could have better served in the rehabilitation of the Mainland after the protracted, bloody Chinese Civil War.

China blinked first. While they professed to enjoy a fathomless chasm of manpower, the Allies, under the gifted leadership of General Ridgway, were grinding them up without pause, until China ultimately realized that Phase Three Chinese Offensive was null and void. China realized that their forces were incapable of ejecting the Allies from the peninsula, and the cost of attempting to do so became so astronomical that they, along with representatives of the NKPA, returned to the bargaining table.[140]

Communist China was subjected to international criticism. It knew full well that a disproportionate number of Chinese prisoners would refuse repatriation to Communist China.[141] Many of the Chinese prisoners were former soldiers of Nationalist China who surrendered to the Communists during the Civil War. It was generally accepted that by surrendering the second time, they would be deemed unreliable and traitorous by the new Chinese government. Forcibly repatriating these subjects to their country of origin would be tantamount to murder. Those questionable prisoners would be subject to torture or death once they were again under the authority of the Communist government.

Through arduous, rancorous, on-off negotiations, the ferocious war eventually wound down and key representatives from both sides of the conflict finally agreed to an armistice on 27 July 1953.[142]

Every soldier on each side of the battlefield huddled in protective foxholes, not wishing to be the last statistic of this bloody conflict. At the agreed upon appointed hour, 10 p.m., both sides fired off pyrotechnics in recognition and celebration of the termination of the three-year brutal conflict. When cessation-of-conflict flares burst open, ripping the starlit sky apart, one American GI curled in his foxhole was heard to murmur, "Who won?"

Virtually every veteran of the Korean War can remember precisely what they were doing on that fateful day when the armistice was signed. Yet, there remain but a handful of veterans alive today who know that the date of 27 July invokes an even more powerful recollection. For it was three years earlier, exactly to the day, that the two battalions of the 29th

---

[140] As Peng was signing the armistice, he was thinking, "Because we have done this once, it means we will do it again and again in the future. This is a happy day for our people." The Chinese People's Volunteer Army and the Korean's People's Army had stood shoulder to shoulder against the strongest armies in the west. "Through three years of fighting together the Volunteers had forged a comradeship in blood with the North Korean people and their army- a friendship which furthered deepened and strengthened our international feelings." Toland, p. 576.

[141] The screen, or polling, of CCF and NKPA POWs began in early April 1952. The results astounded the United Nations. At the half way mark in the polling of the 132,000 military POWs, the U N found that about 40,000 would resist repatriation to the Communists. On the basis of these figures, the UN projected that of the total 132,000 military POWs (plus 38,000 North Korean civilian internees) only a total of about 70,000 would elect to return to Communist control. This could be a great propaganda coup for the UN, but it also posed the danger that the Communists would lose face to such a degree that they would terminate the talks. Blair, p.965.

[142] Blair, p.975.

Infantry Regiment, dispatched from Okinawa, ceased to exist. The 1st Battalion met their horrific fate at the small village of Anui, while the 3rd Battalion, dispatched to the west, in an area called Hadong, was to meet their doom. We few remember.

The date of cessation of armed hostilities is recalled with relief throughout the lands of many nations. Peace was expected to follow. But it was not to be. The armistice signaled a time to embark on a crusade of peace and rebuilding. Instead the conflict continues. In fact, as of this writing, there has been a dramatic escalation of incidents ratcheting to nuclear-threat level.

Subsequent to the armistice, Peng Te-huia returned to China, a national hero, to the gratitude of a thankful nation. In the eyes of the Chinese citizens, Peng was the leader who vanquished the US Army in North Korea. At that time, no other nation in history had been capable of defeating the American Army.[143]

Indubitably, it was the first time in the relatively short history of the US there was resounding defeat of America in a major armed conflict. This defeat eventually led to the ten-year military debacle of the Vietnam War.[144]

Peng relinquished control of the Chinese People's Volunteers and two years later, when the People's Liberation Army was reorganized, General

---

[143] Sadly, the bitter taste of defeat was revisited upon the United States following the Vietnam War. A face-saving armistice was again signed, this time in Paris, France; but reality is reality and a defeat is a defeat. Tactical and political errors that led to the Korean War were repeated. The US rushed to judgment and repeated the same dreadful mistake in the Vietnam War, a conflict that our country became inextricably tied to by virtue of failing to gain the victory of the unification of Korea. It is crucial to curtail these misguided adventures in the future, and to that end, it is my fervent aspiration that I have provided adequate data to remind us to question America's foreign policies. Author.

[144] To a great extent Vietnam began as an attempt to restore American military pride, as an effort to recoup the prestige that had been lost in Korea. And when things began to go wrong in Vietnam, memories of Korea perversely made American military leaders all the more determined to continue, certain that they could profit from their military mistakes and thus do things right the second time around. Tragically, the Korean War failed to teach the United States the vital lessons—about Asian nationalism as distinct from international Communism, about the impossibility of fighting a "moral" war against guerillas, and about the futility of technological warfare against an enemy largely independent of mechanized transport—that might have spared the nation the fiasco of Vietnam. Whelan, p. xiv.

Peng was one of ten generals promoted to the esteemed rank of Marshal, an illustrious honor for his dauntless daring, as well as evidence of his prolonged benevolent association with Mao. At the time, Peng was second in seniority of the original army group.

Mao, symptomatic of megalomaniacal leaders, firmly believed that his innate abilities as a guerrilla commander transformed into a credo that he was an omnipotent leader in all aspects of government. This resulted in many failed endeavors, one of which was the Great Leap Forward, causing the deaths of millions of citizens by famine. Some historians place the loss of life at 30 million innocent souls. Mao resorted to the unworkable tenets of collective farming, which swiftly bankrupted the nation and caused massive, unchecked starvation. Mao learned nothing from the same ill-planned and utterly failed procedure in the Soviet Union.

General Peng's loyalty to Mao was for naught. Mao Tse-tung apparently forgot that it was Peng and Peng alone who agreed with and supported the Chairman's plan of war in North Korea. Moreover, it was General Peng who unquestioningly implemented Mao's battle plans, formulated in Peking far from the war zone. Regretfully, Peng failed to discern Mao's transformation in personality. Peng's tradition of speaking his mind continued, based on the belief he had that right, since he was a loyal devoted disciple of Mao.

Chairman Mao didn't quite see it that way. Peng was seditious in the eyes of Mao, who conveniently forgot the early days of the revolution, when Peng was an equal, empowered to lead his own forces against Chiang Kai-shek.

Mao stripped Peng of command and banished him to a labor camp in far-off Sichuan province. Mao trusted but one person in his Politburo and that person was Prime Minister Chou En-lai. Chou, a sophisticated, urbane diplomat, was respected internationally. Chou was the personification of the New China which generally brought international respect and acceptance of Mao's regime. But more important, Chou was the one person that Mao perceived as being entirely loyal in that Chou did not aspire to a higher calling. Chou's foremost allegiance was to Mao, and he was content to represent China on the world stage, as the official spokesman for Mao and his philosophy.

It was Chou who sounded the alarm to the world in regard to foreign forces crossing into North Korea. He insisted that China had every right to intervene militarily in North Korea, to protect China's territory adjacent to the border. His warnings fell on deaf ears in Washington, which relied primarily on the word of General MacArthur, who maintained that China would not dare to intervene.

Mao's spiral into demented and obsessive belief that his subordinates were attempting to wrest control of the country from him, forced him to take dramatic action to insure his control. Mao Tse-sung appealed directly to the proletariat, who persistently showed collective adulation of him. That misplaced, collective loyalty was the catalyst that spawned the dreaded, infamous Cultural Revolution. Mao, while keeping a tight rein to protect his power, transferred the authority of the state to rebellious, restless students who earlier had frequently contested the legitimacy of the new Communist government.

An abundance of information has been recorded relative to the insidious methods of Mao's illogical Cultural Revolution movement which eventually became contaminated, causing the very soul of China to implode. Despite his extraordinary, revered standing with the people, Peng was not immune nor excluded from the brutality of the Red Guards.

An editorial committee published Peng's memoirs in 1982, eight years after he died at the inhumane hands of the notorious Red Guards:

> Peng Dehuai's refusal to admit any crime infuriated his interrogators. They kicked him until his ribs were fractured and lungs injured. Beatings sent him unconscious to the floor.
>
> He fought to the last. It is said that the noise he made banging on the table and shouting at his investigators shook the house.
>
> "I fear nothing; you can shoot me!" he roared. "Your days are numbered. The more you interrogate, the firmer I'll become."
>
> Peng De-huai was interrogated until he was bedridden. He was deprived of the right to sit, to rise up, to drink water, to go to the toilet or to turn over in bed. By the time he died on November 29th, 1974, he had gone through over 130 interrogations. Spurr, p. 315.

General Peng's demise affected the American public not at all. Nonetheless, veterans of the Battle of the Chongchon, American and Allied prisoners of war, and everyone who stood and fought the Chinese soldiers, generally conceded a very important particular. The Chinese warriors by and large were dedicated, fierce fighters. The role of the infantryman on both sides of the echelon is to kill as many adversaries as possible, lest the favor is returned in kind. Yet, there were numerous accounts of humane treatment by the Chinese soldiers. Wounded, captured Americans were frequently released by Chinese captors and allowed to return to Allied military control. Repatriated American prisoners of war testified that treatment and food doled to Allied prisoners by Chinese captors was noticeably better than they received under the harsh regime of the NKPA.

An international outcry in respect to the brutal handling and inordinate deaths of Allied prisoners by the North Koreans caused the Chinese to relieve the NKPA of responsibility for the prison camps. The newly-founded Chinese Communist government was more cognizant of international concern than the perverse, secretive society of North Korea. In the words of one former American prisoner of war, "It was heaven on earth when the Chinks took over!"

The omnipotent shadow of General Peng covered more than the responsibility of fielding and guiding Chinese troops in battle. By his comportment, General Peng set the standard for civilized conduct of his charges, and the rate of unspeakable atrocities significantly lessened in comparison to the brutal NKPA. Indeed, the war-time interaction by both sides of the respective governments in this conflict has affected the political climate today. America is still at war with the People's Democratic Republic of Korea. We are at peace with the Chinese Communist government, thanks to the superb and professional leadership of Generals Peng and Ridgway, who together embodied principles of civilized behavior, though ironically on blood soaked battlefields.

~~

Now an account of General Walton *Johnnie* Walker is in order. Walker, nicknamed after the scotch whiskey brand, had been the commanding general of the US 8th Army since the conclusion of World War II. During momentous battles in World War II, Walker served with distinction under his mentor and friend, General Patton in the European Theater of operations (ETO). Later Walker was to become General Peng's primary antagonist, until his (Walker's) untimely, violent death.

When the occupation of Japan was initiated as a condition of surrender following the cessation of World War II, Walker was charged with the responsibility of training and maintaining the various American infantry divisions under 8th Army command, primarily on the principal Japanese island of Honshu. Sufficient space to conduct military training operations was severely limited and as a result, various American occupational units were literally scattered haphazardly from one location on Honshu to another. Added to that were draconian fiscal cutbacks to the budget of the Department of Defense.

Walker tried to make do with what he had, but he didn't have much. World War II combat veterans were rotated home to a grateful nation, discharged from the armed forces. Replacement troops were generally very young, uneducated school dropouts who yearned to see another part of the world before embarking on a civilian career.

When those inexperienced teenage soldiers arrived in occupied Japan, it was a heavenly experience. Everyone employed a shoe-shine boy or a lady in waiting at little cost, while field training was slight to nonexistent. Additionally the 8th Army was widely dispersed, and component divisions within the 8th Army were inconveniently separated. No coherent training was implemented because of time, distance, and budget constraints, and no one seemed concerned.

Hide out and don't be seen was the unofficial order from NCOs who practiced what they preached. The unofficial place of duty was the local beer hall in towns off post where proprietors and bar-girls profited from idle post personnel.

When the Korean War exploded, political debris fell all over the western world. A frenzy to do something, anything to stem the flood of invading NKPA was placed at the top of every political agenda. Those adolescent, beer-drinking, cigarette-smoking, insufficiently combat-trained soldiers were hurriedly called upon to end this naked aggression, perpetrated by the well-organized and exceptionally-trained NKPA. President Truman picked up the gauntlet and the rest is history.

General Walker was called upon, and he was determined to stop the enemy dead in their tracks. The operation was to begin at a key rail center southwest of Seoul, the recently fallen capitol of South Korea. To that end, GHQ Tokyo ordered an immediate airlift operation to transport occupation soldiers to the war zone. However, there was a problem of coordination between the two services. The Air Force, now an independent service, was at a crossroads with the Army. Ongoing high-level personality and territorial clashes relating to command and/or coordination negated any effective cooperation between the two services.

The Air Force loathed the role of ferrying Army assault troops for operational and tactical purposes, and as a result, they gave the Army the lowest priority. Ideal flying weather was a requisite for the Air Force because of the responsibility of carrying a significant aggregate of troops and combat equipment. Sufficient well-maintained landing fields were necessary to accommodate the approximately two dozen Douglas C-54s, but aircraft were either unavailable or their use drastically curtailed as a result of grave budget limitations on the Department of Defense. A large portion of these aircraft were grounded for maintenance because of fatigued parts, notably caused by numerous flights delivering tactical supplies to the outgunned ROK Army and evacuating American dependants from the war zone on return flights.

As a result of Air Force insufficiencies, only a minor complement of approximately 450 raw, untrained troops were flown to Korea, then rushed by train to the war zone. The remainder of the unit comprised of about half of a battalion, two rifle companies and a couple of heavy weapons platoons were dispatched by sea.[145]

Eighth Army military equipment was either non-existent or written off as unusable. Left over from World War II, nothing functioned, and it was an excuse to do nothing. Riflemen in the infantry never fired their weapons in occupied Okinawa, and the same lack of training standards existed throughout the Far East Command.

Being forced into the Korean War abruptly ended the soft, pleasant life in Japan and Okinawa, as ineffective, inexperienced adolescent troops were plugged into the breach of Korea in early July 1950 to stop the hemorrhaging of the ROK Army, and to stand against the mighty North Korean invaders. The ROK troops were found to be as untrained and as ill-equipped as the volunteer peacetime American occupation soldiers.

Military analysts, critical of General Walker's initial piece-meal troop commitments to the armed conflict, attempted to justify the supposition by pointing to the overwhelming volume of body bags carrying thousands of dead young Americans back home to final resting places. Actually it was General MacArthur who called up these various combat units throughout the Far East. It was Walker who placed them into defensive chasms as soon as the unqualified, immature troops arrived. There was no margin to spare.

---

[145] General Dean, determined to hold strategic Taejon as long as possible, was only too aware on July 12 that the reinforcements landing in Korea from Japan were by no means prepared for war. In the summer of 1949 General Walker had begun a training program to get Eighth Army troops into combat readiness after their long period of occupation duties. Although most of his troops had progressed through battalion training, none had had advanced to regimental, division or army levels; nor had any maneuvers been carried out, since there was no space to do them in crowded Japan.

The equipment that arrived in Korea was old and worn. Some vehicles had to be towed to the LST's (landing ships, tank) bound for Pusan. Most radios were inoperative, and many weapons, from M-1's to mortars, were not fit for combat. The first troops arriving did not even have cleaning supplies for their weapons. Toland, p. 91.

Task Force Smith was pulverized at Osan, and the two battalions of the Okinawan-based 29th Infantry Regiment at Anui and Hadong were nearly annihilated. Yet, at this juncture, there was no alternative to the constrictions placed by the lack of readiness. To delay until sufficient forces could be fielded was to allow time for the enemy to conquer the territory. The Republic of Korea would have been lost had the Army hesitated in the commitment of piece-meal units.

That was the war that was thrust upon General Walker, and although he readily accepted the challenge, he did not realize that he would end up fighting the war from the rear in Tokyo as well as from the front in South Korea. At the commencement of hostilities, General Walker assembled the high level division commanders of the fighting infantry forces and he spoke to them strictly and candidly, given the grievous alternative.

> "I want you to forget about our successes in World War Two," he said. "Remember the failures. We're like those Americans that faced the Japanese in the early days. Few of our commanders have combat experience. Our troops are poorly trained and in lousy shape. Equipment is in a sorry state.
>
> We lack adequate communications. The supply system is suffering from growing pains. And fire support is almost nonexistent. Many of you think we're better than the enemy. We're not! That's being proven right now north of Taejon. But we're going to turn things around." Toland, p. 94.

Still, the argument for being prepared ruled supreme. The *what ifs* came to light. America emerged as one of two world powers following World War II, but then slipped into indifference following the victorious conclusion of the War. Resting complacently on its laurels because it was the sole nation to possess the atomic bomb, the US was jolted into global reality when the same components of the bomb were acquired by the USSR. Students of military history believe that the US should never have committed to war in Korea in that unprepared military condition.[146]

In fairness to General Walker, the blame for the Korean debacle should have been equally proportioned to all involved. President Truman initiated this terrible calamity by first drastically slashing the military budget, with the blessings and consent of Congress. Then, without due consideration, the President ordered untrained, ill-equipped and under-

---

[146] The occupation of Japan was a big drain on army resources in the post war years. As Truman cut military budgets deeper and deeper the Army was hard pressed to support MacArthur with adequate forces. Complicating this problem was another, closely linked: the occupation of nearby South Korea. Blair, p. 36.

strength troops into combat.

Little credit was given to General Walker's vast accomplishments, particularly during the awful, incessant siege of the Pusan Perimeter. Walker was the ugly stepchild, living under the monumental shadow of his commander, MacArthur.

> From the outset Johnnie Walker's relationship with Douglas MacArthur and GHQ was distant and cool, and it remained that way. Perhaps Walker, no diplomat, disliked MacArthur and could not - or would not - disguise his feelings. Perhaps he was intimidated by MacArthur's soaring intellect and oratorical eloquence or put off by his obsessive search for the limelight, or having served and idolized Patton, perhaps Walker found all other bosses lacking. Blair, p. 36.

It appeared MacArthur felt that Walker could not accomplish any assignment correctly, even though this author concluded, reinforced by tireless research, that it was Walker, and solely Walker, who masterminded the eventual triumph of the Pusan Perimeter. Despite the drastic shortage of men and munitions he had to defend against a superior, overwhelming enemy power.

At age 61 on 3 December, during his command of 8th Army, which was to be his final tour of duty, General Walker was toiling far more hours a day than a man in his forties. The general flew an average of over four hours a day, every day, to reconnoiter and chart the shifting enemy positions during the first phase of the bloodiest fighting of the war.[147]

Once, during a daily reconnaissance flight to reconnoiter enemy troop movement, his pilot, Captain Mike Lynch, on orders of Walker, stalled the two-seat observation plane by cutting the single engine to glide silently over the heads of fleeing American soldiers. Walker leaned out of the gliding airplane and screamed at the top of his lungs:

> "Get back there you yellow sons of bitches! Get back there and fight!!" He turned to Lynch. Have you got three stars on the plane?" No, but I've got one of your star flags. Lynch stuck the flag out as they clipped the tops of trees in a creek bed. He now had the motor idling as Walker kept yelling, and put on power just before it stalled. The men were running, many without helmets and weapons. Lynch could hear someone shriek, "They're going to kill us!" After twenty minutes the plane was drawing enemy fire. "Jesus Christ, said Lynch, "we can't do this anymore!" Besides, the shouting of Walker had no effect. The men were petrified. Toland, p. 165

---

[147] General Walker had three reconnaissance planes at his disposal, one of which lacked the markings of the insignia of rank of the three-star general. Author.

Never in contemporary military history has so much documentation been presented about conflict between military tacticians.[148] The 8th Army Commander, lauded in World War II as a brilliant strategist, was relegated to a role of mediocrity by MacArthur, who deemed Walker to be incompetent. It begs the question as to how a commanding officer could be acknowledged and valued as a brilliant military strategist in one major world conflict by exceptional military superiors, but later, in another combat theater, would be judged as an ineffectual commander.

The 1st Provisional Marine Brigade was committed to battle in early August 1950, during what was to become the primary defensive phase of the Korean War, the Pusan Perimeter. While the ever shrinking Perimeter, now about half the size of Rhode Island, would aid Allied defenders by drawing them closer together for a strengthened, unified front, there was a deplorable lack of reserve units to be rushed to the vanguard whenever the enemy would breach the defensive line. Every soldier on line knew the consequences. They were to stand or die.

A brief explanation is in order in respect to combat tactics of the enemy. The offensive tactics of the NKPA were to forge a unified, suicidal, massive attack along the entire defensive echelon—the sole intent was to rupture the protective line. However, once a chasm was open to the enemy, the NKPA lacked the resources of massive manpower to persist in the drive because they had committed their entire cadre of combat soldiers to simultaneous attack throughout the entire front. The NKPA also lacked sufficient reserve units to follow through.

Conversely, Chinese Communist attack forces concentrated numerically superior forces in what they perceived to be weak areas, often times targeted at defending ROK units. Once a defensive line was breached, the Chinese poured thousands of eager soldiers standing in reserve through shattered lines with the objective of rushing south while avoiding engagement with their enemy. Once to the rear of a particular battle site, the Chinese initiated flanking attacks east and west, and ultimately surrounded

---

[148] From the very beginning Walker's assessment of NKPA intentions had clashed with those of MacArthur, whose contact with Eighth Army, except for infrequent visits, had been through his staff. This was a new experience for Walker. While commanding George Patton's Ghost Corps, Walker had earned a reputation as being one of America's finest tactical commanders. He was used to talking personally to Patton, Bradley, and, on occasion, Eisenhower during critical phases of World War II. Walker had another problem. As one of Eisenhower's close friends, he was privy to MacArthur's failures as a tactician in the past. From his arrival in Korea, Walker never doubted his own fate of how he might be treated by history. But he was too much a soldier to let it bother him. Toland, p. 162.

beaten units, allowing the Chinese to annihilate entire units piecemeal. Allied reinforcements rushing to the aid of beleaguered trapped Allies were repulsed by steel curtains of firepower.

Even though several thousand enemy troops frequently overran American positions and broke through the Pusan Perimeter, General Walker, by strategic planning, was able to redirect forces to block gaps where enemy had ruthlessly crashed through. In those instances, when lines were ultimately stabilized, insurgent forces were trapped and attackers vanquished.

Came the monsoons, and with them, the NKPA 7th Division, under cover of a sopping quilt of brutal, undulating rain. Charging through fragile defensive lines hastily vacated by the Marine 1st Provisional Brigade, the enemy 7th struck viciously in full force. Lightly armed defenders engaged in horrific battles continuing all night on land turned to insufferable quagmire. As the superiorly-numbered, armed and trained enemy divisions broke through, the frail, lightly-manned Perimeter began to crumble. There were no reserve units remaining to plug into this breached defense line held by the Americans. The American 7th Infantry Division, pulled from occupation duties in Japan, was to rendezvous with the 1st Marine Division at Pusan for the strike at Inchon, while Walker's under strength besieged forces were fighting desperately to hold.

MacArthur ordered Walker to issue the Stand or Die ultimatum to his 8th Army. MacArthur not only rebuffed Walker's frequent requests for additional reinforcements to bolster the Perimeter, MacArthur in fact, *stripped* the Pusan Perimeter of the Marine Brigade! It was imperative for MacArthur to ensure the success of the Inchon landing at any cost, knowing a triumphant, amphibious landing would be the crown jewel of his career. The General left nothing to chance in respect to the imminent outcome, other than the few thousand lives of embattled soldiers on line at the Perimeter. Kim Il-sung was resolute in his obsession to break through and liberate Pusan, thereby uniting the entire peninsula under the flag of Communism.

Enemy combatants concealed by thick blankets of rain swarmed through the hills but were systematically cut down by valiant young ROKs and Americans, knowing their backs were to the sea. There was no more retreating. This was where they would Stand or Die.

> The next day, September 7th, survivors of the People's 7th Division were escaping over the Nam River near its junction with the Naktong, while Americans were burying more than two thousand North Korean dead discovered be-

hind their lines. Walker's casualties had been heavy, but those inflicted on the enemy were far more serious. The outnumbered, outgunned enemy had fought fiercely but to no avail. The Pusan Perimeter was intact. The crisis was over. Toland, p. 174.

In reality, the fighting continued to rage far beyond 7 September. Author Toland erred in respect to the date of 7 September, but he corrected himself with the following clarification, in consideration that the Inchon landing struck in force on 15 September 1950.

Whereas Inchon units had met scattered resistance, perimeter troops were encountering fanatical forces in prepared positions on dominant terrain. Every attack was fiercely resisted. Toland, p. 205.

Clearly, General Walker was placed in an inescapable box. Added to this sorry state of affairs, MacArthur continued to vocalize displeasure in respect to his perception of the competency of General Walker.[149]

To speak disparagingly to subordinate personnel of the immediate commander was equally disquieting. If MacArthur was not confident of Walker's abilities, he should have removed him at the appropriate time. Moreover, in reality, Walker's performance before and when the Perimeter was formed, was nothing short of brilliant; but because of MacArthur's ego, Walker was forced into disquieting shadows. General MacArthur believed that if the conflict strayed into troubled waters, it was Walker's blunder. If the Perimeter held, it was because of the unquestionable, gifted military tactics of MacArthur, who authorized Walker's tactics. MacArthur was delusional, for the history of the Korean War painted an entirely different portrait of him than he saw of himself.

That MacArthur excised essential troops from the struggling, intrepid remnants of the 8th Army at the Pusan Perimeter, leaving the fate of isolated, outnumbered soldiers to the battle-hardened enemy, was unconscionable. In order to assure the accomplishment of his Inchon dream, MacArthur ensured that sufficient troops were on hand to accomplish his mission, without regard of the nonstop bloody conflict at the Perimeter.

Author Clair Blair, in an adroit account of the Korean War, stoked the smoldering fires of controversy in respect to the command presence of General Walker:

---

[149] "We have been bastard children lately, and as far as our engineering equipment is concerned we are in pretty bad shape." He added, "I don't want you to think that I am dragging my heels, but I have a river across my whole front." Toland, p. 210.

Walker's generalship in Korea was to draw mixed reviews. He was not physically or mentally imposing. He did not have a "command presence" or a clever mind or a glib tongue. He was not a warm person. He rarely smiled; He had no sense of humor. He was a "fighter," but except for his closest advisors, he was not well liked. On the whole the nickname the press gave him in Korea - Bulldog Walker - seemed a fitting one, except in one regard: He would not challenge his superior, MacArthur. In that relationship he groveled, lest he lose his job. Blair, p. 555.

However, John Toland provided an entirely different assessment of the personality of General Walker, during the general's thankless command of the 8th Army:

Walker had saved his army, but few appreciated the importance of his accomplishments. He never received credit for conducting one of the finest mobile defenses in military history. His successor, General Matthew B. Ridgway, identified one reason why Walker never gained recognition. MacArthur, he wrote, hungered for praise and this "led him on some occasions to claim or accept credit for deeds he had not performed, or to disclaim responsibility for mistakes that were clearly his own".

Years later, a British author, Callum MacDonald, came to Walker's defense. "As for Walker, his crime was to be associated with an embarrassing defeat in an army with a cult of winning. It is difficult to believe that any other general could have done any better. Toland, p. 374.

It is difficult to gain an uncorrupted perspective of General Walker; he is both lauded and criticized, shown in contrast by conflicting opinions of knowledgeable authors. The outcome is left to the ashes of history as to who may ultimately rule on his successes or shortcomings. Military analysts and authors writing about the Forgotten War praise Walker for his gallant stand at the Perimeter, as well as for his ethical courage to stand against MacArthur's 24 November order. By subsequently countermanding MacArthur's injunction for the 8th Army to race without due diligence to the Manchurian border, Walker had to have saved the lives of thousands of American soldiers.

It is of interest to note that during the entire war, both the NKPA and the Chinese Communist Volunteers lacked the sophistication of electronic intelligence or any other means to gather hard, vital enemy information. Enemy guerrilla forces scattered throughout and behind Allied forces were on a crusade to demoralize the Allies by hit-and-run tactics. However, they lacked the means of radio communication with their forces, and, as a result, the non-uniformed combatants were unable to provide intelligence regarding troop movements and battle plans of the Allies.

Communist China and the US re-established diplomatic relations in 1972, as a result of President Nixon's historic trip to China. Détente provided the means for the interchange of military information among former adversaries relative to the Korean Conflict. It was during that period that the Chinese Communist government acknowledged that insignificant intelligence information was gained from prisoners of war, since the majority of captured American and ROK soldiers knew little of objectives and tactics, being primarily aware of only the unit in which they served.

The indiscreet and damaging handling of Allied military information in respect to strategies, military intentions and maneuvers made classified information available to the CCF. The enemy simply monitored AFRS (Armed Forces Radio Service).[150] This practice of blatant disregard for secrecy was unprecedented in American history, as it presented the CCF leaders with a wealth of military information to assist them in pressing on with the conflict.

MacArthur fired the commencement shot on 24 November 1950—his personal directive which ordered the 8th Army to race, without due caution to the Yalu River, reminiscent of the Oklahoma Land Rush of 18 May 1889. But instead of gaining free land to homestead, the young American and Allied soldiers found death on forsaken, blood-soaked battlefields.[151]

Concurrent with the final invasion order, MacArthur personally and publicly broadcast his battle intentions via public radio, outlining his strategy for international consumption and thereby inadvertently alerting the CCF to his strategy.

The offensive drive north with the ultimate goal of securing the last vestige of North Korean territory, despite incessant warnings from the new government of Communist China, was at best, foolhardy, and ill conceived. The foray ultimately led to an unequivocal Allied military rout of immeasurable proportions.

The initial military disaster visited upon Allied units through enemy

---

[150] In Tokyo, MacArthur released a special communiqué to the UN and the world. Seldom before in the history of warfare had a senior commander ever divulged his attack plans to the enemy. But there was no one who could have stopped him. He had become an unchallenged Caesar answerable only to himself. Toland, p. 28.

[151] But these security details were minor compared with what followed when MacArthur returned to Tokyo. He released another of his ill-advised communiqué's that not only boasted that a major offensive was under way but revealed his general strategy....

Seldom in any war had a commanding general so foolishly revealed his hand. Blair, pp. 434-5.

force and firepower was unexpectedly cancelled by a mysterious general withdrawal from the arena of conflict. The CCF was in remission. MacArthur fallaciously deduced that the opponents panicked and retreated behind the political sanctuary of the Yalu River, abandoning the destiny of North Korea to the inept control of the shattered NKPA.

Walker held a contrarian view. The enemy prisoners of war from a plethora of disparate units spelled trouble. Captured enemy soldiers were bold enough to boisterously proclaim: *Many, many soldiers are coming!*

Tortured by the conflict of his reasoning and pitted against his commander's intentions, and with the survival of his 8th Army at stake, Walker ultimately opted to contravene MacArthur's order. He ordered a token, short offensive, to placate MacArthur and the General's overriding obsession to forge his troops to the border. Then Walker reconsolidated his Army, refusing to dispatch his units headlong into the abyss of the unknown. Walker was too little and too late. The CCF caught the unsuspecting 8th Army and overwhelmed Allies at the Battle of the Chongchon.

Harsh, bone-chilling winters of the Koreas are as unforgivably ruthless as the humid and torrid summers, with both seasons clashing and vying for the supreme title of the most miserable location in the world in which to war. Now, on dreary, cold 23 December, General Walker, retreated from North Korea, and set up a secondary defensive line in South Korea, approximately 12 miles north of the South Korean capitol of Seoul. It was vital that Seoul be held. The capitulation of the northern capitol, Pyongyang, was a setback for America, and loss of the southern capitol would prove American forces as impotent, a paper tiger.

The 8th Army acquiesced to the armies of Chairman Mao in North Korea, uttering a silent prayer that the Chinese Communist Forces would respectfully halt their attack at the previously recognized border, the 38th Parallel. Walker was unaware at the time of the Chinese rout that Mao had closed the book on his Phase Two Chinese Offensive, pronouncing another phase successfully concluded. Now, Mao was prepared to implement Phase Three Chinese Offensive through his surrogate, General Peng.

Walker and his Army waited silently and apprehensively for the forthcoming assault by the CCF. Allied intelligence, now realistically and frightfully aware of CCF strength, predicted the major frontal attack along the entire defensive line would occur on Christmas Eve. Chairman Mao and General Peng were intent on delivering a deadly holiday present to the battle-exhausted, UN forces. Mao was willing to sustain a very high casualty rate in order to drive the allies from the peninsula, and to date he showed no sign of altering that drastic commitment.

The burden for holding this defensive line against the oncoming CCF Red Tide fell on General Walker, who was mandated to prevent the loss of the South Korean capitol of Seoul to the enemy.

This reversal of fortune for the Allies was a political and tactical blunder of epic proportions, now shamefully heralded to the world. The American Army was further south at this point than where they were situated on 9 October, that fateful day when Allied armies ventured into North Korea. Momentous repercussions resulted from that irrational decision. Some estimates put the Allied fatality rate in excess of 60,000 young men of all nationalities. Perhaps as much as a billion dollars worth of weapons, vehicles and supplies were lost to the enemy. And now defenders faced the dishonor of being repelled from the Peninsula.

MacArthur was of no help. He was busy, hunkered down with his staff at his Dai Ichi Headquarters in Tokyo, planning for the complete evacuation of all UN and ROK troops from the Korean Peninsula.

This 23 December 1950 was a morning not unlike the typical dreary wet, cold and miserable winter days in The Land of the Morning Calm. This day was absent any premonition. With only the need to wait for the enemy, combat or reconnaissance patrols would be a frivolous and futile endeavor. The Reds were coming and there was nothing standing in the way to impede them. The 8th Army would have to hold. The heirs of Genghis Khan would advance swiftly and attack fearlessly during the black night, eliminating any possibility of retaliatory air support.

Walker perhaps had a premonition of dire circumstance as he climbed into his jeep that fateful morning. He was to meet the same fate as General George S. Patton. Ironically, both generals had little to look forward to in a post-war climate.[152]

---

[152] On December 22 General Walton Walker hurried into the Eighth Army's general officer's mess.... Brigadier General Francis W. Farrell, the Commander of the Korean Military Advisory Group, remembered, "I was there that day with some of my Koreans and I was wolfing down my food and ready to be on my way."

Walker was not known to outsiders as an introspective man; hence Farrell was surprised when the General suddenly began talking about his Second World War idol, General George S. Patton. "I find it ironic," Walker said, "That a man who lived as Patton did would die in a traffic accident." Farrell heard the remark and thought nothing of it. Then Walker finished his food, summoned his jeep driver, and set out to present unit citations to the 20th* Division and the British Commonwealth's 27th Brigade and a Silver Star to his son, Captain Sam Walker, a 20th Division company commander. Goulden, p. 424.

*Typographical error. There was no 20th Division. Perhaps author Goulden referenced the 24th or the 25th Divisions. Author.

The general had an extraordinarily light schedule that portentous day before his strategies would be tested by the arrival of the estimated 115,000 Chinese Communist troops. General Joe Tyner, Walker's trusted aide, learned that Walker's son, Sam, a platoon leader in the 19th Regiment of the 24th Infantry Division, was awarded the Silver Star the day previous. Tyner suggested that it would be fitting for the General to personally present the valorous award to his son.

The jeep, with Walker seated in his customary front passenger seat, aide Joe Tyner seated behind him, and a weapons operator manning a mounted 30-caliber machine gun to Tyner's left, headed northwest on the icy dirt road. The assembly was en route to the Uijongbu sector, about 14 miles north of Seoul. The jeep was driven by Walker's driver since World War II, Master Sergeant George Belton. Southbound traffic was stopped, mired by heavy traffic. Belton abruptly veered from his lane and accelerated rapidly north in the southbound sector, to *double-column* it (Army parlance) into the on-coming traffic.

Despite the usual red light flashing and siren wailing from Walker's jeep, without warning a weapons carrier driver assigned to a ROK 6th Division unit heading south pulled from the traffic-snarled southbound lane, intending to pass. The ROK vehicle's front bumper barely clipped the side of the commander's jeep, but the force was severe enough to cause Walker's jeep to lose control, veer from the road, catapult through the air and land in a deep snow bank where it overturned upon impact. The occupants were thrown clear, sustaining serious injuries, as Walker's grab bar, used to steady him when he stood in the speeding jeep, crushed his head. He was pronounced dead at the scene.[153]

General Walker's blood had barely cooled before MacArthur was on the telephone to Army Chief of Staff J. Lawton Collins, who in turn notified Truman, Marshall and Secretary of the Army, Frank Pace. By protocol, the next in line to assume command of the Eighth Army was General John Coulter, Commanding General, X Corps. The deceased General's designated replacement from Eighth Army was not a consideration. Coul-

---

[153] General MacArthur gave Walker in death the praise he had denied him in life. He told correspondents in Tokyo that he had "recently recommended a promotion for Walker to the four-star rank of full general." If MacArthur, in fact, had done so, he had neglected to say anything about the matter to anyone in the Defense Department. The truth was that MacArthur and other brass, including General Collins, had been looking for an opportunity to fire Walker for four months. But the spunky general died with both his rank and his Eighth Army intact, even if battered. Goulden, p. 425.

ter lost to Ridgway.

~~

A unanimous resolution among American leaders, civilian and military, selected General Matthew B. Ridgway as the commander to succeed deceased General Walker.

General Ridgway, one of the most infallible and exceptional generals in the history of the US Army, arrived in Korea on 26 December 1950, taking immediate command of the 8th Army.

Ridgway inherited a grim, demoralized, near-beaten Army, lacking basic equipment to stay alive, and reluctant to fight. Moreover it was the General's professional view that some commanders lacked the ability to lead and inspire troops.[154]

When General Ridgeway accepted command, one of his first priorities was to formulate an immediate tour of the battlefield, talking to, and inspiring troops, dejected survivors of the brutal Chinese incursion. Single handedly, Ridgway cajoled, re-supplied and rebuilt his demoralized, near defeated, American 8th Army, turning it back into a major force, capable of standing against the enemy once again.

Because of the charisma and exceptional ability of General Ridgway, the Phase Three Chinese Offensive, designed to push the Americans and UN allies from the peninsula, failed miserably. With relatively light losses to the 8th Army, particularly in comparison to the devastating Pusan Perimeter 8th Army debacle, Ridgeway's troops held defensive positions time and again against overwhelming odds. Chinese forces were massacred so many times trying to break through the bulkhead of ROKs and Americans that it became known grimly as *The Meat Grinder*.

Ridgway took to the offensive in the spring of '51 and succeeded in pushing the Chinese armies back to the area of the 38th Parallel, and in the process, liberating Seoul once again. The military operation then ceded to the international diplomatic arena.

---

[154] The new commander was dismayed to discover the lack of essential winter clothing and equipment, the poor food and lack of comforts available to the troops. "The leadership I found in many instances sadly lacking and I said so out loud." Ridgway was unimpressed, to put it politely, by "the unwillingness of the army to forego certain creature comforts, its timidity about getting off the scanty roads, its reluctance to move without radio and telephone equipment, and its lack of imagination in dealing with a foe whom they soon outmatched in firepower and dominated in the air and on the surrounding seas." He met the British General Leslie Mansergh and told him that "training was needed, and touched on the problem of pampered troops, I [Mansergh] said that all ranks felt the absence of information and were in a vacuum. He said he could tell me nothing, because he knew nothing except to 'stand and fight.'" Hastings, p. 190.

Truman's administration desired to advance the American Army farther into enemy territory to establish a stronger negotiating position, but there was an outcry of reluctance among the UN allies who had their forces engaged in Korea. The President deferred to the pressure of the Allies against carrying the UN offense north of the 38th Parallel.[155]

Most American military historians of the Korean Conflict aver that it was the Chinese Communist Government who initially approached the Soviet Envoy to the UN to request assistance in brokering a cease-fire agreement between the Chinese Communist government and the US. Other historians claim that it was the sole benevolence of the Soviet Union under the auspices of the UN, who independently suggested a cease-fire in respect to the Korean matter.[156]

Neither premise was correct. The CCF rejected signals for cease-fire proposals by the US, channeled through third-party countries. When those efforts ended in failure, the US attempted then to initiate negotiations with the Chinese Communist government through the use of media. The Communists were not in favor of compromise, unless immediate concessions were agreed to. The first demand from the CCF was for immediate withdrawal of all foreign troops from the country. The American Army at the time was positioned well inside the eastern border of North Korea, contrary to later wording of a cease-fire proposal.

The Truman Administration believed, with good cause, that an agreement to such a controversial proposal would result in utter defeat for the Republic of Korea. Chinese influence would surely orchestrate the reconstruction of the NKPA, with sufficient aid to promote a decisive defeat of the southern country.

Truman was at a loss for a solution, recognizing that his American Army was hopelessly bogged down in a fruitless, unwinnable war in the wretched diminutive Asian country, while the Soviet Union was firmly entrenched in East Europe. Counter measures against the Soviets by the

---

[155] As Acheson (Secretary of State) and Lei (Secretary of the United Nations) knew, at the time that the Eighth Army, poised on Line Kansas, several miles north of the 38th Parallel in the center was preparing to advance farther yet to Line Wyoming, which was almost twenty miles north of the parallel. Thus, Lie and Acheson's public declaration of a willingness to negotiate a cease-fire at or near or along the 38th Parallel was at best deceptive and at worst false. The statements would return to haunt all parties. Blair, p.911.

[156] At Acheson's request, Kennan made an informal call on the Soviet ambassador to the UN, Jacob Malik, on May 31st. ...Kennan frankly stated that although he had no official position in the U.S. government, he had come to "talk about a possible ceasefire in Korea" and he wondered if Malik might be willing to do so. Blair, p. 911.

US should have been put in place.

Implementing brilliant field tactics, General Ridgway executed precise field operations which drained the manpower pool of the CCF.[157] The 8th Army Commander frequently ordered a limited offensive of perhaps 20 miles or so. Once an objective was seized, his troops would dig in and revert to defense. At a given time, just prior to a CCF counter attack, Ridgway called for an orderly withdrawal, his Army returning to original southern positions. Enemy flooded into the void by the hundreds of thousands, believing that they had the 8th Army on the run, and that they could now defeat them. Ridgway then ordered the terrain to be saturated with bombardment by heavy artillery, coupled with voracious interdiction by the Allied Air Forces. Thousands of enemy were slain, with no appreciable losses to the Allies.

The continuance of the war approached genocide under Mao's orders. Mao said ousting the Allies from the peninsula was the primary goal, and only through the commitment of overwhelming hordes of infantry could the objective be attained.

The inflexible position of Mao resulted in a near revolt, leading to his dismissal of loyal generals. He ousted them because of their resistance to his intractable belief that guerilla tactics, no matter the cost in human life, won over the principles of conventional warfare. All former leaders, veterans and colleagues of Mao Tse-tung during the early revolutionary days and the Long March were later summarily discharged without honor.

Following the death of Mao, Friday, 9 September 1976, the PLA (People's Liberation Army), revisited the concept of guerilla style warfare. They questioned the tactics of pitting mass infantry against a superiorly-armed opponent. The conclusion was a startling reversal and setback for the revolutionary doctrine espoused by Mao. Mao's gifted Prime Minister, Chou En-lai, who died earlier, in January of the same year, left a painful and political void.

The failed Cultural Revolution, though it killed less people than the 1958 *Great Leap Forward*, nevertheless impacted China much more dras-

---

[157] The UN offensive resumed in March of 1951. Seoul fell once again to UN forces on March 14. The Chinese, by now thoroughly alarmed, poured fresh armies into Ridgway's meat grinder. They tried to retake Seoul in April, overwhelming a battalion of the British regiment, the Gloucester's, and attacked once more in May, in massive strength on the central and eastern sectors Both attacks were held. Ridgway returned to the offense, mauling the Chinese so badly that thousands of their fleeing, demoralized troops surrendered; peace feelers were put out by the Soviet delegate to the United Nations. Armistice talks dragged on for two more years, punctuated by sporadic fighting, until a cease-fire agreement was signed on July 27, 1953. Spurr, p. 313.

tically. The movers and shakers of the country, the military, educational, governmental specialists were defrocked of authority and dispatched to Chinese Gulags, sentenced to toil in the fields and pig farms with indeterminate sentences.

Deng Xinoping was such a person. Despite Deng's unswerving loyalty to Mao since the early revolutionary days, Deng was sacked and turned over to the Red Guards for punishment, where he was subjectively humiliated by being paraded through the streets of Peking wearing a dunce cap. After the public degradation Deng was sentenced to toil at hard labor in the fields of rural China.

Amazingly for Deng, but particularly fortunate for China, Deng made a come-back, and in time, set China on a course of free trade, and eventually, some semblance of a fledging Democracy.

And in that venue, contemporary military leaders examined and supposed that the implementation of swarms of suicidal infantrymen was unproductive and passé. The clear acknowledgment of failed practices of guerilla warfare also undermined the credibility of Mao, and his remarkable legacy from then on was open to question.

Finally, the North Korean Army was even less than what the CCF labeled the American Army, a Paper Tiger. The NKPA with only a few thousand survivors, was a spent, toothless, impotent adversary, lacking virtually all implements to continue to wage war. Kim Il-sung most assuredly would have lost control and power over the country, and would have had to flee into exile. Stranded soldiers would return to their villages, take up the scythe once again and there would be peace in the country.

Now, students of military history must ask themselves what was gained and what was lost by the misadventure of entering into the treacherous whirlpool called North Korea. More importantly, why wasn't someone held specifically responsible for these tragic results and terrible losses after the war was concluded?

General MacArthur retired from public view as a national hero. President Truman regained the respect of the public, and is perceived as honest and straightforward. Still they have blood on their hands.

BIBLIOGRAPHY

Alexander, Bevin. *The First War We Lost*. New York, Hippocrene Books, 1986.

Ambrose, Stephen E. *The Victors*. New York, Simon & Schuster, 1998.

Ambrose, Stephen E. *Americans at War*. Mississippi, University Press of Mississippi, 1997.

Appleman, Roy E. *South to the Naktong, North Yalu*. Washington, D.C., Center of Military History, United States Army, 2000.

Appleman, Roy E. *Disaster in Korea*. Texas, Texas A&M University Press, 1989.

Axelrod, Alan and Phillips, Charles. *The Macmillan Dictionary of Military Biography*. New York, Macmillan, 1998.

Barclay, C.N. *The First Commonwealth*, Edinburgh, Thomas Nelson, 1954.

Blair, Clay. *The Forgotten War*. New York, Times Books, 1987.

Bradley, Omar and Clay Blair. *A General's Life*. New York, Simon & Schuster, 1983.

Brady, James. *The Marines of Autumn*. New York, St. Martin's Press, 2000.

Brady, James. *The Coldest War*. New York, Pocket Books, 1990.

Callaghan, Peter. "Famous photo caught war's haunted eyes," *The News Tribune South Sound/Local*, May 29, 2005, B 01Column

Cumings, Bruce. *The Origins of the Korean War*. Princeton University Press, 1981.

Department of State. *Foreign Relations of the United States: The Conference at Cairo and Terhan*, Washington, Dept. of State Publication 7187, 1961.

Domes, Jurgen. *Peng Te-huai The Man and the Image*. California, Stanford University Press, 1985.

Fehrenbach, T.R. *This Kind of War*. New York, Macmillan, 1963. 50th Anniversary Edition, United States, Brassey's, 2000.

Gale, James S. *Korea in Transition*. New York, Educational Department, The Board of Foreign Missions of the Presbyterian Church in the U.S.A.,1909.

Gamble, Harold L. *Korea, I Was There*. North Carolina, Professional Press, 2001.

Goulden, Joseph C. *Korea. The Untold Story of the War*. New York, Times Books, 1982.

Hamby, Alonzo L. *Man of the People*. Oxford, England, Oxford University Press, 1995.

Hastings, Max. *The Korean War*. New York, Touch Tone Book, 1987.

Higgins, Marguerite. *War in Korea*. New York, Doubleday, 1951.

Higgins, Trumbull. *Korea and the Fall Of MacArthur*. New York, Oxford University Press, 1960.

Hirshson, Stanley, P. *General Patton*. New York, HarperCollins Publishers, 2002.

Holmes, Richard. *Acts of War*. New York, The Free Press, 1985.

Kim, Il Sung. *Works 19*. Pyongyang, Korea, Foreign Languages Publishing House, 1964.

MacArthur, Douglas A. *Reminiscences*. New York, McGraw Hill, 1964.

Manchester, William. *American Caesar*. Massachusetts, Little, Brown and Company, 1978.

Manchester, William. *The Arms of Krupp*. Massachusetts, Little, Brown and Company, 1964.

Marshall, S.L.A. *The River and the Gauntlet*. Tennessee, The Battery Press, no date given.

Massie, Robert K. *Nicholas and Alexandra*. New York, Atheneum, 1967.

McGovern, James. *To the Yalu*. New York, William Marrow, 1972.

O'Ballance, Edgar. *Korea, 1950-1953*. Connecticut, Archon Books, 1969.

Paik, Sun Yup. *From Pusan to Panmunjom*. Canada, Brassey's Press, 1992.

Paschall, Rod. *Witness to War: Korea*. New York, Berkley Publishing Group, 1995.

Ridgeway, Matthew B. *The Korean War*. New York, Da Capo Press, 1967.

Sandler, Stanley. *The Korean War: No Victors, No Vanquished*. Kentucky, University Press of Kentucky, 1999.

Spurr, Russell. *Enter the Dragon*. New York, Newmarket Press, 1988.

Burns, Will. *Dry Gulched*. Stars and Stripes, 1950.

Stilwell, Winifred, A. *The Stilwell Papers*. New York, William Sloan Associates, 1948.

Sun Tzu. *The Art of War*. New York, Oxford University Press, 1963.

Tanner, Stephen. *Epic Retreats*. Rockville Centre, New York, Sarpedon, 2000.

Toland, John. *In Mortal Combat*. New York, William Morrow and Company, 1991.

Turbak, Gary. *Hell at Hadong*. VFW Magazine, June-July, 2000.

Terry, Addison, *The Battle for Pusan*. California, Presidio Press, 2000.

Whelan, Richard. *Drawing The Line*. Boston, Little Brown and Company, 1909.

Whitney, Courtney. *MacArthur*. New York, Knopf, 1956.

Williams, Harry T. *The History of American Wars*. New York, Knopf, 1981.

ABOUT THE AUTHOR

The author endured savage battles and fourteen traumatic days behind enemy lines, and his intense Korean War combat experiences are revisited and recorded.

Special emphasis is placed on a chance encounter which resulted in the writer being aided by North Korean civilians, who themselves were recently-escaped political prisoners. Details are given about their flight and how they ultimately smuggled the writer to safety 12 December 1950 under very trying and dangerous conditions.

During the course of the author's escape, he fell through the ice of a body of water, which eventually led to frostbite, and then severe gangrene in both feet. Upon his return to military control, he was emergency evacuated to a military hospital in Osaka, Japan. Ten days later, he was returned to the Zone of Interior and subsequently hospitalized at the Percy Jones Army Hospital, Battle Creek, Michigan.

Additionally, the author was severely affected by reactions to diseases and parasites contracted while fleeing the enemy. In his medical history are recorded diagnoses of hepatitis B and parasites—ascaris and trichinosis.

While in the recovery stage from injuries and diseases, the writer elected to take the GED (General Education Development) test and successfully completed the five-phase test.

Following release from the hospital after approximately eight months, the writer was reassigned to Fort Riley, Kansas, an infantry installation, where an additional major operation was performed on his right ankle, to treat the ancillary effects of gangrenous frostbite.

He volunteered for an additional year of military service and was reassigned to the US occupation forces in Japan. Following approximately two years foreign duty, he rotated home to be honorably discharged on 12 September 1953.

The writer applied for a high school diploma based on the successful completion of the GED tests, and he was granted the diploma in 1954, despite a lack of a high school education. The certificate allowed the writer to enroll in a community college in February 1954. He ultimately received a Bachelor's' degree from California State University at Long Beach in January 1971.

Concurrently, the writer applied for a law enforcement position, and was sworn as a Deputy Sheriff, Los Angeles County, on August 1956. He served 15 years in the Patrol Division.

He received a lifetime teaching credential from the University of California at Los Angeles (UCLA) in 1971, certifying him to teach at the Community College and adult education level in the field of Police Science. The author taught several years at the Community College and Adult Education level in southern California. In 1972, he graduated from Pepperdine University with a master's degree in Public Administration. During his law enforcement career he continued his education through management and law enforcement seminars and courses, and retired in 1982 at the rank of lieutenant.

In early 1994, the author was diagnosed with severe Post Traumatic Stress Disorder, as a result of his war experiences, exacerbated by his law enforcement career. The Department of Veterans Affairs awarded him 100% disability compensation for PTSD and physical wounds. The writer was awarded the Combat Infantry Badge, the Military Order of the Purple Heart with two oak leaf clusters (signifying a 2nd and 3rd award), the American Prisoner of War Medal, the Korean Service Medal with three campaign stars, and numerous other citations.

In a ceremony in September 2005, at Fort Benning, Georgia, the author was awarded the US Army Infantry's highest medal, the Order of Saint Maurice.

He is retired and resides on Fox Island, Washington and can be contacted at anui1950@juno.com.

INDEX

A

Acheson, Dean, Secretary of State, 377, 402, 403, 404, 405, 438
Action
    Battle of Chin-ju Pass, 42, 52, 53, 55, 77
        the Notch, 43, 47, 50, 51, 139
    Battle of the Chongchon, 208, 360, 363, 434
    Chonchong, 208
    Gauntlet, 361, 443
    Hagaru, 364
    Kujang-dong, 361
    Kunu-ri, 356, 360, 361, 364
    Onjong, 350
    Strait of Korea, 116, 285, 397
    Udong-ni, 364, 366
    Wonson Harbor, xiii, 357
AFRS (Armed Forces Radio Service), 433
Allies, 7, 78, 117, 145, 172, 174, 175, 178, 179, 183, 222, 230, 233, 290, 292, 308, 314, 315, 338, 350, 351, 353, 360, 362, 367, 370, 383, 384, 417, 418, 419, 420, 430, 433, 434, 435, 438, 439
Almond, Lieutenant General Ned, 146, 155, 349, 357, 358, 360, 367, 369
Ammunition, 12, 14, 15, 31, 37, 41, 47, 51, 65, 86, 87, 88, 89, 91, 93, 100, 106, 107, 109, 110, 113, 116, 119, 126, 128, 132, 181, 188, 192, 193, 196, 200, 202, 247, 268, 297, 361, 362, 363, 364
Anju, 218, 220, 230, 238, 247, 293
Antong, now known as Dandong, 285, 368, 384, 411
Anui, xii, 7, 11, 14, 16, 19, 21, 22, 27, 31, 36, 37, 38, 39, 40, 41, 42, 46, 55, 61, 63, 67, 74, 78, 81, 83, 84, 87, 90, 91, 92, 95, 97, 108, 111, 122, 130, 139, 141, 150, 154, 168, 180, 193, 202, 204, 230, 241, 283, 299, 421, 427
Armament
    30-caliber Light Medium Machine Gun, 12, 14, 47, 93, 107, 131, 132, 182, 195, 228, 436
    Aircraft
        B-29, 286
        Corsairs, 315
        Douglas C-54, 426
        F-86 Jet, 224, 295, 297, 298, 382
        Helicopter, 224, 225, 297, 331
        MiG-15, 286
        Sikorsky Helicopter, 61
    Anti-personnel Land Mines, 93
    BAR, 124, 126, 174, 179, 181, 182, 183, 185, 195, 199
    Grenade
        Concussion, 95
        Fragmentation, 22, 74, 87, 94, 100, 102, 107, 113, 159
        Hand Grenade, 14, 15, 22, 37, 41, 74, 87, 93, 100, 102, 107, 113, 152, 153, 159, 166, 169, 180, 228
        Mark IIIA-1, 107
        Rifle Grenade, 184, 200
        Stick Grenade, 184

Machine Gun, 12, 17, 50, 59, 73, 83, 89, 93, 98, 99, 102, 124, 145, 166, 195, 196, 228, 295, 296, 297, 311, 337
Napalm, 295, 303, 304
Rifle
    75-mm Recoilless, 50
    Degtyarev Antitank, PTRD-1941, 213
    M-2 Carbine, 83, 131, 169
    Sokolov, 89
Ruptured Cartridge Extractor, 101
Tank
    Sherman, 47, 53, 195, 196
    T-34 Russian, 10, 45, 53, 142, 143, 170, 404
Tracer, 14, 28, 101, 181, 297, 298, 300, 362
Trip Flare, 93
White Phosphorous Rocket (William Peter), 86, 93

B

Baker Company, 6, 7, 8, 11, 12, 14, 15, 36, 37, 38, 39, 41, 45, 46, 47, 48, 49, 54, 55, 56, 66, 67, 68, 72, 76, 77, 78, 82, 86, 87, 89, 91, 93, 94, 100, 101, 103, 104, 105, 106, 116, 128, 129, 150, 188
Banzai, 88, 91, 95, 97
    Manzai, 88
Belton, Master Sergeant George, 436
Bradley, General Omar General and later Chairman of the Joint Chiefs of Staff, 385, 429, 442
Bradley, Omar, General and later Chairman of the Joint Chiefs of Staff, 347, 380
Braun, Otto, 407
Bruner, Sergent First Class Riley, 24, 25, 27, 28, 29, 30, 31, 33, 34, 35, 36, 37, 40, 43, 56, 130, 131, 132, 134, 135, 136, 241, 245
Buckley, Corporal Arthur W., 194
Buildings
    Tule Reed, 16

C

Cagle, 102
Canton, 411
Central Intelligence Agency, 387
China Lobby, 359, 380
Chinese Communist Forces
    Volunteers, 121, 175, 183, 186, 200, 202, 235, 239, 240, 285, 293, 348, 349, 356, 362, 364, 384, 405, 412, 414, 415, 417, 420, 422, 433
Chinese Communist Forces—CCF, iii, vii, xiii, 175, 176, 177, 178, 179, 181, 182, 183, 187, 189, 190, 194, 205, 208, 222, 229, 233, 235, 237, 250, 267, 269, 284, 292, 293, 310, 312, 328, 330, 338, 343, 348, 349, 350, 351, 352, 353, 354, 355, 356, 357, 358, 360, 361, 364, 365, 366, 368, 369, 375, 381, 384, 385, 407, 408, 410, 412, 414, 417, 418, 419, 420, 433, 434, 435, 438, 439, 440
Chin-ju, xii, 3, 4, 5, 7, 14, 19, 37, 41, 42, 44, 45, 47, 55, 56, 61, 63, 76, 78, 84, 87, 90, 108, 111, 113, 117, 122, 154, 166, 180
Chin-ju Pass, xii, 44, 47, 55, 61, 63, 78, 108, 111, 113, 122, 154, 166, 180
Chinnampo, 309, 314, 317, 319, 325, 327, 328, 329, 332, 396
Chokyong Range, 178

446 INDEX

Chokyuryong Mountains, 207, 211, 296
Chosin Reservoir, xiii, 175, 349, 359, 360, 364, 368
Chou En-lai, 348, 405, 412, 413, 414, 422, 440
Collins, General J. Lawton, 437
Compass, 175, 209, 213, 236, 237, 239, 247, 258, 267, 283, 291, 364
Cosmoline, 2, 3
Coulter, General John, 437
C-Rations, 7, 37, 56, 58, 148, 157, 159, 160, 171
Cu Xi, 393

D

Dai Ichi—MacArthur's Tokyo Headquarters, 435
Dandong, formerly known as Antong, 368
Dean, General William Frishe, 141, 142, 143, 377, 402, 404, 426
DeLashment, Lieutenant, 101, 172, 196, 197
Deng Xinoping, 440
Desfor, Max, iii, 308, 342
Disease
    Ascaris, 260, 288
    Frostbite, 180, 241, 250, 256, 264, 358, 445
    Gangrene, 279, 284, 296, 306, 309, 333, 365, 445
    Hepatitis, 57, 115, 260, 445
    Malaria, 115
    Trichinosis, 445
Draft, 67, 97
Dressler, 102

E

Eighth Army, 35, 81, 96, 138, 160, 175, 247, 257, 269, 326, 349, 359, 360, 362, 369, 426, 429, 436, 437, 438
Equipment
    Compass, 175, 209, 213, 236, 237, 239, 247, 258, 267, 283, 291, 364
    SCR 300 Radio, 91
    Sno-pac Boots, 207, 237, 254, 256
Escape
    Anju, 218, 220, 230, 238, 247, 293
    Anui, xii, 7, 11, 14, 16, 19, 21, 22, 27, 31, 36, 37, 38, 39, 40, 41, 42, 46, 55, 61, 63, 67, 74, 78, 81, 83, 84, 87, 90, 91, 92, 95, 97, 108, 111, 122, 130, 139, 141, 150, 154, 168, 180, 193, 202, 204, 230, 241, 283, 299, 421, 427
    Ipstok, 175, 327

F

First Battalion, xii, 5, 6, 7, 11, 37, 40, 44, 45, 47, 54, 55, 76, 159, 354, 421
First Field Army, 415
First Provisional Marine Brigade, 429
Fisher, Henry, 107, 149, 189, 257
Formosa—now Taiwan, 186, 374, 375, 377, 378, 379, 380, 385, 403, 406, 408, 411

G

Gap, The, 98, 359, 360
Gauntlet, The, 361, 443
Gay, Major General Hobart, 355
Geneva Convention, 205, 274, 304
Graves Registration, 76, 267
Great Leap Forward, 422, 440
Grunt, 108

H

Hadong, ix, xii, 7, 11, 14, 38, 39, 42, 84, 95, 146, 421, 427, 444
Hagaru, 364
Hainan Island, 411
Hamchang, 172, 189
Hamhung Harbor, 358
Hamm, 56
Harriman, Averell, 379
Hawaii, 244, 400
Hirohito, 401
Housing
    Hooch, 162, 163, 229, 263, 281, 290
    Quonset Hut, 147
Huagpu—see Whampoa, 414
Hughes, Lieutenant John C., 4, 11, 12, 13, 22, 25, 27, 37, 38, 52, 53, 55, 63, 66, 67, 68, 72, 74, 76, 78, 79, 81, 83, 84, 108, 112, 136, 137, 138, 141, 149, 150, 156, 164, 165, 171, 172, 177, 180, 188, 189, 191, 192, 268
Hungnam, xiii, 365, 366

I

Ida Company, ix, 348
Inchon, xii, 96, 117, 139, 144, 146, 164, 305, 317, 358, 395, 404, 408, 430, 431, 432
Infantry, xii, 8, 13, 39, 44, 45, 55, 66, 76, 87, 94, 97, 105, 126, 129, 130, 139, 152, 159, 175, 176, 188, 189, 208, 247, 305, 351, 356, 362, 367, 368, 436
Ipstok, 175, 327
Isoroku Yamamoto, 400
IX Army, 357, 364

J

Jargon
    Grunt, 108
    Non-com, 40, 41, 108, 172
Johnson, Louis, Secretary of Defense, 377, 378
Jones, Bob, 49, 50, 56, 166, 169, 170, 171, 193, 333, 445

K

Kaesong, 146, 147, 150, 154
Kangson, 307
Keiser, Major General Laurence, 361

Kiangsi Province, 407
Killed in Action (KIA), 39, 56, 217, 354
Kim Chaek, General, 91, 117
Kim Il Sung, 305, 402, 403
KMAG—Korean Military Advisory Group, 147, 352
Korean Military Advisory Group, 147, 352
Koto-ri, xiii, 365
Kujang-dong, 361
Kunu-ri, 356, 360, 361, 364
Kuomintang, 186, 404, 407, 408, 410, 414
Kwanju, 13
Kwantung Army, 400, 401

L

Liaodong Peninsula, 396
Lin Paio, 407, 414
Lin Po-cheng, 410
London, Jack, 395
Long March, 220, 357, 407, 440
Lynch, Captain Mike, 428

M

M-1, 2, 3, 9, 24, 37, 41, 50, 73, 101, 107, 114, 122, 128, 131, 132, 144, 148, 151, 158, 166, 181, 182, 184, 185, 197, 202, 338, 426
M-2 Carbine, 83, 131, 169
MacArthur, General Douglas, vi, xii, xiii, 81, 83, 96, 142, 160, 175, 187, 229, 348, 349, 351, 353, 356, 357, 358, 359, 360, 363, 367, 368, 369, 370, 372, 373, 374, 376, 377, 378, 379, 380, 381, 382, 383, 384, 385, 386, 387, 388, 389, 404, 405, 408, 409, 410, 411, 412, 415, 416, 417, 419, 423, 427, 428, 429, 430, 431, 432, 433, 434, 435, 437, 441, 443, 444
MacArthur, speech to Veterans of Foreign Wars, 379
Malik, Jacob—Soviet Ambassador to UN, 438
Manchuria, 44, 117, 144, 145, 160, 163, 171, 174, 222, 237, 262, 272, 285, 350, 357, 363, 367, 368, 370, 381, 382, 384, 391, 393, 394, 395, 396, 397, 399, 400, 401, 405, 406, 407, 408, 409, 410, 411, 412, 414, 416
Mansergh, General Leslie, 437
Manzai—Banzai, 88
Mao Tse-tung, vi, vii, 162, 174, 285, 290, 303, 328, 330, 349, 356, 367, 374, 380, 404, 405, 407, 411, 412, 413, 414, 415, 416, 418, 422, 423, 435, 439, 440
Map, xi
Marshall, George C., General and later Secretary of Defense, 359, 378, 383, 385, 386, 388, 437, 443
Martin, Joe—House Minority Leader, 385
MASH, 59
Meat Grinder, The, 438
Michaelis, Colonel John, 66
Milburn, Major Gen. Frank W., 355
Military Branches
    Air Force, 145, 146, 158, 186, 197, 198, 212, 218, 227, 234, 238, 242, 253, 276, 285, 286, 294, 295, 296, 300, 302, 307, 318, 319, 325, 381, 382, 425, 426, 439
    Coast Guard, 189

Marines, xiii, 155, 349, 358, 364, 365, 366, 367, 368, 394, 442
Navy, 317, 357, 364, 388, 397, 398
US Army, 239, 344, 386
Military Units
   187th Airborne Regiment, 144, 145
   British
      27th Commonwealth Brigade, 123
   G-2 Intelligence, 126, 161, 234, 242, 383
   Graves Registration, 76, 267
   Infantry, xii, 8, 13, 39, 44, 45, 55, 66, 76, 87, 94, 97, 105, 126, 129, 130, 139, 152, 159, 175, 176, 188, 189, 208, 247, 305, 351, 356, 362, 367, 368, 436
      19th Regiment, 47, 436
      1st Battalion, xii, 7, 11, 37, 40, 44, 45, 47, 54, 55, 76, 159, 354, 421
      25th Division, xii, xiii, 66, 81, 82, 129, 146, 150, 159, 172, 175, 257, 303, 358, 362, 436
      25th Infantry (Tropic Lightning), 175
      27th Regiment, xii, 362
      29th Infantry, ix, xii, 2, 3, 4, 5, 13, 22, 38, 39, 42, 45, 53, 63, 76, 129, 145, 150, 202, 421, 427
      29th Regiment, ix, xii, 2, 3, 4, 5, 9, 13, 14, 22, 38, 39, 42, 44, 45, 53, 63, 76, 129, 145, 150, 202, 421, 423, 427
      34th Infantry, 2, 9, 22
      35th Regiment, xii, xiii, 107, 129, 159, 175, 176, 180, 189, 193, 214, 257, 356, 362
      3rd Platoon, 67, 78, 81, 110, 121, 149, 156, 163, 164, 197
      4th Platoon, 12
      7th Infantry Division, 117, 175, 352, 430
      A Company, 6
      Baker Company, 6, 7, 8, 11, 12, 14, 15, 36, 37, 38, 39, 41, 45, 46, 47, 48, 49, 54, 55, 56, 66, 67, 68, 72, 76, 77, 78, 82, 86, 87, 89, 91, 93, 94, 100, 101, 103, 104, 105, 106, 116, 128, 129, 150, 188
      Cacti Regiment, 175
      King Comapany, viii, 129, 137, 138, 142, 143, 147, 149, 150, 161, 164, 171, 177, 178, 179, 180, 181, 182, 186, 187, 189, 190, 192, 194, 196, 199, 268, 327
      L Company, 146
      Task Force Smith, xii, 4, 13, 141, 142, 427
Miller, Sergeant Benjamin, 107, 108, 113, 118, 119, 121, 122, 125, 126, 149, 158, 159, 160, 164, 165, 166, 167, 168, 169, 170, 171, 172, 173, 187, 189, 192
Missing in Action (MIA), 56, 217
Moats, Ken, 11
Mobile Army Surgical Hospital (Mash), 59
Mobile Army Surgical Hospital (MASH), 55, 62
Molatov, Prime Minister, 402
Mukden—now known as Shenyang, 396, 416
Munitions
   Degtyarev Antitank, 14.5 mm., 213
Musselwhite, Sergeant Willie, 8, 9, 35, 56

N

Naktong River, 381
Napalm, 156, 295, 303, 304, 312, 313
National Security Agency, 387
New China, 415, 416, 418, 422

450   INDEX

Nieh Yen-jung, 162
Nineteenth Regiment, 47, 436
Nixon, President Richard M., 359, 373, 433
No Gun Ri, 17
No Man's Land, 215, 233, 242, 328, 330
Norris, Al, 101
North Korea, i, iii, v, vi, ix, xii, xiii, 4, 6, 11, 13, 14, 17, 18, 22, 23, 24, 27, 28, 29, 31, 38, 39,
    41, 42, 44, 45, 47, 48, 50, 53, 55, 56, 58, 67, 76, 78, 81, 82, 84, 85, 87, 88, 89, 91, 92, 95,
    97, 98, 102, 103, 104, 105, 106, 109, 110, 114, 116, 117, 118, 125, 126, 130, 131, 132,
    134, 135, 138, 139, 140, 141, 142, 144, 146, 147, 156, 158, 159, 160, 163, 164, 166, 172,
    175, 178, 183, 187, 188, 189, 190, 198, 200, 201, 202, 205, 206, 208, 212, 214, 218, 219,
    220, 221, 222, 223, 224, 237, 246, 248, 249, 257, 262, 264, 265, 266, 267, 268, 270, 271,
    272, 273, 274, 275, 277, 278, 279, 280, 284, 285, 286, 290, 292, 293, 294, 298, 302, 303,
    305, 306, 310, 315, 316, 317, 320, 322, 325, 327, 328, 330, 331, 333, 334, 337, 338, 339,
    348, 351, 352, 353, 356, 357, 358, 360, 361, 363, 364, 365, 367, 368, 370, 374, 379, 380,
    381, 383, 384, 385, 390, 393, 394, 402, 403, 404, 405, 408, 409, 410, 412, 413, 414, 415,
    416, 417, 419, 420, 421, 422, 423, 424, 426, 431, 434, 435, 439, 440, 441, 445
North Korean People's Army, iii, xii, 2, 6, 9, 13, 18, 24, 29, 33, 41, 42, 45, 47, 66, 67, 76, 77,
    78, 81, 87, 88, 89, 90, 92, 94, 95, 101, 102, 103, 105, 106, 107, 111, 112, 115, 116, 117,
    118, 125, 137, 138, 140, 141, 142, 143, 144, 145, 146, 147, 150, 164, 170, 172, 174, 183,
    189, 190, 202, 205, 214, 222, 230, 237, 272, 305, 339, 374, 376, 377, 379, 383, 404, 405,
    409, 411, 413, 415, 420, 424, 425, 429, 430, 433, 434, 439, 440
    FourthDivision, 42
    Sixth Division, 11, 18, 24, 41, 42, 44, 45, 49, 51, 89, 94, 103, 111, 114, 117, 139, 150, 189,
        200, 349, 350, 351, 352, 356, 436
    Third Division, 9
Notch, The, 43, 47, 48, 50, 51, 139

O

Observation Post (O.P.), 155
Okchon, 2
Okinawa, 2, 3, 4, 7, 10, 12, 13, 15, 19, 32, 52, 56, 67, 93, 102, 114, 129, 130, 149, 150, 152,
    154, 160, 202, 322, 421, 426
Onjong, 350
Operation Yo-Yo, 357
Osan, 13, 141, 427

P

Pace, Frank —Secretary of the Army, 387, 437
Paik Sun-up, Major General, 349
Pan Mun Jom, 147
Pannikar, K.M.—Indian Ambassador to China, 405
Pappert, Sergeant Edgar, 12, 13, 15, 16, 17, 27, 37, 40, 55, 56, 194, 195
Pearl Harbor, 362, 400
Peng Te-huai, General, 175, 330, 352, 356, 357, 412, 414, 416, 417, 419, 422, 423, 424, 435
Pierce, Bill, 169, 174, 199
Plass, Master Sergeant Frank C., 355
Port Arthur, 393, 395, 396, 397, 400
Provisional Korean government, 400
Pu Yi, 393

Puller, Colonel Lewis B., 358, 364
Pusan
    Pusan Perimeter, xii, 3, 5, 45, 54, 56, 59, 62, 67, 76, 78, 87, 106, 107, 116, 117, 132, 135, 138, 141, 143, 146, 214, 223, 269, 303, 305, 379, 381, 412, 419, 426, 428, 429, 430, 431, 432, 438, 443, 444
Putzier, Private Eugene, 229
Pyongyang, iii, ix, xii, 144, 145, 266, 275, 285, 287, 292, 294, 303, 305, 306, 307, 308, 309, 310, 314, 315, 317, 319, 342, 407, 435, 443

Q

Quonset Hut, 147

R

Radlow, Sam, 247
Ranching Rebellion, 407
Red Cross, 362
Reed, Jim, 67, 118, 119
Republic of Korea, xiii, 6, 41, 42, 54, 77, 78, 107, 112, 117, 119, 126, 138, 145, 146, 150, 158, 166, 167, 168, 175, 190, 208, 247, 274, 305, 310, 316, 317, 333, 335, 337, 338, 349, 350, 351, 352, 353, 354, 356, 357, 358, 362, 370, 374, 404, 405, 408, 409, 410, 415, 424, 426, 430, 435, 436, 439
Rhee, Syngman, xii, 118, 315, 316, 351, 352
Ridgway, Matthew, xiii, 208, 285, 307, 386, 387, 420, 424, 432, 437, 438, 439
Roosevelt, President Theodore, 398
Roslof, Edward E., 3

S

Safe Conduct, 142
Scott, Rodney, 193, 197
Seoul, xii, 42, 143, 144, 266, 269, 295, 305, 317, 392, 399, 416, 425, 434, 435, 436, 438, 439
Seventh Fleet, 380, 411
Sharp Swords, The, 354
Shenshi Province, 407
Shenyang—formerly known as Mukden, 396, 416
Sinanju, 160, 368
Sinuiju, 285, 381
Smith, Major General Oliver P., 357, 367
South Korea, iii, xii, 13, 17, 18, 21, 41, 42, 54, 67, 68, 78, 87, 116, 118, 123, 141, 144, 146, 158, 204, 205, 217, 269, 270, 271, 272, 273, 278, 305, 315, 316, 320, 325, 330, 333, 334, 336, 338, 339, 344, 348, 352, 354, 357, 374, 375, 376, 377, 384, 385, 402, 403, 404, 405, 406, 408, 411, 412, 414, 425, 427, 428, 434, 435
Stalin, Joseph, vi, 369, 370, 374, 375, 402, 403, 404
Stevens, iv, viii, 52, 63, 229
Stimson, Secretary of State Henry L., 387
Strait of Korea, 116, 285
    Strait of Tsushima, 116, 285, 397
Strait of Tsushima, 116, 285, 397
Stratemeyer, General George E., 381
Suddaby, Lieutenant Reed, 48, 86, 88, 89, 93, 104, 116, 164, 172, 189, 192, 194, 195
Sukchong, 247

Sun Yat-Sen, 393
Sung Shin-lun, General, 357
Surrender, 19, 92, 100, 101, 103, 143, 149, 164, 172, 179, 201, 202, 212, 221, 223, 231, 256, 260, 316, 355, 385, 391, 396, 409, 424

T

T-34 Russian Tanks, 10, 45, 53, 142, 143, 170, 404
Taebaek Mountains, 269, 328
Taedong River, iii, 305, 307, 308, 309, 317, 328, 342
Taegu, 59
Taejon, iii, 9, 13, 42, 141, 142, 143, 272, 339, 426, 427
Taro, Katsura—Prime Minister of Japan, 399
Task Force Smith, xii, 4, 13, 141, 142, 427
Thirty-eighth Parallel, 6, 144, 146, 273, 285, 292, 305, 321, 338, 350, 351, 368, 390, 392, 402, 404, 405, 408, 412, 416, 435, 438
Thirty-fourth Infantry, 2, 9, 22
Togo, Admiral Heihachiro, 397
Topography
    Chokyuryong Mountains, 207, 211, 296
    Chonchong River, 208
Townsend, Sergeant, ix
Tracer, 14, 28, 101, 181, 297, 298, 300, 362
Transportation
    Deuce-and-a-half, 4, 41, 52, 76, 106, 121, 122, 228, 288, 334
    Douglas C-54, 426
    Half-track, 83
    Tagasaka Maru, 290
Treaty of Portsmouth, 44, 398
Truman, President Harry S., vi, xii, 144, 218, 222, 370, 372, 373, 374, 375, 376, 377, 378, 379, 380, 381, 382, 383, 384, 386, 387, 388, 389, 402, 405, 406, 407, 411, 412, 425, 428, 437, 438, 439
Tsar Nicholas Romanoff II, 397
Tsushima, 350, 397, 398
Tule Reed, 16, 24, 298, 299
Tumen River, 390
Twenty-fifth Infantry Division, xii, xiii, 66, 81, 82, 129, 146, 159, 175, 257, 358, 362, 436
Twenty-ninth Infantry Regiment, ix, 3, 5, 13, 38, 39, 42, 45, 53, 63, 129, 145, 150, 202, 421, 427
Tyner, General Joe, 436

U

Udong-ni, 364, 366
Uijongbu, 436
Uiju, 396
UN, xii, xiii, 24, 59, 189, 190, 292, 382, 384, 406, 412, 416, 420, 433, 438, 439

V

Vandenberg, Air Force Chief of Staff Hoyt, 381
Veterans of Foreign Wars, 379
Vinegar Joe--General Joseph W. (Vinegar Joe) Stilwell., 443

W

Wake Island, xii, 326
Walker, General Walton (Johnnie), xiii, 40, 81, 87, 103, 305, 306, 349, 360, 367, 369, 424, 425, 426, 427, 428, 429, 430, 431, 432, 434, 435, 436, 437
Whampoa Military Academy, 357, 414
Wilkin, John, 107
Willoughby, Major General Charles A., 360
Wong Lichan, Colonel, 117
Woolfolk, 107
Worrill, Frederick, 197

Y

Yalu River, iii, xiii, 144, 161, 162, 175, 222, 246, 267, 285, 286, 306, 340, 348, 352, 356, 357, 358, 368, 369, 381, 382, 383, 384, 396, 405, 414, 433, 434, 442, 443
Yellow Sea, 323, 391
Yudam, 357

ISBN 141207244-1